Time Out

Florence

timeout.com/florence

Published by Time Out Guides Ltd, a wholly owned subsidiary of Time Out Group Ltd.
Time Out and the Time Out logo are trademarks of Time Out Group Ltd.

Previous editions 1997, 1999, 2001, 2003, 2005.

10 9 8 7 6 5 4 3 2 1

This edition first published in Great Britain in 2008 by Ebury Publishing
A Random House Group Company
20 Vauxhall Bridge Road, London SW1V 2SA

Random House Australia Pty Limited 20 Alfred Street, Milsons Point, Sydney, New South Wales 2061, Australia
Random House New Zealand Limited 18 Poland Road, Glenfield, Auckland 10, New Zealand
Random House South Africa (Pty) Limited Isle of Houghton, Corner Boundary Road & Carse O'Gowrie, Houghton 2198, South Africa

Random House UK Limited Reg. No. 954009

For further distribution details, see www.timeout.com

ISBN: 978184670 0293

A CIP catalogue record for this book is available from the British Library

Printed and bound by Firmengruppe APPL, aprinta druck, Wemding, Germany

The Random House Group Limited supports The Forest Stewardship Council (FSC), the leading international forest certification organisation. All our titles that are printed on Greenpeace approved FSC certified paper carry the FSC logo. Our paper procurement policy can be found at www.rbooks.co.uk/environment

Time Out Guides Limited
Universal House
251 Tottenham Court Road
London W1T 7AB
Tel + 44 (0)20 7813 3000
Fax + 44 (0)20 7813 6001
Email guides@timeout.com
www.timeout.com

Editorial
Editor Daniel Smith
Deputy Editor Anna Norman
Consultant Editor Nicky Swallow
Sub Editors Edoardo Albert, Cyrus Shahrad
Listings Editor Heather Sockol
Proofreader Tamsin Shelton
Indexer Sally Davies

Managing Director Peter Fiennes
Financial Director Gareth Garner
Editorial Director Ruth Jarvis
Deputy Series Editor Dominic Earle
Editorial Manager Holly Pick
Assistant Management Accountant Ija Krasnikova

Design
Art Director Scott Moore
Art Editor Pinelope Kourmouzoglou
Senior Designer Henry Elphick
Graphic Designer Gemma Doyle
Junior Graphic Designer Kei Ishimaru
Digital Imaging Simon Foster
Advertising Designer Jodi Sher

Picture Desk
Picture Editor Jael Marschner
Deputy Picture Editor Katie Morris
Picture Researcher Helen McFarland
Picture Desk Assistant Troy Bailey

Advertising
Sales Director Mark Phillips
International Advertising Manager Kasimir Berger
International Sales Consultant Ross Canadé
International Sales Executive Charlie Sokol
Advertising Sales (Florence) *The Florentine*
Advertising Assistant Kate Staddon

Marketing
Group Marketing Director John Luck
Marketing Manager Yvonne Poon
Sales and Marketing Director North America Lisa Levinson

Production
Group Production Director Mark Lamond
Production Manager Brendan McKeown
Production Controller Caroline Bradford
Production Coordinator Susan Whittaker

Time Out Group
Chairman Tony Elliott
Financial Director Richard Waterlow
Group General Manager/Director Nichola Coulthard
Time Out Magazine Ltd MD Richard Waterlow
Time Out Communications Ltd MD David Pepper
Time Out International MD Cathy Runciman
Group Art Director John Oakey
Group IT Director Simon Chappell

Contributors
Introduction Daniel Smith. **History** Nicky Swallow. **Florence Today** Linda Falcone. **Art** Sophia Cottier. **Renaissance Reborn** Maddalena Delli. **Architecture** Sophia Cottier (*Bland ambition* Maddalena Delli). **Food & Wine** Adrian Smith (*New wave whites* Daniel Smith). **Where to Stay** Nicky Swallow. **Sightseeing Introduction** Daniel Smith. **Sightseeing** Lizzie Fane (*Seeing beyond the façade* Sophia Cottier; *Rogues' gallery, Fictional Florence* Julia Burdet). **Restaurants & Wine Bars** Nicky Swallow. **Cafés, Bars & Gelaterie** Julia Burdet. **Shops & Services** Julia Burdet. **Festivals & Events** Maddalena Delli. **Children** Maddalena Delli. **Film** James Douglas. **Galleries** Julia Burdet. **Gay & Lesbian** Bruno Casini. **Music: Classical & Opera** Nicky Swallow. **Music: Rock, Pop & Jazz** Beth de Felici. **Nightlife** Julia Burdet. **Sports & Fitness** Beth de Felici (*The crying game* Daniel Smith). **Theatre & Dance** Maddalena Delli. **Getting Started** Daniel Smith (*Shingle belles* Nicky Swallow). **Florence & Prato Provinces** Maddalena Delli. **Pistoia Province** Paul Lay. **Pisa** Daniel Smith. **Pisa & Livorno Provinces** Daniel Smith, Nicky Swallow. **Siena** Christine Webb. **Siena Province** Christine Webb (*Gold comfort farm, Unter der toskanischen Sonne* Natasha Foges). **Lucca** Paul Lay (*Tuscany's Toontown* Maddalena Delli). **Massa-Carrara & Lucca Provinces** Paul Lay. **Arezzo** Daniel Smith (*Market force* Christine Webb). **Arezzo Province** Christine Webb. **Southern Tuscany** Kate Singleton. **Directory** Julia Burdet.

Maps john@jsgraphics.co.uk.

Photography by Gianluca Moggi, except: page 10 akg-images/Rabatti – Domingie; page 16 akg-images; page 18 Palazzo Reale de Pisa, Pisa, Italy/The Bridgeman Art Library; page 32 Photo Scala, Florence (right), akg-images/Erich Lessing (left); page 135, 146 Jonathan Perugia.

All illustrations by Simon Foster.

The Editor would like to thank Robin Davis, Nina Douglas, David Howells, Melissa Ormiston at *Italy Magazine*, Fabrizio Quochi, Alessandra Smith and all contributors to previous editions of *Time Out Florence*, whose work forms the basis for parts of this book.

Contents

Introduction 6

In Context 9

History 10
Florence Today 23
Art 26
Renaissance Reborn 32
Architecture 36
Food & Wine 43

Where to Stay 49

Where to Stay 50

Sightseeing 71

Introduction 72
Duomo & Around 75
Santa Maria Novella 93
San Lorenzo 96
San Marco 99
Santa Croce 103
Oltrarno 107
Outside the City Gates 112

Eat, Drink, Shop 117

Restaurants & Wine Bars 118
Cafés, Bars & Gelaterie 140
Shops & Services 148

Arts & Entertainment 169

Festivals & Events 170
Children 175
Film 178
Galleries 181
Gay & Lesbian 183
Music: Classical & Opera 186
Music: Rock, Pop & Jazz 190
Nightlife 193
Sport & Fitness 200
Theatre & Dance 205

Tuscany 209

Getting Started 210
Florence & Prato Provinces 214
Pistoia Province 219
Pisa 222
Map: Pisa 224
Pisa & Livorno Provinces 230
Siena 235
Map: Siena 236
Siena Province 247
Lucca 260
Map: Lucca 261
Massa-Carrara & Lucca Provinces 270
Arezzo 276
Map: Arezzo 277
Arezzo Province 283
Southern Tuscany 290

Directory 299

Getting Around 300
Resources A-Z 304
Vocabulary 317
Glossary 318
Further Reference 319
Index 320
Advertisers' Index 326

Maps 327

Tuscany 328
Greater Florence 331
Florence Overview 332
Street Maps 334
Street Index 336

Introduction

Is there anywhere in the world that trades as heavily on its past as Florence? This small Tuscan city offers visitors the greatest collection of Renaissance art in the world, and boasts a character list that reads like a *Who's Who* of the period's greatest artists and thinkers – Dante, Galileo, Leonardo, Machiavelli, Michelangelo...

In a great many respects, Florence has hardly altered since these prestigious residents were alive. Local pride is just as strong, the surrounding countryside is still as beautiful, and the city's major landmarks are as impressive now as when they were first built.

But some things do change. Traffic issues abound – both vehicular jams and an attraction-clogging seven million annual visitors – and the tramline being built to deal with the problems is not exactly a popular measure. However, on the plus side, the new Alinari photography museum marks the high point of a long-needed restoration of piazza Santa Maria Novella, and Florentines now have a new park to frolic in, the Giardino Bardini. And while we're talking enjoyment, a string of new restaurant, bar and club openings in the district of Santa Croce means that it's now rivalling the Oltrarno – once way ahead of the other neighbourhoods in the coolness stakes – in terms of atmosphere and attractions.

The past, though, continues to make its presence felt. Florence has had to rethink the way it plays *calcio storico*, a historical 'football' game so violent authorities had to suspend it. On a more cerebral level, new investigations into a Leonardo fresco thought lost forever were well underway as we went to press, while the rediscovery of elements of Michelangelo's façade for the church of San Lorenzo have led to a flurry of activity outside the Medicis' spiritual headquarters. We present our findings on pages 32 to 35, but the arty focus continues throughout the book. We've updated the art and architecture chapters, supplied pointers on analysing the Duomo's façade and exposed some of art's greatest rogues. We've even investigated the city's arty hotels.

You've come to see the greatest repository of Renaissance art in the world and you should make the most of your time here. As Michelangelo himself said, 'The greater danger for most of us lies not in setting our aim too high and falling short, but in setting our aim too low, and achieving our mark.' Start planning your return trip now.

● Florence is one of 30 destinations included in *Time Out Italy*, our new guide to the best of the country, published in 2008.

ABOUT TIME OUT CITY GUIDES

This is the sixth edition of *Time Out Florence*, one of an expanding series of more than 50 guides produced by the people behind the successful listings magazines in London, New York, Chicago, Sydney and many more cities around the world. Our guides are all written and updated by resident experts who have striven to provide you with all the most up-to-date information you'll need to explore Florence, whether you're a local or a first-time visitor.

THE LOWDOWN ON THE LISTINGS

Above all, we've tried to make this book as useful as possible. Addresses, telephone numbers, websites, transport information (where necessary), opening times, admission prices and credit card details have all been included in the listings, as have details of other selected services and facilities. However, owners and managers of venues can change their arrangements at any time. Before you go out of your way, we strongly advise you to call and check opening times and other particulars. While every effort has been made to ensure the accuracy of the information contained in this guide, the publishers cannot accept responsibility for any errors it may contain.

PRICES AND PAYMENT

Our listings detail which of the four major credit cards – American Express (AmEx), Diners Club (DC), MasterCard (MC) and Visa (V) – are accepted by individual venues. Many businesses will also accept other cards, such as Maestro and Carte Blanche, as well as travellers' cheques issued by a major financial institution.

The prices we've supplied should be treated as guidelines, not gospel. Fluctuating exchange rates and inflation can cause charges, particularly in shops and restaurants, to change rapidly. If prices vary wildly from those we've quoted, ask whether there's a good reason,

then please email to let us know. We aim to give the best and most up-to-date advice, and we always want to know if you've been badly treated or overcharged.

THE LIE OF THE LAND

To make both book and city easier to navigate, we've divided Florence into areas and assigned each one its own section in the Sightseeing part of the book. These area designations have also been used in addresses throughout the guide, and are illustrated on the overview map on pages 332 and 333.

Central Florence is very compact and it's often easy to walk between destinations. For this reason, we have given bus information only for addresses beyond the old city walls: in the central area, a combination of walking a short distance and using the four electric bus circuits (marked on the maps on pages 334 and 335) should get you everywhere quickly.

MAPS

For addresses given in the Florence section of this book, we've included references to the fully indexed colour street maps on pages 334 and 335 of this guide. Precise locations of hotels (❶), restaurants and wine bars (❶) and cafés, bars and *gelaterie* (❶) have been pinpointed on these maps where possible. The map section (which starts on page 328) also includes a transport map and a street index. Maps for destinations in our Tuscany section (*see pp209-297*) are in the chapters themselves.

TELEPHONE NUMBERS

The area code for Florence is 055, which must be dialled in full (including the zero) at all times, whether calling from within Italy (including Florence itself) or from abroad. Numbers preceded by 800 can be called free of charge from Florence.

As with Florence listings, phone numbers for listings in our Tuscany section are given in their entirety as dialled locally and throughout Italy.

The country code for Italy is 39. To dial numbers as given in this book from abroad, use your country's exit code (00 in the UK, 011 in the US) or the + symbol (on many mobile phones), followed by the country code, followed by the number as listed.

For more on phones, including information on free and premium-rate numbers, *see p313*.

ESSENTIAL INFORMATION

For all the practical information you might need for visiting the city, including customs and immigration information, disabled access, emergency telephone numbers, the lowdown on the local transport network and a list of useful websites, turn to the Directory at the back of this guide. It starts on page 300.

LET US KNOW WHAT YOU THINK

We hope you enjoy *Time Out Florence*, and we'd like to know what you think of it. We welcome tips for places that you consider we should include in future editions, and take notice of your criticism of our choices. You can email us at guides@timeout.com.

Advertisers

We would like to stress that no establishment has been included in this guide because it has advertised in any of our publications and no payment of any kind has influenced any review. The opinions given in this book are those of Time Out writers and entirely independent.

There is an online version of this guide, along with guides to more than 50 other international cities, at **www.timeout.com**.

In Context

History 10
Florence Today 23
Art 26
Renaissance Reborn 32
Architecture 36
Food & Wine 43

Features

The Renaissance 15
Medici cabinet 16
Purple haze 24
Art attack 27
Statues of stature 28
Where to see it 30
Don't miss Architecture 37
Bland ambition 41
New wave whites 46

History

How a tiny Etruscan outpost became the birthplace of the modern world.

Practically the whole of Florence's reputation rests on its history – a tale that stretches back to an almost forgotten European civilisation and takes in some of the most monumental cultural shifts of the last 500 years.

From around the eighth century BC, much of central Italy was controlled by the Etruscans, who may have been natives or may have drifted in from Asia Minor. Whatever their origins, they settled in Veio and Cerveteri, close to Rome, and further north – in what is now Tuscany – around Volterra, Populonia, Arezzo, Chiusi and Cortona. They entirely overlooked the site that we now know as Florence, making hilltop Fiesole their northernmost stronghold.

Tantalisingly little evidence remains of Etruscan civilisation – the culture that was clobbered out of existence by the Romans. One of the main reasons for this is that the Etruscans constructed everything from wood – everything, that is, except their tombs; their graves, and the objects recovered from them, constitute most of the artefacts used to piece together their history. With so little to go on, mythologisers have had a field day. The enchanting frescoes of feasts, dancing and hunting that adorn many of the tombs led DH Lawrence to conclude that 'death to the Etruscan was a pleasant continuance of life'. Others believe that the Etruscans were terrified of mortality, that the seemingly carefree paintings were a desperate plea for the gods to show mercy on the other side.

Despite the scarcity of evidence, historians have come to understand the Etruscan civilisation pretty well. The Etruscans were certainly a religious people, but they were also partial to a good war, against either other tribes or rival Etruscan cities. Their civilisation reached its peak in the seventh and sixth centuries BC, when their loose federation of cities dominated much of what is now southern Tuscany and northern Lazio. Women played an unusually prominent role in society, apparently having as much fun as – if not more than – the men. Writing in the fourth century BC, Theopompos said: 'Etruscan women take particular care of their bodies and exercise often, sometimes along with the men, and sometimes by themselves. It is not a disgrace for them to be seen naked. They do not share their couches with their husbands but with other men who happen to be present… They are expert drinkers and very attractive.'

Etruscan cities grew wealthy on the proceeds of mining and trading copper and iron. Their art and superbly worked gold jewellery display distinctive oriental influences, adding credence to the theory that the Etruscans migrated to Italy from the East, though such influences could have been due to their extensive trading in the eastern Mediterranean. At the end of the seventh century BC, the Etruscans captured the small town of Rome and ruled it for a century before being expelled. The next few hundred years witnessed city fighting city and tribe battling tribe until the emerging Roman republic overwhelmed all by the third century BC.

THE EMERGENCE OF TUSCANY

In 59 BC, Julius Caesar established a colony for army veterans along the narrowest stretch of the Arno, and Florentia was born. Strategically located at the heart of Italian territory, it grew into a flourishing commercial centre, becoming the capital of a Roman province in the third century AD. In the fifth century, the Roman Empire in the West finally crumbled before the pagan hordes (some of whom were no less cultured than the dissolute Romans they displaced). Italian unity collapsed as Ostrogoths, Visigoths, Huns and Lombards rampaged through the peninsula.

The Goths who swept into central Italy in the fifth century were dislodged by the Byzantine forces of the Eastern emperor in conflicts that left the area badly battle-scarred. The Goth King Totila seized Florence again in 552, only to be ejected two decades later when the Lombards stormed across the Alps and established a regional HQ at Lucca.

In the eighth century, Charlemagne and his Frankish forces crushed the last of the Lombard kings of Italy. To thank him for his intervention and ensure his future support (a move that backfired badly, leading to centuries of conflict between pontiff and emperors), Pope Leo III crowned Charlemagne Holy Roman Emperor. Much of the country then came under the (at least nominal) control of the emperor. In practice, local warlords carved out feudal fiefs for themselves and threw their weight around.

The imperial margravate of Tuscany began to emerge as a region of some promise during the tenth and 11th centuries, when it came under the control of the Canossa family. Initially, the richest city was Lucca, but it was Pisa's increasingly profitable maritime trade that brought the biggest impetus of ideas and wealth into the region.

As a prosperous merchant class developed in cities all over Tuscany, the region sought to throw off the constraints and demands of its feudal overlords. By 1200, the majority had succeeded (Florence, Siena and Lucca had been established as independent city states, or *comuni*, by the redoubtable Matilde di Canossa on her death in 1115). Tuscany became a patchwork of tiny but increasingly self-confident and ambitious independent entities. The potential for conflict was huge, and by the 13th century it had crystallised into an intractable and seemingly interminable struggle between Guelphs and Ghibellines.

GUELPHS VS GHIBELLINES

The names Guelph and Ghibelline came from the Italian forms of Welf (the family name of the German emperor Otto IV) and Waiblingen (a castle belonging to the Welfs' rivals for the role of Holy Roman Emperor, the Hohenstaufen) respectively, but by the time the appellations crossed the Alps into Italy (probably in the 12th century), their significance had changed.

'Guelph' became attached primarily to the increasingly influential merchant classes. In their continuing desire to be free from imperial control, they looked around for a powerful backer. The only viable candidate was the emperor's enemy, the pope, who by this time had recognised the error of creating a rival ruler and was peddling the theory that the fourth-century Roman emperor Constantine (who sat by in his new Eastern capital at Constantinople, as the Western Empire fell from the hands of the last Roman emperors into the ruthless ones of barbarian invaders) had assigned not just spiritual but also temporal power in Italy to the papacy. The Guelphs could thus add a patriotic and religious sheen to their own self-interest.

Anyone keen to uphold imperial power and opposed to papal designs and rising commercial interests – mainly the old nobility – became known as Ghibellines. That, at least, was the theory. It soon became clear, however, that self-interest and local rivalries were of far greater importance than theoretical allegiances to emperor or pope.

Although bad feeling had been simmering for decades, the murder of Florentine nobleman Buondelmonte dei Buondelmonti is seen as the spark that ignited flames across Tuscany. On his wedding day in 1215, Buondelmonte was stabbed to death by a member of the Amidei family for having previously jilted an Amidei maiden. The subsequent trial dissolved into a test of wills (and soon of arms) between the pro-Empire Amidei and the pro-*comune* faction mourning the demise of the groom. The Ghibelline Amidei prevailed with help from Emperor Frederick II in 1248, but were ousted with Guelph aid two years later, when a semi-democratic government by the merchant class, known as the *piccolo popolo*, was established.

Live your dreams
in the leading Tuscany Spa Resort

Ten years on, Ghibellines from Siena dislodged the *piccolo popolo* and came close to razing the town; a decade later, the Guelphs were back in the driving seat, with the major craft guilds running the show through an administration called the *secondo popolo*. In 1293, the body passed a regulation effectively banning the nobility from government in Florence, giving power to a *signoria* (government) made up of representatives of the guilds.

The situation was no less complex in other Tuscan towns: Lucca was generally Guelph-dominated, while Siena and Pisa tended to favour the Ghibellines, but this had as much to do with mutual antagonisms as deeply held beliefs. Siena started off Guelph, but couldn't bear the thought of having to be nice to its traditional enemy, Florence, so swapped to the Ghibelline cause. Similarly, the Guelph/Ghibelline splits within cities were more often class- and grudge-based than ideological.

Throughout the 14th century, power ebbed and flowed between the two (loosely knit) parties across Tuscany and from city to city. When one party was in the ascendant its supporters would tear down its opponents' fortified towers (the Guelphs' with their square crenellations, the Ghibellines' with swallow-tail ones), only to have its own towers levelled as soon as the pendulum swung back.

Once firmly in command of Florence at the end of the 13th century, the Guelphs started squabbling internally. In around 1300, open conflict broke out between the virulently anti-Imperial 'Blacks' and the more conciliatory 'Whites'. After various to-ings and fro-ings, the Blacks booted the Whites out for good. Among those sent into exile was Dante Alighieri.

Eventually, the Guelph/Ghibelline conflict ran out of steam. It says much for the energy, innovation, graft and skill of the Tuscans (or for the relative harmlessness of much medieval warfare in Italy) that throughout this stormy period, the region was booming economically.

By the beginning of the 14th century, Florence was one of the five biggest cities in Europe, with a population of almost 100,000. It went through a rocky patch in the middle of the century, when England's King Edward III defaulted on his debts in 1342, bankrupting several Florentine lenders. Six years later a plague epidemic carried off an estimated half of the city's population. But Florence soon bounced back: its currency – the florin, first minted in 1252 – remained one of Europe's strongest; and with fewer illness-prone poor to employ and feed, Florence may even have benefited economically from the Black Death.

The city's good fortune was due in no small part to its woollen cloth industry. Taxes to finance the costly conflict known as the War of the Eight Saints against Pope Gregory XI in 1375-8 hit the *ciompi* (wool carders) hardest, and they revolted, gaining representation in city government. By the mid 1380s, however, the three guilds formed in the wake of the uprising began to lose ground to the *popolo grasso*, a small group of the wealthiest merchant families, who had united with the Guelphs to form an oligarchy in 1382. The *popolo grasso* held sway in the *signoria* for 40 years, during which time intellectuals and artists were becoming increasingly involved in political life.

'Florence turned to a fire-and-brimstone-preaching monk who claimed paintings made the Virgin Mary look like a harlot.'

Not all of Florence's business community backed the *popolo grasso*. Banker Cosimo de' Medici's stance against the extremes of the *signoria* gained him the support both of other dissenting merchants and the *popolo minuto* of the less influential guilds. Cosimo's mounting popularity alarmed the *signoria*, and the dominant Albizzi family had him exiled on trumped-up charges in 1433. A year later he returned to Florence by popular consent and, with handy military backing from his allies in Milan, was immediately made first citizen, becoming 'king in all but name'. For most of the next 300 years, the dynasty remained more or less firmly in Florence's driving seat (*see p16* **Medici cabinet**).

A FAMILY AFFAIR

Cosimo's habit of giving large sums to charity and endowing religious institutions with artworks helped make Florence a centre of artistic production. And by persuading representatives of the Eastern and Western Churches to try to mend their schism at a conference in Florence in 1439, he hosted Greek scholars who could sate his hunger for classical literature.

This artistic and intellectual fervour gathered steam through the long 'reign' of his grandson Lorenzo il Magnifico, which saw Florence become, for a while, the intellectual and artistic centre of the Renaissance that was about to transform Christendom. Under his de facto leadership, Florence enjoyed a long period of relative peace, aided to some extent by

The Renaissance

The Renaissance is a massive source of pride for Florence. For centuries the city has basked in its afterglow, and the world has basked with it. The Florentines have learned to live alongside the perennial swarms of tourists and have grown accustomed to the sight of tour guides marching about their city. Even the most cursory overview of this seminal period in the city's past can substantially increase a visitor's understanding, not just of the history of Florence, but of its architecture, its culture and, above all, its citizens.

The guiding doctrine of the Renaissance (*Rinascimento*, literally 'rebirth') was Humanism – the revival of the language, learning and art of the ancient Greeks and Romans and the reconciliation of this pagan heritage with Christianity. Although the most visible manifestation of the Renaissance in Florence was the astonishing outpouring of art in the 15th century, it was classical studies that sparked the new age.

The groundwork had been done by a handful of men: Dante (1265-1321), Petrarch (1304-74) and Boccaccio (1313-75) had all collected Latin manuscripts, which shaped their approach to writing. But it was mounting Florentine wealth that paid for dedicated manuscript detectives such as Poggio Bracciolini (1380-1459) to dig through neglected monastery libraries across Europe.

A few classical works had never been lost, but those that were known were usually corrupt. The volume of unknown works unearthed was incredible. First came the discovery of Quintilian's *The Training of an Orator*, which detailed the Roman education system, Columella's *De Re Rustica* on agriculture, key texts on Roman architecture by Vitruvius and Frontinus, and Cicero's *Brutus* (a justification of Republicanism). And whereas before very few Greek works were known in Western Europe, suddenly, almost simultaneously, most of Plato, Homer, Sophocles and many other classics were discovered.

The Renaissance focus on a pre-Christian age didn't mean that God was under threat. Just as the Renaissance artists had no compunction about enhancing the beauty of their forms and compositions with classical features and allusions, so Renaissance Humanists sought explanations beyond the Scriptures that were complementary to accepted religion rather than a challenge to it. Much effort was made to present the wisdom of the ancients as a precursor to the ultimate wisdom of God.

Nor did the Renaissance fascination with things semi-scientific – Leonardo's anatomical drawings, for example, or the widespread obsession with the mathematics of Pythagoras – necessarily mean that this was a scientific age. The 15th century was an era when ideas were still paramount and science, as a process of deduction based on observation and experimentation, didn't really get going until the 17th century. In medicine, the theory of the four humours still held sway. Astronomy and astrology were all but synonymous. Mathematics was an almost mystical art, while alchemy, the attempt to transform base metals into gold, flourished.

It was magnificent while it lasted, but Florence's pre-eminence in art and ideas was abruptly snuffed out on the death of Lorenzo il Magnifico in 1492; the invasion by Charles VIII of France in the 1490s and Savonarola's Bonfire of the Vanities (*see p27* **Art attack**) saw to that. In the early 16th century, the cutting-edge switched to Rome, where Michelangelo, Bramante and Raphael were in the process of creating their finest works. Thence, after Emperor Charles V sacked Rome in 1527, to Venice, where masters such as Palladio and Titian practised. But the period left Florence with some of the most important masterpieces and artefacts in the world, thankfully still in existence today, and enjoyed by millions of visitors to the city each year.

For more about three big Renaissance names, *see pp32-35*.

Lorenzo's diplomatic skills in minimising squabbles between Italian states.

This isn't to say that all went smoothly: Lorenzo's relations with Pope Sixtus IV were famously bitter, resulting in excommunication and war; the pope also backed the Pazzi Conspiracy, an assault financed by a rival banking clan, the Pazzi, in which Lorenzo was injured and his brother Giuliano killed during Easter Sunday mass in 1478. Moreover, Lorenzo was more scholar-prince than all-round leader: his lack of economic prowess was to bankrupt the family business and come close to doing the same to his city-state. Though his personal

Medici cabinet

Lorenzo 'Il Magnifico' de' Medici.

The name Medici (pronounced with the stress on the 'e') is all but synonymous with Florence and Tuscany, where a largely well-judged legacy of patronage funded some of the world's greatest artworks. The name's etymology suggests that the family's origins probably lie in the medical profession, though their later wealth was built on banking. Many of their bodies are interred in the Capella Medicee (*see p96*).

Giovanni di Bicci (1360-1429)

The fortune Giovanni di Bicci quietly built up through his banking business – boosted immensely by handling the papal account – provided the basis for the Medici's later clout. Sat on the committee that appointed Ghiberti to make the Baptistry doors.

Cosimo 'il Vecchio' (1389-1464)

Cosimo, Giovanni di Bicci's son, ran Florence informally from 1434, presiding over one of its most prosperous and prestigious eras. An even more astute banker than his father, he spent lavishly on charities and public building projects, introducing a progressive income tax system and balancing the interests of the volatile Florentine classes relatively successfully. In addition to all these achievements, Cosimo was also an intellectual: he encouraged new Humanist learning and developments in art, built up a wonderful public library (the first in Europe) and financed scholars and artists. The name il Vecchio ('the Elder') was a mark of respect.

Piero 'il Gottoso' (1416-69)

All the Medici suffered from gout, but poor Piero the Gouty's joints gave him such gyp that he had to be carried around for half his life. During his short spell at the helm he proved a surprisingly able ruler: he crushed an anti-Medici conspiracy, maintained the success of the Medici bank and patronised the city's best artists and architects.

popularity endured until his death in 1492, it didn't spill over to his son Piero di Lorenzo, who in 1494 handed Florence to the French king Charles VIII as he passed through on the way to conquer Naples – and then fled.

In a violent backlash against the splendour of Lorenzo's times, Florence turned for inspiration and guidance to a fire-and-brimstone-preaching monk who railed against paintings that made the Blessed Virgin Mary 'look like a harlot' and against Humanist thought, which he said would prompt the wrath of the one true and very vengeful God. Girolamo Savonarola (1452-98) perfectly captured the end-of-century spirit, winning the fanatical devotion not only of the poor and uneducated but of the leading minds of Lorenzo's magnificent court. Artists and art patrons willingly threw their works and finery on to the monk's Bonfire of the Vanities in piazza della Signoria in 1497 (*see p27* **Art attack**).

For Savonarola, Charles VIII represented the 'sword of the Lord': the city's capitulation was a just punishment. Savonarola set up a semi-democratic government, firmly allied to him, then allowed his extremist tendencies to get the better of him, alienating the Borgia pope Alexander VI and getting excommunicated. Had Florence been in a better economic state, the pope's gesture may have had little resonance; as it was, the region was devastated by pestilence and starvation. Resentment turned on Savonarola, who was summarily tried and burned at the stake in piazza della Signoria in May 1498.

The republic created after his death was surprisingly democratic but increasingly ineffective, making stronger leadership look

Lorenzo 'il Magnifico' (1449-92)

Cosimo's grandson Lorenzo (*pictured right*) was the major Medici, famous in his own time and legendary in later centuries. His rule marked the peak of the Florentine Renaissance, with artists such as Botticelli and the young Michelangelo producing superlative works under his patronage. Lorenzo was a gifted poet, and gathered round him a supremely talented group of scholars and artists. The climate of intellectual freedom he fostered was a major factor in some of the Renaissance's greatest achievements, and his tactful leadership significantly contributed to bringing peace to Italy. As a businessman, though, he wasn't a patch on his predecessors and the Medici bank suffered a severe decline. Lorenzo maintained a façade of being no more than *primus inter pares* ('first among equals'), but he could be ruthless with his enemies.

Piero di Lorenzo (1471-1503)

Piero couldn't live up to his father Lorenzo: ruthless, charmless and tactless, he had a violent temper, no sense of loyalty and a haughty wife. His father described him as foolish, and he did nothing to help his cause when he surrendered the city to the French in 1494. He spent the rest of his days skulking around Italy, trying to persuade unenthusiastic states to help him regain power in a Florence that had no wish to see his mug again.

Giovanni; Pope Leo X (1475-1521)

Lorenzo il Magnifico's second son wasn't as inept as his brothers; the night before his birth his mother dreamed she would have not a baby but a huge lion. Lorenzo decided early on that Giovanni was destined for a glittering ecclesiastical career, and serious papal ear-bending ensured he became a monk at eight and a cardinal at 16. He elbowed his way into the papacy in 1513. Pope Leo was a likeable, open character and, though lazy, he was a generous host and politically conciliatory. But his exploitation of the sale of indulgences prompted Martin Luther's momentous schism.

Giuliano, Duke of Nemours (1478-1516)

The third son of Lorenzo and an improvement on his brother Piero only in the sense that he was more nonentity than swine, Giuliano was ruler of Florence in name only, being little more than a puppet of his brother, Cardinal Giovanni, who went on to become Pope Leo X.

Giulio; Pope Clement VII (1478-1534)

Lorenzo's illegitimate nephew, Giulio had honours heaped on him by his cousin, Pope Leo. Though neither this nor his disagreeable personality didn't endear him to other cardinals, he swung the papacy in 1524. Pope Clement was notorious for his indecision, irresolution and disloyalty. He abandoned his alliance with Charles V only to regret it when the emperor's troops sacked Rome in 1527. ▶

enticing to disaffected Florentines. In 1502, Piero Soderini, from an old noble family, was elected *gonfalonier*- (banner bearer)-for-life, along the model of the Venetian doge. His pro-French policies brought him into conflict with the pro-Spanish pope Julius II, who had Cardinal Giovanni de' Medici whispering policy suggestions in his ear. In 1512, Soderini went into exile. Giuliano de' Medici, Duke of Nemours, was installed as Florence's most prominent citizen, succeeded by his nephew Lorenzo, Duke of Urbino. The family's already considerable clout was reinforced in 1513 when Giovanni became Pope Leo X.

The Medici clan got a second crack at the papacy in 1524, when Giulio, Lorenzo's illegitimate nephew, became Clement VII. Renowned for his vacillating nature, Clement withdrew his support from Europe's most powerful ruler, the Habsburg emperor Charles V, then dithered for months without reinforcing Rome's fortifications; in 1527, Charles dispatched some troops to show the Medici pope who was boss, Rome was sacked and Clement was forced to slink back to Charles's side, crowning him Holy Roman Emperor in 1529. Meanwhile, back in Florence, the local populace had exploited the Medici ignominy in Rome to reinstall the republic. It was short-lived: Clement had agreed to crown Charles in exchange for a promise of help to get Florence back into Medici hands. The city fell in 1530.

When Clement installed Alessandro, his son, to power in Florence in 1530 and Charles V made him hereditary Duke of Florence, the city entered one of its most desperate periods. Buoyed by support from Charles, whose daughter he had married, the authoritarian

Medici cabinet (continued)

Ferdinando I de' Medici.

Lorenzo, Duke of Urbino (1492-1519)

The son of Piero di Lorenzo was puny, arrogant, high-handed and corrupt. Few wept when he sdied of tuberculosis and syphilis. His only significant legacy was his daughter, Catherine, who, as wife and then widow of Henri II, wielded considerable power in France.

Alessandro (1511-37)

Thought to be Clement's illegitimate son, Alessandro proved to be a bastard by nature as well as by name, abandoning all pretence of respect for the Florentines' treasured institutions and freedoms. Increasingly authoritarian, he tortured and executed his opponents, while managing to outrage the good Florentine burghers by his appalling rudeness and sexual antics. He had a penchant for dressing in women's clothes and riding about town with his bosom buddy and distant cousin, the equally alarming Lorenzino, with whom he would break into nunneries at night. A deputation of senior figures complained to Charles V, to no avail. Lorenzino ultimately had Alessandro stabbed to death.

Cosimo I (1519-74)

With no heir in the direct Medici line, the Florentines chose this obscure 18-year-old, the grandson of Lorenzo il Magnifico's daughter Lucrezia, thinking they could manipulate him. But they could not have been more wrong in their assessment: cold, secretive and cunning, Cosimo set about ruling with merciless efficiency. His general unpleasantness, however, did not stop him from restoring stability in Florence and boosting the city's international image. He was granted the title Grand Duke of Tuscany by Pope Paul V in 1569.

Alessandro trampled on Florentines' traditional rights and privileges while indulging in some shocking sexual antics.

His successor, Cosimo I, had different, though no less unpleasant, defects; nor was he much cop at reversing Tuscany's gentle slide into the economic doldrums. Still, this dark horse – whom the pope made the first Grand Duke of Tuscany in 1569 – at least gave the city a patina of action, extending the writ of the *granducato* to all of Tuscany except Lucca, and adorning the city with vast new *palazzi*, including the Uffizi and Palazzo Pitti.

A SQUALID END

Cosimo's descendants continued to rule for 150 years: they were fittingly poor rulers for what was a very minor statelet in the chessboard of Europe. The *granducato*'s farming methods were backward; the European fulcrum of its core industry, wool-making, like that of its main service industry, banking, had shifted definitively to northern Europe, leaving it to descend inexorably into depression. Its glory – and a very dusty glory it was – hung on its walls and adorned its palaces, with only the occasional spark of intellectual fervour (such as Cosimo II's spirited defence of Galileo Galilei when the astronomer was accused of heresy) to recall what the city had once represented. One 17th-century visitor described Florence as 'much sunk from what it was… one cannot but wonder to find a country that has been a scene of so much action now so forsaken and so poor'.

The male Medici line came to a squalid end in the shape of Gian Gastone, who died in 1737. His pious sister Anna Maria couldn't wait to offload the *granducato*, handing it over to the

Francesco I (1541-87)
Short, skinny, graceless and sulky, Francesco had little in common with his father Cosimo. He retreated into his own little world at any opportunity, to play with his pet reindeer, dabble in alchemy and invent a new process for porcelain production.

Ferdinando I (1549-1609)
Ferdinando (*pictured right*) was an improvement on his brother Francesco. He reduced corruption, improved trade and farming, encouraged learning, and developed both the navy and the port of Livorno. By staging lavish popular entertainments and giving dowries to poor girls, he became the most loved Medici since Lorenzo Il Magnifico, who – coincidentally – had been born exactly one century before Ferdinando.

Cosimo II (1590-1621)
The son of Ferdinando I, Cosimo protected Galileo from a hostile Catholic Church – the only worthwhile thing he would ever do.

Ferdinando II (1610-70)
Porky, laid-back, moustachioed Ferdinando did little to pull Florence from the backwater into which it had sunk. He loved to hunt, eye up boys and collect bric-a-brac.

Cosimo III (1642-1723)
Though trade was drying up and plague and famine stalked the land, Cosimo – a joyless, gluttonous, anti-Semitic loner who hung out with monks (his sulky wife Marguerite-Louise must take some blame for this) – did nothing to improve Tuscany's lot during his 53 years at the helm. Instead, intellectual freedom took a nosedive, taxes soared and public executions were a more or less daily occurrence.

Gian Gastone (1671-1737)
Cosimo's disaster of a son was forcibly married to Anna Maria Francesca of Saxe-Lauenberg, who dragged him off to her gloomy castle near Prague, where he drowned his sorrows in taverns before escaping back to Florence in 1708. He was shocked to find himself Grand Duke in 1723. In the coherent early years of his rule he tried to relieve the tax burden and reinstate citizens' rights but quickly lapsed into chronic apathy and dissolution. Eventually, he wouldn't even get out of bed and was reduced to having boys entertain him by cavorting about.

Anna Maria (died 1743)
Every visitor to Florence since the mid 18th century has reason to be grateful to the straight-laced, pious Anna Maria, who was Gian Gastone's sister and the very last surviving Medici. In her will she bequeathed all Medici property and treasures to the Grand Duchy in perpetuity, on the sole condition that they never leave Florence.

house of Lorraine, cousins of the Austrian Habsburgs. Grand Duke Francis I and his successors spruced up the city, knocked its administration into shape, introduced new farming methods and generally shook the place out of its torpor.

Napoleon's triumphant romp down the peninsula at the end of the 18th century brought him into possession of Tuscany in 1799, to the joy of liberals and the horror of local peasantry, who drove the French out in the Viva Maria uprising, during which they also wreaked their revenge on unlucky Jews and anyone suspected of Jacobin leanings.

But it wasn't long before the French returned, installing Louis de Bourbon of Parma as head of the Kingdom of Etruria in 1801. Napoleon's sister, Elisa Baciocchi, was made Princess of Piombino and Lucca in 1805, and Grand Duchess of Tuscany from 1809 to 1814 – a time that saw much constitutional reform and much pilfering from Florence's art collections. Many of the works spirited off to Paris were returned to Tuscany after the restoration of the Lorraine dynasty in the shape of Ferdinand III in 1816.

UNIFICATION ACROSS THE NATION
By the 1820s and 1830s, under the laid-back if not overly bright Grand Duke Leopold II, Tuscany enjoyed a climate of tolerance that attracted intellectuals, dissidents, artists and writers from all over Italy and Europe. They would meet in the Gabinetto Scientifico-Letterario in Palazzo Buondelmonti in piazza Santa Trinità, frequently welcoming prominent foreigners such as Heine and Byron.

For a time, Leopold and his ministers kept the influence of the Grand Duke's uncle,

Aftermath of the **1966 flood**. *See p22.*

Emperor Francis II of Austria, at arm's length while playing down the growing populist cry for Italian unification. But by the 1840s, it was clear that the nationalist movement posed a serious threat to the status quo. Even relaxed Florence was swept up in nationalist enthusiasm, causing Leopold to clamp down on reformers and impose some censorship. And in 1848 – a tumultuous year of revolutions – insurrections in Livorno and Pisa forced Leopold to grant concessions to the reformers, and they included a Tuscan constitution.

'American bombers swooped in to destroy Campo di Marte station: 218 civilians died; the station remained in perfect working order.'

When news reached Florence that the Milanese had driven the Austrians out of their city, and that Carlo Alberto, King of Sardinia-Piedmont, was determined to push them out of Italy altogether, thousands of Tuscans joined the cause. In 1849, the pendulum seemed to be swinging back in favour of the better-trained Austrians. But radicals in Florence dug in and bullied the Grand Duke into appointing the activist reformer Giuseppe Montanelli, a professor of law at Pisa University, to head a new government. Montanelli went to Rome to attend a constituent assembly, but the alarmed Pope Pius IX threatened to excommunicate anyone taking part in such a gathering.

Leopold panicked, and fled in disguise to Naples. A provisional government was set up but, in the absence of armed support, collapsed. The Florentines invited Leopold back; he returned in July 1849, but brought Austrian troops to keep order. Grim times followed for a city just recovering from one of its worst ever floods. On his return, Leopold seemed content to be an Austrian puppet and clamped down on the press and dissents; his popularity vanished.

In April 1859, Piedmont's Count Camillo Cavour persuaded Napoleon III's France to join him in expelling the Austrians. The French and Piedmontese swept the Austrian armies before them, while in Florence nationalist demos forced the government to resign. On 27 April, Leopold left Florence and his family for the last time. The following year the Tuscan people voted in favour of unification with the Kingdom of Piedmont.

TRUMPING TURIN

Five years later, with Rome holding out against the forces of unification, Florence was declared capital of Italy, much to the annoyance of the Piedmontese capital of Turin – 200 people died

in riots there when the shift was announced. The Florentines greeted their new king with enthusiasm when he arrived in February 1865 to take up residence in Palazzo Pitti, but the influx of northerners was met with mixed feelings: business boomed, but the Florentines didn't take to Piedmontese flashiness.

Huge changes were wrought to the city. Ring roads encircled the old centre, avenues, squares (such as piazza della Repubblica) and suburbs were built and parks were laid out. Intellectuals and socialites crowded the salons and cafés.

When war with Prussia forced the French (who had swapped sides) to withdraw their troops from Italy in 1870, Rome finally fell to Vittorio Emanuele's troops and Italy was united for the first time since the fall of the Roman Empire. Florence's brief reign as capital ended.

FASCISM AND WAR

Florence began the 20th century pretty much as it ended it – as a thriving tourist centre. In the early 1900s, it drew an exclusive coterie of writers, artists, aesthetes and the upper-middle classes. An English-speaking industry sprang up to cater for the needs of these wealthy foreigners.

The city was neither occupied nor attacked in World War I, though it suffered. Post-war hardship inspired a fierce middle-class rage for order that found expression in the black shirt of Fascism. Groups of *squadristi* were already forming in 1919, organising parades and demonstrations in the streets of Florence.

When Mussolini was elected in 1923, there began in Florence a campaign to expunge the city of foreign elements and influences. Hotels and shops with English names were put under pressure to sever their Anglo-Saxon affiliations. The Florence that had been described as a *ville toute anglaise* by the French social-historian Goncourt brothers was under threat.

Italy entered the war on Germany's side on 10 June 1940. The Florentines were confident that their city would never be attacked from the air: Florence was a museum, a testament to artistic evolution, and its monuments were surely its best protection. Nevertheless, the Fascist regime, perhaps for propaganda reasons, began protecting the city's art. Photos of the period show statuary disappearing inside comically inefficient wooden sheds, while the Baptistery doors were bricked up and many main treasures from the Uffizi and Palazzo Pitti were taken to the Castello di Montegufoni – owned by the British Sitwell family – in the Tuscan countryside for safe keeping.

The Germans occupied Florence on 11 September 1943, just weeks after Mussolini's arrest and the armistice was signed. Only when it became necessary to hinder the Nazis' communication lines to Rome were aesthetic scruples set aside. In September 1943, a formation of American bombers swooped in to destroy Florence's Campo di Marte station: the operation was bungled, leaving 218 civilians dead, while the station remained in perfect working order. Further air raids were banned by orders from the highest levels.

At the beginning of the war Florence had a Jewish population of more than 2,000. The chief rabbi saved the lives of many Jews in the city by advising them to hide in convents or little villages under false names. Three raids were carried out by Nazis and Fascists on the night of 27 November 1943. The largest of them was on the Franciscan Sisters of Mary in piazza del Carmine, where dozens of Jews were concealed. The second train to leave Italy bound for the gas chambers set out from Florence, carrying at least 400 Jews from Florence, Siena and Bologna; not one of them is known to have returned.

By 1944, allied commanding officers had extracted permission from their leaders to attack Florence using only the most experienced squadrons, in ideal weather conditions. On 11 March, the Americans began unleashing their bombers on the city, causing casualties but leaving the *centro storico* and its art intact. On 1 August 1944, fighting broke out in various parts of the city, but poorly armed Florentine patriots couldn't prevent the Germans from destroying all the Arno bridges except the ponte Vecchio. Along with the bridges, the old quarter around the ponte Vecchio was razed to the ground.

The Val d'Orcia and Monte Amiata areas in southern Tuscany were key theatres for partisans, who held out with considerable loss of life until British and US infantry reinforced their lines on the Arno on 1 September 1944. The German army abandoned Fiesole a week later. When the Allies eventually reached Florence, they discovered a functioning government formed by the partisan Comitati di Liberazione Nazionale (CLN). Within hours of the Germans' departure, work started to put the bridges back into place. The ponte Santa Trinità was rebuilt, stone by stone, in exactly the same location.

ORDEAL BY FIRE AND WATER

Two decades later, the Florentine skill at restoration was required again, this time for a calamity of an altogether different nature: in the early hours of the morning of 4 November 1966, citizens awoke to find their homes flooded by the Arno, which had broken its banks, and soon all the main *piazze* were under water. An estimated 15,000 cars were destroyed, 6,000 shops put out of business and almost 14,000 families left homeless (*photos pp20-21*). Many artworks, books and archives were damaged, treasures in the refectory of Santa Croce were blackened by mud, and in the church's nave Donatello's *Cavalcanti Annunciation* was soaked with oil up to the Virgin's knees. As word of the disaster spread around the world, public and private funds were pumped into repairs and restoration.

The city's cultural heritage took another direct hit in May 1993, when a bomb planted by the Mafia exploded in the city centre, killing five people. It caused structural damage to the Uffizi, destroying the Georgofili library and damaging the Vasari Corridor. Not that you'd know it now: in a restoration job carried out in record time, one of the world's most-visited art repositories was returned to its pristine state and tourists began queuing outside again, confirming the modern city's vocation for living off its past.

Florence solemnly commemorated the tenth anniversary of the Uffizi bomb in 2003, and seems to have moved on. After several lean years post 9/11, SARS and recession, tourist numbers seem to be up again. However, while the queues to get into the city's most popular museums are as long as ever, there seems to be a general feeling that people are less willing to part with their money, and restauranteurs and shopkeepers in particular continue to grumble. Many tourists don't seem much happier, faced with rising prices and the appalling euro/dollar exchange rate. But while the tourists are tucking into their ribollita, the Florentines are facing major structural changes to their city. The new traffic system around Porta al Prato more or less functions and has alleviated congestion in the area to a certain extent.

However, it's the ongoing (and seemingly neverending) work on the Tramvia – the new tram system – that's now causing traffic chaos in large sections of the city (including the newly freed-up area around porta al Prato), leaving many seriously disgruntled citizens in its wake. Most Florentines are hugely cynical about the project, doubting that the end result will be worth all the disruption and expense, and unhappy about possible repercussions to their beautiful city. On viale Morgagni (near Careggi Hospital), for example, trees lining the road are being cut down to make way for tracks, causing an outcry.

And while some locals accept the idea of tracks passing through the suburbs, residents are united in opposing plans for the tramway to trundle its ugly way past the Duomo. Protest marches and demonstrations have been organised, but the administration appears unwavering. So much for people power.

Florence Today

Despite rising rents and an increase in vandalism, locals remain as loyal to their city as ever.

Renaissance glory dies hard. The Florentines rediscovered the Greek secrets of beauty and tore the drab cloak of medieval mysteries to shreds. They decided that Man (*sic*) would stand naked and be nothing less than genius. They reckoned he should also be smart – and smart men know where the money goes. The Florentines founded the world's first bank and invented the art of 'moving money' by conjuring up that fine financial practice known today as 'credit'. And though the political history of the Florentine city state can hardly be considered democratic, it was certainly revolutionary for its time. Its ruling banker family managed to harness power for centuries without a drop of noble blood running through its veins. The Medici truly bred a match made in heaven; under their government, sound classical philosophy met solid westward moving finance. Florence became a flourishing garden where art blossomed instead of flowers.

What does this have to do with today? Everything. Florence is still a seductive city whose residents know that the Renaissance hasn't really lost its powers of persuasion. Knowing Florence is still a privilege; belonging to her an exclusive right. Florentines are great hosts – they'll entertain you, feed you well, make you laugh, shock you a bit and surround you with beauty – but they will not lend you their hearts with ease. The reason behind their reserve is simple: the Florentines have Florence; they need not open their doors to any other world. Many a Florentine will agree with the accusations of local snobbery, blaming modern provincialism and ancient grandeur for the elitist nature of their townsmen. 'But, *I'm* not a snob,' most will tell you. 'Personally, I like meeting different people.' They are not lying – but such statements should be qualified. In a bar or café, Florentines are occasionally willing to lay aside their feelings of superiority and engage in conversation. Curiosity and casual acquaintance cost nothing, particularly for men. Conversation is spare change and should be spent freely. Debate, biting wit and good-natured political hoopla are never too deeply buried in their pockets. But earning yourself trust that goes beyond the quick tip of a shared cup of coffee is normally a long slog.

To the Florentine mercantile mind, friendship is like good money; it's either been in the family

Purple haze

It's an accepted custom that you should never wear violet to the theatre in Italy; shades of purple are sure to bring bad luck once the curtain comes up. Worn by Catholic priests since medieval times for both Advent and Lent, purple has come to mean 'penitence', and is often considered a variation of black. In Florence, however, violet is thought of as a lucky colour; it's the hallmark hue of the football team, ACF Fiorentina, and, therefore, the symbol of city-wide pride and sport-based patriotism. In Florence, purple is perfect: it's strong enough to blot out the red, white and green of the Italian flag and its ties to Fascist Italy, and bright enough to rival the brilliant blue worn by national sports teams in Italy.

But the Florentine heart was not always violet. In fact, upon its founding in 1926, La Fiorentina's footballers sported shirts inspired by the city's true civic colours. Half red and half white, the jerseys were designed to recall the *comune*'s flag (red lily on white background), created in 1266. The fact the team wears violet today was a bit of a mistake, according to local folklore: in 1929, a distracted laundry maid wrung out the team's wash and let the colours run together, the story goes. Enchanted by the resulting shade and encouraged by the unaffordable thought of buying new jerseys, Fiorentina adopted violet as its team colour.

How red and white blended into violet rather than pink remains an unsolved mystery. Fans, however, are not too worried about chromatic technicalities. When it comes to football mythology, ACF Fiorentina deserves that leap of faith. Violet is the colour of the iris – the flower that means fidelity. It's also the colour of bruises: the bottom line is that when the game hurts, you've got to keep believing. Florentines aren't blue-bloods and don't bleed red – violet runs through their veins.

for generations, or it's hard-earned and very carefully spent. Sentiment belongs in a savings account – easy access makes it vulnerable. 'We Florentines are exclusive about what we wear, what we eat and how we spend our time,' Paola, a local woman, asserts. 'Should we be less choosy about whom we show affection to?'

Such a sentiment betrays a common central Italian conviction. In Tuscany, emotion is a well-weighed personal choice, not a sudden spontaneous feeling. While southern Italians may gracefully succumb to their emotions, central Italians deftly craft theirs into something that stands with grace. Tuscan love obeys the laws of the artisan, it's a work of craftsmanship that can be moulded at will and chiselled to fit creative whims.

The reserved facet of the local character can partly be explained by Florence's deep-rooted suspiciousness of its neighbouring cities. The Sienese have supposedly been traitorous since 1082; loathing for the Pisans is slightly more recent; while distaste for the Milanese can be traced to the Battle of Anghiari in 1440. And a local tirade on regional relations normally ends with 'those thieving Roman wolves' stealing Florence's status as capital in 1871.

One can easily witness Florentines' 'modern' fear of invasion as the city struggles to uphold its role as cultural mecca to the world. The ratios are noteworthy: 400,000 resident Florentines compared to some six million visiting tourists annually. Florentine efforts to maintain and manage their guests often crowd the headlines of local papers where journalists bemoan the city's 'deterioration'. The San Lorenzo area, with its super-central market, has become a much-mentioned clean-up target as petty crime becomes more common and illegal commerce of counterfeit products spirals out of control. In response to merchants' appeals, City Hall has adopted a 'zero tolerance' policy for illegal immigrant vendors – 70 per cent of whom may be without residency papers or work permits. In September 2007, this move was extended to a crackdown on car windscreen cleaners at traffic lights, making the practice a criminal offence. 'The city says *zero tolleranza*, but the illegal vendors are everywhere,' explains Mauro, a native shopkeeper. 'They lay their counterfeit wares on sheets, but once they've scooped them up and closed the bag, it's a violation of privacy for an officer to carry out a search. If you're fast, you're innocent.'

Questionable commerce is not the only problem plaguing the centre. Evidently, medieval urban planners could not foresee the needs of 21st-century traffic. City Hall proposed its controversial answer to 'car control' in 2004 by beginning to build a low-frame tram system. Supporters estimate that once completed, its three lines will host 71 million trips per year – enough to cut traffic in the centre by 50 per cent. But with years of delays, opponents argue that 'Tramvia' is just another word for trouble, being high on cost and low on innovation; banning cars in exchange for an already obsolete tram system may actually foster pollution rather than fight it.

And while citizens in via Talenti tire of living in a perennial construction zone, areas like Santo Spirito, the beloved bohemian quarter on the other side of the Arno, come to terms with a more human brand of pollution: vandalism. Crimes against the arts are on the up, and the church, short on surveillance funds, has been forced to close its doors for months at a time. Several vandalism attacks against the Fountain of Neptune, in piazza della Signoria, have also attracted international attention. When the sea god's hand was pulled off and suffered 30 fractures under the weight of a drunken youth in August 2005, private sponsors shelled out €11,000 to fix the white giant. 'It's not that tourism promotes vandalism. In fact, the opposite may even be true. It's just that the more people we host, the harder it is to maintain public order,' one city official said.

'The city should thank tourists, not charge them.'

The need for city surveillance cameras, increased police support and more effective litter-control prompted officials to consider passing a 2006 bill known as the 'tourist tax'. In true amusement-park style, visitors would be charged a €5 administrative fee to enter the city gates. Florentines would be exempt from the tax, but commuters would be obliged to purchase their tickets along with visiting travellers. The bill did not gain the approval of the city council, but the public debate that ensued is still alive and well. 'Is it wrong to expect reimbursement for city maintenance? Florence lives on past glory, but sustains costs that belong to this day and age,' one admissions supporter affirms. Opponents, however, voice concern. 'Tourism is a huge money-making industry. The city should thank tourists, not charge them,' a shopkeeper on via Calzaoli argues.

But many Florentines maintain that the real problem is that Florentines can no longer afford to live here. Recent studies show Tuscany is the costliest region in Italy, a worrisome statistic if you consider that average earnings in 2007 were little more than €1,000 per month. And while the majority of Tuscan homes are privately owned, almost a third of the population face monthly rental costs that suck up 80 per cent of their incomes. Spring 2007 saw more than 8,000 Florentine families evicted from their centrally located homes.

'*Firenze non è più dei Fiorentini*' ('Florence no longer belongs to the Florentines') is thus becoming a common phrase, coined to reflect the frustration of citizens who find themselves forced to seek housing outside the city walls. As rental costs and market demands make the six square miles of *centro storico* off-limits to local families, the historic centre has become a haven for the city's brimming foreign student population. Extended-stay visitors with fat foreign wallets, and low-income immigrants who crowd multiple families into tiny central flats, inevitably fuel the age-old fear of invasion.

The Florentine 'closed' attitude towards 'the other' isn't all bad, however. It's the Florentines' fear of invasion that ultimately fosters their unique sense of clarity. People may push from all sides but the Florentines choose their cultural battles and stand firm. 'Welcome tourists from far and wide. Some things are not negotiable.' That's the unwritten rule that should hang above the turnstiles, should they ever choose to charge admission at the gates.

City-based loyalty, for example, is paramount. To the Florentine, Florence is mother and lover. Betrayal, either philosophical or physical, is never cheap. Loyalty to the local football club weighs heavier than allegiance to the national side. Let other Italians revel in World Cup glory – the people dancing on top of cars in piazza Duomo in 2006 were not from Florence; although locals would not openly begrudge the Blue Shirts their title as world champions, their loyalty lies only with ACF Fiorentina. Enemies in league games are rivals even when camouflaged by the Italian uniform. While celebrating Italian success may seem tempting, their city pride never lets them savour such victory for long.

But that's what you get when you live under the wing of such an enchanting town – the quasi obsessive need to constantly pledge your allegiance to it. 'Florence is the world's most beautiful city,' is not an opinion, it's an axiom. 'But is the idea arguable?' you may wonder. Of course it is. All things are arguable in Florence.

And if you do choose to dispute the point, you may be surprised. Florentines very readily admit the downfalls of their city. It's unbearably provincial, and shamefully nostalgic of the past. There's too much traffic, and not enough innovation. It's utterly suffocating in summer, and painfully slow to adopt new policies. And yet – for locals – there's nowhere else to go; its loveliness is the only air worth breathing. When all is said and done, Florence's beauty reigns supreme. Debatable? Yes. Negotiable? Never.

Linda Falcone's book Italian, It's All Greek to Me: Everything You Don't Know About Italian Language and Culture *is published by RDR Books.*

Fra Angelico's **Annunciation** in the **Museo di San Marco**.

Art

The cradle of the Italian Renaissance is unrivalled in the breadth of its artistic treasures.

UNESCO estimates that Italy contains up to 60 per cent of the world's most important works of art, over half of which are located in Florence. Considered the spritual home of the Renaissance, Florence and its environs spawned a huge number of great artists such as Michelangelo, Botticelli, Leonardo and Fra Angelico. The wealthy families of Florence entrusted these artists to decorate their palaces, chapels, and city with sumptuous images that would never be forgotten. This kept Florence at the forefront of the artistic and intellectual world during the 15th and 16th centuries, as poets, artists and philosophers mingled in the city, vying for patronage and fame.

MEDIEVAL MONEY

To find art, you need to follow the money. And in the case of Florence the trail takes you back to the medieval cloth and banking businesses that were the foundations of the city's wealth. In the 1320s, the Bardi, a powerful banking family, commissioned **Giotto** (1267-1337) to decorate their chapel in the church of Santa Croce (*see p103*). Here, Giotto demonstrates the stylistic shift between medieval and early Renaissance painting. Although obscured by tombs and damaged by the 1966 flood, the figures in the *Funeral of St Francis* are set in a believable environment with an outpouring of human emotion. As seen in his design for the Duomo's bell tower, Giotto's style is characterised by clarity and simplicity, rendering his works legible and accessible.

Also in the church of Santa Croce is a painted *Crucifix* by Giotto's predecessor, **Cimabue** (1240-1302). With its ties to the previous Byzantine tradition, this work brings Giotto's naturalism into focus. The Uffizi (*see p88*) provides direct comparisons between the two artists, with Cimabue's *Maestà* (1285-6) hanging beside Giotto's *Ognissanti Madonna* (1300-10).

Ignoring the new naturalism of Giotto, **Andrea Orcagna** (1308-68) fashioned his tabernacle in the church of Orsanmichele (1359; *see p86*) in the more popular Gothic style. This highly decorative structure protected the miracle-working image of the Virgin and is inlaid with marble, lapis lazuli, gold and glass.

THE 'REBIRTH'

The Renaissance refers to a literary, intellectual and artistic movement that flourished in Florence between the 14th and 16th centuries (*see also p15* **The Renaissance**). Artists, writers and scholars reinterpreted the classical heritage of the Roman Empire, rediscovering its philosophy, art, sculpture, architecture and literature. Prior to the 14th century, the Catholic Church had primarily commissioned works of art, but this was set to change. As bankers, merchants, and princes became wealthier, the demand for secular art grew.

The 1401 competition for the east doors of the Baptistery saw **Filippo Brunelleschi** (1377-1446) lose out to **Lorenzo Ghiberti** (1378-1455). In a huff, Brunelleschi left for Rome to study the art of the ancients. But he had the last laugh: on his return to Florence, he built the majestic cupola for the Duomo (1420-36; *see also p80* **Seeing beyond the façade**).

As the demand for art grew, so did the number of workshops, in which apprentices learned to paint and sculpt alongside the masters. The workshop of **Luca della Robbia** (1400-82), for example, generated his signature glazed terracotta reliefs that grace prominent structures in Florence, such as Orsanmichele, Brunelleschi's Spedale degli Innocenti (*see p102*) and the interior of the Duomo (*see p77*).

As a young apprentice in the workshop of Ghiberti, **Donatello** (1386-1466) worked on the Baptistery doors. Like Brunelleschi, he had studied in Rome, and his Orsanmichele statues of *St Mark* (1411) and *St George* (1416), now in the Bargello, demonstrate his ability to create naturalistic drapery over believable bodies.

Commissioned by Cosimo I de' Medici, Donatello's *David* (1430), now also in the Bargello (*see p104*), was the first free-standing life-size nude bronze since antiquity. It was originally designed to stand on the buttress of Florence Cathedral. But in 1416, the Priory of the Republic decided that the statue should become a symbol of the Florentine Republic, so *David* was placed in a more prominent position in Palazzo dei Priori (*see also p28* **Statues of stature**).

Andrea del Verrocchio (1435-88) eventually replaced Donatello as the leading sculptor in Florence, and his *Christ and Doubting Thomas* (1476-83) takes on a new dimension as its figures step out of a niche in the exterior of the Orsanmichele (*see p86*). This skilled composition shows an acute awareness of anatomy. Verrocchio, like Donatello, worked for the Medici (*see p16* **Medici cabinet**), creating the tomb of Piero and Giovanni in the Old Sacristy of San Lorenzo (1469-72), as well as the charming *Putto with Dolphin* fountain (1470) in the Palazzo Vecchio.

Early Renaissance painting took its cue from sculpture, attempting to create the same sense of naturalism on a two-dimensional scale. Brunelleschi's theory of linear perspective became a tool for the realistic representation of distance and depth. Perspective was first applied to painting by artists such as **Masaccio** (1401-28), particularly in his *Trinità* fresco in Santa Maria Novella (1427; *see p95*) and, with the help of **Masolino** (1400-47), the fresco cycle in the Cappella Brancacci (1425; *see p109*). Similarly, **Paolo Uccello** (1396-1475) experimented with foreshortening and a sense of perspective in works such as *The Battle of San Romano* (1435) in the Uffizi, and the fresco of *John Hawkwood* (1436) in the Duomo.

Piero della Francesca (1416-92) was active in Florence in the 1430s, both as a painter and as an author of treatises on perspective and mathematics. His *Legend of the True Cross* fresco cycle (c1453-65), in Arezzo, reveals his adherence to mathematical order by his treatment of natural and architectural elements, which recede into the distance.

Dominican friar **Fra Angelico** (1400-55) also used perspective when creating his sublime frescoes in the monastery (now museum) of San Marco (*see p99*), using them as an extension of reality. His *Annunciation* (1440-41) mirrors the architecture of the monks' cells, adding a new sense of immediacy. The stark style of Fra Angelico reflects the humility of his religious order and the function of the monastery as a place of meditation.

Art attack

Everyone knows that Florence has a higher concentration of art than anywhere else in the world. But an untold number of lost artworks will never be appreciated. We can lay the blame for a number of these losses at the feet of Girolamo Savonarola.

With a beak-like nose and burning eyes, Savonarola was a fanatical Dominican monk famous for his fiery sermons. On 7 February 1497, he called on the people of Florence to cleanse the city of its sins by throwing material objects on to a 'Bonfire of the Vanities'. The bonfire, held in piazza della Signoria, was huge at 18 metres (60 feet) high and 12 metres (40 feet) wide.

Priceless works of art by Botticelli and Michelangelo are known to have been lost here, and rumour has it that the artists threw the paintings on the fire themselves.

Other burned items included gambling tables, pornography, mirrors, cosmetics, women's hats, chess pieces, musical instruments and 'immoral' books. Savonarola met a sticky end on 23 May 1498, when he was publicly hanged and burned in piazza della Signoria, at the exact spot on which he'd held his bonfire.

Statues of stature

The Rape of the Sabine Women

By Giambologna, 1583. Loggia dei Lanzi (see p84).

Undoubtedly one of the most violent sculptures displayed in the Loggia dei Lanzi, Giambologna's *The Rape of the Sabine Women* is a powerful, evocative and artistically accomplished work, said to have been created from the largest piece of marble ever seen in Florence.

The sculpture was commissioned for the loggia by the Grand Duke Francesco I and relates the mythological story of the Sabine women who were ruthlessly raped by Roman officers. It was a story that symbolised Roman power and triumph.

However, Giambologna was more interested in creating a sense of energy and vitality in the spiralling movement of his figures and in the facial expressions of the woman and two men. With his complex group of figures, densely interwoven, twisting dynamically, Giambologna creates a sculpture packed with tension and emotion that can be viewed from all angles.

Mary Magdalene

By Donatello, 1455. Museo dell'Opera del Duomo (see p82).

Gnarled and withered, Mary Magdalene is both grotesque and strangely alluring. Carved out of solid poplar, she's depicted after her 30 years of atonement in the wilderness. She's clothed only in her matted hair, which envelops her scared and emaciated form.

Despite the ugliness of his imagined subject, Donatello portrays Mary Magdalene with incredible sensitivity. Take a careful look at the sculpture: she has beautiful high cheek bones, delicately formed ankles, soft eyes, fine, long fingers, and a slight nose. Her eyes are not focused on any worldly object but, seemingly, on an inner spiritual reality. With her hands slightly raised and her mouth open, it looks as if she's praying.

During some extensive restoration work on the sculpture in the 1960s, it was revealed that Donatello had originally gilded her hair and painted her skin a light brown colour, as though it had been tanned during her time in the wilderness.

The Rape of the Sabine Women.

Mary Magdalene.

David

By Michelangelo, c1501-1504. Galleria dell' Accademia (see p99), plus copies in piazza della Signoria and piazzale Michelangelo.

Undoubtedly *the* most celebrated Renaissance sculpture in Florence, *David* was created from a single block of marble from nearby Carrara that was incredibly narrow and filled with cracks.

David symbolises the beauty and the strength of the human body. His muscles are taut and his veins swell with tension as he contemplates his enemy. His face conveys both concentration and determination before battle.

Michelangelo worked on *David* for three years behind shuttered scaffolding. After Michelangelo had completed his work, the statue was kept hidden for two months until a brass girdle had been made for his waist, in order to keep his manhood hidden from a prudish public.

David was originally intended as an outdoor sculpture, and stood in piazza della Signoria until 1873.

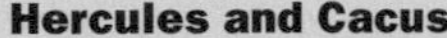

Hercules and Cacus

By Baccio Bandinelli. Piazza della Signoria (see p82).

Criticised for being lumpy and lifeless, *Hercules and Cacus* has courted controversy ever since its installation outside Palazzo Vecchio. Benvenuto Cellini said it resembled 'a sack full of melons', and when the marble block from which it was carved fell into the river in transit, many joked that it had tried to commit suicide.

Commissioned to symbolise Florence's strength and Cosimo de' Medici's return to power, it was designed to complement the sculptures in piazza della Signoria, which included *David* and the *Fountain of Neptune*.

The sculpture depicts Hercules in the moments after he's killed the firebreathing monster, Cacus, during his tenth labour. But Bandinelli has failed to humanise his sculpture or capture any emotion. The torsos look awkward, rigid and proportionally unrealistic.

Unfortunately for Bandinelli, he is remembered more for his difficult character than for the quality of his sculptures.

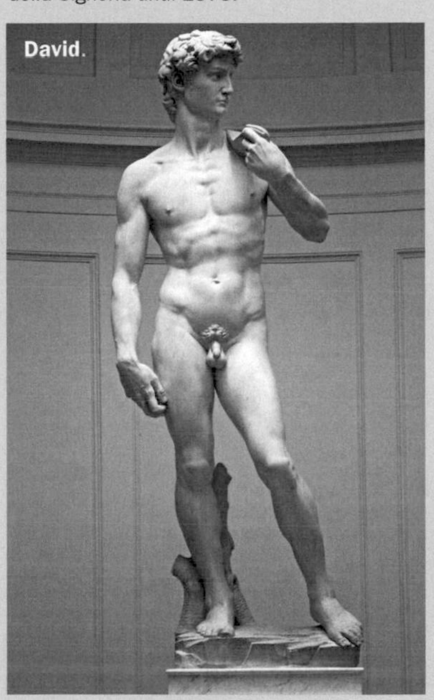

David.

Hercules and Cacus.

Where to see it

Perfect paintings, fab frescoes

Botticelli: *Birth of Venus* and *Primavera*, Uffizi (*see p88*).
Della Francesca: *Legend of the True Cross* fresco cycle, Arezzo (*see p27 and p276*).
Fra Angelico: *Annunciation*, Museo di San Marco (*see p99*).
Giotto: frescoes depicting the life of St Francis, Cappella Bardi di Vernio, Santa Croce (*see p26 and p103*).
Leonardo (with Verrocchio): *Baptism of Christ*, Uffizi (*see p88*).

Stupendous statues

Cellini: *Perseus*, Loggia dei Lanzi (*see p84*).
Donatello: *Saint George*, Bargello (*see p103*).
Giambologna: *The Rape of the Sabine Women*, Loggia dei Lanzi (*see p84*).
Michelangelo: *David*, Galleria dell'Accademia (*see p29 and p99*).
Verrocchio: *Putto with Dolphin*, Palazzo Vecchio (*see p86*).

Lesser-known treasures

Del Sarto: *Last Supper*, Museo del Cenacolo di Andrea del Sarto (*see p113*).
Ghirlandaio: Cappella Sassetti, church of Santa Trinità (*see p91*).
Gozzoli: frescoes in the Cappella dei Magi, Palazzo Medici Riccardi (*see p30 and p96*).
Martini *Annunciation*, Uffizi (*see p88*).
Orcagna: tabernacle, Orsanmichele (*see p86*).

Placing a biblical event in a contemporary Florentine context became acceptable during the Renaissance, providing a new way for lay people to understand and connect with the story. It also became commonplace to depict one's patron in a prominent position. In his painting of the Cappella dei Magi (1459-60) in Palazzo Medici Riccardi (*see p96*), **Benozzo Gozzoli** (1420-97) depicts Lorenzo de' Medici as one of the participants in this lavish procession. Gozzoli also painted himself appearing among the crowd, reflecting a growing self-awareness of 'the artist' during this period. For instance, **Domenico Ghirlandaio** (1449-94) looks out at us from his frescoes in the Cappella Sassetti in the church of Santa Trinità (1483-85; *see p91*).

Filippo Lippi (1406-69), a Carmelite friar, had little interest in creating an illusion of the real world. In his *Madonna with Child and Angels* (1465) in the Uffizi, he depicts a fantastic background scene behind his pearl-adorned Madonna that disregards the laws of perspective and human anatomy.

Filippo passed his linear style on to his pupil, **Sandro Botticelli** (1445-1510). The figures in both *Primavera*, or *Allegory of Spring* (c1482), and *The Birth of Venus* (1476-87), commissioned by the Medici and now in the Uffizi, are infused with grace and idealised beauty, and seem to float just above the ground.

PINNACLE OF ACHIEVEMENT

The artists of the 15th century developed the tools and methods that would characterise the artistic activity in the century that followed. These artists surpassed their own masters in their quest for ideal beauty, balanced proportions and structured compositions.

Leonardo da Vinci (1452-1519) emerged from the workshop of Verrocchio when he helped his master paint the *Baptism of Christ* (1469-80), now in the Uffizi. A true 'Renaissance man', Leonardo was not only a skilled painter but also a sculptor, architect, engineer and scientist. His exploration of the natural world as a scientist also manifested itself in his art, which reflects his sensitive observation of nature. Da Vinci experimented extensively with oils, developing the *sfumato* technique, which creates atmospheric and subtle shading. This can clearly be seen in the carefully structured *Annunciation* (1472) in the Uffizi.

Another quintessential Florentine Renaissance artist was **Michelangelo Buonarroti**, better known as Michelangelo (1475-1564). He was catapulted to fame with his idealised male nude statue, *David* (1501-04; *see p29* **Statues of stature**), quickly lauded as the greatest work of sculpture ever created. Though a copy remains in piazza della Signoria (*see p82*), the original is now in the Accademia, along with the *Slaves* (1527-28) – half-finished sculptures that reveal Michelangelo's method of removing excess stone to reveal the 'pre-existing spirit' of the statue. For more about Leonardo and Michelangelo, *see pp32-35*.

MIND YOUR MANNERISM

The late period of the High Renaissance, dating from 1520 until 1600, is known as Mannerism. The term originates from the Italian *maniera*, meaning 'style' or 'manner', and is characterised by complicated compositions, bright garish colours, exaggerated forms and a heightened sense of drama. To a certain extent this art movement symbolised the anxiety and confusion that was widely felt in Italy as a result of the Protestant Reformation and the weakening power of the Catholic Church. Mannerism is also considered to be a violent reaction against the order and harmony of Renaissance art.

One of the leading artists of this style was **Andrea del Sarto** (1486-1530). A contemporary of Michelangelo and Raphael, del Sarto was an equally graceful painter and skilled draughtsman. His *Madonna of the Harpies* altarpiece (1517) in the Uffizi is a fine example of Mannerist painting, as is his *Last Supper* (1526-7), in the refectory of the monastery of San Salvi.

Giorgio Vasari (1511-74) also belonged to the Mannerist circle. In 1571, he began the fresco that decorates the interior of the Duomo's cupola, which was later completed by the Roman artist **Federico Zuccari**. Vasari is also the architect responsible for the Uffizi, but is perhaps best remembered for his book *The Lives of the Artists*, a collection of biographies.

Florence is also home to a number of pieces of outstanding Mannerist sculpture – some on public display in the piazza della Signoria and in the Loggia dei Lanzi within it – reflecting the military strength of the Medici administration under the Grand Duke of Tuscany, Cosimo I de' Medici. **Benvenuto Cellini's** (1500-71) life-size *Perseus* (1545-54) is a chilling reminder of the duke's authority, combining an appreciation for Renaissance sculptors with the elegance of Mannerism. **Giambologna** (or Giovanni da Bologna; 1524-1608) created the statue of Cosimo I on horseback (1598) as well as *Hercules and Centaur* (1599) and *The Rape of the Sabine Women* (1582; *see p28* **Statues of stature**), both also to be found in the Loggia dei Lanzi.

MODERN MASTERS

Apart from a few Florentines, such as **Ludovico Cardi** ('Cigoli'; 1559-1613), **Cristoforo Allori** (1577-1621) and **Carlo Dolci** (1616-87), the most important artists were working in Rome in the 17th century. The Medici family, however, invited several artists to their court. **Pietro da Cortona** (1596-1669), for instance, decorated the state apartments in Palazzo Pitti in the 1630s). During this time the Florentine *pietra dura* technique of decorating with inlaid marble was developed.

By the 18th century, Florence was an essential stop on the Grand Tour. The Accademia delle Belle Arti (1784) became the centre of artistic activity during the 18th and 19th centuries, when Romantic and Naturalist styles prevailed.

Throughout the Napoleonic occupation of the city (1799-1814) Florence followed the French neoclassicists. A group of artists known as the Macchiaioli met while frequenting Florence's Caffè Michelangelo, united by social, political and artistic discontent. Their name, 'stain-makers', or 'splatterers', refers to their style, comprising patches of colour and inspired by French Impressionism and the Barbizon School. Leading Macchiaioli include **Giovanni Fattori** (1825-1908), **Telemaco Signorini** (1835-1901) and **Silvestro Lega** (1826-95), and their works are housed in the Galleria d'Arte Moderna section of the Palazzo Pitti (*see p107*).

Perhaps the most renowned Florentine artist of the 20th century is **Marino Marini** (1901-80), whose museum is in the former church of San Pancrazio (*see p93*). Marini devoted himself to sculpture around the 1920s, experimenting with terracotta, bronze and coloured plaster.

A number of artists still work in the Florence area. Among them is the painter **Roberto Barni** (born 1939), known for his large monochrome canvases; **Paolo Staccioli** (born 1943), whose ceramic sculpture focuses on human figures and animals on the move; and Tuscan sculptor **Enzo Pazzagli**, who specialises in outdoor sculptures with multiple layers, superimposed on each other. Much of Pazzagli's work can be seen at his Art Park on via Sant'Andrea a Rovezzano.

Fans of contemporary art might not be able to sate their hunger in Florence itself, but a trip to the **Centro per l'arte Contemporanea Luigi Pecci** in Prato (*see p214*) should go some way to doing so.

See also pp32-35 and pp181-82.

Enzo Pazzagli's **Art Park.**

Renaissance Reborn

A hidden Leonardo, an incomplete Michelangelo and the daring of Galileo: three modern Renaissance controversies.

'Art is never finished, only abandoned.' So said Leonardo da Vinci, to many the embodiment of the Renaissance, the age we associate most closely with Florence. He also claimed there were three classes of people: 'those who see, those who see when they are shown, those who do not see.' His words are particularly fitting for modern-day Florence, where the themes of vision and the invisible are the driving forces behind three exciting projects that will raise interest in three of Tuscany's greatest names – **Leonardo**, **Michelangelo** and **Galileo** – to unprecedented levels.

THE FABLED FRESCO

It is a widespread misconception that all of Florence's major Renaissance masterpieces are a result of the enlightened Medici patronage. In fact, the city's most representative individual piece of artwork, Michelangelo's *David*, was commissioned by the Repubblica Fiorentina in 1501 as an embodiment of republican anti-tyranny virtues, at a time when the Medici dynasty had been temporarily overthrown (1494-1512) and exiled, and Piero Soderini was the Gonfalonier of Justice.

A couple of years later the same patron, artist and underlying theme lay behind a project that might well have proved to be the zenith of Renaissance art: two mural paintings for the Council Hall (now called Salone dei Cinquecento or Hall of the Five Hundred) in **Palazzo Vecchio** (*see p86*). The plan would have seen Leonardo da Vinci and Michelangelo Buonarroti working back to back in the great hall, each busy on a huge battle scene: the *Battle* *of Anghiari* for Leonardo, and the *Battle of Cascina* for Michelangelo. Both battles had been fought by Florentine citizens and not mercenary armies; their immortalisation was intended to stir up civic pride and rally the city to the republican cause.

The concurrent painting project would have been 'the ultimate contest between the 52-year-old maestro and the young emergent genius half his age', according to historian Paul Strathern: Leonardo the supreme empiricist, executing an unprecedented marriage of science and art, with no place in his work for God; and Michelangelo, unable to stop thinking about his deity, trying to embody man's spirituality in his work. Given the fierce mutual dislike between the two characters, there is little doubt that they would have gone out of their way to outdo each other – if they hadn't fallen to blows in the meantime.

'Might Vasari have built his new wall at a small distance from the original, in order to protect Leonardo's work?'

Sadly for visitors to Florence, Michelangelo's progress stopped at the preparatory cartoon stage when he was summoned to Rome in 1505 by Pope Julius II to start work on his tomb. Leonardo, however – who had about one year's head start – began his mural in the summer of 1505, probably completing 15 to 20 square metres (160 to 210 square feet) of the centrepiece, a fierce clash of horses depicting the Fight for the Standard. However, parts of the experimental oil-based paint dripped, and the painting was left unfinished when he moved to Milan in 1506.

Contemporary documentary evidence confirms that Leonardo's *Battle* was still visible as late as 1549, when Anton Francesco Doni advised a friend: 'Having ascended the stairs of the Salone Grande, take a diligent view of a group of horses [a portion of Leonardo's battle], which will appear a miraculous thing to you.' In 1563, though, the reinstated Medici rulers asked court architect Giorgio Vasari to remodel the hall, and wipe out anything celebrating the Republic – including, we can only assume, Leonardo's work. Alas, Vasari complied, and all we are left with are a few drawings and copies (see our reconstruction on p32, which uses a copy by Peter Paul Rubens), showing us how distinctively and powerfully the two art titans had tackled their given topics.

Or maybe not. Maurizio Seracini, a biomedical engineer turned art 'diagnostician' (a word he borrows from medicine), has been looking for evidence of Leonardo's mural since 1975, when he started experimenting with alternative uses for medical devices. For 30 years Seracini has been re-engineering a battery of medical and military technology – laser beams, fiber-optics, ultrasound, X-rays, infrared, thermography and UV devices – and turning them towards art.

Experimental and archival research both infer that the East wall (the one you face when entering the Salone dei Cinquecento today) was the one entrusted to Leonardo. Tantalisingly, in 1975 Seracini noticed a green flag in Vasari's *Battle of Marciano* bearing two tiny words in white paint: *'Cerca trova'* ('Seek and you shall find'). Further examination confirmed that the words were coeval with the rest of the painting. Could they be Vasari's clue for posterity? Lo and behold! While mapping the Salone with pulse laser beams and a thermo-scanner Seracini detected a three-centimetre (one-inch) gap right behind Vasari's *'cerca trova'* mural. Might Vasari have built his new brick wall at a small distance from the original, in order to protect Leonardo's work? We know that he saved at least one other art masterpiece by screening it with a wall when making renovations: Masaccio's groundbreaking fresco of the Holy Trinity in the church of **Santa Maria Novella** (*see p95*), which Vasari replaced with a more modern altar, and which was accidentally uncovered in the 19th century.

Seracini desperately needed a way to identify the possible presence of pigments beyond Vasari's wall. The answer came from yet another scientific discipline: at an astrophysics congress, Professor Raymond DuVarney of Emory University, Atlanta, suggested that neutron-activation analysis might reveal traces of chemicals in the hidden paint mixtures – if they exist – by measuring the gamma rays emitted by the different chemical compounds used to make 16th-century paint. Funded by a pool of private sponsors, a device was built and successfully tested on a replica wall. A fine-tuned, portable version of this appliance will send beams of neutrons through Vasari's *'cerca trova'* wall, and should reveal whether it hides anything; and if so, roughly what.

Seracini's theory is supported by a number of eminent academics from around the world. Some experts are more cautious, but even among them Seracini's reputation had a sudden boost in 2001-02, when he revealed the stunning Leonardo drawing hidden beneath the clumsy monochrome paint (applied at a later stage by another hand) in the *Adoration of the Magi* in the **Uffizi** (*see p88*).

As a result, a panel of experts and officials was nominated in May 2007, and as we went to press the Italian culture minister officially announced the final pursuit for Leonardo's lost mural. However, what many fear is that even if Seracini's theory proved correct, little or nothing may be left of the *Battle* on account of Leonardo's experimental technique, which may not have survived intact; experimentation with technique would let Leonardo down, after all, with his masterful but flawed *Last Supper* in Milan's Santa Maria delle Grazie.

But what would Florence's art guardians do if faced with one masterpiece obscured by another? In 1979, two square metres (21.5 square feet) of Vasari's *Battaglia di Torre* were removed from the west wall as part of the search, but nothing was found. Authorities – understandably – are being more cautious about taking another risk. However, if traces of the Leonardo are found, there is little doubt that they would detach Vasari's fresco and remove enough of the wall to have a better look behind.

THE UNFINISHED FAÇADE

Just over a decade after the abortive Salone dei Cinquecento project, Julius II had been replaced as pontiff by Leo X (formerly Giovanni de' Medici, a son of Lorenzo il Magnifico). The influence of this character – whose favourite food was peacock tongues and who owned a pet elephant – would help cement his family's influence in Florence once more.

In 1516, Michelangelo won a competition called by the pope to erect a marble façade for the basilica of **San Lorenzo** (*see p98*), the Medici family church in Florence. A late wooden model in the **Casa Buonarroti** museum (*see p104*) shows how grand Michelangelo's winning project was. He came up with an ingenious solution to a problem that regularly beset Renaissance architects: how to apply classical orders to the irregular heights of basilican churches. His answer was to conceal the three naves behind an imposing marble front on two levels, splendidly decorated with a wealth of freestanding greater than life-size statues. The commission was formally signed in 1518, and the vast extant correspondence and sketches attest to Michelangelo's eagerness: for over two years he personally supervised all the work, including the opening of marble quarries on Monte Altissimo in the territory of **Pietrasanta** (*see p271*). His façade, Michelangelo wrote, would be the 'mirror of architecture and sculpture of all Italy'.

Then, to Michelangelo's great frustration, in 1520 the pope changed his mind and decided to shift his funds to works for the **New Sacristy** (*see p97*) and the **Laurentian Library** (*see p98*) instead. The façade was left in its unfinished state, all the architectural elements already built were dispersed, and the marble already quarried was relocated elsewhere. We know from Vasari's writings that one huge marble column had already been shipped up the Arno from Pietrasanta, and was left lying by the church until it was decided to inter it in the square by the church side on account of the rubbish that kept amassing behind it. San Lorenzo briefly became the focus for a façade project when Anna Maria Luisa, the last Medici (who bequeathed all her family's art treasures to the City of Florence), in the last few years before her death in 1743, considered a new project for the façade, but again the plan failed to materialise.

And so the matter rested, largely undisturbed – until 2007, when the City of Florence decided to honour the anniversary of Anna Maria Luisa's death on 18 February with projections of a 'virtual façade' on San Lorenzo's bare brick front (*photo p35*). Based on three-dimensional models computer generated to Michelangelo's design by architect Paolo Bertoncini Sabatini and Professor Gabriele Morolli of Florence University, the projections were meant to attract sponsors for an even grander display set to happen in 2008: a life-size reconstruction of Michelangelo's façade, in fabric or plastic – probably in front of the current church. Meanwhile, a hotel chain is suggesting a new competition to see how modern contenders would rival Michelangelo's project (on paper, at least).

This resurgence in interest was prompted by the recent discovery in a marble warehouse near Pietrasanta of three columns that might pertain to the set quarried by Michelangelo for his façade: the height, size and marble type match the identikit perfectly. The Teseco Foundation for Art of Pisa, which purchased the three Pietrasanta columns, sent one of them to Florence to be displayed alongside the projections. If we seek the column that lies buried in the square, many believe, we could find out for certain whether these other three are Michelangelo's too.

THE PERSECUTED PISAN

Painters and architects didn't constitute the only manifestations of the new learning during the Renaissance. The spread of Humanism through Italy brought with it the rediscovery of learning in the sciences too. The time is 1609: winds of cultural change are subverting the Renaissance creed that Man is the centre and the measure of all things. In fact, Galileo Galilei, a Pisan mathematician (born just three days before Michelangelo's death) achieves the first experimental proof – counter-intuitive, revolutionary and dangerously heretical – that not even the Earth is the centre of the Universe.

The telescope had been invented by Flemish optician Hans Lippershey, but it was Galileo who ingeniously improved it from a 3x to a 30x magnification, and an estimated 20x in the late months of 1609, when he pointed this unprecedented device to the night sky and started a chain of exceptional discoveries so unsettling that they would eventually cost him the wrath of the Inquisition. With all the evidence showing that planets revolved around the Sun, he could only deduce that Copernicus's heliocentric theory was right.

'Galileo was forced to say he "detested" the notion that the Earth moved round the Sun. But he never said he didn't believe it.'

By 1616, a backlash from the Church had been fully mobilised, and Galileo was told in no uncertain terms that he must refute Copernican ideas or face the Inquisition. However, the scientist was fortunate to have befriended Pope Urban VIII before his appointment as pontiff; Urban granted Galileo the right to propound a Copernican view, as long as it was clear that it was a hypothesis. Galileo, in his enthusiasm, overstepped the mark. In the 1620s, Vatican paranoia reached new levels as it came to terms with the threats it faced from Protestantism, and in 1633 Galileo – who had continued publishing his findings – faced his perhaps inevitable trial for heresy. Sensibly, he avoided torture by claiming he 'abjured, cursed and detested' the notion that the Earth moved round the Sun. But he never said he didn't believe it.

To mark the 400th anniversary of Galileo's first astronomical observations, 2009 has been declared the International Year of Astronomy. Italy, one of the main promoters of the event, will be honouring the genius of Galileo in the three cities where he lived and worked: Padua in the Veneto (where he was professor of mathematics), and, of course, Pisa and Florence.

In Florence, between March and September 2009, **Palazzo Strozzi** (*see p91*) will host Macrocosm, a major exhibition exploring the ways in which the Universe was imagined and represented from antiquity to Galileo's time. The exhibition aims to explore the relations hip between astronomy and astrology, while a special section focuses on the only two original telescopes known to be Galileo's, both from the collections of the **Museo di Storia della Scienza** (*see p86*) in Florence. The science museum itself will undergo a thorough refurbishment, to reopen in the autumn of 2009 as **Museo Galileo**. Meanwhile, a brand-new **Museum of the Universe** is set to open in the Torre del Gallo castle, located south of the city centre on the Arcetri hill, about halfway between Florence's Astrophysical Observatory and the Villa Il Gioiello, where Galileo spent his late years in confinement.

Pisa will concentrate its celebrations on the intricate relationship between Galileo and the arts with an exhibition of paintings, statues, books, etchings and scientific devices in **Palazzo Giuli**, which is being restored to house the **Fondazione Cassa di Risparmio di Pisa**, while a rich programme of plays and films will depict the fortune of Galileo's character and tragic story in European culture. Finally, Pisa will also pair with Kraków in Poland for a tribute to Copernicus and Galileo.

Incredibly, it took the Vatican till 1741 to rehabilitate Galileo, and until 1992 to issue a formal apology, and even then – to widespread outrage – the whole affair was dismissed as an unfortunate 'mutual misunderstanding'. Yet Galileo's only crime was that he sought, and reported what he found.

● *Maddalena Delli is a freelance journalist who lives and works in Florence.*

The 'virtual façade' of **San Lorenzo**.

The **Uffizi**. *See p89.*

Architecture

The Renaissance blueprint laid bare.

The history of Florentine architecture begins in 900 BC, around the time that the Etruscans dominated large parts of central Italy. Many of the architectural features used on buildings from this period later became key elements of Florentine architecture; the arch, in particular, can be traced back to this enigmatic civilisation.

Fiesole (*see p114*), just north of Florence, was the first major town in the area, established between the ninth and eighth centuries BC. It was probably settled to protect both the pass coming out of the Appennines and the crossing point just over the Arno. Extensive sections of walls survive, some constructed with the massive blocks of stone for which the Etruscans have become famous.

Only when the Romans began to absorb Etruscan civilisation was Roman Florence built, probably on a razed Etruscan village. Founded by Julius Caesar in 59 BC, Florentia, as it was then called, was laid out on a grid pattern typical of the Roman cities. Not much of Roman Florence remains above ground, but historians know that the theatre was located just behind Palazzo Vecchio, while the amphitheatre's shape can still be seen in the layout of the streets and buildings of piazza Santa Croce.

Medieval Florence grew up along one of the main axes of Roman Florence (now via dei Calzaiuoli). At one end of the axis was the religious centre with the Baptistery and Santa Reparata, which once stood where the present-day Duomo stands. At the other, where Palazzo Vecchio now stands, was the civil centre of piazza della Signoria. Between the two lay the commercial centre, now known as piazza della Repubblica. A number of towers from medieval times have survived: the oldest is the **Torre della Pagliazza** in via Sant' Elisabetta (off via del Corso). There are others in via Dante Alighieri, in piazza di San Pier Maggiore and in borgo San Jacopo.

As Florence expanded, new walls were built, principally between 1259 and 1333. The newly enclosed area came to include the *borghi* – the service areas for industry and storage that grew along the roads leading out of the medieval towns. These were fairly straight, wide roads, and the owners of the industrial property found themselves sitting on prime land. Many moved their commercial premises outside the walls and constructed large townhouses with gardens in their place – the *palazzi* of the future.

A FLORENTINE STYLE EMERGES

Florence flourished in the tenth and 11th centuries, when a large amount of money was spent on constructing religious buildings, generating an indigenous architectural style. Piazza del Duomo's **Battistero di San Giovanni**, believed to be the oldest building in the city, was completed around the middle of the 11th century, although its foundations are thought to date back to the fourth or fifth century. Famous for Ghiberti's bronze door on the east side, the Baptistery exemplifies what can only be termed the 'Florentine style', characterised by a simple, balanced, sharp-edged design and a wide roof. Catholic noblemen from the city were baptised here up until the 19th century.

A number of prominent Florentine and Tuscan architects worked and developed the Florentine style over the centuries. The most important were, chronologically: **Arnolfo di Cambio** (c1245-1302), **Giotto** (1266/7-1337), **Filippo Brunelleschi** (1377-1446), **Michelozzo di Bartolomeo Michelozzi** (1396-1472), **Leon Battista Alberti** (1404-72), **Giuliano da Sangallo** (c1445-1535), **Il Cronaca** (1454-1508), **Michelangelo Buonarroti** (1475-1564), **Giorgio Vasari** (1511-74), **Bartolomeo Ammannati** (1511-92), **Bernardo Buontalenti** (1531-1608); and later **Giuseppe Poggi** (1811-1901) and **Giovanni Michelucci** (1891-1991).

Many of the city's most prestigious buildings were constructed in marble, much of which came from nearby Carrara. It was originally extracted by hammering pegs made of figwood into the stone, but this method was eventually supplanted by gunpowder in the 19th century. (This harmed the marble, however, causing it to crack and deteriorate.) Half a million tonnes of marble are still quarried annually in Carrara.

ROMANESQUE AND GOTHIC

San Miniato al Monte (*see p115*), constructed in 1018 on the site of a fourth-century chapel, is one of the most beautiful Romanesque structures in Florence. With its wonderful green and white façade, the church is rather simple in design, and its 15th-century campanile remains unfinished. During the Siege of Florence (1529-30), this important religious site was surrounded with fortified walls, which were hastily constructed by Michelangelo.

The 11th-century church of **Santissimi Apostoli** (*see p91*), in piazza del Limbo, is considered one of the most elegant examples of Romanesque architecture in the city. The interior is divided into three aisles, separated by columns made with green marble. It's also believed that this church heavily influenced Brunelleschi in his designs for the church of San Lorenzo. The church was reworked during the 15th century and was only restored to its original Romanesque appearance in the 1930s.

Gothic style dominated new architectural works from the 13th century, with builders using pointed arches to make higher and wider structures. There are four major Gothic churches in Florence, all of which were influenced by the earlier **San Remigio**, a 12th-century French pilgrims' church in central Florence, known for its rather stark exterior that gives way to an altogether livelier interior (a classic Florentine attribute).

The lower portion of the **Santa Maria Novella** (*see p95*) was constructed between 1278 and 1360, and is perhaps the most beautiful structure commissioned by the Dominican monks. It was adorned with three open portals, each surrounded by an arch, and three blind portals located just above these, also with arches.

The **Duomo** (*see p77 and p80* **Seeing beyond the façade**), or Santa Maria del Fiore, to give it its proper name, was designed by

Baptistery
See left and p79.

Biblioteca Mediceo-Laurenziana
See p98.

Cappella dei Pazzi
See p105.

Ponte Santa Trinità
See p40 and p90.

San Miniato al Monte
See left and p115.

Santa Maria Novella station
See p42 and p93.

Santo Spirito
See p38 and p112.

Stadio Artemio Franchi
See p42 and p101.

Arnolfo di Cambio in 1297. It was built to replace the crumbling church of Santa Reparata, and was initially designed to be the largest Roman Catholic church in Europe. However, its design, and subsequently its size, was altered several times, and work practically came to a standstill after Arnolfo's death in 1302. The project was later overseen by a number of other architects, including Francesco Talenti and Giovanni di Lapo Ghini. The Duomo's interior consists of a nave leading down to the centralised space beneath the dome, spawning four bays that open on to side aisles; large crowds of worshippers were thus able to move easily between the different areas.

Santa Croce (*see p105*) is another major Gothic church in the city; begun in 1298, it has also been attributed to Arnolfo. A timbered roof combines with seven bays with pointed arches to give the illusion of loftiness, at the same time drawing the eye down to the altar.

'No longer just skilled labourers, the architects became artists.'

The **Campanile** of Santa Maria del Fiore in piazza del Duomo (*see p75*), designed by Giotto (c1330), constructed with white and green marble, was only completed after his death. As the storeys rise, the windows multiply – a traditional feature of medieval Florentine architecture (*see also p80* **Seeing beyond the façade**).

At the end of the 14th century, renovation work began on the ground-floor loggia of San Michele (or **Orsanmichele**; *see p86*) in Orto's via Calzaiuoli, creating a church for the guilds of Florence. Every guild was allocated a niche on the exterior, for which they were to commission a statue. The originals are no longer in the niches but can be seen in the Museo di Orsanmichele and the Bargello. On the ground floor of this square plan building is the original loggia with its 13th-century arches.

Another notable building is **Palazzo Davanzati** (*see p91*), constructed in the 14th century. Built in sandstone, the palace encompasses four storeys and is decorated with portals and mullioned windows. The top storey contains a loggia with columns and pilasters.

EARLY RENAISSANCE

Florence is a shrine to Renaissance architecture – its centre filled with palaces, monuments and churches constructed with an artistic and cultural intelligence that was unsurpassed at the time. A pilgrimage to Rome to study the ancient structures was seen as a vital part of an architect's training, with particular attention paid to the Colosseum, the Pantheon and the Forum. As the architects absorbed the styles of these classical buildings, a new architectural vocabulary developed encompassing columns, pilasters, entablatures, arches and pediments.

The treatise of the first-century BC Roman architect Vitruvius also formed an important part of Renaissance education, helping to define Renaissance ideals concerning architectural beauty. These ideals subsequently raised the status of the profession – no longer just skilled labourers, the architects became artists (*see also p15* **The Renaissance**). Renaissance architecture is defined by strict mathematical proportions, measurements based on the human body and balanced form. In Florence, the period was dominated by three great architects: Brunelleschi, Michelozzo and Alberti.

Brunelleschi, who gave the Duomo its cupola (the largest such construction since ancient Roman times), went on to design two of the city's finest churches: **San Lorenzo** (1422-69), with its independent Old Sacristy (1422-29), and **Santo Spirito** (1444-81). Less heralded, but equally notable, is his **Capella dei Pazzi** (begun 1422), a small private family building in the garden of Santa Croce, based on perfect proportions. These structures embrace human thought far more than Christian faith and their architectural forms return to ideas that pre-date Christianity. The Duomo's cupola, a symbol of the Renaissance, went on to influence many High Renaissance and Baroque architects; Michelangelo's cupola for St Peter's in Rome, designed more than 100 years later, has roughly the same interior diameter at 42 metres (138 feet).

Brunelleschi's signature style can clearly be seen in piazza della SS Annunziata's **Ospedale degli Innocenti**, begun in 1419. Through a series of arcades with Corinthian columns, friezes, pedimented windows and matching loggias, Brunelleschi created the most unified square in Florence.

It's the architect Michelozzo, however, who is widely credited with developing the form of the Florentine palazzo (or mansion), considered among the most important architectural products of the Renaissance. Michelozzo often worked for Cosimo de' Medici (Cosimo il Vecchio), the founder of the Medici family's fortunes (*see p16* **Medici cabinet**). His most notable construction was Cosimo's town residence, Palazzo Medici, now called **Palazzo Medici Riccardi** (1444; *see p97*). To 21st-century eyes this building looks unpalatial and unwelcoming, constructed with roughly cut stones that project rudely. The regularity of the building, however, its two façades and its strongly rusticated orders heralded a new era in palazzo construction.

Completing the trio is Leon Battista Alberti, a Florentine who mostly worked outside the city. In Florence itself he completed the façade of **Santa Maria Novella** (1470; *see p95*), a handsome white and green marble front crowned with a temple and framed with volutes. He also designed the highly original **Palazzo Rucellai** (*see p94*) in via della Vigna Nuova (c1446-51), on which he first introduced to Florence his innovative system of pilasters and capitals of the three classical orders, which ascend in importance on each storey, and which are separated by ornate friezes. In 1450, Alberti published his *Ten Books on Architecture*, the text that became an indispensable guide for all those designing buildings during the Renaissance and beyond.

LATER RENAISSANCE

The Brunelleschian and Albertian principles continued to be used by architects into the 16th century, with one of the main exponents being Il Cronaca (or Simone del Pallaiolo), whose work was extremely sober in style. Il Cronaca built the **Santo Spirito** vestibule and sacristy (1489-94) and the **Museo Horne** (formerly Palazzo Horne, 1495-1502), an elegant palace with an internal courtyard.

Giuliano da Sangallo, the preferred architect of Lorenzo il Magnifico, was greatly concerned with instilling in his designs a refined classicism that he'd learnt in Rome. The best example of his work is at the beautiful **Medici villa** (*see p215*) at Poggio a Caiano (begun 1480) a simple rectangular block, with a temple portico, plain walls and sharp eaves that project out. The horizontal design is further enhanced by the use of mouldings on the pediment that extend outwards. Despite these impressive designs, however, the focus for architecture at this time shifted distinctly to Rome.

Michelangelo was one of the most important High Renaissance architects, although he came to architecture rather late in his career, at the age of 40. His work spanned the years before, during and after Florence's subjugation by the Habsburg emperor, Charles V, in 1530. Michelangelo took the bold, classicising style that da Sangallo and Il Cronaca had inherited from Alberti, and instilled it with a sense of uncertainty, but also with great energy and rhythm. Rather than making the exteriors of his buildings imitate those of ancient Rome, Michelangelo gave his creations a pagan grounding oriented towards man's emotional state. He believed that architecture should

The imposing sandstone façade of **Palazzo Davanzati**. *See p91.*

be influenced more from an inner creativity rooted in human thought than any religious reasoning. It was this that moved his architecture beyond the Renaissance.

Michelangelo undertook two key projects in Florence for Pope Leo X (formerly Giovanni de' Medici): the **New Sacristy** (*see p97*) and the **Biblioteca Mediceo-Laurenziana** (Laurentian Library; *see p98*), both in the church of San Lorenzo, which had become an important symbol of dynastic power for the pope's family, the Medici.

Another important project designed by Michelangelo is the **Capelle Medicee** (1519-34; *see p96*), adjacent to San Lorenzo. Although it was never entirely completed, it's arguably the best example in existence of Michelangelo's architectural-sculptural designs, where the boundaries between the walls, floors and artwork become blurred. In the Capelle, the design of the building, the melancholy mood of the sculptures and the almost artificial proportions of the human body create a subdued effect that befits its purpose as a place of burial. This is further heightened by the impressive lighting effects that Michelangelo employed: he ensured that the top portion of the Capelle was raised above the neighbouring buildings so the light could shine into the building from a decent height – generating a rather eerie effect. Michelangelo left for Rome in 1534 and did not return.

Both the **Fortezza da Basso** (1534), the strongest side of which faces the city, and the **Forte di Belvedere** (1590), which dominates from just above the ponte Vecchio, were commissioned by the Medici family and are symbolic of the great control that the family exercised over the city and its inhabitants. The vast **Palazzo Pitti** (1457; *see p108*), where the Medici lived in the mid 16th century, pays further tribute to the family's strength: designed by Brunelleschi and Fancelli, it was built with massive blocks of stone, some of which measure six metres (20 feet) in length. The palace was designed to look severe and foreboding to all who passed.

The main court architects at this time were Vasari, Ammannati and Buontalenti. However, all ended up following Michelangelo, and the financial rewards of patronage, to Rome. While in Florence, Vasari, assisted by Buontalenti, designed the **Uffizi Palace** (1560), which was filled with offices and workshops, leaving the top floor for the gallery. He also constructed the corridor that bears his name, running from the Uffizi, across the ponte Vecchio to Palazzo Pitti, and used by the Medici family to avoid the throngs on the street.

In 1557, Ammannati designed the **ponte Santa Trinità** over the Arno to replace a bridge that had collapsed in 1557. He also began the 300-year expansion of Palazzo Pitti. Meanwhile, Buontalenti extended Palazzo Vecchio to its present eastern limits and built the palaces for the Medici at Petraia (1587) and Pratolino (1568, later demolished).

THE LONG DECLINE

During the 17th and 18th centuries, Florence suffered an economic recession. As a result, the arts were neglected and, from 1600 to the death of the last Medici ruler in 1737, not much new building work was commissioned in Florence and the city fell into a state of decline, becoming something of a provincial backwater for the ruling Habsburgs.

During this time, however, many of the Renaissance palaces were enlarged and gardens were added. In this, the Florentine noblemen took their lead from their Roman counterparts, who were adding gardens, complete with fountains and statues, to their town villas, which gave an air of sophistication and complemented the design of the building. Garden design subsequently came to be seen as another form of art. At Palazzo Pitti, an extra 45,000 square metres (484,000 square feet) were added to the **Boboli Gardens** (*see p109*). An amphitheatre was built behind the palace, decorated with interesting statues from Roman mythological stories by Florentine sculptors, and a number of picturesque grottoes with fountains were constructed.

In the 19th century, two railway stations were erected: **Leopolda** (1847) and **Maria Antonia**, near Santa Maria Novella (1848). Only the Leopolda still stands and is now an impressive performance space (*see p192*).

DEVELOPMENT AND DESTRUCTION

Between 1865 and 1870, large parts of the city underwent significant redevelopment as Florence became the capital of the unified Kingdom of Italy. Giuseppe Poggi (1811-1901) had been named the principal town planner and architect by the Florentine authorities in 1864, and his ambitious redevelopment project included constructing wide boulevards, to accommodate carriages, as well as several elegant piazze. **Piazza Beccaria** and **piazza della Libertà** are superb examples of these new city-centre squares, both of which were designed in the neoclassical and neo-Renaissance styles. Both are unfortunately submerged in traffic in present-day Florence.

One of Poggi's most impressive projects was constructing **piazzale Michelangelo** (1875; *see p107*) on the south side of the

Bland ambition

Firenze Nova.

Long gone are the days when an architect could envisage a self-supporting cupola and convince his fellow citizens that the fanciful project might be worth the investment of Florence's gold and reputation. Even in Brunelleschi's time, Florentines were distrusting and quarrelsome; yet dragging out idle debate for decades now seems to have become the institutional method for letting innovative sparks die out and routinely making architectural gurus like Santiago Calatrava, Arata Isozaki and – more recently – Jean Nouvel walk out on their Florentine engagements in various degrees of indignation.

Several major projects that started with high hopes of international standards worthy of this city of culture, like the renovation of the Museo dell'Opera del Duomo, eventually ended up in the hands of local architect Adolfo Natalini – a decent, solid professional, but certainly not a visionary in the Calatrava league. Take his new university campus in the ex-Fiat area in Novoli: though the new edifices are just as dull as the surrounding buildings, they don't even blend in – the originals being 1970s constructs, the modern one mock-1930s. After decades of imaginatively arid and architecturally bland developments in all the new neighbourhoods (Firenze Nova, Isolotto, Le Piagge, Sorgane) surrounding the city, this was yet another wasted opportunity.

A few hundred metres down the viale Guidoni from the university campus, the now virtually complete law courts building (watch out for its skyward spikes on your way to or from the Amerigo Vespucci Airport) is easily Florence's most futuristic edifice. Yet it was designed by Leonardo Ricci almost 30 years ago (Ricci himself died in 1994), and it's made obsolete by today's architectural standards: there's too much concrete, too little natural light and not enough concern for the environment.

Some 50 years after the old tram system was dismantled, Florence is building three new tram lines stretching for about 20 kilometres (12 miles) over 30 stops. While nobody really believes the claim that 35 per cent of commuters will opt for the Tramvia (www.tramvia.fi.it), decreasing city congestion by 50 per cent, there's little denying that the transportation problem needed some drastic measures. Still, the countless tramway building sites – where no detectable progress is made for months on end – have brought the traffic situation to new impossible heights and most Florentines, who voted for the Tramvia back in 1988, are now turning against it. It does not help win public favour that about 700 full-grown trees have been cut down, that costs keep swelling and completion dates shifting.

On a happier note, over the years some enlightened renovation solutions have turned a number of historic Florentine buildings to new use: the former church of San Pancrazio became the (sadly underrated) Marino Marini museum (*see p94*); what was once the Leopolda train station is now an exhibition and events venue; the Oblate convent was converted into a state-of-the-art library; while the Murate complex, formerly a nunnery and more recently a prison, is being turned into a stylish mix of residential and commercial units following Renzo Piano's guidelines.

And the 21st century? It will have to wait, unless – a full 80 years after Giovanni Michelucci's Santa Maria Novella train terminal – Sir Norman Foster's design for the new rail station finally breaks the curse.

river. This large open space offers an excellent view over Florence. He also enlarged a number of boulevards around the piazzale, which continued along the side of the hills facing Florence and the Forte di Belvedere, and then came back down again to the Porta Romana. This wonderful drive of roughly six kilometres (3.5 miles), one of the prettiest in Italy, is also due in great part to Poggi's vision.

Undeveloped land inside the city walls was also set aside for new houses, and parts of the city walls on the north side of the Arno were pulled down (1865-69) – leaving only the gates, which can still be seen today.

In these same years, parts of the old city were also demolished to make way for three covered cast-iron market buildings. This was followed, from 1890 onwards, by some of the most thoughtless devastation of all, which changed the architectural face of Florence. Piazza della Repubblica and its surrounding streets, which had been the centre of the Roman and medieval city, were pulled down so that the city centre could be redeveloped. Then, soon after World War I, the central government in Rome demolished further stretches of the city, in Santa Maria Novella and Santa Croce.

In 1944, only 50 years after the centre of Florence had been gutted, another bout of destruction took place, once again removing scores of irreplaceable ancient buildings. Partly out of fury with their former allies and partly in a hopeless attempt to stem the Anglo-American advance, the Germans blew up almost all the bridges over the Arno (only the ponte Vecchio was spared), along with all the buildings to the immediate north and south of the ponte Vecchio. Ponte Santa Trinità was rebuilt in the 1950s using its original stones that had been raised from the river, but the other three – **ponte alle Grazie**, **ponte alla Carraia** and **ponte alla Vittoria** – were all replaced by more modern designs.

Most of the old centre of Florence had been largely intact at the start of the 20th century, made up of medieval buildings built on foundations dating back to at least ancient Rome. Today, as a result of the periods of destruction described, you can walk all the way from the Duomo, down via Roma, across piazza Repubblica, through via Calimala and via Santa Maria and all the way down the ponte Vecchio without passing more than two or three buildings that are more than a century old. And the newer buildings are, on the whole, banal at best and ugly at worst.

There are a few notable 20th-century buildings in the city, however, including the **Stadio Artemio Franchi** (*see p191*) designed by Pier Luigi Nervi (1891-1979), which was finished in 1932 and built using reinforced concrete. It was later renovated in time for the 1990 FIFA World Cup and is widely considered to be one of the most impressive contemporary structures in Florence. The Fascist interwar period also produced a number of fine, rather grand buildings: a reception building for the Italian royal family called the **Palazzina Reale**, attached to the Santa Maria Novella station, which is now home to the University of Florence department of science; the **Instituto Aeronautica Militare** building in the Cascine Park; and the **Cinema Puccini** in piazza Puccini. Other interesting buildings include the **Santa Maria Novella station**, built in 1936 by Giovanni Michelucci; and the church of **San Giovanni Battista**, built with vision and sensitivity by Michelucci in 1960, at the crossing of the Autostrade del Sole and del Mare. A rather unusual structure, its form reflects both traditional and contemporary church planning, combining the conventional cross-floor arrangement with an innovative exterior that resembles a tent with vertical poles. The church was constructed out of a number of different materials – stone and concrete on the exterior, copper on the roof, and glass, marble and bronze in the interior – and was designed to offer religious facilities to those travelling around the area and in need of spiritual refreshment.

BEST FOOT FORWARD

Florence is currently undergoing some major structural renovations, undertaken by some of the world's foremost architects and engineering companies. Sir Norman Foster has designed the enormous underground terminal of the high-speed Milano–Roma train link, due to be completed in 2010-11. This huge complex will be topped with an arched glazed roof that will hark back to the railway stations of the 19th century. The planned extension to the **Museo dell'Opera del Duomo** (*see p82*) has suffered a series of setbacks and has yet to get off the ground. The work, which will provide an extra 2,000 square metres (21,500 square feet), was due to be completed in 2008-09. And controversial designs for the new **Uffizi** exit by Japanese architect Arata Isozaki were finally given the green light in August 2007. The exit, which will feature a high canopy made out of steel, stone and polycarbonate, is expected to be completed in 2013, ten years after its original deadline.

With both these and a number of further architectural plans that have had varying success (*see p41* **Bland ambition**), it remains to be seen whether Florence is ready for a new wave of architectural innovation.

Chianti. *See p46.*

Food & Wine in Tuscany

Be seduced by fresh, local specialities and some of the best wine in Italy.

Food

THE BASICS

The three main staples of the Tuscan diet are bread, olive oil and wine. Wines are famously substantial and the olive oil peppery, but bread is deliberately bland. Made without salt, it's a neutral canvas for accompanying food. A worthy intention, but an acquired (lack of) taste.

Tuscany claims to have Italy's best olive oil. Even within Tuscany, each region claims superiority, though the consensus is that the finest oil comes from groves located slightly inland, away from the varying temperatures and high moisture levels of the coast. While you're making your way round Tuscany, be sure to seek out oil from small producers, in particular extra virgin oils that have been cold pressed from estate-grown olives.

L'ANTIPASTO

Meals generally start with the *antipasto*: literally, 'before the meal'. In Tuscany the most common *antipasto* is *crostini*, often chicken liver pâté on toast. Cured meats are a regional speciality – usually pork and wild boar. *Prosciutto crudo* comes from a pig haunch buried under salt for three weeks, then swabbed with spicy vinegar, covered with black pepper and hung to dry for a further five months. *Capocollo* is a neck cut cured the same way for three days, covered with pepper and fennel seed, rolled in yellow butcher's paper and then tied up with string. It's ready to eat a few

- For **wine tastings** *see p258.*
- For **wine bars** *see pp118-139.*
- For **food tourism** *see p213.*

Tuscany's very own White Stripes: the *cinta senese* pig.

months later. The most typical Tuscan salami is *finocchiona* (pork with fennel seeds and peppercorns). *Salamini di cinghiale*, or small wild boar salamis, include chilli pepper and a little fatty pork. Look out for *milza*, a pungent pâté made from spleen, herbs, spices and wine. *Antipasti* sometimes includes *prosciutto* or *salame* from the distinctively striped and highly prized *cinta senese* pig.

IL PRIMO

The *primo* (first course) is carbohydrate-based. In most parts of Italy this is pasta or rice, but in Tuscany it's as likely to be a bread-based salad or soup. Old bread is never thrown away, but is mixed with Tuscan staples such as tomatoes, garlic, cabbage and *fagioli* (white beans). These form dishes such as *panzanella* (stale bread soaked in water, squeezed, mixed with raw onion, fresh tomato and basil and dressed with oil, salt and pepper), *ribollita* (rich bean and cabbage soup with bread, made using the local *cavolo nero* or black cabbage), *acqua cotta* (toasted bread rubbed with garlic and covered with crinkly dark green cabbage, then topped with olive oil, and covered with broth – sometimes with an egg broken into it), *pappa al pomodoro* (an exquisite thick soup with onion, garlic, tomatoes, bread, basil and chilli pepper). The ultimate winter ritual is *bruschetta* or *fettunta* (toasted bread rubbed with garlic and soaked in freshly pressed olive oil).

Fresh pasta in Tuscany usually takes the form of *tagliatelle* (flat egg-based ribbons), *pappardelle* (wide flat ribbons), *ravioli* (parcels containing ricotta and spinach) and *tordelli* (from around Lucca, stuffed with chard, meat and ricotta). South you'll find *pici* (flour and water extruded into fattish strings) and, in the Mugello, *tortelli* (stuffed with a potato mixture). Ravioli are typically best eaten with *burro e salvia* (butter and sage) and a sprinkling of parmesan or pecorino. Flat ribbon-like pastas go well with gamey sauces like *lepre* (hare) and *cinghiale* (wild boar), and also *anatra* (duck), as well as *ragù* (made with tomato and minced beef or, occasionally, lamb) and *salsa di pomodoro* (spicy tomato sauce).

IL SECONDO

Cacciagione (game), *salsicce* (sausages) and *bistecca* (beef steak) are the main regional meats, though there is good lamb about (look out for *agnellino nostrale*, meaning young, locally raised lamb). Also common are *coniglio* (rabbit, usually roasted, sometimes with pine nuts, sometimes rolled around a filling such as egg and bacon) and *pollo* (chicken; go for *ruspante*, free-range). During the winter you'll find plenty of slowly stewed and highly spiced *cinghiale*. This species was cross-bred with the domestic pig about 20 years ago, producing a creature so prolific that it has to be culled. Other common game includes *lepre* and *fagiano* (pheasant). The famous *bistecca fiorentina* is a vast T-bone steak, usually served very rare.

IL CONTORNO

To accompany your meat course you're normally offered a side plate of vegetables or a salad. *Bietole* (Swiss chard) is available almost throughout the year. It's scalded in salted water and tossed in the pan with olive oil, garlic and chilli pepper. *Fagiolini* (green beans) are likely to be boiled and dressed with oil and lemon or vinegar. The sublime white Tuscan *fagioli* are served lukewarm with olive oil and a sprinkle of black pepper. *Patatine fritte* (French fries) are available almost everywhere, though boiled potatoes dressed with oil, pepper and capers are often much tastier. *Pomodori* (tomatoes) and *cipolle* (onions) sliced, spiced and baked *al forno* (in the oven) are recommended. To those accustomed to watery lettuce, *radicchio* salads may seem bitter at first. In early summer, artichokes are eaten raw, stripped of their tough outer leaves and dipped into olive oil and salt.

IL FORMAGGIO

The one true Tuscan cheese is pecorino, made with ewe's milk. The sheep grazing on the hillsides are more often than not there for their milk rather than meat or wool.

Thirty years ago each small farm would have enough sheep to provide the household with sufficient rounds of pecorino, which can be eaten *fresco* (up to a month old), *semi-stagionato* (with about a month of ripening) or up to six months later, when the cheese is fully *stagionato*, and thus drier, sharper and tastier. Nowadays, sheep farming and cheese-making are mostly done by Sardinians, who came over to work the land abandoned by the Tuscans drawn to towns and factory employment.

Fresh ricotta, which is made from whey and is thus not strictly speaking a cheese, is soft, mild and wet and should be eaten with black pepper and a few drops of olive oil on top.

IL DOLCE

The Tuscans are only recently coming round to the way of desserts. Christmas classics such as *panforte* are now available year-round, but these days you'll find tiramisù, *torta della nonna* and basic fruit or jam tarts almost everywhere. The Tuscans like to conclude festive meals with a glass of a dry raisin wine called *vin santo*, into which they dunk *cantucci*, little dry biscuits packed with almonds. *Vin santo* is made with a special white grape variety that's dried out in bunches for a month and then crushed to obtain a sweet juice, which is aged for at least five years. You could get five bottles of wine from the grapes you need for one bottle of *vin santo*, so to offer a glass of *vin santo* is to honour a guest with the essence of hospitality.

LA FRUTTA

Cherries, then apricots and peaches, are readily available in summer, grapes in late summer, and apples and pears in early autumn. Although citrus fruits imported from the south now take pride of place in the winter months, the main indigenous fruits are quinces (*mele cotogne*, excellent baked, stewed or jellied) and persimmons (*cachi*). However, for visitors to Tuscany, fruit is perhaps most interesting in sweet/savoury combinations: *il cacio con le pere* (cheese with pears), *i fichi con il salame* (figs with salami), *melone* or *popone con prosciutto* (melon and cured ham).

Wine

The renown of Tuscan winemaking has traditionally derived almost exclusively from one grape variety: the sangiovese. More recently other grape varieties, both local and international, have begun to emerge as blends and varietals, with interesting results. On the red wine shelves, merlots, syrahs and cabernet sauvignons are all as popular as ever, but there are now some fine wines being made with the local ciliegiolo and alicante varieties. Vermentino, meanwhile, is at last lifting a number of Tuscan whites above mediocrity (*see also p46* **New wave whites**).

During the past 15 years, wine production in Tuscany has massively evolved. Look out for orchards of fruit trees interspersed with a few rows of tall, exuberant vines, their tendrils embracing sturdy trees for support: this is viticultural archaeology, destined to disappear entirely before long. Quality has become the watchword: there's not a traditional winemaker left who feels he can do without an oenologist (a wine technician).

The emphasis these days is on densely planted vineyards (*see also p258* **Fine vines**). Vibrant green geometries have replaced the softer contours and mixed hues of the sparsely planted orchards tended by yesteryear's sharecrop farmers. The work ethic is that vines need to be 'stressed' by competition: that way, they'll concentrate on survival, focusing energy on seed production and thus on sturdy, healthy fruit. Bunches of grapes grown on vines that are radically pruned in winter and again in the spring will often be thinned out to improve quality and ensure that ripening proceeds evenly. The goal: relatively low yields with high concentrations of sugars and aromas.

In terms of quality of recent wines, 1995, 1997 and 1999 were excellent years (though most wines from these vintages will be getting a bit old now), as was 2001. Both 2002 and 2003 were difficult vintages and generally best avoided. Indications as we went to press were that 2005 is a great vintage for immediate drinking (particularly for higher end bottles), but 2004s have a better acidity (so a better chance to improve), while 2006 so far holds fantastic promise, and could be an excellent vintage for wines to cellar.

WHAT'S UP, DOC?

With the help of the oeneologists, winemakers have grown more aware of what their own particular vineyards should produce. Such territorial specificity ensures *tipicità*: a distinct character pertaining to a given place.

New wave whites

Think Tuscany and you normally think Chianti, Vino Nobile di Montepulciano, Brunello di Montalcino... in any case, of a rich red swirling in the bottom of your glass, the perfect accompaniment to *bistecca fiorentina*.

However, official statistics for 2005 showed that 53.3 per cent of wine produced in Italy was white, the remaining 46.7 per cent shared between red and rosé. So why hasn't Tuscany had much luck with whites? Partly, white grape varieties in Chianti just don't produce serious quality – trebbiano, for example, is a very basic grape that makes a bland wine. The main issue, though, is the heat: the kind of white grape that can cope with the scorching Tuscan sun is chardonnay, but many farmers consider themselves better off planting the more reliable red sangiovese instead, as chardonnay grapes have proved notoriously hard to pick at optimum ripeness.

Around 15 years ago, a few brave souls began experimenting, and achieved a greater freshness by using cooler fermentation and harvesting the grapes in lower temperatures. Though their successors are not many in number, they are raising the profile of the humble *bianco toscano*.

So which whites should Tuscany currently be most proud of? Late-ripening **vermentino** from Poggio al Tesoro in Bolgheri presents subtle floral perfumes, and Panizzi's **vernaccia di San Gimignano** stands out from its contemporaries as brighter, fresher and more aromatic; this winery also makes a *reserva*, aged in *barriques*. But our favourite is **L'Anima**, from Livernano in Chianti: based on chardonnay and sauvignon blanc, but also including viognier and gewürztraminer, it's one of the most interesting Tuscan whites from the new mould.

To some extent, *tipicità* is defined by the various DOCs (Denominazione di Origine Controllata, which regulate wines from a specific, controlled area); the ultra-select category of DOCGs (Denominazione di Origine Controllata e Garantita); and IGTs (Indicazione Geografica Tipica – table wines from a well-defined area). Each sets out rules and regulations to which producers must adhere. Tuscany has ten DOCGs and almost four times as many DOCs, of which the most famous are **Chianti Classico**, **Brunello di Montalcino** and **Vino Nobile di Montepulciano**.

This trio's reputation tends to overshadow some fine younger siblings: **Bolgheri Rosso** DOC, for example, made in the coastal area north of Grosseto; **Montescudaio** DOC, a little further south; and, yet further, the **Morellino di Scansano** DOC. A little further inland is the **Montecucco** DOC, while two other newer southern Tuscan DOCs are **Capalbio**, on the coast, and **Sovana**, between the southern slopes of Monte Amiata and the coast. Due east and slightly north of here is the fairly extensive and variegated area devoted to **Orcia** DOC, whose flagship in its early years has been Donatella Cinelli Colombini at the Fattoria del Colle, near Trequanda.

The well-established Tuscan whites are the **Vernaccia di San Gimignano** DOC and the **Bianco di Pitigliano** DOC. However, a number of the newer DOCs also embrace white wines, though so far not many can stand up to comparisons with the few Tuscan whites of excellence: **Batàr** pinot bianco, made by Agricola Querciabella at Greve in Chianti, and the **Cabreo La Pietra** chardonnay, made by Ruffino at Pontassieve. For more on Tuscany's white wines, *see above* **New wave whites**.

REASONS TO CELLARBRATE

More attention is now also paid to the cellar. The peasant winemaker of a few years ago now either sells his grapes to larger wineries or has embarked on a programme of investment: spotless new cellars, temperature-controlled steel fermentation tanks, expensive pumps that shift the deep red liquid from one container to another without bruising it, small French oak barrels (*barriques*) for oxygenating and ageing the wine, immaculate bottling equipment and, as often as not, a tasting room.

A number of small growers sell their grapes to the remaining co-operative wineries. With the help of agronomists, who advise the growers, and oenologists, who work in the cellars, the better co-operative winemakers are producing acceptable wines with a good price-to-quality ratio that helps smooth over what might otherwise be perceived as a lack of character. The bigger producers include **Agricoltori del Chianti Geografico**, which produces a fine Chianti Classico; the **Cantina di Montalcino**; the **Cantina Cooperativa del Morellino**, which has a good Morellino di Scansano; Redi, the flagship for the **Vecchia Cantina** co-operative winery at Montepulciano; and **Le Chiantigiane**, producing the white Vernaccia di San Gimignano. Such wines are widely distributed, both at supermarket level in Italy and in wine stores and chains abroad.

At the other end of the spectrum sit the great aristocratic wine dynasties, names such as **Antinori**, **Ricasoli** (owners of Brolio), **Frescobaldi**, **Mazzei** (who own Fonterutoli) and **Folonari** (owners of Ruffino). These giants have gradually expanded from the area south of Florence, where they principally produce Chianti Classico, to other parts of Tuscany, and as far afield as California and Chile.

'The wine press came up with the name Super Tuscan – and the epithet stuck.'

These sizeable winemakers have the clout, financially and socially, to shape palates in anticipation of market trends, as happened with the development of **Galestro** in the late 1970s. In a region that was then largely identified with reds, these producers saw the time was ripe for a white wine in which the emphasis was more on freshness and lightness than aroma and body. The wine was made up largely of the trebbiano toscano grape variety, with small amounts of malvasia del Chianti, vernaccia di San Gimignano, chardonnay, pinot bianco and Rhine-riesling, and production involved pioneering vinification techniques. In 20 years, Galestro has grown to become an acceptable aperitif or accompaniment to summer cuisine.

Other, smaller, quality producers whose names you're likely to see in restaurants and bars include **Fontodi**, **Isole e Olena** and **Castello di Ama** (all from Chianti); **Poliziano** and **Avignionesi** (Montepulciano growers); **Casanova di Neri**, **Argiano**, **Cupano** and **Colle Mattoni** (from Montalcino).

BEST OF THE BUNCH

Still more impressive and influential has been the development from the mid 1980s of the so-called Super Tuscans. The idea behind them was to open up the way for wines that could satisfy changing tastes, especially abroad: at the time, Tuscan table wines were seen as poor, and the production of DOC wines was stultified by excessive strictures and regulations. The far-sighted few who felt there was room for wines that didn't conform to established Tuscan models began experimenting with the grape varieties that had contributed to the renown of French viticulture: cabernets, merlot, chardonnay and sauvignon.

Alongside these enterprising producers came a new generation of highly trained wine technicians, whose wines were beautifully made, highly priced and, for consumers abroad, initially somewhat perplexing. Why should an 'ordinary' wine cost more than certain DOCs? The British and American wine press decreed that reds such as **Tignanello** (sangiovese and cabernet sauvignon) and **Solaia** (cabernet with a small percentage of sangiovese) made by Marchesi Antinori in Chianti deserved the epithet Super Tuscans, and the name stuck.

Similar enthusiasm greeted Nicolò Incisa della Rocchetta's **Sassicaia** (90 per cent cabernet sauvignon, ten per cent cabernet franc) and Lodovico Antinori's **Ornellaia** (90 per cent cabernet sauvignon, ten per cent merlot); both are made at Bolgheri near the northern Maremma coast, an area hitherto devoted entirely to sangiovese and trebbiano. Names to have joined the top ranks in recent years include **Tenuta di Trinoro**, **Siepi**, **Il Blu** and **Solengo**.

The new wines soon spread in range, reaching areas as distant from the original Chianti region as the western foothills of Monte Amiata and Montalcino. Several of the Super

Super Tuscans.

Tuscans have joined the IGT category, some have continued to call themselves *vini da tavola*, and others still have achieved a more specific geographical identity by associating with the newly created DOCs.

ONES TO WATCH

Tuscan wines are currently more varied and interesting than ever before, at least partly thanks to a generation of younger winemakers who are opening up new vistas by fine-tuning a particular feature within a given DOC. These youngsters, better educated and travelled than their fathers, are keen to experiment with new clones, grape varieties, vinification methods and ageing techniques.

'*Enoteche* are happy to give you a "horizontal" tasting (no reference to your final posture).'

At Bolgheri, Eugenio Campolmi's winery (**Le Macchiole**) has made a name for itself with Paleo, Messorio and Scrio, all excellent reds. At Suvereto Rita Tua's winery (called **Tua Rita**) produces Redigaffi and Giusto di Notri. Around Montalcino, the number of *contadini* ('peasant farmers', but the term has no negative connotations) who have become prestigious Brunello producers has grown: Giancarlo Pacenti at the winery that bears his father's name (Pelagrilli di Pacenti Siro); Paolo Bartolommei at the Caprili winery; Vincenzo Abbruzzese at Val di Cava; and Giacomo Neri at Casanova di Neri, the Fattoi family and winery.

Another interesting feature of Tuscan winemaking of late has been the contribution of foreign winemakers who have settled in the region, learned all they could from the locals and then added their own passion, expertise, individuality and insight. Foremost among them is Irish winemaker Sèan O'Callaghan at the **Riecine** winery outside Gaiole in Chianti; others include Martin Frölich, a former lawyer from Germany, at the **Castagnoli** winery near Castellina in Chianti, and the Frenchman Lionel Cousin, who in 2003 bottled his first Brunello at **Cupano**, his small organic winery situated near Montalcino.

GETTING STARTED

The wine map of Tuscany is far more varied than a visit to a UK or US wine shop would ever lead you to believe. It's so rich, in fact, that Tuscany is at the forefront of *il turismo enogastronomico*, whereby tourists devote part of their holiday to visiting wineries and sampling local foods: over 90 per cent of Italy's wine and food tourism focuses on Tuscany. Such tourism is seen as sustainable, as good for the visitor as it is for the local economy and as a lovely way of getting to know the countryside as well as its products. To lure discerning palates to the lesser-known reaches of Tuscan viticulture, the **Movimento del Turismo del Vino** (www.movimentoturismovino.it) has helped set up a number of offices in most of the wine-producing areas. These **Strade del Vino** organise tasting tours, visits to cellars, meals based on local produce and other events. Another event worth a look is **Cantine Aperte**, held on the last weekend of May, when wineries all over the region (and the country) open their doors (and bottles) to visitors.

Visiting wineries entirely under your own steam can be both interesting and frustrating. While most welcome tourists with advance warning, not all have a proper tasting facility, or staff who speak English; nor, indeed, do they have the time to devote to this sort of PR. However, a little research goes a long way. For our picks of wineries open to the public, *see p258* **Fine vines**, but well-run local *enoteche* will be in a position to advise, both by providing tastings on their own premises or phoning their contacts in selected wineries. These shops are usually run by *appassionati* who will happily provide you with a number of glasses for a 'vertical' tasting of different vintages of the same wine, or a 'horizontal' tasting (no reference to your final posture) of wines of the same variety and/or year made by different producers. *Enoteche* also sell wine, by the bottle or the case. Prices may be higher than at the wineries, but you may find smaller wineries have no product left to sell or are so far away it's not worth the effort to get there.

DRINKING OUT

The **Strade del Vino di Toscana** organisation is gradually working with restaurateurs to improve the level of wine expertise of their staff. In an expensive gourmet restaurant you're bound to find a waiter who really knows about the listed wines, though this isn't really the case in simpler eateries. Where suggestions are not forthcoming, you have a few choices. You could arm yourself with the annually updated English edition of the generally reliable *Italian Wines Guide*, published by Slow Food and Gambero Rosso, and pick something from the wine list. You could choose a bottle made by one of the old, established wine estates, or one of the more impressive new ones (*see above*). Or you might do some research into the local DOC and opt for a medium-priced bottle, an approach that often leads the intrepid taster to a gratifying discovery.

Where to Stay

Where to Stay **50**

Features

The best Hotels 53
Painting by room numbers 56
Family guys 67

Helvetia & Bristol. *See p53.*

Where to Stay

More than just a room with a view (though you might well be charged for that).

While room rates remain among the highest in Italy, the positive side to accommodation in Florence is the sheer variety of options. Whether your bed of choice lies in a boutique hotel with a sharp design edge or a homely B&B on the top floor of an ancient palazzo, chances are that you'll find something appealing. Book a bunk in a youth hostel occupying a crumbling villa, a penthouse suite with terrace views, a frescoed boudoir looking on to a private garden or an executive room with all the technical facilities necessary for a business trip; in fact, just about the only thing missing in this city (and this is a firm positive) is big chain hotels.

After several years of fairly lean pickings, the tourists were back in force in the 2007/08 season, leaving the city's hoteliers cautiously optimistic. In fact, there has been a steady stream of new openings since our last edition. Most significant in recent years has been the huge increase in the number of B&Bs, *afittacamere* (rooms to rent) and *residenze d'epoca* (listed buildings with no more than 12 rooms), but as these categories lie outside the star rating system (*see below*), it can be difficult to judge what you're likely to end up with. They range from spartan, gloomy rooms with threadbare towels and no breakfast (yes, B&Bs with no breakfast) to homely pads furnished with antiques where you start the day with warm brioches. The ones listed here are among our favourites, but there are plenty more on offer. Good online resources include www.bedandbreakfast.it, www.bbitalia.it and www.caffelletto.it.

There are also several new hotels in the upper price brackets, and the most keenly anticipated new opening for years was receiving its finishing touches as this guide went to press. After many delays, the long-awaited **Four Seasons Florence** is due to receive its first guests in early spring 2008. Housed in historic Palazzo della Gherardesca, which stands in one of the largest privately owned gardens in Florence, it's the result of a multi-million-euro restoration project and will house 116 luxurious rooms and suites plus multifarious five-star facilities, including a big spa, gym and outdoor pool.

> ❶ Green numbers given in this chapter correspond to the location of each hotel as marked on the street maps. *See pp334-35.*

STAR RATINGS AND FACILITIES

Hotels are officially given a star rating from one to five by the tourist board (some lodgings are excluded from this system; *see above*), but the rating is an indication of the facilities on offer rather than the standards. There can be enormous disparity within any given category so it pays to do your research.

Most hotels price their rooms according to size, view, the amount of natural light they receive, the size and type of bathroom and whether rooms have balconies or terraces. Bedrooms in all the hotels listed here that fall within the star system have phones and en suite bathrooms, with the exception of some of those in the Budget category; where a Budget hotel does offer ensuite facilities, we've mentioned it in the review. Many rooms also have safes and hairdryers. Facilities vary among hotels that come under the other categories, so check before you book if you require something specific. If you don't like the room you've been given, ask to see another one, and don't be put off by grumpy owners. Hotels are required by law to display official maximum room rates in each room; if you feel you've been taken for a ride, there's an office for complaints (*see p304*).

If you're staying in the centre of the city during the long hot summer, a private terrace or balcony – or some kind of outside space – can make a big difference. Alternatively, head for the hills, where, within a short distance of the city centre, you'll find lodgings set in wonderful rural locations. On the subject of fresh air, the Italian smoking ban means that within a hotel, you can't smoke in any public space (unless it has the legally required ventilation and special doors), and you can only smoke in officially designated smoking guestrooms (a rule not always adhered to). However, many hotels have simply banned smoking altogether. If you have strong feelings about smoking in the bedroom, one way or another, always say so at the time of booking.

Very few hotels in the centre of town have their own parking facilities; most have an arrangement with a nearby private garage, though this will be expensive (we have given rates under each hotel). A law requires hotels with three or more stars to have rooms with disabled access – but in some cases, rooms for the disabled are only accessible, absurdly, by a lift that's too narrow to take a wheelchair.

BOOKING AND PRICES

High season for Florence's hotels runs roughly from Easter (the busiest weekend of the year) until late July, and September until early November. It also covers Christmas, New Year, Italian public holidays (*see p315*) and the Pitti fashion fairs in early January. Hotel rooms at these times are at their most expensive and much in demand, so book well in advance. On the other hand, low season (roughly November to February and late July to August, excluding the holiday periods mentioned above) offers great potential for accommodation bargains, especially among the upper-end establishments; budget hotels and B&Bs are less likely to lower their rates significantly. If you are willing to take your chances and are travelling off-season,

Luxury linens and sumptuous sofas at the **Helvetia & Bristol**. *See p53.*

SERRISTORI COUNTRY

In the heart of the florentine Chianti region, just 20 km from Florence and 40 km from Siena, settled on the crest of a rolling hill covered with vineyards and olive orchards, the two abodes (the farmhouse and the villa) which make up Serristori Country have sat facing each other for centuries.
The structure has been divided into 10 comfortable apartments, in accordance with the ancient architectural canons of tuscan farmers, where baked stone and wood are mixed harmoniously. To finish these materials, natural products that were once common place have been used: beeswax, linseed oil, and old whitewashing techniques.

APARTMENTS

Poggio al Frantoio, Strada commenda 2
50028 Tavarnelle Val di Pesa - Firenze, Italy
tel +39 055 2001623 fax +39 055 2347828
www.serristoricountry.com info@serristoricountry.com

SERRISTORI PALACE

A true jewel in the magical settings of piazzale Michelangelo and the enchanting Arno embankmets; just a few steps away from the Ponte Vecchio and Pitti Palace. From its balconies you can almost touch the major monuments of florence: Santa Croce, the Uffizi gallery, Palazzo Vecchio, the Duomo... the renaissance at its most authentic, its history and culture, from the heights of a building which epitomises this atmosphere.
This unique place in the world. Serristori palace is a choice that offers you the opportunity of living in the heart of Florence.

RESIDENCE

Lungarno Serristori, 13 - 50125 Firenze, Italy
tel +39 055 2001623 fax +39 055 2347828
www.serristoripalace.com info@serristoripalace.com

it's worth doing the rounds to see what kind of bargain you come up with. The ITA office in Santa Maria Novella station has a list of Florence hotels and also offers a booking service. Available at tourist offices, the APT booklet *Guida all'Ospitalità* details hotels, *affittacamere*, residences, campsites and hostels in Florence and its province, as well as listing *case per ferie* – religious institutions that offer a number of beds. The majority are cheap, but they're often single-sex and operate curfews.

Prices given here – which are subject to change – are for double rooms with en suite bathrooms and complimentary breakfast, unless otherwise stated. The price ranges from the cost of the cheapest double in low season to the most expensive double in high season; the categories (luxury, expensive, etc) are based on the maximum price. However, given the potential for off-season discounts, these categories are fairly fluid. It's always worth haggling as rates may be lowered if occupancy is down. Most hotels will put at least one extra bed in a double room for a fee; many provide cots for which you may have to pay extra.

Duomo & Around

Luxury

Gallery Hotel Art

Vicolo dell'Oro 5 (055 27263/www.lungarnohotels.com). **Rooms** 74. **Rates** €385. **Credit** AmEx, DC, MC, V. **Map** p334 C3 ❶

Florence's original hip hotel opened in 1999, back when its East-meets-West design aesthetic was refreshingly different from the norm – but it's now no longer the only trendy kid on the block. Located in a tiny piazza near the ponte Vecchio, the place has a cosy library with squashy sofas, thoughtfully supplied with cashmere throws and mountains of arty books to browse. Also here is the stylish Fusion Bar, which serves *aperitivi*, brunches, light lunches and dinners, while the public rooms on the ground floor often double as show-space for contemporary artists and photographers (*see p56* **Painting by room numbers**). The bedrooms are super comfortable, and the bathrooms are a dream.

Bar. Concierge. Disabled-adapted rooms. Internet (dataport). No-smoking rooms. Parking (€32/day). Restaurant. Room service. TV (DVD on request, pay movies).

Helvetia & Bristol

Via de' Pescioni 2 (055 26651/www.royaldemeure.com). **Rooms** 67. **Rates** €100-€530; €26 breakfast. **Credit** AmEx, DC, MC, V. **Map** p334 B3 ❷

Since 2005, a new, energetic young management team has been breathing fresh life into the venerable Helvetia & Bristol, open since the late 1800s. Distinguished past guests include Igor Stravinsky and Bertrand Russell and the place is filled with antiques, fine paintings and prints, but the historic feel has a decidedly hip edge to it nowadays. Oil paintings, velvet sofas and vast *pietra serena* fireplaces characterise the beautiful salon, while background sounds are likely to be jazz or something cool and contemporary. There's an atmospheric, belle époque Winter Garden conservatory for cool-weather breakfasts (served alfresco in summer),

The best Hotels

For an alfresco breakfast
Beacci Tornabuoni (*see p59*), **Hermitage** (*see p54*), **Palazzo Magnani Feroni** (*see p65*) and **Residenza del Moro** (*see p57*).

For a rooftop aperitivo
Antica Torre Tornabuoni (*see p59*), **Hotel Continentale** (*see p54*), **Palazzo Magnani Feroni** (*see p65*), **La Scaletta** (*see p65*) and **Torre Guelfa** (*see p55*).

For overall value for money
Casa Pucci (*see p65*), **Palazzo Galletti** (*see p63*), **Relais Grand Tour** (*see p61*) and **Antica Dimora Johlea** (*see p60*).

For a breath of fresh air
Pensione Bencistà (*see p68*), **Classic Hotel** (*see p67*), **Riva Lofts** (*see p67*) and **Villa Poggio San Felice** (*see p68*).

For cutting-edge design
Riva Lofts (*see p67*) and **Una Hotel Vittoria** (*see p66*).

For stargazing
Relais Santa Croce (*see p63*), **Savoy** (*see p54*) and **Villa San Michele** (*see p66*).

For a blast of the past
Beacci Tornabuoni (*see p59*) and **Pensione Bencistà** (*see p68*).

For a mega-suite
Helvetia & Bristol (*see p53*), **JK Place** (*see p57*), **Relais Santa Croce** (*see p63*) and **Residenza del Moro** (*see p57*).

For being in the thick of it
Helvetia & Bristol (*see p53*) and **Residenza d'Epoca in Piazza della Signoria** (*see p54*).

while the restaurant, done out in vibrant oranges and reds, offers a relaxed atmosphere and an inviting new look at Florentine cooking. The sumptuous decor in the bedrooms has been updated, leaving an air of more discreet luxury, where fine fabrics and period furniture rub alongside fluffy duvets, flat-screen TVs and new 'old-fashioned' bathrooms. All things considered, this is one of central Florence's best smallish hotels. *Photo p51.*
Bar. Business centre. Disabled-adapted rooms. Internet (wireless). No-smoking rooms. Parking (€45/day). Restaurant. Room service. TV (DVD, pay movies).

Hotel Continentale

Vicolo dell'Oro 6r (055 27262/www.lungarno hotels.com). **Rooms** 43. **Rates** €418-€594. **Credit** AmEx, DC, MC, V. **Map** p334 C3 ❸
Another distinguished member of the Ferragamo family's Lungarno group, the Continentale is situated across a small piazza from the Gallery Hotel Art (*see p53*), but has a different feel from its sister. Both boast a contemporary style, but the Continentale is the feminine flipside to the Gallery's more masculine image. Splashes of zingy colour are supplied by some 1960s pieces, but otherwise the design is free of fuss: blonde woods, creamy fabrics, filmy white curtains, and huge glass vases, all illuminated soft pools of light. Bedrooms have modern four-posters and fabulous bathrooms; 'superiors' have full-on views of the river and the ponte Vecchio. There's a spectacular roof terrace and bar, but the best place to chill is the first floor Relax Room, where light filters through slatted blinds, and daybeds afford horizontal views of the crowds.
Bar. Concierge. Disabled-adapted rooms. Gym. Internet (dataport). No-smoking rooms. Parking (€32/day). Room service. TV (DVD).

Lungarno Suites

Lungarno Acciaiuoli 4 (055 27268000/ www.lungarnohotels.com). **Rooms** 44. **Rates** €324-€660 apartment. **Credit** AmEx, DC, MC, V. **Map** p334 C3 ❹
Ideal for travellers who are after the comforts and levels of service typical of a four-star hotel, while maintaining a little more independence, the stylish Lungarno Suites – part of the Ferragamo hotel group, and sharing its design aesthetic – offers fully serviced self-catering apartments of various sizes, situated on the north bank of the Arno. Around half the apartments have river views; those on the top floors have terraces. Each unit has a cleverly hidden and fully equipped kitchen, but you can have your shopping done for you or order meals from the Gallery Hotel Art (*see p53*).
Bar. Disabled-adapted rooms. Internet (high-speed, web TV). No-smoking rooms. Parking (€32/day). Room service. TV (DVD on request, pay movies).

Savoy

Piazza della Repubblica 7 (055 283313/www. hotelsavoy.com). **Rooms** 102. **Rates** €490-€510. **Credit** AmEx, DC, MC, V. **Map** p334 B3 ❺
It may occupy the shell of the 19th-century hotel of the same name, but today's Savoy doesn't bear much of a resemblance to its predecessor. Now one of the city's most popular all-rounders, big with the business, leisure and celebrity brackets, the hotel was added to the ever-expanding Rocco Forte portfolio in the late 1990s. Olga Polizzi, Sir Rocco's interior designer sister, has created a characteristically stylish and calm ambience in the period space, setting dark wood, splashes of colour and some modern art against more neutral beiges and creams. The top-of-the-range Brunelleschi and Signoria suites have their own steam rooms, and there's a rooftop gym. The L'Incontro bar and brasserie is not cheap, but it's great for people-watching.
Bar. Business centre. Concierge. Disabled-adapted rooms. Gym. Internet (wireless, high-speed). No-smoking rooms. Parking (€35-€50/day). Restaurant. Room service. Spa. TV (DVD on request, pay movies).

Expensive

Hermitage

Vicolo Marzio 1, piazza del Pesce (055 287216/ www.hermitagehotel.com). **Rooms** 28. **Rates** €163-€245. **Credit** MC, V. **Map** p334 C3 ❻
This charming and perennially popular little three-star boasts a superb location practically on top of the ponte Vecchio. It's a bit like an upside-down doll's house; the reception and public rooms (painted a rather fetching avocado green) are on the top floors, with the bedrooms (all 28 comfortable, some rather small) located on the lower four floors. All the rooms have jacuzzi baths or showers. Those at the front have amazing views, but can be noisy.
Bar. Concierge. Disabled-adapted rooms. Internet (dataport, high-speed). No-smoking rooms. Parking (€21-€34/day). Room service. TV.

Residenza d'Epoca in Piazza della Signoria

Via de' Magazzini 2 (055 2399546/www.inpiazza dellasignoria.com). **Rooms** 10. **Rates** €280. **Credit** AmEx, DC, MC, V. **Map** p334 C4 ❼
Located just a few steps from piazza della Signoria, this is a hotel for visitors who want to be right in the heart of the cultural action. Most of the rooms have views of the piazza, the best of which can be found in Leonardo and Michaelangelo: rooms are named after famous Florentine residents (with nice touches – the Dante and Beatrice rooms are adjacent). Up the absolutely tiny lift (or the more spacious stairs), rooms are furnished in a fairly traditional, unfussy style, with antiques, canopied beds, oriental rugs, wood floors and pastel walls. Imaginatively fitted bathrooms give a sense of the opulence of a much bigger hotel. Meet your neighbours over a hearty breakfast at the huge oval table on the third floor, or have it delivered to your room.
Bar. Business centre. Internet (dataport, high-speed shared terminal). No-smoking rooms. Parking (€24-€30/day). Room service. TV.

Moderate

B&B Novecento

Via Ricasoli 10, San Marco (055 214138/www.bbnovecentofirenze.it). **Rooms** 6. **Rates** €100-€150. **Map** p335 B4 ❽

Franco and Sawako have been running their cosy six-room B&B with commitment and enthusiasm since 2003 and have an excellent record of return guests. The space occupies the third floor of a building between the Duomo and piazza della SS Annunziata and has the advantage of a small roof terrace where you can enjoy a glass of wine to the spectacular backdrop of Florence's skyline. There's no lift, but your cases will be hauled up by an ingenious pulley system. The pretty rooms are mostly on the small side, but have been carefully furnished with nice touches such as colourful cushions, padded bedheads and firm, orthopaedic mattresses; they all have new, tiled bathrooms. An above-average breakfast is served at your table in the homely breakfast room. Prices are a little over the odds.

Concierge. No-smoking rooms. Parking (€30/day). Room service. TV (satellite).

B&B Novecento.

Dei Mori

Via Dante Alighieri 12 (055 211438/www.deimori.it). **Rooms** 8. **Rates** €100-€120; reduced rates for longer stays. **Credit** MC, V. **Map** p335 B4 ❾

This friendly guesthouse in the heart of the medieval city was one of Florence's first B&Bs, and it's still one of the best. The rooms are keenly priced and comfortable: the ones on the first floor are more traditional (and some don't have bathrooms), while those upstairs are smarter and all en suite. The welcome is exceptionally warm: fresh flowers, bright rugs, cheerful paintings and a comfy sitting room complete with a TV, a stereo and lots of books and magazines. There's a terrace from which you can just see the top of the Duomo.

Internet (dataport). No-smoking rooms. Parking (€25/€30 day). Room service. TV room.

Perseo

Via de' Cerretani 1 (055 212504/www.hotelperseo.it). **Rooms** 20. **Rates** €148. **Credit** AmEx, MC, V. **Map** p334 B3 ❿

Occupying the shell of its rather down-at-heel predecessor, the new-look Perseo opened in April 2006, offering 20 stylish rooms, good prices and a super-central location. The owners have gone for a clean, contemporary look so expect modern wood furniture, a palette of earthy colours, flat-screen TVs, sharp light fittings and sparkling new bathrooms. The sitting room is well supplied with books and magazines while a complimentary *aperitivo*, along with nibbles, is offered to guests each evening.

Bar. Concierge. Disabled-adapted rooms. Internet (dataport). No-smoking rooms. Parking (€26-€32/daily). TV.

Relais degli Uffizi

Chiasso del Buco 16, off chiasso de' Baroncelli (055 2676239/www.relaisuffizi.it). **Rooms** 10. **Rates** €200-€240. **Credit** AmEx, MC, V. **Map** p334 C3 ⓫

Perhaps the best-positioned hotel for the Uffizi and Palazzo Vecchio, this attractive, smart hotel is nevertheless a little tricky to locate, down a tiny alley off the south side of piazza della Signoria. Once you're upstairs, either settle down in the sitting room and enjoy its fab views, or relax in the great comfort of your own room. The ten rooms vary in shape and size but are all spacious; iron beds and parquet floors set the aesthetic tone, which is consolidated by an assortment of well-chosen antiques and paintings. Adjacent to the hotel is Uffizi House, an equally tasteful guesthouse with rates from €80 to €170.

Bar. Concierge. Disabled-adapted rooms. No-smoking rooms. Parking (€28/day). Room service. TV.

Torre Guelfa

Borgo SS Apostoli 8 (055 2396338/www.hoteltorreguelfa.com). **Rooms** 25. **Rates** €170-€190. **Credit** AmEx, MC, V. **Map** p334 C3 ⓬

This popular hotel literally started at the top and worked its way down; the original rooms were all on the top floor, but the hotel now occupies the whole of the 14th-century palazzo, which incorporates the

tallest privately owned tower in Florence. Evening drinks come with stunning views at the tower-top bar. Breakfast is served in a sunny, glassed-in loggia on the third floor, where there's also an elegant sitting room (with Wi-Fi access) with a painted box ceiling. Bedrooms are decorated in pastel colours with wrought-iron beds (including several four-posters); some are huge. Number 15 is a romantic little den with its own roof garden – you'll need to book at least six months in advance for this. The 12 rooms on the first floor are cheaper and simpler; those facing the street are quite dark.
Bar. Concierge. Disabled-adapted rooms. Internet (dataport, shared-terminal, €5/hr, Wi-Fi in sitting room). No-smoking rooms. Parking (€30/day). Room service. TV.

Budget

Cestelli

Borgo SS Apostoli 25 (055 214213/www.hotelcestelli.com). **Rooms** 8. **Rates** €75-€95. **Credit** AmEx, MC, V. **Map** p334 C2 ⓭
The Cestelli is a thoughtful conversion of an old one-star hotel: super-friendly owners Alessandro and Asumi have done a wonderful job in maintaining an old-fashioned feel while updating what was once something of a shabby property. At these rates it's one of the best deals in Florence for simple, pristine, generously sized rooms (even the singles are ample). The building's antique parquet floors have been scrubbed up to great effect, and a

Painting by room numbers

Residenza del Moro.

With all those blank walls, hotels have great potential as art exhibition spaces and Florence can boast a number of places where art (both contemporary and period) plays a major role in the decor. Even when the works concerned are not of major importance, an original painting, lithograph or print on one's bedroom wall makes a nice change from the ubiquitous reproduction of Botticelli's *Primavera*.

Gilberto and Rosa Sandretto are among Italy's foremost collectors of contemporary art, and with homes all over the world, they have plenty of room to hang their hoard. They also own two hotels in Tuscany, the **Albergo Pietrasanta** in the Versilia (*see p272*) and the luxurious **Residenza del Moro** in Florence (*see p57*) where, among the frescoes and stuccos, works by contemporary art heavyweights such as Mario Schiffano, Roni Horn, Lawrence Beck and Anselm Kiefer are prominently displayed.

The owners of **Il Guelfo Bianco** (*see p60*) started collecting in a modest way in the early 1990s in order to avoid filling the rooms with swathes of fabric and banal reproductions. Some 25 years on, the hotel houses their ample collection of mainly Italian contemporary and modern works. The most important pieces hang in the long, narrow reception area where there are paintings by Lucca-born Arturo Carmassi, Florentine Silvio Loffredo and Roman Piero Dorazio. There's also a cheerful, multicoloured assemblage in wood by British artist Joe Tilson.

Some 450 works (mostly prints, etchings and drawings), mainly dating from the early 20th century, hang in the Ferragamo-owned **Lungarno** hotel (*see p64*), a collection that was started by the previous owners in the late 1960s. The most significant pieces are on display in the suites and public areas on the ground floor, where you can ogle works by Picasso, Tuscan 'splatterer' Ottone Rosai and Jean Cocteau.

Art hounds should also keep an eye on what's on offer at the **Gallery Hotel Art** (*see p53*). While it doesn't have a permanent collection of its own, the hotel's sleek, contemporary decor and ample public space provide an interesting backdrop for exhibitions by contemporary artists and photographers curated by the Brancolini Grimaldi gallery (*see p181*).

complementary mix of antique and new furniture presides within. All but three of the eight rooms come with a private bathroom.
Concierge. No-smoking rooms. Parking (€20/day).

Santa Maria Novella

Luxury

Grand Hotel

Piazza Ognissanti 1 (055 27161/www.luxurycollection.com/grandflorence). **Rooms** 107. **Rates** €583-€759; €98 supplement for river view; €39 breakfast. **Credit** AmEx, DC, MC, V. **Map** p334 B1 ⓮

While its rooms are no less luxurious than those at its sister hotel across the piazza, the Grand is decidedly different in character to the Westin Excelsior (*see below*). The reception area is light and airy, while the conservatory, with its stained-glass ceiling, marble floor and *pietra serena* columns, offers old-fashioned opulence; within it is a lounge area and a piano bar. Less oppressive is new eaterie InCanto, offering a modern take on Tuscan food in a contemporary setting. Roughly half of the 107 bedrooms and suites are done up in faux-Renaissance Florentine style, complete with frescoes, painted ceilings and heavy traditional fabrics. If your roommate is canine, you'll be given a dogs' welcome kit.
Bar. Business centre. Concierge. Disabled-adapted rooms. Gym. Internet (dataport, high-speed, wireless in public areas). No-smoking rooms. Parking (€42-€55/day). Restaurants (2). Room service. TV (DVD, pay movies).

Hotel Santa Maria Novella

Piazza Santa Maria Novella 1 (055 271840/www.hotelsantamarianovella.it). **Rooms** 45. **Rates** €190-€520. **Credit** AmEx, DC, MC, V. **Map** p334 B2 ⓯

Owned by clothing manufacturer Rifle, this 45-room hotel is due to open another 25 rooms in an adjacent building by mid 2008. The property is done out in fairly elaborate Empire style, with rich colours, painted wood panelling and fancy marquetry, but contemporary decorative touches mean it never feels too oppressive. Two cosy sitting rooms on the ground floor have open fires, velvet sofas and armchairs, plus original oil paintings on the walls. The bedrooms, kitted out in bright colours with modern, country fabrics, come with canopied beds, silk curtains and plasma-screen TVs; the grand marble bathrooms are equipped with Santa Maria Novella goodies. The breakfast room is a symphony of mirrors, but there's also an intimate little wood-panelled bar on the ground floor and a panoramic terrace bar on the roof.
Bar. Business centre. Concierge. Disabled-adapted rooms. Gym. Internet (dataport, high-speed). No-smoking rooms. Parking (€27-€32/day). Room service. TV.

JK Place

Piazza Santa Maria Novella 7 (055 2645181/www.jkplace.com). **Rooms** 20. **Rates** €350-€650. **Credit** AmEx, DC, MC, V. **Map** p334 B2 ⓰

One of the best small hotels in Florence, the ultra-sophisticated, 20-room JK Place occupies an attractive old townhouse on piazza Santa Maria Novella. Architect/designer Michele Bonan (who has also worked on the Ferragamo hotels; *see p54 and p63*) is responsible for the style, a contemporary take on a neoclassical look, where muted colours beautifully offset fine antiques, old prints, black and white photos and artful flower arrangements. The flicker of candlelight provides a soft glow. No two bedrooms are alike, though all are luxurious and lack nothing in the way of facilities: several of the larger ones overlook the piazza while others are smaller and don't have views. If you're lucky enough to stay in the top-floor penthouse suite, you'll have a 360° sweep of the city from the bathroom. Drinks, snacks and light meals are on offer in the sleek lounge, while an inviting fire burns in the adjacent living room in winter; there's also a roof terrace.
Bar. Concierge. Disabled-adapted rooms. Internet (dataport, high-speed, wireless in public areas). No-smoking rooms. Parking (€32/day). Restaurant. Room service. TV (DVD).

Residenza del Moro

Via del Moro 15 (055 2648494/www.residenzadelmoro.com). **Rooms** 11. **Rates** €539-€850. **Map** p334 B2 ⓱

The splendid *piano nobile* of 16th-century Palazzo Niccolini-Bourbon has been exquisitely restored and now houses this luxurious *residenza* with its 11 rooms and suites. You'll find eleborate stucco work, impressive frescoes and lofty, painted ceilings. The bedrooms vary enormously in shape and size (and price) from the cosy, almost-affordable Biblioteca to the palatial, super-priced Marchese Suite, but all feature precious antiques, rich fabrics and canopied beds made up with fine linens and cashmere blankets. The lovely marble bathrooms are everything you'd expect from such a place. One thing you would not necessarily anticipate is the beautiful hanging garden where breakfast is served when the weather permits. Another surprise is the fine collection of contemporary art that hangs throughout the bedrooms and public spaces. For more on hotel art, *see p56* **Painting by room numbers**).
Bars (2). Business centre. Concierge. Disabled-adapted rooms. Gym. Internet (wireless). No-smoking rooms. Parking (€32/day). Room service. TV (DVD on request).

Westin Excelsior

Piazza Ognissanti 3 (055 27151/www.westin.com/excelsiorflorence). **Rooms** 171. **Rates** €568-€732; €98 supplement for river view; €39 breakfast. **Credit** AmEx, DC, MC, V. **Map** p334 B1 ⓲

While it still offers an element of old-world luxury, the Westin Excelsior has recently introduced some contemporary touches. There's now a fitness area, plus two 'Westin Workout' rooms that have been equipped for the health-conscious guest (yoghurt drinks, tisanes, a massage chair and New Age music on the sound system, for example). In

addition, the restaurant now offers a special menu of low-calorie dishes. All this, however, exists within a very traditional framework: the doormen are dressed in maroon and grey livery, and the grand public rooms have polished marble floors, neoclassical columns, painted wooden ceilings and stained glass. The 171 rooms and suites are sumptuously appointed; some boast terraces with views over the river to the rooftops of the Oltrarno.
Bar. Business centre. Concierge. Disabled-adapted rooms. Gym. Internet (dataport, high-speed, wireless in public areas). No-smoking rooms. Parking (€42-€55/day). Restaurants (2). Room service. TV (multimedia system, pay movies, DVD in suites).

Expensive

Antica Torre Tornabuoni Uno

Via de' Tornabuoni 1 (055 2658161/www.tornabuoni1.com). **Rooms** 12. **Rates** €180-€350. **Credit** AmEx, DC, MC, V. **Map** p334 C2 ⑲
The roof terrace of this 12-room hotel, which occupies the upper storeys of an ancient tower overlooking piazza Santa Trinità, has arguably the most spectacular view of any hotel in Florence. Breakfast and drinks are served here in summer to a backdrop of just about every monument in the city. In cooler weather, the glassed-in loggia is almost as good. While undeniably comfortable, the bedrooms (several of which have private terraces) are not terribly inspiring; however, the views that they enjoy certainly are. Aside from the terrace, though, there are are no public spaces. In early 2008, eight luxurious new suites (most of them vast) are due to open; you'll be paying a premium for these, but the views over the Arno will be stunning.
Bar. Business centre. Concierge. Disabled-adapted rooms. Internet (high-speed). No-smoking rooms. Parking (€20-€30/day). Room service. TV (DVD).

Beacci Tornabuoni

Via de' Tornabuoni 3 (055 212645/www.tornabuonihotels.com). **Rooms** 41. **Rates** €180-€240. **Credit** AmEx, MC, V. **Map** p334 B2 ⑳
Comfortable and characterful Beacci Tornabuoni is situated on the top floors of the 15th-century Palazzo Minerbetti Strozzi and, though surrounded by via de' Tornabuoni's designer shops and offers all mod cons, it has a delightful Edwardian feel. The wonderful flower-filled roof garden is used for breakfast and light dinners in summer; inside, the old parquet floors creak and groan under the weight of the antique furniture. The lovely old reading room smells of floor wax and wood smoke, the latter from a huge old *pietra serena* fireplace.
Bar. Business centre. Internet (dataport, high-speed shared terminal). No-smoking rooms. Parking (€25-€30/day). Restaurant. Room service (24hrs). TV.

Casa Howard

Via della Scala 18 (06 69924555/www.casahoward.com). **Rooms** 12. **Rates** €190-€250; €10 breakfast. **Credit** AmEx, DC, MC, V. **Map** p334 B2 ㉑
The owner of this stylish pied-à-terre has set out to offer comfortable, upmarket accommodation at reasonable rates in the discreet atmosphere of a private home. The 12 rooms here are classy and vaguely eccentric, decorated with strong colours and a mix of antique and custom-made furniture. Visit the website to choose the one you like best: the large, dramatic Drawing Room, perhaps, or maybe the sexy Hidden Room with its sunken bath and deep-red walls hung with Japanese erotic prints. There's even a room for those travelling with a canine companion; the Game Room has a terrace and dog beds. There's a Turkish bath to ease those museum-weary muscles and each floor is supplied with an 'honesty fridge'.
Bar. Concierge. Disabled-adapted rooms. Internet (dataport, high-speed, wireless in public areas). No-smoking room. Parking (€20-€35/day). Room service. TV.

Grand Hotel Minerva

Piazza Santa Maria Novella 16 (055 27230/www.grandhotelminerva.com). **Rooms** 102. **Rates** €155-€440. **Credit** AmEx, DC, MC, V. **Map** p334 B2 ㉒
Once an annexe hosting guests to the adjacent convent, the Minerva has been a hotel since the mid 19th century. However, the interior was revamped in the mid 1990s in bright, modern colours; today, it's staffed by a young, dynamic team, and is one of the nicest hotels in this category; it's also close to the train station. Many of the appealing rooms have sunny views over piazza Santa Maria Novella (it can get noisy in summer), while extras include in-room electric kettles, a kids' package of videos and games and a shiatsu masseuse on request. Pet owners get a special deal (a room with a terrace and a wood floor, cat litter and pet food) as do women travelling alone (room upgrades, special bath goodies, magazines, free room service). There's a small pool and a bar on the panoramic roof garden.
Bar. Business centre. Concierge. Disabled-adapted rooms. Internet (wireless, dataport, high-speed shared terminal). No-smoking rooms. Parking (€27-€31/day). Pool (outdoor). Restaurant. Room service. TV (DVD on request, pay movies).

Budget

Abaco

Via de' Banchi 1 (055 2381919/www.hotelabaco.it). **Rooms** 7. **Rates** €75-€85; €5 breakfast. **Credit** AmEx, MC, V. **Map** p334 B3 ㉓
There's a bit of a climb up to the second floor of this 550-year-old building; once you've made it, you'll find a modest shell housing a handsome hotel. The friendly owner has painstakingly decorated the less-than-grand place in grand style: the seven bedrooms, each named after a Renaissance artist, are decorated in sumptuous fabrics with reproductions of works by the relevant painter on the walls. Gilding adorns the picture and mirror frames, and most of the beds are canopied. Three rooms have their own full bathrooms, while others have only a shower.

Breakfast is free if you pay in cash (and there's a further 10% discount in November and December).
Bar. Concierge. Disabled-adapted rooms. Internet (dataport, high-speed shared terminal). No-smoking rooms. Parking (€24/day). TV.

Ferretti

Via delle Belle Donne 17 (055 2381328/www.hotelferretti.com). **Rooms** 16. **Rates** €55-€105. **Credit** MC, V. **Map** p334 B2 ㉔

This friendly, spotlessly clean little one-star hotel enjoys a great location in a network of quiet, medieval streets between the station and via de' Tornabuoni. All 16 rooms are pleasant (and all have ceiling fans), but the best are at the top of the old building; bright and sunny, they have recently been redecorated and have crisp cotton covers on iron bedsteads and lovely old marble floors. There's a cosy, wood-panelled breakfast room with a free internet point. Only about half the rooms have a private bathroom, so check when you book.
Bar. Concierge. Disabled-adapted rooms. No-smoking rooms. Parking (€25/day).

Scoti

Via de' Tornabuoni 7 (055 292128/www.hotelscoti.com). **Rooms** 11. **Rates** €115. **Credit** AmEx, DC, MC, V. **Map** p334 B2 ㉕

If you want to secure a room in the wonderful Scoti, housed on the second floor of a 15th-century palazzo, book well ahead: it's popular with visitors worldwide. After extensive renovation a couple of years back, the lofty bedrooms are simple but bright and sunny and all en suite; the frescoed salon has retained its air of faded glory. Breakfast is served around a big communal table or in the rooms.
Disabled-adapted rooms. No-smoking rooms. Parking (€28-€30/day). TV room.

San Lorenzo

Moderate

Antica Dimora Johlea

Via San Gallo 72 (055 4627296/www.johanna.it). **Rooms** 6. **Rates** €125-€150. **Credit** MC, V.

Lea Gulmanelli and Johanan Vitta opened the first of their mini-chain of five *residenze* back in 1994. Their latest project is the Antica Dimora Johlea (formerly the Johlea Uno), situated a ten-minute walk north of the central market and now the most upmarket of the group. Classical music and a warm glow set the scene when you enter. The cosy bedrooms, all with four posters, are done out in a riot of strong colours with bright kilims on marble or parquet floors, Indian print covers on the beds and swathes of raw Thai silk. Defying the low rates, all have flat-screen TVs, DVD players, digital radios and electric kettles. Breakfast is served at the top of the house where there's also a sitting room with an honesty bar; from here a wooden staircase leads up to a flower-filled roof terrace with 360° views. If there's no room at this inn, check out the other – cheaper – hotels in the group's portfolio (on the same website): all small, charming and great value.
Bar. Disabled-adapted rooms. No-smoking rooms. Internet (wireless). Parking (€20/day). TV (DVD).

Casci

Via Cavour 13 (055 211686/www.hotelcasci.com). **Rooms** 24. **Rates** €90-€150. Closed 3wks Jan. **Credit** AmEx, DC, MC, V. **Map** p335 A4 ㉖

The super-helpful Lombardi family runs this friendly *pensione*, which occupies a 15th-century palazzo just north of the Duomo, where opera composer Giacomo Rossini lived from 1851 to 1855. The open-plan bar and breakfast area has frescoed ceilings and shelves stocked with guidebooks; the 24 bedrooms are comfortable and come with up-to-date bathrooms. Bedrooms at the back look on to a beautiful garden; two sizeable family rooms sleep up to five. There's now Wi-Fi throughout the hotel.
Bar. Concierge. Disabled-adapted rooms. Internet (wireless). No-smoking rooms. Parking (€23/day). Room service. TV.

Il Guelfo Bianco

Via Cavour 29 (055 288330/www.ilguelfobianco.it). **Rooms** 40. **Rates** €160-€180. **Credit** AmEx, MC, V. **Map** p335 A4 ㉗

Inhabiting two adjacent 15th-century townhouses, this pleasant, efficiently run hotel lies just north of the Duomo. The 40 bedrooms and one self-catering apartment (sleeping four) have been thoughtfully decorated in traditional style; the more capacious rooms allow for an additional two beds, making them a good choice for families. The walls throughout are hung with the owner's impressive contemporary art collection (*see p56* **Painting by room numbers**). The rooms that front on to via Cavour have been soundproofed, but those at the back are still noticeably quieter. Two attractive courtyards offer respite from the city noise; one is used for breakfast in warm weather.
Bar. Concierge. Disabled-adapted rooms. Internet (wireless, high-speed shared terminal, €5/hr). No-smoking rooms. Parking (€26-€32/day). Room service. TV (pay movies).

Locanda degli Artisti

Via Faenza 56 (055 213806/www.hotelazzi.it). **Rooms** 29. **Rates** €75-€120. **Credit** AmEx, DC, MC, V. **Map** p334 A2 ㉘

Housed on the first two floors of a rambling old palazzo near the station, the Locanda degli Artisti is an interesting and comfortable little hotel with good prices and a lovely terrace. The big reception area has a retro vibe and you'll probably be greeted by classical music or jazz on the sound system. Eco-friendly materials and natural colours have been used in the 29 bright, sunny bedrooms, and organic produce is served at breakfast. If you're prepared to pay a little over the odds for a touch of luxury, the Suite Blu has a big jacuzzi bath.
Bar. Disabled-adapted rooms. Internet (dataport shared teminal). No-smoking rooms. Parking (€15/day). TV (DVD some rooms).

Relais Grand Tour

Via Santa Reparata 21 (055 283955/www.florencegrandtour.com). **Rooms** 9. **Rates** €95-€110. **No credit cards.**

Those 17th-century folk well-heeled enough to undertake the Grand Tour would have been delighted to rest their overexcited heads at one of the luxurious suites of this hotel, named in the journey's honour. A former 16th-century house, the imaginatively restored B&B is run by welcoming couple Cristina and Giuseppe. The Mirrors Suite (use your imagination) is much loved by honeymooners, while the extraordinary Theatre Suite occupies an authentic private playhouse – the bed is on the stage, faced by several rows of seats (fashion shows are sometimes put on here). An assortment of croissants is left in a basket outside the room each morning on request. The first-floor rooms are less extravagant, but thoroughly presentable and correspondingly cheaper.
Internet (dataport, high-speed in suites, shared terminal). No-smoking rooms. Parking (€23-€28/day). TV (on request).

San Marco

Expensive

Loggiato dei Serviti

Piazza della SS Annunziata 3 (055 289592/www.loggiatodeiservitihotel.it). **Rooms** 38. **Rates** €170-€205. **Credit** AmEx, DC, MC, V. **Map** p335 A5 ㉙

This is one of the most beautiful three-star hotels in Florence, housed in a 16th-century former convent that looks over lovely piazza della SS Annunziata to Brunelleschi's famous portico. Inside is a tasteful and stylish combination of original architectural features, wonderful antique furniture and the modern comforts of an upmarket hotel. The 38 bedrooms, five of which are housed in an annexe in via dei Servi, vary in size and style; the four suites are ideal for families. Breakfast is served in a bright, elegant room with vaulted ceilings, while drinks can be ordered in the cosy bar area. Be aware of the live music events plus bar and restaurant set up in the square in summer: one man's entertainment is another's lost sleep.
Bar. Concierge. Disabled-adapted rooms. Internet (dataport, shared terminal). No-smoking rooms. Parking (€24-€30/day). Room service. TV.

Residence Hilda

Via dei Servi 40 (055 288021/www.residencehilda.com). **Rooms** 10. **Rates** €190-€350 apartment. **Credit** AmEx DC, MC, V. **Map** p335 A5 ㉚

Boasting a prime location just five minutes' walk north of the Duomo, Residence Hilda offers stylish self-catering accommodation ranging from small units for two people to larger apartments for five. All of the cool, super-modern apartments come with well-equipped kitchen units that can be hidden away behind sliding doors when required. The furnishings throughout are stylishly spare, with Philippe Starck chairs and other modern classics sitting on blonde wood floors. Staff will even deliver your shopping.

Antique chairs and modern comforts at **Casa Rovai**. *See p63.*

Internet (dataport, high-speed, shared terminal). No-smoking rooms. Parking (€24-€30/day). TV (satellite).

Santa Croce

Luxury

Relais Santa Croce

Via Ghibellina 87 (055 2342230/www.relaisanta croce.com). **Rooms** 24. **Rates** €295-€385. **Credit** AmEx, DC, MC, V. **Map** p335 C5 ㉛

This hotel offers contemporary style and personalised service in the shell of grand, 18th-century Palazzo Ciofi-Jacometti. The public rooms on the first floor are suitably grandiose – especially the vast music room, with its lofty, frescoed ceilings, wonderful old parquet floor and stucco panels. The bedrooms, meanwhile, have clean, modern lines with quirky design details (including amazing light fittings). Two Royal Suites offer the full VIP treatment; past incumbents of the spectacular Verazzano Suite include Kate Moss, Dave Gilmore and Marilyn Manson. Rear-facing rooms on the upper floors have views over a jumble of red-tiled rooftops to the façade of the Santa Croce church. The Relais shares its entrance with one of Italy's most celebrated restaurants, the Enoteca Pinchiorri (*see p127*), but a more reasonably priced alternative is the hotel's own restaurant (though it's only reasonably priced in comparison to its neighbour).

Bar. Business centre. Concierge. Disabled-adapted rooms. Internet (high-speed, wireless). No-smoking rooms. Parking (€30/day). Restaurant. Room service. TV (pay movies).

Moderate

Casa Rovai

Via Fiesolana 1 (055 2469856/www.casarovai.com). **Rooms** 6. **Rates** €90-€150. **Credit** AmEx, MC, V. **Map** p335 B5 ㉜

This reasonably priced, retro-stylish little guesthouse occupies the first floor of a 16th-century building not far from the lively Sant'Ambrogio market. Expect 19th-century *terrazzo* floors, traditional cream and dove-grey paintwork, the odd fresco, and a mix of late 19th- and early 20th-century furniture picked up at flea markets and auction houses, plus stylish, modern leather sofas and chairs. The six bedrooms (a couple of which have painted ceilings) vary in shape and size, but all are comfortable and have contemporary bathrooms. Continental breakfast is included in the room rate, but for an extra €5 you can order eggs, prosciutto and cheeses. *Photo p61.*

Concierge. Internet (high-speed). No-smoking rooms. Parking (€5/day). TV.

Palazzo Galletti

Via Sant'Egidio 12 (055 3905750/www.palazzo galletti.it). **Rooms** 9. **Rates** €110-€260. **Credit** AmEx, MC, V. **Map** p335 B5 ㉝

Offering excellent value and situated on a busy street just a few minutes' walk east of the Duomo, Palazzo Galletti occupies the first floor of an 18th-century mansion built around an internal courtyard. All the elements of a grand palazzo are here (weathered old *cotto* floors, lofty arched ceilings, elegant paintwork in soothing pastels,

Get the VIP treatment at **Relais Santa Croce**.

frescoes, the odd chandelier), but the overall effect is not at all pompous thanks to the addition of some carefully chosen ethnic and contemporary design details. All but two of the nine lovely bedrooms face on to the quiet *cortile* (yard) and have a tiny terrace. Even the smallest rooms are a good size, while the two entirely frescoed suites are vast. Hotel guests are offered special rates at the new ground-floor Soulspace spa (*see p166*).
Bar. Concierge. Disabled-adapted rooms. Internet (high-speed). No-smoking rooms. Parking (€20/day). Spa (ground floor). TV.

Le Stanze di Santa Croce

Via delle Pinzochere 6 (347 2593010 mobile/www.viapinzochere6.it). **Rooms** 6. **Rates** €160. **Credit** MC, V. **Map** p335 C5 34
The diminutive, three-floor townhouse that houses this little B&B has a great location, just off piazza Santa Croce, and you'll receive a genuinely friendly welcome from the owner, Mariangela. The four comfortable double bedrooms at Le Stanze have been individually furnished with pretty fabrics, lively colours and a well considered mix of old and new furniture; one has a romantic wrought-iron four-poster. Breakfast is served on a lovely flower-filled terrace where guests can hang out all day and help themselves from a well-stocked 'honesty fridge'. Mariangela is a relaxed host and a great cook; she bakes fresh cakes daily for breakfast and offers cooking courses.
Internet (dataport). No-smoking rooms. Parking (€18-€24/day).

Budget

Dalì

Via dell'Oriuolo 17 (055 2340706/www.hoteldali.com). **Rooms** 10. **Rates** €65-€80. **Credit** MC, V. **Map** p335 B5 35
Run with genuine care by an enthusiastic young couple, Samanta and Marco, this little gem just east of the Duomo offers spotless, bright and homely rooms at budget prices and – a miracle in central Florence – free car parking. Only four of the ten rooms have private bathrooms, but all are thoughtfully decorated and furnished with hand stencilling, pretty bedcovers and old bedheads; all have ceiling fans. Those fronting on to the busy street can be a bit noisy, but double glazing helps; rooms at the back overlooking the courtyard are sunny and quiet. Breakfast is not provided, but there are electric kettles and fridges in all the rooms.
No-smoking rooms. Parking (free). TV (some rooms).

Oltrarno

Luxury

Lungarno

Borgo San Jacopo 14 (055 27261/www.lungarnohotels.com). **Rooms** 74. **Rates** €310-€385. **Credit** AmEx, DC, MC, V. **Map** p334 C2 36
The most coveted rooms in this stylish hotel, housed in a 1960s building incorporating a medieval tower, have terraces overlooking the Arno. However, even

Grand but not grandstanding: **Palazzo Galletti**. *See p63.*

if you can't secure a river view, you can enjoy the waterside setting from the breakfast room and lounge/bar, or the outside seating area on the river. More classic in feel than other Ferragamo-owned hotels such as the Gallery Hotel Art (*see p53*) and the Continentale (*see p54*), the Lungarno has been decorated in a cream and navy-blue colour scheme, but some lovely mahogany and cherrywood antique furniture, plus a collection of fine prints and drawings (*see p56* **Painting by room numbers**), lends a reassuringly traditional touch. Bedrooms are stylish and comfy but, with the exception of a couple of spacious suites, not that big. The Borgo San Jacopo restaurant (*see p132*) a few doors down serves excellent food in a calm, elegant setting.
Bar. Concierge. Disabled-adapted rooms. Internet (wireless, dataport). No-smoking rooms. Parking (€35/day). Restaurant. Room service. TV (DVD on request).

Palazzo Magnani Feroni

Borgo San Frediano 5 (055 2399544/www.florencepalace.it). **Rooms** 12. **Rates** €380-€800 suite. **Credit** AmEx, DC, MC, V. **Map** p334 C1 37
Expect top-class service and facilities with prices to match at this grand palazzo just south of the river. All but one of the 12 big suites have separate sitting rooms elegantly furnished with squashy sofas, armchairs and antiques. The most charming room of all is actually the smallest: a romantic junior suite with floor-to-ceiling frescoes and a little private garden. The bathrooms are super-smart and equipped with slippers, robes and heated towel rails: you can even choose the smell of your soap. The fabulous roof terrace – complete with a bar serving light meals – offers views of the whole city.
Bar. Concierge. Gym. Internet (wireless, dataport). No-smoking rooms. Parking (€40-€47/day). Room service. TV (DVD, pay movies).

Moderate

Annalena

Via Romana 34 (055 222402/www.annalenahotel.com). **Rooms** 20. **Rates** €80-€155. **Credit** AmEx, MC, V. **Map** p334 D1 38
The Annalena is housed in a 15th-century building located just opposite the back entrance to the Boboli Gardens. At various times it has been used as a refuge for young widows and lodgings for refugees from Mussolini's Fascist police. Today, it has a pleasantly old-fashioned atmosphere and, after a period of decline, has just been taken over by enthusiastic, helpful new management, which is determined to bring the place up to scratch. It's brightened up the huge, atmospheric salon that serves as lounge, bar and breakfast room, while the pleasant, oft-spacious bedrooms have been given a lick of paint; future plans include updating the bathrooms. The best rooms are at the back overlooking the gorgeous Annalena gardens and have terraces scented with jasmine.
Bar. Internet (wireless). No-smoking rooms. Parking (€13-€25/day). Room service. TV.

La Scaletta

Via de' Guicciardini 13 (055 283028/214255/www.hotellascaletta.it). **Rooms** 15. **Rates** €85-€140. **Credit** MC, V. **Map** p334 D3 39
A change of management in 2005 swept away the figurative cobwebs of the old-style Scaletta, housed in a grand 15th-century palazzo between the ponte Vecchio and Palazzo Pitti, in favour of cleaner – even stylish – lines. The 16 buttermilk-painted bedrooms have elegant matching curtains and bedspreads, modern wrought-iron bedheads and nice old wardrobes. Most are quiet; nos.21, 22 and 23 overlook the Boboli Gardens, while those on noisy via Guicciardini boast effective double glazing. All rooms now have bathrooms. There are no fewer than three roof gardens/terraces that offer breathtaking views of Boboli and the city skyline; one has a bar that's open in the evenings.
Bar. Concierge. No-smoking rooms. Parking (€25-€30/day). TV.

Budget

Casa Pucci

Via Santa Monaca 8 (055 216560/www.casapucci.artwork-inform.com). **Rooms** 5. **Rates** €90-€110. **Map** p334 C1 40
Signora Pucci's cosy ground-floor apartment, not far from buzzy piazza Santo Spirito, occupies part of an ex-convent dating from the 15th century. Three of the five rooms lead off a cool, plant-filled courtyard garden where a huge rustic table is laid in the mornings for summer breakfasts. The whole place has a nice, lived-in feel, from the big kitchen (which guests are free to use) to the spacious, homely rooms furnished with family antiques and paintings. Romantics should go for room five with its four-poster bed and stone fireplace. A faithful clientele of return guests – plus amazingly low prices – means that you need to book well ahead. *Photo p66.*
Disabled-adapted rooms. Internet (wireless in public area). No-smoking rooms. TV.

Istituto Gould

Via de' Serragli 49 (055 212576). **Open** *Office* 8.45am-1pm, 3-7.30pm Mon-Fri; 9am-1.30pm, 2.30-6pm Sat. **Rooms** 42. **Rates** €56-€64. **Credit** MC, V. **Map** p334 D1 41
Run by the Valdese Church, Istituto Gould offers excellent budget accommodation in a well-kept 17th-century palazzo with a serene courtyard, stone staircases, terracotta floors, a tantalisingly lovely garden (unfortunately, not accessible to guests) and lots of atmosphere. There are now some 41 rooms on site: two-thirds are doubles, while the others accommodate a maximum of four. All rooms but two (a triple and a quad) now have private bathrooms. If you want to avoid noisy via de' Serragli, ask for a room at the back; some have access to a terrace. You need to check in during office hours, but once that's done, you get your own key.
No-smoking hotel.

Casa Pucci. *See p65.*

Outside the City Gates

Luxury

Una Hotel Vittoria

Via Pisana 9 (055 22771/www.unahotels.it). **Rooms** 84. **Rates** €450-€466. **Credit** AmEx, DC, MC, V.

Milan-based architect/designer Fabio Novembre's exuberant Una Hotel Vittoria (housed in the shell of a 19th-century warehouse just outside Porta San Frediano) is geared towards an upmarket business clientele, but will appeal to anyone looking for something completely different decor-wise. The building is filled with Novembre's idiosyncratic designs; the huge swooping mosaic that greets you in the entrance hall is based on a 19th-century floral brocade while the long, curving wooden table in the restaurant (designed for communal eating) was influenced by the refectory tables found in Tuscan monasteries. The spacious bedrooms are equipped with a plethora of gadgetry. They lead off black-painted corridors where each door is framed in gold leaf and sports an 'old master' portrait; effectively, you walk through the painting to enter the room. Once inside, the beds are tucked into cosy alcoves and backed by oversized bedheads studded with star-like fibre optic lights that change colour. Anyone with a modest disposition should book elsewhere; only glass separates the mosaic bathrooms from the rest of the room.

Bar. Business centre. Concierge. Disabled-adapted rooms. Internet (wireless, €20/day). No-smoking rooms. Parking (€20/day). Restaurant. Room service. TV (DVD on request, pay movies).

Villa San Michele

Via Doccia 4 (055 5678200/www.villasanmichele.com). Bus 7. **Rooms** 46. **Rates** €840. Closed late Nov-late Mar. **Credit** AmEx, DC, MC, V.

The rooms in this fabulous yet understated hotel, much beloved on the celebrity circuit, are among the most expensive in Italy. Housed in a 15th-century monastery, Villa San Michele enjoys a superb location, nestled in a beautiful terraced garden on the hillside just below Fiesole. Understated elegance and good taste, combined with subtle nods to the past, inform the style, which is always luxurious but never ostentatious. The views down to the city are splendid: dinner under the loggia at sunset is an unforgettable experience, though the bill will be too. Service throughout the property is immaculate.

Bar. Business centre. Concierge. Gym. Internet (dataport, high-speed). No-smoking rooms. Parking (free). Pool (outdoor). Restaurants (3). Room service. Spa. TV (DVD, pay movies).

Expensive

Relais Marignolle

Via di San Quirichino a Marignolle 16 (055 2286910/www.marignolle.com). No bus. **Rooms** 9. **Rates** €235-€275. **Credit** AmEx, MC, V.

Set in rambling grounds on a south-facing hillside at Marignolle (a few kilometres south of Porta Romana), the Bulleri family's classily converted farmhouse is a great base from which to make the most of elegant country living while still keeping the sights of the city within easy reach. Sun pours into the large, bright living room, where comfortable armchairs and sofas, an open fire and an honesty bar encourage lingering. Breakfast is served on a veranda, open in summer and glassed in over the colder months. The nine bedrooms vary in shape and size, but all are decorated along the same tasteful lines, with stylish country fabrics, padded bedheads, pristine white paintwork and dark parquet floors. Signora Bulleri serves light meals on request and holds cooking classes. The attractive pool is another nice perk.

Bar. Concierge. Internet (wireless). No-smoking rooms. Parking (free). Pool (outdoor). Room service. TV.

Riva Lofts

Via Baccio Bandinelli 98 (055 7130272/www.rivahotel.it). **Rooms** 9. **Rates** €190-€550. **Credit** AmEx, MC, V.

A welcome jolt has been given to Florence's predominantly traditional hotel scene by the December 2006 opening of Riva Lofts, the project of renowned local architect Claudio Nardi. It occupies a small complex of 19th-century artisan workshops on the Arno a 20-minute walk west of the ponte Vecchio. The heart of Riva is the big, open-plan living room with high vaulted ceiling and exposed brick where guests can help themselves from the honesty bar, and relax and chat in front of the huge fire. The use of natural elements (wood, stone) throughout warms the clean lines and spare design, and furniture is an eclectic mix of modern classics and vintage pieces. The nine suites (all but one with kitchen) range in size from 30sq m to 100sq m (320-1,080sq ft); top of the pile are the two spectacular lofts themselves, huge spaces infused with light from tall, arched windows. All rooms have super-contemporary bathrooms and electronic gadgetry; thoughtful extras include an exercise mat and weights. For recreation, there's a garden with a heated pool made of pale sandstone, walks along the riverbank, and bikes (vintage, of course) to get you into town. *Photo p68.*

Bar. Business centre. Concierge. Disabled-adapted rooms. Internet (wireless, dataport). No-smoking rooms. Parking (free). Pool (outdoor). Restaurant. TV (DVD).

Moderate

Classic Hotel

Viale Nicolò Machiavelli 25 (055 229351/www.classichotel.it). Bus 11, 36, 37 to Porta Romana. **Rooms** 20. **Rates** €120-€166. **Credit** AmEx, MC, V.

Family guys

If there's one name that's dominating today's hotel and hospitality scene in Florence, it's Fratini. Two separate branches of this family of textile magnates have bought up swathes of real estate in the city and great chunks of the Tuscan countryside too.

Sandro Fratini, manufacturer of Rifle jeans, opened the four-star **Hotel Santa Maria Novella** (*see p56*) in late 2003 and quickly expanded into the adjacent building. He has subsequently bought up several more *palazzi* on the eastern side of the square and work is currently underway on another two hotels, one of which, the watch-themed Hotel L'Ò, will be ready to receive its first guests in 2008. The opening of the second hotel, on piazza Santa Maria Novella, will follow shortly after, offering some 200 rooms.

The other side of the family, Sandro's cousins Corrado and Marcello, own the RDM Fingen Group. The managing director is Jacopo Mazzei, member of the aristocratic winemaking dynasty. Mazzei is said to be the vision behind RDM's hotel and property projects, the most high-profile of which is Florence's **Four Seasons** hotel (*see p50*), due to open in spring 2008, a multi-million-euro investment that promises to offer the most luxurious accommodation in town.

Mega-bucks are also pouring into another city-centre project, hyped as Florence's 'first and only fractional-ownership property' (whatever you do, don't call it a timeshare). **Palazzo Tornabuoni** (www.palazzotornabuoni.com), a 15th-century residence once owned by Pope Leo XI, is located smack bang in the middle of designer clothes land and will be a high-end residence club whose members (including, it is rumoured, Brooke Shields) buy into one of 36 luxuriously appointed and fully serviced apartments for a certain number of weeks a year.

RDM Fingen also has its fingers in several pies outside Florence. Its development in the **Val di Luce** (a vast swathe of mountainside near the ski resort of Abetone; *see p220*) includes a four-star hotel and spa (due to open for Christmas 2008) and around 150 apartments. Last (for the moment), but very certainly not least, is the purchase of the ex-Club Med property at Donoratico, in Livorno Province. Together with Bulgari (maker of glitzy jewellery and owner of super-luxury hotels in Milan and Bali), RDM is planning to open a five-star resort and private members' club with a state-of-the-art spa on 500 metres (1,640 feet) of private beach. The talk is of a 2010 opening.

If you want the convenience of being able to walk into town (or catch a bus), but also like the idea of staying amid a little bit of greenery, then try the very civilised Classic Hotel. Set in a lush garden just five minutes' walk south-west of the old city gate at Porta Romana, this attractive villa has been tastefully refurbished. Breakfast is served either in a basement room or, more pleasantly, in a conservatory leading to a garden full of mature trees and shrubs. Romantics should consider booking the annexe suite with its own terrace.

Bar. Concierge. Disabled-adapted rooms. Internet (dataport). No-smoking rooms. Parking (free). Room service. TV (DVD on request).

Pensione Bencistà

Via Benedetto da Maiano 4, Fiesole (055 59163/ www.bencista.com). Bus 7. **Rooms** 40. **Rates** €139-€154. **Credit** MC, V.

The characterful old Bencistà has taken a few halting steps towards the 21st century (a website, credit cards, a lift) in recent years, but not so many as to destroy the delightful old-world atmosphere of the place. Housed in a former convent and run as a *pensione* by the Simoni family since 1925, it has a fabulous setting on the hillside just below Fiesole. Public rooms are furnished with antiques; one has a fireplace and shelves stuffed with old books. Bedrooms are off a warren of passageways and staircases. No two are alike – those at the front enjoy unrivalled city views as does the flower-filled terrace. The restaurant overlooks the city and serves homely, traditional food; half-board rates are available but no longer obligatory.

Bar. Business centre. Disabled-adapted rooms. Internet (high-speed shared terminal in public area). No-smoking rooms. Parking (free). Restaurant. Room service. TV room.

Villa Poggio San Felice

Via San Matteo in Arcetri 24 (055 220016/www. villapoggiosanfelice.com). **Rooms** 5. **Rates** €150-€200; €250 suite. **Credit** AmEx, MC, V.

The hills immediately surrounding Florence are dotted with elegant old houses, of which the mellow 15th-century Villa Poggio San Felice is a prime example. Set in a beautiful, rose-filled garden with a small pool and views of the city, it was rescued from decay by the descendants of a Swiss hotel magnate, who were careful not to spoil it with heavy-handed over-restoration. There are five guest bedrooms; one of them, La Camera dei Nonni, has a big terrace overlooking the city. All in all, it offers peace, quiet and the atmosphere of a cultured private home a ten-minute drive from downtown Florence. There's a daily, complimentary shuttle service to and from the city centre.

Bar. Concierge. Gym. Internet (dataport). No-smoking rooms. Parking (free). Pool (outdoor). Room service. TV room.

Hostels

Hostel Archi Rossi

Via Faenza 94r, Santa Maria Novella (055 290804/ www.hostelarchirossi.com). **Open** 6.30am-2am daily. **Rooms** 15. **Rates** €18-€25/person in dormitory; €50-€80 doubles. **Credit** MC, V.

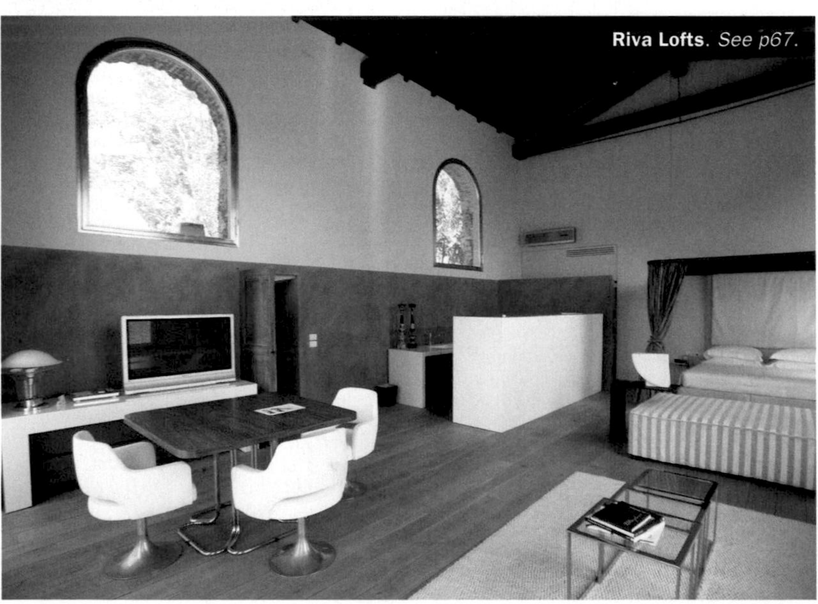

Riva Lofts. *See p67.*

The reception of this hostel is covered with garish renditions of famous frescoes, done by guests. The maximum number of beds in the spacious, light rooms is nine, but many are smaller and some have private bathrooms. Just ten minutes' walk from the station, it's a good choice for early departures or late arrivals. There are now 147 beds in total, including four doubles in an annexe, which have private bathrooms, TV, minibar and internet access. The management allows mixed-sex rooms as long as everyone knows each other. Facilities for the disabled are unusually good, and there's a lovely garden. Guided tours of the city in English are offered free of charge.
Bar. Disabled-adapted rooms. Internet (shared terminal). No-smoking hostel. TV room.

Ostello per la Gioventù

Viale Augusto Righi 2-4, Outside the City Gates (055 601451/www.iyhf.org). Bus 17A, 17B. **Rooms** 10. **Rates** €18 single; €60 double; €69 triple; €80 quad. **Credit** MC, V.

If you visit Florence during the torrid summer, head for the hills and this YHA youth hostel, which lies just below Fiesole. It may be some way from the action, but its location, in the impressive Villa Camerata will keep you cool. Most of the 322 beds are in dorms with shared bathrooms, but there are some doubles, triples and quads with private baths plus bungalows sleeping two people and camping facilities. You have to be a member of the YHA to join, but if you aren't one already, you can join on the spot for an extra €3 a day (for the first six days). There's no curfew.
Bar. Disabled-adapted rooms. Internet (high-speed shared terminal in public area, €3.50/hr). No-smoking hostel. Restaurant. TV room.

Ostello Monaco 34

Via Guido Monaco 34, Santa Maria Novella (055 321018/www.ostellomonaco34.com). **Rooms** 18. **Rates** €28-€35/person. **Credit** AmEx, MC, V.

Offering stylish budget accommodation and excellent facilities, this 50-bed hostel opened in July 2007 on a noisy street just west of the train station. Until very recently, the 1960s building was made up of five residential floors and the rooms (doubles, triples and quads) are still arranged so that each floor is self-contained, with bedrooms sharing a large, well-equipped kitchen and two bathrooms. The smart red, dark grey and beige colour scheme and modern linear furniture make it all quite stylish and, amazingly for these prices, rooms all have flat-screen satellite TVs and air-conditioning. There's also Wi-Fi throughout. Good double glazing takes care of the traffic noise, but a couple of rooms on the top floor are windowless.
Disabled-adapted rooms. Internet (wireless). No-smoking rooms. TV.

Campsites

Camping facilities in Italy are generally reliable. Bear in mind that most campsites become packed in summer, and can be very noisy.

Camping Michelangelo

Viale Michelangelo 80, Outside the City Gates (055 6811977). Bus 12, 13. **Open** *Office* 7am-midnight daily. **Rates** €10.30 person; €5.20 concessions; free under-4s; €6.40 tent; €35 house tent; €13.80 camper van. **Credit** MC, V (minimum €100).

This campsite just below piazzale Michelangelo has spectacular views of the city, yet is only a short walk from the centre. There's room on site for 240 tents and caravans, allowing for a maximum capacity of about 950 people. There are also 150 'house tents' for two people, with proper beds. Facilities are good (with a bar, a restaurant, a supermarket, an internet point, a kids' playground, a disco).
Bar. Restaurant.

Camping Panoramico

Via Peramondo 1, Outside the City Gates (055 599069/www.florencecamping.com). Bus 7. **Open** *Office* 8am-10pm daily. **Rates** €10.50-€10.80 person; €15.75-€16 tent; €15.75-€16 camper van. **Credit** AmEx, MC, V (minimum €52).

This 120-pitch site is the most picturesque site within easy reach of Florence (it's about five miles north of the city centre). In addition to the pitches, 21 self-catering bungalows accommodate up to four people, and there are also some caravans to rent. Facilities include a bar, a restaurant, a supermarket and a pool. The campsite also puts on a free, twice-daily shuttle service to and from Fiesole.
Bar. Disabled-adapted bathrooms. Internet (high-speed shared terminal). Pool (outdoor). Restaurant. TV room.

Long-term accommodation

Renting a flat through an agency inevitably involves commission charges, and the minimum stay is usually a week. To avoid these charges, search through the hundreds of websites advertising holiday lets, or look in the holiday sections of UK newspapers; it's worth doing a bit of research to compare prices. The following firms employ English-speaking staff.

Florence & Abroad

Via San Zanobi 58, San Lorenzo (055 487004/ www.florenceandabroad.com). **Open** 10am-5pm Mon-Fri. **No credit cards**.

This well-established agency offers both long and short-term accommodation for students and visitors to Florence. It also handles properties in Tuscany.

Your Agency In Florence (YAIF)

Via della Vigna Nuova 9, Santa Maria Novella (055 274871/www.home-reservation-service.com). Bus 6. **Open** 10am-6pm Mon-Fri. **Credit** AmEx, DC, MC, V. **Map** p334 B2 ㊷

YAIF specialises in student accommodation and short-term holiday rentals (by the day, week and month). Expect to pay from around €900 per month for a *monolocale* (one-room flat) in low season.
Other locations Piazza Santo Spirito 2r, Oltrarno (055 2748782).

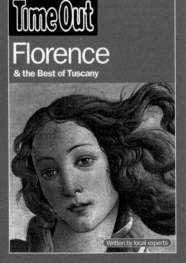

Sightseeing

Introduction	**72**
Duomo & Around	**75**
Santa Maria Novella	**93**
San Lorenzo	**96**
San Marco	**99**
Santa Croce	**103**
Oltrarno	**107**
Outside the City Gates	**112**

Features

The best Sights	73
Finding your niche	74
Seeing beyond the façade	80
Rogues' gallery Cellini	87
Rogues' gallery Torrigiani	94
Rogues' gallery Lippi	98
Fictional Florence	101
Walk Up the garden path	110

Piazza della Signoria. *See p83.*

Introduction

The fine art of planning ahead.

From the top of Brunelleschi's stunning dome to the waters of the Arno, Florence is packed with works of great finesse. From Michelangelo's *David* and Botticelli's *Birth of Venus*, to the incomparable Baptistery doors and the gold shops lining the ponte Vecchio, aesthetic pleasures are everywhere. If you've chosen to visit Florence then there's a high chance that you're a lover of the more refined things in life. You'll be spoiled for choice here, and you should simply concern yourself with ensuring that you get the most enjoyment from your pilgrimage. And while there's a lot to be said for wandering the streets and soaking up the atmosphere – taking in gorgeous, art-studded churches, fascinating museums and *gelateria* as you find them – for a truly satisfactory experience it pays to be organised.

Florence's virtually unrivalled wealth of artistic gold – there are more works here per square metre than anywhere else on the planet – has been known to attract a visitor or two. Something like seven million visitors cram into this small 'Renaissance City' annually, hoping that some of the glory of a Leonardo or Fra Angelico will rub off on them. If you have an itinerary planned, know which sights need pre-booking to guarantee access, and try to gain a basic knowledge of the city centre, you'll be one step ahead of the game.

ORIENTATION AND GEOGRAPHY

With a historic centre roughly a fifth the size of Rome's, Florence is easily navigable. Most major sights are within walking distance of any other central point and it's practically impossible to get lost, with the often-visible dome of the Duomo and the River Arno's four central bridges acting as reference points. The majority of the main sights and museums are clustered north of the two central bridges (ponte Vecchio and ponte Santa Trinità), in the area around the Duomo. Most of the other important sites are in the areas around this rectangle: Santa Maria Novella, San Lorenzo, San Marco, Santa Croce and Oltrarno. We have used these neighbourhood designations throughout this guide, with the rest of the city's attractions covered in the chapter Outside the City Gates.

So many artworks, so little time: work out your route in advance to get the most out of them.

The main central area of Florence sits in the river valley and so is virtually flat, but the surrounding hills rise steeply on both sides, creating challenging walks and rewarding views that are easily accessible on foot or by bus. For a self-guided walk within the Boboli Gardens, *see p110* **Up the garden path**; for a walk past Florence's literary and filmic points of references, *see p101* **Fictional Florence**.

MUSEUMS AND GALLERIES

During the summer, around Easter and on public holidays, Florence spills over with visitors: the sights are crowded and huge queues can form at the main museums. The best times to visit are the in-between seasons, from January to March (avoiding Easter), and from October to mid December. If you're intending to visit all the main museums, it may be worth going for the week in spring or early summer when state museums give free entrance (*see below and p172*).

Many of Florence's unrivalled museums have private collections at their core, whether that of a mega-family such as the Medici (**Uffizi**, **Palazzo Pitti**) or of a lone connoisseur (the **Bardini**, **Horne** and **Stibbert** museums). Other major museums were founded to preserve treasures too precious to expose to the elements (the **Accademia**, the **Bargello** and the **Museo dell'Opera del Duomo**). The main city-run museums are the **Cappella Brancacci**, the **Cenacolo di Santo Spirito**, the **Museo di Firenze com'era**, the **Palazzo Vecchio** and the **Museo Bardini**.

For one week of the year (Settimana dei Beni Culturali), entrance to all the state museums is free. This week is generally in late spring/ early summer, but the exact dates vary from year to year and often aren't decided until the last minute (call 055 290832 for details). For general information on the state museums and for booking, call Firenze Musei on 055 294883. The state museums are the **Pitti** museums, the **Uffizi**, the **Accademia**, the **Bargello**, the **Museo di San Marco**, the **Opificio delle Pietre Dure**, the **Cappelle Medicee** and the **Museo Archeologico**.

Firenze Musei strongly recommends booking for the Uffizi and the Accademia, and, at busy times of year, for the Pitti museums; this could save you a two-hour wait. At more popular times of the year there are long waits (weeks, even months) to get tickets for the Uffizi, even by pre-booking, so reserve as soon as you can. Booking costs €3 and tickets are collected from a window beside the normal ticket office, or, in the case of the Palazzo Pitti, from an office in the right-hand wing before you reach the main entrance. Pay when you pick up the tickets. Don't expect to be able to book tickets there directly: you will be told to phone the central number. Last issuing times for tickets vary (and we have given the closing time, not last admission, in our listings). Try to get to the ticket office an hour before the museum closes.

Art lovers should be aware that works of art are often loaned to other museums or to exhibitions, and restoration can be carried out with little or no notice, so it's always a wise idea to call first if you want to view a specific piece.

Temporary exhibitions are regularly held at a few locations in Florence, among them the Palazzo Vecchio, the Palazzo Medici Riccardi, the Fortezza da Basso and the Palazzo Strozzi. See *Firenze Spettacolo* magazine, *The Florentine*,

The best Sights

Outdoor sights

The **ponte Vecchio** (*see p84*), seen from the lovely **ponte Santa Trinità** (*see p90*); the panoramic views from the **Campanile** (*see p79*); Alberti's façade of **Santa Maria Novella** (*see p95*); the unique church of **Orsanmichele** (*see p85*); the **synagogue** (*see p106*); the **Vasca dell'Isolotto** in the **Boboli Gardens** (*see p109*) – enter via the lesser-known entrance on via Romana.

Indoor sights

Michelangelo's **David** (*see p99*); Botticelli's **Primavera** (*see p89*); Fra Angelico's **Annunciation** and Ghirlandaio's **Last Supper** in the **Museo di San Marco** (*see p99*); the magnificent map room in the **Palazzo Vecchio** (*see p83*); Donatello's heart-wrenching **Mary Magdalene** in the **Museo dell'Opera del Duomo** (*see p75*); the **Brancacci Chapel** frescoed by Masaccio, Masolino and Filippino Lippi in **Santa Maria del Carmine** (*see p110*); the **Chapel of the Magi** frescoed by Benozzo Gozzoli in the **Palazzo Medici Riccardi** (*see p97*).

Well-kept secrets

The mesmerising **Sala dei Pappagalli** in the **Palazzo Davanzati** (*see p90*); the amazing inlays of semi-precious stones in the **Opificio delle Pietre Dure** (*see p102*); the bronze miniature collection on the second floor of the **Museo Bargello** (*see p104*); Andrea del Sarto's **Cenacolo** (Last Supper) in **San Salvi** (*see p31*); the Brownings-related mini-museum in the fascinating **Casa Guidi** (*see p107*); shoes for all seasons in the **Museo Ferragamo** (*see p90*).

Florence & Tuscany News (for both, *see p309*) or local newspapers for details.

THEY DON'T LIKE MONDAYS

For non-Italians it can be a shock – and a spanner in the planning works – to find that some of Florence's major museums close on Monday. These include the Uffizi, Accademia and the Galleria Palatina in the Palazzo Pitti. If it's the first, third or fifth Monday of the month, you could go to the Bargello or the Museo di San Marco, or if it's the second or fourth, the Cappelle Medicee or some of the museums of the Palazzo Pitti.

TOURIST INFORMATION

Apart from the tourist offices (*see p314*), the city police have information points in piazza della Repubblica, on via Calzaiuoli and borgo San Lorenzo, and at the southern end of the ponte Vecchio, from where they give directions and basic information about the main sights in various languages. Many of the city's minor sights – churches, palazzi and monuments – also have signs posted beside them detailing their history and distinguishing features, making a DIY tour that much easier. In addition, you'll see big plaques with useful maps mounted in many squares and other strategic positions.

GUIDED TOURS

There's not a great deal to choose between Florence's various tour companies, all of which offer a range of itineraries, with English-language options, covering the main monuments and museums on foot or by bus. The highly reputable **Association of Tourist Guides** (055 2645217, www.florencetouristguides.com), the **Association of Florentine Tourist Guides** (055 4220901, www.florenceguides.it) and the **Cultural Association of Guides** (055 7877744, www.firenze-guide.com) all have a vast selection of standard tours. Two firms that provide a little more variety are **Walking Tours of Florence** (055 2645033, mobile 329 6132730, www.italy.artviva.com; *see also p201*) and **CAF** (055 283200, www.caftours.com), with both offering a wide choice of interesting options. **Context Florence** (06 4820911, www.contextflorence.com) uses expert scholars rather than tour guides, and limits groups to six, so you can be sure of a personal service.

If you prefer to do it yourself when it comes to sightseeing, the best ways in which to see the city are to hire a bike or moped (*see p303*), or to take a ride on the **busini** – electric buses that cover the central areas of the city. Another bus option is an official tour: **City Sightseeing Firenze** (piazza Stazione 1, 055 290451), 9.30am-6pm Mon-Sun, €20, €10 concessions, no credit cards) run two lines, of one and two hour lengths, departing from Santa Maria Novella train station and the Line B departure at Porta San Frediano. Tickets are valid for 24 hours.

Finding your niche

The Italian tradition of creating shrines to the Madonna, Jesus or the saints on street corners is particularly strong in Florence.

This high concentration of conventicles is partly due to the early 14th-century episodes of armed conflict in the city between the orthodox followers of the Church and the so-called Patarine heretics, a Ghibelline-supported reform movement advocating action against corruption in the clergy and named after the street in Milan from where their most active members hailed.

To prove their devotion (and avoid the potentially nasty repercussions of being branded heretics), many individuals, trades, guilds and confraternities built tabernacles in conspicuous positions, often on the corner of their home or centre. The tabernacle was usually built as an *edicola*, a frame for the icon itself, normally of stone. It often came with a 'roof' to protect the artwork, and a mantle on which to place offerings. The icon itself could be a fresco, painting, relief, tile or sculpture, and sometimes famous artists were hired to create the venerable image and boost the cachet of the sponsor in the eyes of the Church. The result is an art heritage of sometimes astonishing value. The shrines listed below are among the most noteworthy.

Piazza dell'Unità Italiana *corner with via Sant'Antonio.* **Map** p334 A2.
Via Arte della Lana *corner with via di Orsanmichele.* **Map** p334 C3.
Via degli Alfani *corner with borgo Pinti.* **Map** p335 B5.
Via Ricasoli *corner with via de' Pucci.* **Map** p335 A4.
Via della Spada *near San Pancrazio.* **Map** p334 B2.
Via de' Tornabuoni *corner with via della Vigna Nuova.* **Map** p334 B2.

Duomo & Around

Dome is where the art is.

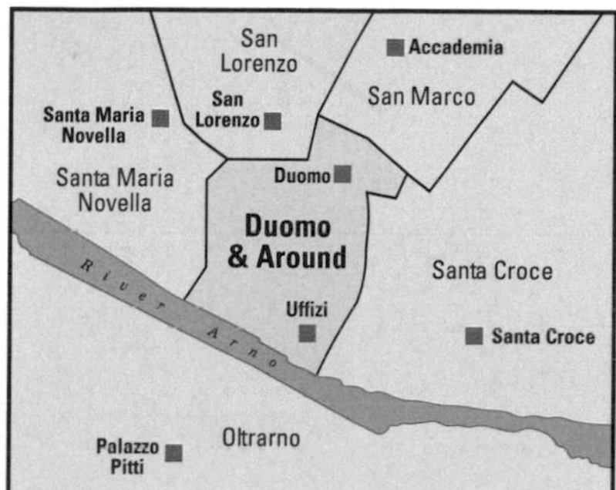

A creative confluence of business, religion and civic duty, the centre of Florence showcases the various forces at work on the city at its most crucial moments in history. The area covered in this chapter takes in both the religious heartland around the magnificent cathedral, and the former administrative hub surrounding Palazzo Vecchio. Stretching from the streets just north of the Duomo to the ponte Vecchio, the area corresponds almost exactly to the city walls of the ninth century, now bordered on the east by via del Proconsolo, which follows the line of the even more ancient Roman walls (still visible on the corner of this street and via Dante Alighieri), and on the west by via de' Tornabuoni, well known for its designer shops. As the original nucleus of Florence, it's the ideal place to start your explorations.

Around piazza del Duomo

The trio of stunning religious buildings at the heart of piazza del Duomo form an obvious landmark: the spacing and uniformity of their surroundings were carefully dictated in order to preserve their dignity. The glorious **Duomo** (*see p77*) is one of the most recognised landmarks in Europe but never fails to astound: nestled in the piazza at the heart of Florence's historic centre, the cathedral is so enormous that there's no spot nearby from where you can see the whole thing, though a walk through the surrounding streets will be punctuated by glimpses of its red-tiled dome.

In piazza del Duomo, visitors in awe of the cathedral's magnitude gape up at the intricately patterned marble, delicate carvings and the mammoth dome, even more impressive seen in the close proximity forced by the narrowness of the road on its northern flank. The areas outside the entrance and around the south of the Duomo are pedestrianised, while mopeds and buses roar around the north and east sides. Inside the cathedral is the **Crypt of Santa Reparata** (*see p78*), the original church built on this site in the fifth century, while on the south side of the Duomo is the entrance to the dome itself, the spectacular **Cupola** (*see p79*). The **Campanile** (*see p79*), Giotto's elegant bell tower, is also south of the Duomo, level with its façade.

In piazza San Giovanni, named after John the Baptist, the octagonal **Baptistery** (*see p79*) faces the main doors of the Duomo. This large square, always thronging with tourists, also houses the tiny **Museo di Bigallo** (*see p82*). South from the façade of the Duomo is via de' Calzaiuoli, a heaving, pedestrianised shopping street flanked by self-service restaurants, shops and *gelaterie*, while to the west of the Baptistery is via de' Cerretani, a busy shopping street and traffic thoroughfare that's home to **Santa Maria Maggiore**, an 11th-century parish church. Following the curve of the piazza on the north side of the Duomo, the **Museo dell'Opera del Duomo** (*see p82*), which houses many of the Duomo's treasures, is on the north-east of the square.

Near the Museo dell'Opera del Duomo is a round marble slab embedded in the pavement with no inscription to identify it. It marks the exact spot where the gilt copper ball and cross (made by Verrocchio in 1469 and containing holy relics) fell from the top of the Duomo's lantern after being struck by lightning on 17 July 1600. (It was replaced by an even larger bronze ball two years later.) Slightly further around the piazza in a clockwise direction at the base of a flat column belonging to piazza del Duomo, at no.54, a plaque indicates the 'Sasso di Dante', or Dante's stone. Although now a shopfront, this is the place where the poet was said to sit in summer.

Situated on the same side of the piazza are Luigi Pampaloni's huge 19th-century sculptures of Filippo Brunelleschi, the creator of the great dome, and Arnolfo di Cambio, the first architect of the cathedral. They show

each artist holding their relevant plans and tools and looking directly at the parts of the Duomo they worked on.

Running down from the south-west corner of the Baptistery is the more upmarket via Roma, which opens into the pompous **piazza della Repubblica**. This ungainly square was built in 1882, when the so-called Mercato Vecchio ('old market', and part of the Jewish ghetto) was demolished and rebuilt in a massive clean-up after a cholera outbreak. The only remnant from before that time is the huge **Colonna dell'Abbondanza**, a column that used to mark the spot where two principal Roman roads crossed, and which was reinstated to its original position after World War II.

Vasari's delightful **Loggia del Pesce**, with its ceramic marine creature *tondi*, was once the central meeting place of the square, but has been moved to piazza de' Ciompi in Santa Croce (*see p103*). In the medieval period, the area covered by the whole of piazza della Repubblica was given over to a huge market where you could change money, buy a hawk or falcon, pay over the odds for a quack remedy, or pick up a prostitute (distinguished by the bells on their hats and gloves). Further back, the ancient Roman Forum once occupied a quarter of the piazza, and the Campidoglio and Temple of Jupiter covered the rest. The sun-trap square is now flanked by pavement cafés, and dominated at night by street artists and strollers.

Duomo (Santa Maria del Fiore)

055 2302885/www.duomofirenze.it. **Open** 10am-5pm Mon-Wed, Fri; 10am-4pm Thur; 10am-4.45pm Sat (except 1st Sat of mth, 10am-3.30pm); 1.30-4.45pm Sun. **Admission** free. **Map** p335 B4.

Florence's most important religious building is a truly awe-inspiring sight. It not only dominates the skyline but it represents the geographical, cultural and historical centre of the city and is the result of years of work spanning over six centuries. A hugely successful and expanding wool industry gave the Florentine population such a boost in the 13th century that several new churches had to be built; Santa Croce (*see p105*) and Santa Maria Novella (*see p95*) were among them, but the most important of all was Santa Maria del Fiore, or the Duomo, which replaced the small church of Santa Reparata (*see p78*). The project marked the first time that a guild of laymen had been entrusted with financing the city's development – traditionally, this responsibility had fallen to monks and priests. It thus marks the point at which religious architecture became a civic duty.

The building was commissioned by the Florentine Republic as an opportunity to show Florence off as the most important Tuscan city. The competition to find an architect was won by Arnolfo di Cambio, a sculptor from Pisa who had trained with Nicola Pisano, and the first stones were laid on 8 September 1296 around the exterior of Santa Reparata. Building continued for the next 170 years – despite the attack of bubonic plague in 1348 that killed half the population of Florence – with guidance and revision from three further architects, though the church was consecrated 30 years before its completion in 1436 (at which time it was the largest cathedral in Europe).

The rich exterior, in white Carrara, green Prato and red Maremma marbles, reflects the variety of time periods that work on the building covered, with a huge variation in the styles of the inlaid patterns. The visionary Francesco Talenti had sufficient confidence to enlarge the cathedral and prepare the building for Brunelleschi's inspired dome, which wasn't completed until 1436 – 140 years after construction had first started on the cathedral.

A workshop on via dello Studio, overlooked by the **Duomo**.

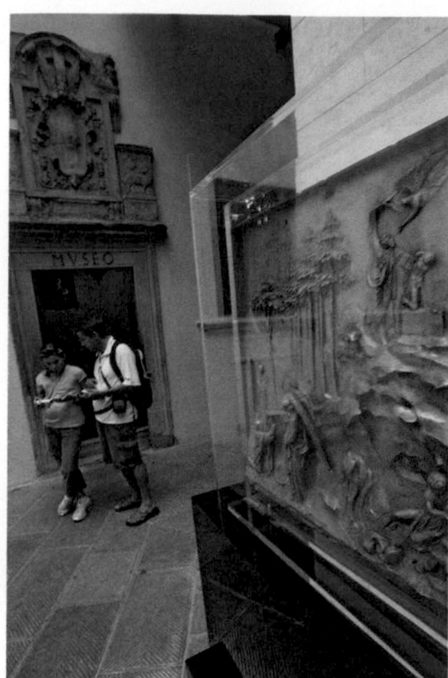

Museo dell'Opera del Duomo. *See p82.*

Remarkably, when this dome was conceived (as the highest ever built at the time), Brunelleschi – the man who would work out how to pull off the feat, hadn't even been born. The last significant change came in the 19th century, when Emilio de Fabris designed a neo-Gothic façade (*see p80* **Seeing beyond the façade**). After his death, Luigi del Moro was left to crown the façade.

After the splendid exterior, the interior looks somewhat dull, though decorating one of the world's largest cathedrals was never going to be easy. It's actually full of fascinating peculiarities: notably, the clock on the Paolo Uccello inner façade, which marks 24 hours, operates anti-clockwise and starts its days at sunset (it's between four and six hours fast). The clock is surrounded by the so-called Heads of the Prophets peering out from four roundels and showing the distinct influences of Ghiberti and Donatello.

Also by Uccello is a monument to Sir John Hawkwood, painted in 1436 as a tribute to the English soldier who led Florentine troops to victory in the Battle of Cascina of 1364. The fresco has given rise to debate about whether its perspective and the movement of the horse's right legs are wrong, or an original treatment of perspective construction, learned from Masaccio and considered by some to be visionary and even a forerunner to Cubism. Beyond Andrea del Castagno's 1456 monument to Niccolò da Tolentino, illustrating the heroic characteristics of a Renaissance man, is Domenico di Michelino's *Dante Explaining the Divine Comedy*, featuring the poet in pink and the new Duomo vying for prominence with the Mountain of Purgatory.

A couple of strides put you directly underneath the dome, the size of which is even more breathtaking inside than out. The lantern in the centre is 90m (295ft) above you and the diameter of the inner dome is 43m (141ft) across, housing within it one of the largest frescoed surfaces in the world. Brunelleschi had intended for the inner cupola to be mosaic, to mirror the Baptistery ceiling. However, interior work only began some 125 years after his death in 1572, when Cosimo de' Medici commissioned Giorgio Vasari to carry out the work; together with Don Vincenzo Borghini, who chose the iconographic subjects, they decided to fresco the surface instead.

The concentric rows of images were started by Vasari, whose subtle treatment of colour and form drew inspiration from Michelangelo's Sistine Chapel, but he died two years later before completing the project, and was succeeded by Federico Zuccari, who worked for a further five years until its completion. Zuccari had a much more flamboyant (and more crude) dry-painting style, believing that the distance from which the visitor would view the cupola wasted the delicacy of Vasari's wet fresco technique, especially as featured faces included some of the best-known personalities of the time. Zuccari's most crucial contribution to the cycle is the rendering of Dante's vision of Hell inspired by Signorelli's frescoes in Orvieto Cathedral.

Crypt of Santa Reparata

Open 10am-5pm Mon-Wed, Fri; 10am-3.30pm Thur; 10am-4.45pm Sat (except 1st Sat of mth, 10am-3.30pm); 1.30-4.45pm Sun. **Admission** €3. **No credit cards. Map** p335 B4.

By the 13th century, Santa Reparata had served as the city's main church for some 900 years and desperately needed to be replaced, especially as, after a period of rapid population expansion, it had become too small to serves the needs of the community. It was decided in 1293 that a new cathedral was to be built over the top of the original church (the original date of which is unknown, but between the 5th and seventh centuries). The entrance to this is inside the Duomo itself. The intricate mosaic floor of the church was built only 30cm (12in) above the Roman remains of houses and shops, some of which are on display in the crypt. Also here is the tomb of Brunelleschi, although no trace has ever been found of those of Arnolfo di Cambio and Giotto, both also supposedly buried here. Local legend has it that some of the land needed for the building of the much bigger Duomo was occupied by the Florentine Bischeri family, who, when they continued to refuse the ever-bigger sums of money they were offered to relocate, were unceremoniously kicked out of their palazzo with no compensation. This led to the Florentine expression '*bischero*' (a gullible fool).

Excavations to the building in the mid 1960s to 1970s unearthed the original crypt and medieval ruins, which are now on view for visitors.

Cupola/Dome

Open 8.30am-6.20pm Mon-Fri; 8.30am-5pm Sat (except 1st Sat of mth, 8.30am-3.20pm). **Admission** €6. **No credit cards**. **Map** p335 B4.

The spectacular 37,000-tonne dome constructed with more than four million bricks is, as Alberti put it, 'a structure so immense, rising above the skies [that it is] broad enough to cover with its shadow all the peoples of Tuscany'. But the dome isn't just visually stunning: as the first octagonal dome in history to be built without a wooden supporting frame, it really is an absolutely incredible feat of engineering. Brunelleschi had dreamed of completing the cupola ever since his childhood. He won the commission with the more experienced Lorenzo Ghiberti, riding on the back of his success with the Baptistery doors, but he soon found that while he was doing the crucial work, Ghiberti was taking all the glory. So Brunelleschi pulled a sickie, halting work, and got the recognition he deserved.

Brunelleschi first considered designing the classic semi-spherical dome used in existing churches around Italy, but the sheer size of the structure precluded the traditional method of laying tree trunks across the diameter in order to build around them. In the end Brunelleschi made the dome support itself by building two shells, one on top of the other, and by laying the bricks in herringbone-pattern rings to integrate successive layers that could support themselves. The design risked becoming a victim of its own success: the ribs around the dome were in danger of 'springing' open at the top, so a heavier lantern than normal was designed to hold them in place.

Just as innovative as the design were the tools used and the organisation of the work. Brunelleschi devised pulley systems to winch materials and workers up to the dome. Between the two shells of the dome, he installed a canteen so the workforce wouldn't waste time going to ground level to eat, bringing construction time down to a mere 16 years (1420-36). A separate side entrance gives access to the top of the dome (463 steps, about 20 minutes up and down) with fantastic city views, though the climb is not recommended for the faint-hearted or those with limited mobility. In March 2007, two peregrine falcons nested and raised their young in the cathedral's cupola, while twitchers worldwide watched the hatching online via 'birdcam'. It's clearly not just tourists who are attracted to the architecture.

Campanile

055 2302885. **Open** 8.30am-6.50pm daily. **Admission** €6. **No credit cards**. **Map** p335 B4.

The cathedral's three-floor, 414-step bell tower was designed by Giotto in 1334, though his plans weren't followed faithfully (the original drawing is in the Museo dell'Opera del Duomo in Siena; *see p241*). Andrea Pisano, who continued the work three years after Giotto's death, took the precaution of doubling the thickness of the walls, while Francesco Talenti, who saw the building to completion in 1359, inserted the large windows high up the tower. Inlaid, like the Duomo, with pretty pink, white and green marble, the Campanile is decorated with 16 sculptures of prophets, patriarchs and pagans (the originals are in Florence's Museo dell'Opera del Duomo; *see 82*), bas-reliefs designed by Giotto and artfully executed by Pisano recounting the *Creation and Fall of Man* and *Redemption Through Industry*; you can make out Eve emerging from Adam's side and a drunken Noah. The steps to the top are steep and narrow, but great views await. *Photo p83.*

Baptistery

Open 12.15-6.30pm Mon-Sat; 8.30am-1pm Sun. **Admission** €3. **No credit cards**. **Map** p334 B3.

The pan-European overhaul of intellectual endeavour that we now call the Renaissance started on this spot when, in the winter of 1400, the Calimala guild of cloth importers held a competition to find an artist to create a pair of bronze doors for the Baptistery's north entrance. Judging works by seven artists, Brunelleschi among them, they gave the commission to Ghiberti, then just 20 years old. (Brunelleschi later got revenge with superior work on the cupola but never sculpted again.) You can compare two of the finalists' magnificent entries in the Bargello (*see p104*). The 28 relief panels on the three-tonne, 6m-high (20ft) doors tell the story of Christ from the Annunciation to the Crucifixion; the eight lower panels show the four evangelists and four doctors of the Church. The deep pictorial space and an emphasis on figures makes many scholars believe that these doors contain the very first signs of Renaissance art.

No sooner had the north doors been installed than the Calimala commissioned Ghiberti to make another pair: the even more remarkable east doors – described by Vasari as 'undeniably perfect in every way' – took the artist and his workshop (including Michelozzo and Benozzo Gozzoli) 27 years to complete. They're known, since Michelangelo coined the phrase, as the 'Gates of Paradise' (although 'paradise' is, in fact, what the area between a baptistery and its church is called). The doors you see are copies (the originals are in the Museo dell'Opera del Duomo; *see 82*), but the casts are good enough that it's not difficult to appreciate Ghiberti's extraordinary work, especially his fine use of the recently-discovered principles of perspective.

The very first set of Baptistery doors were those on the south side, completed by Andrea Pisano in 1336, after only six years of work. The doors are composed of 28 Gothic quatrefoil-framed panels depicting stories from the life of St John the Baptist and the eight theological and cardinal virtues. The Latin inscription on top of the door translates as 'Andrea Pisano made me in 1330'.

For centuries, the likes of Brunelleschi and Alberti believed the Baptistery was converted from a Roman temple dedicated to Mars. Other scholars reckoned that the Roman site on which the octagonal church was built was the Praetorium, while still more thought its ancient origins were as a bakery. In fact, the Baptistery of St John the Baptist, patron

Continues p82.▶

Seeing beyond the façade

How to read the Duomo's exterior.

The sculptures and reliefs on the Duomo façade

This façade was added to the Duomo between 1871 and 1887. Dedicated to the Virgin Mary, it is also distinctly patriotic. Over the middle door is a relief of Mary holding a flowered sceptre – a symbol of royalty and deity. According to 15th-century religious documents, the flowered sceptre symbolises Christ, who grew on the stalk (Mary) that flourished from the root, the House of David. On this relief, Mary is also flanked by John the Baptist, who had become the patron saint of Florence after the city had converted to Christianity.

Above this level, in between the tympanum and the ornate rose window, is a gallery of niches containing busts of various Florentine artists, humanists and rich merchants. Although primarily a way for these important personalities to pay their respects to the Virgin Mary, an appearance on the façade was also a vital status symbol for these wealthy men, ensuring that they would be remembered and venerated for their generosity and charity. Above this level, the 12 Apostles are represented.

The dome

Containing four million bricks and weighing in at 37,000 tonnes, Brunelleschi's dome is a feat of Renaissance engineering – its octagonal design with a double wall was an unprecedented achievement at the time. The dome was also built without the support of any scaffolding – which naturally worried the Florentine authorities – and during construction Brunelleschi even installed a canteen to cut workers' travel time up and down (as well as regulating the wine they consumed). The dome is topped by a lantern with a gilt copper ball and a cross that contains holy relics. These were hoisted up using machinery designed by Leonardo da Vinci. The original copper ball was hit by lightning in 1600 and replaced.

The bronze doors

The Duomo's doors (1899-1903) are decorated with scenes from the life of the Virgin Mary. Though the sober and slightly lifeless bronze doors of the Duomo are no match for Ghiberti's stunning Gates of Paradise, their figures are beautiful and sinuous, exuding an air of translucency. Each door is complemented by a mosaic lunette, designed by Barbarino. These represent (right to left): local artists, merchants, and humanists honouring Christ; Christ with Mary and John the Baptist; and Charity among the Florentine noblemen who had established the city's charitable foundations. In this way, Florentine civic duty became inextricably linked with the construction of the cathedral.

The Campanile statues

Between 1334 and 1435, 16 statues of Old Testament prophets were placed in niches above the lozenges. As the statues were designed to be seen from afar, their depictions and attributes were dramatic and deliberately ugly. The postures and stern expressions of the prophets mirror the fiery messages God had given them to relate on earth.

Arguably the most impressive is the so-called *Zuccone*, by Donatello, who stands drawing in his chin, implicitly condemning human inadequacy. Zuccone (actually called Habakkuk) lived in the seventh century BC and is best known for providing Daniel with food in the lion's den. Jeremiah, also by Donatello, is equally frightening, symbolising the continued conflict between morality and sin.

The lozenges on the second storey of the Campanile

The second storey of the Campanile is decorated with a series of lozenges (rhombus-shaped panels) containing a number of allegorical images relating to the liberal arts and theology. These images thematically support the sculptural reliefs on the storey below. The images decorating the southern side are particularly impressive, with marble allegorical figures on blue ceramic backgrounds, to represent the virtues. Look out for the planets, the moon and the sun on the west side. The Seven Sacraments, as decreed by the Church, are illustrated on the north side. Although these are presented realistically rather than allegorically, they symbolise the journey that every faithful Florentine must go on in order to achieve divine life and forgiveness of sin.

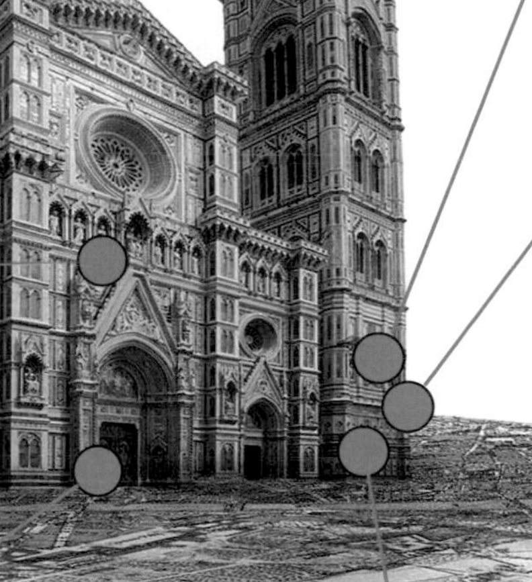

Illustration by Simon Foster

The sculptural reliefs on the lower part of the Campanile

On this level you can see a series of hexagonal panels designed by the Pisano studio, depicting the history of mankind. This history begins with the creation of man, with Noah portrayed on the west side as the first farmer. The south side is dedicated to the arts and sciences, with panels on medicine, hunting, legislation and wool-making. The west side details the liberal arts, the north side the creative arts. These figurative narratives are located on the Campanile's base in order to illustrate to the Florentine public the disciplines considered necessary for an efficient, peaceful and happy society.

Sightseeing

▶ Continued from p79.
saint of Florence, was built to an octagonal design between 1059 and 1128 as a remodelling of a sixth- or seventh-century version. In between, it functioned for a period as the cathedral for Florence (then Florentia) in place of Santa Reparata, the church on whose site the Duomo now stands (*see p77*). The octagon reappears most obviously in the shape of the cathedral dome, but also on the buttresses of the Campanile, which constitute its corners. It's also the shape of the remains of the original font where children, including many of the Medici family and the poet Dante, were brought for a double baptism: both as a Christian and as a Florentine. The font near the exit that you can see today was installed in 1658, and the reliefs that decorate it are attributed to Andrea Pisano or his school.

Today, the striped octagon is best known for its gilded bronze doors, though the interior is worth visiting for the dazzling *Last Judgement* mosaic lining the vault ceiling, with the 8m-high (26ft) mosaic figure of *Christ in Judgement* dominating the apse (1225). The mosaics depicting Hell are thought to have inspired Dante's *Inferno*. The geometrically patterned marble mosaic floor showing oriental zodiac motifs was begun in 1209, around the same time as the western side of the Baptistery was enlarged. Squeezed between two columns, the tomb of Antipope John XXIII (Baldassare Coscia) was designed by Donatello and his student Michelozzo in the 1420s.

Museo di Bigallo

Piazza San Giovanni 1 (055 2302885). **Open** 10am-2pm, 3-7pm Tue-Sun. **Admission** €5. **No credit cards. Map** p334 B3.

The city's smallest museum is housed in a beautiful Gothic loggia built in 1358 for the Misericordia, a charitable organisation that cared for unwanted children and plague victims. The loggia was later renovated for another fraternity, the Bigallo, and the Misericordia moved to piazza del Duomo (no.19), from where it still works as a voluntary medical service. The main room has frescoes depicting the work of the two fraternities, though the two scenes on the left wall as you enter were damaged in the 18th century. The *Madonna della Misericordia*, a fresco of 1342 from the workshop of Bernardo Daddi, a pupil of Giotto, has the Virgin suspended above the earliest known depiction of Florence, showing the Baptistery, the original Arnolfo façade to the domeless Duomo, the original Santa Reparata with its two bell towers, and an incomplete Campanile.

Museo dell'Opera del Duomo

Piazza del Duomo 9 (055 2302885/www.operaduomo.firenze.it). **Open** 9am-6.50pm Mon-Sat; 9am-1pm Sun. **Admission** €6. **No credit cards. Map** p335 B4.

Built on the site of the 15th-century cathedral workshop, where Michelangelo carved his famous *David*, the Museum of the Cathedral Works still contains the tools and machinery used to build the Duomo, the original wooden models of the cathedral and its cupola in various stages of development, as well as sculptures and artwork from the Duomo complex deemed too precious and vulnerable to be left to the mercy of the elements. It is one of the city's most interesting museums, though the explanatory panels can sometimes make for hard reading.

In the first rooms are Gothic sculptures from the exteriors of the Baptistery and the original but never-finished Duomo façade, including a classical-style *Madonna* with unsettling glass eyes by Arnolfo di Cambio, the cathedral's first architect. There are also pieces from Santa Reparata and a collection of relics. Halfway up the stairs is the *Pietà Bandini*, a heart-rending late work by Michelangelo showing Christ slithering from the grasp of Nicodemus. The sculpture was intended as Michelangelo's tombstone; he sculpted his own features on the face of Nicodemus, showing how his obsession with the story had become too much for him to bear. In true tortured artist style, frustrated with the piece, he smashed Christ's left arm.

The originals of Donatello's *Prophets* from the exterior of the Campanile are upstairs in the main chamber, notably *Habakkuk* (affectionately called *Lo Zuccone* by Florentines, meaning 'marrow head'), a work of such realism that Donatello himself is said to have gripped it and screamed, 'Speak, damn you, speak!' This room also houses two enormous and joyful *cantorie* (choir lofts). One is by Donatello, with cavorting *putti* (small, angelic boys); the other, by Luca della Robbia, is full of angel musicians. Beyond are bas-reliefs for the Campanile, most carved by Pisano to Giotto's designs.

Donatello was the first artist to free sculpture from its Gothic limitations: in the room leading off to the right of the main chamber is an extreme example of the artist's unprecedented use of naturalism: an emotive wood sculpture of Mary Magdalene, dishevelled and ugly, with coarse, dirty hair so realistic you can almost smell it. Although it was undergoing restoration on our visit, at the back of this room there is usually a stunning dossal (altar-frontal) made from 400kg of silver and worked on by Michelozzo, Verrocchio, Antonio del Pollaiolo and Bernardo Cennini, among others.

Going straight back through the main chamber is a new corridor displaying the pulleys and ropes used to winch building materials (and workers) up to the inside of the dome. There is also the death mask of Brunelleschi and an 18th-century sedan chair cleverly built in a curved form so that two servants were able to carry Grand Duke Cosimo III de' Medici up the spiral steps to the top of the Dome without getting stuck. Back on the ground floor, under the glass roof of the courtyard, are the ten original bronze panels from the east door of the Baptistery, the so-called *Porta del Paradiso* (Gates of Paradise) sculpted by Lorenzo Ghiberti over the 27 years between 1425 and 1452 and often considered to be the work of art that initiated the Renaissance. *Photo p78.*

Around piazza della Signoria

Frequently packed with perspiring tour groups it may be, but the piazza della Signoria is the place to go to discover Florence's alternative central square, a public gathering point and former administrative district. Lined with tourist-trap restaurants and cafés, Florence's civic showpiece square is nevertheless delightful, especially in the early morning before the groups arrive or by the loggia late in the evening, where talented buskers perform nightly.

The piazza is dominated by **Palazzo Vecchio** (*see p86*). The crenellated and corbelled building, completed at the end of the 13th century as the seat of the Signoria (the top tier of the city's government), looms down over the piazza and is visible from almost any point in the city. The palazzo still houses the main local government offices, but is also home to the **Associazione Musei dei Ragazzi** (*see p85*) and the **Quartieri Monumentali** (*see p86*), once the main quarters of the Medici.

The piazza itself started life in 1268, when the Guelphs regained control from the Ghibellines and demolished their rivals' 36 houses in the area. However, they left the neighbouring houses intact, hence the unusual asymmetrical shape of the square. Over the next few centuries, the piazza remained the focus of civic – though not necessarily civilised – activity. It didn't take much to ignite a crowd: on one occasion, in the 14th century, a scrap in the piazza led to a man being eaten by the mob.

It was here that the religious and political reformer Girolamo Savonarola lit his so-called Bonfire of the Vanities in 1497 (*see p27* **Art attack**). Savonarola ended up burned at the stake on 23 May 1498, on the exact spot of his prophetic bonfire (marked by a plaque in front of the Neptune fountain). However, the piazza has also been the seat of civic defence. Whenever Florence was threatened by an external enemy, the bell of Palazzo della Signoria (known as the *vacca*, or cow, after its mooing tone) was tolled to summon the citizens' militia. Part of their training included playing *calcio storico* on the piazza, a version of rugby that's still played in piazza Santa Croce every June (*see p173 and p203* **The crying game**).

When, in the mid 1980s, it was decided that the piazza's ancient paving stones should be taken up and restored, the Sovrintendenza dei Beni Archeologici, which oversees the city's archaeological works, took the opportunity to carry out excavations on the area. Ruins from 12th-century Florence were discovered beneath the piazza, built over the thermal baths of Roman Florentia and parts of the Etruscans' outpost. The authorities ordered further excavation, and there was even talk of an underground museum. Local government, however, objected, fearing their showpiece piazza would become a building site.

The project ultimately resulted in an utter shambles. The company engaged to restore the paving stones apparently catalogued the position of the stones using chalk, which was washed away on the first rainy day. It also managed to 'lose' some of the slabs, now rumoured to grace the courtyards of various Tuscan villas. The decision to replace the paving with artificially aged stones and reseal the Roman site was deplorable but predictable.

Dominating the piazza are a copy of Michelangelo's **David** (the original is in the Galleria dell'Accademia; *see p99*) and an equestrian bronze of **Cosimo I** by Giambologna, notable mainly for the horse cast as a single piece. Giambologna also created sexy nymphs and satyrs for Ammannati's Neptune fountain (nicknamed 'il Biancone' or 'big whitey'), a Mannerist monstrosity of which Michelangelo is reputed to have wailed, 'Ammannati, what beautiful marble you have ruined.' Even Ammannati admitted it was a failure, in part because the block of marble used for Neptune lacked width, forcing him to give the god narrow shoulders and keep his right arm close to his

A view from the **Campanile**. *See p79.*

Sightseeing

body. This statue has suffered a lot of damage over the years, the last time being in August 2005 when a man from Empoli drunkenly climbed the statue and fell. In 32 seconds of action captured on CCTV, he pulled off the right hand, broke the trident, and landed painfully on a marble shell in the fountain, necessitating almost a year of restoration work.

Beyond the fountain are copies of Donatello's *Marzocco* (the original of this heraldic lion, one of Florence's oldest emblems, is in the Bargello; *see p104*) and *Judith and Holofernes* (the original is in Palazzo Vecchio; *see p86*). Like *David*, Judith was a symbol of the power of the people over tyrannical rulers: a Jewish widow who inveigled her way into the camp of Holofernes, Israel's enemy, she got him drunk and cut off his head. Beyond *David* is *Hercules and Cacus* by Bandinelli, much ridiculed by the exacting Florentines and described by rival sculptor Benvenuto Cellini as a 'sack of melons' (*see also p28* **Statues of stature**). On one of the cornerstones at the edge of Palazzo Vecchio nearest the loggia is the etched graffiti profile of a hawk-nosed man reputed to be a portrait of a prisoner by Michelangelo (*photo below*).

Cellini himself is represented by another monster-killer: a fabulous *Perseus*, holding the snaky head of Medusa, standing victorious in the adjacent **Loggia dei Lanzi**, and testament to the artist's pig-headed determination: most considered it would be impossible to cast, but after several failed attempts, Cellini finally succeeded by burning his family furniture to fan the furnace (*see also p87* **Rogues' gallery**). Also in the loggia is Giambologna's spiralling marble *Rape of the Sabine Women* (1582), a virtuoso attempt to outdo Cellini (*see also p28* **Statues of stature**).

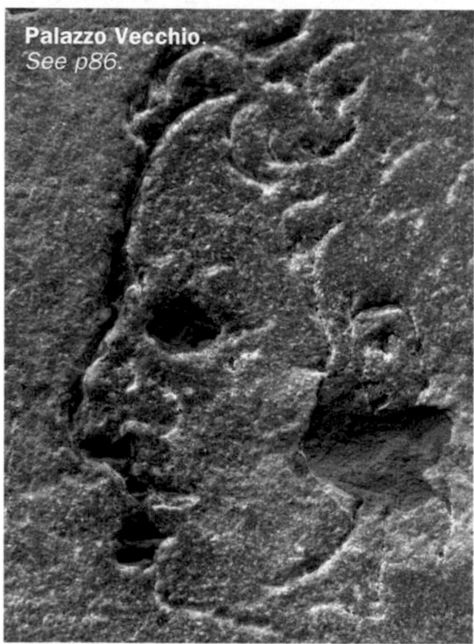
Palazzo Vecchio. *See p86.*

The loggia itself, the name of which derives from the *lanzichenecchi* (a private army of Cosimo I), was built in the late 1300s to shelter civic bigwigs during ceremonies. By the mid 15th century, it had become a favourite spot for old men to gossip and shelter from the sun.

Leading down to the river from piazza della Signoria, the daunting piazzale degli Uffizi is home to the world-renowned Galleria degli Uffizi (the **Uffizi**; *see p88*). Also here is the separate entrance to the **Corridoio Vasariano** or Vasari Corridor. Halfway down the piazzale on the right, in via Lambertesca, is the entrance to the **Collezione Contini-Bonacossi** (*see p85*) and the Georgofili library, where a Mafia bomb exploded in 1993.

Turning left from the riverbank leads you to the **Museo di Storia della Scienza** (*see p86*). Via Castellani heads north from the museum to piazza San Firenze and its imposing law courts; just north of the piazza, in via Proconsolo, is the entrance to the **Badia Fiorentina** (*see 85*), its elegant stone tower visible for the first time in years after a painfully drawn-out restoration. Opposite, on the corner with via Ghibellina, is the foreboding National Museum, the sculpture-laden **Bargello** (*see p104*). We're now well and truly in Danteland; just behind the Badia is the **Museo Casa di Dante** (*see p85*), while opposite the house is the **Chiesa di Dante**, the delightful little church where Dante's beloved Beatrice is buried.

Back at the river end of the Uffizi and on the right is the landmark **ponte Vecchio**, north of which is the mainly modern architecture of via Por Santa Maria, much of which had to be rebuilt after the German bombing at the end of World War II. In a piazza just off the east side of the street is the **Museo Diocesano di Santo Stefano al Ponte** (*see p86*), a tiny church museum.

At the top of via Por Santa Maria, a busy shopping street, is the **Mercato Nuovo** (literally the 'new market', but often called the 'straw market', or Mercato della Paglia), a fine stone loggia erected between 1547 and 1551 on a site where there had been a market since the 11th century. It now houses stalls selling leather and straw goods and cheap souvenirs, but back in the 16th century it was full of silk and gold merchants. The market is popularly known as the Porcellino, or piglet, after the bronze statue of a boar, a copy of a bronze by Pietro Tacca that in turn was a copy of an ancient marble now in the Uffizi. It's considered good luck to rub the boar's nose and put a coin in its mouth: proceeds go to a children's charity, and legend says the donor is assured a return trip.

A block further up via Calimala (named after the Greek for 'beautiful fleece') on the right is the portico-and-ramparts grandeur of **Palazzo dell'Arte della Lana**, the Renaissance home to the filthy-rich guild of clothmakers. This fairytale castle is connected by an arched overpass to the church of **Orsanmichele** (*see p86*), the main entrance to which is on via de' Calzaiuoli, the pedestrian thoroughfare between piazza della Signoria and the Duomo.

On the corner of the palazzo facing Orsanmichele is the stunning Gothic **Madonna of the Trumpet** tabernacle, complete with spiral columns, a pointed arch, family crest decorations, and a long and complex history. The tabernacle started life in the 13th century on the corner of the Old Market and Calimala, housing the supposedly miracle-working *Madonna* painting (later destroyed by fire). It was replaced in 1335 by *Enthroned Madonna and Child, Saints John the Baptist and John the Evangelist and Angels* by Jacopo di Casentino; *Coronation of the Virgin and Saints* by Niccolò di Pietro Gerini was added in 1380.

Associazione Musei dei Ragazzi

Palazzo Vecchio, piazza della Signoria (entrance from via de'Gondi) (055 2768224/www.musei ragazzifirenze.it). **Open** 9am-5pm Mon-Wed, Fri, Sat; 9am-2pm Thur; 9am-7pm Sun. **Admission** €6. **No credit cards. Map** p335 C4.

One for the kids, though this is more educational activity-running establishment than museum. For children aged three to seven, there's a playroom with a dressing-up corner, a puppet theatre and building blocks, all with a Renaissance theme; for older children (target audience: eight to 88) there's a series of workshops, talks by experts, meetings with historical characters such as Eleonora di Toledo and Cosimo I, visits on 'secret routes', and multimedia activities, based in museums around town.

Badia Fiorentina

Via Dante Alighieri (055 264402). **Open** *Cloister* 3-6pm Mon. *Church* 3-6pm Mon; 7am-6pm Tue-Sat. **Admission** donation to Eucharist. **Map** p335 C4.

A Benedictine abbey founded in the tenth century by Willa, the mother of Ugo, Margrave of Tuscany, the Badia Fiorentia was the richest religious institution in medieval Florence. Willa had been deeply influenced by Romuald, a monk who travelled around Tuscany denouncing the wickedness of the clergy, flagellating himself and urging the rich to build monasteries; it was Romuald who persuaded Willa to found the Badia in 978.

When Ugo was a child, his exiled father returned to Florence and invented a novel paternity test by expecting the boy to recognise the father he'd never seen in a room of men. Happily for his mother, Ugo succeeded. The people decided he must have had divine guidance, and he was considered a visionary leader. Ugo lavished money and land on what was then known as the Badia Florentia, and was eventually buried there in a Roman sarcophagus (later replaced by a tomb made by Renaissance sculptor Mino da Fiesole) that's still housed in the abbey.

It was here in 1274, just across the street from his probable birthplace, that the eight-year-old Dante fell in love at first sight with Beatrice Portinari. He was devastated when her family arranged her marriage, at the tender age of 17, to Simone de' Bardi, and absolutely crushed when she died seven years later. Poor Dante attempted to forget his pain and anguish by throwing himself into war.

The Badia has been rebuilt many times since Dante's day, but still retains a graceful Romanesque campanile and an exquisite carved ceiling. The Chiostro degli Aranci dates from 1430 and is frescoed with scenes from the life of San Bernardo. Inside the church, Bernardo is celebrated once again, in a painting by Filippino Lippi. The Cappella dei Pandolfini is where writer Giovanni Boccaccio held the first public reading of the works of Dante.

Collezione Contini-Bonacossi

Uffizi, entrance on via Lambertesca (055 294883). **Open** guided group visits by appt only. **Admission** free. **Map** p334 C3.

An impressive collection donated to the state by the Contini Bonacossi family in 1974. Exhibits include renderings of the *Madonna and Child* by Duccio, Cimabue and Andrea del Castagno, and a roomful of works by artistic VIPs (like Bernini and Tintoretto). El Greco, Velázquez and Goya are numbered among the foreigners who are considered prestigious enough for the collection.

Museo Casa di Dante

Via Santa Margherita 1 (055 219416/www.museo casadidante.it). **Open** 10am-6pm Tue-Sat; 10am-4pm 1st Sun of mth; 10am-1pm, 2nd & 3rd Sun of mth. **Admission** €4. **No credit cards. Map** p335 B4.

Housed in the building where Dante is thought by some to have lived, this museum, dedicated to the father of the Italian language, reopened after three years of renovation in June 2005. If you go expecting to see the poet's belongings, original works or in fact anything original at all, you'll be disappointed. What the museum does offer, however, is an extensive amount of information about the political, economic and cultural environment of Dante's time, mostly in the form of brightly coloured factual posters lining the walls on all three floors. There are miniature-model reconstructions of battles and of ancient Florence, an example of a medieval bedroom, costumed mannequins and clear illustrations of Heaven, Hell and Purgatory taken from the poet's most famous work, *The Divine Comedy*.

Museo Diocesano di Santo Stefano al Ponte

Piazza Santo Stefano 5 (055 2710732). **Open** *Summer* 4-7pm Fri. *Winter* 3.30-6.30pm Fri; also by appointment. Closed mid July-Sept. **Admission** free. **Map** p334 C3.

A tiny, little-known museum hidden from the tourist trail in a square north of the ponte Vecchio. Among the religious icons and church relics are a few big surprises: a *Maestà* by Giotto, *San Giuliano* by Masolino and the *Quarate Predella* by Paolo Uccello.

Museo di Storia della Scienza

Piazza dei Giudici 1 (055 265311/www.imss.fi.it). **Open** *Summer* 9.30am-5pm Mon-Sat. *Winter* 9.30am-5pm Mon, Wed-Sat; 9.30am-1pm Tue; 10am-1pm 2nd Sun of mth. **Admission** €6.50. **No credit cards. Map** p335 C4.

Galileo Galilei's scientific instruments are the big draw here, but even without them, this would be one of the most interesting museums in Florence. Galileo's fascinatingly crafted compass and his leather-bound telescope (which, conversely, seems singularly unimpressive) are in the two rooms dedicated to the heretical stargazer. A morbid reliquary in the shape of his middle right finger is also on display, offering unintentionally ironic echoes to the honour more usually bestowed on saints.

In the next rooms are a collection of prisms and optical games. Art continues to mingle with science in Room 7, devoted to armillary spheres and dominated by a model commissioned by Federico II in 1593. Most of the spheres have the earth placed at the centre of the universe, surrounded by seven spheres of the planets.The second floor has an eclectic mix of machines, mechanisms and models, including a 19th-century clock (*pianola*) that writes a sentence with a mechanical hand, and a selection of electromagnetic and electrostatic instruments (Room 14). The display of amputation implements and models of foetuses adorning the walls are rather grisly. For information about events in Florence and Tuscany to commemorate the 400-year anniversary of Galileo's discovery, *see pp32-35*.

Orsanmichele & Museo di Orsanmichele

Via dell'Arte della Lana (055 284944/284715). **Open** *Church* 10am-7pm Tue-Sun. *Museum* tours 9am, 10am, 11am daily. Phone to check. Closed 1st & last Mon of mth. **Admission** free. **Map** p334 C3.

Most famous for the statues in the 14 niches that surround the building, Orsanmichele has become a relic of the extreme dedication and pride of Florentine trades, and a reminder that a competitive climate often heralds the greatest art. There's no spire and no overt religious symbols: Orsanmichele may not look much like a church, but it is – although one with a difference, melding as it does the relationship between art, religion and commerce.

In 1290, a loggia intended as a grain store was built to a design by Arnolfo di Cambio, the original architect of the Duomo, in the garden (*orto*) of the Monastery of San Michele (hence, 'Orsanmichele'). The loggia burned down in 1304, along with a painting of the Madonna that, from 1292, had been said to perform miracles. Such was the effect of her miracles that people flocked from every corner of Tuscany to worship her. When the building was reconstructed in the mid 1300s by Talenti and Fioravante, the painting was replaced and honoured by the creation of a marvellously elaborate glass and marble tabernacle by Andrea Orcagna. However, this was then replaced in 1347 by Bernardo Daddi's *Coronation of the Madonna with Eight Angels*, which is still in place today.

During reconstruction of the building, two upper floors were added for religious services. From the outset, the council intended the building to be a magnificent advertisement for the wealth of the city's guilds, and in 1339 each guild was instructed to fill one of the loggia's 14 niches with a statue of its patron saint. Only the wool guild obliged, so in 1406, after the building's conversion into a church, the council handed the guilds a ten-year deadline.

Six years later, the Calimala cloth importers, the wealthiest of all the guilds, commissioned Ghiberti to create a life-sized bronze of John the Baptist. It was the largest statue ever cast in Florence, and its arrival spurred the other major guilds into action. The guild of armourers was represented by a tense *St George* by Donatello (now in the Bargello; *see p104*), one of the first psychologically realistic sculptures of the Renaissance, while the Parte Guelfa guild had Donatello gild their bronze, a *St Louis of Toulouse* (later removed by the Medici in their drive to expunge all memory of the Guelphs).

All the statues in the external niches today are copies. However, the originals can be found on the first floor of the museum, displayed on a platform in the same order in which they once appeared around the church. And on the second floor is a collection of statues of 14th-century saints and prophets in arenaria stone. They were on the external façade of the church until the 1950s, when they were saved from the elements and moved to the Opificio delle Pietre Dure (*see p102*).

The church and museum do not always stick to the opening hours posted, so it's advisable to phone to check the hours before making a special trip.

Palazzo Vecchio Quartieri Monumentali

Piazza della Signoria (055 2768224/www.comune.firenze.it). **Open** 9am-7pm Mon-Wed, Fri, Sat; 9am-2pm Thur; 9am-7pm Sun. **Admission** €6. **No credit cards. Map** p335 C4.

The most important civic square in Florence is dominated by Florence's town hall; the imposing power of Palazzo Vecchio's austere and commanding walls were built to Arnolfo di Cambio's late 13th-century plans as seat to the Signoria – the city's ruling body as priors of the main guilds of the Medici. The building represented the immense strength of the city at this time.

The Medici enjoyed their own nine-year stay (1540-49) and instigated a Mannerist makeover of the interior from 1555 to 1574. However, the rustic stone exterior of the building and Arnolfo's tower, the highest in the city at 94m (308ft), remained largely intact. The tower, set just off-centre in order to incorporate a previous tower and to fit in with the irregularity of the square, and topped by two of the main symbols of Florence (a lion holding a lily), saw the imprisonment of Savonarola and Cosimo il Vecchio in a room euphemistically called the Albergaccio ('bad hotel'). From 1565, Palazzo Vecchio lost some of its administrative exclusivity to the Pitti Palace and the Uffizi. However, it later became the seat of the Italian government's House of Deputies from 1865 to 1871, when Florence was the first capital of the Kingdom of Italy. You might recognise one balcony from a rather gruesome scene in the Sir Anthony Hopkins film *Hannibal* (*see p101* **Walk**).

The Salone dei Cinquecento (Hall of the Five Hundred), where members of the Great Council met, should have been decorated by Michelangelo and Leonardo, not the zestless scenes of victory over Siena and Pisa by Vasari that cover the walls. Leonardo abandoned the project; Michelangelo had only finished the cartoon for the Battle of Cascine when he was summoned to Rome by Pope Julius II. Many believe da Vinci's sketches lie beneath the Vasari mural; to read more about the controversy, *see pp32-35.* One of Michaelangelo's commissions did end up here, however: the *Genius of Victory*, a statue thought to have been carved, along with the better-known *Slaves*, for the pope's never-finished tomb.

Off the Salone is the Studiolo di Francesco I, the office where Francesco hid away to practise alchemy. Also decorated by Vasari, it includes a scene from the alchemist's laboratory and illustrations of the four elements. From the vaulted ceiling, Bronzino's portraits of Francesco's parents, Cosimo I and Eleonora di Toledo, look down. The Quartiere di Eleonora, the apartments of the wife of Cosimo I, has two entirely frescoed chapels; the first was partly decorated by Bronzino, who used intense pastel hues to depict a surreal *Crossing the Red Sea*, while the Cappella dei Priori is decorated with fake mosaics and an idealised *Annunciation.*

Rogues' gallery Cellini

Benvenuto Cellini (1500-1571)

Cellini's delicate sensibility, expressed in his exquisite goldsmithing and sculpting, eluded him in his personal life. His autobiography reveals either a self-confessed murderer or a deluded braggart with homicidal fantasies, with the smart money on both. Cellini was exiled from Florence as a teenager for his part in a violent brawl and went to Siena, where the silver lining was an apprenticeship with Fracastoro. There would be many more forced moves, with Cellini upping sticks for Pisa, Bologna, Mantua, Fontainebleau, Paris, Florence again – where he created his masterpiece *Perseus* (*pictured*) – and Rome, where, he later boasted, defending the city from attack, he shot dead the marauding Constable of Bourbon. It seems he got away with the revenge killing of his brother's murderer, but crossed the line with his attack on a city notary. He had to leg it to Naples, but was reinstated as Rome's favoured medal-maker when Pope Paul III acceded the papal throne. A ruck with the pope's son meant yet another period of quiet reflection in a safe house. When he was finally imprisoned, it was ironically on the trumped-up charge of stealing the pope's tiara jewels. In 1549, he returned to his native Florence in high dudgeon to lead a tiresomely ordinary life as an artist and chronicler of his own exploits.

Beyond here is the garish Sala d'Udienza, with a carved ceiling dripping in gold; more subtle is the Sala dei Gigli, so named because of the gilded lilies that cover the walls. Decorated in the 15th century, it has a ceiling by Giuliano and Benedetto da Maiano, and some sublime frescoes of Roman statesmen by Ghirlandaio opposite the door. Donatello's original *Judith and Holofernes*, rich in political significance, is also here. Finally, go through into the Map Room where you can inspect the gigantic 16th-century globe by Egnazio Danti and, from the same period, 53 beautifully hand-decorated maps of countries and continents.

For an insight into Palazzo Vecchio's workings, book yourself on to the Visita ai Percorsi Segreti (Secret Passageways Tour) to see private rooms not usually open to the public and to climb on to the roof of the building where the lifts and pulleys that hold up the wooden panelled ceiling of the Sala dei Cinquecento are hidden. Other tours on offer include An Invitation to Cosimo's Court (good for children) and the Tour of the Quartieri Monumentali. This last guided visit ends in Bianca Cappello's special chamber, a room cunningly designed so the duchess would be able to see the goings-on in the Salone dei Cinquecento without being seen herself. Ask at the ticket office for more information. *Photo p84.*

Uffizi

Piazzale degli Uffizi 6 (055 2388651/www.uffizi.firenze.it). **Open** 8.15am-6.50pm Tue-Sun. **Admission** €6.50; €3.25 concessions. Small extra charge for special exhibitions. *Advance booking* via Firenze Musei (055 294883); booking charge €3. **No credit cards. Map** p335 C4.

Statues outside the Uffizi commemorate many of the most interesting artists and scholars in Florence's history but these pale into insignificance when you enter this stunning temple of Renaissance art. The quantity and quality of the paintings on display make this without a doubt the greatest treasure trove of Renaissance art in the world. Plans to double the gallery's display space, allowing long-hidden works to come out of storage, are finally under way, with designs by Japanese architect Arata Isozaki for a new exit wing approved in August 2007.

In the meantime the queues remain, and even booking in advance isn't foolproof: during peak times you need to reserve up to a couple of months in advance. Whether you book in advance or not, aim to arrive either when the museum opens or at lunchtime, when the tour groups are less prevalent. To see the whole collection takes a lot of time and energy: it's best to jump to the rooms in which you're most interested or, better still, to plan a return visit. Allow three hours for the unmissables. Several groups run guided tours (*see p104*); there are also audio tours in six languages for €4.65 (single headset) or €6.20 (double headset) from the ticket office.

The building was designed by Vasari in the mid 16th century as a public administration centre for Cosimo I (hence 'Uffizi', meaning 'offices'). To make way for the *pietra serena* and white plaster building, inspired by Michelangelo's Laurentian Library in San Lorenzo, most of the 11th-century church of San Piero Scheraggio was demolished. By 1581, Francesco I had already begun turning the top floor into a new home for his art collection; a succession of Medici added to the collection, culminating in the

Piazza della Signoria: Florence's civic showpiece. *See p83.*

bequest of most of the family's artworks by the last important familymember, Anna Maria, in 1743.

The chronological collection begins gloriously in **Room 2**, with three *Maestàs* by Giotto, Cimabue and Duccio; all were painted in the 13th and early 14th centuries, and all are still part of the Byzantine tradition. **Room 3** is 14th-century Siena, evoked most exquisitely by Simone Martini's lavish gilt altarpiece *Annunciation*. Such delight in detail reached its zenith in the international Gothic movement (**Rooms 5** and **6**) and, in particular, the work of Gentile da Fabriano (1370-1427), whose ornate *Adoration of the Magi*, known as the Strozzi Altarpiece because it was commissioned by Palla di Noferi Strozzi for the sacristy of Santa Trinità, has been restored to its original sumptuous grandeur.

It comes as something of a surprise, then, to find a strikingly contemporary *Virgin and Child with St Anne* by Masolino and Masaccio (1401-28) in **Room 7**. Masaccio painted the Virgin, whose severe expression and statuesque pose make her an indubitable descendant of Giotto's *Maestà*. In the same room is the *Santa Lucia dei Magnoli* altarpiece by Domenico Veneziano (1400-61), a Venetian artist who had a remarkable skill for rendering the way light affects colour. His influence on pupil Piero della Francesca's work is clear in the younger artist's portraits of the Duke and Duchess of Urbino. Paolo Uccello (1396-1475) is represented by the *Battle of San Romano*: a work of tremendous energy and power, it's part of a triptych; the other thirds are in London's National Gallery and the Louvre in Paris.

Rooms 8 and **9** are dominated by Filippo Lippi (*see also p98* **Rogues' gallery**) and the Pollaiolo brothers. The Madonna in Lippi's *Madonna with Child and Angels* is a portrait of the beautiful Lucrezia Buti, painted with their son Filippino. Antonio Pollaiolo's small panels of the *Labours of Hercules* demonstrate his familiarity with the skeletal form and musculature.

The two most famous paintings in the Uffizi and in Italy are in **Room 10**. Botticelli's *Birth of Venus*, the epitome of Renaissance romance, depicts the birth of the goddess from a sea impregnated by the castration of Uranus. It's an allegory of the birth of beauty from the mingling of the physical world (the sea) and the spiritual (Uranus). Scholars have been squabbling about the true meaning of Botticelli's *Primavera*, or *Allegory of Spring*, since it was painted in 1482. Many now agree that it was intended to represent the onset of spring and to signify the triumph of Venus (centre) as true love, with the Three Graces representing her beauty and Zephyr, on the right, as lust, pursuing the nymph Chloris, who is transformed into Flora, Venus's fecundity. If you look closely at Botticelli's *Portrait of a Young man with Medal* (1475-6) you'll see that the golden disc is not, in fact, painted but inlaid, making the portrait the only collage in the entire gallery.

In **Room 15** are several paintings by Leonardo da Vinci, including a collaboration with his master Verrocchio, *The Baptism of Christ*. Da Vinci painted the angel in profile, and parts of the landscape in this composition, and it's said that Verrocchio never painted again because his work couldn't match up to Leonardo's. The octagonal **Room 18**, known as La Tribuna, was designed to display some of the greatest masterpieces in the Medicean collection. It's dominated by portraits by Agnolo Bronzino, most strikingly that of Eleonora di Toledo; assured, beautiful and very Spanish in an opulent gold and black brocade gown. The oval **Room 24**, which was originally a treasure chamber, is home to the world's biggest collection of miniatures.

In **Room 25**, the gallery makes its transition to Mannerism led by Michelangelo's *Holy Family* (Doni Tondo), which shows the sculptural bodies, virtuoso composition and luscious palette that characterised the new wave. Florentine works in the same room include Mariotto Albertinelli's *Visitation*, with Elizabeth's saffron-coloured shawl glowing in what was the artist's only masterpiece. Next you'll come to the Pontormo- and Rosso Fiorentino-dominated **Room 27**; once again, Michelangelo's legacy is visible, most notably in *Moses Defends the Daughters of Jethro* by Rosso Fiorentino. Also by the same artist is the *Portrait of a Young Woman*, with the ubiquitous musical angel detail. The works by Titian in **Room 28** include his masterpiece *Venus of Urbino*, whose questionably chaste gaze has disarmed viewers for centuries. For more Venetian works, skip to Rooms 31-35, but don't miss the challenging *Madonna with the Long Neck* by Parmigianino en route in **Room 29**.

At this point it's very easy to become confused by the room numbers. Rooms 36-37 and 39-40 don't actually exist, 'room' 38 is a statue-lined area at the top of the stairwell and room 41 is a restoration laboratory. **Room 42**, also known as the Sala delle Niobe, is lined with four monumental canvases by Rubens and displays a collection of recently restored statues from the Villa Medici gardens in Rome. It's difficult to believe that these Roman copies of Greek originals are, in fact, 2,000 years old, as their dramatic poses depicting the myth of Niobe are reminiscent of 17th-century Baroque theatricality.

Downstairs, most of the first floor is reserved for the Uffizi's temporary exhibitions, but in the middle you'll find rooms 47-51. **Room 47** is home to a particularly grisly rendering of *Judith and Holofernes* by the 17th-century Caravaggio-esque female artist Artemisia Gentileschi. Caravaggio himself is represented by his famous *Medusa* (who is more shocked-looking than horror-inspiring), a *Bacchus* and a *Sacrifice of Isaac*, all of which demonstrate his masterly treatment of light. More Caravaggio-esque artists such as Manfredi and Gherardo delle Notti employ his use of chiaroscuro (dramatic light contrasts) to the paintings in the final four rooms of the corridor. It's this final collection that suffered most from the last terrorist attack. At 5am on 27 May 1993 a Mafia-related car bomb exploded outside the west wing of the Uffizi (a gnarled olive tree has been placed in the exact spot to remember the five people

Sightseeing

who were killed). In all, 32 paintings were damaged and three completely destroyed in the blast, which also severely hit the Sala delle Niobe. Ironically enough, most of the damage done to the paintings was from the shattering of their protective glass screens, which ripped the canvases to shreds. The restoration of Gherardo delle Notti's *Adoration of the Magi* is still taking place.

Note that paintings may be moved or go on loan at any time, so if you've set your heart on seeing a particular masterpiece, phone first to check it's here.

Around via de' Tornabuoni

Sightseeing

The Strozzi family were banking rivals of the more famous Medici; it's the gargantuan stones of fortified **Palazzo Strozzi** (*see p91*) that dominate the elegant shopping mecca of via de' Tornabuoni. The walls of the building (up to and around the main entrance in piazza Strozzi) are set with horse-tethering rings and torch holders and embellished with the three crescent-moon motifs of the family crest. The main street itself sweeps down from piazza Antinori to piazza Santa Trinità and the Santa Trinità bridge. It's crowned by **Palazzo Antinori**, an austere mid 15th-century palace of neat stone blocks that's been inhabited by the Antinori winemaking family since 1506. The rather garish **San Gaetano** opposite is one of the only completely Baroque churches in Florence.

Heading south towards the river, passing all manner of designer names, you'll come to piazza Santa Trinità. Just before the square is via Porta Rossa, with the Renaissance house museum **Palazzo Davanzati** (*see below*). At the far end of via Porta Rossa, on the right, the road widens into a square. The ramparts and Gothic leaded windows of the **Palagio di Parte Guelfa** date back to the 13th century, and have been modified by, among others, Brunelleschi and Vasari. The imposing building, once the headquarters of the Guelphs, is now used as a library and meeting rooms. Running parallel to via Porta Rossa is borgo Santissimi Apostoli, a narrow street in the middle of which is piazza del Limbo, so called because it occupies the site of a graveyard for unbaptised babies. The tiny church is **Santissimi Apostoli** (*see p91*).

Piazza Santa Trinità itself is little more than a bulge dominated by the curved ramparts of **Palazzo Spini Feroni**, home to and the shoetastic **Museo Ferragamo** (*see below*), and by an ancient column taken from the Baths of Caracalla in Rome, a gift to Cosimo I from Pope Pius I in 1560. The statue of Justice on top was designed by Francesco del Tadda. The first palazzo after via de' Tornabuoni is **Palazzo Bartolini-Salimbeni** by Baccio d'Agnolo.

Opposite Palazzo Spini Feroni, on the west side of via de' Tornabuoni, is the church of **Santa Trinità** (*see p91*).

The ponte Santa Trinità, an elegant bridge with an elliptical arch, links piazza Santa Trinità with **Oltrarno** (*see pp107-11*). First built in 1252 on the initiative of the Frescobaldi family, it was rebuilt in 1346 and again in 1567. It's this version, built by Ammannati (perhaps to a design by Michelangelo) that stands today; it's considered by many to be the most beautiful bridge in the world. The statues at either end represent the four seasons, and were placed there in 1608 to celebrate Cosimo II's marriage to Maria of Austria. Having been bombed on the night of 3 August 1944 by retreating Germans, the bridge was rebuilt in 1955 in the same position and to the same design. The head of the most famous statue, *Spring*, by Pietro Francavilla, which graces the north-east side of the bridge, remained lost until 1961, when a council employee dredged it up during a routine clean-up and claimed the reward offered for its return years before by a US newspaper.

Museo Ferragamo

Piazza Santa Trinità 5r (055 3360456/455/www.ferragamo.it). **Open** 10am-6pm Mon, Wed-Sun. **Admission** €5. **Map** p334 C2.

Down some steps from the eponymous shop (*see p164* **Brand new**) and into the medieval basement (where it was moved in December 2006) this museum is as elegant and stylish as the shoes on display. In the first chamber you can see order forms signed by famous actors and actresses, including John Wayne, and wooden 'lasts' (foot shapes) used to design shoes for Ava Gardner and Drew Barrymore. The rest of the museum is filled with a choice selection of the company's 10,000 shoes, boasting many pairs created for the likes of Marilyn Monroe, Judy Garland and Audrey Hepburn, and, if nothing else, affording an opportunity for shoe fetishists to drool over some of the world's most beautiful footwear.

Palazzo Davanzati/Museo dell'Antica Casa Fiorentina

Via Porta Rossa 13 (055 2388610/www.polomuseale.firenze.it). **Open** 8.15am-1.50pm daily. Closed 1st, 3rd & 5th Mon, 2nd & 4th Sun of mth. **Admission** free. **Map** p334 C3.

After years of renovation, the Ancient Florentine House Museum is partially open again. On the first floor are the painted Sala dei Pappagalli, the Salone Madornale and the Studiolo, displaying carved Renaissance furniture, paintings, tapestries, an incredible 16th-century strongbox and a permanent exhibition about spinning, weaving, embroidery and lace. The building itself is a wonderful example of a 14th-century palazzo for well-to-do Florentines; the little *cortile* with a view up to all of the different levels has a stone staircase leading to the first floor (as high as the noble guests would be visiting) and wooden stairs thereafter. There is a well beneath the building accessed by buckets that were lowered down a hollow column (like a dumb-waiter) from the kitchens, which were hidden high up on the (inaccessible) third floor to keep smoke and smells out of the way. Until the restoration is completed in early 2008, access to the museum is free and guided visits to part of the second floor are available on the hour, every hour, from 10am to 1pm (inclusive) to see the Sala da Pranzo and bedrooms.

Palazzo Strozzi

Piazza Strozzi (Institute Gabinetto Vieusseux 055 283962). **Open** *Library* 9am-1.30pm, 3-6pm Mon, Wed, Fri; 9am-6pm Tue, Thur. *Exhibitions* times vary. **Admission** *Ground-floor courtyard* free. *Exhibitions* vary. **Map** p334 B3.

Flanked on two sides by Florence's most chic and stylish shopping streets, Palazzo Strozzi is without a doubt one of the most magnificent of the hundred or so palaces built in the city during the 15th century. Behind the imposing rusticated stone walls lies the Humanist Institute's Renaissance book and manuscript collection and, just as we went to press, CCCS – the Centro di Cultura Contemporanea Strozzina – which will host contemporary art in the palazzo's cellar space. Given the auspicious setting, this could prove to be one of the most exciting new openings in Florence for many years.

In 1489, work began on the construction of the palazzo by order of Filippo Strozzi, whose family had been exiled from Florence in 1434 for opposing the Medici. However, they'd made good use of the time, moving south and becoming bankers to the King of Naples, and had amassed a fortune by the time they returned to Florence in 1466. Filippo began buying up property in the centre of Florence eight years later, until he had acquired enough real estate to build the biggest palace in the city.

An astrologer was asked to choose an auspicious day to lay the foundation stone; 6 August 1489 tied in nicely with a new law that tax-exempted anyone who built a house on an empty site. When Filippo died in 1491, he left his heirs to complete the project, which eventually bankrupted them, but the palace remained in the family up until 1937 when it became the seat of an insurance company and was finally handed over to the state in 1999.

Santa Trinità

Piazza Santa Trinità (055 216912). **Open** 8am-noon, 4-6pm Mon-Sat; 4-6pm Sun. **Admission** free. **Map** p334 C2.

This plain church was built in the 13th century over the ruins of two earlier churches belonging to the Vallombrosans. The order was founded in 1038 by San Giovanni Gualberto Visdomini, who spent much of his life attempting to persuade pious aristocrats to surrender their wealth and live a life of austerity. The order became extremely wealthy and powerful, reaching a peak in the 16th and 17th centuries, when its huge fortress abbey at Vallombrosa, in the Casentino countryside north of Arezzo, was built. Santa Trinità's façade was made at the end of the 16th century by Bernardo Buontalenti (who created the Boboli Gardens' Grotta Grande; *see p110* **Walk**) but the church is well worth a visit for the Cappella Sassetti alone. This famous chapel was luminously frescoed by Ghirlandaio in 1486 with scenes from the life of St Francis, including one set in the piazza della Signoria and featuring Lorenzo il Magnifico and his children.

Santissimi: La chiesa dei Santissimi Apostoli

Piazza del Limbo 1 (055 290642). **Open** 10.15am-noon, 4-7pm Mon-Sat; 10.15am-noon Sun. **Admission** free. **Map** p334 C3.

The design of Santissimi Apostoli, like that of the early Christian churches of Rome, is based on that of a Roman basilica. It's one of the oldest churches in Florence, retaining much of its 11th-century façade. The third chapel on the right holds an *Immaculate Conception* by Vasari; in the left aisle is an odd glazed terracotta tabernacle by Giovanni della Robbia. The church holds pieces of flint reputed to have come from Jerusalem's Holy Sepulchre, awarded to Pazzino de' Pazzi for his bravery during the Crusades: he was the first to scale the walls of Jerusalem, though his nickname, 'Little Mad Man of the Mad Men', suggests his actions may have been more foolish than brave. These flints were used on Easter Day to light the 'dove' that set off the fireworks display at the Scoppio del Carro (*see p170*). Note that the church has a tendency to close in the afternoon without notice.

The site of the **Mafia bomb**. *See p89.*

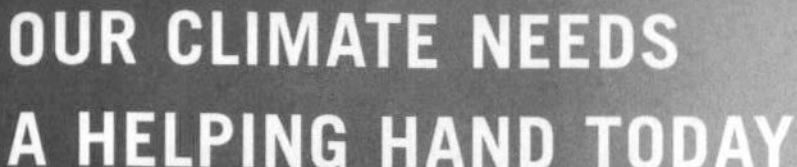
OUR CLIMATE NEEDS
A HELPING HAND TODAY

Santa Maria Novella

The old Dominican stronghold is emerging from a makeover with more visitor appeal than ever.

Santa Maria Novella was one of two buildings of any substance (the other being Santa Croce) that lay immediately outside the city walls in the 13th century. Many visitors think of Santa Maria Novella in functional terms – it is, after all, where coaches and trains arrive, and where most car-hire firms can be found. However, there's another, more tranquil side to this area where artistic treasures include the church and the new Alinari Photography museum; the latter, plus the nearly completed restoration work on piazza Santa Maria Novella, suggest the district's cultural cachet is only set to increase.

The area's three main streets, running parallel to each other, are each different in feel. Workaday via Palazzuolo (home to the Oratorio dei Vanchetoni at no.17, a beautiful 1602 building that occasionally opens to the public for free concerts) is sandwiched between elegant borgo Ognissanti and traffic-heavy via della Scala, home to the famous **Farmacia Santa Maria Novella** (*see p164*).

Santa Maria Novella station was designed by Giovanni Michelucci in 1935. Its bold form is not to everyone's taste, but the building is regarded as a masterpiece of modernism. As we went to press, the station's façade was under wraps for restoration, scheduled for completion in March 2008.

A short walk south of the station, Leon Battista Alberti's exquisite, precision-built façade for the church of **Santa Maria Novella** (*see p95*) looks out on to the grassy (but scruffy, even before the building works began) piazza of the same name, which held annual chariot races on the feast day of Florence's patron saint, John the Baptist, from 1563 to 1852. The course was marked by two obelisks for the chariots to lap, which are still in the piazza, resting on turtles sculpted by Giambologna. Opposite the church, on the southern side of the square, is the newly restored **Loggia di San Paolo**, a late 15th-century arcade built to the model of Brunelleschi's Loggiato degli Innocenti in San Marco (*see p99*). This is where the new **Museo Nazionale Alinari della Fotografia** (*see p94*) opened in October 2006.

Piazza Santa Maria Novella has been the subject of long-running disputes between local residents, hotel owners and the city police, whose opinions over the degree of safety and civic care are, to say the least, at odds with one another. By day the square is a bustling and pretty tourist mecca, but nights can be dodgier. The opening of smart hotels such as JK Place (*see p57*) spruced up the eastern side of the square a number of years ago, but problems remain with drug dealers after dark. An ongoing overhaul of the piazza will brighten it up with flowerbeds, as well as creating a larger pedestrianised zone.

In stark contrast, walk a little south of the piazza, where the triangle formed by via de' Fossi, via della Spada and via della Vigna Nuova is not just a friendly, lively area during the day, but also generally safe for night-time window-shopping. The area is cluttered with antiques emporia, designer clothes shops, cafés and *trattorie*; next to each other in the centre of the triangle are fine Palazzo Rucellai (not open to the public), the **Capella Rucellai** and the adjacent modern art museum, the **Museo Marino Marini** (for both, *see p94*).

Alberti had already designed Palazzo Rucellai in via della Vigna Nuova for the Rucellai family when he created the façade of Santa Maria Novella. The palazzo's subtle frontage was inspired by Rome's Colosseum: the pilasters that section the bottom storey have Doric capitals, those on the middle level come with Ionic capitals, and those on the top storey are based on the Corinthian style. There's no rustication: Alberti considered it fit only for tyrants, of whom there were plenty at the time. The Rucellai were wool merchants who had grown rich by importing a Mallorcan red dye derived from lichen and known as *oricello*, from which their surname derives. The charming Orti Oricellari garden at the far end of via della Scala was where the family grew their crop.

Up past piazza Goldoni, lungarno Vespucci and borgo Ognissanti open out into piazza Ognissanti, flanked by swanky hotels and topped by the church of **Ognissanti** (*see p95*), the cloister of which houses the **Cenacolo di Ognissanti** (*see below*). Further up, elegant residential roads lead out on to the main avenues, Porta al Prato and the mammoth park of **Parco delle Cascine** (*see p113*).

Cappella Rucellai

Via della Spada (055 216912). **Open** 10am-noon Mon-Sat. **Admission** free. **Map** p334 B2.

It's not so much a case of blink and you'll miss this tiny chapel; more that if you oversleep or linger over breakfast, you'll find it's already closed for the day. Once part of the church of San Pancrazio (now the Museo Marino Marini, *see below*), the chapel retains the church's charming bell tower and contains the tombs of many members of the extended family of 15th-century wool magnate Giovanni Rucellai, including that of his wife Iacopa Strozzi. It's worth a visit to see Alberti's Temple of the Santo Sepolcro, commissioned in 1467 by Giovanni to be built to the same proportions as the Holy Sepulchre of Jerusalem in an attempt to ensure his own salvation.

Cenacolo di Ognissanti

Borgo Ognissanti 42 (055 2398700). **Open** *Last Supper* 9am-noon Mon, Tue, Sat. **Admission** free. **Map** p334 B1.

The Ognissanti's (*see p95*) lovely cloister, accessed via a separate entrance on borgo Ognissanti, is painted with frescoes illustrating the life of St Francis. The cloister's main point of interest, however, is Ghirlandaio's most famous *Last Supper*, dated 1480, housed in the refectory. There's also a museum of Franciscan bits and bobs.

Museo Marino Marini

Piazza San Pancrazio (055 219432/www.museomarinomarini.it). **Open** *Summer* 10am-5pm Mon, Wed-Fri. *Winter* 10am-5pm Mon, Wed-Sat. Closed Aug. **Admission** €4. **No credit cards**. **Map** p334 B2.

The original Albertian church on this site, San Pancrazio, was redesigned to accommodate the works of prolific sculptor and painter Marino Marini (1901-80). It's now a huge, bright and modern exhibition space filled predominantly with sculptures on the theme of horse and rider; the central exhibit is the 6m (20ft) *Composizione Equestre*. The second floor houses a series of other bronze and polychrome plaster pieces, including the hypnotic *Nuotatore* (Swimmer), and some fabulous colourful paintings and sculptures of dancers and jugglers created during the early 1950s.

Museo Nazionale Alinari della Fotografia

Piazza Santa Maria Novella 14a (055 216310/www.alinarifondazione.it). **Open** 9.30am-7.30pm Mon, Tue, Thur, Fri, Sun; 9.30am-11.30pm Sat. **Admission** €9; €7.50 each for 2 or more visitors, children, and visitors during happy hour (last hour before closing). **Map** p334 B2.

The Alinari National Museum of Photography opened in October 2006 with more than four million pictures in its archives, and has found immediate success with both Florentines and visitors. The first two rooms are reserved as a temporary exhibition space; the actual museum begins behind them with an introduction to the history of Italian and world photography from 1839 to the present day. The displays include video screens, functional camera obscuras, clearly laid-out displays of photographs and negatives, binoculars that turn photographs three-dimensional and a vast collectors' dream of cameras. Reconstructions of many photographs using plastic and textiles, and explanatory panels written in braille, make it possible for the museum to be appreciated by blind visitors.

Rogues' gallery Torrigiani

Pietro Torrigiani (1472-1528)

Torrigiani was the bullyboy artist credited with bringing the Renaissance to Britain. A contemporary of Michelangelo, he studied with him in the sculpture school of Lorenzo de' Medici, where the best artistic talents in the city were nurtured. The younger Michelangelo managed to usurp Torrigiani's position as teacher's pet within days of arriving. On a sketching visit to the Brancacci Chapel, Torrigiani picked a fight with 'that Buonarotti' as he called him, and in the ensuing brawl Michelangelo's hooter was shattered. 'I felt the bone and the cartilage yield upon my fist as if they had been of crisp wafer,' the assailant recalled.

Banished in disgrace, Torrigiani became a mercenary for a time before winding up in the English Tudor court. He seemed to thrive working for like-minded hooligans, and was commissioned to create both the effigy for Henry VII's tomb in Westminster Abbey and Henry VIII's tomb monument. Having moved to Spain, his hell-raising finally got up the wrong thugs' noses and he died of starvation in an Inquisition prison.

Ognissanti

Borgo Ognissanti 42 (055 2398700). **Open** 9am-12.30pm, 4-7.30pm daily. **Admission** free. **Map** p334 B1.

The church of Ognissanti (All Saints) was founded in the 13th century by the Umiliati, a group of monks from Lombardy. The monks introduced the wool trade to Florence and thus brough with them great properity; without them, perhaps, there would have been no Florentine Renaissance. The Umiliati were so rich by the 14th century that they commissioned Giotto to paint the *Maestà* for their high altar; 50 years later, they got Giovanni da Milano to create a flashier altarpiece with more gold. Both are now in the Uffizi (*see p89*). Ognissanti was also the parish church of the Vespucci, a family of merchants that included 15th-century navigator Amerigo, who sailed to the Venezuelan coast in 1499 – and had two continents named after him.

The church has been rebuilt numerous times and is now visited mainly for paintings by Ghirlandaio, including *St Jerome* and the *Madonna della Misericordia*, which includes a portrait of Amerigo Vespucci: he's the young boy dressed in pink. To see Ghirlandaio's masterful *Last Supper* you have to go back outside and through the next door. Other frescoes include a *St Augustine* by Botticelli and a *St Jerome* by Ghirlandaio. In the Chapel of St Peter of Alcantara, look out for the tomb of Botticelli, marked with his family name of Filipepi.

Santa Maria Novella

Piazza Santa Maria Novella (055 2645184/219257/ www.smn.it). **Open** 9am-5pm daily. **Admission** €2.50. **No credit cards. Map** p334 A2.

Called Novella (New) because it was built on the site of the ninth-century Santa Maria delle Vigne, the church dominates the piazza with its huge, geometrical façade. Santa Maria Novella was the Florentine seat of the Dominicans, an order fond of leading street brawls against suspected heretics. The piazza outside was enlarged in 1244-45 to accommodate the crowds that came to hear St Peter the Martyr, one of the viler members of the saintly canon.

The pièce de résistance of the church is its magnificent Alberti façade. In 1465 the architect incorporated the Romanesque lower storey into a refined Renaissance scheme, adding the triangular tympanum and the scrolls that mask the side nave exteriors in an exercise of consummate classical harmony. The church interior, however, was designed by the order's monks and is fittingly severe.

The church also houses the *Crocifisso* by Giotto, a simple wooden crucifix. It was finally returned to the church in 2001 after a 12-year restoration and placed in the centre of the basilica where the Dominicans had originally positioned it in 1290.

Until Vasari had them whitewashed in the mid 16th century, the church walls were covered with frescoes. Fortunately, Masaccio's *Trinità* of 1427 on the left nave remains (*see also pp32-35*), a triumph of trompe l'œil, with God, Christ and two saints

Giotto's *Crocifisso* at **Santa Maria Novella**.

appearing to stand in a niche watched by the patrons Lorenzo Lenzi and his wife. The sinister inscription above the skeleton on the sarcophagus reads: 'I was what you are and what I am you shall be.'

In 1485, the Dominicans let Ghirlandaio cover the walls of the Cappella Tornabuoni, behind the altarpiece, with scenes from the life of John the Baptist, featuring lavish contemporary Florentine interiors and a supporting cast from the Tornabuoni family all wearing beautiful clothes – effectively making the work part-advertisement, as the family were cloth merchants. Ghirlandaio also found time to train a young Michelangelo while working on the chapel. At about the same time, Filippino Lippi was at work next door in the Cappella di Filippo Strozzi, painting scenes from the life of St Philip. A wooden crucifix by Brunelleschi, the envy of Donatello, is to the left of the altarpiece.

To compare Masaccio's easeful use of perspective with the contorted struggles of Paolo Uccello, visit the Chiostro Verde (green cloister) to the left of the church (via a separate entrance). Uccello's lunettes can be considered either visionary experiments of modern art or a complete perspective mess, depending on your tolerance of artistic licence. Off the Chiostro you'll find the Cappellone (or Cappella) degli Spagnoli, named after the Spanish wife of Cosimo I, Eleonora di Toledo, and decorated with vibrant scenes by Andrea di Bonaiuto. Look out for the odd-looking cupola on the Duomo fresco: it's the artist's own design for the dome, ultimately rejected in favour of Brunelleschi's plan.

San Lorenzo

The original Medici neighbourhood is one of the city's most vibrant enclaves.

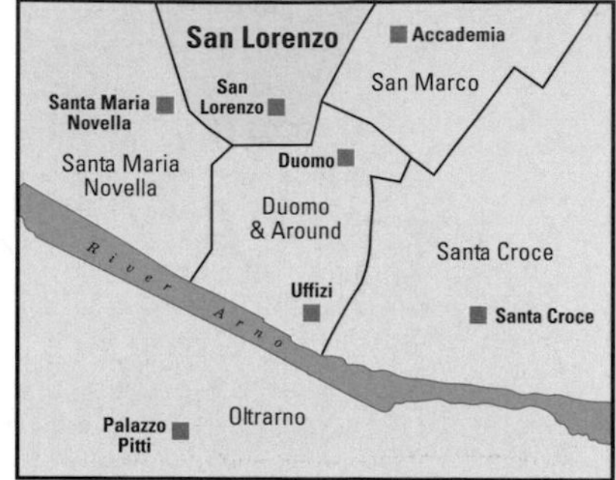

Teeming with life, San Lorenzo is loved and hated in equal measure. The incongruously unfinished façade of San Lorenzo church itself and the chapel of the Medici family may be rather serious affairs, but this area is marked out by the hectic, frenetic activity generated by the huge central market, the high number of tourists, and the plethora of shops, delis, cafés and doughnut stands.

The **market** of San Lorenzo constitutes the hub of the area, and spreads its tentacles over a wide swathe of *piazze*, snaking north from the church of **San Lorenzo** (*see p98*). The street stalls around here sell cheap clothes, mediocre leather goods and tacky souvenirs, which all but conceal the entrance to the bustling Mercato Centrale; *see p150* **Playing the markets**.

Roads lead off the *piazze* in a star shape. Head north-east from piazza San Lorenzo up via de' Ginori, alongside the gardens at the back of **Palazzo Medici Riccardi** (*see p97*), and past craft shops up to the corner of via San Gallo and via XXVII Aprile. The Benedictine refectory of **Cenacolo di Sant'Apollonia** (*see p97*) is on the left, while the **Chiostro dello Scalzo** (*see p97*) is situated north of piazza San Marco. Coming back down via Cavour, you'll pass the tacky gimmick that is the new **Serial Killer & Death Penalty Museum** (no.51r, 055 210188, www.serialkiller museum.com) – it might make a good place to dump any bored teenagers for an hour. In stark contrast is the nearby entrance to Palazzo Medici Riccardi with its beautiful family chapel painted by Benozzo Gozzoli. Following the walls of the palazzo round to the right you'll once more find yourself in piazza San Lorenzo.

Travelling south from this piazza will lead you past busy shoe and clothes shops in borgo San Lorenzo. If you head north-west from the **Cappelle Medicee** (*see below*) in piazza di Madonna degli Aldobrandini at the back of San Lorenzo church, you pass along via Faenza, with the **Interactive Museum of Medieval Florence** (no.13r, 055 282432, www.oscuro medioevo.com) on the corner, another naff money-spinner. Heading north-east up via Sant'Antonino takes you past tiny food stores and back towards the Mercato Centrale.

If you continue up via Faenza and cross dingy via Nazionale, you'll come to the **Cenacolo di Fuligno** (*see p97*) on the right. Heading north-east up via Nazionale, the roads widen into piazza dell'Indipendenza, where the grand *palazzi* herald the beginnings of a more genteel area. The double square, with a main road running through the middle, bald grass and a couple of trees, is a bad excuse for a park but it does at least take you a step closer to the duck pond and flowerbeds of the gardens of the otherwise unspectacular (albeit massive) **Fortezza da Basso** (*see p113*).

Cappelle Medicee

Piazza di Madonna degli Aldobrandini 6 (055 2388602). **Open** 8.15am-4.20pm Tue-Sat, 1st, 3rd, 5th Mon & 2nd, 4th Sun of mth. **Admission** €6. **No credit cards**. **Map** p334 A3.

The spectacular Medici mausoleum is the most splendid and fascinating part of the basilica of San Lorenzo. Up the curling stairs at the back of the entrance chamber (containing the family's reliquaries and memorial plaques) is the grand Cappella dei Principi (Chapel of the Princes), which was constructed from huge hunks of porphyry and ancient Roman marbles hauled into the city by Turkish slaves, and houses six sarcophagi of the Medici grand dukes. The floor plan of the Cappella dei Principi was based on that of Florence's Baptistery and, possibly, that of the Holy Sepulchre in Jerusalem. It had been hoped that the tombs would be joined by that purporting to be of Christ, but the authorities in Jerusalem refused to sell it. This mausoleum was commissioned in 1602 but, amazingly, the beautifully intricate inlay of marble and precious stones wasn't fully completed by the workers of the Opificio delle Pietre Dure until an external pavement was finished in 1962, at which point the Medici dynasty had been over for 220 years.

Although it's closed to the public, the discovery of the crypt in 1994 caused much excitement, especially the sensational unearthing of a stone under the chapel's altar that concealed its entrance. The exhumation of 49 Medici bodies ensued and enabled scientists to determine in what manner many of them died. It was originally thought that Francesco I de' Medici and his mistress Bianca Cappella, who died within hours of each other, had suffered from malaria: it has now been proven that they had in fact undergone acute arsenic poisoning – probably at the hand of Francesco's jealous brother Ferdinando.

Out of the Cappella dei Principi, a passage to your left leads to Michelangelo's Sagrestia Nuova (New Sacristy). This chamber, begun in 1520, makes a stark contrast to the excesses of the Cappella dei Principi. It's dominated by the tombs of Lorenzo il Magnifico's relatives: grandson Lorenzo, Duke of Urbino, and son Giuliano, Duke of Nemours who grew up alongside Michelangelo. The tombs were designed by the artist with the allegorical figures of Night and Day, and, opposite, Dawn and Dusk reclining on top; their gaze directs the visitor's eyes to a sculpture of a Madonna and child on a facing wall. Also here, under the sacristy, is the incomplete tomb of Lorenzo il Magnifico and his brother Giuliano. The chapel's coffered dome was designed to contribute to Michelangelo's allegory within the tomb of the inevitability of death, symbolising the 'sun' of salvation. The Sagrestia Nuova was finished by Giorgio Vasari, Michelangelo himself having been hauled off to Rome to finish the Sistine Chapel. The great man was furious at having to leave the city – 'I cannot live under pressure from patrons, let alone paint' – but he'd worked long enough on the project to leave it as one of his masterpieces.

Cenacolo del Conservatorio di Fuligno

Via Faenza 42 (055 286982). **Open** 9am-noon & by appointment Tue, Thur, Sat. **Admission** free. **Map** p334 A3.

The harmonious fresco on the refectory wall of the ex-convent of St Onofrio was discovered in 1845, and was at first thought to be the work of Raphael. In fact, it is one of the best of Perugino's works: a *Last Supper* from about 1490. In the background is a representation of the Oration of the Garden in the characteristically Umbrian landscape, a giveaway of the Perugian-born painter's roots.

Cenacolo di Sant'Apollonia

Via XXVII Aprile 1 (055 23885). **Open** 8.30am-1.50pm Tue-Sat, 1st, 3rd, 5th Mon & 2nd, 4th Sun of mth. **Admission** free.

The works in this Benedictine refectory, such as the frescoes of the Passion of Christ, were covered over during the Baroque period and only came to light in the late 19th century. The most important is Andrea del Castagno's *Last Supper*.

Chiostro dello Scalzo

Via Cavour 69 (055 2388604). **Open** 9am-1pm Mon; by appointment only other days. **Admission** free. **Map** p3359 A4.

The 'Cloister of the Barefoot', so called because the monk holding the cross in the re-enactments of the Passion of Christ traditionally went shoeless, is frescoed with the monochrome chiaroscuro episodes from the life of St John the Baptist by Andrea del Sarto. Built to a design by Sangallo around a double courtyard with spindly Corinthian columns, it's a must-see epitome of delicacy and understatement.

Palazzo Medici Riccardi

Via Cavour 1 (055 2760340/www.palazzo-medici.it). **Open** 9am-7pm Mon, Tue, Thur-Sun. **Admission** €5. **No credit cards**. **Map** p335 B4.

In true Medici fashion, the family's 15th-century Renaissance palace is strategically placed. The family bought a string of adjacent houses on via Larga (now via Cavour) in the mid 14th century when it was a fairly broad road in a peaceful residential area – but in close proximity to the Duomo, and merely a few steps from their church, San Lorenzo (*see p98*). They ensured not only that their home (until they moved into Palazzo Vecchio in 1540) was in a position of power but that it would subtly intimidate any opposition with its strongbox-like appearance. Not wishing to appear too ostentatious, however, Cosimo il Vecchio rejected Brunelleschi's design as too extravagant and plumped for one by Michelozzo, who had recently proved his worth as a heavyweight architect in the rebuilding of the San Marco convent complex. Michelozzo designed a façade with a heavily rusticated lower storey in the style of many military buildings, a smoother and more refined first storey and a yet more restrained second storey.

The building was expanded and revamped in the 17th century by the Riccardi, its new owners, but

San Lorenzo market.

Sightseeing

retains Michelozzo's charming chapel. Almost entirely covered with frescoes by Benozzo Gozzoli, a student of Fra Angelico, the chapel features a vivid *Journey of the Magi*, which is actually a portrait of 15th-century Medici. In another room, off the gallery, is Fra Filippo Lippi's winsome *Madonna and Child*. Don't miss the new interactive technology on the ground floor (in what was once the chamber of Lorenzo the Magnificent) where you stand under a little metal dome and point with a dramatic gesture at a large, flat screen in front of you. Without touching anything, you can select parts of the chapel upstairs to find out more about them.

Sightseeing

San Lorenzo

Piazza San Lorenzo (055 2645184). **Open** 10am-5.30pm Mon-Sat. *Summer* 10am-5.30pm Mon-Sat; 1.30-5.30pm Sun. **Admission** €2.50. **No credit cards. Map** p334 A3.

Built on the site of Florence's cathedral from the end of the fourth to the ninth century – and thus occupying the spot of Florence's oldest church – San Lorenzo's sheer size more than compensates for its very plain exterior. It was built between 1419 and 1469 to a design by Brunelleschi (largely completed by Manetti, his erstwhile assistant, who made several design alterations), and was the first church to which the architect applied his theory of rational proportion. It sprawls, heavy and imposing, between piazza San Lorenzo and piazza di Madonna degli Aldobrandini, with a dome almost as prominent as that of the Duomo.

Despite the fortune spent on the place, the façade was never finished, hence the digestive biscuit-like bricks. In 1518, the Medici pope Leo X commissioned Michelangelo to design a façade – the models are in the Casa Buonarroti (*see p104*) – and ordained that the marble should be quarried at Pietrasanta. Michelangelo disagreed, preferring high-quality Carrara marble. In the end, it didn't matter: the scheme was cancelled in 1520. Recently, there has been great excitement about this absent façade: a column built for the project was discovered buried in the piazza and others – that some now believe were destined for San Lorenzo – were found in Pietrasanta. The basilica hosted six nights of a projected 'virtual façade' in March 2007. For a more thorough examination of Michelangelo's plans, the happenings around the church in 2007 and the proposals for the future, *see p32-35*.

A couple of artworks in the church merit a closer look. Savonarola snarled his tales of sin and doom from Donatello's bronze pulpits, but the reliefs are also powerful: you can almost hear the crowds scream in the *Deposition*. On the north wall is a *Martyrdom of St Lawrence* by Mannerist painter par excellence Bronzino. In the second chapel on the right is another Mannerist work, a *Marriage of the Virgin* by Rosso Fiorentino, while the north transept holds an *Annunciation* by Filippo Lippi (*see also below* **Rogues' gallery**), which displays a clarity of line and a depth of perspective that make it perfect for this interior.

Opening off the north transept is the Sagrestia Vecchia (Old Sacristy): another Brunelleschi design, it has a dome segmented like a tangerine and proportions based on cubes and spheres, along with a fabulous painted *tondo* by Donatello. The doors, also by Donatello, feature martyrs, apostles and Church fathers; to the left of the entrance is an elaborate tomb made out of serpentine, porphyry, marble and bronze containing the remains of Lorenzo il Magnifico's father and uncle, by Verrocchio.

Reached via the door to the left of the façade, Michelangelo's architectural classic, the Biblioteca Mediceo-Laurenziana (Laurentian Library), was built to house the Medici's large library. It still contains priceless volumes, papyri, codices and documents, though not all of them are on permanent display. The entrance corridor has a stunning red and cream inlaid mosaic floor, while the library itself displays Michelangelo's predilection for the human form over any classical architectural norms. However, it's in the vestibule leading into the reading room that the true masterpiece of the library is to be found. The highly original three-sweep stairwell in *pietra serena* was a ground-breaking design, the first example ever of the expressive Mannerist style in architecture and one of the most elegant staircases ever built.

Rogues' gallery Lippi

Filippo Lippi (1406-1469)

From the ethereal aura of Filippo Lippi's frescoes you'd be forgiven for thinking butter wouldn't melt. Not so: it seems Giorgio Vasari's comment that 'Fra Filippo was extremely fond of cheerful company and lived for his own part in a very joyous fashion' was an outrageous euphemism. The friar would get so hot under the collar his patron Cosimo de' Medici often kept him locked in his Medici Palace painting studio to stop him downing brushes to head off in search of a bit of skirt. Things came to a head when lusty Lippi met a young novice nun, Lucrezia Buti, and asked her to model for him. After a round of kiss chase in the Santa Margherita convent of Prato, he spirited her away, fending off the pursuing nuns; Filippo Lippi lived a life of unwedded bliss, producing many little Lippis including the equally renowned Filippino.

San Marco

Museums galore – and Michelangelo's masterpiece.

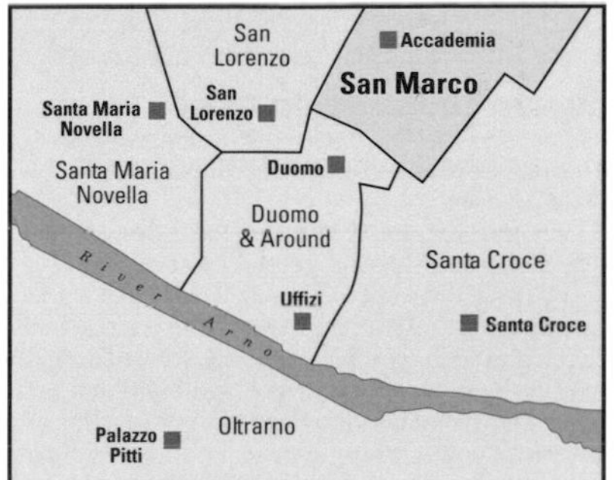

The diverse museums in this visitor-friendly district contain fascinating displays of weird and wonderful things. From Egyptian mummies and flying machines to Renaissance masterpieces and prehistoric gems (not to mention a certain statue), each collection vies for the attention of the visiting hordes. However, it's far from just a tourist centre: head to the nigh-on perfect porticoed square of Santissima Annunziata and it'll become apparent that the area thrives on the crowds of students from the nearby faculties – and that it's still an active centre of religious worship. But when it comes to famous attractions, San Marco has all the other outer districts trumped, housing as it does Michaelangelo's *David* in the **Galleria dell'Accademia** (*see below*). Despite all the action, though, there's a paucity of decent restaurants here, but there is the **Focacceria Pugi** (*see p159*) – renowned for selling the best *schiacciata con l'uva* (flat bread with grapes).

The **piazza della Santissima Annunziata** (abbreviated to SS Annunziata) is dominated by the powerful equestrian statue of Grand Duke Ferdinando I by Giambologna. On the eastern side is the **Spedale degli Innocenti** (*see p102*). Opened in 1445 as the first foundling hospital in Europe, it was designed by Filippo Brunelleschi and marks the advent of Renaissance town planning: Brunelleschi had designed it to fit into his greater plan for a perfectly symmetrical piazza – to be modern Europe's first – but died before realising his dream. The powder-blue medallions in the spandrels, each showing a swaddled baby, are by Andrea della Robbia.

Passing under the northernmost arch of the Spedale is via della Colonna, highlighted by the **Museo Archeologico** (*see p100*). On the southernmost corner of the piazza you'll find the **Bottega dei Ragazzi** (*see p102*), where children can enjoy Florence-themed creative workshops. Walking south down via dei Servi towards the Duomo will bring you to the **Museo Leonardo da Vinci** (*see p100*). On the western side of the square is upmarket hotel Loggiato dei Serviti (*see p63*); the church of **Santissima Annunziata** (*see p102*) is to the north. West takes you to piazza San Marco, a hub for buses and site of the church of **San Marco** (*see p102*).

Beside San Marco is the **Museo di San Marco** (*see p100*). Round the corner from the queues extending from the Accademia is the **Opificio delle Pietre Dure** (*see p102*), dedicated to the art of inlaying gems in mosaics. North of the piazza is the mineral department of the city's **Museo di Storia Naturale** (*see p102*); just around the corner is the exotic **Giardino dei Semplici** (*see p100*).

Galleria dell'Accademia

Via Ricasoli 58-60 (055 2388609). **Open** 8.15am-6.50pm Tue-Sun. **Admission** €10, €13 with reservation. **No credit cards. Map** p335 A4.

Despite the fact that the Accademia contains a huge number of magnificent and historic works, the queue snaking around the corner is for one reason above all: Michelangelo's monumental *David* (1501-04; *see also p29* **Statues of stature**), still gleaming from a 2003 €400,000 clean-up – his first bath in 130 years.

David started life as a political icon portraying strength and resolve, to encourage Florentines to support their fledgling constitution. However, having carved it from a 5m-high (16ft) slab of marble, Michelangelo undoubtedly considered it a monument to his genius. He intended it to stand high up on the Duomo, and so gave *David* a top-heavy shape so that it would look its best from the beholder's viewpoint (notice the slightly oversize head and hands). However, in 1873, when the statue was moved from piazza della Signoria (where a copy still stands) following acts of vandalism, the authorities decided to keep the plinth low so visitors could witness its curves close-up; hence it's a little out of proportion.

Other Michelangelo works line the walls of the *David* salon; among them are his *Slaves*, masterly but unfinished sculptures struggling to escape from marble prisons. They were intended for Pope Julius II's tomb, a project Michelangelo was forced to abandon in order to paint the Sistine Chapel ceiling in Rome. On the right of *David* is the unfinished *Pietà Palestrina*, often attributed to Michelangelo.

The gallery also houses a mixed bag of late Gothic and Renaissance paintings on the ground floor, and a fabulous collection of musical instruments from the Conservatory of Luigi Cherubini.

Giardino dei Semplici

Via Micheli 3 (055 2757402). **Open** 9am-1pm Mon, Tue, Thur, Fri, Sun; 9am-5pm Sat. **Admission** €4. **No credit cards. Map** p335 A4.

The Giardino dei Semplici, containing vegetable varieties with medicinal properties, was planted by landscape gardener Il Tribolo in 1545 for Cosimo I to cultivate and research exotic plants. Essential oils were extracted, perfumes distilled and cures and antidotes sought for various ailments and poisons.

Museo Archeologico

Via Gino Capponi 1, piazza della SS Annunziata (055 23575/www.comune.fi.it/soggetti/sat). **Open** 2-7pm Mon; 8.30am-7pm Tue, Thur; 8.30am-2pm Wed, Fri-Sun. **Admission** €4. **No credit cards. Map** p335 A5.

It's easy to come to Florence and get completely submerged in the Renaissance but the archaeological museum, housed in Palazzo della Crocetta, explains what happened before the Golden Age. The recently renovated museum now boasts an impressive entrance hall, an enormous temporary exhibition space and a new Etruscan money display, La Mostra di Monete. Guided tours run every 45 minutes from 9am – meet at the checkpoint in Room 15 on the first floor. Elsewhere you'll find jewellery, funerary sculpture, urns and bronzes dating from the fifth century BC, as well as the fabulous Chimera, a mythical beast that's part lion, part goat and part snake. Also present is the first-century BC Etruscan bronze *Orator,* famous and historically important because the speaker in question is wearing a Roman toga. The first rooms house Egyptian artefacts (including sarcophagi complete with creepy shrivelled bodies) from prehistoric eras through to the Copta period (310 AD). Outside is a beautiful garden lined with Etruscan tombs and monuments (only open on Saturdays).

Santissima Annunziata. *See p102.*

Museo Leonardo da Vinci

Via de' Servi 66-68r (055 282966). **Open** 10am-7pm daily. **Admission** €6. **Credit** AmEx, MC, V. **Map** p335 A4.

The painter, sculptor, musician, engineer, inventor, scientist and all-round genius Leonardo da Vinci justly has a museum to himself. The museum offers an attractive, interactive insight into the machines that featured in da Vinci's codes. Several of his most extraordinary inventions have been built from studies taken from his drawings: flying machines, a hydraulic saw, a printing machine and even a massive tank measuring 5.3m by 3m (17ft by 10ft) and weighing 2 tonnes. Most of the exhibits can be touched, moved and even dangled from, making the place immensely popular with kids.

Museo di San Marco

Piazza San Marco 1 (055 2388608). **Open** 8.15am-1.40pm Tue-Fri, 1st, 3rd & 5th Mon of mth; 8.15am-6.40pm Sat; 8.15am-7pm 2nd & 4th Sun of mth. **Admission** €4. **No credit cards. Map** p335 A5.

The Museo di San Marco is not only a fascinating coming-together of religion and history, but a wonderful place to rest and take in the general splendour. Housed in the monastery where he lived with his fellow monks, the museum is largely dedicated to the ethereal paintings of Fra Angelico (aka Beato Angelico), one of the most important spiritual artists of the 15th century, who would never lift a brush without a prayer and who wept whenever he painted a crucifixion. You're greeted on the first floor by one of the most famous images in Christendom, an other-worldly *Annunciation*, but the images Fra Angelico and his assistants frescoed on the walls of the monks' white vaulted cells are almost as impressive. Particularly outstanding is the lyrical *Noli Me Tangere*, which depicts Christ appearing to Mary Magdalene in a field of flowers, and the surreal *Mocking of Christ*, in which Christ's torturers are represented simply by relevant fragments of their anatomy (a hand holding a whip, a face spitting).

The cell that was later occupied by Fra Girolamo Savonarola (*see also p27* **Art attack**) is adorned with portraits of the rabid reformer by Fra Bartolomeo. You can also see his black wool cloak and his cilith, which was tied around the thigh to cause constant pain in reminder of the suffering of Christ. Near the cells reserved specially for Cosimo de' Medici is the beautiful library designed by his favourite architect, Michelozzo, in 1441.

Walk Fictional Florence

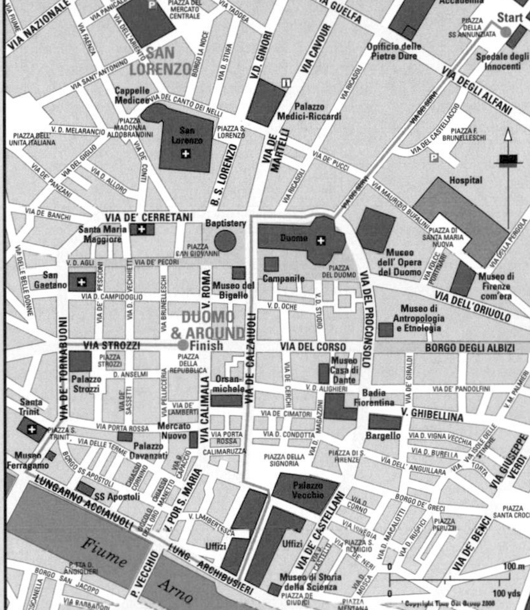

Set off from the Spedale degli Innocenti in piazza della SS Annunziata. The courtyard of the foundling hospital sets the scene for Joan Plowright's Mary Wallace to rescue the illegitimate Luca from an orphanage fate in Franco Zeffirelli's *Tea with Mussolini*, while Giambologna's Grand Duke Ferdinand I statue is the starting point for Judi Dench's Eleanor Lavish to whisk Maggie Smith's Charlotte Bartlett off to see the sights in *A Room with a View*. The exquisite piazza also plays a cameo role, complete with horses, carts and cabbage leaves, in Jane Campion's *Portrait of a Lady*, based on the book by Henry James.

Follow via de' Servi down to piazza del Duomo, where in the same film Nicole Kidman's independently minded Isabel Archer rides in her carriage to a less independent destiny with John Malkovich's Gilbert Osmond. Skirt round the north of the Duomo between the Baptistery and the façade steps, where Charlton Heston's Michelangelo lovingly contemplates the cathedral's carved images in *The Agony and the Ecstasy*, and continue down via de' Calzaiuoli to via de' Tavolini where, in Irving Stone's novel, Michelangelo is seconded to Ghirlandaio's studio.

Arriving at piazza della Signoria, admire the world's most gruesome Renaissance square – in fact and fiction. This is where Savonarola made his Bonfire of the Vanities. Helena Bonham-Carter's *Room with a View* young aristo Lucy Honeychurch swoons here after witnessing a murder, and, on the balcony of Palazzo Vecchio, Anthony Hopkins's Dr Hannibal Lecter brings a whole new meaning to 'letting it all hang out', at the expense of police inspector Giancarlo Giannini's innards, in *Hannibal*.

Cut through piazzale degli Uffizi, where Asia Argento's detective Anna Manni was 'rescued' after suffering a severe bout of artistic overkill in *The Stendhal Syndrome*. When you reach the river, turn right into lungarno degli Archibusieri, where at no.4 is the hotel where James Ivory found his *Room with a View* location (though the views in the film are actually from lungarno Torrigiani, and in EM Forster's book the Pensione Bertollini was on lungarno delle Grazie).

Carry along the riverbank, past the ponte Vecchio to the curved ramparts of Ferragamo's Palazzo Spini Ferroni, and turn right into via de' Tornabuoni. At no.8 is Palazzo Aldoviti Sangalletti, once home to Gran Caffè Doney and daily meeting place for I Scorpioni, the genteel group of 1930s expats remembered in *Tea with Mussolini*. In the film, Farmacia Inglese, now a shoe shop, was used for the setting, but truffle parlour Procacci, shown in a scuffle with the Blackshirts, is still here.

For a final macabre touch, turn right into via Strozzi, which ends with the perpendicular portico of via Pellicceria on the right, stalking ground for a hungry Hannibal Lecter.

On the ground floor, in the Ospizio dei Pellegrini (pilgrims' hospice), are more works by Fra Angelico. The *Tabernacle of the Madonna dei Linaiuoli*, his first commission from 1433 for the guild of linen makers, is here: painted on wood carved by Ghiberti, it contains some of his best-known images, the polichrome musical angels. Also here are a superb *Deposition* and a *Last Judgement*. The small refectory is dominated by a Ghirlandaio *Last Supper* (1479-80), where the disciples pick at a frugal repast of bread, wine and cherries against a symbolic background of orange trees, a peacock, a Burmese cat and flying ducks.

Museo di Storia Naturale – Sezione Mineralogia

Via la Pira 4 (055 216936/www.unifi.it/msn). **Open** 9am-1pm Mon, Tue, Thur, Fri, Sun; 9am-5pm Sat. **Admission** €5. **No credit cards. Map** p335 A4.
This clearly explained collection makes gem-lovers drool. It's packed full of strange and lovely stones, including 12 huge Brazilian quartzes.

Istituto degli Innocenti – La Bottega dei Ragazzi

Via de' Fibbiai 2 (piazza della SS Annunziata) (055 2478386/www.istitutodegliinnocenti.it). **Open** 9am-1pm, 3-7pm Mon-Sat. **Admission** (Reservation advised) €10, 3 admissions; €20, 6 admissions; €50, 8 admissions. **Map** p335 A4.
The Children's Workshop was set up in 2006, and although it caters predominantly for Italians, four different creative workshops are available for English-speaking children aged three to 11. The sessions cover history, animals and Florentine art.

Opificio delle Pietre Dure

Via degli Alfani 78 (055 265111). **Open** 8.15am-1.45pm Mon-Wed, Fri, Sat; 8.15am-7pm Thur. **Admission** €2. **No credit cards. Map** p335 A4.
Pietra dura is the craft of inlaying gems or semi-precious stones in intricate mosaics and you'll see fine examples in all the grandest palaces and most expensive shops of Florence. The Opificio (workshop) was founded by Grand Duke Ferdinando I in 1588; it's now an important restoration centre, but also provides a fascinating insight into this typically Florentine art, with its mezzanine exhibitions of tools and stones, and its displays of the methods used for the cutting and polishing of the stones through to the inlaying and mosaic techniques.

San Marco

Piazza San Marco (055 287628). **Open** 8.30am-noon, 4-6pm Mon-Sat; 4-6pm Sun. **Admission** free. **Map** p335 A4.
The amount of money lavished by the Medici family on San Lorenzo (*see p98*) is nothing compared with that spent on the church and convent of San Marco. After Cosimo il Vecchio returned from exile in 1434 and organised the transfer of the monastery of San Marco from the Silvestrine monks to the Dominicans from Fiesole, he went on to fund the renovation of the decaying church and convent by Michelozzo. Cosimo also founded a public library that greatly influenced Florentine humanists; meetings of the Florentine Humanist Academy were held in the gardens. Ironically, later in the 15th century, San Marco became the base of religious fundamentalist Fra Girolamo Savonarola, who burned countless humanist treasures in his notorious Bonfire of the Vanities (*see p27* **Art attack**).

Inside the church you can see the Giambologna's 16th-century nave with side chapels. He completed the Cappella di Sant'Antonino in 1589 where you can now, creepily, see the whole dried body of the saint.

The altarpiece *Madonna and Child* (1440s) is by Fra Angelico, whose other more famous works can be seen in the Museo di San Marco next door (*see p100*). Two missing panels from the painting were curiously discovered behind a door in an elderly Englishwoman's house in Oxford in 2006.

Santissima Annunziata

Piazza della SS Annunziata (055 266181). **Open** 7am-12.30pm, 4-6.30pm daily. **Admission** free. **Map** p335 A4.
Despite Brunelleschi's perfectionist ambitions for the square it crowns, Santissima Annunziata – the church of the Servite order – is a place of popular worship rather than perfect proportion. Highlights include a frescoed Baroque ceiling and an opulent shrine built around a miraculous *Madonna*, purportedly painted by a monk in 1252 and, as the story goes, finished overnight by angels. Surrounding the icon are flowers, silver lamps and pewter body parts, *ex votos* left in the hope that the Madonna will cure the dicky heart or gammy leg of loved ones.

Michelozzo was the directing architect and built the Villani and Madonna chapels, and the oratory on the left side of the church. In 1453, after almost ten years of work and not much progress, directorship was handed to Antonio Manetti. When Manetti ran into financial difficulty, the governing priests ceded the venture to the Gonzaga family. In 1477, Leon Batisti completed the church with slight modifications. The atrium was frescoed early the following century by Pontormo, Rosso Fiorentino and, most strikingly, Andrea del Sarto, whose *Birth of the Virgin* is set within the walls of a Renaissance palazzo with cherubs perched on a mantelpiece. *Photo p101.*

Spedale degli Innocenti

Piazza della SS Annunziata (055 2037308/www.istitutodeglinnocenti.it). **Open** 8.30am-7pm Mon-Sat; 8.30am-2pm Sun. **Admission** €4. **No credit cards. Map** p335 A5.
Housed in the recreation room of Brunelleschi's foundlings hospital, this collection received a substantial blow in 1853, when several important works were auctioned off (for a relative pittance) to raise money for the hospital. The remaining pieces include an unsurprising concentration of Madonna and Bambino pieces, including a Botticelli and a vivid Luca della Robbia. The high point, however, is Ghirlandaio's *Adoration of the Magi*, commissioned for the high altar of the hospital's church.

Santa Croce

The museums look after the history, so the atmosphere can be very much about today.

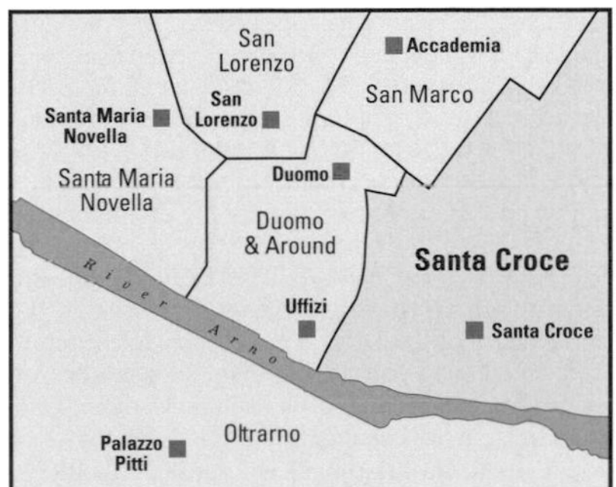

The largest of Florence's medieval parochial areas has, like much of the centre, a heady air of history and learning – it encompasses the impressive church with which it shares its name, the city's synagogue, the national library and several fascinating museums. But it's not hard to have fun here too, with some of the best ice-cream in the city (*see p146-47*), a lively market, excellent shopping and two world-class restaurants, **Cibrèo** and **Enoteca Pinchiorri** (for both, *see p127*); in terms of new openings and a general feeling of buzziness, Santa Croce is beginning to rival the Oltrarno for the title of Florence's most exciting neighbourhood.

Central **piazza Santa Croce** is a natural meeting and greeting spot where children play and adults rest their weary feet. But it's not always so relaxing: the sui/homicidal football game *calcio storico* is played here every June (although it was suspended in 2006 and 2007; *see also p173 and p203* **The crying game**) and from the end of November there's a wonderful, vibrant Christmas market. The **Sinagoga & Museo di Arte e Storia Ebraica** (*see p106*) lies in northern Santa Croce, just south of the elegant piazza d'Azeglio, while the **Museo di Antropologia e Etnologia** (*see p104*) can be found at the corner of borgo degli Albizi and via del Proconsolo; south of here, piazza San Firenze houses the sculpture-packed **Bargello** (*see p104*).

South of the Bargello in piazza San Firenze, the ornate Baroque church of San Firenze houses the city's law courts (until they move to Firenze Nuova). In via dell'Oriuolo, off via Proconsolo and east of the Duomo, is the **Museo di Firenze com'era** stuffed with the city archives, and, nearby, the **Museo Fiorentino di Preistoria** (for both, *see p105*). In borgo Pinti, east of the Duomo, watch out for the hard-to-find entrance to the church of **Santa Maria Maddalena dei Pazzi** (no.58). Just north of the river you return to piazza Santa Croce, with its imposing Gothic church of **Santa Croce** and attached **Museo dell'Opera di Santa Croce & Cappella dei Pazzi** (for both, *see p105*). Lining the pedestrianised square is a mix of shops and restaurants with outside tables. On the south side is the frescoed sepia façade of **Palazzo d'Antella**: decorated in 1620, it now houses smart rental apartments. Outside the church is Enrico Pazzi's 1865 statue of Dante.

At the head of piazza Santa Croce, via de' Benci is dotted with crafts shops and bohemian restaurants running down towards the Arno, past the eclectic **Museo Horne** (*see p105*), to the **ponte alle Grazie**. Like most of the bridges in central Florence, this one has a fascinating history; it was blown up just before the Germans' retreat at the end of World War II and was only rebuilt in 1957. The bridge gets its name from one of these chapels, devoted to Santa Maria delle Grazie, which was popular with distraught lovers seeking solace.

Continuing east you'll come across a square dominated by the **Biblioteca Nazionale**. Built to house the three million books and two million documents that were held in the Uffizi until 1935, the national library has two towers with statues of Dante and Galileo. In mock disrespect, Florentines nicknamed the twin towers 'the asses' ears'.

North-west of the parish square lie myriad winding streets mostly given over to leather factories and tiny souvenir shops. Until recently, the area north of the church of Santa Croce itself, stretching up past the **Casa Buonarroti** (*see p104*) in via Ghibellina to piazza de' Ciompi, was the rough-and-ready home to rival gangs of bored Florentine youths. Increasingly yuppified, it now yields trendy *trattorie* and wine bars. Piazza de' Ciompi was named after the dyers' and wool workers' revolt of 1378, and is taken over by a junk and antiques market during the week and a huge day-long flea market on the last Sunday of the month (*see p150* **Playing the market**). It's dominated by the **Loggia del Pesce**, built by Vasari in 1568 for the Mercato Vecchio, which previously occupied the site of piazza della Repubblica. It was taken apart in the 19th century and re-erected here.

Further east is piazza Ghiberti, home of the fruit and vegetable market of Sant'Ambrogio (*see p150* **Playing the market**), the world-famous Cibrèo restaurant and the shops, bars, *pizzerie* and restaurants of borgo La Croce. Borgo La Croce extends as far as piazza Beccaria and rests at the east city gate, Porta alla Croce, in the middle of the avenues circling the historic centre of the city.

Bargello

Via del Proconsolo 4 (055 2388606/www.sbas.firenze.it/bargello). **Open** 8.15am-1.50pm Tue-Sat, 1st, 3rd & 5th Mon of mth, 2nd & 4th Sun of mth. **Admission** €4. **No credit cards. Map** p335 C4.

This imposing, fortified structure has had so many different purposes over the years that although it's now most famous for containing Florence's main set of sculptures, the building itself and its history are equally fascinating. The Bargello started life as the Palazzo del Popolo in 1250 and soon became the mainstay of the chief magistrate, or *podestà*. The bodies of executed criminals were displayed in the courtyard during the 14th century; in the 15th century, law courts, prisons and torture chambers were set up inside. The Medici made it the seat of the *bargello* (chief of police) in the 16th century.

The **Bargello**: ideal for sculpture vultures.

Officially the Museo Nazionale del Bargello, the museum opened in 1865 to celebrate Florence becoming the capital of Italy, and now holds Florence's most eclectic and prestigious collection of sculpture, with treasures ranging from prime pieces – among the most famous works are Michelangelo's *Drunken Bacchus* and *Brutus* (the only bust he ever sculpted), Giambologna's fleet-footed *Mercury* and the *Davids* of Donatello – to Scandinavian chess sets and Egyptian ivories. The Salone Donatello contains the artist's two triumphant *Davids* (the more famous of which is undergoing on-site restoration until the end of 2008) and a tense *St George*, the original sculpture that once stood outside the Orsanmichele. Also fascinating are the two bronze panels of the Sacrifice of Isaac, sculpted by Brunelleschi and Lorenzo Ghiberti for a competition to design the north doors of the Duomo Baptistery. Back out on the grand loggia you can see Giambologna's bronze birds that used to spout water in a Medici grotto, including a madly exaggerated turkey. On this floor you can also find the little frescoed Magdalen Chapel, which contains the oldest confirmed portrait of Dante, painted by Giotto. The easily missable second floor has a fascinating selection of small bronze statues and Andrea del Verrocchio's *Lady with a Posy* (1474), which may have been carved in collaboration with his student Leonardo da Vinci.

Casa Buonarroti

Via Ghibellina 70 (055 241752/www.casabuonarroti.it). **Open** 9.30am-2pm Mon, Wed-Sun. **Admission** €6.50. **No credit cards. Map** p335 C5.

In 1612, Michelangelo Buonarotti the Younger took the decision to create a building in order to honour the memory of his rather more famous great-uncle. Even though Michelangelo (1475-1564) never actually lived here, this 17th-century house, owned by his descendants until 1858, has a collection of memorabilia that gives an insight into Florence's most famous artistic son. On the walls are scenes from the painter's life, while the pieces collated by the artist's great-nephew Filippo include a magnificent wooden model for the façade of San Lorenzo (*see also p32-35*) and two important original works: a bas-relief *Madonna of the Stairs* breastfeeding at the foot of a flight of stairs, and an unfinished *Battle of the Centaurs*.

Museo di Antropologia e Etnologia

Via del Proconsolo 12 (055 2396449). **Open** 9am-1pm Mon-Fri, Sun; 9am-5pm Sat. **Admission** €4. **No credit cards. Map** p335 B4.

Among the eclectic mix of artefacts from all over the world on display here are a collection of Peruvian mummies, an Ostyak harp from Lapland in the shape of a swan, an engraved trumpet made from an elephant tusk from the former Belgian Congo, Ecuadorian shrunken heads featured alongside a specially designed skull-beating club, and a Marini-meets-Picasso equestrian monument.

Museo Fiorentino di Preistoria

Via Sant'Egidio 21 (055 295159/www.museo fiorentinopreistoria.it). **Open** 9.30am-12.30pm Mon, Wed, Fri, Sat; 9.30am-4.30pm Tue, Thur; guided tours by appointment. **Admission** €3. **No credit cards. Map** p335 B4.

Florence's Museum of Prehistory traces humanity's development from the Paleolithic to the Bronze Age, but – predictably, as most evidence is found in caves – it has to content itself with various displays of photographs and illustrations. The first floor follows hominid physical changes, and also examines Italy's prehistoric art. The second floor includes a fascinating collection of stone implements.

Museo di Firenze com'era

Via dell'Oriuolo 24 (055 2616545). **Open** 9am-1.30pm Mon-Wed; 9am-6.30pm Sat. **Admission** €2.70. **No credit cards. Map** p335 B5.

This charmingly named museum ('Florence As It Was') traces the city's development through collections of maps, paintings and archaeological discoveries. There are rooms devoted to Giuseppe Poggi's plans from the 1860s to modernise Florence by creating Parisian-style boulevards; the famous lunettes of the Medici villas painted in 1599 by Flemish artist Giusto Utens; and the history of the region from 200 million years ago to Roman times. New exhibits include a model of 'Florentia' that shows how the city may have been in Roman times, with a Roman theatre buried below Palazzo Vecchio. Also interesting is the huge reproduction of the famous *Pianta della Catena*, a 19th-century copy of a 1470 engraving showing the first topological plan of Florence.

Museo Horne

Via de' Benci 6 (055 244661/www.museohorne.it). **Open** 9am-1pm Mon-Sat. **Admission** €5. **No credit cards. Map** p335 C4.

The 15th-century Palazzo Corsi-Alberti was purchased in the 1800s by English architect and art historian Herbert Percy Horne, who restored it to its Renaissance splendour. When he died in 1916, he left his palazzo and vast collection to the state. Objects range from ceramics and Florentine coins to a coffee grinder and a pair of spectacles. Upstairs is a damaged wooden panel from a triptych attributed to Masaccio. Also here is an *Exorcism* by the Maestro di San Severino and, the pride of the collection, a gold-black *Santo Stefano* by Giotto.

Museo dell'Opera di Santa Croce & Cappella dei Pazzi

Piazza Santa Croce 16 (055 2466105/www.opera disantacroce.it). **Open** 9.30am-5.30pm Mon-Sat; 1-5.30pm Sun. **Admission** €4 (incl museum & chapel). **No credit cards. Map** p335 C5.

Brunelleschi's geometric tour de force, the Cappella dei Pazzi, was planned in the 1430s and completed almost 40 years later. The chapel is based on a central square, topped by a cupola flanked by two barrel-vaulted bays. The pure lines of the interior are decorated with Luca della Robbia's painted ceramic roundels of the 12 apostles and the four evangelists. The chapel opens on to the cloisters of Santa Croce (*see below*), resulting in a calm, almost detached atmosphere.

Across the courtyard is a small museum of church treasures; the collection includes Donatello's pious bronze *St Louis of Toulouse* from Orsanmichele (*see p84*). The backbone of the collection is in the former refectory, with Giotto's godson Taddeo Gaddi's imposing yet poetic *Tree of Life* above his *Last Supper* (unfortunately, in very bad condition). In equally poor condition is Cimabue's *Crucifixion*, which hung in the basilica until it was damaged in the flood of 1966. There's also a small permanent exhibition of the woodcuts and engravings of the modern artist Pietro Parigi. Access to the museum and chapel is through Santa Croce (*see below*).

Santa Croce

Piazza Santa Croce 16 (055 2466105). **Open** 9.30am-5.30pm Mon-Sat; 1-5.30pm Sun. **Admission** €5 (incl museum & chapel). **No credit cards. Map** p335 C5.

The richest medieval church in the city, Santa Croce has a great deal to offer, even to visitors long tired of church-hopping. The Museo dell'Opera di Santa Croce is housed here, along with the delightful chapter house known as the Cappella dei Pazzi (for both, *see above*) and two beautiful cloistered courtyards, not to mention the church itself, which is crammed with illustrious tombs and cenotaphs. The coloured

Santa Croce: resting place of Michelangelo.

marble façade is impressive, but at first sight the interior seems big and gloomy, with overbearing marble tombs clogging the walls. Not all of them contain bodies: Dante's, for example, is simply a memorial to the poet, who is buried in Ravenna.

In the niche alongside Dante's is the tomb of Michelangelo, by Vasari. The artist had insisted on burial here when the time came, as he wanted 'a view towards the cupola of the Duomo for all eternity', and had worked on his obsession, the *Pietà* (now in the Museo dell'Opera del Duomo; *see p80*) to adorn his tomb. It is said that he would have disliked the finished tomb because, despite being an impressive mixture of painting, sculpture and architecture, the whole is too ostentatious and complicated for a memorial tomb (unlike his own serene Sagrestia Nuova in the Capelle Medicee; *see p97*). Further into the church are the tombs of Leonardo Bruni by Bernardo Rossellino, Vittorio Alfieri and Ugolino della Gherardesca, best known for brain-eating in the *Divine Comedy*. Back at the top of the left aisle is Galileo's tomb, a polychrome marble confection created by Foggini more than a century after the astronomer's death, when the Church finally permitted him a Christian burial (*see also p32-35*).

It's something of a paradox that while the church is filled with the tombs of the great and the grand, it formerly belonged to the Franciscans, the most unworldly of the religious orders. They founded it in 1228, ten years after arriving in the city. A recently established order, they were supposed to make their living through manual work, preaching and begging. At the time, the area was a slum, home to the city's dyers and wool workers, and Franciscan preaching, with its message that all men were equal, had a huge impact on the poor folk who lived there. Indeed, in 1378, inspired by the Franciscans, the dyers and wool workers revolted against the guilds.

As for the Franciscans, their vow of poverty slowly eroded. By the late 13th century, the old church was felt to be inadequate and a new building was planned: intended to be one of the largest in Christendom, it was designed by Arnolfo di Cambio, architect of the Duomo and Palazzo Vecchio, who himself laid the first stone on 3 May 1294. The building was financed partly by confiscated Ghibelline property.

The church underwent various stages of restoration and modification, with one of Vasari's infamous remodernisations robbing it of some frescoes by Giotto's school in favour of heavy classical altars. Fortunately, he left the main chapels intact, though subsequent makeovers completely destroyed the decorations of the Cappella Tosinghi-Spinelli. Among the remaining gems are the fabulous stained-glass windows at the east end (behind the high altar) by Agnolo Gaddi, the marble tomb of Leonardo Bruni and the Cavalcanti tabernacle (both flanking the side door on the south wall).

At the eastern end of the church, the Bardi and Peruzzi chapels, which were completely frescoed by Giotto, are masterpieces. That said, the condition of the frescoes is not brilliant – a result of Giotto painting on dry instead of wet plaster and daubing them with whitewash – and were only rediscovered in the mid 18th century. The most striking of the two chapels is the Bardi, with scenes from the life of St Francis in haunting, virtual monotone, the figures just stylised enough to make them otherworldly yet individual enough to make them human. On the far side of the high altar is the Cappella Bardi di Vernio, frescoed by one of Giotto's most interesting followers, Maso di Banco, in vibrant colours. Don't miss the leather school behind the church (accessible from via San Giuseppe; *see p158*). *Photo p105.*

Sinagoga & Museo di Arte e Storia Ebraica

Via Farini 4 (055 2346654). **Open** *Apr, May, Sept, Oct* 10am-1pm, 2-5pm Mon-Thur, Sun; 10am-1pm Fri. *June-Aug* 10am-6pm Mon-Thur, Sun; 10am-2pm Fri. *Oct-Mar* 10am-4pm Mon-Thur, Sun; 10am-2pm Fri. **Admission** €4. **No credit cards. Map** p335 B5.

Built in 1870, following the demolition of the ghetto, this synagogue is an extraordinarily ornate mix of Moorish, Byzantine and Eastern influences, with its walls and ceilings covered in polychrome arabesques. The Museum of Jewish Art and History, which was extended up on to a second floor in March 2007, holds a collection tracing the history of Jews in Florence, from their supposed arrival as Roman slaves to their official introduction into the city as money-lenders in 1430. Exhibits include documented stories, jewellery, ceremonial objects and furniture, photos and drawings, many of which depict the ghetto that occupied the area just north of piazza della Repubblica.

Sinagoga and Museo di Arte e Storia Ebraica.

Oltrarno

How the other half lives: quiet parks, lively bars and Bohemian enclaves.

Spanning the width of the city centre along the southern banks of the Arno and extending down to Porta Romana in an oblique triangle is the Oltrarno (literally, 'beyond the Arno'). This eclectic area is a beguiling, contradictory world of ornate *palazzi* with splendid gardens, church squares and tumbledown artisan workshops.

To the west are the salt-of-the-earth parishes of **San Frediano** and **Santo Spirito**, which taper south to the old stone gate and hideous 'balancing women' statue of Porta Romana. At the heart of the Oltrarno is the gargantuan rusticated **Palazzo Pitti** (*see p108*), with its various museums and **Boboli Gardens** (*see p109*), while to the south-east is the sleepy parish of **San Niccolò** and the steep picturesque country lanes leading uphill to the panoramic **piazzale Michelangelo**.

The parish of San Frediano is dominated by piazza del Carmine, a social hub by night and home to the **Santa Maria del Carmine** church and the **Brancacci Chapel** (for both, *see p110*). This area still very much belongs to the locals.

Piazza Santo Spirito is the heart of its own bohemian neighbourhood, bustling with the comings and goings of locals, whether furniture restorers or restaurateurs. A morning market is held in the square from Monday to Saturday, with a flea market on the second Sunday of the month and an organic food market every third Sunday of the month. In winter this is a lively but low-key space, but on summer evenings the square's bars and restaurants and the steps of **Santo Spirito** church (*see p110*) are packed to the gills, with an open-air bar in the piazza in 2007, and concerts and events laid on in previous years.

Running south between Santo Spirito and a maze of narrow streets to the east is the grand **via Maggio** with its fabulous antiques shops and massive stone crests representing their original noble owners. At its river end is a delightful triangular house with a fountain and tiny garden room where the street joins borgo San Jacopo. Backing directly on to the river, this street mixes medieval towers, hip clothes shops and 1960s monstrosities built to replace houses bombed in the war, and leads to the southern end of the ponte Vecchio. Heading south-west down from the bridge is via Guicciardini, with its expensive paper, crafts and jewellery shops (and tourist tat shops, too, sadly) and the small church of **Santa Felicità** (*see p110*). Passing the grandeur of the Medici's Palazzo Pitti it ends in a square dominated by Palazzo Guidi, housing Casa Guidi, where Robert Browning and Elizabeth Barrett Browning wrote some of their most famous works. Here via Maggio and via Guicciardini join to become via Romana, a long, extremely straight thoroughfare leading to Porta Romana, lined with picture framers and antiques shops, and home to the gory **La Specola** museum (*see p111*) and the second entrance to Boboli.

South-east of the ponte Vecchio are the *costas* (meaning 'ribs'). These pretty, narrow lanes snake steeply uphill towards the **Forte di Belvedere** (*see p108*), giving surprise glimpses of different angles of the city at each turn. Halfway up costa San Giorgio is one of the two entrances to the spectacular, newly opened **Giardino Bardini**, while the other is in via de' Bardi, a quiet street running uphill behind the riverbank, which leads into lungarno Serristori and the **Casa Museo Rodolfo Siviero** (*see p108*). Behind lies **San Niccolò**, leading as far as Porta di San Niccolò in piazza Poggi. This is a quiet area with a village feel until the evening, when the wine bars and *osterie* along via de' Renai open up, overlooking the riverside piazza Demidoff. The **Museo Bardini** (piazza de' Mozzi 1, 055 2342427) is undergoing a torturous restoration that should end in 2009 with the birth of the **Galleria Corsi**, featuring paintings from the 14th to 19th centuries.

Casa Guidi

Piazza San Felice 8 (UK number 01628 825925). **Open** *Apr-Nov* 3-6pm Mon, Wed, Fri. **Admission** by donation. **Map** p334 D2.

English poets Robert Browning and Elizabeth Barrett Browning came to Florence in April 1847 after a clandestine marriage, and for 14 years an apartment in this house was their home. Now owned by the Landmark Trust and partly rented out as a holiday home, key rooms of the apartment where they lived and wrote are open for visits during certain months. A few of the pieces in the flat are originals, including the piano used by their son Pen.

Casa Museo Rodolfo Siviero

Lungarno Serristori 1-3 (055 2345219/guided tours 055 293007). **Open** 9.30am-12.30pm Mon; 3.30-6.30pm Sat. **Admission** free. **Map** p335 D5.

This was previously the house of government minister Rodolfo Siviero, dubbed the 'James Bond of art' for his efforts to prevent the Nazis plundering Italian masters. The pieces he saved were returned to their owners but Siviero left his own private collection to the Regione Toscana on condition they would be open to the public. Among the 500 pieces on display are paintings and sculptures by friends of Siviero including de Chirico, Annigoni and da Messina.

Cenacolo di Santo Spirito

Piazza Santo Spirito 29 (055 287043). **Open** 9am-2pm Tue-Sun. **Admission** €2.20. **No credit cards**. **Map** p334 D1.

Orcagna's 14th-century fresco *The Last Supper*, housed in a former Augustinian refectory, was butchered by an 18th-century architect commissioned to build some doors into it. Only the fringes of the fresco remain, though there's a more complete (albeit heavily restored) *Crucifixion* above it. The small Museo della Fondazione Romano here houses an eclectic collection of sculptures given to the state in 1946 on the death of sailor Salvatore Romano.

Artisan hub: **piazza Santa Spirito**. *See p107.*

Forte di Belvedere

Via San Leonardo (055 27681). **Open** phone for details. **Admission** free. **Map** p334 D3.

This star-shaped fortress was built in 1590 by Bernardo Buontalenti to protect the city from insurgents and was then used as a strongroom for the Medici Grand Dukes' treasures. After a painfully drawn-out restoration, the fort is open once again for temporary art exhibitions, shows and events.

Giardino Bardini

Via de' Bardi 1r, costa San Giorgio 2 (055 290112). **Open** *Nov-Feb* 8.15am-4.30pm daily. *Mar* 8.15am-5.30pm daily. *Apr, May, Sept, Oct* 8.15am-6.30pm daily. *June-Aug* 8.15am-7.30pm daily. Closed last Mon of the mth. **Admission** €9 (incl Museo degli Argenti, Museo del Costume, Museo delle Porcellane & Giardino di Boboli). **No credit cards**. **Map** p335 D4.

First created in the 1200s by the Mozzi family, this intriguing garden has just been opened after five years of painstaking restoration. The garden is divided into three distinct areas: the Baroque steps, leading to a terrace with amazing views; the English wood, a shady haven of evergreens; and the farm park, with a dwarf orchard, rhododendron collection and 'tunnel' of wisteria and hydrangea.

Palazzo Pitti

Piazza Pitti 1, via Romana (055 2654321/www.palazzopitti.it). **Open** 8.15am-6.50pm Tue-Sun. **Admission** €11.50. **Map** p334 D1.

The Pitti Palace was built in 1457 for Luca Pitti, a Medici rival, supposedly to a design by Brunelleschi that had been rejected by Cosimo il Vecchio as too grandiose. However, it also proved too grandiose for the Pitti, who, gallingly, were forced to sell to the Medici. Its ornate, opulent rooms now hold the vast Medici collections plus later additions in the various museums detailed below.

Galleria d'Arte Moderna

055 2388616. **Open** 8.15am-1.50pm (last entry 1.15pm) Tue-Sat, 2nd, 4th Mon of mth & 1st, 3rd, 5th Sun of mth. **Admission** €5 (incl Museo del Costume). **No credit cards**.

The 30 rooms on the second floor of the Pitti were royal apartments until 1920; today they're given over to Florence's Modern Art museum. The collection covers neoclassical to early 20th-century art, with highlights including Giovanni Dupré's bronze sculptures of Cain and Abel (Room 5) and Ottone Rosai's simple *Piazza del Carmine* in Room 30. Rooms 11, 12, 18 and 19 showcase the work of the Macchiaioli school, the early Italian Impressionist group who were ridiculed for painting-by-dots (*macchie*), and house works by Giovanni Fattori and Telemaco Signorini.

Galleria Palatina & Appartamenti Reali
055 2388614. **Open** 8.15am-6.50pm Tue-Sun. **Admission** €11.50. **No credit cards.**
The gallery has 28 rooms of paintings, which are hung four- or five-high on its damask walls. You'll want to linger longest in the five planet rooms, named after Venus, Mercury (Apollo), Mars, Jupiter and Saturn. The Sala di Venere (Venus), crowned by a gilded stucco ceiling, is dominated by a statue of Venus by Canova, but also contains Titian's regal *La Bella*. The Sala di Apollo houses the nine *Muses* and is crowded with works by Rosso Fiorentino and Andrea del Sarto. The Sala di Marte (Mars) is closed for restoration; Rubens's *Four Philosophers* and the other works from this room are on show in the Sala delle Nicchie. The best place to look in the Sala di Giove (Jupiter) is up, in order to admire the lofty depiction of Jupiter with his eagle and his lightning. Look too for Raphael's lover, the so-called 'baker girl' Margherita Luti, in his *La Velata*. Finally, the Sala di Saturno (Saturn) contains some of Raphael's best-known works: among them the *Madonna of the Grand Duke*, which shows a distinct Leonardo influence, and his last painting, *Holy Family*, seemingly inspired by Michelangelo.

Giardini di Boboli
055 2651816/2651838. **Open** *Nov-Feb* 8.15am-4.30pm daily. *Mar, June-Aug, Oct* 8.15am-7.30pm daily. *Apr, May, Sept* 8.15am-6.30pm daily. Closed 1st & last Mon of mth. **Admission** €6 (incl Museo degli Argenti, Museo del Costume, Museo delle Porcellane & Giardino Bardini). **No credit cards. Map** p334 D1-D3.
Boboli is the best loved of the few green spaces and parks in the city centre, and despite the entrance fee is a popular oasis, particularly on hot summer days. Far to the left of the main entrance is a fountain showing Cosimo I's obese dwarf as a nude Bacchus, heralding the walkway that leads to Buontalenti's grotto with Bandinelli's statues of Ceres and Apollo, casts of Michelangelo's *Slaves* and a second grotto adorned with frescoes of classic Greek and Roman myths and encrusted with shells. The ramps take you to the amphitheatre, where Jacopo Peri's and Giulio Caccini's *Euridice* was staged for the Medici in 1600. At the top of the hill is the Museo delle Porcellane (*see below*), entered through the Giardino dei Cavalieri. *See also p110* **Up the garden path**.

Museo degli Argenti
055 2388709. **Open** *Oct-May, Sept* 8.15am-6.30pm daily. *June-Aug* 8.15am-7.30pm daily. Year-round closed 1st & last Mon of mth. **Admission** €6 (incl Museo delle Porcellane, Museo del Costume, Giardino di Boboli & Giardino Bardini). **No credit cards.**
This extravagant two-tier museum section of the Pitti Palace houses not just silver, but an astonishing hoard of treasures amassed by the Medici, from tapestries and rock crystal vases to a breathtakingly banal collection of miniature animals.

Museo delle Carrozze
055 2388614. **Open** by appointment only.
While plans are being made to move this fairytale collection of carriages that once belonged to the Medici, Lorraine and Savoy houses into the former Medici stables, anyone with a Cinderella complex can arrange a visit by appointment.

Museo del Costume
055 2388713. **Open** 8.15am-6.30pm (last entry 6.15pm) Tue-Sat, 2nd, 4th Mon of mth & 1st, 3rd, 5th Sun of mth. **Admission** €9 (incl Museo degli Argenti, Museo delle Porcellane, Giardino di Boboli and Giardino Bardini). **No credit cards.**
The sumptuous Costume Museum is in the Palazzina della Meridiana, which periodically served as residence to the Lorraine family and the House of Savoy. Collections of formal, theatre and everyday costumes from the museum's 6,000 pieces and from a period spanning five centuries are shown in rotation, changing every two years. Some of the more important get-ups are permanently on display, among them Cosimo I's and Eleonora di Toledo's clothes, including her grand velvet creation from Bronzino's portrait.

Museo delle Porcellane
055 2388709. **Open** as per Boboli Gardens; *see above*. **Admission** €6 (incl Museo degli Argenti, Museo del Costume, Giardino di Boboli & Giardino Bardini). **No credit cards.**
This outhouse at the top of the Boboli Gardens was once a reception room for artists, built by Leopoldo de' Medici. The museum has ceramics used by the

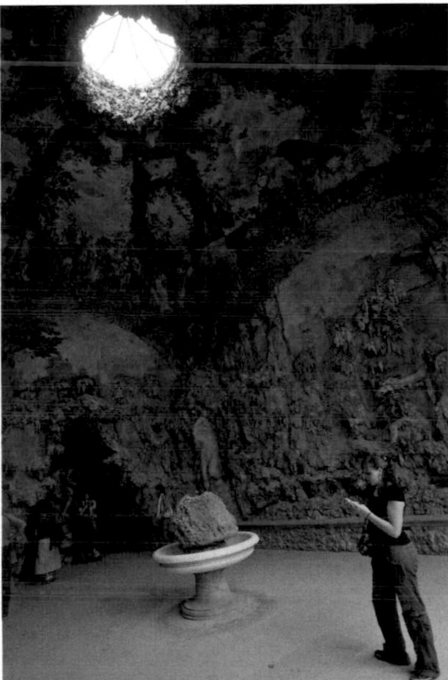

The Boboli Garden's **Buontalenti Grotto.**

Walk Up the garden path

Start at the via Romana entrance to the Boboli Gardens. Immediately ahead of you is a small grotto sheltering statues of Adam and Eve. At the top of the hill, turn left and then right on to the viale de Platani and continue uphill. About halfway along this covered path is the entrance to the **Botanical Gardens**, also called the **Giardino degli Ananassi** after the pineapples once grown here. Continue on the same path to the **viale dei Cipressi** ('il Viottolone'), an avenue lined with glorious, lichen-covered statues. Turn right here.

At the bottom of the viale dei Cipressi lies the gorgeous **Isolotto**, a small island sitting in a circular moat laid out in 1612. In the middle is the *Fountain of Oceanus*, designed by Il Tribolo for Cosimo II. Beyond the Isolotto is the semicircular, English-style lawn known as the **Hemicycle**. Turn right to join viale della Meridiana once again, passing the lovely green and white **Orangery**. You emerge with the Meridiana wing of Palazzo Pitti on your left and a colossal Roman *vasca* (basin) on your right.

Take one of the steep paths that climb the hill and get splendid views of Florence. Follow the path on the left side of the tree-lined lawn, past a bronze sculpture by Igor Mitoraj. To the right is the viale dei Cipressi. Walk straight on past the row of old houses on your right to an elegant stairway that sweeps up to the walled **Giardino del Cavalieri**. From here the views are purely rural: villas, the odd tower, olive groves and cypress trees.

Back at the bottom of the steps, the path immediately to the right brings you to **Abundance**, an enormous statue clutching a sheaf of golden corn. Instead of going down the steps, take the path that hugs the walls of Forte di Belvedere until you come to the back gate of the fort. From here, follow the path opposite past the pale peppermint green **Kaffeehaus**, a rococo gem built in 1775 for Pietro Leopoldo, and straight on down a steep path, which brings you out above the huge **amphitheatre**. This faces the rear façade and entrance of the Pitti Palace, where you'll find the **Fontana del Carciofo**, a superb Baroque fountain, named after the bronze artichoke that once topped it.

Head around to the right, and a wide gravel path leads to a small rose garden dominated by Baccio Bandinelli's *Jupiter*. The little path to the right ends at the small **Grotticina di Madama**, dominated by bizarre statues of goats and the first of the several grottoes for which the garden has become famous.

Back at *Jupiter*, follow the railings to the end and descend the steps to the wonderful **Grotta Grande** or the **Grotta di Buontalenti**. It's not always possible to walk into the chambers, but you can see through the railings. The Grotta di Buontalenti was built between 1557 and 1593 by heavyweights Vasari, Ammannati and Buontalenti. The last curiosity before leaving is a statue of Pietro Barbino, Cosimo I's pot-bellied dwarf.

various occupants of Palazzo Pitti and includes the largest selection of Viennese china outside Vienna, but most visitors are more interested in the views.

Santa Felicità

Piazza Santa Felicità (055 213018). **Open** 9am-12.30pm, 3.30-6.30pm Mon-Sat; 9am-1pm Sun (except 9am & noon services). **Admission** free. **Map** p334 D2.

This church occupies the site of the first church in Florence, founded in the second century AD by Syrian Greek tradesmen. The oldest surviving part is the portico, built in 1564; the interior mainly dates back to the 18th century. Most who come here do so to see Pontormo's *Deposition* altarpiece in the Cappella Barbadori-Capponi.

Santa Maria del Carmine & Cappella Brancacci

Piazza del Carmine (055 2768558/bookings 055 2768224/558). **Open** *Chapel* 10am-5pm Mon, Wed-Sat; 1-5pm Sun. Phone to book. **Admission** €4. **No credit cards. Map** p334 C1.

This blowsy Baroque church is dominated by a huge single nave adorned with pilasters and pious sculptures overlooked by a ceiling fresco of the Ascension, but this is not what visitors queue in droves for. The Brancacci Chapel, frescoed in the 15th century by Masaccio and Masolino, miraculously escaped the fire and is one of the city's greatest art treasures. Masaccio died aged just 27, but reached his peak with this cycle of frescoes, especially the tangibly grief-stricken Adam and Eve in the *Expulsion from Paradise*, a fresco that entranced Michelangelo.

Santo Spirito

Piazza Santo Spirito (055 210030). **Open** *Winter* 8am-noon, 4-5pm Mon, Tue, Thur, Fri; 8am-noon Wed. *Summer* 8am-noon, 4-6pm Mon, Tue, Thur, Fri; 8am-noon Wed. **Admission** free. **Map** p334 C2.

Behind the exquisitely simple 18th-century cream façade is one of Brunelleschi's most extraordinary works. There was an Augustinian church on this site from 1250, but in 1397 the monks decided to replace it, eventually commissioning Brunelleschi to

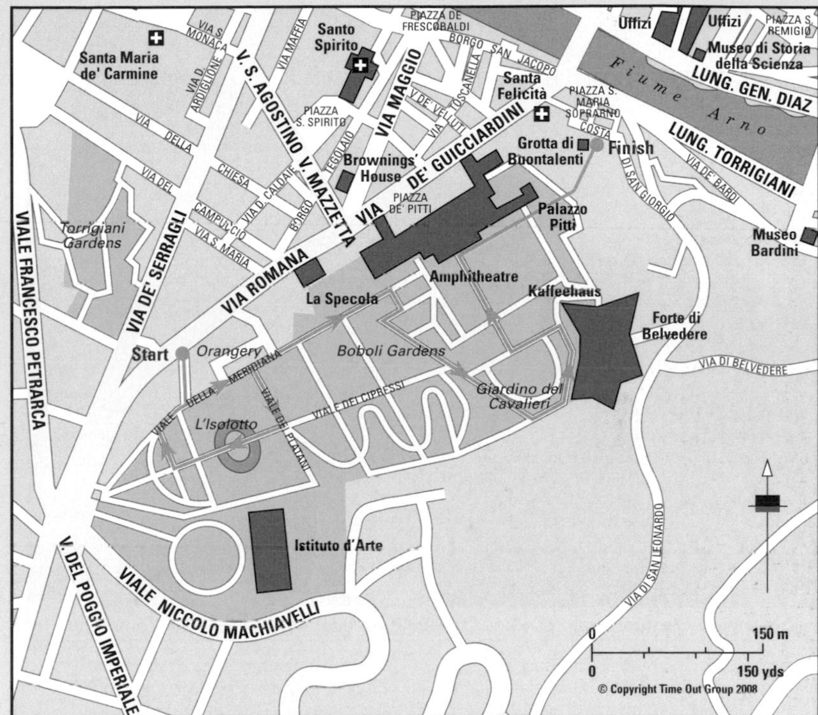

design it. Work started in 1444, two years before the great master died, and the façade and exterior walls were never finished. Vasari wrote that if the church had been completed as planned, it would have been 'the most perfect temple of Christianity' and it's easy to see why – Santo Spirito's structure is a beautifully proportioned, Latin cross church lined with a colonnade of dove grey-coloured *pietra serena* pilasters sheltering 38 chapels. Left of the church is the refectory housing the Cenacolo di Santo Spirito museum (*see p108*). The church is open on weekends to worshippers but recent staffing problems mean it's worth calling first to make sure the official opening hours for visits are being kept to.

La Specola

Via Romana 17 (055 2288251/guided visits 055 2346760/www.msn.unifi.it). **Open** 9am-1pm Mon, Tue, Thur, Fri, Sun; 9am-5pm Sat. **Admission** €4. **No credit cards**. **Map** p334 D1.

A dream day out for older kids with horror fixations, La Specola is the zoology department of the Natural History Museum. The first 23 rooms are crammed with stuffed and pickled animals including many famously extinct species, and up to here the museum can also be fun for younger children. From Room 24 onwards, however, the exhibits are more gruesome. A *Frankenstein*-esque laboratory is filled with wax corpses on satin beds, each a little more dissected than the last, and walls are covered with realistic body parts crafted as teaching aids in the 18th and 19th centuries.

Villa Bardini

Via de' Bardi 1r (055 2638599/www.bardini peyron.it). **Open** 10am-4pm daily. Closed 1st & last Mon of the month. **Admission** €5. **No credit cards**. **Map** p335 D4.

The newly restored Villa Bardini is home to a permanent exhibition of the fabulously extravagent creations of couturier Roberto Capucci. A new museum in the villa of the works of Italian artist Pietro Annigoni is due to open in spring 2008, preceded by a new bar/restaurant.

Outside the City Gates

Escape the throngs.

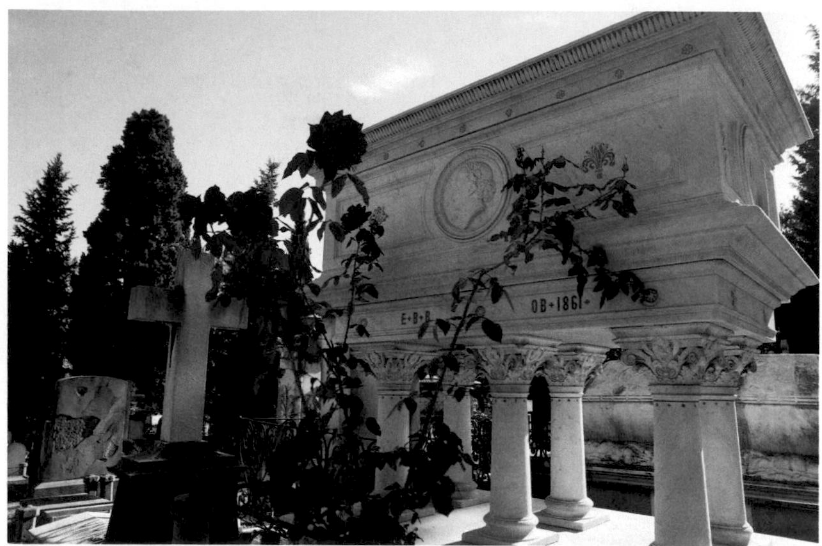

Keeping Anglo-Florentine relations alive: the **Cimitero degli Inglesi** (English Cemetery).

The historic centre of Florence is home to the densest concentration of art treasures and sights in the world, but it's surprisingly small. This makes exploring beyond the area delineated by the eight surviving city gates easy even without your own means of transport, and the rewards are fabulous views, sublime countryside and fascinating cultural sights.

North of the river, the old stone gates are linked by the *viali*, traffic-clogged multi-lane arteries circling the city. To the north, the roads leading to **Fiesole** and **Settignano** are dotted with charming country houses. Travelling east is a more mixed experience of genteel suburbia and semi-industrial plots. **Firenze Nova**, the satellite city and administrative centre, constructed on reclaimed land north-west of the centre, has breathed new, though generally uninspiring, life into the area. Further out in this direction, dull housing and industrial development have claimed swathes of land, creating urban eyesores such as **Brozzi** and **Campi Bisenzio**, though there are still ancient convents and elegant villas on the hills, and the old town area of **Sesto Fiorentino** has a charm of its own.

The gently winding, tree-lined avenues forming an umbrella round the south of the city are much more picturesque than the northern *viali* and are worth a drive or a bus-ride in themselves. Head south of the historic centre for the best walks, views and sights; as the hills practically rise from the banks of the Arno, you can walk in minutes from the town into real countryside dotted with villas, cypress and olive trees. This proximity to nature is one of the most unusual and attractive physical characteristics of Florence, but also has its downside: being situated in a basin the resulting climate is hot and humid in summer, and cold and damp in winter.

The efficient ATAF bus network has good services to the suburbs: most of the places listed in this chapter are directly on a city bus route or a short walk from a bus stop.

North of the river

To the west, **Porta al Prato** and the hellish traffic of the *viali* mark the edge of the city centre. Just south of the old gate, skirting the northern bank of the Arno for a full three kilometres (two miles) is the green oasis of the **Parco delle Cascine**, a public park backed by woods that were once full of deer. Its name comes from *cascina*, meaning 'dairy farm', which is the role the area played under the Medici. It later became a hunting park and a space for theatre and public spectacles. Shelley wrote his 'Ode to the West Wind' here in 1819, while in 1870 the body of the Maharaja of Kolhapur (who died in Florence) was burned on a funeral pyre at the far end of the park, on a spot now marked by an equestrian statue. The first major changes to the park for centuries have been made with the building of the new Tramvia (*see p301*), which has encroached on the eastern entrance and shifted the huge Tuesday-morning market further downriver.

The Cascine is the city's lung, the only large park and a popular destination for a day out, especially at weekends, with cycling children, in-line skaters, joggers, picnickers and others simply out for a stroll. There's a riding school, a swimming pool, a race track where horse racing and polo matches are held and tennis courts, and in summer the park is used as a venue for club nights, theatre and gigs (*see p195*). It's safe enough when summer night-time events are held, but be aware that the area is decidedly seamy at night, with prostitutes touting for business along the park's main roads and the adjoining *viali*.

Coming back towards the centre of town, five minutes' walk from Santa Maria Novella train station along viale Rosselli is the massive pentagonal stone **Fortezza da Basso** (*see also p96*), designed by Antonio da Sangallo. It was commissioned in 1534 by Alessandro de' Medici, who met his death within its ugly walls, and is a prototype of 16th-century military architecture; restored in the 1990s, it's now Florence's main exhibition centre. Just north of the fortress lies Florence's decorative **Russian Orthodox church**, with its five polychrome onion domes (via Leone X). Completed in 1904, it's a reminder that the city was once popular with wealthy Russians (Dostoevsky, Tchaikovsky and Gorky among them) as a retreat from the harsh winters back home. You can arrange for a guided tour (available in English or Italian; 055 2477986/290148) or visit during mass (6pm Sat, 10.30am Sun).

Directly north of here is the eccentric **Museo Stibbert** (via Stibbert 26, 055 486049, www.museostibbert.it, 10am-2pm Mon-Wed, 10am-6pm Fri-Sun, €6). Its bizarre collection, covering everything from arms and armour to snuff boxes, formerly belonged to Frederick Stibbert (1838-1906), a brother-in-arms with Garibaldi. Stibbert was born to an English father and Italian mother, who left him her 14th-century house. He then bought the neighbouring mansion and had the two joined together to house his collection. Among the 50,000 items crammed into the 64 rooms and shown in rotation are Napoleon's coronation robes (Stibbert was a fan), a hand-painted harpsichord, a collection of shoe buckles, chalices, crucifixes and even an attributed Botticelli. The rambling garden has a lily pond, stables, a neoclassical folly by Poggi where lemon trees were kept, and ancient Greek- and Egyptian-inspired temples.

Piazza della Libertà, the focal point of northern access to the city, is dominated by constant traffic jams and the massive and rather graceless triumphal arch built to mark the arrival in Florence of the eighth Grand Duke of Tuscany in 1744.

Heading south-east towards **piazza Beccaria** and the **Porta alla Croce** is the **Cimitero degli Inglesi** (English Cemetery; piazzale Donatello 38, 055 582608 afternoons, closed Mon afternoons, Tue mornings and all day Sat & Sun, admission by donation). Designated in 1827 and later given its oval shape by Giuseppe Poggi (he of the harmonious sweeping *viali* south of the river and piazzale Michelangelo; *see p114*), the atmospheric graveyard is worth a visit. Reflecting the prevalence of English artists living in Florence in the 19th century, Frederic, Lord Leighton, Roddam Spencer Stanhope and William Holman Hunt are among those who designed and sculpted the lichen-covered gravestones and tombs. The cemetery houses the remains of many famous Anglo-Florentines, as well as Swiss, Russians and Americans. Among them are poet Elizabeth Barrett Browning, novelist Fanny Trollope and sculptor Hiram Powers.

East of this is the **Stadio 'Comunale' Artemo Franchi** (*see p200*), Pier Luigi Nervi's football stadium near Campo di Marte station. Built in 1932 and enlarged for the 1990 World Cup, it has a capacity of 66,000 and is used for football matches as well as the odd rock concert. A short walk south-east of here is the **Museo del Cenacolo di Andrea del Sarto** (via San Salvi 16, 055 238 8603, closed Mon, free). A refectory-cum-museum, it was part of the Vallombrosan monastery of San Salvi, and is chiefly notable for housing Andrea del Sarto's celebrated lunette-shaped Mannerist *Last Supper*.

It's a bus ride north-west of here to visit the **Villa della Petraia** (via della Petraia 40, 055 452691, closed 2nd & 3rd Mon of mth, free entrance), acquired by the Medici family in 1530. Sitting on a little hill, the villa and grounds stand apart from the surrounding industrial mess. Originally a tower belonging to Brunelleschi's family, the fabulous formal

Sightseeing

terraced gardens by Il Tribolo are among the select few immortalised in Giusto Utens's lunettes. Just down the hill from La Petraia is another Medici pad, **Villa di Castello** (via del Castello 40, 055 454791, closed 2nd & 3rd Mon of mth, free entrance). The villa is known mostly for its Il Tribolo gardens and for Ammanati's miserable-looking sculpture *Allegory of Winter*, as well as the extravagant Grotta degli Animali, a grotto filled with animal and bird statues and stone water features, planned by Il Tribolo and finished by Vasari.

Fiesole & around

The foundation of Fiesole precedes that of Florence by centuries and could be credited with the city's very existence – this stubborn Etruscan hill town proved so difficult for the Romans to subdue that they were forced to set up camp in the river valley below. When they eventually took Fiesole, it became one of the most important towns in Etruria, remaining independent until the 12th century, when Florence finally vanquished it in battle. It soon took on a new role as a refined suburb where Florentine aristocrats could escape the heat and hoi polloi; the road leading up to the town winds by beautiful villas and gardens built as a result and still highly desirable addresses. Today, around 14,000 people live in Fiesole.

Piazza Mino, the recently restored main square, is named after the 15th-century sculptor Mino da Fiesole, and is lined with cafés and restaurants, some with direct views over Florence. It's dominated by the immense honey-stone campanile of the 11th-century **Duomo** (055 59400, Nov-Mar 7.30am-noon, 2-5pm daily; Apr-Oct 7.30am-noon, 3-6pm daily); inside it sit columns topped with capitals dating from Fiesole's period under Roman occupation. The nearby **Museo Bandini** (via Portigiani 1, 055 59477/598720, €13 incl Teatro Romano & Museo Archeologico) houses an array of Florentine paintings dating from the 13th to 15th centuries and, after recent restoration, two new rooms displaying previously unshown works from the Bandini collection, including a number of Andrea della Robbia terracottas.

Down the hill, more relics of Roman Fiesole can be seen at the 3,000-seat **Teatro Romano** (via Portigiani 1, 055 59477, closed Tue in winter, admission incl in Museo Bandini ticket). Built in 1 BC, the amphitheatre still stages a mix of concerts and plays in summer; a complex here is home to the remains of two temples, partially restored Roman baths and a stretch of Etruscan walls. The **Museo Archeologico** (listings as per Teatro Romano, *see above*; admission incl in Museo Bandini ticket, *see above*) houses finds from Bronze Age, Etruscan and Roman Fiesole, and the Costantini collection of Greek vases.

There are some lovely walks around Fiesole, the best of which is down steep, twisting via Vecchia Fiesolana to the hamlet of San Domenico. To the left on the way down is the **Villa Medici**, built by Michelozzo for Cosimo il Vecchio and the childhood home of Anglo-American writer Iris Origo. At the bottom of the hill is the 15th-century church and convent where painter Fra Angelico was a monk. It now houses his delicate *Madonna and Angels* (1420), while in the chapter house of the adjacent monastery is one of his frescoes (ring the bell at no.4 for entry). Opposite the church is a lane leading down to the **Badia Fiesolana** (via Roccettini 9, 055 59155, closed Sat afternoon & Sun, free), Fiesole's cathedral until 1028. The façade incorporates the original front of the older church, with its elegant green and white marble inlay. Enter via the cloister if the church doors are closed.

The village of **Settignano** lies on the hill to the east of Fiesole and has views to rival or surpass its hilltop neighbour. There's no public transport to Settignano from Fiesole, though it's an easy bus ride from Santa Maria Novella station (bus 10). The walk between the two through woods is long but picturesque and it's an easy drive. Despite its lack of cultural landmarks, Settignano makes for an almost tourist-free trip out of town, and its history is littered with eminent names: sculptors Desiderio da Settignano and the Rossellino brothers were born here, and Michelangelo spent part of his childhood at the building now known as **Villa Michelangelo** (known locally as Villa Buonarotti; via della Capponcina 65).

South of the river

South of the Arno, steep lanes rise sharply from the riverbank, lined with high walls and impenetrable gates protecting beautiful villas. From the city centre up the *costas* and long flights of mossy steps to the vantage points on the hills are short but testing walks, punctuated by views of olive groves, cypress trees and the odd view through walls and round corners of the city itself.

The most famous viewpoint in Florence is probably from **piazzale Michelangelo**, on the hill directly above piazza Poggi. Considered the city's balcony, this is a large, open square with vistas over the entire city to the hills beyond. Its stone balustrade is perennially crowded with tourists buying souvenirs and taking photos. Laid out in 1869 by Giuseppe Poggi, the piazzale is dominated by a bronze replica of Michelangelo's *David* and crammed all day with coaches. Buses 12 and 13 take the scenic route in opposite directions round Poggi's *viali*, but it's also a pleasant walk along via San Niccolò to Porta San Miniato, then up via del Monte alle Croci, and left up the long flight of stone steps winding between handsome villas and gardens. Alternatively, take the rococo staircase that Poggi designed to link piazzale Michelangelo with the piazza in his name below.

From piazzale Michelangelo it's a short walk to the exquisite **San Miniato al Monte** (via delle Porte Sante 34, 055 2342731, free). The church façade is delicately inlaid with white Carrara and green Verde di Prato marble and the glittering gold mosaic dates from the 13th century. There has been a chapel on this site since at least the fourth century; this is also the spot where, according to legend, St Miniato picked up his decapitated head and walked from the banks of the Arno up the hill, where he finally expired. The chapel was replaced with a Benedictine monastery in the early 11th century, built on the orders of reforming Bishop Hildebrand. The church's interior is one of Tuscany's loveliest, its walls a patchwork of faded frescoes and its choir raised above a serene 11th-century crypt. One of the church's most remarkable features is the marble pavement in the nave, inlaid with the signs of the zodiac and stylised lions and lambs. It's worth timing your trip to coincide with the Gregorian chant sung daily by the monks (4.30pm winter, 5.30pm summer).

A 20-minute walk west of Porta Romana is a less visited but just as gorgeous viewpoint, the hamlet of **Bellosguardo** ('beautiful view'). On the way up is a vantage point just before the piazza di Bellosguardo that affords a glimpse of every important church façade in central Florence. At the top of the hill sits a higgledy-piggledy group of old houses and grand villas grouped around a shady square; the only sign of modern life, apart from the inevitable cars, is a postbox on a wall. The most impressive of the villas is the **Villa Bellosguardo**, down a little turning to the left. It was built in 1780 for the Marchese Orazio Pucci (ancestor of fashion designer Emilio Pucci) and bought, more than a century later, by the great tenor Enrico Caruso, who lived here for three years before his death in 1921.

About five kilometres (three miles) south-west of Porta Romana, the **Certosa del Galluzzo** looms like a fortress above the busy Siena road (via Buca di Certosa 2, Galluzzo, www.cistercensi.info, admission by donation, bus 36 or 37). The imposing complex was founded in 1342 as a Carthusian monastery by Renaissance big-wig Niccolò Acciaiuoli and is the third of six built in Tuscany in the 14th century. It's been inhabited since 1958 by a group of Cistercian monks, whose 12 cells surround the main cloister, each with a well, a vegetable garden and a study. The main entrance leads into a courtyard and the church of San Lorenzo, said to be by Brunelleschi.

San Miniato al Monte.

Eat, Drink, Shop

Restaurants & Wine Bars 118
Cafés, Bars & Gelaterie 140
Shops & Services 148

Features

The best Restaurants 120
For those who can stomach it… 124
A woman's place? 131
What's on the menu? 134
The best Cafés 141
Coffee: the local low-down 142
A brew with a view 146
The best Shops 149
Playing the market 150
Where to shop 155
Cast-off culture 158
Brand new 164

San Lorenzo market. *See p96.*

Restaurants & Wine Bars

A new generation of *trattoria* owners are adding even more flavour to Florence's culinary culture.

According to local lore, the eating scene in Florence has always been *difficile*. In a city that is so geared towards tourists, standards are bound to slip and the Florentines themselves suffer for it. As the older generation of cooks – which once provided the backbone of rustic, unpretentious eateries in the city – moves on to the great stove in the sky, who is going to take over the family business? In some cases, the next generation is committed enough to the principals of authentic, no-nonsense *cucina casalinga* (home-style cooking) to keep things going, but others, with dollar signs firmly in their sights, sell out to a shoddy imitation of the real thing that packs 'em in and spits 'em out before you can say 'bruschetta'.

Luckily, among the faux straw wine flasks and the red-checked tablecloths, there are still some wonderfully unreconstructed *trattorie* and *osterie* where the mamma figure (maybe together with her son or daughter) continues to prepare the sort of rustic recipes that have been handed down through the generations and that make up the basis of Florentine *cucina tradizionale* (for a modern take on mamma figures, *see p131* **A woman's place?**). You have to look hard, but the locals know where these places are and so do we: our favourites are listed below.

Alongside the sort of diehards described above, a new generation of *trattoria* is emerging, places that are based on the unfussy principles of the traditional family-run eaterie, but where the chefs are adding a contemporary element to their cooking. They are also paying more attention to sourcing ingredients properly and the overall result is very successful, and often reasonably priced. These types of place, along with the old-style joints, are very popular these days as Florentines continue to rail against the rising cost of eating out.

❶ Purple numbers given in this chapter correspond to the location of each restaurant or wine bar as marked on the street maps. *See pp334-35.*

While a meal at a good, convivial *trattoria* can be a richly rewarding experience, you may want to splash out and try something a bit different. In this case, go for one of the restaurants where chefs are experimenting with today's fashion for *cucina rivisitata* (literally 'revisited') bringing a fresh approach and new emphasis to traditional recipes. This is the kind of cooking that needs to be executed with intelligence and a sense of restraint, but done properly, it's an interesting alternative (albeit a more expensive one) to *ribollita*.

These days, the coolest areas in town to hang out (and with the highest concentration of bars, *enoteche* and restaurants) are around Santo Spirito in the Oltrarno and in Santa Croce, and it's therefore no surprise that quite a high proportion of the places listed in this chapter fall into these two locations. There's also a fair number of listings outside the centre of town, restaurants that involve a bus or taxi ride. But the extra effort (and expense) will be rewarded by a virtually tourist-free experience.

THE RESTAURANT

Be warned: Florence is, above all else, a tourist city, and at too many restaurants, sloppy cooking and high prices are the norm. This guide aims to list the very best eateries in and around town, but it's also worth looking out for windows displaying the recommendation stickers of respected Italian restaurant guides, like Gambero Rosso's *Ristoranti d'Italia*, *Veronelli*, *L'Espresso*, or Slow Food's *Osterie d'Italia*. Failing that, try to pick places where there are plenty of locals, and avoid anywhere that advertises a fixed-price *menù turistico* written in several languages.

Eating out is a very social affair in Florence, especially in the evenings, and restaurants tend to be informal and quite lively. You can wear casual dress in all but the very smartest establishments, and children are almost always welcome. The majority of restaurants are happy to produce a plate of *pasta al pomodoro* to satisfy unadventurous taste buds, and you can also ask for a half portion (*una mezza porzione*).

Quite a few restaurants carry high chairs (*una seggiolona*). Booking is advisable, especially at weekends or if you want to dine at an outdoor table during the summer months.

THE MENU

An increasing number of more upmarket restaurants now offer some kind of fixed menu (and we're not talking about the ubiquitous *menù turistico* here). Usually called *menù degustazione*, it consists of a series of courses that allows diners to try the house specialities. Such menus tend to represent good value. For help with sorting through the menu, *see pp43-48* and *p134* **What's on the menu**.

THE WINE LIST

The price of your meal will be heavily influenced by what goes into your glass and even many *trattorie* nowadays have more choice than just the house plonk. However, most budget and moderately priced restaurants do offer *vino della casa* (house wine) in quarter-litre, half-litre or litre flasks, which is invariably cheaper than buying by the bottle. It might be anything from ghastly gut-rot to quaffable country wine. If in doubt, order a *quartino* to try; if it's undrinkable, ask for the wine list.

While the *liste dei vini* in Tuscany are unsurprisingly dominated by *vini toscani*, other regional wines – and even the odd non-Italian label – are now being given more cellar space. For guidelines on choosing wines, *see pp45-48*.

PIZZA

While pizza isn't a typically Florentine dish, pizzerias are very popular among the locals (especially young people) – firstly because they make for a cheap, casual meal out and secondly because they tend to stay open late. Most pizzerias don't serve exclusively pizza either; there's nearly always a wide selection of *primi* and various salads on the menu and some places serve complete meals too. A Florentine pizza traditionally has a thin, crisp base but, these days, most of the pizzas to be found in the city are of the Neapolitan variety with (ideally) light, puffy bases. Either way, make sure it's baked in a wood oven (*forno a legna*) rather than in the gas or electric equivalent. Pizza is an evening meal in Florence; very few pizzerias worth their *mozzarella di bufala* serve at lunchtimes.

VEGETARIANS

The days are (almost) gone when waiters would look aghast at the words *sono vegetariano* ('I'm vegetarian'). While there are few strictly vegetarian restaurants in Florence, non meat-eaters, particularly those who eat fish, are better off here than in many parts of, say, France or Germany. Indeed, reflecting a general trend in Italy towards more healthy eating habits, a number of new fish restaurants have opened in Florence since the last edition of this guide. Most restaurants offer vegetable-based pasta and rice dishes, as well as plenty of salads

It's all about the simple pleasures... seasonal and top-quality fodder at **'Ino**. *See p123.*

and vegetable side dishes (*contorni*), while an increasing number of more upmarket places serve a specifically vegetarian option.

SMOKING

Smoking was banned in public places in Italy in early 2005, and it's now no longer possible to smoke in a restaurant unless it has a separate room with the legally required ventilation system. Few do, so you'll have to go and join the other puffers on the street.

THE BILL

For restaurants and wine bars, we give the average price per person for a three-course meal (antipasto or *primo*, *secondo*, *contorno* and *dolce*) excluding drinks or extras. The price in a pizzeria covers an average pizza plus a *birra media*. Most pizzerias also serve more substantial fare and prices will rise accordingly. In wine bars where only snacks are on offer, we have not given an average; prices might range from 50¢ for a *crostino* to €12 for a plate of French cheeses.

Bills usually include a cover charge (*pane e coperto*) per person of anything from €1.50 to an outrageous €5; the average is about €2.50. This covers bread, and should also reflect the standard of service and table settings. There's also a service charge, which must by law be included in the bill (though it's sometimes listed separately). Some places now include cover and service in the price of the meal. One consolation is that you're not expected to leave a hefty tip. You can leave ten per cent if you're truly happy with your service, or, in a modest place, perhaps round up the bill by a euro or so.

Although prices have risen horribly since the arrival of the euro, eating out in Florence is still cheaper than in London or New York. The restaurants here have been chosen either for their value for money or simply because the food is great. Some are located out of the centre of town, but the food makes them worth the journey.

WINE BARS AND ALTERNATIVE EATS

There are various types of wine bar in Florence. Tiny street booths (known as *fiaschetteria*, *vineria* or *mescita*) with virtually no seating, serving basic Tuscan wines and rustic snacks, sit alongside comfortable, traditional drinking holes, which compete with new, upmarket *enoteche* that offer a huge range of labels from all over Italy and beyond and something more sophisticated in the way of food.

Wine bars offer one of several alternatives to full restaurant dining in Florence. *Rosticcerie* (rotisseries) serve everything from antipasti and roasted meats to desserts; those listed here give

The best Restaurants

For fish and seafood

L'Arte Gaia (*see p137*), **Borgo San Jacopo** (*see p132*), **Filipepe** (*see p133*), **Portofino** (*see p138*), **Povero Pesce** (*see p138*) and **Ricchi** (*see p133*).

For vegetarians

Ruth's (*see p129*), **Il Vegetariano** (*see p126*) and any pizzeria.

For a romantic meal

Borgo San Jacopo (a table on the terrace; *see p132*), **Cavolo Nero** (*see p132*), **Filipepe** (*see p133*) and **Targa** (*see p138*).

For a bit of local colour

Da Mario (*see p125*), **Da Nerbone** (*see p125*), **Da Rocco** (*see p130*), **Ruggero** (*see p138*) and **Da Sergio** (*see p125*).

For great wine lists

Beccofino (*see p130*), **Cibrèo** (*see p127*), **Enoteca Pinchiorri** (*see p127*), **Il Guscio** (*see p133*), **Oliviero** (*see p121*), **Ora d'Aria** (*p129*), **Pane e Vino** (*p133*) and **Targa** (*see p138*).

For perfect pizza

Santa Lucia (*see p139*) and **Vico del Carmine** (*see p139*).

For a bistecca alla Fiorentina

Alla Vecchia Bettola (*see p137*), **Beccofino** (*see p130*), **Il Latini** (*see p124*), **Da Mario** (*see p125*) and **Trattoria del Carmine** (*see p136*).

For an alfresco experience

Beccofino (*see p130*), **Bibe** (*see p137*), **Cavolo Nero** (*see p132*), **Napoleone** (*see p133*), **Portofino** (*see p138*), **Ricchi** (*see p133*) and **Trattoria 4 Leoni** (*see p136*).

For a snack between sights

Boccadama (*see p126*), **Canova di Gustavino** (*see p121*), **Cantinetta dei Verrazzano** (*see p121*), **Coquinarius** (*see p121*), **I Fratellini** (*see p121*), **Dei Frescobaldi** (*see p121*), **'Ino** (*see p123*) and **Le Volpi e L'Uva** (*see p137*).

For a good-value lunch

Cibreino (*see p127*), **Fusion Bar** (*see p121*), **Il Guscio** (*p133*) and **Sant'Agostino 23** (*p136*).

the option of eating in or taking away. You can also find traditional tripe stands (*tripperie*) in various parts of the city (*see p124* **For those who can stomach it...**) – stand-up affairs where you can fill up for a few euro. In addition, many bars now offer a limited choice of hot and cold dishes at lunchtimes. The quality of the food isn't always the highest, and there may or may not be seating, but it's a cheap and speedy alternative to a restaurant.

Duomo & Around

Restaurants

Fusion Bar

Gallery Hotel Art, vicolo dell'Oro 2 (055 27263). **Open** 7pm-midnight Mon-Sat; 7-10pm Sun. **Average** €40. **Credit** AmEx, DC, MC, V. **Map** p334 C3 ❶

Fitting in beautifully with the East-meets-West design ethos of the hotel that hosts it, this bar and restaurant is a stylish place to come for a quiet, light lunch, or an evening cocktail accompanied by nibbles or dinner. A set price (€16) help-yourself buffet is laid out on the bar at midday, featuring dishes with a fusion element. In the evening, there's a full menu of Japanese and fusion dishes, some of which are more convincing than others. Go for one of two set menus (€35 and €50), or order à la carte from the likes of sushi, sashimi, tempura and noodle dishes, tuna tartare, confit of duck with orange soy sauce and satay-marinated saddle of rabbit. Brunch is served at weekends.

Oliviero

Via delle Terme 51r (055 212421). **Open** 7.30pm-midnight Mon-Sat. Closed Aug. **Average** €50. **Credit** AmEx, DC, MC, V. **Map** p334 C3 ❷

Once a favoured haunt of (among others) Sophia Loren and Maria Callas, Francesco Altomare's restaurant still has a curious retro vibe in spite of a recent refit: the revolving door, the wood-panelled bar, the silent grand piano and the rather formal service all hark back to La Dolce Vita. The food, however, is not only great but very much in keeping with today's fashion for reinterpreting traditional recipes (in this case, mainly from Tuscany and southern Italy) resulting in dishes that are carefully thought out and never over-fussy. Menus (one quite traditional, the other offering *cucina contemporanea*) range through fish and meat options with some vegetarian choices. A glass of complimentary prosecco comes with the menu, where you'll find the likes of bay-spiked duck terrine, spinach and ricotta *gnudi* with truffles and beef fillet with Brunello-poached pears. There's an excellent cheeseboard and a fine wine list weighted towards Tuscany.

Wine bars

Canova di Gustavino

Via Canova 29 (055 2399806). **Open** noon-12.20am daily. **Credit** AmEx, DC, MC, V. **Map** p335 C4 ❸

A useful address if you require a light meal or a glass of wine in the area near the Duomo, this colourful, brick-vaulted *enoteca* (property of the Lanciola wine estate near Impruneta) is an offshoot of the fancier restaurant next door; the 800-strong wine list is available in both venues. To sop it all up there's a selection of salads, crostoni, cheeses and cold meats.

Cantinetta dei Verrazzano

Via de' Tavolini 18-20r (055 268590/www.verrazzano.com). **Open** *Sept-June* 8am-9pm Mon-Sat. *July, Aug* 8am-4pm Mon-Sat. **Credit** AmEx, DC, MC, V. **Map** p335 B4 ❹

Owned by the Castello da Verrazzano, one of the major wine estates in Chianti, the wood-panelled rooms of this '*cantinetta*' are continually crowded with smartly dressed Florentines and discerning tourists. On one side is a bakery and coffee shop (serving the Piansa coffee blend), while on the other is a wine bar serving (very good) estate-produced wines by the glass or bottle. Snacks include focaccia straight from the wood oven (the one with creamy cheese and sweet baby peas is recommended) and an unusual selection of *crostini*.

Coquinarius

Via delle Oche 15r (055 2302153/www.coquinarius.com). **Open** 9am-11pm Mon-Sat; 9am-4pm Sun. Food served from noon Mon-Sat. Closed Aug. **Credit** AmEx, DC, MC, V. **Map** p335 B4 ❺

A useful address in an area largely devoid of decent places to eat, this cosy little wine bar and café tucked away behind the Duomo is great for a quiet lunch or an informal evening meal: unusually, the full menu is available between noon and 11pm. Bare brick walls and soft jazz provide the background for good pastas (such as pecorino and pear ravioli), carpaccio, imaginative salads and platters of cheeses and meats. The own-made cakes are truly divine, but you could also pop across the road to Grom (*see p147*) for some of the best ice-cream in town.

I Fratellini

Via Ghibellina 27r (055 2347389). **Open** 8am-5pm Mon-Fri. **No credit cards. Map** p335 C4 ❻

There used to be loads of these hole-in-the-wall *vinai* (wine merchants) in Florence; nowadays, I Fratellini, founded back in 1875, is one of very few left in the city. There's nowhere to sit down: just join the locals standing in the road (there's not much traffic) or squatting on the pavement for a glass of cheap and cheerful plonk or something a bit more special. Help it down with a liver-topped *crostino* or a great slab of *porchetta* (rosemary roast pork) on a hunk of bread.

Dei Frescobaldi Ristorante & Wine Bar

Vicolo de' Gondi, off via della Condotta (055 284724). **Open** 7pm-midnight Mon; noon-midnight Tue-Sat. Closed 3wks Aug. **Credit** MC, V. **Map** p335 C4 ❼

This cosy wine bar showcases wines from the formidable Frescobaldi estates of Tuscany, Umbria, Friuli and even as far afield as Chile and California, where they collaborate with wine producer Robert Mondavi; unusually, all of the wine stocked here can be ordered by the glass as well as the bottle. Snacks include terrines, pâtés, marinated anchovies, cheeses and salamis, but you can also choose from the full menu offered in the smart restaurant next door (average €30). The wine bar makes a relaxed setting for the likes of warm octopus salad, pumpkin and scallop risotto and duck breast with prunes. Outdoor seating is also available in fine weather.

Snacks & quick meals

'Ino

Via de' Georgofili 3r-7r (055 219208/www.ino-firenze.com). **Open** 11am-8pm Tue-Sun; noon-5pm Sun. **Credit** MC, V. **Map** p334 C3 ❽

A useful address for a post-Uffizi/Palazzo Vecchio gastronomic break, 'Ino is a classy, contemporary sandwich bar and deli. Located a few steps from where the Mafia placed its bomb in 1993, it offers panini and other goodies made with top-notch ingredients, sourced from all over the country by owner Alessandro Frassica. Sandwiches (to eat in, perched at the counter, or to take away) are made to order and filled according to seasonal availability; the price of each (from €4) includes a glass of wine. The deli/shop (*see p161*) is stocked with cured meats, local cheeses, olive oils, vinegars, wines and other tempting goodies, and there's a range of sweet stuff that makes excellent gifts. *Photo p119.*

Santa Maria Novella

Restaurants

Cantinetta Antinori

Piazza degli Antinori 3 (055 2359827). **Open** 12.30-2.30pm, 7-10.30pm Mon-Sat. Closed 3wks Aug. **Average** €40. **Credit** AmEx, DC, MC, V. **Map** p334 B2 ❾

Well-heeled tourists rub shoulders with business types and ladies who lunch at this classic restaurant/wine bar, which opened in 1965. It occupies an elegantly vaulted ground-floor room of the 15th-century Palazzo Antinori, the historic home of one of Tuscany's foremost wine-producing families. Waiters in white jackets and black bow ties bring out textbook versions of Florentine classics, such as *pappa al pomodoro, salsiccie e fagioli* (sausage and beans), tripe and fillet steak. Very civilised, if a little on the expensive side.

Garga

Via del Moro 48r (055 2398898). **Open** 7.30-10.30pm Tue-Sun. **Average** €55. **Credit** AmEx, DC, MC, V. **Map** p334 B2 ❿

Bohemian in everything but its prices, this *trattoria* is perennially popular, particularly among well-heeled visitors. Ebullient owner Giuliano Gargani (who has been known to regale customers with operatic arias) presides over his colourful kingdom with its quirky decor (with garish frescoes and an eccentric clutter of objects) while chatty staff serve up well-executed pastas, meats and fish dishes. The menu features such luscious dishes as *taglierini del Magnifico* with a sauce of cream, parmesan, orange and lemon zest, and veal escalope with avocado;

Ora d'Aria. *See p129.*

For those who can stomach it...

In an era when food is becoming more standardised and the ever more stringent Italian health and hygiene laws are strangling individual gastronomic endeavour, Florence's *trippai* (tripe vendors) are standing firm against a sea of change. Once a dying breed, these traditional food vendors are nowadays often manned by a new generation of 'offalophiles', proudly carrying on an ancient Florentine culinary tradition.

The average visitor to Florence, when faced with a tripe stand, would be forgiven for not knowing what was brewing. The mobile stalls are laden with a series of bubbling cauldrons and heated trays, the contents of which are not for the faint-hearted. *Lampredotto* is probably the scariest item on the menu; the lining of the last stomach of the cow is simmered for hours in stock and served either in a *panino* with salt, pepper and maybe a lick of garlicky green salsa verde or with its broth in a little dish to be eaten with a plastic fork. Tripe (*trippa*) is served in these parts *alla fiorentina*, that is, in rich tomato sauce topped with a sprinkling of parmesan. It's also eaten cold mixed with pickles and dressed with olive oil, salt and pepper. Other offerings vary from stall to stall, but watch out for such delights as boiled *nervetti* (tendons), stewed *budelline* (intestines) and *lingua* (tongue).

This Florentine-style fast food is cheap (a *panino con lampredotto* and a plastic cup of plonk will only set you back a few euros), healthy and has a fan base that transcends all social boundaries. You're likely to be munching your cow tummy sarnie in the company of factory workers, builders, Senegalese street vendors, shop assistants and slick-suited business types; it's a great way to sample Florentine street life.

Trippai normally open from around 8.30am to 7pm Monday to Friday; some also open on Saturdays. The stalls nearest the city centre are at the following locations: under the Loggia del Porcellino; on the corner of via de' Macci and borgo La Croce; via Maso Finiguerra near the corner of via Palazzuolo; piazza de' Cimatori.

the atmosphere may not be particularly Tuscan, but the standard of the cooking is undeniably high, if also highly priced (you'll pay €8 for a tomato and rocket salad). Co-owner Sharon Oddson also runs popular cooking classes.

Il Latini

Via de' Palchetti 6r (055 210916). **Open** 12.30-2.30pm, 7.30-10.30pm Tue-Sun. Closed last wk Dec & 1st wk Jan. **Average** €40. **Credit** AmEx, DC, MC, V. **Map** p334 B2 ⓫

You'll inevitably have to queue to get in (no bookings are taken after 8pm) and, once inside, it'll be noisy and you'll probably be sharing a table with other customers, but that's all part of the fun, and the punters (both Italians and tourists) just keep piling in to this rustic eaterie, run by the Latini family since 1950. Vegetarians should keep well away, however: the thing here is the meat, great hunks of it. Skip the mediocre pasta dishes and go for one of the soups (the *pappa al pomodoro* is particularly good) for a first course, before tucking into the hefty *secondi* – this is a good place for *bistecca*. If you order *arrosto misto*, a vast platter of roast meats will arrive at the table defying all but the most prodigious appetites. The Latini are prolific producers of a fine, sludgy-green olive oil, and some decent wines: the house red is very drinkable.

Pizzerie & rosticcerie

Rosticceria della Spada

Via della Spada 62r (055 218757/www.laspada italia.com). **Open** noon-3pm, 6-10.30pm daily. **Average** €18. **Credit** AmEx, MC, V. **Map** p334 B2 ⓬

This centrally located *rosticceria* has been selling delicious dishes to go for a good many years, but now you can also eat in, and plenty do. The menu is more or less the same whether you choose to sit in or take away, but you'll pay about 50% less if you decide to do the latter. There are good pastas (try the lasagne), roast meats and vegetables and a truly delicious *melanzane alla parmigiana.*

Snacks & fast food

Amon

Via Palazzuolo 28r (055 293146). **Open** noon-3pm, 6-11pm Tue-Sat. **No credit cards. Map** p334 B2 ⓭

When Amon first started selling Egyptian specialities in 1987, there were few other places in Florence where you could get ethnic food. Amazingly, the place has only changed hands once since then and is still going strong in spite of plenty of new competition from doner kebab joints. Everything is made in-house, from pitta breads to the veal kebab, and it's all both delicious and cheap (doner kebabs cost €3.30, falafel €2.80).

Bar Galli

Via de' Banchi 14r (055 213776). **Open** noon-3.30pm Mon-Sat. Japanese food served 12.30-3pm & 7-10.30pm Tue-Sat. **Credit** MC, V. **Map** p334 B2 ⓮

The tourist-worn strip between the station and the Duomo is a gastronomic desert, but salvation is at hand in the form of this busy bar, which, alongside the usual pastries, panini and selection of (above-average) hot and cold dishes, offers a menu of delicious Japanese fare. The setting in the bar's back room is spartan (Formica-topped tables and ugly strip lighting) and the choice is limited to such homely dishes as ramen noodles and soups with the odd additional rice dish (the evening menu is a bit more elaborate), but it's very good and it's cheap. A steaming bowl of noodles costs from €7, the set evening menus from €10 and a bottle of cold Asahi is €4.

San Lorenzo

Restaurants

Da Mario

Via Rosina 2r (055 218550). **Open** noon-3.30pm Mon-Sat. Closed 3wks Aug. **Average** €15. **No credit cards. Map** p334 A3 ⓯

Be prepared to queue for a table at this tiny, cramped eaterie, in which four generations of the Colsi family have reigned for 50 years. Your fellow lunchers (who might even be sharing your barewood table) will include stallholders, businessmen, students and tourists, an egalitarian mix all drawn by the excellent Florentine home cooking and cheap prices: try the earthy *zuppa di fagioli e cavolo nero* (bean and black cabbage soup), a terrific *bollito misto* (mixed boiled meats) served with a biting garlic and parsley salsa verde and, for a supplement, the excellent *bistecca.* It doesn't get much better for the price.

Da Sergio

Piazza San Lorenzo 8r (055 281941). **Open** noon-3pm Mon-Sat. Closed Aug. **Average** €20. **Credit** MC, V. **Map** p334 A3 ⓰

Hidden away behind the market stalls, this family-run eaterie opened in the early 1900s selling just wine and olive oil. Today, it oozes authentic, old-fashioned Florentine atmosphere and makes a less frantic alternative to Da Mario (*see above*) as a place to sample genuine home cooking. Two airy rooms house large tables (you may find yourselves sharing) with crisp white tablecloths. Begin with *minestrone di verdura, ribollita* or *minestra di farro* (spelt soup), before moving on to a roast or *bistecca alla fiorentina.* There's tripe on Mondays and Thursdays and fresh fish (including superb *seppie in inzimino* – sweet tender squid stewed with Swiss chard) on Tuesdays and Fridays.

Wine bars

Casa del Vino

Via dell'Ariento 16r, San Lorenzo (055 215609/ www.casadelvino.it). **Open** 9.30am-5.30pm Mon-Fri; 10am-3.30pm Sat. Closed Aug. **Credit** AmEx, MC, V. **Map** p334 A3 ⓱

The only seating at this crowded and authentic wine bar, hidden behind the stalls of the San Lorenzo market, is on benches backed up against the wine cabinets. No matter: punters continue to pile in for a glass of good plonk and some delicious panini and *crostini* to accompany it. Bottles for all budgets sit on lovely old carved wood shelves that line the room; you'll find fairly priced wines from all over Italy, plus labels from further afield and plenty of choice by the glass.

Snacks & fast food

Nerbone

Mercato Centrale (055 219949). **Open** 7am-2pm Mon-Sat. Closed Aug. **Average** €10. **No credit cards. Map** p334 A3 ⓲

This food stall/*trattoria*, located on the ground floor of the covered central market and dating back to 1872, is a good place to find local colour. It's packed from breakfast time with market workers: even if you can't face a *lampredotto* (cow's intestine) sarnie and a glass of rough red plonk at 7am, the locals can, and it only costs them €3.50. Plates of simple pasta and soups (from €4) offer alternatives at lunchtime.

San Marco

Restaurants

L'Accademia

Piazza San Marco 7r (055 217343/www.ristorante accademia.it). **Open** noon-3pm, 7-11pm daily. **Average** €30. **Pizza** €15. **Credit** AmEx, DC, MC, V. **Map** p335 A4 ⑲

Sure, it's geared towards tourists, but nonetheless, L'Accademia is a useful spot in an area where there aren't many good eating choices. With a few exceptions (fillet steak cooked in an intense brachetto wine sauce with glazed shallots, for example), the more ambitious options on the menu are the least successful, so it's best to go for more reliable staples such as pasta with mixed seafood. The pizzas are a decent choice too. The wine list is surprisingly comprehensive, prices are reasonable and the Iacovitti brothers are cheerful hosts.

Il Vegetariano

Via delle Ruote 30r (055 475030). **Open** 12.30-2.30pm, 7.30-10.30pm Tue-Fri; 7.30-10.30pm Sat, Sun. Closed 3wks Aug. **Average** €25. **No credit cards.**

One of only a few dedicated vegetarian restaurants in Florence, Il Vegetariano offers wholesome fare and excellent value for money.The menu offers plenty of variety, including a choice of ethnic dishes, and generous portions. There's a fabulous salad bar and the wines are all organic. The one drag about a meal here? Actually getting the food is a bit of an ordeal: take your pick from the menu on the blackboard, pay at the desk, get a written receipt and then get your food from the counter.

Santa Croce

Restaurants

Baldovino

Via San Giuseppe 22r (055 241773/www.baldovino.com). **Open** *Apr-Oct* 11.30am-2.30pm, 7-11.30pm daily. *Nov-Mar* 11.30am-2.30pm, 7-11.30pm Tue-Sun. **Average** €30. **Pizza** €15. **Credit** AmEx, MC, V. **Map** p335 C5 ⑳

Scottish restaurateur David Gardner's colourful decor and flexible menus (have a full meal, snack or a pizza or salad) appeal to everyone from students to tour groups (who tend to eat early and get back on the bus). The food is decent rather than good, and the service can be haphazard, but prices are reasonable, there's plenty of choice and the wine list is full and varied. Across the road, the same owners run the smaller, quieter Baldoria, which serves casual, snacky-type food, plus pizzas and pastas.

Boccadama

Piazza Santa Croce 25-26r (055 243640). **Open** *Summer* 8.30am-11pm daily. *Winter* 8.30am-3pm

Creative impulses are never in short supply at aesthetically pleasing **Filipepe**. *See p133.*

Mon; 8.30am-11pm Tue-Sun. **Average** €30. **Credit** AmEx, DC, MC, V. **Map** p335 C5 ㉑
Under the same management as Finisterrae across the square, this inviting restaurant and wine bar is open all day: visit for breakfast or coffee, a light lunch (salads, pastas, bruschettas and so on) or a more creative full dinner (like beetroot-flavoured pasta with duck and black olive sauce, pork fillet with thyme on a bed of honeyed mushrooms). Wine by the glass is rather limited for a place that stocks over 400 labels. Nevertheless, thanks to its location, Boccadama is swamped with tourists (particularly for lunch) during the summer, when the terrace comes into its own.

Cibreino

Via de' Macci 122r (055 2341100). **Open** 12.50-2.30pm, 7-11.15pm Tue-Sat. Closed Aug. **Average** €30. **No credit cards. Map** p335 C6 ㉒
If your budget won't stretch to Cibrèo (*see below*), nip next door to its *trattoria* sibling. You can't book tables (prepare to queue or arrive early), the atmosphere is rustic and often overcrowded, there are no complimentary extras and the menu has a little less choice. But the food is of the same excellent standard, the bill will be less than a third of what you would pay in the more famous restaurant, and you still get the added extra of witnessing weak-stomached experience-hunters blanch when a chicken's head arrives on their plate.

Cibrèo

Via Andrea del Verrocchio 8r (055 2341100). **Open** 12.50-2.30pm, 7-11.15pm Tue-Sat. Closed Aug. **Average** €75. **Credit** AmEx, DC, MC, V. **Map** p335 C6 ㉓
Located at the heart of the bustling Sant'Ambrogio market area, Cibrèo has become something of a Florentine institution. The dishes at the flagship of chef/patron Fabio Picchi's little gastronomic empire (that also includes a bar, a *trattoria*, a theatre with buffet-style food and a cookbook) are a modern interpretation of Florence's traditional *cucina povera* (poor-man's food), with prime ingredients and heavy use of fresh herbs and spices to create intense flavours. There's no menu (and no pasta or coffee), but a chummy waiter will sit at your table in the elegant, wood-panelled room to take you through the options. A series of delicious antipasti arrives automatically with a glass of wine to be followed by *primi* such as a remarkable yellow pepper soup and soft polenta dressed with intensely herby melted butter. *Secondi* are divided between meat and fish; classics include a melting *coda di vitella in umido* (stewed ox tail) and *collo di pollo ripieno* (stuffed chicken neck) served with an unctious mayonnaise. Desserts are fabulous (the flourless chocolate cake has become a classic), and the wine list is everything you might expect. Cibrèo provokes extreme opinions: some think it's the best restaurant in Florence, while others claim it's overrated, over-priced and over-full of tourists. *See also above* Cibreino and *p144* Caffè Cibrèo.

Enoteca Pinchiorri

Via Ghibellina 87 (055 242757/www.enotecapinchiorri.com). **Open** 7.30-10pm Tue; 12.30-2pm, 7.30-10pm Thur-Sat. Closed Aug. **Average** €270. **Credit** AmEx, MC, V. **Map** p335 C5 ㉔
Generally acknowledged to be one of Italy's great temples to gastronomic excellence (and, it must be said, one of the country's most expensive restaurants), Enoteca Pinchiorri won back its third Michelin star in 2004. Although chef Annie Féolde (*see p131* **A woman's place?**) no longer does any cooking, she oversees the kitchen and runs front-of-house where the atmosphere is of the formal, luxuriously old-fashioned kind. You can choose à la carte, but there are several set menus (which represent the best value), including one based on Tuscan traditions and another with more creative options; each involves at least eight or nine tiny but superbly executed courses. Then there's the stellar cellar: Giorgio Pinchiorri has amassed a collection of wines that's second to none and offers one of the world's great wine lists. Wherever you eat – inside the palazzo or in the gorgeous, jasmine-scented courtyard – it all looks fabulous; service is elegant and prices are very high. Men are now required to wear jackets.

Del Fagioli

Corso de' Tintori 47r (055 244285). **Open** noon-2pm, 7-10.30pm Mon-Sat. **Average** €22. **Credit** MC, V. **Map** p335 C5 ㉕
Opened by Luigi ('Gigi') Zucchini just after the flood in 1966, this is one of those unpretentious time-worn places where little has changed over the years. It offers genuine Florentine traditional cooking and such standards as *ribollita*, *pappa al pomodoro* and *bollito misto con salsa verde* (mixed boiled meats served with a bright green parsley sauce). Gigi is still cooking and his *involtini* (thin rolls of beef stuffed with cheese, ham and artichokes) are delicious. There's warm apple cake to finish.

La Giostra

Borgo Pinti 12r (055 241341/www.ristorantelagiostra.com). **Open** 1-2.30pm, 7.30pm-midnight Mon-Fri; 7.30pm-midnight Sat, Sun. **Average** €70. **Credit** AmEx, DC, MC, V. **Map** p335 B5 ㉖
Run with eccentric charm by elderly chef/proprietor Principe Dimitri Kunz d'Asburgo Loreno and his twin sons, La Giostra is not a particularly princely place; too many tables are squeezed into a small room (although the recent opening of the new and rather more elegant fireplace room has helped to alleviate the overcrowding), with walls covered with pics of visiting celebs and a ceiling draped with fairy lights. The place is always full of tourists, and prices are high – but the food is very good, verging on excellent. The restaurant is well known for its *primi*, which include *taglierini* with white Umbrian truffles and divine ravioli stuffed with brie and served with sautéed artichokes. Follow this with veal in truffle sauce or Wiener schnitzel. Don't order too much: there's a complimentary plate of nibbles to start, and

Eat, Drink, Shop

portions are huge. If you happen to have room for dessert, however, try the rich, gooey *Sachertorte* made from an old Habsburg family recipe. The wine list features big names for big prices.

Kome

Via de' Benci 41r (055 2008009/www.kome firenze.it). **Open** noon-3pm, 7pm-midnight Tue-Sun. **Average** €40 (less at the *kalten*). **Credit** AmEx, DC, MC, V. **Map** p335 C5 ㉗

Boasting Florence's first *kalten* (conveyer belt) and Italy's only *yakiniku* (barbecue), the 'Grain of Rice' is making waves both for its Japanese and Asian specialities and its stunning decor. Kome is the brainchild of Carlo Caldini, a historic figure on Florence's nightlife scene and an architect who has created a warm, contemporary space. Downstairs, you perch on avocado-green bar stools under a swooping gold ceiling to select good sushi, sashimi, nighiri and other Japanese classics (€2.50-€6) from the belt while excellent light tempura, miso soup and various 'fries' are made to order. On the more functional upper floor, a gas barbecue is set into each table. If you choose one of the set menus (€36-€58), a series of hors d'oeuvres and a soup arrive, followed by a plate of raw fish, chicken or beef fillet that you cook yourself and then eat with sauces by folding into a lettuce leaf. There's a large basement bar too where – hallelujah! – you can smoke.

Ora d'Aria

Via Ghibellina 3Cr (055 2001699/www.oradaria ristorante.com). **Open** 7.30-11.30pm Mon-Sat. **Average** €50. **Credit** AmEx, MC, V.

This cool, minimalist restaurant, at the eastern end of via Ghibellina, opposite the old prison (the name refers to the inmates' fresh-air break) is quietly but confidently making waves among local foodies. Young Tuscan chef Marco Stabile has impeccable credentials (including a period at Michelin-starred Arnolfo in Colle Val d'Elsa) and his dishes are executed with real skill. Menus, featuring fish, seafood and meat options and sunny, Mediterranean flavours, are based strictly on the freshest of seasonal ingredients. There are several tasting menus (one of which, at a very reasonable €45, intelligently offers half portions), which range between 'traditions' and 'innovations' so alongside pigeon-stuffed tortelli and beef tartare you'll find juicy prawns in spun sugar, and tuna steak with caramelised tomatoes, watercress and ginger. For dessert, there's a sinful dark chocolate flan with a molten liquid centre. Own-made breads are varied and delicious and everything is beautifully presented. With an excellent and fairly priced wine list, which includes heavyweight vintages from Tuscany, Piemonte and France, this is arguably the best-value gourmet dining experience to be had in Florence. *Photo p123.*

Osteria de' Benci

Via de' Benci 13r (055 2344923). **Open** 1-2.45pm, 7.30-10.45pm Mon-Sat. **Average** €30. **Credit** AmEx, DC, MC, V. **Map** p335 C4 ㉘

There's a great atmosphere to this lively *trattoria*, complementing the impressive size and flavour of its meat. You'll pay about €20 for a Chianina fillet, but it'll be worth it – it's vast, cooked over an open fire and served *al sangue* (rare). The bean and garlic soup is pretty bland, but if traditional local specialities like *ribollita* and *trippa alla fiorentina* are available, you won't be disappointed. Pasta dishes are interesting (tortellini with saffron and rocket, spaghetti with red radicchio and shavings of mullet roe) and desserts are strong – try the excellent chocolate flan with bitter orange marmalade. Service can be brusque when it's busy, but such popularity can only be a good sign.

Ruth's

Via Farini 2A (055 2480888). **Open** 12.30-2.30pm, 7.30-10.30pm Mon-Thur; 12.30-2.30pm Fri. **Average** €25. **Credit** AmEx, DC, MC, V. **Map** p335 B6 ㉙

Located next to the synagogue, Ruth's serves great-value kosher vegetarian food as well as fish dishes. The dining area is a pleasant, modern and bright room with a full view of the open kitchen. The cooking has palpable Middle Eastern and North African influences, resulting in dishes such as falafel and other typical meze, fish or vegetable couscous, and fish *brik* (deep-fried flaky pastry parcels) served with a Tunisian salad, along with a range of pastas and salads.

La Vie en Rose

Borgo Allegri 68r (055 2346943/www.lver.it). **Open** 7-11pm Mon-Sat. **Average** €26. **Credit** MC, V. **Map** p335 B6 ㉚

Over the years, this cute little restaurant flanking Florence's famous flea market has undergone several changes of identity, but today's young French owner seems to have settled in with a valid formula offering good food with an Italo-French stamp at excellent value. There's only room for a handful of tables in the spare, narrow room, where the walls are painted deep-red and the lighting is low. Opt for one of the set menus (€22 and €32) or choose from the short *carta*; we were impressed by a light, mint-spiked courgette and ricotta *tortino* (pastry-less flan), a pretty pink beetroot risotto, steak tartare and a tart lemon cream that made a perfect, summery end to the meal. The only criticism was that the wine list was limited, unbalanced and too expensive, but we are assured this is due to change. Note that this is officially a *circolo* or club, so you have to take out (free) membership the first time you go.

Wine bars

All'Antico Vinaio

Via de' Neri 65r (no phone). **Open** 8am-8pm Tue-Sat; 8am-1pm Sun. Closed Aug. **Credit** AmEx, MC, V. **Map** p335 C4 ㉛

This small, no-frills neighbourhood *vineria* is often packed with locals – especially in the evenings, when there's time to mull over the day's proceedings with a *gottino* (a stubby glass) of wine and a delicious artichoke-topped *crostino*. Food comes from the *rosticceria* over the road (the establishments share an owner): soups and hearty pasta in the winter and rice salads and carpaccio in summer. The panini are also good. As a visitor, you may not be able to join in the chat, but it's a good place to soak up some atmosphere.

Pizzerie & rosticcerie

Caffè Italiano

Via Isola delle Stinche 13r (055 289020/www.caffe italiano.it). **Open** 12.30-2.30pm, 7.30pm-11am Tue-Sun. Closed 3wks Aug. **Average** €15. **Credit** MC, V. **Map** p335 C5 ㉜

There's almost no choice – marinara, margherita or Napoli – and just four bare tables, but the pizzas at this annexe to the upmarket Osteria del Caffè Italiano are authentic and delicious, their light and puffy bases topped with San Marzano tomatoes and proper *mozzarella di bufala*. After 10.30pm, the overflow is seated at the elegant restaurant.

Il Pizzaiuolo

Via dei Macci 113r (055 241171). **Open** 12.30-3pm, 7.30pm-12.30am Mon-Sat. Closed Aug. **Average** €15. **Credit** MC, V. **Map** p335 C6 ㉝

Il Pizzaiuolo lost its tip-top reputation when it changed hands a couple of years ago, but the place still turns out more-than-decent versions of the delicious Neapolitan variety. For an authentic taste of Naples, try the pizza topped with *salsiccia e friarelli* – sausage and a kind of bitter greens typical to the Campania region. Delicious Neapolitan pasta dishes include spaghetti Gaeta with tomato, olives and capers, or *trofie* (a kind of pasta) with pesto and cherry tomatoes. Finish the meal off with a *babà al rhum* (a rum-flavoured Neopolitan dessert). The small, white-tiled room is always packed (and often very noisy), so booking is a must here and be prepared that you may find yourself sharing a table with strangers.

Rosticceria Giuliano Centro

Via de' Neri 74r (055 2382723). **Open** 8am-3pm, 5-9pm Tue-Sat; 8am-3pm Sun. Closed 2wks July. **Average** €13. **Credit** AmEx, MC, V. **Map** p335 C4 ㉞

An appetising display of food is displayed on the counter at this *rosticceria*. More unusual dishes include spicy chicken wings and seafood salad, but there's also good lasagne, succulent roasts, grilled veg and some fresh-looking salads. Takeaway food is sold by weight; you pay about 15% more to eat in, at the back of the shop.

Trattoria I Fratellini

Via Ghibellina 27r (055 2347389). **Open** 8am-5pm Mon-Fri. **Average** €10. **No credit cards. Map** p335 C6 ㉟

Seemingly caught in a time warp, this atmospheric cross between a wine bar, *rosticceria* and grocer's shop, has been run by the Bisazzi family since the 1950s – and it's still one of the best bargains in town. Walk through the long, wood-panelled shop to the food counter and real fire, choose whatever takes your fancy, and either take it away or eat in it at one of the wooden tables at the back. *Primi* cost between €3 and €4, while *secondi* (including spit-roasted chicken) will set you back a maximum of €5. Make sure you sample Simona's superbly creamy tiramisù to finish. At €1.30 for 250ml, the house wine is also a snip.

Snacks & fast food

Da Rocco

Inside Sant'Ambrogio market, piazza Ghiberti (no phone). **Open** noon-2pm, 7-10.30pm Mon-Sat. **Credit** MC, V. **Map** p335 C6 ㊱

The bustling Sant'Ambrogio market is a much more local affair than its larger San Lorenzo counterpart, and Rocco's glorified food kiosk is where many of the neighbourhood shoppers end up for a quick lunch after their purchases. Located right in the middle of the covered part of the market, the place serves up cheap and cheerful versions of rustic local classics such as *pappa al pomodoro*, *spezzatino* (a kind of beef stew), pasta with ragù and tripe salad. You will probably have to queue up and there's no service to speak of, but the food is tasty and satisfying and the bill will likely come as a pleasant surprise; pastas cost €2.50 and mains will only set you back €3.10.

Oltrarno

Restaurants

Beccofino

Piazza degli Scarlatti 1r (055 290076/www.beccofino.com). **Open** 7-11.30pm Tue-Sun. **Average** €45. **Credit** MC, V. **Map** p334 C2 ㊲

When David Gardner opened Beccofino in 1999, its combination of contemporary decor, innovative food and serious wines was unique in town. After initial success, the restaurant slipped into something of a decline, but a relaunch in 2006 seems to have put things back on track. The menu has been streamlined towards food that celebrates the best of Tuscany. Anglo-Italian chef Roby Papin's curriculum includes stints with Marco-Pierre White, Gordon Ramsay and, closer to home, at Enoteca Pinchiorri (*see p127*), and his cooking aims to exalt both local recipes and their seasonal ingredients. An autumn meal included potato-stuffed tortelli with a mixed mushroom sauce, spaghetti with artichokes, capers, olives and anchovies and roast lamb in an almond and rosemary crust. You can also plump for a plain old *bistecca alla Fiorentina*, confident that the prized Chianina meat will be properly sourced. The heavyweight wine list includes an unusually good choice by the glass.

A woman's place?

The heart of many an Italian household is its kitchen, a place traditionally dominated by a homely Mamma figure producing great vats of wholesome food for the family according to recipes that she has learnt from her mother and her grandmother before that. This rose-tinted picture is somewhat fading from view these days, but there are still plenty of women fulfilling the role. Young women are used to watching their mothers cook and they learn easily, so it's ironic that female chefs are still an anomaly in Italy.

There is, however, a handful of gutsy women in Florence who have made a name for themselves in this highly competitive, progesterone-led business although, significantly, none of those featured here received a formal chef's training.

Annie Feolde of **Enoteca Pinchiorri** (*see p127*) won her third Michelin star (the first woman outside France to do so) in 1992; it was taken away two years later but re-awarded in 2006. She didn't set out to be a starred chef, but began cooking to complement her husband's celebrated wine collection in 1972. What started off as little 'bites' to go with drinks soon became a buffet, and the rest, as they say, is history. Feolde is not surprised that few women make it to the top of this 'very, very tough' business, but she herself actually prefers male kitchen staff claiming that they are less likely to 'disturb the calm'. So much for the Sisterhood.

Benedetta Vitali's kitchen and restaurant, on the other hand, are dominated by women, two of whom are her business partners. The problem with men, she says, is that they need to be *stelle* (stars) and this upsets the equilibrium. Vitali trained as an architect, but co-founded (along with ex-husband Fabio Picchi) **Cibrèo** (*see p127*) in the late 1970s, and has managed to bring up four children and forge a successful career as chef, restauranteur, author and teacher. She opened **Zibibbo** (*see p139*) in 1999 and maintains that clients have different expectations from a female chef; they don't necessarily expect 'grand cuisine' but they do expect good food.

One-time fashion designer **Beatrice Segoni** had never even boiled an egg when she married a man who owned a restaurant on the Adriatic coast, but learnt fast under the guidance of such illustrious (male) chefs as superstar Giancarlo Vissani. Her big break came in 2004 when she cooked for Bill Clinton at the G8 summit; she was then invited to take up the helm of **Borgo San Jacopo** (*see p132*), the Ferragamo-owned restaurant in Oltrarno.

Just down the street, **Da Camillo** (*see p132*) started life as a modest *osteria* in 1942 to give work to the women in the family who would have otherwise remained unemployed in the lean war years. By the early '50s, it was a fully fledged *trattoria*, hugely popular with the arty set of the day. Another self-taught chef, **Chiara Masiero** inherited the business from her parents and started cooking for clients in 1993, adding her own creative ideas to the traditional dishes. She too has raised a family under the shadow of long and anti-social hours away from home, something, she says, that's only possible if you have a supportive partner who's prepared to concede the limelight. And that's not always easy in Italy.

Benedetta Vitali.

Chiara Masiero.

Beatrice Segoni.

Borgo San Jacopo

Borgo San Jacopo 62r (055 281661/www.lungarnohotels.com). **Open** 7.30-10.30pm Mon, Wed-Sun. **Average** €60. **Average** €50. **Credit** AmEx, DC, MC, V. **Map** p334 C2 ㊳

The Hotel Lungarno's restaurant is well respected in Florence for both its classy yet ultimately informal ambience and its delicious, unfussy food. Chef Beatrice Segoni (*see p131* **A woman's place?**) hails from the Marche on the Adriatic coast and several fish dishes from her home territory are featured among the regional food on the menu; the *brodetto di pesce*, for example, is a typical Marchigiana fish soup. Punchy meat options include a *millefoglie* of duck breast and pigeon with artichokes. The restaurant occupies a long, narrow space with a gallery stretching from the street to the river; a huge arched window allows for plenty of watery views, but you'll have to fight for one of only four tables on the tiny terrace, from where views of the ponte Vecchio are incomparable.

Da Camillo

Borgo San Jacopo 57r (055 212427). **Open** 7.30-10.20pm Tue-Sun. **Average** €45. **Credit** MC, V. **Map** p334 C2 ㊴

You may pay over the odds to eat at this delightfully unreconstructed Florentine *trattoria* (the favoured haunt of the Florentine aristocracy since the 1940s), but the food is top notch and always prepared with the very best, properly sourced seasonal ingredients. Chiara Masiero's (*see p131* **A woman's place?**) long and varied menus feature Florentine classics, influences from Romagna (thanks to her Bolognese father) plus the results of her own experimenting, such as *ceciata di maiale* (a hearty stew of pork, chickpeas and spinach), duck with orange and black olives and a fabulous, booze-infused terrine of foie gras. Friday's menus always include lots of fish. There's a fairly hefty mark-up on the wines, but the *vino della casa* (from the family farm) is good and affordable. Pasta, bread and batters (for deep-frying) are all available in gluten-free versions.

La Casalinga

Via de' Michelozzi 9r (055 218624). **Open** noon-2.30pm, 7-9.30pm Mon-Sat. Closed 3wks Aug. **Average** €20. **Credit** DC, MC, V. **Map** p334 D2 ㊵

This bustling, family-run *trattoria* has been part of the Oltrarno scene for decades, managing to maintain its authentic atmosphere in spite of the onslaught of tourists. Prices have remained relatively low and the cooking is wholesome and reliable. Still, some dishes are better than others: avoid the ubiquitous *tortellini alla panna* in favour of such local specialities as *minestrone di riso e cavolo* (thick, warming soup with black cabbage and rice), roast guinea fowl and apple cake.

Cavolo Nero

Via dell'Ardiglione 22 (055 294744/www.cavolonero.it). **Open** 7.30-10.30pm Mon-Sat. **Average** €40. **Credit** AmEx, MC, V. **Map** p334 C1 ㊶

Since 1993, this intimately lit, inviting restaurant has been nestled on the narrow Oltrarno street where Filippo Lippi was born. Originally the food was stoically Florentine, but today chef/owner Arturo Dori's menus (divided equally between fish and meat) have evolved to offer unfussy 'contemporary Italian' cooking that's often very good indeed. He and his wife Michela (who makes the desserts) run their outfit with charm and enthusiasm

Napoleone.

and have a firm local fan base. Dishes come from all over Italy, but Mediterranean flavours dominate; try creamy goat's cheese wrapped in crisp filo pastry served with tapenade, roast *baccalà* on a sweet onion purée, lamb cutlets with spicy fig compote and a triumphant soft chocolate torte to finish. The wine list is long and fairly priced.

Filipepe

Via di San Niccolò 39r (055 2001397/www.filipepe.com). **Open** 7.30pm-1am daily. Closed 2wks Aug. **Average** €40. **Credit** AmEx, DC, MC, V. **Map** p335 D5 ㊷

Funky, chic decor provides a sensual setting for the unusual food at this great restaurant, and although prices have risen since the last edition of this guide, it's still one of the best deals in town. The two chefs hail from Calabria in southern Italy and their regularly changing menus of *sapori mediterranei* (Mediterranean tastes) feature punchy, sunny flavours. Dishes are divided into *freddo e crudo* (cold and raw) and *caldo* (hot) sections with no formal structure, so you can mix and match as you wish. The food is beautifully presented and there's always something interesting and unusual on offer: choose from the likes of carpaccio of *ombrina* (a white fish) with asparagus and fresh coriander; pasta with sardines, sultanas and pine nuts (a typical Sicilian dish); and seared tuna with a whipped balsamic mousse. Desserts are a feast for both eye and palate (there's often a wonderful tart lemon torte), and the wine list is interesting and well priced. All pasta dishes are available in a gluten-free version. *Photo p126.*

Il Guscio

Via dell'Orto 49 (055 224421). **Open** noon-2pm, 8-11pm Mon-Sat. Closed Aug. **Average** €30. **Credit** AmEx, DC, MC, V.

The atmosphere at this popular eaterie is that of a new-generation *trattoria* (it's one of the city's best) while the menu offers carefully prepared versions of dishes that hail from Tuscany's traditional rural cuisine, with the odd variation. Francesco Gozzini runs front-of-house while his wife and mother prepare the likes of potato soup with courgette flowers and octopus and own-made tagliatelle with pigeon and guinea fowl sauce. In summer, the menu leans towards fish and seafood such as the *padella* of seafood that comes served in its pan straight from the stove, while in winter, hearty meat choices prevail; the fillet of beef cooked in *vin santo* and topped with a slab of liver pâté is a favourite. Desserts are good and the wine list features over 530 labels from Italy and beyond, starting at just €10. Pop in for a quick *divino panino* or a bowl of soup at lunchtimes (the only choices) – the price (€5) includes a glass of wine and a coffee.

Napoleone

Piazza del Carmine 24 (055 281015). **Open** 7pm-1am daily. **Average** €35 (less for pizza). **Credit** AmEx, MC, V. **Map** p334 C1 ㊸

This hybrid restaurant/pizzeria has been one of the Oltrarno's more popular hangouts since it opened in 2005. While the food is no better than average (and the service isn't great), it's a fun, buzzy place to spend an evening, either on the large summer terrace with its multicoloured fairy lights or in the chic, moody interior – a large space divided into a series of intimate rooms. The menu is much too long to be taken too seriously, but if you choose carefully, you can eat well here. The restaurant is well known for its steak – you could cut the succulent *tagliata* with a *grissino* (breadstick) and it comes topped with *rucola* and parmesan shavings or with a tart, balsamic vinegar-based sauce. The thin-crust pizzas are good too. After dinner you can continue your Oltrarno entertainment just across the piazza at nightlife stalwart La Dolce Vita (*see p197*).

Olio e Convivium

Via Santo Spirito 4 (055 2658198/www.conviviumfirenze.com). **Open** Food served noon-3pm Mon; noon-3pm, 5.30-10.30pm Tue-Sat. Closed 3wks Aug. **Average** €30. **Credit** AmEx, MC, V. **Map** p334 C2 ㊹

Well-heeled locals call into this upmarket grocer to buy delicious food to go (*see p161*), but two cosy restaurant rooms – with chequerboard floors, sparkling crystal, shelves stacked with wine, olive oil and other edibles – make fine spots in which to enjoy a quiet meal. Specials are chalked up on a board, and feature the likes of taglierini with lobster, broad bean and pecorino risotto and roast pork with prunes. Wines are expensive.

Pane e Vino

Piazza Cestello 3 (055 2476956/www.ristorantepaneevino.it). **Open** 7.30pm-midnight Mon-Sat. Closed 2wks Aug. **Average** €35. **Credit** DC, MC, V. **Map** p334 C1 ㊺

Pane e Vino has earned a faithful following among Florentine foodies who appreciate the consistently high standards of cooking and the keen prices. Occupying a former warehouse near the river, the menu features Tuscan-based dishes alongside influences from other parts of Italy: more adventurous and creative dishes have been appearing on the menu of late. Expect the likes of broad bean soup topped with a sauté of chicory, parmesan crème brûlée, cocoa-stuffed ravioli and skewered rabbit flavoured with Tuscan herbs and a suggestion of curry. If you find fresh dates stuffed with caramel mascarpone on the dessert menu, go for it – they're superb. There are two set menus: a six-course set menu *degustazione* at €45 and a three-course menu *tradizionale* at €30. The honest mark-ups on the unusual wine list and the late hours are added perks. On the downside, service can be sloppy and bordering on the rude.

Ricchi

Piazza Santo Spirito 8-9r (055 215864). **Open** 7-10.30pm Mon-Sat. **Average** €18. **Credit** MC, V. **Map** p334 D2 ㊻

What's on the menu?

Cooking techniques & descriptions

Affumicato smoked; **al forno** cooked in an oven; **arrosto** roast; **brasato** braised; **fatto in casa** home-made; **griglia** grilled; **fritto** fried; **nostrale** locally grown/raised; **ripieno** stuffed; **ruspante** free-range; **vapore** steamed.

Basics

Aceto vinegar; **burro** butter; **bottiglia** bottle; **focaccia** flat bread made with olive oil; **ghiaccio** ice; **miele** honey; **olio** oil; **pane** bread; **panino** sandwich; **panna** cream; **pepe** pepper; **sale** salt; **salsa** sauce; **senape** mustard; **uovo** egg.

Antipasti

Antipasto misto mixed hors d'œuvres; **bruschetta** bread toasted and rubbed with garlic, sometimes drizzled with olive oil and often topped with tomatoes or white Tuscan beans; **crostini** small slices of toasted bread; **crostini toscani** are smeared with chicken liver pâté; **crostoni** big *crostini*; **fettunta** the Tuscan name for *bruschetta*; **prosciutto crudo** cured ham, either *dolce* (sweet, similar to parma ham) or *salato* (salty).

Primi

Acquacotta cabbage soup usually served with a *bruschetta*, sometimes with an egg broken into it; **agnolotti** stuffed triangular pasta; **brodo** broth; **cacciucco** thick, chilli-spiked fish soup (Livorno's main contribution to Tuscan cuisine); **cecina** flat, crispy bread made of chickpea flour; **fettuccine** long, narrow ribbons of egg pasta; **frittata** type of substantial omelette; **gnocchi** small potato and flour dumplings; **minestra** soup, usually vegetable; **panzanella** Tuscan bread and tomato salad; **pappa al pomodoro** bread and tomato soup; **pappardelle** broad ribbons of egg pasta, usually served with *lepre* (hare); **passato** puréed soup; **pasta e fagioli** pasta and bean soup; **pici** (thick, irregular spaghetti); **ribollita** literally a twice-cooked soup of bean, bread, cabbage and veg; **taglierini** thin ribbons of pasta; **tordelli/tortelli** stuffed pasta; **zuppa** soup; **zuppa frantoiana** literally, olive press soup – another bean and cabbage soup, distinguished as it's served with the very best young olive oil.

Fish & seafood

Acciughe/alici anchovies; **anguilla** eel; **aragosta** lobster; **aringa** herring; **baccalà** salt cod; **bianchetti** little fish, like whitebait; **bonito** small tuna; **branzino** sea bass; **calamari** squid; **capesante** scallops; **coda di rospo** monkfish tails; **cozze** mussels; **fritto misto** mixed fried fish; **gamberetti** shrimps; **gamberi** prawns; **gefalo** grey mullet; **granchio** crab; **insalata di mare** seafood salad; **merluzzo** cod; **nasello** hake; **ostriche** oyster; **pesce** fish; **pesce spada** swordfish; **polpo** octopus; **ricci** sea urchins; **rombo** turbot; **San Pietro** John Dory; **sarde** sardines; **scampi** langoustines; **scoglio** shell- and rockfish; **seppia** cuttlefish or squid; **sgombro** mackerel; **sogliola** sole; **spigola** sea bass; **stoccafisso** stockfish; **tonno** tuna; **triglia** red mullet; **trota** trout; **trota salmonata** salmon trout; **vongole** clams.

Meat, poultry & game

Agnellino young lamb; **agnello** lamb; **anatra** duck; **animelle** sweetbreads; **arrosto misto** mixed roast meats; **beccacce** woodcock; **bistecca** beef steak; **bresaola** cured, dried beef, served in thin slices; **caccia** general term for game; **capretto** kid; **carpaccio** raw beef, served in thin slices; **cervo** venison; **cinghiale** wild boar; **coniglio** rabbit; **cotoletta/ costoletta** chop; **fagiano** pheasant; **fegato** liver; **lepre** hare; **lardo** pork fat; **maiale** pork; **manzo** beef; **ocio/oca** goose; **ossobuco** veal shank stew; **pancetta** like bacon; **piccione** pigeon; **pollo** chicken; **porchetta** roast pork; **rognone** kidney; **salsicce** sausages; **tacchino** turkey; **trippa** tripe; **vitello** veal.

Herbs, pulses & vegetables

Aglio garlic; **asparagi** asparagus; **basilico** basil; **bietola** Swiss chard; **capperi** capers; **carciofi** artichokes; **carote** carrots; **castagne** chestnuts; **cavolfiore** cauliflower; **cavolo nero** black cabbage; **ceci** chickpeas; **cetriolo** cucumber; **cipolla** onion; **dragoncello** tarragon; **erbe** herbs; **fagioli** white Tuscan beans; **fagiolini** green, string or French beans; **farro** spelt (a hard wheat), a popular soup ingredient around Lucca and the Garfagnana; **fave** or **baccelli** broad beans (although *fava* in Tuscany also means the male 'organ', so use *baccelli*); **finocchio** fennel; **fiori di zucca** courgette flowers; **funghi** mushrooms; **funghi porcini** ceps; **funghi selvatici** wild mushrooms; **lattuga** lettuce; **lenticchie** lentils; **mandorle** almonds; **melanzane** aubergine (UK), eggplant (US); **menta** mint; **patate** potatoes; **peperoncino** chilli pepper; **peperoni** peppers; **pinoli** pine nuts; **pinzimonio** selection of raw vegetables to be dipped in olive oil; **piselli** peas; **pomodoro** tomato; **porri** leeks; **prezzemolo** parsley; **radice/ ravanelli** radish; **ramerino/ rosmarino** rosemary; **rapa** turnip; **rucola/rughetta** rocket (UK), arugula (US); **salvia** sage; **sedano** celery; **spinaci** spinach; **tartufato** cut thin like a truffle; **tartufo** truffles; **zucchini** courgette.

Fruit

Albicocche apricots; **ananas** pineapple; **arance** oranges; **banane** bananas; **ciliegie** cherries; **cocomero** watermelon; **datteri** dates; **fichi** figs; **fragole** strawberries; **lamponi** raspberries; **limone** lemon; **macedonia di frutta** fruit salad; **mele** apples; **melone** melon; **more** blackberries; **pere** pears; **pesche** peaches; **pompelmo** grapefruit; **uva** grapes.

Desserts & cheese

Cantuccini almond biscuits; **castagnaccio** chestnut flour cake, made around Lucca; **cavallucci** spiced biscuits from Siena; **gelato** ice-cream; **granita** flavoured ice; **mandorlata** almond brittle; **panforte** cake of dried fruit from Siena; **pecorino** sheep's milk cheese; **ricciarelli** almond biscuits from Siena; **torrone** nougat; **torta** tart, cake; **zabaglione** egg custard mixed with Marsala; **zuppa Inglese** trifle.

Drinks

Acqua water, *gassata* (fizzy) or *liscia/ naturale* (still); **birra** beer; **caffè** coffee; **cioccolata** hot chocolate; **latte** milk; **succo di frutta** fruit juice; **tè** tea; **vino rosso/ bianco/rosato** red/white/rosé wine; **vin santo** dessert wine.

General

Posso vedere il menù? May I see the menu? **Mi fa il conto, per favore?** May I have the bill, please?

Eat, Drink, Shop

Just as this guide was going to press, we heard that chef Pierluigi Campi was leaving Ristorante Ricchi which, thanks to him, has become one of the best places to eat fish in Florence. However, while a question marks hangs over the future of the restaurant in the evenings (Campi just cooked dinner), Ricchi remains an excellent place for a reasonably-priced lunch. The menu changes daily, but there are always several pasta choices (try the lasagne with taleggio cheese and *radicchio rosso*), *secondi* such as roast beef and roast potatoes and a selection of generous salads. In warm weather, you can eat on the terrace to the backdrop of one of the city's most characterful piazzas. If you want to eat on the cheap, a selection of hot dishes is served in the adjacent bar.

Sant'Agostino 23

Via Sant'Agostino 23 (055 210208). **Open** noon-2.30pm, 7.30-10.30pm Mon-Sat. **Average** €30. **Credit** AmEx, MC, V. **Map** p334 D1 ㊼

A welcome addition to the Oltrarno eating scene comes in the form of this tastefully modernised neighbourhood *trattoria*, which serves up Florentine and Italian specialities; *tagliolini* with grated tuna roe, grilled *baccalà* (salt cod) with a rosemary-spiked chickpea purée, tripe, *orecchia di elefante* (literally 'elephant ear', a kind of super-thin Wiener schnitzel) and a fine hamburger and chips. The daily changing lunchtime *menu del pellegrino* (that's 'pilgrim') offers great value at €10 for a *primo*, *secondo* and water.

Il Santo Bevitore

Via di Santo Spirito 64-66r (055 211264/www.santobevitore.com). **Open** 12.30-3pm, 7.30-11.30pm daily. Closed 3wks Aug. **Average** €30. **Credit** AmEx, MC, V. **Map** p334 C1 ㊽

This restaurant/wine bar, which occupies a large, vaulted room just south of the river, has become hugely popular with a young crowd recently and is always packed in the evenings. Lunchtimes, when there's a more limited menu and place settings are laid on paper mats, are quieter. The food is reliable, even very good at times, and prices are fair; the varied and nicely priced wine list (supplied by excellent Millesimi, *see p160*) is another attraction. As well as the ever-present wooden platters laden with selections of cheeses and cold meats, there's fresh pappardelle with lamb and artichoke sauce, potato soufflé with aromatic butter, and tartare of Chianina beef.

Al Tranvai

Piazza Torquato Tasso 14r (055 225197). **Open** noon-2.30pm, 7-11pm Mon-Sat. **Average** €25. **Credit** AmEx, DC, MC, V.

Given the bitter arguments that are raging among Florentines for and against the city's new Tramvia (*see p301*), the *tram-mobilia* that characterises this lovely little *trattoria* has assumed a certain irony. Local artisans continue piling in to the place from their nearby workshops, especially at lunchtimes, for the wholesome, down-to-earth cooking and great prices. Dishes hail from the *cucina popolare* tradition: *ribollita* and *pappa al pomodoro* (or *panzanella* in summer), tripe and *lampredotto* (cow's intestine), *lesso rifatto con le cipolle* (a tasty beef and onion stew) and squid *in inzimino* (with Swiss chard). Puds are own-made and the house plonk is just fine.

Trattoria del Carmine.

Trattoria del Carmine

Piazza del Carmine 18r (055 218601). **Open** noon-2.30pm, 7.30-10.30pm Mon-Sat. Closed 3wks Aug. **Average** €22. **Credit** AmEx, DC, MC, V. **Map** p334 C1 ㊾

This pleasantly rustic, good-value neighbourhood *trattoria* is a step up, in terms of both food and service, from some of the other budget options in the area. The clientele is a mix of regular locals and tourists and the menu is divided between a seasonally inspired *menù del giorno* and a long, fixed menu. Tuscan standards (*ribollita*, spinach and ricotta ravioli, excellent *bistecca* and so on) are always on offer, while daily specials might include own-made tagliatelle with porcini mushrooms or swordfish steaks.

Trattoria 4 Leoni

Via de' Vellutini 1r (055 218562/www.4leoni.com). **Open** noon-2.30pm, 7-11pm Mon, Tue, Thur-Sun; 7-11pm Wed. **Average** €35. **Credit** AmEx, DC, MC, V. **Map** p334 D2 ㊿

Once a simple local eaterie, the Four Lions is trendier (and more expensive) these days. Set on delightful little piazza delle Passera, the interior is done out in vibrant colours, with exposed brickwork, rustic tables and chairs, and a sometimes intrusive level of background music. It buzzes with a mixed crowd of tourists and locals who chow down on a menu of acceptable Tuscan-based food; potato-stuffed tortelli *alla Mugellana*, *pepposa* (a peppery beef stew) and the classic *gran fritto dell'aia*, a mix of deep-fried chicken, rabbit and vegetables, which, on Friday, is substituted by a fishy version. In summer, meals are served under big, white umbrellas in the charming square.

Alla Vecchia Bettola

Viale Ariosto 32-34r (055 224158). **Open** noon-2.30pm, 7.30-10.30pm Tue-Sat. Closed 3wks Aug. **Average** €25. **Credit** MC, V.

This popular *trattoria*, situated on a busy ring road, first opened in 1979 and is a real locals' favourite; there's usually a queue, and the noise levels in the single tiled room rise as the evening progresses. The traditional menu of hearty, rustic dishes includes daily specials alongside such regulars as *penne alla Bettola* (with tomato, chilli pepper, vodka and a dash of cream) and a superb beef carpaccio topped with artichoke hearts and shaved parmesan, while offal fans can enjoy tripe and *lampredotto*. The *bistecca* is succulent, delicious and vast.

Wine bars

Pitti Gola e Cantina

Piazza Pitti 16 (055 212704). **Open** *Summer* 10am-midnight Tue-Sun. *Winter* 12.30-4pm, 7-9pm Tue-Sun. **Credit** AmEx, MC, V. **Map** p334 D2 51

Dark-green paintwork and marble-topped tables lend this little wine bar a classy, classic feel. Right opposite Palazzo Pitti (a little terrace gets the full view), it's often packed with tourists and prices are on the high side, but the atmosphere is very pleasant and there's a good choice of wines, heavily weighted towards Tuscany. Snacks include Dario Cecchini's famous *tonno del Chianti*: not tuna fish at all, but pork marinated in white wine and herbs.

Le Volpi e l'Uva

Piazza de' Rossi 1r (055 2398132/www.levolpieluva.com). **Open** 11am-9pm Mon-Sat. **Credit** AmEx, MC, V. **Map** p334 D3 52

In winter, the only seats at this squeeze of an *enoteca* are at the bar, where you'll probably find yourself in the company of local wine aficionados. In summer, there's much more room thanks to the terrace. Much of what's on offer will be unfamiliar to all but the most clued-up oenophiles: owners Riccardo and Emilio search out small, little-known producers from all over Italy, with an eye on value for money. A limited but delicious selection of nibbles includes Italian and French cheeses, cured meats, panini *tartufati* (stuffed with truffle cream), smoked duck and rich pâtés. *Photo p138.*

Pizzerie & rosticcerie

La Mangiatoia

Piazza San Felice 8-10r (055 224060). **Open** noon-3pm, 7-10pm Tue-Sun. **Average** €18. **Credit** AmEx, DC, MC, V. **Map** p334 D2 53

La Mangiatoia, a combination of *rosticceria* and pizzeria, is popular with a mix of local Santo Spirito residents, students and tourists, thanks to its rock-bottom prices and good, honest home cooking. Order takeaway food from the counter in the front, or go through to one of a series of rooms behind the shop, where, aside from standard *rosticceria* fare (lasagne, spit-roast chicken, roast meats), there's a daily menu of specials and good pizzas.

Outside the City Gates

Restaurants

L'Arte Gaia

Via Faentina 1 (055 5978498). Bus 1A. **Open** 8-10.30pm Tue, Sun; noon-2.30pm, 8-10.30pm Wed-Sat. Closed 2wks Aug. **Average** €35. **Credit** AmEx, MC, V.

Situated on a small bridge crossing a scruffy tributary of the Arno just below Fiesole, this modern, welcoming restaurant specialises in fresh fish and seafood. It's a little hard to get to, but the effort will be rewarded by an excellent fish meal and an honest bill. Wood floors, crisp white tablecloths and soft lighting provide the background to colourful and punchy cooking: expect dishes such as smoked tuna and melon (an interesting alternative to the more usual *proscuitto e melone*), mint-spiked red mullet and aubergine kebabs, *fregole* (a kind of Sardinian pasta) with clams and mussels and *polpo Arte Gaia*, deliciously sweet marinated and grilled octopus. Puds are a little disappointing. At €35 and €39, the four-course set menus are great value.

Bibe

Via delle Bagnese 1r (055 2049085). Bus 36, 37, then taxi. **Open** 7.30-10pm Mon, Tue, Thur, Fri; 12.30-2pm, 7.30-10pm Sat, Sun. Closed last wk Jan, 1st wk Feb & 1st 2wks Nov. **Average** €28. **Credit** AmEx, MC, V.

Occupying an old farmhouse about 3km (2miles) south of Porta Romana, and entered through a small bar and grocer's shop, family-run Bibe is a good place to soak up the atmosphere of a rustic country restaurant without having to travel too far from the city. From the menu, try deep-fried courgette flowers stuffed with ricotta cheese, or sublime herb-infused *zuppa di porcini e ceci* (porcini mushroom soup with chickpeas). *Secondi* are classic Tuscan dishes; deep-fried chicken, rabbit and brains is a speciality. The puddings and the wine list are several notches above your average rustic eaterie. It's a shame that the flower-filled terrace is often blighted by mosquitos and traffic noise.

Omero

Via Pian de' Giullari 11r (055 220053). Bus 13, 38. **Open** noon-2.30pm, 7.30-10.30pm Mon, Wed-Sun. Closed Aug. **Average** €40. **Credit** AmEx, DC, MC, V.

The entrance to Omero, located in the quiet, exclusive hamlet of Pian de' Giullari, is on a narrow cobbled street, but if you walk through to the back of the grocer's that fronts the restaurant, you'll emerge into a sunny room with great views of the rural surroundings; come at lunchtime for maximum effect. (Downstairs is not so nice.) The menu features traditional Florentine food, reliable, if not particularly exciting, and served at high prices. Never mind: you're here for the old-fashioned atmosphere, the respectful service and the wonderful location.

Portofino

Viale Mazzini 25-27r (055 244140/www.ristoranteportofino.it). **Open** 12.30-3pm, 7.30-11pm Tue-Sat; 12.30-3pm Sun. **Average** €40. **Credit** AmEx, DC, MC, V.

Proof of the fact that some of Florence's better eateries are in the suburbs, this relatively new fish restaurant is located near Campo di Marte train station. There's a roadside terrace for summer meals, but a table in the stylish interior will be quieter. Fish and seafood dominate here (although a nod is given to meat eaters) and very good it is too. Tuscan-based flavours are given a creative twist, so expect courgette flowers stuffed with sole and prawns, tender chunks of sweetest squid nestling on a bed of chickpea purée dusted with smoked mullet roe, basil-flavoured *taglierini* with baby calamari, clams and *bottarga*. Mains include tuna steak in a sesame crust and sea bass fillet with cherry tomatoes and capers. Puds are delicious and the wine list (not surprisingly dominated by whites) is fairly priced. Shame about the naff background sounds.

Wine buffs unite: **La Volpi e L'Uva**. *See p137.*

Povero Pesce

Via Pierfortunato Calvi 8r (055 671218/www.poveropesce.it). **Open** noon-3pm, 7-11pm daily. **Average** €35. **Credit** DC, MC, V.

Simple, unpretentious and good-value fish and seafood dishes make up the backbone of the menu at this fish-only *trattoria* located near the football stadium. With its modern, vaguely nautical-themed interior and keen prices, it's become very popular and is often full, especially in the evenings. The menu changes daily, based as it is on market availability and what the chef thinks looks good, but a typical meal might feature a starter of the house *antipasto misto* (you'll get five or six little tasters), *spaghetti alle vongole* (clams) or *bavette all' astice* (lobster) and grilled swordfish. A tart *sorbetto al limone* is a good way to finish. The wine list is quite limited and on the pricey side.

Da Ruggero

Via Senese 89r (055 220542). Bus 11, 36, 37. **Open** noon-2.30pm, 7.30-10.30pm Mon, Thur-Sun. Closed mid July-mid Aug. **Average** €25. **Credit** AmEx, DC, MC, V.

This tiny *trattoria*, run by the Colsi family for over 30 years, is one of the best places in Florence to eat genuine home cooking. The thing is, the locals all know it, so don't risk the trek to Porta Romana without booking. The menu of traditional dishes changes with the seasons, but always includes a hearty soup or two and an excellent spicy *spaghetti alla carattiera*. Among the roast meats, try the tasty pigeon or go for the exemplary *bollito misto* (mixed boiled meats) served with tangy, parsley-fresh salsa verde.

Salaam Bombay

Viale Rosselli 45r (055 357900). Bus 22. **Open** 7.30-10pm Mon-Fri; 7.30pm-midnight Sat, Sun. **Average** €25. **Credit** AmEx, DC, MC, V.

When you need a spicy change from *pasta e fagioli*, head to one of Florence's few Indian restaurants. Tapestries adorn the walls of the single, galleried room; sit upstairs if you want to look down on the buzzy action below. The menu offers the sort of safe but decently cooked standards found on the menus of most Indian restaurants in Italy: tandooris and mughlai dishes, vegetarian options, great naans and own-made mango chutney. It's good value.

Targa

Lungarno Cristoforo Colombo 7 (055 677377/www.targabistrot.net). Bus 14. **Open** 12.30-2.30pm, 7.30-11pm Mon-Sat. Closed 1st 3wks Aug. **Average** €45. **Credit** AmEx, DC, MC, V.

Gabriele Tarchiani's riverside 'Bistrot Fiorentino' has a particularly inviting interior – with lots of wood and glass, low lighting and plenty of greenery – and a relaxed vibe. Local flavours and traditions dominate the seasonal menu, but there are also dishes from further afield: marinated *baccalà* (salt cod) with chickpeas, rigatoni with broccoli, fresh tuna and cherry tomatoes and rack of lamb. One of Tarchiani's classics is the hot chocolate soufflé: make sure you leave room. On the whole, the food is very good indeed. The cheeseboard is impressive and the hefty tome of a wine list is superb.

Zibibbo

Via di Terzollina 3r (055 433383/www.zibibbonline.com). Bus 14. **Open** 12.30-3pm, 7.30-10pm Mon-Sat. Closed Aug. **Average** €35. **Credit** AmEx, DC, MC, V.

Located just north of Careggi hospital, this bright, sunny restaurant may be some way from the centre of town, but the food absolutely justifies the effort. This is the domain of Benedetta Vitali, co-founder and former chef at Cibrèo (*see p127* and *p131* **A woman's place?**). Her superb, unfussy cooking finds roots in both Florentine and southern Italian traditions ('zibibbo' is a Sicilian white grape), using only fresh, seasonal ingredients. A faithful and mostly local clientele comes to sample the likes of soft liver pâté with orange peel in port, tender octopus and potato salad, spaghetti with mussels and clams, and stuffed duck cooked in honey with a plum sauce. The wine list is interesting with plenty of curiosities (from all over the world) along with the big guns. Lunchtimes are more casual and, for a quick snack, you can have a sandwich or a plate of pasta at the bar.

Wine bars

Fuori Porta

Via Monte alle Croci 10r (055 234 2483/www.fuoriporta.it). Bus D. **Open** 12.30-3.30pm, 7pm-12.30am Mon-Sat. Closed 2wks Aug. **Average** €25. **Credit** AmEx, MC, V.

Florence's best-known wine bar is situated in a lovely neighbourhood at Porta San Miniato and has a terrace overlooking the old city gate. It's a relaxed spot for a glass and a snack at lunchtimes; evenings are buzzier. At any time, there are between 500 and 650 labels on the list, with about 50 available by the glass and 250cl carafe, which rotate roughly every week. Tuscan and Piedmontese reds dominate, but other Italian regions are also well represented and there are also formidable choices of grappas and Scotches. The daily menu has excellent pastas, *carpacci* and salads; the classic snack here is one of the delicious *crostoni*, a kind of open cheese-topped grilled sandwich.

Pizzerie & rosticcerie

Santa Lucia

Via Ponte alle Mosse 102r (055 353255). Bus 30, 35. **Open** 7.30pm-midnight Mon, Tue, Thur-Sun. Closed Aug. **Average** €15. **No credit cards.**

It may be a bit of a trek (a ten-minute walk northwest of Porta al Prato), but many Florentines reckon the pizza at Santa Lucia to be the best in town (although it now has a serious contender for that honour, *see below* Vico del Carmine). Pizzas are authentically Neapolitan – with a light and puffy base, and the sweetest tomatoes and milkiest mozzarella on top – and so is the atmosphere. If you don't want pizza, terrific fish dishes include *spaghetti allo scoglio* (with mixed seafood) and octopus in spicy tomato sauce; the bill will be hiked up accordingly. Book in advance or be prepared to queue.

Vico del Carmine

Via Pisana 40-42r (055 2336862). **Open** 7-11pm Mon-Sat. **Average** €18. **Credit** MC, V.

Noise phobics should give the Vico del Carmine a wide berth. Done out as a typical street in old Naples (complete with washing lines strung across a balcony), this pizzeria and restaurant is always full, and, for many, the cacophony adds to the atmosphere. Punters pile in for what is possibly the best pizza in town, baked in an authentic Neopolitan pizza oven with ingredients that are strictly sourced from the Campania region (as are most of the wines). The pizzas come with a light, puffy crust and a miraculously un-soggy base. Highly recommended is the remarkable *a chiummenzana*; the folded-over crust is stuffed with ricotta while the base is topped with smoked scamorza cheese and cherry tomatoes. Less remarkable (but perfectly decent) are the pasta and fish choices.

Stock up on omega-3s at **Povero Pesce**.

Cafés, Bars & Gelaterie

Excellent espressos for the coffee cognoscenti.

Caffè Florian. *See p142.*

When it comes to coffee in Florence you can forget about global branding; this city has always prided itself on its diversity and independence. Simple corner places with the buzz of local workers throwing back espressos at the bar for a quick hit of caffeine; genteel, gilded affairs where the cutlery is silver plated and a coffee at a table with a view costs more than the barman's hourly wage; rustic bars with students sitting at the benches with piles of books and a *caffelatte*, and all the possible combinations in between. These have been joined in recent years by cafés that could be straight out of *Wallpaper** and there's even rumoured to be a new Nespresso café opening on via de' Tornabuoni, completing the Florentine café repertoire from greasy Joe to George Clooney hangout.

Italians take their coffee seriously, and the comparative merits of the brew itself influence the decision of where to stop for the next. But Florentine café society isn't just about coffee. Although breakfast is almost always still a simple cappuccino and brioche, the 'light lunch' can encompass all manner of buffets, gourmet menus and brunch offerings. Tea and cake is also an increasingly popular afternoon diversion, and the early-evening *aperitivo* sees true feasts of free snacks and home-made dishes offered to drinkers (*see p194* **The aperitivo awards**). Hybrids straddling bars, cafés, restaurants and bistros have been springing up like mushrooms in recent times, blurring the traditionally clear-cut descriptions and hours that were forced on many venues by the previously stringent licensing regulations.

Classic bars come in several guises, but this still depends on their licence. In café-bars you can usually sit down for a full lunch; in bar-*tabacchi* you can also buy cigarettes, bus tickets and stamps; in *latterie* you can pick up milk and dairy products; and in *drogherie* you can stock up on groceries. In other shops, especially *pasticcerie* and *gelaterie*, there's often also a bar. In bigger bars and cafés you pay for coffee at the till before you order it from the barman with your receipt, unless you want to sit down. And bear in mind that location is everything when it comes to the bill: it usually costs far less if you stand at the bar rather than sit at a table, and you often pay more to sit outside, especially at one of the more touristy spots.

❶ Pink numbers given in this chapter correspond to the location of each café, bar or *gelateria* as marked on the street maps. *See pp334-35.*

Duomo & Around

Astor Caffè

Piazza del Duomo 20r (055 284305). **Open** noon-2am daily. **Credit** AmEx, DC. **Map** p335 B4 ❶
Astor's huge central skylight creates the perfect environment for its regular exhibitions of local photographers and bas-relief sculptors. Perch on a padded bar stool in this vast contemporary chrome-and-glass bar for an *aperitivo*, or linger for a lunch of smoked trout and orange salad or steaming olive and cherry tomato pasta. There's jazz in the downstairs bar some evenings; upstairs, sip cocktails, eat a full dinner or check your emails at the internet point. *See also p197.*

Bar Perseo

Piazza della Signoria 16r (055 2398316). **Open** 7.30am-midnight Mon-Sat. Closed 3wks Nov. **Credit** AmEx, DC. **Map** p334 C3 ❷
Even though it doesn't have the charm of the more celebrated Rivoire (*see below*), this bar overlooks the city's most famous Renaissance square, along with its namesake – Cellini's *Perseus*, in the Loggia dei Lanzi. Inside, the centrepiece is a sculptural art deco chandelier, but most eyes are drawn to the mountains of own-made ice-cream topped with cherries, berries and chocolate curls. *See also p146* **A brew with a view**.

Caffè Rivoire

Piazza della Signoria 5r (055 214412/www.rivoire.it). **Open** 8am-midnight Tue-Sun. Closed last 2wks Jan. **Credit** AmEx, DC, MC, V. **Map** p334 C3 ❸
Founded in 1872 as a chocolate factory, Rivoire is the most famous and best loved of all Florentine cafés. Its chocolates are divine – try the puffed rice and *gianduja* (hazlenut and almond-flavoured chocolate) – and its own-brand coffee is among the best in the city. The outside tables have views of Palazzo Vecchio and the Loggia dei Lanzi. One downside: your wallet will be hit hard for the privilege. *See also p146* **A brew with a view**.

Caruso Jazz Café

Via Lambertesca 14-16r (055 281940/www.caruso jazzcafe.com). **Open** 9.30am-3.30pm, 6-11pm Mon-Sat. **Credit** AmEx, DC, MC, V. **Map** p334 C3 ❹
Huge papier mâché sculptures of Florentine landmarks and cherubs adorn this vaulted bar, tucked behind the piazza della Signoria. The artist owner has created a friendly, easygoing atmosphere in this much-loved watering hole. As well as the simple lunch and tea menus and the jazz acts that play some evenings (*see 191*), there are four computers offering internet access.

Chiaroscuro

Via del Corso 36r (055 214247). **Open** 7.30am-9.30pm daily. **Credit** MC, V. **Map** p335 B4 ❺
Chiaroscuro's expert barmen consider themselves coffee connoisseurs, and the risk of being served a below-par brew here is practically non-existent. Coffee is also sold freshly ground by weight and there's a range of coffee makers and machines. There's usually room to sit down, even at busy lunchtimes. The buffet *aperitivo* is a safe bet.

Colle Bereto

Piazza Strozzi 5r (055 283156/www.collebereto.com). **Open** *Summer* 8am-midnight Mon-Sat. *Winter* 8am-9pm Mon-Sat. Food from noon. **Credit** AmEx, MC, V. **Map** p334 B3 ❻
Colle Bereto is a smart bar with a prime location: outside is a ludicrously luxurious covered terrace with red and white sofas and armchairs overlooking the monumental Palazzo Strozzi. The menu is a standard affair, but best of all are the tiny fruit tarts with whipped yoghurt fillings. *See also 197.*

Gilli

Piazza della Repubblica 36-39r (055 213 896). **Open** 8am-midnight Mon, Wed-Sun. **Credit** AmEx, DC, MC, V. **Map** p334 B3 ❼
With the loss in recent years of many of the city centre's most beloved shops and bars to make room for international designer flagship stores, continuing murmurings abound about the future of historic Gilli. Its closure would be a blow to its loyal clientele and to impressed visitors. Gilli's belle époque interior is original, its seasonally themed sweet window displays wickedly tempting and its rich, flavoured hot chocolates legendary. Outside seating year-round.

Procacci

Via de' Tornabuoni 64r (055 211656). **Open** 10.30am-8pm Mon-Sat. Closed Aug. **Credit** AmEx, MC, V. **Map** p334 B3 ❽
One of the few traditional shops on this thoroughfare to survive the onslaught of designer names, the small wood-lined bar and shop is a favourite with nostalgic Florentines. In season (Oct-Dec), truffles arrive daily at around 10am, filling the room with their soft musty aroma (the speciality is melt in the mouth truffle and butter brioche.

The best Cafés

For breakfast
I Visacci (*see p144*).

For mid-morning coffee
Caffè Rivoire (*see p141*).

For snacks
Procacci (*see p141*).

For a sit-down lunch
Rose's (*see p143*).

For Sunday brunch
Il Rifrullo (*see p145*).

La Terrazza, Rinascente

Piazza della Repubblica 1 (055 219113/www.rinascente.it). **Open** 10am-9pm Mon-Sat; 10.30am-8pm Sun. **Credit** AmEx, DC, MC, V. **Map** p334 B3 ❾
The rooftop terrace café at this department store affords some of the most stunning views of the city; the splendour of Brunelleschi's cupola at such close quarters more than makes up for the mediocre menu and the patchy service. Come at sundown, when you can experience the city bathed in pink light. *See also p146* **A brew with a view**.

Santa Maria Novella

Amerini

Via della Vigna Nuova 63r (055 284941).
Open 8.30am-8.30pm Mon-Sat. Closed 2wks Aug. **Credit** AmEx, MC, V. **Map** p334 B2 ❿
Smart but cosy, Amerini is such a lunchtime favourite that you're sometimes asked to endure the classic café faux pas of unknown companions being seated at your small table. Choose from sandwiches such as grilled vegetables with brie, or order a bowl of fresh pasta. Breakfast time and afternoons are more relaxing, so you can sample luscious lemon tart relatively undisturbed.

Caffè Florian

Via del Parione 28r (055 284291/www.caffeflorian.com). **Open** 9am-8pm daily. **Credit** AmEx, DC, MC, V. **Map** p334 C2 ⓫
The Venice icon recently opened this pretty, genteel sister café in a small backstreet off via de' Tornabuoni. Tisanes and coffees are served with dainty petit fours that look too good to eat, and the savouries are exquisite morsels with truffle or delicious cheeses. *Photo p140.*

Caffè Megara

Via della Spada 15-17r (055 211837). **Open** 8am-2am daily (lunch noon-3pm). **Credit** AmEx, DC, MC, V. **Map** p334 B2 ⓬
Always full at lunchtimes with tourists and loyal regulars who know the great menu has daily specials. Pasta dishes are always a safe bet and the *bruschette* are enormous. Megara gets even busier when big matches are on. Smooth jazzy sounds play out in the evenings and in summer a hatch serves *aperitivo* snacks to the tables outside.

Caffè San Carlo

Borgo Ognissanti 32-34r (055 216879/www.caffesancarlo.com). **Open** 7.30am-midnight Mon-Sat. **Credit** AmEx, MC, V. **Map** p334 B1 ⓭
Pre-lunch and dinner aperitifs are the big draws in this stylish and lively small bar. In good weather, the French windows are opened up, wine barrels are used as serving tables and the canopied outside area becomes a miniature socialising hub.

Caffè Vitali

Via del Moro 51r (055 285486). **Open** 8am-10pm Mon-Sat. **Credit** V. **Map** p334 B2 ⓮
Rustic café with a quiet, hidey-hole mezzanine floor and chirpy service. The slightly tacky neon shop sign and touristy fixed menus belie the high quality of the pastas and seasonal dishes.

Giacosa Roberto Cavalli

Via della Spada 10r (055 2776328). **Open** *Summer* 7.30am-midnight Mon-Sat. *Winter* 7.30am-8.30pm Mon-Sat. Closed 2wks Aug. **Credit** AmEx, MC, V. **Map** p334 B2 ⓯
Alongside Florentine designer Cavalli's clothing shop is his café, complete with leopard-skin pouffes, catwalk shows beamed on a plasma screen and plenty of attitude. The store took over the via Tornabuoni corner space of the much-loved Giacosa café, and in the central bar room Cavalli continues to serve hot lunches and sweet treats.

Noir

Lungarno Corsini 12-14r (055 210751/www.noirfirenze.com). **Open** noon-2am daily. **Credit** AmEx, DC, MC, V. **Map** p334 C2 ⓰

Coffee: the local low-down

Cappuccino The breakfast of choice, never drunk after mid morning; '*ben caldo*' means piping hot.
Espresso A strong hit of black coffee taken at the bar and after dinner.
Doppio espresso Double, usually served with a raised eyebrow.
Macchiato caldo Espresso with hot froth.
Macchiato freddo Espresso with a dash of cold milk, for lightweights.
Caffelatte The acceptable face of post-breakfast cappuccino, served in a glass with a creamy head but no froth.
Latte macchiato Hot milk with a flick of the wrist of espresso.
Caffè lungo About double the height of an espresso, so weaker.
Caffè americano A big cup full of diluted espresso – the nearest thing Italy has to filter coffee.
Caffè ristretto A very short shot of full-bodied espresso, often barely covering the bottom of the cup.
Caffè corretto An espresso 'corrected' with a shot of any spirit – makes a perfect 'hair of the dog'.

Gaming nerds galore at **Area 51**. *See p145.*

Fans of the old Capocaccia will have got used to its regular, increasingly daring makeovers. The latest incarnation of this riverfront venue has pushed the design envelope to the edge. The new name is a not-so-subtle clue, as Gothic revival Noir is almost entirely black. The frescoed ceilings have survived, and the new get-up works best in the evenings for the legendary *aperitivo*, but daytime punters can nab a table on the outside terrace. Sunday brunch is still a hit, with a choice of options including eggs benedict and salmon bagels as well as a 'Babette's feast' buffet. *See also p198 and p146* **A brew with a view**.

Rose's

Via del Parione 26r (055 287090/www.roses.it). **Open** 9am-1.30am Mon-Sat (brunch 12.30-3.30pm Sat); 6pm-1.30am Sun. Closed 2wks Aug. **Credit** AmEx, MC, V. **Map** p334 C2 ⓱

This spacious restaurant-bar, with soothing cornflower-blue velvet decor, is invariably packed with a young crowd from local offices. Breakfast means fresh brownies and apple strudel. Lunch specialities are burgers and fish carpaccios, followed by carrot cake; at night, it's the hippest sushi bar in town.

San Lorenzo

BZF (Bizzeffe)

Via Panicale 61r (055 2741009/www.bzf.it). **Open** 4pm-midnight Tue-Sun. Closed June-Aug. **Credit** MC, V. **Map** p334 A3 ⓲

A stunning 13th-century convent with an intellectual spirit. The bar is adjoined to the bookshop, internet terminal and an art space. As well as hosting jazz gigs and serving grown-up brunches, BZF organises regular lectures and debates. A range of coffees and teas from around the world is served, and there's a strong food menu: try the divine pumpkin soup, cheeseboards or American-style sweets. Sunday brunch has accompanying jazz sounds and traditional roasts. *See also p181.*

Nabucco

Via XVII Aprile 28r (055 475087). **Open** 6.30am-10pm Mon-Sat. **Credit** AmEx, DC, MC, V.

Despite an almost constant influx of students, it's generally easy to get a seat at one of the many tables or bar stools lining the huge windows of this spacious, pleasant café-wine bar. Unusually, just about every type of wine is available by the glass as well as the bottle, and prices here are reasonable, with lots of choice for under €3. Tasting sessions are held on Wednesday evenings between September and May.

Nannini Coffee Shop

Via Borgo 7r (055 212680). **Open** 7.30am-7.30pm Mon-Fri, Sun; 7.30am-8.30pm Sat. **Credit** MC, V. **Map** p334 B3 ⓳

Perennially bustling, Nannini is perfect for coffee and *panforte* (a sticky Sienese cake made with dried fruits and nuts) after a visit to the nearby central market. Sweets from Siena are the bar's speciality, including *cantuccini* (almond biscuits) and *ricciarelli* (choc-covered marzipan petits fours).

Porfirio Rubirosa

Viale Strozzi 18-20 (055 490965). **Open** 7pm-2am Mon-Sat. Closed 2wks Aug. **Credit** MC, V.

This chic bar is the watering hole of choice during the trade shows in the Fortezza da Basso, just across the avenue. Lunch on truffle mozzarella or smoked tuna salad, lounge on the balcony mezzanine with a slice of passion fruit cheesecake at teatime, or come back in the evening to make a night of it. *See also p199.*

San Marco

Robiglio

Via de' Servi 112r (055 214501/www.robiglio.it). **Open** 7.30am-7.30pm Mon-Sat. Closed 3wks Aug. **Credit** AmEx, MC, V. **Map** p335 A5 ⓴

The sublime hot chocolate served here is so thick that the spoon stands up in it, and the delicious pastries are a Florentine institution. Robiglio's sister café located on via Tosinghi (no.11r, 055 215013) has outside tables in summer.

Zona 15

Via del Castellaccio 53-55r (055 211678/www.zona15wine.it). **Open** 11am-3am Mon-Fri; 6pm-3am Sat, Sun. **Credit** AmEx, DC, MC, V. **Map** p335 A4 ㉑

Hemingway.

Looking rather like a futuristic American diner, this decidedly hip café-cum-wine bar's leather and chrome stools hug a massive central spotlit bar area. Walls are clad in oyster mosaics and crowned by dramatic vaulted ceilings. The *aperitivo* tapas menu, based on Basque recipes, is available daily from 6pm, while the decent wine menu offers around 200 different options.

Santa Croce

Caffè Cibrèo

Via Andrea del Verrocchio 5r (055 2345853). **Open** 8am-1am Tue-Sat (lunch 1-2.30pm). Closed 2wks Aug. **No credit cards. Map** p335 C6 ㉒
This delightful café has exquisite carved wood ceilings, antique furniture, a candlelit mosaic and outside tables, but also a knack for making everything it presents look as beautiful as the bar itself. As you'd expect from an outpost of Cibrèo (*see p125*), the savoury dishes are both inventive and refined, but the desserts, like the rich, dense chocolate torte and the cheesecake with bitter orange sauce, are also amazing.

Caffellatte

Via degli Alfani 39r (055 2478878). **Open** 8am-midnight Tue-Sat; 9am-midnight Sun. **No credit cards. Map** p335 B5 ㉓
The lattes in this small café, done out with rustic wooden tables and chairs, are among the best in Florence. But if they're too dull for you, the *cappuccione* comes piping hot in a giant bowl with honey and Turkish cinnamon. The pastries and cakes are made in the café's organic bakery.

La Loggia degli Albizi

Borgo degli Albizi 39r (055 2479574). **Open** 7.30am-8.30pm Mon-Sat. Closed Aug. **Credit** AmEx, MC, V. **Map** p335 C5 ㉔
With some of the best pastries and cakes in town, La Loggia degli Albizi is the perfect stop-off after some hard shopping. Try the *torta della nonna* (crumbly pastry filled with baked pâtisserie cream).

Nuove Poste

Via Giuseppe Verdi 73r (055 2480424). **Open** 7am-1pm daily. **Credit** AmEx, MC, V. **Map** p335 B5 ㉕
This corner bar would be fairly bog standard were it not for the huge outdoor canopied seating area on the pedestrian concourse. It's right on the crossroads of streets leading to Santa Croce, the Duomo and Sant'Ambrogio, so a strategically useful pit stop.

I Visacci

Borgo degli Albizi 80r (055 2001956). **Open** 10.30am-2.30am Mon-Sat. **Credit** MC, V. **Map** p335 B4 ㉖
Cosy up in one of the padded alcove sofa seats in this cutesy bar, decked out in different-coloured stripes. The best cappuccinos in the city are served here; the mellow music may also help to lull you into a longer stay. The lunchtime menu hits the right notes: cheap hot *crostoni* (open sandwiches), salads, omelettes and cold meat plates.

Oltrarno

Cabiria

Piazza Santo Spirito 4r (055 215732). **Open** 8.30am-1.30am Mon, Wed-Sun. **No credit cards. Map** p334 D2 ㉗
A long-standing artsy haunt, popular with students. Inside, scarlet walls are punctuated with the paintings and photographs of visiting exhibitions and there's an enclosed outside terrace. Hot focaccias with rocket and creamy sheep's cheese are served at lunchtime and the barman shakes up a mean aperitif at noon and 7pm. *See also p197 and p146* **A brew with a view**.

Caffè degli Artigiani

Via dello Sprone 16r (055 291882/www.oltrarno-firenze.net). **Open** *May-Sept* 8am-4pm Mon; 8am-midnight Tue-Sat. *Oct-Apr* 8.30am-10.30pm Mon-Sat. **Credit** MC, V. **Map** p334 C2 ㉘
This charming, laid-back gem of a café is worth seeking out for its country cottage atmosphere (think low ceilings and beautifully carved antique chairs). Staff are friendly and multilingual and a couple of outside tables appear in warm weather.

Caffè Ricchi

Piazza Santo Spirito 9r (055 215864/www.caffericchi.com). **Open** *Summer* 7am-1.30am Mon-Sat. *Winter* 7am-10pm Mon-Sat. Closed last 2wks Aug, last 2wks Feb. **Credit** MC, V. **Map** p334 D2 ㉙

Ricchi is on the traffic-free piazza Santo Spirito, a charming setting for alfresco drinking. The place does a good lunch menu that changes daily. If it rains, the side room is a great place to relax with a coffee and a cake. *See also p130 and p146* **A brew with a view**.

Hemingway

Piazza Piattellina 9r (055 284781/www.hemingway.fi.it). **Open** 4.30pm-1am Mon-Thur; 4.30pm-2am Fri, Sat; 3.30pm-1am Sun (brunch noon-2.15pm). Closed mid June-mid Sept. **Credit** AmEx, DC, MC, V.

This charming café has a huge selection of quality teas, unusual tea cocktails and at least 20 types of coffee, but it's best known for its chocolate delectables: the owner belongs to the Chocolate Appreciation Society, and the café's *sette veli* chocolate cake once won the World Cake Championship. Hemingway's high tea (6-7.30pm) tempts with ten different sweet delights; there's also a Sunday brunch (book in advance).

Libreria Café La Cité

Borgo San Frediano 20r (055 210387/www.lacitelibreria.info). **Open** 10.30am-1am daily. **No credit cards**. **Map** p334 C1 ㉚

La Cité has given this part of the Oltrarno a true Left Bank feel. The mezzanine café area of this bookshop and cultural centre is in rustic reclaimed woods with metal bolts and serves home-baked cakes, freshly made fruit and veg juices and Fairtrade coffees. Afternoon and early-evening tastings of – mostly organic – wines, oils and cheeses from local producers are organised regularly, often with live jazz in the background. *See also p151.*

Il Rifrullo

Via San Niccolò 55r (055 2342621/www.ilrifrullo.com). **Open** 8am-2am daily. Closed 2wks Aug. **Credit** AmEx, DC, MC, V. **Map** p335 D5 ㉛

Set in peaceful San Niccolò, this long-time favourite of Florentines is decked out in pale stained woods and cool greens. The atmosphere is usually sleepy and laid-back during the day, but the mood mutates for the evening *aperitivo*, when the music comes on, the back rooms open to accommodate the crowds and plates of snacks and cocktails are served on the charming summer roof garden in warmer weather. Sunday brunch is another crowd-puller, with its full roasts and a bar groaning with miniature glasses of tiramisù, cheesecake and fruit salad.

Outside the City Gates

Area 51

Il Magnifico, Warner Village, via del Cavallaccio (335 8014085 mobile/www.area51.it). Bus 1. **Open** 8am-4am daily. **No credit cards**.

More 'internet' than 'café', Area 51 is the biggest gaming centre in the country. More than 40 PCs are set up for all the latest games, with the option to bring your own disc to be set up if the place doesn't already have it. *Photo p143.*

Libreria Café La Cité.

Gelaterie

Florentines like to claim that *gelato* was invented in the city, and, whether this is a delusional belief or not, it would be bad luck to end up with even a mediocre ice-cream in Florence. To find the best, look out for '*produzione proprio*', or '*artigianale*', as this means the ice-cream is home-made. In summer, many bars install ice-cream corners, with a small selection of locally made flavours. Some of the smaller places that make their own *gelato* close in winter, but it's still easy to find one open year-round on the main thoroughfares in the cold months, when hot fudge and chocolate sauces are often served on top.

Carabé

Via Ricasoli 60r, San Marco (055 289476). **Open** *Summer* 9am-1am daily. *Winter* 9am-8pm daily. Closed mid Dec-mid Jan. **No credit cards. Map** p335 A4 ㉜

The Sicilian owners of this *gelateria* near the Accademia are third-generation ice-cream makers and proud of their heritage. They excel in the island's specialities – one crunchy *granita* is flavoured with almond milk, fresh lemons are brought in weekly from Sicily to make a tangy ice-cream/sorbet cross-breed and the *cremolata* is made with the pulp of seasonal soft fruits. One of the few places in the city to offer authentic *cassata* (cream *gelato* pyramid blocks with candied fruit) and *cannoli* (the round ricotta-filled snaps immortalised as weapons in *The Godfather III*).

A brew with a view

La Terrazza, Rinascente.

The aesthetic elements of Florence have always been one of its greatest attributes; beauty abounds in and around the city, meaning that even the unspectacular cafés and bars often have views worth writing home about. In the centre, keeping coffee, lunch and tea breaks within sight of historic buildings, churches and art is a time-effective way to soak up the city's visual delights. And, luckily, there's a good sprinkling of ideally positioned bars.

The few tables outside **Noir** (*see p143*) come with a view of the precarious-looking houses on the ponte Vecchio, and the *Spring* and *Summer* statues at the north end of the elegant ponte Santa Trinità.

From the tables outside **Astor Caffè** (*see p141*) is a humbling ant's-eye view of the kaleidoscopic green, pink and white marble of the massive walls of the Duomo bearing down from its terracotta dome. For a bird's-eye view of the Cupola itself and of Giotto's Campanile, take the lift to **La Terrazza** café (*see p142*), up from the top floor of La Rinascente department store.

Cabiria (*see p144*) and **Caffè Ricchi** (*see p144*) both have tables overlooking the exquisite plain cream façade of Brunelleschi's Santo Spirito church. **Colle Bereto** (*see p141*) faces Palazzo Strozzi's monumental stones set with original iron tethering rings and embellished with the crescent moons of the Strozzi family crest. Also on view for contemporary art buffs is the bronze horse and cherub rider of sculptor Mario Ceroli.

In the cradle of Florence's 'alfresco art' square, piazza della Signoria, are **Caffè Rivoire** (*see p141*) and **Bar Perseo** (*see p141*). From Rivoire you get a head-on view of the famous clock tower of Palazzo Vecchio, with the copy of Michelangelo's *David* at its foot. Bar Perseo faces the city's most original landmark, the Loggia dei Lanzi, with Cellini's bronze masterpiece *Perseus* and Giambologna's ground-breaking *Rape of the Sabine Women*.

Meanwhile, on the outskirts of the city, the cafés and bars dotted on the hills at piazzale Michelangelo, Settignano and Fiesole afford fabulous views of the centre.

It's big decisions all round at **Grom**, with a wealth of tempting flavours.

Gelateria dei Neri

Via de' Neri 22r, Santa Croce (055 210034). **Open** *Summer* 11am-midnight daily. *Winter* 11am-midnight daily. **No credit cards. Map** p335 C4 ❸❸

A gem for those who want to sample the Florentine frozen assets but have an intolerance to milk – it's one of the few parlours to serve soya ice-cream alongside the classic creamy *gelati.*

Gold/La Carrozza

Piazza Pesce 3/5r, Duomo & Around (055 2396810). **Open** *Summer* 10am-midnight daily. *Winter* 10.30am-7.30pm Tue, Thur-Sun. **No credit cards. Map** p334 C3 ❸❹

On summer nights, crowds congregate at the hatch of this classic *gelateria* in a prime position between the ponte Vecchio and the Uffizi. Specialities are exotic seasonal fruit flavours, from papaya *gelato* to lime sorbet, but the coffee flavour is also a revelation – a small cup has similar properties to a double espresso.

Grom

Via del Campanile (corner of via delle Oche), Duomo & Around (055 216158/www.grom.it). **Open** *Summer* 10.30am-midnight daily. *Winter* 10.30am-11pm daily. **No credit cards. Map** p335 B4 ❸❺

Everything about this newcomer – and strong contender for best *gelateria* in Florence – is comfortingly traditional, from the limestone flagging and metal jars to the *gelataio*'s apron. Flavours of the month may be the refreshing milk and fresh mint in the summer, or zingy ginger (*zenzero*) in winter. Fortunately, the sensational Crema di Grom, made with organic eggs, soft cookies and Valrhona Ecuadorian chocolate, is served year-round.

Perchè No!

Via dei Tavolini 19r, Duomo & Around (055 239 8969/www.perchenofirenze.it). **Open** *Summer* 11am-midnight daily. *Winter* noon-7.30pm Mon, Wed-Sun. **No credit cards. Map** p334 C3 ❸❻

This is a favourite with the locals – many have been coming for generations. Not by chance, it is often cited as the best *gelateria* for the more traditional flavours – *crema* (vanilla), pistachio and chocolate.

Vestri

Borgo degli Albizi 11r, Santa Croce (055 2340374/www.vestri.it). **Open** *Summer* 10am-8pm daily. *Winter* 10am-8pm daily. Closed Aug. **Credit** DC, MC, V. **Map** p335 B5 ❸❼

Primarily a gourmet chocolate shop, in summer Vestri installs a few metal churns, from which are served up exquisite own-made ice-cream concoctions. The flavours are few but ingenious and adventurous – white chocolate with wild strawberries, chocolate and *peperoncino* (Italian chillies) and bitter chocolate with Cointreau.

Vivoli

Via Isola delle Stinche 7r, Santa Croce (055 292334/www.vivoli.it). **Open** *Summer* 7.30am-midnight Tue-Sun. *Winter* 7.30am-9pm Tue-Sun. Closed mid Aug. **No credit cards. Map** p335 C5 ❸❽

Local institution Vivoli has clung on jealously to its long-standing but increasingly threatened reputation as the best *gelateria* in Florence. The wickedly rich chocolate orange and divine *riso* (rice pudding) are still up there with the best of them. So too are its famous *semi-freddi* – which are creamier and softer than ordinary *gelato*.

Shops & Services

Florence is becoming increasingly fashion conscious – but don't worry, you can still buy Duomo-shaped chocs for your friends at home.

Save the Queen Circus. *See p151.*

Shopping in Florence is increasingly a 'painting by numbers' experience. The central streets were once like mini-villages, with a mishmash of shops – galleries, pharmacies, boutiques and bakeries – sat side by side. The influx of big designer names in upmarket areas (*see also p164* **Brand new**) has, however, created a multi-magnet effect, with shops of similar types being drawn to each other. This may have made shopping in the city less of an instantly ecletic experience, but it also makes it easy to head in the right direction (*see p155* **Where to shop**).

OPENING HOURS AND INFORMATION

Supermarkets and larger stores in the city centre tend to stay open throughout the day (*orario continuato*), but most shops still operate standard hours, closing at lunchtime and on Monday mornings. The standard opening times are 3.30pm to 7.30pm on Monday, and 9am to 1pm then 3.30pm to 7.30pm Tuesday to Saturday, with clothes shops sometimes opening around 10am. Food shops usually open earlier in the morning, close at 1pm and reopen at 5pm, and are closed Wednesday afternoons. Many of the central stores stay open for at least part of Sunday; several more open on the last Sunday of the month.

Hours alter slightly in mid June until the end of August, when most shops close on Saturday afternoons. Small shops tend to shut completely at some point during July or August for a week to a month. The opening times listed here apply most of the year – we have noted closures of more than two weeks whenever possible – but they can vary, particularly in the case of smaller shops. Visitors from outside the EU are entitled to a VAT rebate on purchases of goods over €160. Look for the 'tax-free' signs in shop windows; *see also p310*.

General

Department stores

COIN

Via de' Calzaiuoli 56r, Duomo & Around (055 280531/www.coin.it). **Open** *Jan-Mar* 10am-7.30pm Mon-Sat; 11am-7.30pm Sun. *Apr-Dec* 10am-8pm Mon-Sat; 11am-8pm Sun. **Credit** AmEx, DC, MC, V. **Map** p334 B3.

Furnishings are the strong point of this mid-range store, with bright contemporary homeware and regular consignments of Far Eastern furnishings.

Principe

Via del Sole 2, Santa Maria Novella (055 292764/ www.principedifirenze.com). **Open** 10.30am-7.30pm Mon; 9.30am-7.30pm Tue-Sat. *Sept-June* also 11am-7.30pm last Sun of mth. **Credit** AmEx, DC, MC. **Map** p334 B2.

Stuffy staff run this grande dame of a department store. Highlights include bedlinens in Egyptian cotton, bath and kitchen accessories and quality toiletries.

La Rinascente

Piazza della Repubblica 1, Duomo & Around (055 219113/www.rinascente.it). **Open** 10am-9pm Mon-Sat; 10.30am-8pm Sun. **Credit** AmEx, DC, MC, V. **Map** p334 B3.

This classic store has casual and designer clothes, the most extensive cosmetics and perfume department in the city, a decent lingerie section and smart bedding supplies. The rooftop café, reached via the top floor, has fantastic views (*see p142*).

Malls

I Gigli

Via San Quirico 165, Outside the City Gates (055 8969250/www.igigli.it). **Open** 9am-10pm daily. **Credit** Varies depending on shop.

An authentic covered mall about 30 minutes by bus from the centre of town, with over 120 Italian and international chains and restaurants.

Markets

See p150 **Playing the market**.

Specialist

Books & magazines

English-language

It's generally easy to find English-language titles in Florence, but you'll find that prices are higher than back home.

BM American British Bookstore

Borgo Ognissanti 4r, Santa Maria Novella (055 294575/www.bmbookshop.com). **Open** 9.30am-7.30pm Mon-Sat. **Credit** AmEx, DC, MC, V. **Map** p334 B1.

A good collection of books in English, many with Italian and Florentine themes. Some used books and a range of children's titles are stocked, as well as an odd array of gifts. *See also p176.*

McRae Books

Via de' Neri 32r, Santa Croce (055 2382456/ www.mcraebooks.com). **Open** 9am-7.30pm daily. **Credit** AmEx, MC, V. **Map** p335 C4.

This excellent bookstore specialises in English titles, from travel guides and maps to bestselling novels, art history, cookery and current affairs titles. There's also a small range of CDs, DVDs and used books.

General

Edison

Piazza della Repubblica 27r, Duomo & Around (055 213110/www.libreriaedison.it). **Open** 9am-midnight Mon-Sat; 10am-midnight Sun. **Credit** AmEx, DC, MC, V. **Map** p334 B3.

The best Shops

For gifts

Glamorous tassels from **Passamaneria Toscana** (*see p166*), hand-crafted ceramics from **Sbigoli Terrecotte** (*see p166*), marbled paper from **A Cozzi** (*see p162*), a hand-blown glass oil pourer from **Moleria Locchi** (*see p163*), or soaps, perfumes and tonics from the **Officina Profumo-Farmaceutica di Santa Maria Novella** (*see p164*).

For food and drink

Tiny pots of truffles and truffle butter from **Procacci** (*see p161*), chocolate Duomos and *David*s from **Dolceforte** (*see p161*), cheeses preserved in jars of oil from **Mariano Alimentari** (*see p161*), local pâtés and mostarda from **'Ino** (*see p161*), peppery extra-virgin olive oils from **I Sapori del Chianti** (*see p161*), and Chianti Classici, Super Tuscans and nut liqueurs to wash it all down from **Alessi** (*see p160*).

For clothing

Light crinkle cotton dresses for summer Flake ad moments from **Lisa Corti** (*see p154*), mix 'n' match men's shirts and ties at **AteSeta** (*see p153*), discount garb from **Il Guardaroba** (*see p153*), and full-priced designer credit card dynamite with attitude at **Luisa** (*see p153*).

For accessories

Shoe fetishes fulfilled with cheap chic from **Otisopse** (*see p159*), leather gloves in a range of colours to make Pantone proud from **Madova** (*see p155*), classic leather bags and cases in awe-inspiring settings at the **Scuola del Cuoio** (*see p157*), statement costume jewellery from **Angela Caputi** (*see p157*), and 1960s underwear from Florentine designer **Emilio Cavallini** (*see p157*).

Playing the market

Mercato Centrale.

Markets are a shopping staple for the inhabitants of Florence, a treasure trove for visitors and another good excuse for a day out. The annual arrival of the German Christmas market in piazza Santa Croce, the autumn farmers' market in piazza SS Annunziata and the book fair in piazza Santa Croce are greeted with as much excitement as they would have been centuries ago. Then there are the monthly markets to fill the gaps, as well as the weekly and the daily markets that appear in even the tiniest of squares to provide regular fixes of browsing opportunities.

In **piazza Santo Spirito** at the monthly flea market (8am-6pm, every 2nd Sun of mth) you can pick up old photos, furniture, frames and jewellery. Another monthly in the piazza is the **Fierucola** (8am-6pm, every 3rd Sun of mth), a farmers' market with stalls selling organic foods and wines, honey, handmade clothing and toys, cosmetics and natural medicines.

The biggest weekly event is a market held on the riverbanks in a park some way from the city centre, but worth making a morning of at the **Cascine** (8am-1pm, Tue). In the gardens just west of the city centre, hundreds of stalls line the main avenue, viale Lincoln, selling groceries, new clothes, agricultural supplies, toys and practically everything else that a market worth its salt should have. On Thursdays, the plant and flower market under the loggia of via Pellicceria (10am-7pm, though most stalls shut down at lunchtime) adds a welcome sweet-smelling green space to the city centre, albeit temporarily.

Piazza Santo Spirito has a small daily weekday morning market with stalls selling food and clothes, as do many city squares and corners, but for a cornucopia of sights, sounds and, most of all, smells, there's the 19th-century covered market in **piazza del Mercato Centrale** (7am-2pm, Mon-Sat and Sat afternoons; entrances on the piazza itself and on via del Ariento). Downstairs is packed with kiosks selling meats, fresh fish, cheeses and bakery goods, while upstairs is dedicated to stalls with pyramids of seasonal fruit and vegetables right out of the ground or straight off the trees. Foodies can also head to the **Sant'Ambrogio** market in piazza Ghiberti (7am-2pm, Mon-Sat) for cheap, fresh farmers' produce.

Snaking from piazza San Lorenzo around the church is the main **San Lorenzo** market (8.30am-7pm, Mon-Sat), a loud bustle of market-goers milling around the leather goods, clothes and souvenirs. Another busy central daily market is the **Mercato Nuovo** (9am-7pm, Mon-Sat), in the covered Loggia del Mercato Nuovo just off via Calimala. Also known as the Mercato del Porcellino in honour of the bronze boar statue whose nose you should rub if you want a return visit to Florence, this is a great place to find bags, scarves and pashminas, souvenirs and gifts. A much quieter experience on the other side of town is the flea market, the **Mercato delle Pulci**, in piazza dei Ciompi (9am-7pm, Mon-Sat) where you can browse through the bric-a-brac for that elusive antique find.

This multi-storey superstore sells books, maps, magazines, calendars and CDs. The travel section includes lots of guides in English. Internet terminals, a café and a lecture area are further attractions.

Feltrinelli International

Via Cavour 12-20r, San Marco (055 219524/ www.feltrinelli.it). **Open** 9am-7.30pm Mon-Sat. **Credit** AmEx, DC, MC, V. **Map** p335 A4.
This modern bookshop has strong art, photography and comic-book sections, plus a huge selection of titles in English, language-teaching books, original-language videos and a gift section.

Libreria Café La Cité

Via San Frediano 20r, Oltrarno (055 210387/ www.lacitelibreria.info). **Open** 10.30am-1am daily. **Credit** AmEx, MC, V. **Map** p334 C1.
As much of a cultural centre as a bookshop, La Cité organises creative writing sessions, readings, debates and presentations, as well as promoting young and new authors. Most activities are held in Italian, but international guest writers are occasionally invited. *See also p145.*

Libreria Martelli

Via de' Martelli 22r, Duomo & Around (055 2657603/www.libreriamartelli.it). **Open** 9am-8pm Mon-Sat; 10am-8pm Sun. **Credit** MC, V. **Map** p335 B4.
This big, light and airy store has an excellent range of books in various languages, including English. The selection of travel guides is particularly strong.

Specialist

Alinari

Largo Alinari 15, Santa Maria Novella (055 2395232/www.alinari.it). **Open** 9am-1pm, 2-6pm Mon-Fri; 10am-1pm, 2-6pm Sat. Closed 3wks Aug. **Credit** MC, V. **Map** p334 A2.
One of the world's first and most famous photographic firms, established in 1852. Photography books and exhibition catalogues are stock; prints can be ordered from its archives.

Fashion Room

Via de' Palchetti 3-3A, Santa Maria Novella (055 213270/www.fashionroom.it). **Open** 9.30am-1pm, 3-7.30pm Mon-Fri; 10am-1pm, 3-6pm Sat. **Credit** AmEx, DC, MC, V. **Map** p334 A2.
An unrivalled collection of books, catalogues and magazines on interior design, architecture and fashion, including hard-to-find limited-editions and coffee-table tomes.

Franco Maria Ricci/Babele

Via delle Belle Donne 41r, Santa Maria Novella (055 283312). **Open** 3.30-7.30pm Mon; 10am-1pm, 3.30-7.30pm Tue-Sat. **Credit** AmEx, DC, MC. **Map** p334 B2.
A delightful art bookshop and arts and crafts gallery stocking mainly limited editions, numbered prints and handmade stationery.

Libreria delle Donne

Via Fiesolana 2B, Santa Croce (055 240384). **Open** 3.30-7.30pm Mon; 9.30am-1pm, 3.30-7.30pm Tue-Fri. Closed Aug. **Credit** MC, V. **Map** p335 B5.
A good reference point for women in Florence, not just for its books but also for the useful noticeboard that has details on local activities.

Used

Paperback Exchange

Via dell Oche 4r, Duomo & Around (055 293460/ www.papex.it). **Open** 9am-7.30pm Mon-Fri; 10am-7.30pm Sat. Closed 2wks Aug. **Credit** AmEx, MC, V. **Map** p335 B5.
This old favourite stocks thousands of new and used English-language fiction and non-fiction titles, specialising in art, art history and Italian culture. The noticeboard has information about literary events, courses, accommodation and language lessons. Second-hand books can be traded.

Children

For children's toys, *see p176.*

Fashion

Children's clothes can be more expensive than the adult versions in Italy, so check the tags. Via Gioberti (Outside the City Gates) also has a concentration of children's clothing shops.

Petit Bateau

Via della Vigna Nuova 74r, Santa Maria Novella (055 215167/290457). **Open** 10am-7.30pm Mon-Sat. **Credit** AmEx, DC, MC, V. **Map** p334 B2.
This French chain sells well-made clothes in natural fibres with simple motifs. Adult sizes are available for some of the T-shirts. Surprisingly easy on the wallet.

Sarà

Via della Spada 42r, Santa Maria Novella (055 281048). **Open** 3.30-7.30pm Mon; 10am-1pm, 3.30-7.30pm Tue-Sat. **Credit** AmEx, MC, V. **Map** p334 B2.
Stylish maternity clothes in crinkled silks and cottons, plus baby and children's clothing and footwear.

Save the Queen Circus

Via de' Tornabuoni 49r, Santa Maria Novella (055 213231/www.savethequeen.com). **Open** 10am-7pm Mon-Sat, last Sun of mth. **Credit** AmEx, DC, MC, V. **Map** p334 B2.
A fantasy space for kids with multicoloured rocking horses and swings hanging from the ceilings. The brightly coloured clothes for girls are for modern-day princesses, with price tags to match. *Photo p148*

Electronics & photography

Bongi

Via Por Santa Maria 82-84r, Duomo & Around (055 2398811/www.otticabongi.com).

Open 3.30-7.30pm Mon; 10am-7.30pm Tue-Sat. **Credit** AmEx, DC, MC, V. **Map** p334 C3.
One of the best-stocked photographic shops in the city centre, offering a wide range of new and used equipment for sale, digital photo reprographics services and print developing.

Foto Ottica Fontani

Viale Strozzi 18-20A, San Lorenzo (055 470981/ www.otticafontani.com). **Open** 9am-1pm, 3-7.30pm Mon-Sat. **Credit** V. **Map** p334 B3.
Photography enthusiasts in Florence make a beeline for this shop, where the prices for processing and developing are the lowest in town.

Repairs

Meridianet

Borgo San Frediano 5r, Oltrarno (055 2645507/ info@meridianet.it). **Open** 11am-1pm, 3.30-9pm Mon-Fri; 3.30-9pm Sat, Sun. **No credit cards.** **Map** p334 C1.
Services include home visits for computer technical support. There's also an internet point inside the store. Prices tend to be very fair.

Fashion

For vintage clothing, *see p158* **Cast-off culture**.

Designer

For high-profile openings, *see p164* **Brand new**.

Gerard Loft

Via de' Pecori 36r, Duomo & Around (055 282491/ www.gerardloft.com). **Open** 2.30-7.30pm Mon; 10am-7.30pm Tue-Sat. **Credit** AmEx, DC, MC, V. **Map** p334 B3.
Hip clothing with men's and women's lines by the likes of Marc Jacobs, Chloé and Helmut Lang.

Luisa

Via Roma 19-21r, Duomo & Around (055 217826/ www.luisaviaroma.com). **Open** 10am-7.30pm Mon-Sat; 11am-7pm Sun. **Credit** AmEx, DC, MC, V. **Map** p334 B3.
Renowned for its inventive window displays, this multi-level store features designer collections from Issey Miyake, Roberto Cavalli and others.

Matucci

Via del Corso 71r, Duomo & Around (055 2396420). **Open** 3.30-8pm Mon; 10am-7.30pm Tue-Sat. **Credit** AmEx, DC, MC, V. **Map** p334 B4.
Collections by Armani, Diesel, Boss and Versace. Womenswear is just down the road at no.46r.

Michele Negri

Via de' Pescioni 1r, Duomo & Around (055 212781/ www.michelenegri.com). **Open** 10.30am-7.30pm daily. **Credit** AmEx, DC, MC, V. **Map** p334 B3.
The new flagship store of one of Florence's most famous home-grown menswear designers. Suits and shirts are fairly staid but well made – the rarity here is the bar within the shop. Womenswear is also sold.
Other locations Via Roma 24r, Duomo & Around (055 216524); via Porta Rossa 54r, Duomo & Around (055 215606).

Miu Miu

Via Roma 8r, Duomo & Around (055 2608931/ www.miumiu.com). **Open** 10am-7.30pm Mon-Sat; 10am-7pm Sun. **Credit** AmEx, DC, MC, V. **Map** p334 B3.
Miuccia Prada's concession to the younger and less moneyed fans of her feminine style.

Raspini

Via Roma 25-29r, Duomo & Around (055 213077/ www.raspini.com). **Open** 3.30-7.30pm Mon; 9.30am-1.30pm, 3.30-7.30pm Tue-Fri; 9.30am-7.30pm Sat. **Credit** AmEx, DC, MC, V. **Map** p334 B3.
A one-stop shop for Romeo Gigli, Armani, Prada, Miu Miu, Anna Molinari, D&G and many others.
Other locations Via Por Santa Maria 72r, Duomo & Around (055 213901); via Martelli 3-7, Duomo & Around (055 2398336).

Discount

Il Guardaroba

Via Giuseppe Verdi 28r, Santa Croce (055 2478250). **Open** 3.30-7.30pm Mon; 9.30am-7.30pm Tue-Sat. **Credit** AmEx, DC, MC, V. **Map** p335 C5.
Il Guardaroba deals in designer end-of-lines and past seasons' stock with good deals to be had.
Other locations throughout the city.

General

A Piedi Nudi nel Parco

Borgo degli Albizi 46r, Santa Croce (055 2340768). **Open** noon-8pm Mon; 10am-8pm Tue-Sat. **Credit** AmEx, DC, MC, V. **Map** p335 B5.
These sister shops take their name from the 1960s film *Barefoot in the Park*, but the style is more neo-1970s, with beautifully cut, long, fluid and asymmtrical styles with a decorative twist, in understated colours and high-quality fabrics.
Other locations Borgo San Jacopo 38r, Oltrarno (055 2658221).

AteSeta

Via de' Calzaiuoli 1r, Duomo & Around (055 214959/www.ateseta.com). **Open** 9.30am-8pm daily. **Credit** AmEx, DC, MC, V. **Map** p334 C3.
Row upon row of mix 'n' match men's shirts and ties.
Other locations Via Porta Rossa 21r, Duomo & Around (055 283301); via Cerretani 33r, Duomo & Around (055 215085); via Por Santa Maria 1r, Duomo & Around (055 2382851).

BP Studio

Via della Vigna Nuova 15r, Santa Maria Novella (055 213243/www.bpstudio.it). **Open** 3-7pm Mon; 10am-2pm, 3-7pm Tue-Sat. **Credit** AmEx, DC, MC, V. **Map** p334 B2.

Delicate knitwear, rosebud-edged chiffon skirts and mohair stoles from young designers are shown at this upmarket but youthful store.

Eredi Chiarini

Via Roma 16r, Duomo & Around (055 284478/ www.eredichiarini.com). **Open** 3.30-7.30pm Mon; 10am-7.30pm Tue-Sat. **Credit** AmEx, DC, MC, V. **Map** p334 B3.

A favourite with Florentines, who love its effortlessly stylish polos, softly tailored jackets and cool wool suits. Womenswear is nearby at via Porta Rossa 39r.

Ethic

Borgo degli Albizi 37r, Santa Croce (055 2344413). **Open** 3-8pm Mon, Sun; 10am-8pm Tue-Sat. **Credit** AmEx, DC, MC, V. **Map** p335 B5.

Unique clothing store with low to mid-range prices as well as a cutting-edge selection of CDs and a home section with curtains, cushions and accessories.

Lisa Corti

Via de' Bardi 58, Oltrarno (055 2645600/www.lisa corti.com). **Open** 3.30-7.30pm Mon; 10am-7.30pm Tue-Sat; 11am-1.30pm, 2.30-7pm Sun. **Credit** MC, V. **Map** p334 D3.

Gorgeous shirts and dresses in printed crinkle cottons, pleated two-tone scarves and silk bags. **Other locations** Via San Niccolò 97r, Oltrarno (055 2001200); piazza Ghiberti 33, Santa Croce (055 2645600).

Liu Jo

Via Calimala 14r, Duomo & Around (055 216164/ www.liujo.it). **Open** 3.30-7.30pm Mon; 10am-7.30pm Tue-Sat; 11am-1.30pm, 2.30-7pm Sun. **Credit** AmEx, DC, MC, V. **Map** p334 B3.

Net dresses, pretty vest-tops, dressy combat gear and high wooden mules from this hip designer. **Other locations** Via della Vigna Nuova, Santa Maria Novella (055 2654692).

Massimo Rebecchi

Via della Vigna Nuova 26r, Santa Maria Novella (055 268053). **Open** 3.30-7.30pm Mon, last Sun of mth; 10am-1.30pm, 3-7.30pm Tue-Fri; 10am-7.30pm Sat. **Credit** AmEx, DC, MC, V. **Map** p334 B2.

Quality jumpers and casual suits for men and women.

Miss Macis

Borgo Pinti 38r, Santa Croce. **Open** 3.30-7.30pm Mon; 10am-7.30pm Tue-Sat. **Credit** AmEx, DC, MC, V. **Map** p334 C3.

Women's and children's dresses, hats and belts in fun prints with flowers, dots and stripes.

Miss Trench

Via Porta Rossa 16r, Duomo & Around (055 287601). **Open** 3.30-7.30pm Mon; 10am-7.30pm Tue-Sat. **Credit** AmEx, DC, MC, V. **Map** p334 C3.

Rock-chick chic, plus a smattering of Miss Sixty accessories, such as bags and sequinned belts.

Quelle Tre

Via de' Pucci 43r, Duomo & Around (055 293284). **Open** 10am-7.30pm Mon-Sat; 10am-7pm Sun. **Credit** AmEx, DC, MC, V. **Map** p335 A4.

Graziella Jewels Sculptures. *See p157.*

Where to shop

If you're aiming to pep up your wardrobe, Italian-style, go to **via de' Tornabuoni** and **via della Vigna Nuova**, which boast the lion's share of the designer big guns; head for the main streets around **piazza della Repubblica** for the chains such as Benetton, Sisley and Zara; go east of the Duomo to **via de' Neri** or north to **borgo San Lorenzo** and the **San Lorenzo market** for bargain-basement clothes shops; and to **via Porta Rossa** or over a bridge to **borgo San Jacopo** and the surrounding streets for independent boutiques.

Traditional jewellers are famously to be found on the **ponte Vecchio** in tiny 16th-century shops (be sure to pass by at night to see them closed up with fabulous wooden and wrought-iron shutters), and also in **via Por Santa Maria**, while more contemporary and designer pieces can be found in the streets and *lungarni* between here and **via de' Tornabuoni. Via del Corso**, **via Porta Rossa** and **piazza del Duomo** will kit you out with footwear, while **via del Parione** is a good place to start for quality leather goods.

Via Maggio and **via de' Serragli** are lined with wonderful antiques shops, as is **via de' Fossi**, which has also become the hub for a fast-growing trend in the city: contemporary interior design studios. The side streets around **piazza Santo Spirito** are home to what is left of a once full well of artisan craftsmen carrying out their age-old skills of furniture and picture restoration, marquetry, inlay, gilding, carving, bookbinding and paper-making.

Kooky clothing and accessories in colourful combinations of different textures and prints.
Other locations Via Santo Spirito 42r, Oltrarno (055 219374); dressmaking by appointment at via de' Giandonati 15, Outside the City Gates (055 2321214).

Replay

Via de' Pecori 7-9r, Duomo & Around (055 293041). **Open** 10am-7.30pm Mon-Sat; 2.30-7.30pm Sun. **Credit** AmEx, DC, MC, V. **Map** p334 B3.
Men's and women's casualwear par excellence.
Other locations Via Por Santa Maria 27r, Duomo & Around (055 287950).

Sandro P 2

Via de' Tosinghi 7r, Duomo & Around (055 215063). **Open** 3-7.30pm Mon; 10am-1pm, 3.30-7.30pm Tue-Sat. **Credit** AmEx, DC, MC, V. **Map** p334 B3.
One of Florence's hippest men's and unisex clothing shops, with the latest from New York and London.

Tommy Hilfiger

Piazza Antinori 3d, Duomo & Around (055 2741041). **Open** 3-7pm Mon; 10am-7pm Tue-Sat. **Credit** AmEx, DC, MC, V. **Map** p334 B3.
The bright king of casual for men and women; yet there's nothing casual about this new shop, with its swanky sofas, chandeliers and glass skylight.

Fashion accessories & services

Cleaning & repairs

Lucy & Rita

Via de' Serragli 71r, Oltrarno (055 224536). **Open** 7am-1pm, 2.30-7pm Mon-Fri. Closed 2wks Aug. **Credit** AmEx, DC, MC, V. **Map** p334 D1.
A generally reliable dry-cleaners in Oltrarno, which also offers regular service washes.

Silvana e Ombretta Riparazioni

Borgo San Frediano 38r, Oltrarno (368 7571418 mobile). **Open** 9am-noon, 3.30-6.30pm Mon-Fri. Closed Aug. **No credit cards**. **Map** p334 C1.
Repairs and alterations to clothes.

Vincenzo Arezzo

Via delle Terme 8r, Duomo & Around (055 280177). **Open** 10am-12.30pm, 3-7pm Mon-Fri. **No credit cards**. **Map** p334 C3.
Shoe repairs, though usually not while you wait.

Walter's Silver & Gold

Borgo de' Greci 11Cr, Santa Croce (055 2396678/ www.waltersilverandgold.com). **Open** 9.30am-5.30pm daily. Closed Nov. **Credit** AmEx, DC, MC, V. **Map** p335 C4.
English-speaking Walter is able to repair all types of jewellery. Italian-made chains, bracelets, earrings and rings are also sold.

Wash & Dry

Via Ghibellina 143r, Santa Croce (055 580480/ www.washedry.it). **Open** 8am-10pm daily. **No credit cards**. **Map** p334 A3.
A self-service launderette chain that has eight centrally located branches.

Gloves

Madova

Via de' Guicciardini 1r, Oltrarno (055 2396526/ www.madova.com). **Open** 9.30am-7pm Mon-Sat. **Credit** AmEx, MC, V. **Map** p334 C3.
Madova makes gloves in every imaginable style and colour in its factory, just behind this tiny shop.

Eat, Drink, Shop

Jewellery

The **ponte Vecchio** and **via Por Santa Maria** are the places to go for traditional and antique gold and silver jewellery.

Angela Caputi

Borgo SS Apostoli, Duomo & Around (055 292993/ www.angelacaputi.com). **Open** 10am-1pm, 3.30-7.30pm Mon-Sat. **Credit** AmEx, DC, MC, V. **Map** p334 C3.
Colourful costume jewellery in plastics, resin and crystal. Styles are exuberant, with ethnic, art deco and psychedelic patterns.

Antica Orologeria Nuti

Via della Scala 10r, Santa Maria Novella (055 294594). **Open** 4-7pm Mon; 9am-12.30pm, 4-7pm Tue-Sat. Closed Aug. **Credit** AmEx, DC, MC, V. **Map** p334 B2.
Fabulous antique and reproduction art deco and art nouveau jewellery, plus an eclectic collection of lantern, long-case, bracket and mantel clocks.

Aprosio e Co

Via Santo Spirito 11, Oltrarno (055 290534/www. aprosio.it). **Open** 9.30am-1.30pm, 3-7pm Mon-Sat. **Credit** AmEx, DC, MC, V. **Map** p334 C2.
An aloof dog guards the intricate necklaces, bracelets, earrings, evening bags and belts, all made from tiny glass beads, at this sleek showroom.

Graziella Jewels Sculptures

Lungarno degli Acciaiuoli 74r, Duomo & Around (055 211498/www.gruppograziella.it). **Open** 10am-7pm daily. **Credit** AmEx, DC, MC, V. **Map** p334 C3.
This shop is so stunning that it outshines even its sumptuous jewellery. The spiralling silver, silver gilt and gold chunky swirl rings and flower bracelets encrusted with tiny diamonds and semi-precious stones are shown in glass 'safes' set into black walls, while a gold resin bench inset with fibre optics ripples down the middle of the room. *Photo p154.*

Parenti

Via de' Tornabuoni 93r, Santa Maria Novella (055 214438/www.parentifirenze.it). **Open** 3-7pm Mon; 9am-1pm, 3-7pm Tue-Sat. Closed Aug. **Credit** AmEx, DC, MC, V. **Map** p334 B2.
A slightly daunting-looking emporium with Baccarat rings, art deco pieces and 1950s Tiffany jewellery.

Pomellato

Via de' Tornabuoni 89-91r, Santa Maria Novella (055 288530/www.pomellato.it). **Open** 10am-7pm Mon-Sat. **Credit** AmEx, DC, MC, V. **Map** p334 B2.
The gilt ceiling in this swish shop reflects a golden glow on to the cabinets. Within them are rings with gems the size and colours of fruit gums, contemporary watches and the Dodo line of animal pendants.

Lingerie & underwear

Emilio Cavallini

Via della Vigna Nuova 24r, Santa Maria Novella (055 2382789/www.emiliocavallini.com). **Open** 3-7pm Mon; 10am-7pm Tue-Sat. Closed 2wks Aug. **Credit** AmEx, DC, MC, V. **Map** p334 B2.
Cavallini's trademark wacky tights are stocked here, plus lines of black and white clothing, and lingerie with Warhol Marilyn and motif prints.

Intimissimi

Via de' Calzaiuoli 99r, Duomo & Around (055 2302609/www.intimissimi.it). **Open** 10.30am-8pm Mon; 9.30am-8pm Tue-Sat; 10.30am-8pm Sun. **Credit** AmEx, MC, V. **Map** p334 B3.
Well-priced cotton lingerie is the speciality at Intimissimi, though there are also jersey vests and trousers, silk satin pyjamas and boa-trimmed tops.
Other locations Via de' Panzani 22, Santa Maria Novella (055 2608636); piazza Madonna degli Aldobrandini 3, San Lorenzo (055 210540).

La Perla

Via della Vigna Nuova 17-19r, Santa Maria Novella (055 217070/www.laperla.com). **Open** 3-7.30pm Mon; 10am-2pm, 3-7.30pm Tue-Sat. **Credit** AmEx, MC, V. **Map** p334 B2.
Luxury lingerie, swimwear and boudoir apparel, in pastel silks, devoré and handmade lace.

Luggage & bags

Il Bisonte

Via del Parione 31r, Santa Maria Novella (055 215722/www.ilbisonte.net). **Open** 9.30am-7pm Mon-Sat. **Credit** AmEx, DC, MC, V. **Map** p334 B2.
A renowned, long-established outlet for top-tier soft leather bags and accessories and rugged cases.

Bojola

Via de' Rondinelli 25r, Duomo & Around (055 211155/www.bojola.it). **Open** 3.30-7.30pm Mon; 9am-7.30pm Tue-Sat. **Credit** AmEx, DC, MC, V. **Map** p334 B2.
Top-notch craftsmanship and high-quality hides add up to the city's best classic-style leather goods.

Coccinelle

Via Por Santa Maria 49r, Duomo & Around (055 2398782/www.coccinelle.com). **Open** 10.30am-7.30pm daily. **Credit** AmEx, DC, MC, V. **Map** p334 C3.
Smart, contemporary leather bags in seasonal colours, crafted in smooth durable leather.

Scuola del Cuoio

Via San Giuseppe 5r, Santa Croce (055 244533/ www.leatherschool.com). **Open** 9.30am-6pm Mon-Sat; 10am-6pm Sun. **Credit** AmEx, DC, MC, V. **Map** p335 C5.
At this leather school in the cloisters of Santa Croce (*see p104*), you can watch the craftsmen making bags and accessories. The prices add further appeal.

Segue

Via degli Speziali 6r, Duomo & Around (055 288949/ www.segue.it). **Open** 10am-7.30pm Mon-Sat; 1-7.30pm Sun. **Credit** AmEx, DC, MC, V. **Map** p334 B3.
The full Benetton range of smart bags and luggage, plus seasonal accessories, such as funky umbrellas.

Cast-off culture

Until very recently, fashion-conscious Italians wouldn't have been seen dead in second-hand clothes. Charity shop chic is still considered well beyond the pale, but Florentines have finally embraced cast-off culture in a suitably snobby form: vintage. Perhaps partly thanks to the Hollywood craze for vintage Valentino, this trend has caught on in such a big way in image-obsessed Florence that the city now hosts the biggest fair of vintage pieces in Italy, twice yearly in February and July at the Stazione Leopolda (055 2466198).

One designer who was way ahead of the game was **Elio Ferraro**. His shop in Santa Maria Novella (via del Parione 47r, 055 290425, www.elioferraro.com) stocks vintage designer gear and furnishings at heart-stopping prices, sourced from Ferraro's extensive worldwide contacts. Clothes may be by Chanel, Dior or Schiaparelli, or more recent design divas like Romeo Gigli and Vivienne Westwood, while the eccentric selection of original 1950s and '60s furniture and accessories includes pieces by icons Fornasetti, Giò Ponti and Ettore Sottsass.

A whole clutch of new shops has recently opened, to join the few veterans. **Boutique Nadine** (lungarno degli Acciaiuoli 22r, 055 287851) holds vintage 1940s and '50s stock, including Gucci bags, Louis Vuitton trunks, Pucci dresses and costume jewellery, as well as some old but unused stock, probably dug out from dusty storerooms and still in the original packaging. Relative newcomer **Maison Dumitru** (borgo Pinti 25r, 055 7189417) sells more obscure-name authentic vintage clothing and accessories and nearby **Soqquadro** (borgo Pinti 13r, 055 2347502) is a great place to source 1960s furniture, lighting and retro homewares.

Elio Ferraro.

The resident kitten in **Ceri Vintage** (via de' Serragli 26r, 055 217978) plays in a setting resembling Breakfast at Tiffany's, with 1960s prints, posters and postcards, leather suitcases and chic cocktail dresses. Round the corner, **Pitti Vintage** (sdrucciolo de' Pitti 19r, 055 2302676, www.pittivintage.it), seems to have a near monopoly on the attic and wardrobe clear-outs of classy Florentines, with regularly replenished rails of clothing dating back as far as the early 1900s. Some 'vintage' pieces, though, date from eras as recent as the 1980s.

Other shops are taking more liberties with their interpretation of 'vintage', and such is the success of this retro revisit that even designer shops are jumping on the bandwagon. Raspini Vintage (via Calimaruzza 17r, www.raspinivintage.it) has big savings on previous seasons' designer stock from the main Raspini stores (*see p153*).

Shoes

Bologna

Piazza del Duomo 13-15r, Duomo & Around (055 290545). **Open** 9.30am-7.30pm Mon-Sat; 3-7.30pm Sun. **Credit** AmEx, DC, MC, V. **Map** p335 B4.
Weird and wonderful men's and women's styles at Florence's favourite shoe store.

Calvani

Via degli Speziali 7r, Duomo & Around (055 2654043). **Open** 2.30-7.30pm Mon; 10am-7.30pm Tue-Sat; 3-7pm Sun. **Credit** AmEx, DC, MC, V. **Map** p334 B3.
Men's and women's shoes in hip styles and colours from young designers such as Roberto del Carlo.

Divarese

Piazza del Duomo 47r, Duomo & Around (055 212890). **Open** 9am-7.30pm Mon-Sat; 11.30am-6.30pm Sun. **Credit** AmEx, DC, MC, V. **Map** p335 B4.
Well-made, mid-range shoes for men and women.

Geox

Via Panzani 4r, Duomo & Around (055 283606/ www.geox.it). **Open** 10am-7.30pm Mon-Sat; 11am-7.30pm Sun. **Credit** AmEx, DC, MC, V. **Map** p334 B3.
The 'breathing' shoes that have taken the footwear market by storm; good for traipsing around the city.
Other locations Via Calimala 11r, Duomo & Around (055 2645016).

Marco Candido

Piazza del Duomo 5r, Duomo & Around (055 215342). **Open** 3-7.30pm Mon; 10am-7.30pm Tue-Sat; noon-7.30pm Sun. Closed Sun Feb, July, Aug. **Credit** AmEx, DC, MC, V. **Map** p335 B4.
Sexy but stylish modern shoes and boots for women, and classic but modern shoes for men.

Otisopse

Via Porta Rossa 13r, Duomo & Around (055 2396717). **Open** 2-8pm Mon; 10am-1pm, 2-7.30pm Tue-Sat; 11am-7.30pm Sun. **Credit** AmEx, DC, MC, V. **Map** p335 B4.
Wearable styles for men and women all at €59. There are mocassins, simple pumps and courts, and the odd find from Hobbs. The outlet at piazza N Sauro 17r stocks previous seasons' stock for even less.
Other locations Via de' Neri 58r 14r, Santa Croce Duomo & Around (055 2645036).

Peppe Peluso

Via del Corso 5-6r, Duomo & Around (055 268283). **Open** 2-8pm Mon; 10am-8pm Tue-Sat; 11am-7.30pm Sun. **Credit** AmEx, DC, MC, V. **Map** p335 B4.
A pair of shoes or boots from the vast (men's and women's) ranges here may or may not last the season, but at these bargain prices, who cares? The branch opposite (no.6r) has even cheaper footwear.

Stefano Bemer

Borgo San Frediano 143r, Oltrarno (055 222558/ www.stefanobemer.it). **Open** 9am-1pm, 3.30-7.30pm Mon-Sat. Closed Aug. **Credit** AmEx, DC, MC, V. **Map** p334 C1.

A world of wine: **Obsequium**. *See p160.*

Well-heeled Florentine men come here for handmade luxury shoes. The branch does a ready-to-wear line.
Other location Via Camaldoli 10r (055 222462).

Food & drink

For markets, *see p150* **Playing the market**.
For takeaway roasts, *see pp120-139* Rosticcerie.

Bakeries

Focacceria Pugi

Piazza San Marco 10, San Marco (055 280981/ www.focacceria-pugi.it). **Open** 7.45am-8pm Mon-Sat. **Credit** MC, V. **Map** A4.
An institution since 1924, and justly famed for its *schiacciata* – a delicious flat bread with olive oil or grapes.
Other locations Via San Gallo 62r, San Lorenzo (055 475975); viale de Amicis 49r, Outside the City Gates (055 669666).

Il Forno di Stefano Galli

Via Faenza 39r, San Lorenzo (055 215314). **Open** 7am-8pm daily. **No credit cards. Map** p334 A3.
Great for early-morning pastries and brioches.
Other locations throughout the city.

Forno Top

Via della Spada 23r, Santa Maria Novella (055 212461). **Open** 7.30am-1.30pm, 5-7.30pm Mon-Sat. **No credit cards. Map** p334 B2.

Tasty sandwiches, hot focaccia, fabulous carrot or chocolate and pear cakes, and seasonal specialities. **Other locations** Via Orsanmichele 8r, Duomo & Around (055 216564).

Sartoni

Via della Spada 24r, Duomo & Around (055 212570). **Open** 7.30am-1.30pm, 5-7.30pm Mon-Sat. **Credit** AmEx, MC, V. **Map** p335 B4.
A central pit stop stocking slices of delicious hot pizza, filled focaccia and apple pies.

Drinks

For more on wine, *see pp45-48.* Most wine bars (*see pp120-139*) also sell by the bottle to take away; for wineries out of town, *see p258* **Fine vines**.

Alessi

Via delle Oche 27r, Duomo & Around (055 214966/ www.enotecaalessi.it). **Open** 9am-1pm, 3.30-7.30pm Mon-Sat. **Credit** AmEx, DC, MC, V. **Map** p335 B4.
This fabulous *enoteca* is piled high with cakes, biscuits and chocs. Coffee is ground on the spot.

Millesimi

Borgo Tegolaio 35r, Oltrarno (055 2654675/ www.millesimi.it). **Open** 2-8pm Mon; 11am-8pm Mon-Fri. Closed 2wks Aug. **Credit** AmEx, MC, V. **Map** p334 D2.
Home to one of the biggest selections in town, Millesimi offers a wide range of wines from Piemonte as well as Tuscan labels, and has the best choice of wines from France (the owner is French).

Obsequium

Borgo San Jacopo 17, Oltrarno (055 216849). **Open** 10.30am-7.30pm Mon-Sat. **Credit** AmEx, MC, V. **Map** p334 C2.
A treasure trove for wine-lovers, in a 12th-century tower. As well as an incredible cellar of fine and everyday wines, spirits and liqueurs, the place stocks all manner of drink-themed gadgets. *Photo p159.*

General

A clutch of new mini-supermakets has sprung up around the city centre, including on via Romana, corso dei Tintori and around the San Lorenzo market. Some of the best and most convenient include **Esselunga** (via Pisana 130-132, Outside the City Gates, 055 706556), **Pegna** (via dello Studio 8, Duomo & Around, 055 282701), **Margherita Conad** (via L Alamanni 2-8r, Santa Maria Novella, 055 211544) and **Standa** (via Pietrapiana 42-44, Santa Croce, 055 2347856).

Pâtisseries

Most *pasticcerie* serve breakfast, coffee and snacks, plus takeaway cakes and savouries.

Dolcissimo.

Bottega della Frutta

Via de' Federighi 31r, Santa Maria Novella (055 2398590). **Open** 8am-7.30pm Mon, Tue, Thur-Sat; 8am-1.30pm Wed. Closed Aug. **Credit** MC, V. **Map** p334 B2.
Alongside fruit and vegetables, this charming shop sells wines, vintage balsamic vinegars, truffle-scented oils and speciality sweets. You'll need to be prepared to queue, however.

Dolci e Dolcezze

Piazza Beccaria 8r, Santa Croce (055 2345458). **Open** 8.30am-8pm Tue-Sat; 9am-1pm, 4.30-7.30pm Sun. Closed 2wks Aug. **No credit cards**.
This pâtisserie is famous for its delectable, flourless chocolate cake, but you may also be tempted by the strawberry meringue. Savouries are just as good.

I Dolci di Patrizio Cosi

Borgo degli Albizi 11r, Santa Croce (055 2480367). **Open** 8.30am-7.30pm Tue-Sat; 9am-1pm Sun. Closed Aug. **No credit cards**. **Map** p335 B5.
A huge range of sweet treats. Delicious hot dough-nuts (*bomboloni caldi*) are served at 5pm.

Dolcissimo

Via Maggio 61r, Oltrarno (055 2396268/ www.caffeitaliano.it). **Open** 8am-1pm, 2-8pm Tue-Sat; 9am-2pm Sun. **Credit** MC, V. **Map** p334 D2.
A delightful shop from another age. Exquisite chocolates are displayed in gilded cabinets, and glass cake stands hold delicious-looking concoctions, including an unmissable chocolate and pear cake.

Sugar e Spice

Via de' Servi 43r, Duomo & Around (055 290263). **Open** 10am-7.30pm Mon-Fri. Closed Aug. **No credit cards. Map** p334 A4.
Own-made, American-style sweets and cakes, including muffins. There's also a bar.

Specialist

Dolceforte

Via della Scala 21, Santa Maria Novella (055 219116/www.dolceforte.it). **Open** 10am-1pm, 3.30-8pm Mon-Sat. **Credit** AmEx, MC, V. **Map** p334 B2.
Connoisseur chocolates, plus novelty-shaped treats such as chocolate Duomos. In hot months, melting stock is replaced with jams, sugared almond flowers and jars of *gianduja*, a chocolate hazelnut spread.

'Ino

For listings, *see p123.*
A gourmet's dream kitchen-cupboard store, with wines, chocolates, cured meats, cheeses and pots of pâtés, chutneys and jams in unusual flavours.

Mariano Alimentari

Via del Parione 19r, Santa Maria Novella (055 214067). **Open** 8am-3pm, 5-7.30pm Mon-Fri; 8am-3pm Sat. Closed 3wks Aug. **Credit** AmEx, MC, V. **Map** p334 C2.
This tiny, rustic food shop-cum-sandwich bar offers focaccia filled with marinated aubergines and oil-preserved pecorino, and an array of delicacies. Have a coffee at the bar or in the vaulted wine cellar.

L'Olandese Volante

Via San Gallo 44r, San Lorenzo (055 473240). **Open** 10am-1pm, 3.30-8pm Mon-Sat. Closed 3wks Aug. **Credit** MC, V. **Map** p335 A4.
Northern European specialities, including Dutch cheeses with cumin, mustard seeds or herbs, smoked herrings, gourmet chocs and caramel-filled wafers.

Olio e Convivium

Via Santo Spirito 4, Oltrarno (055 2658198/ www.conviviumfirenze.it). **Open** 10am-2.30pm Mon; 10am-2.30pm, 5.30-10.30pm Tue-Sat. **Credit** AmEx, MC, V. **Map** p334 C2.
A wonderful place for Tuscan olive oils and wines, sweet and savoury preserves and superlative treats, although you're likely to pay more here than at the various food markets in the city. There's also a restaurant/wine bar (*see p133*).

Peter's Tea House

Piazza San Pancrazio 2r, Santa Maria Novella (055 2670620/www.peters-teahouse.it). **Open** 3.30-7pm Mon; 10am-1pm, 3.30-7pm Tue-Sat. Closed 3wks Aug. **Credit** AmEx, MC, V. **Map** p334 B2.
Hundreds of different types of tea from around the world, alongside biscuits to dunk in them and a range of tea-themed gift sets.

Procacci

Via de' Tornabuoni 64r, Duomo & Around (055 211656). **Open** 10.30am-8pm Mon-Sat. **Credit** AmEx, MC, V. **Map** p334 B2/C2.
Famous for its truffle panini, Procacci also sells the 'white gold' and its black cousin. Other nice gifts are the chocs in Duomo-shaped boxes. *Photos p162-63.*

I Sapori del Chianti

Via de' Servi 10, San Marco (055 2382071/www. isaporidelchianti.it). **Open** 10.30am-8pm daily. **Credit** AmEx, MC, V. **Map** p334 B2.
The 'flavours of Chianti' sold here come in the form of wines, grappas, olive oils and salamis, plus jars of pesto, condiments and vegetables in olive oil.

Sugar Blues

Via dei Serragli 57r, Oltrarno (055 268378). **Open** 9am-1.30pm, 4.30-8pm Mon-Fri; 9am-1.30pm Sat. *Sept-June* also 4.30-8pm Sat. **Credit** MC, V. **Map** p334 D1.
A great source of organic health foods and produce, eco-friendly detergents and ethical beauty products.
Other locations Via XXVII Aprile 46-48r, San Lorenzo (055 483666).

Vestri

Borgo degli Albizi 11r, Santa Croce (055 2340374/ www.vestri.it). **Open** 10.30am-8pm Mon-Sat. Closed Aug. **Credit** MC, V. **Map** p335 B5.
Handmade chocolates with chilli pepper, cinnamon and more prosaic fillings, as well as a full range of pralines and bars. The upmarket shop is beautifully designed to evoke a luxurious experience all-round, and it's an excellent bet for gifts for sweet-toothed friends. Flavoured hot chocolates are served in winter, with rich ice-creams the speciality in summer. *See also pp146-147* Gelaterie.

Known for its truffle-based offerings, **Procacci** is also a draw for the sweet-toothed. *See p161.*

Gifts & souvenirs

Handmade marble paper

A Cozzi

Via del Parione 37r, Santa Maria Novella (055 294968). **Open** 3.30-7.30pm Mon; 10am-1pm, 3.30-7.30pm Tue-Sat. **Credit** AmEx, DC, MC, V. **Map** p334 B2/C2.
A bookbinder's workshop and showroom with a wonderful selection of books with swirled-coloured paper covers, and some bound in leather.

Giulio Giannini e Figlio

Piazza Pitti 36r, Oltrarno (055 212621/www.giulio giannini.it). **Open** 10am-7.30pm Mon-Sat; 11am-6.30pm Sun. **Credit** AmEx, DC, MC, V. **Map** p334 D2.
Family-run firm stocking marbled paper, leather desk accessories and greetings cards.

Il Papiro

Via Cavour 55r, San Marco (055 215262/www.il papiro.it). **Open** 9am-7.30pm Mon-Sat; 10am-6pm Sun. **Credit** AmEx, DC, MC, V. **Map** p335 A4.
A chain of olde-worlde shops with bright paper desk accessories, photo frames, playing cards and more.
Other locations throughout the city.

Il Torchio

Via de' Bardi 17, Oltrarno (055 2342862). **Open** 2.30-7pm Mon; 10am-1.30pm, 2.30-7.30pm Tue-Sat. **Credit** AmEx, MC, V. **Map** p335 D4.
Watch bookbinding in action, and stock up on handmade paper boxes, stationery and albums.

General

La Bottega dell'Olio

Piazza del Limbo 2r, Duomo & Around (055 2670468). **Open** *Mar-Sept* 10am-7pm Mon-Sat. Closed 2wks Jan. *Oct-Feb* 3-7pm Mon; 10am-1pm, 2-7pm Tue-Sat. **Credit** AmEx, DC, MC, V. **Map** p334 C3.
All things olive oil, from soaps and delicacies to olive-wood breadboards and pestles and mortars.

Carte Etc

Via de' Cerchi 13r, Duomo & Around (055 268302/ www.carteetc.it). **Open** 10am-7.30pm daily. **Credit** AmEx, MC, V. **Map** p335 B4.
Exquisite glass and stationery, unusual postcards of Florence and handmade greetings cards.

Cartoleria Ecologica La Tartaruga

Borgo degli Albizi 60r, Santa Croce (055 2340845). **Open** 1.30-7.30pm Mon; 9.30am-7.30pm Tue-Sat. **Credit** MC, V. **Map** p335 B5.
Unusual stationery, toys and gifts made of recycled paper, wood and papier mâché.

La Fabrique

Borgo degli Albizi 40r, Santa Croce (055 2340333). **Open** 3.30-7.30pm Mon; 10am-7.30pm Tue-Sat. **Credit** AmEx, MC, V. **Map** p335 B5.

The sort of shop that has teenage girls and the young at heart squealing with delight. Costume jewellery, colourful beaded bags, hair accessories and pretty items for the home.

G Veneziano

Via de' Fossi 53r, Santa Maria Novella (055 287925). **Open** 3-7pm Mon; 9am-1pm, 3-7pm Tue-Sat. Closed Aug. **Credit** AmEx, DC, MC, V. **Map** p334 B2.

Friendly, upmarket place to find Venetian glass jewellery, bottle-stoppers and plates, funky printed crockery, flower-embroidered cushions and tablecloths and a quirky Barbapapa range of gifts.

Lungarno Details

Lungarno degli Acciaiuoli, Duomo & Around (055 287367/www.lungarnohotels.com). **Open** 10.30am-1.30pm, 3.30-7.30pm Mon-Fri; 10.30am-1.30pm Sat. **Credit** AmEx, DC, MC, V. **Map** p335 A4.

So many guests of the Lungarno Suites above (*see p54*) asked where they could find items from their hotel apartments that this shop was opened below. On sale are furniture, framed photos, lighting, food gifts and beautifully packaged candles and toiletries by Sicilian company Ortigia. *Photo p165.*

Mandragora ArtStore

Piazza del Duomo 50r, Duomo & Around (055 292559/www.mandragora.it). **Open** 10am-7.30pm Mon-Sat; 10.30am-6.30pm Sun. **Credit** AmEx, DC, MC, V. **Map** p335 B4.

Decent reproductions by local artists of famous Florentine works of art, on furnishings, scarves, bags and ornaments, plus great books, cards and prints.

Moleria Locchi

Via Burchiello 10, Outside the City Gates (055 2298371/www.locchi.com). **Open** 9am-1pm, 3-6.30pm Mon-Fri. **Credit** MC, V.

It's worth the trek to visit this unique old-fashioned glass and lead crystal workshop. Moleria Locchi offers a restoration service and creates bespoke replacements for glass objects like chandeliers. *Photo p167.*

Signum

Borgo de' Greci 40r, Santa Croce (055 280621/ www.signumfirenze.it). **Open** 9am-7.30pm Mon-Sat; 10am-7pm Sun. **Credit** MC, V. **Map** p335 C4.

This delightful shop, housed in an ancient wine cellar, stocks an appealingly wide range of gifts, among them miniature models of shop windows and bookcases, and Murano glass inkwells and pens.

Other locations Lungarno Archibusieri 14r, Duomo & Around (055 289393); via de' Benci 29r, Santa Croce (055 244590).

Stationery & art supplies

Le Dune

Piazza Ottaviani 9r, Santa Maria Novella (055 214377). **Open** 9am-7pm Mon-Fri; 9am-1pm Sat. Closed 2wks Aug. **Credit** V. **Map** p334 B2.

A small stationery and gift shop with a good choice of greetings cards. The shop also offers photocopying, photo developing and faxing services.

Pineider

Piazza della Signoria 13r, Duomo & Around (055 284655/www.pineider.com). **Open** 10am-7pm daily. **Credit** AmEx, DC, MC, V. **Map** p335 C4.

Pineider is famous for its high-quality writing paper and accessories and top-notch office leather goods.

Romeo

Via della Condotta 43r, Duomo & Around (055 210350). **Open** 10am-7.30pm Mon-Sat. **Credit** AmEx, MC, V. **Map** p335 C4.

The interior of this lovely stationery shop is filled to the ceiling with Spalding's full range, Aurora pens and Giorgio Fedon's smart coloured leather bags.

Zecchi

Via dello Studio 19r, Duomo & Around (055 211470/www.zecchi.com). **Open** 8.30am-12.30pm, 3.30-7.30pm Mon-Fri; 8.30am-12.30pm Sat. Closed 3wks Aug. **Credit** AmEx, MC, V. **Map** p335 B4.

The best shop in town for art supplies, with everything from pencils to gold leaf.

Health & beauty

Complementary medicine

Erboristeria Inglese

Via de' Tornabuoni 19, Duomo & Around (055 210628/www.officinadetornabuoni.it). **Open** 3.30-8pm Mon; 10am-8pm Tue-Sat. Closed 2wks Aug. **Credit** AmEx, MC, V. **Map** p334 B2.

From a 15th-century palazzo, the very knowledgeable Donatella sells handmade gifts, perfumes and candles from Diptyque, herbal remedies and Dr Hauschka toiletries and cosmetics. She can also recommend alternative medicine practitioners. There's no main shop window so look for the raised entrance set off the street.

Farmacia del Cinghiale

Piazza del Mercato Nuovo 4r, Duomo & Around (055 212128). **Open** 9am-1pm; 3.30-7.30pm Mon-Fri; Sat according to rota. **Credit** MC, V. **Map** p334 C3.
Named after the famous wild boar statue in the square opposite, Cinghiale was founded in the 18th century by the herbalist Guadagni, and still makes its own herbal remedies and cosmetics.

Münstermann

Piazza Goldoni 2r, Santa Maria Novella (055 210660/www.munstermann.it). **Open** 9am-1pm, 4-8pm Mon-Fri. **Credit** AmEx, DC, MC, V. **Map** p334 B2.
This charming shell-shaped corner icon was opened in 1897, a stone's throw from the ponte Vecchio, and still has its original shop fittings. It stocks pharmaceutical and herbal medicines, toiletries, silver pillboxes, hair accessories and bathroom oddities. Its own-brand products (body lotions, hand creams, shampoos, fragrances) use high-quality, natural ingredients.

Officina Profumo-Farmaceutica di Santa Maria Novella

Via della Scala 16, Santa Maria Novella (055 216276/www.smnovella.it). **Open** 9.30am-7.30pm Mon-Sat; 10.30am-6.30pm Sun. Closed Sun Feb & Nov, 2wks Aug. **Credit** AmEx, DC, MC, V. **Map** p334 B2.
One of the most beautiful shops in Florence, an ancient herbal pharmacy with a 13th-century frescoed chapel. The world-renowned products include pomegranate perfume, orange blossom water, soaps reputed to be the best in the world and the calming Acqua di Santa Maria Novella.

Hairdressers & barbers

All hairdressers and barbers in Florence are closed on Mondays.

Gabrio Staff Olimpo

Via de' Tornabuoni 5, Santa Maria Novella (055 214668). **Open** 9.30am-7pm Tue-Sat. Closed 2wks Aug. **Credit** AmEx, DC, MC, V. **Map** p334 C2.
This unisex hair and beauty centre is set in an amazing atelier. Staff dish out buffet snacks to clients at lunchtime. Cuts cost from €60.

Jean Louis David

Lungarno Corsini 52r, Santa Maria Novella (055 216760). **Open** 9am-7pm Tue-Sat. Closed 2wks Aug. **Credit** AmEx, DC, MC, V. **Map** p334 C2.

Brand new

Paris, New York... Florence! This city is increasingly seen as a major European shopping destination as well as a cultural hub. Big-name branding is the name of the game and top design companies are prepared to pay matching big-buck prices to acquire prestigious addresses for their flagship stores. When their rental contracts have come up for renewal, many small or family-run shops, bars and galleries in the three or four main designer thoroughfares have found it impossible to keep up with the bidding – closing down entirely, or moving to quieter streets.

Recent new kids on via Strozzi's block are **Bottega Veneta** (no.6, 055 284735, www.bottegaveneta.com), **Dolce & Gabbana** (nos.12-18r, 055 281003, www.dolcegabbana.it), **Louis Vuitton** (piazza degli Strozzi 1, 055 266981, www.louisvuitton.com) and **Bulgari** (corner of via de' Tornabuoni 61-63r, 055 2396786, www.bulgari.com). In the last few years via de' Tornabuoni has also seen retro chic **Pucci** (nos.20-22r, 055 2658082, www.emiliopucci.com), flashy **Roberto Cavalli** (no.83r, 055 2396226, www.robertocavalli.it), **Max Mara** (nos.66-70r, 055 214133, www.maxmara.com) and refined **Armani** (no.48r, 055 219041, www.giorgioarmani.com) join **Versace** (nos.13-15r, 055 282638, www.gianniversace.com) and the rest of the gang on the main designer artery.

When it comes to via de' Tornabuoni, if it's not a new store, then it's an expanding one; **Gucci** (no.73r, 055 264011, www.gucci.it), **Prada** (nos.51-53r, 67r, 055 283439, www.prada.it) and **Ferragamo** (nos.4-14r, 055 292123, www.salvatoreferragamo.com) are designer stores on this street that have all upped their floorspace or frontage over recent years.

The story is similar on via Roma, with **Hugo Boss** on nearby piazza della Repubblica (no.46r, 055 2399168, www.hugoboss.com), **Michele Negri** (*see p153*) and others joining multi-designer emporia **Luisa** (via Roma 19-21r, 055 217826, www.luisaviaroma.com) and **Raspini** (via Roma 25-29r, 055 213077, www.raspini.com).

If you can't afford the hotel, you can at least buy a piece of it: **Lungarno Details**. *See p163.*

A women's wash and cut at Jean Louis David is €35; men are also welcome, and there's a student discount of 20% (don't forget to bring your ID). If you're feeling brave and adventurous, call ahead to book a free haircut in the salon's school.

Opticians

Camera and optical lenses go hand in hand in Italy: photography shops (*see p151*) sell glasses and opticians sell basic photo equipment.

Pisacchi

Via della Condotta 22-24r, Duomo & Around (055 214542). **Open** 4-7.30pm Mon; 9am-1pm, 4-7.30pm Tue-Sat. **Credit** AmEx, DC, MC, V. Closed 2wks Aug. **Map** p335 C4.
As well as providing eye tests, this contact lens specialist sells prescription glasses and sunglasses.

Pharmacies

Farmacia all'Insegna del Moro

Piazza San Giovanni 20r, Duomo & Around (055 211343). **Open** 24hrs daily. **Credit** AmEx, MC, V. **Map** p334 B3.
Some English spoken.

Farmacia Comunale No.13

Santa Maria Novella train station, Santa Maria Novella (055 216761/289435). **Open** 24hrs daily. **Credit** AmEx, DC, MC, V. **Map** p334 A2.
English spoken.

Farmacia Molteni

Via de' Calzaiuoli 7r, Duomo & Around (055 215472/289490). **Open** 24hrs daily. **Credit** AmEx, DC, MC, V. **Map** p334 C3.
English spoken.

Shops

Profumeria Aline

Via de' Calzaiuoli 53, Duomo & Around (055 219073/www.profumeriaaline.com). **Open** 3.30-7.30pm Mon; 9am-7.30pm Tue-Sat. **Credit** MC, V. **Map** p335 B4.
A well-stocked perfumery and cosmetics shop, set in a prime location. There's a beauty centre at no.7 (055 2398292), and the loyalty card enables you to build up a cumulative discount.
Other locations Via Vacchereccia 11r, Duomo & Around (055 294976); piazza San Giovanni 26-27, Duomo & Around (055 212864).

Sephora at Laguna

Via Martelli 10, Duomo & Around (055 2381922). **Open** 11am-8pm Mon; 9.30am-8pm Tue-Sat; 3-7.30pm Sun. **Credit** AmEx, MC, V. **Map** p335 B4.
This Florentine outlet of the highly regarded French beauty chain is relatively small, but it still sells many other cult labels alongside the famous Sephora own-brand line.

Spas & salons

Freni

Via Calimala 1, Duomo & Around (055 2396647). **Open** 1-7.30pm Mon; 9am-7.30pm Tue-Fri; 9am-1pm Sat. **Credit** MC, V. **Map** p334 A3.
If your feet give out after tramping around all those museums, come here to revive them with a pedicure. Facials, manicures and massages are also offered.

Hito Estetica

Via de' Ginori 21, San Lorenzo (055 284424). **Open** 9am-7.30pm Mon-Fri; 9am-7pm Sat. **Credit** AmEx, MC, V. **Map** p335 A4.

A range of natural treatments and pampering for men and women, including Ayurvedic techniques. Prices start at around €40 for a facial.

International Studio

Via Porta Rossa 82r, Duomo & Around (055 293393). **Open** 1-8pm Mon; 10am-8pm Tue-Sat. **Credit** MC, V. **Map** p334 C3.

A solarium, hair and beauty centre, box office and showcase for *objets d'art*, all rolled into one.

Soul Space

Via Sant'Egidio 12, Santa Croce (055 2001794/ www.soulspace.it). **Open** 10am-7pm Mon-Sat. **Credit** MC, V. **Map** p334 C3.

A luxurious new spa with pool, garden, real hammam, relaxation room with a fireplace, and a range of spa treatments including hot stone therapies. *Photo p168.*

Wave

Via Santo Spirito 27, Oltrarno (055 2654650/ www.waveitalia.net). **Open** noon-7pm Mon; 10am-7pm Tue-Fri; 9am-2pm Sat. **Credit** V. **Map** p334 C1.

A swanky new hair and beauty centre, with Ayurvedic and other speciality treatments.

House & home

For antiques, head to via Maggio, via dei Serragli and via dei Fossi.

Ceramics & glass

La Bottega dei Cristalli

Via de' Benci 51r, Santa Croce (055 2344891/ www.labottegadeicristalli.com). **Open** 10am-7.30pm daily. Closed mid Jan-mid Feb. **Credit** AmEx, DC, MC, V. **Map** p335 C5.

A lovely range of Murano and Tuscan-made glass plates, picture frames, lamps and chandeliers, and tiny glass 'sweets' and bottles.

La Botteghina del Ceramista

Via Guelfa 5r, San Lorenzo (055 287367). **Open** 10am-1.30pm, 3.30-7.30pm Mon-Fri; 10am-1.30pm Sat. Closed 2wks Aug. **Credit** AmEx, DC, MC, V. **Map** p335 A4.

Superb hand-painted ceramics in intricate designs and vivid colours.

Sbigoli Terrecotte

Via Sant'Egidio 4r, Santa Croce (055 2479713/ www.sbigoliterrecotte.it). **Open** 9am-1pm, 3-7.30pm Mon-Sat. **Credit** AmEx, DC, MC, V. **Map** p335 B5.

Handmade Tuscan ceramics and terracotta in traditional designs are the order of the day here.

Florists

Al Portico

Piazza San Firenze 1, Duomo & Around (055 213716/www.semialportico.it). **Open** 8.30am-7.30pm Mon-Sat; 10am-1pm Sun. **Credit** AmEx, DC, MC, V. **Map** p335 C5.

An extraordinary shop in the Renaissance courtyard of a magnificent palazzo, with trees, fountains, huge plants and flowers. The owner is happy to show customers round, even if they don't want to buy.

Other locations Piazza della Signoria 36, Duomo & Around (055 2608658).

La Rosa Canina

Via dell'Erta Canina 1r, Outside the City Gates (055 2342449/www.larosacaninafioristi.it). Bus 23. **Open** 9.30am-1.30pm, 4.30-9.30pm Tue-Sat; 9.30am-1.30pm Sun. **Credit** V.

On a stroll up to piazzale Michelangelo, take time to admire the lovely displays of plants and flowers.

General

Arte sì di Paola Capecchi

Via de' Fossi 23r, Santa Maria Novella (055 2645504). **Open** 3.30-7.30pm Mon; 10am-1pm, 3.30-7.30pm Tue-Sat. Closed 3wks Aug. **Credit** AmEx, DC, MC, V. **Map** p334 B2.

More gallery than shop, this mezzanine space is dotted with outlandish design *objets* and furniture: think silver and frosted pink leather dining chairs, or a papier mâché throne. Capecchi herself is an interior designer so opening hours can be erratic.

Bartolini

Via de' Servi 30r, San Marco (055 211895/www.dinobartolini.it). **Open** 3.30-7.30pm Mon; 10am-1pm, 3.30-7.30pm Tue-Sat. Closed 2wks Aug. **Credit** AmEx, MC, V. **Map** p335 A4.

This charming kitchen shop has extensive selections of cutlery and crockery, plus accessories ranging from garlic mincers to kitchen sinks.

Frette

Via Martelli 23r, San Marco (055 211369/www.frette.com). **Open** 3-7pm Mon; 10am-7pm Tue-Sat. Closed 3wks Aug. **Credit** AmEx, DC, MC, V. **Map** p335 A4.

The full range of bedding, towels and robes so beloved of boutique hotels the world over.

Lisa Corti Home Textiles Emporium

Piazza Ghiberti 33r, Santa Croce (055 2001860/ www.lisacorti.com). **Open** 3.30-7.30pm Mon; 10am-7.30pm Tue-Sat; 11am-1.30pm, 2.30-7pm Sun. **Credit** AmEx, DC, MC, V. **Map** p335 C6.

Brightly coloured cushions, bedspreads, quilts and curtains, in silks and cottons and with an oriental feel. Designer Lisa Corti has also created a small range of furniture and pottery.

Other locations Via de' Bardi 58, Oltrarno (055 2645600).

Passamaneria Toscana

Piazza San Lorenzo 12r, San Lorenzo (055 214670/ www.passamaneriatoscana.com). **Open** 9.30am-7.30pm Mon-Sat; 10am-7.30pm Sun. **Credit** AmEx, DC, MC, V. **Map** p334 B2.

This shop sells all kinds of soft furnishings: everything from rich brocade cushions to embroidered Florentine crests, wall hangings and tassels.

Repairs

Ferramenta Masini

Via del Sole 19-21r, 18-20r, Santa Maria Novella (055 212560). **Open** 9am-1pm, 3.30-7.30pm Mon-Fri; 9am-1pm Sat. **Credit** AmEx, DC, MC, V. **Map** p334 B2.
Two friendly shops, under the same management, with plugs and adaptors, hardware, a key-cutting service and door and lock repairs.

Specialist

Arredamenti Castorina

Via Santo Spirito 13-15r, Oltrarno (055 212885/ www.castorina.net). **Open** 9am-1pm, 3.30-7.30pm Mon-Fri; 9am-1pm Sat. Closed Aug. **Credit** V. **Map** p334 C1.
An extraordinary old shop in Oltrarno, full of all things baroque, including gilded mouldings, frames, cherubs, trompe l'œil tables and fake malachite and tortoiseshell obelisks.

Borgo degli Albizi 48 Rosso

Borgo degli Albizi 48r, Santa Croce (055 2347598/ www.borgoalbizi.com). **Open** 3.30-7.30pm Mon; 10am-1pm, 3.30-7.30pm Tue-Sat. **Credit** AmEx, DC, MC, V. **Map** p335 B5.
Opulent chandeliers and glass pear-drop lamps made with antique or new crystals. You can also order items to your own design.

Casa della Cornice

Via Sant'Egidio 26r, Santa Croce (055 2480222). **Open** 9am-1pm, 3-7.30pm Mon-Fri; 9.30am-1pm Sat. **No credit cards. Map** p335 B5.
A huge catalogue of traditional and contemporary picture frames in silver and gold leaf.

Music & entertainment

CDs, DVDs & records

Alberti

Borgo San Lorenzo 45-49r, San Lorenzo (055 294271). **Open** 3.30-7.30pm Mon; 9am-7.30pm Tue-Sat. **Credit** AmEx, MC, V. **Map** p334 B3.
The oldest record shop in the city has a vast repertoire of pop, dance, jazz and indie CD recordings, some vinyl, a variety of DVDs and a great selection of portable DVD and CD players.
Other locations Via de' Pucci 16r, San Marco (055 284346).

Data Records

Via de' Neri 15r, Santa Croce (055 287592/www. superecords.com). **Open** 3.30-7.30pm Mon; 10am-1pm, 3.30-7.30pm Tue-Sat. Closed 2wks Aug. **Credit** AmEx, DC, MC, V. **Map** p335 C4.
Staff here are true music buffs with a local reputation for being able to find the unfindable. Home to over 80,000 titles, new and used, with an emphasis on psychedelia, blues, R&B, jazz and soundtracks.

Ricordi

Via Brunelleschi 8r, Duomo & Around (055 214104). **Open** 9.30am-7.30pm Mon-Sat; 3-7.30pm last Sun of mth. **Credit** AmEx, DC, MC, V. **Map** p334 B3.
Ricordi has the best choice of DVDs and CDs in town, with original-language films and classical, jazz, rock and dance sections. Ricordi also sells instruments, sheet music and scores.

Moleria Locchi. *See p163.*

Soul Space – the perfect retreat after pacing the streets. *See p166.*

Eat, Drink, Shop

Twisted

Borgo San Frediano 21r, Oltrarno (055 282011). **Open** 9am-1pm, 3-7.30pm Mon-Sat. **Credit** AmEx, DC, MC, V.
A specialist jazz centre with rare recordings and more mainstream sounds. The stocked artists span 1950s trad jazz right through to acid and nu jazz.

Video & DVD rental

Blockbuster

Viale Belfiore 6a, Outside the City Gates (055 330542/ www.blockbuster.it). Bus 2, 14, 28. **Open** 11am-11pm Mon-Thur, Sun; 11am-midnight Fri, Sat. **Credit** V.
Stocks some mainstream films in English.
Other locations Via di Novoli 9-11, Outside the City Gates (055 333533).

Punto Video

Via San Antonino 7r, San Lorenzo (055 2398485). **Open** 9am-1pm, 3-8pm Mon-Sat. **Credit** AmEx, DC, MC, V. **Map** p334 A2.
Punto has over 500 titles in English.

Sports & fitness

See also pp200-204.

Il Rifugio

Piazza Ottaviani 3r, Santa Maria Novella (055 294736/www.rifugiosport.it). **Open** 9.30am-7.30pm Mon-Sat. **Credit** AmEx, DC, MC, V. **Map** p334 B2.
Vast selections of sporting equipment and accessories, as well as trainers and sports clothing. Staff are friendly and helpful.
Other locations Piazza della Stazione 1, Santa Maria Novella (055 289328).

Universo

Piazza del Duomo 6-8r, Duomo & Around (055 284412/www.universosport.it). **Open** 10am-7.30pm Mon-Sat. **Credit** AmEx, DC, MC, V. **Map** p335 B4.
Very central sports equipment shop, with specialist and designer sports clothing.

Ticket agencies

When booking tickets for events by phone, ensure that all the arrangements for collection or delivery are clearly specified.

Box Office

Via Alamanni 39, Santa Maria Novella (055 210804/www.boxol.it). **Open** 3.30-7.30pm Mon; 10am-7.30pm Tue-Fri; 10am-2pm Sat. **Credit** MC, V. **Map** p334 A1.
Box Office sells tickets for concerts, plays and exhibitions in Italy and abroad.

Travellers' needs

For luggage, *see p157*; for mobile phone rental, *see p313*; for computer repairs, *see p153*; for banks, *see p310*; for shipping services, *see p304.*

Travel agents

Biemme

Via delle Belle Donne, Santa Maria Novella (055 294329). **Open** 2.30-6.30pm Mon-Sat. **Credit** MC, V. **Map** p334 B2.
The staff here are experts at finding the best deals for holidays and flights, train and boat tickets.

CTS (Student Travel Centre)

Via de' Ginori 25r, San Lorenzo (055 289570/ www.cts.it). **Open** 9.30am-1pm, 2.30-6pm Mon-Sat. **Credit** MC, V. **Map** p335 A4.
The official student travel centre, offering discounted air, coach and train tickets, some to under-25s only, some to students only and some for all. Obligatory membership is €10 for students and €11 for non-students.

Arts & Entertainment

Festivals & Events	170
Children	175
Film	178
Galleries	181
Gay & Lesbian	183
Music: Classical & Opera	186
Music: Rock, Pop & Jazz	190
Nightlife	193
Sport & Fitness	200
Theatre & Dance	205

Features

Top five Festivals	170
Just for kicks	177
The Tuscan king of comedy	180
Torre adore	185
Seasonal settings	189
The best Venues	191
The aperitivo awards	194
Winter of content	199
The crying game	203

Stadio Artemio Franchi. *See p200.*

Festivals & Events

From jousts and pageants to food and wine, Tuscany's vibrant events reveal the heart of the local psyche.

Feast on Tuscany's art treasures, soothing landscape and culinary delights all you want, but for an insight into the deeper layers and finer textures of this charming land and its indomitable people, you really ought to time your visit to experience at least one of the many local festivals. Far from the skin-deep theatricality you might expect, events such as Siena's **Palio** (*see p173* and *p244* **The Palio**) still speak volumes about the Tuscan character, and the subtle balance between religious and civic powers both past and present. The Tuscans' wry and bold sense of humour also surface glaringly: take the subjects of the floats in the **Viareggio Carnival** (*see p174*), for example, which often feature caricatures of politicians and celebrities. On the other hand, any country *sagra* (food festival) will demonstrate how life in Tuscany is still geared towards the countryside and the natural rhythm of the seasons.

The main issue with festivals in Florence and Tuscany is that few of them are widely publicised. Tourist offices are grouped by province and are unlikely to know what's on elsewhere, so keep an eye out for posters and flyers instead. Although many of the websites listed below are in Italian only, their photos, maps, dates and prices (where applicable) will be helpful all the same. Note that the telephone numbers may only be operational in the direct run-up to the event. For music-only festivals, *see p189* and *p192*; for film festivals, *see p179*; for theatre and dance events, *see p207*.

Top five Festivals

For a party
Carnevale di Viareggio (*see p174*).

For tradition
Palio delle Contrade (*see p173*).

For food & wine
Boccaccesca (*see p174*) and **Cantine Aperte** (*see p172*).

For culture
Settimana dei Beni Culturali (*see p172*).

For sport
Mille Miglia (*see p172*).

Spring

Festa della Donna
Date 8 Mar.

For International Women's Day, women are traditionally presented with yellow mimosa flowers. In the evening, restaurants and clubs get packed with girlie gangs set on having a wild night out.

Holy Week
Date wk leading up to Easter.

Many Tuscan towns celebrate Holy Week with religious processions, often in period costume. The most impressive of them involves almost 600 performers and takes place in the evening of Good Friday at Grassina by Bagno a Ripoli, just outside Florence (055 646051/www.rievstoricagrassina.it).

Scoppio del Carro
Piazzale della Porta al Prato to piazza del Duomo, Florence. **Date** Easter Sun.

At 9.30am on Easter morning, a parade of costumed musicians, flag-throwers and dignitaries escort a wooden cart, laden with fireworks and pulled by four white oxen, from via il Prato (watch for the three-storey wooden doors on the left of the Hotel Villa Medici) to a jam-packed piazza del Duomo. Meanwhile, another parade departs from the church of Santissimi Apostoli (*see p91*) with a holy fire kindled with the flints from the Holy Sepulchre. At 11am, during mass, a dove-shaped rocket shoots along a wire from the high altar to the carro outside, starting the fireworks. If all goes smoothly, it's said that the year's harvest will be good.

Mostra Mercato di Piante e Fiori
Giardino dell'Orticoltura, via Vittorio Emanuele 4, Outside the City Gates, Florence (055 2625385). Bus 4. **Date** late Apr/early May, early Oct.

Growers from all over Tuscany proudly exhibit and sell their plants and blooms at these spectacular horticultural shows, which are laid out around a grand 19th-century glasshouse.

Maggio Musicale Fiorentino
Teatro del Maggio Musicale Fiorentino, corso Italia 16, Santa Maria Novella, Florence (055 213535/www.maggiofiorentino.com). **Date** late Apr-early July.

Get out your best armour for Easter's colourful **Scoppio del Carro**.

Founded in 1933, Florence's 'Musical May' is universally acclaimed as one of the best festivals in Italy for opera, concerts and dance performances. It closes with two free jamborees (one ballet, one music) in piazza della Signoria.

Settimana dei Beni Culturali

Throughout Italy (055 290832). **Date** 1wk in Apr/May.

'Culture Week' means free admission to state museums and archaeological sites, including the Uffizi, Bargello, Accademia and Palatina galleries in Florence, as well as special events (concerts, talks, guided visits and exhibitions). Queues are less daunting than one might expect, possibly because dates keep shifting every year and few manage to time their visit accordingly.

Artigianato e Palazzo

Palazzo Corsini sul Prato, via della Scala 115, Florence (055 2654589/www.artigianatoepalazzo.it). **Date** wknd in mid May.

Master artisans demonstrate their skills and sell their wares at this upmarket craft show in one of Tuscany's finest Italianate gardens.

Festa del Grillo

Parco delle Cascine, Outside the City Gates, Florence. Bus 17C. **Date** 6th Sun after Easter.

On the feast of Ascension, Florentine families used to come to the Cascine park for a picnic, and part of the fun was chasing (or buying) crickets and taking them home in brightly painted little cages. Live crickets have been replaced by chirping mechanical devices, and this traditional event now has the feel of a general market.

Amico Museo

Throughout Tuscany (www.regione.toscana.it/amicomuseo). **Date** 3wks in May.

Special and late openings and events to familiarise the crowds with the region's lesser-known and local museums. Pick up a brochure from any tourist office.

Genio Fiorentino

Florence & around (055 2760061/www.geniofiorentino.it). **Date** 2wks in May.

An eclectic programme of arts and music events celebrating Florence's cultural heritage. Events explore the elusive Florentine mentality, which over the centuries has fostered an endless string of 'geniuses' in science, poetry, exploration, art and politics.

Mille Miglia

Across Tuscany (030 280036/www.millemiglia.it). **Date** Sat in late May.

Almost 400 vintage cars take part in this three-day, 1,600km (1,000 mile) race. The teams wind along the Cassia road for the length of Tuscany, on their way back from Rome to Brescia on the Saturday, passing through Siena around noon and entering Florence (through Porta Romana, en route to piazza della Signoria) early in the afternoon. Then it's onwards to Bologna via the Mugello.

Cantine Aperte

Throughout Italy (0577 738312/www.movimentoturismovino.it). **Date** last Sun in May.

Wine-producing estates, many of which would not normally be open to the public, show their cellars to visitors and hold tastings.

Summer

Around the end of May, Tuscany's open-air venues emerge from hibernation. In Florence, outdoor cinemas screen movies (*see p180*), open-air bars double as music venues (*see pp193-195*) and many clubs move dancefloors under the stars. Cloisters and squares host classical concerts, as locals take to the city's squares and gardens.

Estate Fiesolana

Fiesole (800 414240/www.estatefiesolana.it). Bus 7. **Date** mid June-early Sept.

An assorted mix of performing arts shows in scenic settings like the Roman theatre and the Maiano stone quarries. The Vivere Jazz Festival stands out for the quality of its guests.

Giugno Pisano

Pisa (050 910393). **Date** 16, 17 & last Sun in June.

On 16 June, eve of the feast of Pisa's patron saint, 70,000 candles are lit on the façades of the palaces along the Arno for the charming Luminara di San Ranieri. The following day, at 6.30pm, the Palio di San Ranieri boat race takes place between the town's ancient quarters. To round off the 'Pisan June' events, Il Gioco del Ponte – a 16th-century 'push-of-war' (a reverse tug-of-war) – is fought on the last Sunday of the month on the ponte di Mezzo between teams from the two sides of the Arno. Processions start at 4.30pm and the competition begins two hours later. A historic regatta (Regata Storica) between the Ancient Maritime Republics of Pisa, Genoa, Venice and Amalfi also takes place in May or June every year; Pisa next gets to play host in 2010.

Giostra del Saracino

Piazza Grande, Arezzo (0575 377462/www.giostradelsaracino.arezzo.it). **Date** penultimate Sat in June; 1st Sun in Sept.

This ancient jousting tournament was first recorded in 1535. Five centuries later, it's still plenty of fun. The procession of horses, knights and their escorts arrives in the piazza at 9.30pm in June, and at 5pm in September. Then the action begins, with four couples of riders representing the four city quarters trying to achieve the highest score by hitting a dummy of an Arab soldier (the Saracino). The days leading to the challenge are also rich in events (check the website for dates). About a week before, in a solemn ceremony, the lances and starting order are cast by lot, and the prize (the Golden Lance) is brought to the Cathedral. There follow four or five nights of unofficial trial runs, followed by a 'dress rehearsal' of the pageant and a Giostra run by the junior jousters.

Festa Internazionale della Ceramica

Montelupo (0571 518993). **Date** 8 days in mid-late June.

The town's reputation as a prime manufacturing centre for ceramics dates from the Middle Ages. This festival celebrates the craft with exhibitions, markets, workshops and demonstrations of techniques.

Calcio Storico

Piazza Santa Croce, Florence (055 290832). **Map** p335 C5. **Date** June.

With the 2006 and 2007 events cancelled due to excessive violence, the future of Florence's rugby-like calcio storico looks a little uncertain (*see p203* **The crying game**). Two preliminary matches are normally played in early June, while the final is normally held on 24 June, a city holiday (*see below*). Teams representing the city's ancient quarters (Santa Croce, Santa Maria Novella, Santo Spirito and San Giovanni) parade through the streets before settling old rivalries in a no-holds-barred 27-a-side match played by bare-chested lads in colourful medieval breeches.

Festa di San Giovanni

Florence. **Date** 24 June.

A public holiday in Florence. A huge fireworks display takes place at 10pm from near Piazzale Michelangelo to honour the city's patron saint. Best enjoyed from the Lungarni (just follow the crowds).

Palio delle Contrade

Piazza del Campo, Siena (0577 280551/www.palio.comune.siena.it). **Date** 2 July & 16 Aug.

Although this bareback, breakneck race is staged primarily for the natives, it's a major attraction for visitors, and held twice over the summer. The horses' safety is a controversial issue – the animals are adored but several have been fatally injured in the past – but there's little denying that this is Tuscan pageantry at its best. Trial races are run prior to the two main dates, the last at 9am on the days themselves. At 2.30pm, the horses and jockeys of the ten participating *contrade* (out of 17) are blessed in their neighbourhood's church. At 5pm the procession enters the shell-shaped piazza del Campo, and after some elaborate flag-throwing and maybe a couple of false starts, the race – three laps of the square – gets going around 7pm and is all over in 90 seconds. It's free to stand, but get there by 4pm and take a sun hat. Tickets for balconies overlooking the piazza are sold in the bars and cafés that line it, but they're hard to come by and expensive. *See also p244* **The Palio**.

On the Road Festival

Pelago (055 8327301). **Date** early July.

A four-day (Thur-Sun) competitive showcase of street performers and buskers in a pretty country village. The action starts at 6pm.

Medieval Festival

Monteriggioni (0577 304810/www.monteriggioni medievale.com). **Date** 2 wknds in mid July.

This re-enactment, in period dress, of medieval town life and warfare features food, drink and craft stalls, plus music, dancing and other performances. A different theme is chosen each year.

Giostra dell'Orso

Pistoia (0573 21622/www.giostradellorso.it). **Date** 25 July.

Pistoia's annual festival culminates in the city's cathedral square at 9.30pm on St James's feast day after a month of concerts, markets and pageantry. The joust sees 12 riders, three for each city quarter, gallop in pairs and attempt to spear with a lance two 'bears' (wooden dummies in checked cloaks).

Effetto Venezia

Livorno (0586 204611/www.comune.livorno.it). **Date** early Aug.

A ten-day run of shows and concerts in Livorno's 'Venetian quarter', so called because of its canals. Restaurants and street stalls stay open late serving *cacciucco* (spicy fish stew) and other tasty morsels. Don't miss a boat tour of the Fossi Medicei.

Calici di stelle

Throughout Tuscany (www.movimentoturismovino.it). **Date** 10 Aug.

About 50 Tuscan 'Città del vino' participate in this 'wine under the stars' event – held on the night of San Lorenzo – by hosting a fascinating combination of wine tastings and meteor gazing from historic piazze and courtyards throughout Tuscany. Details of the specific events are advertised on the website listed above from July. Music and fireworks add to the convivial atmosphere.

Tuscan Sun Festival

Cortona (0575 630353/www.tuscansunfestival.com). **Date** 8 days early Aug.

Bestselling author Frances Mayes is the co-director of this cultural festival, which launched in 2003 and attracts an international line-up. The programme features concerts by high-profile musicians, alongside art and culinary events and lectures.

Volterra AD 1398

Volterra (0588 86099/www.volterra1398.it). **Date** last 2 Sun in Aug.

Life as it would have been in 1398 is painstakingly recreated throughout the old city centre of Volterra, with markets, open workshops, musicians, jugglers, commoners, clergymen, soldiers and nobles. Crafts and refreshments can only be bought with 'grossos' – the medieval local currency – so change up your euros before taking a wander.

Bravio delle botti

Montepulciano (0578 757575/www.bravio dellebotti.it). **Date** last Sun in Aug.

Champions from the eight city neighbourhoods compete in an exhausting wine barrel-rolling contest up the steep and winding route to piazza Grande. The race starts at 7pm, but colourful celebrations take place over the week leading up to the event.

La Rificolona

Florence. **Date** 7 Sept.

In the past, country folk used to walk to Florence on the eve of the Nativity of the Virgin Mary, as a pilgrimage as well as for the fair that's still held in piazza SS Annunziata. They carried paper lanterns, or *rificolone*, to light their way. Today, children still parade through the city proudly swaying their colourful candlelit paper lanterns.

Ostensione della Sacra Cintola & Corteggio Storico

Prato. **Date** 8 Sept.

The Holy Girdle of the Virgin, allegedly the belt that Mary handed to St Thomas on ascending into Heaven, was brought to Prato from the Holy Land around 1141. The relic is displayed from Donatello's pulpit on the cathedral façade on four other occasions annually – Easter Sunday, 1 May, 15 August and Christmas Day – but 8 September is the grandest celebration, accompanied by parading and drum-beating.

Autumn

Boccaccesca

Certaldo (0571 663384/www.boccaccesca.it). **Date** 1st 2wknds in Oct.

Over two long weekends (Fri to Sun), the charming medieval setting of Certaldo hosts this much-acclaimed celebration of the finest Tuscan produce, with wine, olive oil and the unique local onions.

Sagra del Tordo

Montalcino (0577 849331). **Date** last wknd in Oct.

After all the customary blessing, dancing and parading in medieval costume for this 'feast of the thrush', two champions for each of the town's four neighbourhoods compete in an archery tournament in the grounds of a 14th-century stronghold. Later, attention turns to the succulent fowl and meat roasting on the coals, and to a glass of the celebrated Brunello wine.

Florence Marathon

Florence (055 5522957/fax 055 5536823/www.firenzemarathon.it). **Date** last Sun in Nov.

The race kicks off at 9am from piazzale Michelangelo and finishes in piazza Santa Croce. Anyone over 18 can enter; applications can be made online, by fax or by post up to the day before the race. A health certificate must be also be presented. *See also p204.*

Winter

Nativities

Throughout Tuscany. **Date** Dec-Jan.

As Christmas approaches, the Italian tradition of Nativity scenes is embraced in various ways and places. Many churches set up cribs, the main ones in Florence being in the Duomo, at San Lorenzo, Santa Croce, Chiesa di Dante and Santa Maria de' Ricci. Some country villages also stage *presepi viventi* – live re-enactments of the Nativity.

Christmas Market

Date 1st 2wks in Dec. **Open** 10am-10pm daily.

This picturesque German-style 'Weihnachtsmarkt' has become an irresistible destination for the Florentines' Christmas shopping sprees.

Christmas

Christmas in Florence is marked by the usual suspects of shopping, decorations, eating and drinking and special events throughout December. An ice-skating rink is set up at the Parterre on piazza della Libertà, while piazza della Repubblica hosts a huge Christmas tree and an information booth on ongoing events. Meanwhile, the Amici degli Uffizi puts up a free themed exhibition displaying major artworks from the Uffizi deposits, and free concerts of all music genres are held daily. Some restaurants are open on Christmas Day, but you'll find more choice on 26 December.

New Year's Eve

With restaurants and clubs charging preposterous figures for dinner and dancing parties, increasing numbers of Italians spend the long festive night of San Silvestro among friends and family at home, with a gigantic meal (including the mandatory stuffed pigs' trotters and lentils) and a fair supply of firecrackers and sparklers to 'burn' the past year and welcome in the new. An inexpensive and fun option is the many street parties and free concerts put on in several Tuscan towns.

La Befana (Epiphany)

Date 6 Jan.

La Befana, a ragged old woman riding a broomstick, rewards well-behaved children with stockings full of toys and sweets, while naughty kids just get a sockful of coal. Many small towns around the region hold street parties in celebration, while in Pistoia La Befana gets stuck up the cathedral belfry due to a failure of her broom, and firemen perform a spectacular rescue. Fun for children.

Carnevale di Viareggio

Viareggio (0584 962568/www.ilcarnevale.com). **Date** late Jan-early Mar.

Most Tuscan towns have *carnevale* celebrations, ranging from parades of elaborate floats to simple fancy-dress parties. In Florence, children dress up and scatter confetti along lungarno Amerigo Vespucci. However, the biggest carnival in the region dates back to 1873 and is held in the seaside town of Viareggio on the three Sundays before Shrove Tuesday (at 3pm), on Mardi Gras (again at 3pm) and on the following Sunday (from 5pm, followed by the award ceremony for the best floats and a fireworks display). The parades consist of over-the-top processions of gigantic papier mâché satirical floats that take 100 people the best part of a year to assemble. You can buy seats in one of the stands flanking the Lungomare, but, as long as you watch out for your valuables, it's more fun to be among the revelling crowds.

Children

Dazzling views, Pinocchio puppets and engaging activities – you won't have to rely on the ice-cream to keep them sweet.

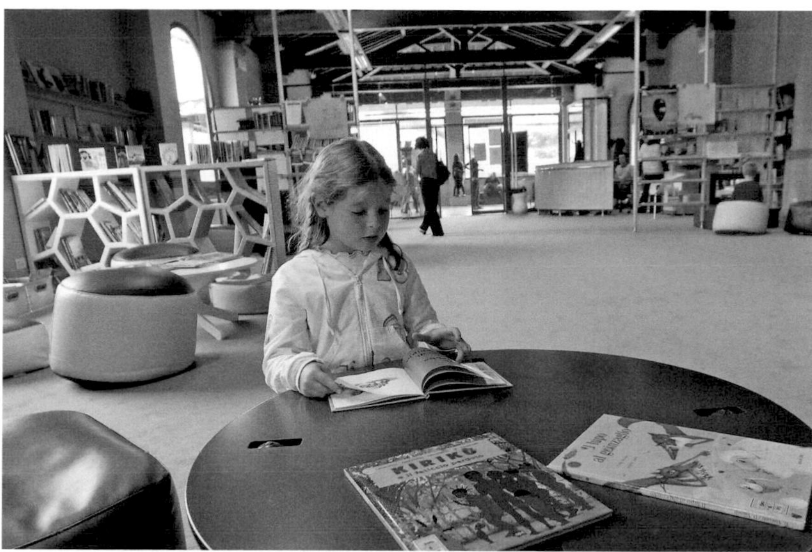

Let them learn about the city in their own time at **Biblioteca delle Oblate**. *See p176.*

One vital trick to make your family holiday in Tuscany a successful one is timing your visit outside the peak tourist season, so you won't need to fret about your kids getting lost in the crowds; Florence is a fairly child-sized – and child-friendly – place, and your main concern should be making sure your kids have *fun*. Their sense of the place will improve dramatically if you show them the city from above early on and pinpoint the main sights on a good, visual map: climb the stairs to the top of the **Cupola** or **Campanile** (*see p75*), or catch a bus to **piazzale Michelangelo** (*see p114*).

The good news is that under-18s can enter all state-owned museums (listed on www.polo museale.firenze.it) free of charge, although it may be worth paying the advance booking fee for the busiest museums in order to avoid the frequently long queues. Museum bookshops often stock relevant activity books and special children's guidebooks, so these are worth checking out before you start your visit. The **Associazione Musei dei Ragazzi** (*see p85*) runs activities and guided visits for children and families in several galleries, including at least a dozen different programmes in Palazzo Vecchio alone, while other institutions have children's workshops. Again, phone ahead to book wherever possible.

In addition to **La Befana** festival in January (*see p174*), children take the spotlight at **Carnevale** in February and **La Rificolona** in September (for both, *see p174*). On a sultry summer day, head for an outdoor swimming pool (*see p204*) or plan an outing to the beach or the countryside.

For shops selling children's clothes, *see p151*.

Bookshops & libraries

Most of the largest bookshops in town, including **Edison** and **Feltrinelli International** (for both, *see p151*), stock a fair selection of videos, games and children's books. The **Paperback Exchange** (*see p151*) occasionally runs readings of children's books in English on Saturday afternoons. For **Libri Liberi**, *see p177* **Teatrino del Gallo**.

Arts & Entertainment

Biblioteca delle Oblate

Via dell'Oriuolo 26, Duomo & Around (055 2616512/www.bibliotecadelleoblate.it). **Open** 8.30am-6.30pm Mon-Fri; 8.30am-1.30pm Sat & 16 July-31 Aug. **Admission** free. **Map** p335 B4.
The new city library has an attractive, open-plan room on the top floor designed for children. Books in several languages can be taken directly from the shelves, while games and DVD cartoons may be requested from the desk by an adult free of charge.

BM American British Bookstore

Borgo Ognissanti 4r, Santa Maria Novella (055 294575/www.bmbookshop.com). **Open** 9am-7.30pm Mon-Sat. *Apr-June, Sept, Oct, Dec* 9am-7.30pm Mon-Sat; 10.30am-7pm Sun. **Credit** AmEx, DC, MC, V. **Map** p334 B1.
A tiny independent with one of the best collections of English titles in Florence, including a wide range of new and collectable children's books. Specialists in Italian traditions and folklore.

Toy shops

Bartolucci

Via Condotta 12r, Duomo & Around (055 221779/www.bartolucci.com). **Open** 9.30am-7.30pm daily. **Credit** AmEx, MC, V. **Map** p335 C4.
Individually crafted pinewood rabbit-clocks and cat-lamps, spring guns and rocking horses, as well as Vespa replicas and Pinocchio puppets, all the result of three generations' worth of Bartolucci expertise.
Other locations Borgo dei Greci, 11a-r, Santa Croce (055 2398596).

Città del Sole

Via dei Cimatori 21r, Duomo & Around (055 219345/www.cittadelsole.com). **Open** 3.30-7.30pm Mon; 10am-7.30pm Tue-Sat. Closed 1wk Aug. **Credit** AmEx, MC, V. **Map** p335 C4.
Educational toys, board games and puzzles.

Dreoni Giocattoli

Via Cavour 31-33r, San Marco (055 216611/www.dreoni.it). **Open** 3.30-7.30pm Mon; 9am-1pm, 3.30-7.30pm Tue-Sat. Closed Mon morning in winter, Sat afternoon in summer. **Credit** AmEx, DC, MC, V. **Map** p335 A4.
A model car collector's heaven, this gallery is also the place to go for Carnevale and Halloween costumes.

Natura e...

Via dello Studio 30r, Duomo & Around (055 2657624/www.natura-e.com). **Open** *Summer* 10am-2pm, 3-7.30pm Mon-Fri; 10am-2pm Sat. *Winter* 10am-2pm, 3-7.30pm Mon-Sat. **Credit** MC, V. **Map** p335 B4.
Nature-lovers of all ages will find anything from scientific toys to outdoor trekking gear.

Eating out

Bustling family *trattorie* and *pizzerie* that make dishes to order are the most suitable choices for children with less adventurous palates. Just ask for a simple *pasta al pomodoro* (with tomato sauce), or a half portion (*mezza porzione*) of what you're ordering. For lunch, instead of heading for the ubiquitous fast-food options, try buying picnic goodies at a market (*see p150* **Playing the market**) and head for a park (*see below*). For the best ice-cream parlours in Florence, *see p146*.

Il Cucciolo

Via del Corso 25r, Duomo & Around (055 287727). **Open** 7.30am-8.30pm Mon-Sat. Closed 3wks Aug. **No credit cards. Map** p335 B4.
This bar is popular with Florentine children due to the *bomboloni* (doughnuts), made on the upper floor then dropped down a tube and served hot.

Mr Jimmy's American Bakery

Piazza Pitti 6, Oltrarno (055 2480999/www.mr-jimmy.com). **Open** 10am-8pm Mon-Sat. Closed Aug. **Credit** AmEx, DC, MC, V. **Map** p335 D5.
International bakery specialising in American-style pies, cakes and pastries as well as Neapolitan seasonal sweets. Home delivery available.

I Tarocchi

Via dei Renai 12-14r, Oltrarno (055 2343912). **Open** 12.30-2.30pm, 7pm-1am Tue-Fri. **Average** €12. **Credit** AmEx, DC, MC, V. **Map** p335 D4/5.
Child-friendly pizza and pasta portions, in an informal room with long tables. High chairs available.

Leisure activities

Gardens & parks

Boboli Gardens

For listings, *see p108*.
The Boboli Gardens' labyrinths, grottoes, fountains, statues and hiding places make great diversions for children, while parents can enjoy magnificent views.

Parco Carraia

Entrance off via dell'Erta Canina, San Niccolò, Outside the City Gates. Bus 23.
This little-known park is just a stroll up from Porta San Miniato but feels miles away from the city. You'll find swings, picnic facilities and green space.

Parco delle Cascine

Entrance nr ponte della Vittoria, Outside the City Gates. Bus 17C.
Stretching west of the city on the right bank of the Arno, Florence's largest park hosts regular fairs and markets. It's at its busiest on Sundays, with parties playing football and families picnicking. Playgrounds dot the park, and in-line skates can be hired.

Play centres

La Bottega dei Ragazzi

Via dei Fibbiai 2, San Marco (055 2478386/www.istitutodeglinnocenti.it). **Open** 9am-1pm, 3-7pm Mon-

Sat. Closed Aug. **Admission** €10 for 1 entrance; €50 for 8 entrances. **No credit cards**. **Map** p335 A5.
Learn-through-play 90-minute workshops in Italian, English, French and Spanish for children aged three to 11, from 10am to noon and 5pm to 6.30pm Monday to Saturday. Workshops do not require the presence of parents and focus either on art history and techniques or on issues such as children's rights, multiculturalism and recycling. There's also a free playroom with games and books for children accompanied by an adult (9am-1pm and 3-6pm Mon-Sat).

Canadian Island

Via Gioberti 15, Outside the City Gates (055 677567/ www.canadianisland.com). Bus 3, 6, 14. **Open** *June, July, Sept* 8am-5pm Mon-Fri. *Oct-May* 8am-2pm, 3.30-6.30pm Mon-Fri; 9am-1pm Sat. Closed Aug. **Admission** €30 afternoon. **No credit cards**.
Childcare for kids aged between three and 12 by responsible, English- and Italian-speaking adults. They also organise summer sleepover and day camps in the Tuscan countryside.

Mondobimbo Inflatables

Parterre, via Mafalda di Savoia (by piazza della Libertà), Outside the City Gates (055 5532946). **Open** *June-July* 10am-1pm, 4.30-11.30pm daily; *Sept-May* 10am-1pm, 3.30-7.30pm daily. Closed Aug. **Admission** €5 day ticket. **Credit** MC, V.
Huge bouncy castles, whales, dogs and snakes for under-tens. Children must wear socks.

Museo Fiorentino di Preistoria

For listings, *see p104*.
Would-be cave dwellers can learn to paint, weave and make pots. There's a regular programme of activities, but workshops lasting one to three hours can also be scheduled on demand on Mondays and Saturdays (9.30am-12.30pm) or Tuesdays and Thursdays (1.30-4.30pm) for a fee of €40 to €70.

St James's American Church

Via Bernardo Rucellai 9, Santa Maria Novella (055 294417/www.stjames.it). **Open** 9am-1pm Mon-Fri (office). *Activities* phone to check. **No credit cards**. **Map** p334 A1.
Child- and family-oriented activities, as well as English-language Sunday School and nursery care. Also provides referrals for dependable babysitters, while the undercroft is available for parties.

Theatre

For the children's shows at **Teatro Cantiere Florida**, *see p206*.

Teatrino del Gallo

Via San Gallo 25-27r, San Lorenzo (055 2658324/ www.teatrinodelgallo.it). **Open** see website for show times. Closed 3wks in Aug. **Tickets** €5 children; €7 adults. **Credit** AmEx, DC, MC, V. **Map** p335 A4.
The lemon house and garden of the Libri Liberi bookshop host a regular afternoon programme of puppet and theatre shows for kids aged three to 13.

Out of town

Bambimus Museo d'arte per bambini

Santa Maria della Scala, piazza del Duomo 2, Siena (0577 46517/www.comune.siena.it/bambimus). **Open** 10.30am-6.30pm daily; school visits some mornings, phone to check. **Admission** €6. **No credit cards**. **Map** p334 C2.
Starting from its own permanent collection, this museum's activities provide an introduction to art appreciation for children over three. In Italian, but with English and French support.

Giardino Zoologico

Via Pieve a Celle 160, Pistoia (0573 911219/www.zoodipistoia.it). **Open** *Summer* 9am-6.30pm Mon-Fri; 9am-7pm Sat, Sun. *Winter* 9am-5pm daily. Last entry 1hr before closing. **Admission** €10.50; €8.50 3-9s; free under-3s. **No credit cards**.
The park is home to over 600 animals, including around 65 species of mammals, 40 species of birds and 30 of reptiles.

Parco Preistorico

Peccioli, via Cappuccini 20, Pisa (0587 636030/ 635430/www.parcopreistorico.it). **Open** *Apr-Aug* 9am-7pm daily. **Admission** *Apr-Aug* €4. *Sept-Mar* €4 adults, €3 children. **No credit cards**.
About 40km (25 miles) south-east of Pisa, this park has life-size models of dinosaurs, a play area and picnic facilities. Free overnight stay for motor caravans.

Just for kicks

Budding champions will be enthralled by Florence's football museum, housed in a converted barn adjoining Casa Italia in Coverciano. 'Casa Italia' is the nickname for the central training grounds of the Italian national football team and technical headquarters of FIGC, the Italian Football Association. Exhibits in the museum range from the actual World Cups won by Italy to a vast collection of football-related postage stamps, as well as the shirts of Italian and international footballers. The huge multimedia databank with photos and video footage from 1898 to the present day provides an entertaining insight into the country's best-loved sport.

Museo del Calcio

Viale Palazzeschi 20, Coverciano, Outside the City Gates (055 600526/www.museodelcalcio.it). Bus 17 to the Viale Volta Terminus. **Open** 9am-1pm, 4-6pm Mon-Fri, 9am-1pm Sat. Closed Aug. **Admission** €3, incl audio guide; €1.50 6-14s; free under-6s.

Film

The city evokes a plethora of romanticised film sets, but Florence's alfresco cinema scene keeps things real.

Romanticised, picture-perfect scenes from *A Room with a View* have burned an image of Florence into the collective psyche of the English-speaking world and beyond. Although Merchant-Ivory's adaptation of the Edwardian classic is now over two decades old, it still strikes a chord with visitors who, like Lucy Honeychurch, come to Florence to be transfigured by Giotto's frescoes in Santa Croce. Ridley Scott's *Hannibal* represents the polar perspective, being the movie that best captures the psychopathic, dark medieval heart of Florentine history, through its allusion to the Pazzi conspiracy. For a prettified version of wartime Florence, meanwhile, Franco Zeffirelli's *Tea with Mussolini* is your film, with its English stiff upper lip resistance to Fascist bully boys.

Other celluloid depictions of Florence are offered in Jane Campion's version of Henry James's *The Portrait of a Lady*, in *Up at the Villa* – a lesser-known adaptation of a Somerset Maugham story starring Sean Penn – and in Anthony Minghella's multiple award-winning *The English Patient*, which revisits wartime Italy and captures the magic of ancient Tuscan churches, isolated villas and quaint hill towns. Adaptations of two of Shakepeare's tales, Kenneth Branagh's *Much Ado About Nothing* and Michael Hoffman's *A Midsummer Night's Dream,* make the most of the backdrop offered by the unique Tuscan landscape for their comic romps. Best forgotten is the sentimental *bella Toscana* nonsense of *Under the Tuscan Sun*, with its ghastly San Franciscan interloper trying to ingratiate herself with the locals in a self-serving bid for mid-life transformation.

A rather more suave character was making an impression on Tuscany in 2007 – Daniel Craig's James Bond was shooting the 22nd film in the franchise in Siena as we went to press.

GETTING A SEAT

Florence's cinematic circuit is not generally accessible for non-Italian-speakers, while Italians are generally loath to sit through a subtitled film. The fairly recent Warner Village 11-screen multiplex **Il Magnifico** (via del Cavallacio, 055 7870000, www.warnervillage.it, bus 1), slightly out of town, has been drawing cinemagoers away from the city centre and the consequence has been predictable, if unfortunate: some of the old cinemas in the city centre can no longer maintain their customer base, so some are turning into bingo halls while others just lie idle and abandoned. Nonetheless, the very central **Odeon Cinema**, with its Original Sound programme (*see below*), continues to show international films in their original languages (*versione originale*) three nights a week. More varied programmes, including subtitled films, are offered at film clubs (*cineclubs*; *see p179*).

Italians have an aversion to booking, especially for the cinema, so expect chaos on Friday and Saturday nights for new releases. You may also find yourself invaded by people looking for the best seats for the next show before your show has finished. When the *posto in piedi* light is lit, the tickets sold are standing-room only. If you speak Italian, check the cheaper matinées offered at many main cinemas on weekdays before 6.30pm or all day Wednesday, when it costs €5 instead of the standard €7.20. (The reduction doesn't usually apply to original-language screenings.) For information, check *La Maschera*, an information sheet on display at most bars that contains movie and theatre listings. *The Florentine* (*see p309*) also has cinema listings for anglophones. For festivals and other special events, check local listings such as *Firenze Spettacolo* or in the local supplement of the national daily *La Repubblica*.

Online resources include www.mymovies.it and *La Repubblica*'s cinema-search website (www.repubblica.it/trovacinema).

Cinemas

British Institute Cultural Programme

Lungarno Guicciardini 9, Oltrarno (055 267781/ www.britishinstitute.it). **Open** *Lectures* from 6pm. *Screenings* from 8.30pm. **Tickets** €5 plus €5 membership. **No credit cards. Map** p334 C2.

The British Institute runs a Talking Pictures programme on Wednesday evenings. A movie is sandwiched between an introduction and a discussion, all in English. It also runs courses in Italian cinema.

Odeon Original Sound

Piazza Strozzi 2, Duomo & Around (055 295051/ 295331/www.cinehall.it). **Open** *Box office* times vary. Closed Aug. **Tickets** €7.20. **No credit cards. Map** p334 B3.

Catch a flick under the stars at **Cinema Arena di Marte**. *See p180.*

Mondays, Tuesdays and Thursdays are big draws for English-speakers at this stunning art nouveau cinema. Films on current release in English are screened, sometimes with Italian subtitles. There's a discount of up to 40% with a club card for eight films from a programme of 13 (€36); alternatively, use the voucher from the previous Sunday's *La Repubblica* for 30% off.

Cineclubs

Part of the attraction of Florence's film clubs is the value for money they offer, especially for students, although you normally have to buy membership first.

CineCittà

Via Pisana 576, Scandicci, Outside the City Gates (055 7324510). Bus 6. **Shows** times vary. **Tickets** €3-€5. **Membership** €1. **No credit cards.**

Hollywood action pictures and festivals of obscure Italian films. Some screenings are shown in their original language or with subtitles.

Cineteca di Firenze

Via R Giuliani 374, Outside the City Gates (055 450749/www.cinetecadifirenze.it). Bus 2, 18, 28. **Shows** times vary. **Tickets** €4-€5. **Membership** €3. **No credit cards.**

Cycles of films showcasing various actors, some in their original language.

Stensen Cineforum

Viale Don Minzoni 25C, Outside the City Gates (055 576551/5535858/www.stensen.org). Bus 1, 7, 12. **Shows** usually 9.15pm Thur-Sat (except in summer), but phone to check. **Tickets** prices vary. **No credit cards. Map** p334 B2.

The Stensen screens Italian and foreign films, but only for holders of season tickets. It also runs lectures and debates. The Korea Filmfest (www.koreafilmfest.com), usually held in March, showcases contemporary and classic South Korean cinema.

Seasonal cinema

The two major international film festivals, usually screening in original language, are in Florence and Fiesole. In November or December the **Festival dei Popoli** (055 244778) screens dramas and documentaries – centring around a social issue – in clubs and cinemas throughout Florence. The **Premio Fiesole ai Maestri del Cinema** (055 597107, www.comune.fiesole.fi.it), held in July/August in Fiesole's open-air Roman theatre, pays homage to the works of one director. Recent honorands have included Ken Loach, Bernardo Bertolucci and Spike Lee.

In addition, recent years have seen **France Cinema** (055 214053, www.francecinema.it) grow in importance. The festival is usually held in November at the French Institute (piazza Ognissanti 2, 055 2398902) and the Teatro della Compagnia (via Cavour 50r, 055 217428). The annual **River to River** Indian film festival (055 286929, www.rivertoriver.it) is held in December; films are mostly in English, or the original language with English subtitles.

Italians regard cinemagoing in the summer months as an eccentricity reserved for mad dogs and Englishmen. However, a pleasant alternative for Italian-speakers (though international films are sometimes shown in their original languages) or those wanting to sample local life are the area's open-air cinemas, which show recent films from June to September. Shows start as darkness falls – around 9pm to 9.30pm depending on the month – and a couple of cinemas run double bills, with the second film finishing around 1.30am.

Open-air screens

Arena Raggio Verde

Palacongressi Firenze, viale Strozzi, Outside the City Gates (055 4973222/www.ateliergroup.it). **Dates** late June-late Aug. **Tickets** vary. **No credit cards.**
This stunning amphitheatre-style cinema, overlooking a 16th-century villa, runs nightly double bills during summer. Phone ahead for further details.

Cinema Arena di Marte

Palazzetto dello Sport di Firenze, viale Paoli, Outside the City Gates (055 289318/www.ateliergroup.it). Bus 10, 20, 34. **Dates** late June-late Aug. **Open** 8pm (shows 9.30pm daily). **Tickets** €5. **No credit cards.**
One of the two screens at this major outdoor venue shows cult and non-mainstream films (some in their original languages); the larger screen runs the previous year's major blockbuster movies. There's a good outdoor restaurant too. *Photo p179.*

Cinema Chiardiluna Arena

Via Monte Oliveto 1, Outside the City Gates (055 218682). Bus 12, 13. **Dates** June-Sept. **Open** 8pm (shows 9.30pm) daily. **Tickets** €5. **No credit cards.**
Surrounded by woodland, Chiardiluna is cooler than the other outdoor cinemas, but you should still take mosquito repellent. The movies are generally recent commercial releases, with some double bills.

Forte di Belvedere

Porta San Giorgio, Oltrarno (055 2625908/www.fiesta.com/www.firenze-oltrarno.net). **Dates** late June-late Aug. **Admission** free.
Restoration work at this star-shaped fortress in the Boboli Gardens (*see p107*) has finished, and a full programme of events, including open-air screenings, is in place. It's worth the trek up the steep hill, where films are screened on the breezy terrace. Screen size has been sacrificed for more bar and restaurant space.

The Tuscan king of comedy

'I want to kiss you all!' he said, before clambering over the back of the big-screen bigwigs' seats and French-kissing Sophia Loren on the way to collecting a second Oscar for *Life is Beautiful* (*La vita è bella*), the first Best Actor gong ever awarded to a lead in a foreign film. The irony, of course, is that the ebullient, irrepressible, half-crazed Roberto Benigni, the greatest clown Italy has seen since Totò, won the prize for what is by far his most serious film, the bittersweet story of a father determined to save not just his young son's life but his childish innocence amid the desperation of a Nazi concentration camp.

A true Tuscan by birth and nature, Benigni was born in Misericordia, near Arezzo, and was brought up in Vergaio, near Prato. He encapsulates the stereotypical *toscanaccio* character: left-wing, highly cultured yet unapologetically vulgar. His stand-up shows, TV turns and interviews revolve around a tirade of hilarious jibes at politicians in general and former Prime Minister Silvio Berlusconi in particular (he's long been a critic of the conservative ruling elite). He can recite from memory Dante's *Divine Comedy* in its entirety and now has a touring show called *Tutto Dante,* which weaves his serious and scholarly side into his comedy routines. His film parts, such as Walter Matthau's hard-to-shake *Little Devil* and a taxi driver detailing his sheep fetish to a shocked priest in *Night on Earth,* are all too convincing.

Buoyed by the popularity brought to him by the controversial *Life is Beautiful* both here and abroad, Benigni sank a mountain of money into his dream project: a live-action version of *Pinocchio.* His love for the tale was nurtured during a childhood spent practically next door to the wooden boy's home town of Collodi; 'I've been waiting for my nose to grow for 20 years,' Benigni quipped. Although the movie broke box office records in Italy, it was mercilessly slated abroad for being clumsily dumbed down; the film won two David di Donatello awards (Italian Oscars) for Best Set and Best Costume Design, but Benigni was awarded the prize for Worst Actor at the 2003 Golden Raspberry Awards. Yet Benigni isn't one to be down for long, and he bounced back, appearing in Jim Jarmusch's *Coffee and Cigarettes* (2003), and in the rather poorly received *La Tigre e la Neve* (*The Tiger and the Snow*; 2005), starring and directed by the man himself. Benigni's international movie career appears to have hit a rough patch of late; but, like him or loathe him, it's unlikely he'll be out of the picture for long.

Galleries

With so much focus on the art of the past, Florence's increasingly vibrant contemporary scene is often overlooked – but it shouldn't be.

Leave your stylistic preconceptions at the door of **57 Rosso Art Gallery**.

Contemporary art in Florence is increasingly an outdoor affair. The early demise of Quarter – the much-fanfared contemporary art centre – and continuing delays for a major public art forum at the former Meccanotessile factory have led to a change in emphasis. Private donations and public acquisitions are now proudly displayed in main city squares and gardens. The city's most crucial contributions to contemporary art continue to come from the restaurants, bars and hotels that show the work of local and even international artists. **BZF (Bizzeffe**; *see p143*), **Astor Caffé** (*see p141*), **Rex Café** (*see p199*), **Gallery Hotel Art** (*see p53*) and **Caruso Jazz Café** (*see p141*) are among those putting on regular, gallery-worthy exhibitions. *See also p56* **Painting by room numbers**.

Gallery spaces

57 Rosso Art Gallery

Via de' Fossi 57r, Santa Maria Novella (055 2741486/www.57rossoartgallery.com). **Open** 9.30am-1pm, 3-7pm Mon-Sat. **Credit** MC, V. **Map** p334 B2.

A sparkling white space showing contemporary sculpture, paintings, drawings and installations. The unpretentious owners choose artists on the basis of merit in any style or medium; the result is a uniquely eclectic mix.

Base

Via San Niccolò 18r, Oltrarno (055 2207281/679378/www.baseitaly.org). **Open** 5-8pm Mon-Sat. **No credit cards**. **Map** p335 D4.

A centre of excellence for Tuscany-based artists specialising in film, installation and digital art.

BrancoliniGrimaldi

Vicolo dell'Oro 12r, Duomo & Around (055 2396263/www.isabellabrancolini.it). **Open** 10am-7.30pm Mon-Fri. Closed Aug. **No credit cards**. **Map** p334 C3.

A dozen emerging artists from all over the world are chosen for their originality and outlandish styles for this gallery, part of the Ferragamo Gallery Hotel Art and Lungarno Suites complex, situated beside the group's Continentale hotel (*see p54*).

Falteri

Via della Spada 38r, Santa Maria Novella (055 217740/www.falteri.it). **Open** 10am-1pm, 4-7.30pm Tue-Sat. **No credit cards**. **Map** p334 A2.

A small gallery specialising in master prints and drawing from the early 1500s to the first half of the 20th century. Since the move to its current home, the gallery has started to broaden its horizons, holding exhibitions of contemporary painters, such as Antonio Biancalani and Ana Kapor.

Fondazione Pitti Immagine Discovery

Via Faenza 111, San Lorenzo (055 36931/www.pittimmagine.com). **Open** 9am-1pm, 2-5pm Mon-Fri. **Credit** AmEx, MC, V. **Map** p334 A2.

Pitti Immagine stages major fashion, textiles and interiors shows in Florence. It also offers exhibitions – anything from installations to displays of fashion photography – in the Pitti building on via Faenza.

Forte Belvedere

Via San Leonardo, Oltrarno (www.comune.firenze.it/www.fi-esta.com). **Open** times vary. **No credit cards. Map** p334 D3.

The newly reopened fort, with its panoramic views, hosts a series of exhibitions of modern and contemporary art. The inaugural show brought together pieces from 15 of the city's top galleries, but with slightly disappointing results. However, the location alone makes it a prime spot for future exhibitions, for which we have higher hopes.

Galleria Alessandro Bagnai

Via Salutati 4r, Outside the City Gates (055 6802066/www.galleriabagnai.it). **Open** 10am-1pm, 3-7pm Mon-Sat, Sun by appointment. Closed Aug. **No credit cards. Map** p334 D2.

Bagnai has moved to a calm, cavernous space, with skylights creating good viewing light. The gallery is outside the centre, but worth making the trip to see Tuscan sculptor Roberto Barni's nonchalant bronze men, Paolo Grassino's proud but legless reindeer, Dormice's defiant bimbo paintings, and work from modern and contemporary art icons.

Galleria Biagiotti Arte Contemporanea

Via delle Belle Donne 39r, Santa Maria Novella (055 214757/www.artbiagiotti.com). **Open** 2-7pm Tue-Sat. Closed Aug. **No credit cards. Map** p334 B2.

Carole Biagiotti runs this stunning 15th-century converted atrium gallery like a fairy godmother, supporting young international artists. Installations are a favourite, and have previously featured elephants in 'un-gilded' cages and even the artists themselves in 'live' works. Pieces often sell to collectors unseen.

Galleria Il Ponte

Via di Mezzo 42B, Santa Maria Novella (055 240617). **Open** *Sept-June* 4-7.30pm Tue-Sat. *July* 4-7.30pm Mon-Fri. Closed Aug. **No credit cards. Map** p335 B6.

Modern and contemporary abstract painters and sculptors feature in major retrospectives at this respected gallery and art publishing house. Recent shows have seen the gallery broaden its horizons to include younger up-and-coming artists.

Galleria Pananti

Via Maggio 15, Oltrarno (055 2741011/www.pananti.com). **Open** 9.30am-1pm, 3-7pm Mon-Fri. Closed Aug. **No credit cards. Map** p334 C5.

One of the most important art hubs of the city, this gallery and auction house hosts major contemporary shows and retrospectives of modern artists, with an emphasis on figurative photography and painting.

Galleria Paradigma

Via de' Fossi 41r, Santa Maria Novella (055 2776265/www.galleriaparadigma.it). **Open** 10.30am-12.45pm, 3.30-7pm Mon-Fri. **Credit** MC, V. **Map** p334 B2.

A prestigious yet understated gallery showing 20th-century art and *objets*. Highlights are Paolo Staccioli's Etruscan-inspired vases and iridescent female figures, and Pino Chierchi's bright, totemic glass discs.

Galleria Santo Ficara

Via Ghibellina 164r, Santa Croce (055 2340239/www.santoficara.it). **Open** 9.30am-12.30pm, 3.30-7.30pm Mon-Sat. Closed Aug. **Credit** AmEx, DC, MC, V. **Map** p335 C5.

The walls of this important city-centre gallery, with its tall vaulted ceilings, are hung with works by established artists with an international market, such as 1950s Gruppo Forma member Carla Accardi.

Galleria Tornabuoni

Borgo San Jacopo 53r, Oltrarno (055 284720/www.galleriatornabuoni.it). **Open** 3.30-7.30pm Mon; 9.30am-1pm, 3.30-7.30pm Tue-Sat. **Credit** AmEx, DC, MC, V. **Map** p334 B2.

This important Florentine gallery was forced out of via de' Tornabuoni by rising rents. It's fallen on its feet with its new home (though has kept the old name). The gallery still works with iconic local artists such as Guiliano Tomaino and Francesco Musante.

Ken's Art Gallery

Via San Niccolò 23r, Oltrano (055 242895/www.kensartgallery.com). **Open** 10am-1pm, 3-8pm Mon-Sat. **Credit** AmEx, DC, MC, V. **Map** p334 C3.

Walter Bellini's exciting gallery was one of the first in the city to exhibit mixed media. The contemporary pieces are all by Florence-based artists.

Mirabili

Lungarno Guicciardini 21r, Oltrarno (055 294257/www.mirabili.it). **Open** 3-7.30pm Mon; 9.30am-1pm, 3-7.30pm Tue-Sat. Closed Aug. **Credit** AmEx, DC, MC, V. **Map** p334 C2.

The collections of furniture, *objets* and artworks here have been exhibited in high-profile international spaces. Artists include Ettore Sottsass and Max Ernst.

Poggiali e Forconi

Via della Scala 35A, Santa Maria Novella (055 287748/www.poggialieforconi.it). **Open** *June-Sept* 9.30am-1.30pm Mon-Sat. Closed 2wks Aug. *Oct-May* 9.30am-1.30pm, 3-7pm Mon-Sat. **Credit** AmEx, MC, V. **Map** p334 B2.

This series of arched spaces showcases the works of some of Italy's best-known young artists. Shows have featured Livio Scarpella's brash nudes.

Gay & Lesbian

The city's gay golden age has passed – but head to the coast for the renaissance.

Mama Mia. *See p185.*

Though Florence has been popular with gay writers, artists and travellers for centuries, it was only in 1970 that the city got its first proper gay disco, **Tabasco** (*see p184*), which is still going strong today. Around the same time, the **Fronte Unitario Omosessuale Rivoluzionario Italiano (FUORI** – Italian for 'out'), Tuscany's first gay and lesbian organisation, was set up. Other landmarks include the opening of the gay cultural space **Banana Moon** in borgo degli Albizi in 1977 and the founding of the regional chapter of **ArciGay/Lesbica**, the leading organisation for gay political initiatives in 1980s Italy. In the 1990s, it split into two groups: **IREOS** (www.ireos.org), a social, cultural and information centre, and more political **Azione Gay e Lesbica** (www.gayelesbica.it).

Florence has lost quite a few of its gay and lesbian entertainment offerings in the last few years, and the scene is less active than in the golden years of the 1980s. On weekends, many people go to larger cities, like Bologna or Rome.

No problems should arise from holding hands in the street in Florence and Tuscany, but anything much more overt in public is less acceptable (outside the gay resorts). Men have several cruising options, though some can be dangerous. The Parco delle Cascine, for instance, is active from sunset till late, but local cognoscenti warn against it. Another popular area is the Campo di Marte (in western Florence), where most cruising takes place in cars. The park at viale Malta near the football stadium is active too, but subject to frequent incursions from police checking IDs.

The age of consent in Italy is 18; clubs and bars check ID. For some venues you will need an ArciGay/Lesbica membership card, which currently costs €14 per year and is available at any of the venues that require it (noted below).

Florence

Bars

Bar 85

Via Guelfa 85r, San Lorenzo (055 216050/www.bar 85.eu). **Open** 5pm-3am Mon-Thur; 5pm-6am Fri, Sat. **Admission** €6; membership free. **Credit** AmEx, DC, MC, V. **Map** p335 A4.

A new bar in Florence with a 'leather' vibe, geared to a mature crowd. Music caters to all tastes.

BK Bar – Butterfly Kiss

Via Alfieri 95, Sesto Fiorentino, Outside the City Gates (055 4218878/www.bkbar.com). Bus 2, 28. **Open** 7am-2am daily. **Admission** free. **No credit cards.**

This pub may not be centrally located but it's nonetheless highly popular with women, who come for the parlour games, themed performances and photography exhibitions.

Crisco

Via Sant'Egidio 43r, Santa Croce (055 2480580/ www.crisco.it). **Open** 11pm-3am Mon, Wed, Thur, Sun; 10pm-6am Fri, Sat. Closed 2wks mid Feb. **Admission** free membership. **Credit** MC, V. **Map** p335 B5.

A well-known, long-standing bar offering videos (mostly X-rated), special events, parties and a variety of performances. The exclusively male crowd is mixed but leathermen and bears prevail.

Muna
Via Maffia 31r, Oltrarno (055 287198/www.muna ciello.it). **Open** 8pm-2am daily. **Admission** free. **Credit** AmEx, MC, V. **Map** p334 C1.
A small, new locale in the central Santo Spirito area, defined by minimalist design and cocktails. It's also a good place for dinner, in the Mediterranean-style restaurant O'Munaciello that Muna adjoins.

Piccolo Caffè
Borgo Santa Croce 23, Santa Croce (055 2001057/ www.piccolofirenze.com). **Open** 6.30pm-2.30am daily. **Admission** free. **Credit** AmEx, DC, MC, V. **Map** p335 C5.
Attracting a very mixed crowd, the Piccolo gets especially packed on Fridays and Saturdays. Check out the frequent art exhibitions and live shows.

YAG B@R
Via de' Macci 8r, Santa Croce (055 2469022/www. yagbar.com). **Open** 8pm-3am daily. **Admission** free. **Credit** AmEx, DC, MC, V. **Map** p335 C6.
This spacious, futuristic dance bar draws a young crowd of both genders, often here as a first stop on the club-hopping route. Current tunes dominate, and internet access and video games are also to hand.

Clubs

Azione Gay e Lesbica at Auditorium FLOG
For listing, *see p191* Auditorium FLOG.
Once a month on a Friday, a megafest of DJs, cabaret acts and bands draws a huge and diverse crowd out to this Poggetto venue in support of Azione Gay e Lesbica (*see below*). It's also a great place to stock up on literature and information on all the latest goings-on in the local gay community.

Fabrik
Viale del Lavoro, 19, Calenzano (349 8906645 mobile/ www.fabrikfirenze.it). Bus 2, 28. **Open** 10pm-4am Tue-Sun. **Admission** €12 with ArciGay membership. **No credit cards**.
About 15km (nine miles) from Florence, Fabrik constitutes two storeys of post-industrial decor, featuring a video-bar and an open-air garden. There's a cruising area with roomy cabins and a darkroom.

Tabasco Disco Gay
Piazza Santa Cecilia 3r, Duomo & Around (055 213000/www.tabascogay.it). **Open** 10pm-6am Tue-Sun. **Admission** €13 Tue-Fri; €15 Sat. **Credit** AmEx, MC, V. **Map** p335 C5.
Founded more than 35 years ago, Tabasco was Florence's first gay club, and has stood the test of time, remaining popular among tourists and young locals of both sexes. Music is mostly techno.

Tenax
Via Pratese 46, Peretola, Outside the City Gates (055 308160/www.tenax.org). Bus 29, 30. **Open** 10pm-4am Sat. Closed mid May-Sept. **Admission** €25 women; €30 men. **Credit** AmEx, MC, V.
Saturday nights at this trendy Peretola club go by the name of Nobody's Perfect. But that doesn't stop an international fashion crowd going all out to look flawless – so make sure you dress the part.

Saunas

Florence Baths
Via Guelfa 93r, San Lorenzo (055 216050/www. tabascogay.it). **Open** 2pm-2am Mon-Thur, Sun; 2pm-4am Fri, Sat. **Admission** €13 Mon-Fri; €14 Sat, Sun. **Membership** €16/yr. **Credit** AmEx, MC, V. **Map** p334 A3.
Florence's only sauna offers excellent dry and steam rooms, a jacuzzi (always cold), a bar, and TV and private rooms. It's usually best to arrive in the late afternoon or the early evening.

Services

Associazione Italiana Transessuali
Arci Il Progresso, via Vittorio Emanuele 135, Calenzano (347 3086110 mobile). **Open** 4-8pm Mon.
Support association for identity disorders.

Azione Gay e Lesbica
Via Pisana 32-34r, Oltrarno (055 220250/www. azionegayelesbica.it). **Open** 6-8pm Mon-Fri. Closed 3wks in Aug. **Map** p334 D2.
In addition to the Azione Gay e Lesbica parties it runs, this organisation has a library and offers easy HIV-testing and community information.

IREOS Queer Community Service Center
Via de' Serragli 3-5, Oltrarno (055 216907/ www.ireos.org). **Open** 5-8pm Mon-Thur, Sat. **Map** p334 D1.
IREOS hosts a social open house every Wednesday evening, offering referrals for HIV testing, psychological counselling and self-help groups. It also organises hikes and other day-trips, as well as running the Florence Queer Festival (www.florence queerfestival.it) in September and October. The festival showcases recent films and documentaries on gay, lesbian and transgender issues, and well as organising plays, literature and music events and photography exhibitions.

Bed & breakfasts

The following are gay-friendly options. The **Relais Grand Tour** (*see p63*) is also a great option. For the centrally located, friendly B&B **Dei Mori**, *see p55*.

MartinDago
Via de' Macci 84, Santa Croce (055 2341415/www. martindago.com). **Rates** €120. **Credit** AmEx, DC, MC, V. **Map** p335 C6.
Situated in the Santa Croce area, this recently opened B&B has frescoed ceilings in the bedrooms.

Torre adore

Torre del Lago.

Italy's answer to Spain's Sitges is to be found in the Versilia Riviera, specifically **Torre del Lago Puccini** (named in honour of composer/ former resident Giacomo Puccini, but often just called Torre del Lago), near Viareggio. The town has become something of a gay mecca in recent years, with a host of gay-friendly and gay-owned clubs and bars and several annual events – including Italy's **Mardi Gras** celebration in mid August, **Bears on the Beach** at the end of June (dedicated to bears and their admirers) and **Les Week e Miss Gaya** (lesbian week) in mid July. The organisation Friendly Versilia (www.friendlyversilia.it) has further information.

During the daytime, **Mama Mia Beach**, in the north of the resort and about 100 metres from the club of the same name, is a very elegant bathing spot, equipped with umbrellas, cabins and bar.

Nightlife in Torre del Lago centres on the lively Europa boardwalk, which attracts thousands nightly to its clubs; the most popular include **Mama Mia**, with its waterside terrace (viale Europa 5, 389 6262642 mobile, www.mamamia.tv); trendy **Boca Chica** (viale Europa 1, 338 5951208 mobile, www.bocachica.dj); hotspot **Priscilla**, with drag queen performances (viale Europa 7, 0584 341804, www.priscillacaffe.it); new chill-out space **Adagio** (viale Europa 11, 392 9232446 mobile, www.adagiolounge.com); and **Frau Disco** (viale Europa, 0584 342282).

If you want to start partying early, head to Viareggio for the **Voice Music Bar** (viale Margherita 63, 0584 943321); the club opens in the morning (9.30am-midnight), hosting parties and small raves into the night.

Accommodation is reasonably plentiful. Gay-friendly options include **Caffeletti** (via Pardini 34C, 347 1964685 mobile, www.caffeletti.com, €80), close to the beach, popular gay venues and the Torre del Lago nature reserve; **B&B Fate e Folletti** (via Garibaldi 33, 0584 350546, www.fateefolletti.com, €64-€84), housed in a beautiful central building; and **Le Villi** (viale Puccini 178, 0584 340355, www.levilli.com, €80-€130), a relaxing, colourful spot with a Mediterranean vibe.

Soggiorno Gloria

Via Nazionale 17, San Lorenzo (055 288147/www.soggiornogloria.eu). **Rates** €80. **Credit** AmEx, DC, MC, V. **Map** p334 A3

A pleasant and comfortable hotel with big, bright rooms and generous balconies overlooking the old heart of Florence near the train station. Reception staff can be rather nonchalant.

Radio

Controradio FM 93.6

055 7399970/www.controradio.it.

Every Thursday at 12.30pm, Italian-speakers should tune into *La casalingay*.

Tuscany

In Pisa, **Colours** (via Mossoti 10, 050 500248, www.colors.fm, admission free, closed Mon & Tue) is a mixed high-tech DJ bar, while sauna, steam, jacuzzi and private room facilities can be found at **Sauna Siesta Club 77** (via di Porta A Mare 25-27, 050 2200146, www.siestaclub77.com, admission €12, €10 concessions, closed Sept-Apr, 2wks mid July).

In Lucca, **Hub** (via di Poggio 29, Ponte San Pietro, 389 6262642 mobile, www.hub.fm, admission €10, closed Sun-Fri, 1st 2wks June & 1st 2wks Sept) is a great place for a boogie, pumping out house, funk, techno and more.

Music: Classical & Opera

The city's classical music scene may not be cutting edge, but the wealth of historic settings more than makes up for it.

Florence's classical musical life focuses around the **Teatro del Maggio Musical Fiorentino** (*see p187*), one of the foremost opera houses in Italy. Opera has a special place in the heart of many Italians, and if you get the chance to catch a production at the Maggio, go for it. A performance of a Puccini or Verdi opera by a good Italian orchestra and chorus is almost always a worthwhile experience.

With the odd exception, though, productions are unlikely to be avant-garde. Conservative Florentines – like most Italians – don't take kindly to directors messing with their favourite operas, and any experimenting is likely to be met with slating critiques and boos from the audience. It wasn't always this way, however. Back in the 15th century, Florence was on the cutting edge of musical culture thanks to a group of intellectuals known as the Florentine Camerata who began experimenting with the setting of words to music. Pieri and Caccini's *Euridice*, widely considered to be the world's first opera, was performed in the Boboli Gardens in 1600 and Florence's musical importance continued into the early 17th century; after this time, the country's musical focus shifted northwards, with the Venetian school of composition becoming admired as the country's most progressive.

Back in the present, Florence plods on with a steady, if not particularly exciting, line-up of classical music events. There's lots on offer in the way of symphonic and chamber concerts, with two resident symphony orchestras, a clutch of smaller groups and a world-class chamber music series. Smaller events are promoted on fly posters and in local media. From June to October there are concerts in churches, plus outdoor concerts at villas, gardens and museums, some of them free. Keep an eye open for summer performances in the magical Boboli Gardens; the standard isn't always the highest, but the setting is superb.

Not all these events are well advertised, but tourist offices usually have information. For events taking place outside Florence, *see p189* **Seasonal settings**.

TICKET INFORMATION

For main ticket agencies, *see p168*. Many hotels and travel agents also book tickets for the biggest venues. Tickets for the Teatro del Maggio can be hard to come by, as many seats are taken by holders of season tickets. Advance bookings for the opera and concert seasons (Sept-Mar) open around mid September. Tickets for the **Maggio Musicale Fiorentino** (*see p187*) go on sale in early April. You can book online (www.maggiofiorentino.com) up to a week before the performance. Phone bookings through the theatre's ticket office can't be paid for with credit cards; those through the call centre (199 112112, only within Italy) can.

If you can't get a seat in advance, turn up on the night for the chance of a return or one of the restricted-vision seats that go on sale an hour before the start of each performance. For chamber concerts and Orchestra Regionale Toscana concerts, tickets are usually available on the door half an hour beforehand. Note that not all theatres accept card payments.

TICKET PRICES

At the Teatro del Maggio, tickets for the opening night of an opera range from €30 to €60 in the upper circle, and from €55 to €90 for a box or stalls seat. Repeat performances cost a little less. Symphonic concerts cost from €25 to €35 and ballets from €15 to €25. Restricted-view seats are around €11 to €25.

Tickets for the Orchestra Regionale Toscana concerts at the Teatro Verdi cost €12 to €15, while the Amici della Musica series at the Teatro della Pergola costs €12 to €25 per seat. One-off concerts don't usually cost more than €15, and some outdoor events are free.

Venues

Accademia Bartolomeo Cristofori

Via di Camaldoli 7r, Oltrarno (055 221646/www.accademiacristofori.it). **Open** by appointment only.

Named after the inventor of the piano, the academy houses a fine private collection of early keyboard instruments. Chamber concerts and seminars are held in a beautiful little hall next door.

Teatro della Pergola. *See p188.*

Chiesa Luterana

Lungarno Torrigiani 11, Oltrarno (055 2542775/ tourist office 055 290832). **Map** p335 D4.

Organ recitals and other chamber music, often involving early repertoire, are held at Florence's Lutheran church all year and are usually free.

Chiesa di Santo Stefano al Ponte

Piazza Santo Stefano 5, Duomo & Around (tourist office 055 290832). **Map** p334 C3.

Located just north of the ponte Vecchio, this large, deconsecrated church hosts regular concerts.

Scuola Musica di Fiesole

Villa La Torraccia, via delle Fontinelle 24, San Domenico, Fiesole (055 597851/www.scuolamusica.fiesole.fi.it). Bus 7, then 10min walk. **Open** 8.30am-8.30pm Mon-Sat.

One of Italy's most famous music schools occupies a 16th-century villa in beautiful grounds. Founded by the charismatic viola player of the Quartetto Italiano, Piero Farulli, it's the home of the Orchestra Giovanile Italiana, the country's number one youth orchestra. Farulli is now in his dotage, but his teaching legacy is very much alive. The annual Festa della Musica, a musical open day with concerts and workshops by pupils, is held on 24 June, while the Concerti per gli Amici series takes place in the 200-seat auditorium from September/October to June.

Teatro Goldoni

Via Santa Maria 15, Oltrarno (055 229651/Teatro Comunale 055 213535). **Open** *Box office* 1hr before performance. **Map** p334 D1.

This divine little theatre in the Oltrarno dates from the early 18th century and seats only 400 people. A long drawn-out restoration was finally finished in the late 1990s and the theatre is now partially under the direction of the Teatro del Maggio (*see below*). It's used – though not regularly enough – for chamber music, small-scale opera and ballet.

Teatro del Maggio Musicale Fiorentino

Corso Italia 16, Santa Maria Novella (box office 055 213535/phone bookings 199 112112 within Italy/ 0424 600458 from abroad/www.maggiofiorentino.com). **Open** *Phone bookings* 8am-8pm Mon-Fri; 8am-3pm Sat. *Box office* 10am-4.30pm Tue-Fri; 10am-1pm Sat; 1hr before performance.

The Maggio Musicale Fiorentino festival (hosted by the Teatro del Maggio) celebrated its 70th anniversary in 2007. It's been going almost non-stop since 1933. Now the bad news: the theatre is still in deep financial trouble thanks to the reduction in state funding and an increased dependency on inadequate private contributions (there are very few tax breaks in Italy for sponsors of the arts). The theatre has gargantuan overheads: it sustains a full orchestra, chorus and ballet company, plus armies of staff. Some cutting back has been going on in the past couple of years, but the unions make it hard.

Financial worries aside, the theatre has a lot going for it and there has been an attempt over the past year or so to revamp and modernise its rather stuffy image. The charismatic Zubin Mehta hit 70 in 2007, but he is showing no signs of retiring as principal conductor. When on form, the Teatro del Maggio's resident orchestra and chorus are on a level with La Scala in Milan. However, lack of funds means that big-name conductors and soloists are often padded out with mediocre unknowns who just don't get the same results. While few risks are taken in terms of repertoire, the highlight of recent years has been the fabulous 2007/08 staging of Wagner's marathon Ring Cycle, a co-production with the Palau de les

Florence's grandest classical venue: **Teatro del Maggio Musicale Fiorentino**. *See p187.*

Arts in Valencia. Long-term plans include a projected brand new theatre to be built in a vast space owned by the state railways just east of Porta al Prato. But that's rather a long way off.

The theatre's performing year is divided roughly into three parts: January to March is the concert season, with performances on Fridays, Saturdays and Sundays (the programme changes each week); October to December is the opera and ballet season, with about four operatic productions, a couple of ballets and the odd concert; and the Maggio Musicale Fiorentino festival runs for two months from late April/early May. The latter offers a mix of opera, ballet, concerts and recital programmes, and culminates in a free open-air concert and free dance extravaganza in piazza della Signoria.

The theatre building itself, constructed in 1882 and renovated in 1957, is architecturally unexciting. Of the 2,000-odd seats, the best acoustics are to be had in the second gallery (they are also the cheapest), but if you want to strut your stuff alongside the designer outfits of *Firenze per bene*, you need to fork out for an opening night in the stalls or one of the *palchi* (boxes). *See also p206.*

Teatro della Pergola

Via della Pergola 18-32, San Marco (055 2264316/ www.pergola.firenze.it). **Open** *Box office* 9.30am-6.45pm Mon-Sat; 10am-12.15pm Sun. **Season** Oct-Apr. **Map** p335 B5.

Inaugurated in 1661, the exquisite, intimate Pergola is one of Italy's oldest theatres. Richly decorated in red and gold and with three layers of boxes, it's ideal for chamber music and small-scale operas. The excellent series of chamber music concerts promoted by the Amici della Musica (*see below*) is held here, while the Teatro del Maggio also occasionally uses it for opera during the Maggio festival (*see p207*). *Photo p187.*

Teatro Verdi

Via Ghibellina 99, Santa Croce (055 212320/www. teatroverdifirenze.it). **Open** *Box office* 10am-1pm, 4-9pm Mon-Sat. **Season** Sept-June. **Map** p335 C5.

This large theatre was extensively revamped in 2004 for its 150th anniversary. A wood floor was added in the auditorium and new splendid red velvet seats were installed. They may be by Poltrona Frau, but they are extremely uncomfortable, with less legroom than a holiday charter flight. Teatro Verdi is the home of the Orchestra della Toscana (*see p189*) and is the orchestra's principal Florence venue. *See also p207.*

Performance groups/ promoters

Amici della Musica

Via Pier Capponi 41 (055 608420/607440/ www.amicimusica.fi.it).

This organisation, founded in 1906, promotes world-class chamber music concerts, mostly at the gorgeous Teatro della Pergola (*see above*), from September through to late April/early May. The annual series always features some of the world's great string quartets and recitalists such as Andras Schiff (a Florence resident), Alfred Brendel, and the Emerson and Alban Berg string quartets. Early music groups of the calibre of Fabio Biondi's Europa Galante and Jordi Savall also appear regularly. Afternoon and evening concerts are usually held on Saturdays and Sundays.

L'Homme Armé

055 695000/www.hommearme.it.

Until recently, the repertoire of this small, semi-professional chamber choir has ranged from medieval to Baroque, but they have recently introduced an interesting contemporary element. It gives about ten concerts a year in Florence (no fixed venue) and runs excellent courses on aspects of early music.

Orchestra da Camera Fiorentina

055 783374/www.orcafi.it.

This young chamber orchestra, under its principal conductor Giuseppe Lanzetta, plays a series of concerts mostly at Orsanmichele (*see p86*) between February and September. The venue means that in the summer season, they attract a good tourist-based audience, but standards are mixed. Concerts are usually held on Sunday and Monday evenings.

Orchestra della Toscana

055 2340710/www.orchestradellatoscana.it.

If you're looking for something creative, try to catch a concert given by the Orchestra della Toscana. Founded in 1980 with the brief of taking classical music into Tuscany, it has a dynamic management team and artistic director, who are responsible for a wider repertoire than that of the Maggio orchestra. Particular emphasis is given to rarely heard 19th-century music, early 20th-century composers and contemporary works, but there's plenty more besides. International names frequently appear as soloists and conductors, and during the season (November/December-May) the orchestra gives two or three concerts a month in Florence at the Teatro Verdi (*see p188*), and up to 40 in other Tuscan towns.

Festivals

In addition to the festivals listed below, *see also p170* **Maggio Musicale Fiorentino** and *p173* **Effetto Venezia**. For **Estate Musicale Chigiana, Puccini Opera Festival** and **Incontri in Terra di Siena**, *see below* **Seasonal settings**.

Christmas Concert

Teatro Verdi (055 2340710/tickets 055 212320). **Map** p335 C5. **Date** 24 Dec.

This annual concert by the Orchestra Regionale Toscana doesn't necessarily include 'Christmas Music', but there is usually something good on offer.

New Year Concert

Teatro Comunale (055 597851). **Date** 1 Jan.

Put on by the Scuola di Musica di Fiesole. Call the above number for free tickets.

Settembre Musica

Teatro della Pergola & other venues (055 608420/www.amicimusica.fi.it). **Date** Sept.

A month of early music concerts, by young or up-and-coming ensembles with the odd bigger name.

Seasonal settings

There's something about hearing music in the setting of a beautiful church or cloister, a historic piazza, an elegant villa or a tiny, restored theatre that is compelling even for people who don't normally 'do' classical music and opera. Tuscany is a great place to indulge such urges, as seasons and festivals spring up all over the place, particularly in summer. Some of these events have a high-enough profile to be well advertised, while others often go unnoticed by anyone not in the know. So read the local press and posters and search out the smaller, one-off performances, as well as the better-known seasons listed below.

Events worth looking out for include the **Estate Musicale Chigiana** series of concerts in Siena and at such gorgeous venues as the nearby abbeys of San Galgano and Sant'Antimo (July-Aug, 0577 22091); the **Tavernelle Val di Pesa** concerts at the Badia in Passignano monastery (late May, tourist office 055 8077832); the **Barga Opera Festival**, which features productions of little-known operas (July-mid Aug, 0583 723250); the **Incontri in Terra di Siena** chamber music festival based at La Foce in the Val d'Orcia (late July, 0578 69101, www.lafoce.com); the **Puccini Opera Festival**, during which several of the Lucca-born composer's favourite operas are performed on the lakeside near his villa in Torre del Lago (0584 359322); and the **Tuscan Sun Festival** (*see p173*), inaugurated in 2003 on the back of Francis Mayes' bestseller *Under the Tuscan Sun*, and featuring high-profile conductors and singers for two weeks of music in Cortona.

Concerts are held in Pisa's spectacular Duomo for the **Anima Mundi** festival of Sacred Music under the artistic direction of Sir John Eliot Gardiner (Sept-Oct, 050 3872229, www.opapisa.it).

Local tourist offices can supply further information about these and other events.

Music: Rock, Pop & Jazz

What goes on when the sun goes down.

'Take me, take me, Vasco, I'm yours.' **Stadio Artemio Franchi.**

In contrast to some of its mightier Italian neighbours – Rome, Milan, Turin – Florence is often left off the touring itineraries of major musical acts. Yet, mainly thanks to the large student population, it offers a surprisingly good array of nightly activities for a provincial city of its size, with plenty of options to satisfy the musical appetites of both visitors and residents.

One of the best ways to find out about events is to pick up the latest addition of *Firenze Spettacolo*. This monthly Italian-language magazine showcases what's hot in Florence. And don't fret if your language skills aren't up to scratch, as there's a huge event calendar in English with information on live gigs, from international musicians and rock bands to local home-grown jazz musicians and beatniks. It's also worth picking up a copy of free local English-language newspaper the *Florentine* (*see p309*), which has a great spread of upcoming live events and concerts; or drop into one of the city's record shops (*see p167*) to pick up flyers. For jazz events, it's also worth contacting gig-promoter **Musicus Concentus** (piazza del Carmine 19, 055 287347), which can give information on forthcoming events.

To book tickets for concerts (regardless of genre), call the venue directly or contact the Box Office ticket agency (*see p168*).

Bigger venues

Palasport Mandela Forum

Viale Paoli 3, Outside the City Gates (055 678841/ www.mandelaforum.it). Bus 3. **Tickets** prices vary. **No credit cards**.

This 7,000-capacity hall is where Florence houses major touring artists – Italian stars like Zucchero and international acts such as Michael Bublé.

Sala Vanni

Piazza del Carmine 19, Oltrarno (055 287347/ www.musicusconcentus.com). **Tickets** prices vary. **No credit cards**. **Map** p334 C1.

Sadly underused, this large warehouse-like auditorium is a great place to hear good progressive jazz and contemporary classical groups. The venue hosts a sparse but excellent series of concerts organised by Musicus Concentus in autumn and winter.

Saschall-Teatro di Firenze

Via Fabrizio de André, nr lungarno A Moro 3, Outside the City Gates (055 6504112/www.saschall.it). Bus 14. **Tickets** prices vary. **Credit** AmEx, DC, MC, V.

This tent-shaped, 4,000-capacity venue hosts a variety of mainstream acts from Italy and abroad. The upper balconies have seating, but choose the main standing hall downstairs if you're there for sound rather than comfort. Saschall's annual events include a St Patrick's Day knees-up.

Stadio Artemio Franchi

Viale Manfredo Fanti 14, Campo di Marte, Outside the City Gates (055 667566). Bus 10, 11, 17. **Tickets** prices vary. **No credit cards.**

When not even the Palasport Mandela Forum (*see p190*) is big enough, this football stadium moonlights as a music venue; it's hosted acts such as Italian megastars Vasco Rossi and Renato Zero.

Smaller venues

Admission to the following venues is free unless otherwise stated.

Ambaciata di Marte

Via Mannelli 2, Outside the City Gates (055 6550786/www.ambaciatadimarte.org). Bus 3, 6, 10, 20, 44. **Open** times vary, but usually 10pm-2am Mon-Sat. Closed July, Aug. **Tickets** €5 annual membership. **No credit cards.**

One of the newest additions to Florence's music scene, Ambaciata di Marte is a one-stop locale for upcoming bands. Showcasing an impressive stage for local alternative groups, it also has a sound studio that can be rented out. Drinks prices are reasonable.

Auditorium FLOG

Via M Mercati 24B, Outside the City Gates (055 487145/www.flog.it). Bus 4, 8, 14, 20, 28. **Open** 10pm-late Tue-Sat. Closed June-Aug. **Tickets** €10-€15. **No credit cards.**

At FLOG, music runs from rock to Tex-Mex rockabilly, with Fridays for reggae and ska, and a DJ after the bands. Dance parties and theatrical shows take place early in the week, and the venue hosts the Rassegna Internazionale Musica dei Popoli (*see p192*) and Azione Gay e Lesbica parties (*see p184*).

Caruso Jazz Café

Via Lambertesca 14-16r, Duomo & Around (055 281940/www.carusojazzcafe.com). **Open** 9.30am-3:30pm, 6pm-midnight Mon-Sat. **Credit** AmEx, DC, MC, V. **Map** p334 C3.

This cavernous bar is a magnet for talented jazz musicians, including many famed Italians. Every Thursday and Friday jazz echoes around the bar's brick vaults in a buzzy atmosphere.

Dolce Vita

Piazza del Carmine 6r, Oltrarno (055 284595/ www.dolcevitaflorence.com). **Open** 5pm-2am Tue-Sun. Closed 2wks Aug. **Credit** AmEx, MC, V. **Map** p334 C1.

Dolce Vita is a club that lives up to its name. One of the city's swankier clubs, it's filled with beautiful people dancing to live Brazilian, jazz and contemporary music on Wednesdays and Thursdays. The drinks prices are a little steep, but the atmosphere, decor and scenery make up for it. There's no official dress code, but showing up in jeans and a T-shirt will incur plenty of unwelcome glances.

Girasol

Via del Romito 1, Outside the City Gates (055 474948/www.girasol.it). Bus 14. **Open** 7pm-2am Tue-Sun. Closed June-Aug. **No credit cards.**

One of the most colourful bars in Florence, Girasol tops the list when it comes to Latin (particularly Brazilian) sounds, playing live music pretty well nightly. Instructors from local dance schools occasionally give free lessons in tango and samba to get you in the mood. Drinks are on the pricey side, but the exotic mixes blend in perfectly with the colourful decor. Girasol is in the process of a minor renovation, adding a pizzeria for 2008.

Golden View

Via de' Bardi 58r, Oltrarno (055 214502/www. goldenviewopenbar.com). **Open** 11.30am-2am daily. **Credit** AmEx, DC, MC, V. **Map** p335 D4.

The uninspiring decor of this restaurant and bar is more than made up for by the direct views afforded of the ponte Vecchio and Uffizi. The jazz comes from pianist Antonio Figura, who performs on Mondays, Wednesdays and Sundays in duos and trios.

Jazz Club

Via Nuova de' Caccini 3, Santa Croce (055 2479700/www.jazzclubfirenze.com). **Open** 9pm-2am Mon-Fri; 9pm-3am Sat. Closed July, Aug. **Tickets** €8.50 membership. **No credit cards. Map** p335 B5.

One of the few places in Florence where you can hear live jazz almost nightly, this hard-to-find club is worth searching out. From Tuesday to Saturday, it hosts an array of popular local jazz bands, and it has also welcomed notable international acts such as

The best Venues

For cult acts
Tenax (*see p192*).

For great acoustics
Saschall-Teatro di Firenze (*see above*).

For jazz
Pinocchio Jazz (*see p192*).

For Latin/samba
Girasol (*see above*).

For rock/cult
Sintetika (*see p192*).

jazz musician/actor Peter Weller (probably better known for his role in the first two *Robocop* films than playing the trumpet on stage). Every Monday there's a live jam session where you can hop on stage with the house band accompanying.

Loonees

For listings, *see p198.*
Loonees brims nightly with tipsy foreign students, random punters and locals on the pull. Sounds range from reggae- and rock-covers to Italian pop and blues. Two bars offer free shots with every beer, which may help assuage more critical ears; the two-for-one happy hour is from 8pm to 10pm. *See also p198.*

Pinocchio Jazz

Viale Giannotti 13, Outside the City Gates (055 680362/www.pinocchiojazz.it). Bus 8, 23, 31, 32, 80. **Open** 9pm-2am Sat. Closed May-Oct. **Tickets** €10 membership; entrance with membership €10-€15. **Credit** MC, V.
Pinocchio Jazz hosts internationally recognised jazz stars such as Chris Speed, Anthony Coleman and Richard Galliano, as well as Italian artists. Later in the evening, the atmosphere becomes more mellow, with soft jazz filling the air. The Pinocchio Jazz Live Festival is held from January to March, showcasing the best of Italian jazz musicians, plus a smattering of international talent, every Saturday night.

Porto di Mare Eskimo Club

Via Pisana 128, Outside the City Gates (328 7593125/www.palcodautore.com). **Open** 8pm-3am nightly. Closed Aug. **Credit** MC, V.
This club is perfect if you're planning a simple night out. Starting at the top floor of the three-tiered club is a rustic pizzeria that makes a great *penne alle Calabrese*. On the second floor is a quaint pub with a large TV screen and comfy chairs. Head down to the basement to catch a live show – local rock and folk musicians play seven days a week.

Sintetika

Via Luigi Alamanni, 4, Santa Maria Novella (333 3591575/www.sintetikalive.it). Bus 2, 14. **Open** 11.30pm-4am. Days vary, call for info. **Tickets** €8 membership. **No credit cards**. **Map** p334 A1.
With a rapidly increasing number of local rock bands sprouting up, and no dedicated venue in which to house them, Sintetika stepped up to accept the challenge. This is one of very few clubs in Florence that plays only live music. Still in its infancy, the hours of operation are as varied as the musicians it hosts, who run the gamut from the Pinball Wizard through to hard-core punkers Devocka. Though the bar is fairly basic, the service and prices will be a welcome relief from the main city bars. It can be tricky to find: look for the crowd that seems to be loitering outside a garage door opposite a Box Office outlet.

Stazione Leopolda

Via Fratelli Rosselli 5, Outside the City Gates (055 89875/3245485/www.stazione-leopolda.com). Bus 1, 9, 12, 16, 17. **Tickets** prices vary. **Credit** MC, V.
This huge disused station is beloved of street-chic designers, who host catwalk shows here, but it's also occasionally called into service by artists such as jazz pianist Stefano Bollani and Liars, a US noise-rock band. The Fabbrica Europa performing arts festival is held here (*see p207*).

Tenax

Via Pratese 46, Outside the City Gates (055 308160/ www.tenax.org). Bus 29, 30. **Open** 10.30pm-4am Thur-Sat. Closed mid May-Sept. **Tickets** prices vary. **Credit** AmEx, MC, V.
New Order played here in the 1980s, with Basement Jaxx visiting in the '90s, and Tenax's cultish line-ups are still strong in the 21st century, with acts such as Ani DiFranco and Tricky. The club has a huge raised dancefloor and antechambers stuffed with computers, pool tables and bars for post-gig entertainment. Upstairs are more bars and café-style seating areas with balconies. Great acoustics. *See also p196.*

Summer music venues

From June to September, acts play on a variety of open-air stages. Of note are the nightly **Jazz&Co** events in piazza della SS Annunziata (see www.firenzejazz.it).

Festivals

Tuscany in the summer is a great place to catch some quality music festivals covering almost every genre of music. Mid July alone sees three of the best festivals in the region take place. **Pistoia Blues Festival** (www.pistoia blues.com) stages a number of open-air blues concerts, with big-names like Patti Smith and Joe Cocker heading the bills. **Italia Wave Love Festival** (www.italiawave.it) – formally Arezzo Wave – was moved to Sesto Fiorentino, outside Florence, in 2007. Providing four days of non-stop music in almost every genre, it starts early in the morning with laid-back music, progressing to a full-on rave in the wee hours. If you're willing to travel a little further out of the city gates, the **Porretta Soul Festival** (www.porrettasoul.it), going for some 20 years, is always a big affair. Held in Porretta Terme, a small spa town 30 kilometres (19 miles) north of Pistoia, past performers have included the likes of Booker T. Porretta lies in the Tuscan-Emilian Apennines, with a wonderful natural surrounding of beech, pine and chestnut woods.

Festivals are not just held in the summer, however; the most noteworthy autumn event is **Musica dei Popoli** (www.musicadeipopoli.com), held at FLOG (*see p191*). Starting the first weekend in October, this world music festival has varied artists playing their original folk sound, and is not to be missed.

Nightlife

As night falls, be privy to another type of Florentine culture, led by *apertivi* and alfresco drinking.

See that girl, watch that scene at **Central Park**. *See p195.*

Italians may be creatures of habit, but the popularity of the *aperitivo* phenomenon (*see p194* **The aperitivo awards**) has led to a seismic shift in Florentine nightlife patterns. Instead of going home for dinner after work then venturing out at 9pm or 10pm, it's now the done thing to go straight from work to one of the many bars serving complimentary buffets with drinks – and then move on somewhere else.

The late-night club is the loser in this new timetable, and not by chance several city-centre clubs have closed down in the last couple of years, while others have morphed into bar/ clubs serving early-evening *aperitivi* in the hope of roping punters in for the night.

That's not to say clubbing has died a death. It's just treated less as nightly entertainment and more as an occasion, along with one-off events at venues such as the **Stazione Leopolda** (*see p192*) and paying villa parties on the hills.

Most clubs charge an admission fee that includes a drink, but some clubs still use the unpopular card system. At these venues, you're given a card that's stamped whenever you buy drinks or use the cloakroom. You then hand the card in at the till and pay before leaving. Some smaller clubs are members-only, but these will almost always give out free membership.

Note that opening times and closing days of bars and clubs are notoriously vague and erratic, and phones that are answered are the exception. Musical genres often vary with the day of the week – check flyers, English-language newspaper the *Florentine* or *Firenze Spettacolo* for information.

SUMMER CLUBBING

From the end of May to the beginning of September most Florentine nightlife shifts from crowded underground clubs to outdoor venues in piazze, gardens and villas. Most have free admission and stay open until the small hours. Each summer brings new openings to replace previous closures, as well as the return after absence of established venues. Two of the most popular places in previous years, Parterre (piazza della Libertà) and Le Rime Rampanti (above piazza Poggi), are current non-shows but may reappear, while another, Vie di Fuga, is now a year-round restaurant.

Temporary bars set up in streets and squares are also a hot summer phenomenon, with piazza Santo Spirito usually playing host to nightly

The aperitivo awards

Putting a few free snacks on the bar has always been a mark of Italian hospitality, but now almost any bar worth its salt serves up a full free buffet with its pre-dinner drinks (which generally cost between €5 and €10). This is the nationwide *aperitivo* craze, which started in Milan and has spread steadily southwards. Reminiscent of the medieval races to build the tallest towers, a keen competitive spirit has now been stirred up among the main Florentine nightlife bars, with all competing to provide the most exciting, gourmet, imaginative or just plain enormous feast.

The biggest *aperitivo*, and contender for most popular, is at **Noir** (previously Capocaccia; *see p198*); a huge buffet of hot and cold snacks is followed by pasta, risottos and main dishes. When these have been demolished, the sweets are rolled out – tiramisù, fruit salads, brownies and cheesecakes. There are a few variations – Tuesday is sushi and ethnic food and Thursday is Tuscan food, and there's a DJ set almost every evening. For an *apertivo* that looks almost too good to eat, meanwhile, walk up the riverbank to the **Fusion Bar Shozan** in the Gallery Hotel Art (*see p53*), where snacks of authentic sushi and tempura are beautifully presented on lacquered black plates, lined up on the blue backlit bar. Prize for best *aperitivo* with a view goes to another Ferragamo joint – the Sky Lounge terrace bar of the **Hotel Continentale** (*see p54*). Take the lift up to the fifth floor for a breathtaking 360-degree sunset panorama. Silver medal goes to the rooftop bar of the **Grand Hotel Minerva** (*see p60*), where the marinated tuna, king prawns, gazpacho and squid-ink risotto are served poolside. There's no buffet but drinks come with crudités and delicacies like artichoke dips and truffle canapés. Most atmospheric *aperitivo* is served at **Slowly** (*see p199*), where the coloured lanterns and LED-lit floor and bar lead to a balconied room with gold-leaf luminaire and a central pedestal laden with platters of hot and cold delicacies brought from the bar's kitchens.

Many bars have seasoned the evening's snacks with live music or DJ sets that go on well into the night to make it worth sticking around. Two of the best bets if you want to settle in for the night are **Twice** (*see p196*) and **Rex** (*see p198*). In its early-evening bar incarnation, Twice does a Tuscan buffet with wine tastings from 7pm, while its club nights kick off at 11pm. Rex serves up a 'Mediterranean' feast from 6pm, bizarrely including chapatis with dips, as well as the more authentically local cold meats, cheeses and focaccias. The night gets even hotter after the chocolate fondue has been licked, with DJs and live bands till late.

gigs and events. Other one-off events are organised in piazza Pitti, the Boboli Gardens and Forte Belvedere, and the Stazione Leopolda is increasingly used as a summer venue. The return in 2007 of the **Ippodromo delle Mulina at the Cascine** (via del Pegaso, bus 17C) was big news, with roots, reggae, rock, dance or house music playing every night from 11pm till late. Jazzy nights at the **Sant'Ambrogio Summer Festival** also run from June to July in piazza Ghiberti (www.firenzejazz.it) and the newest summer venue was at the loggia del Pesce in piazza dei Ciompi, with a bar and restaurant, and music swinging from bossanova and samba to jazz and blues. For riverside seats, head to **Teatro sull'Acqua** (lungarno Pecori Giraldi, 055 2343460) or **Lido** (*see p198*) – sprawling bar-cum-clubs on the riverbank.

Bear in mind that the local council grants permission to these summer-only venues on a year-by-year basis, so the situation can change at any time. Check the local press for details.

Clubs

Central Park

Via Fosso Macinante 2, nr ponte di Vittoria, Outside the City Gates (335 8183400). Bus 1, 9, 26. **Open** *Summer* 11.30pm-4.30am Tue-Sat. *Winter* 11pm-4am Fri, Sat. **Admission** €16-€25. **Credit** AmEx, MC, V.

The greatest of summer disco venues, Central Park comes into its own in hot weather, when the huge garden areas with bars and outdoor dancefloors provide the perfect environment for sun-frazzled dancing legs. The music is progressive by Florentine standards. You might heed the siren call of trance, techno, garage, drum 'n' bass and deep house classics, or strike lucky when the organisers have arranged an Amnesia from Ibiza night. Frankie Knuckles turned up in 2007. Then again, you might stumble upon mediocre live acts and play-by-rote hits. Thursdays (featuring some of the best drum 'n' bass in Italy) and Fridays are usually good bets. Saturdays see an influx of out-of-towners. *Photo p193.*

Doris

Via de' Pandolfini 26r, Santa Croce (055 2466775/ www.dorisfirenze.it). **Open** *Bar* 7-10pm Tue-Sun. *Club* 11.30pm-4am Tue-Sun. **Admission** €10. **Credit** AmEx, MC, V. **Map** p335 B5.

This venue has old-timers recounting nostalgic tales of the down 'n' dirty heaving dancefloor and cinema chill-out room of the '90s. It recently reopened as the sweet as cherry pie-sounding Doris, and things have changed. The three rooms have been brought bang up to date with an über-design makeover of white sofas and pendant lamps, and there's a two-tier opening system to accommodate the *aperitivo* craze early evening before the club night kicks in. In a particularly welcome move, the management has also managed to wangle a smokers' corner.

ExMud

Corso dei Tintori 4, Santa Croce (055 2638583/ www.exmud.it). **Open** 11.30pm-4am Tue-Sun. **Admission** €10. **Credit** AmEx, MC, V. **Map** p335 C5.

Now reopened, ExMud has been welcomed back with open arms. A warren of passageways and rooms in a stone basement, this is, on a good night, everything a great underground nightclub should be. Expect hot, sweaty and rocking fun, with a young cosmopolitan crowd boogying to international DJs spinning house, garage, drum 'n' bass or liquid funk. Hit a bad night, on the other hand, and you'll be listening to hardcore Italian electronica played to empty dancefloors.

Faces

Via de' Geppi 3r, Oltrarno (055 293006/www. facesclub.it). **Open** 10pm-2am Tue-Sat. Closed June-Sept. **Admission** free. **Credit** AmEx, MC, V. **Map** p335 C4.

Tucked away in a nondescript alley near the river, Faces is a tiny club with loyal regulars, so nights have a bit of a house-party feel. Saturdays see popular DJ Nate Maestrum lording it with his house, hip hop and R&B set. Other evenings can feature anything from 1980s tracks to radio anthems.

Full-Up

Via della Vigna Vecchia 23r, Santa Croce (055 293006). **Open** 11pm-4am Tue-Sat. Closed June-Sept. **Admission** free. **Credit** AmEx, MC, V. **Map** p335 C4.

With the demise of Dolce Zucchero, the winner is old-hand Full-Up. Friendly staff from the defunct DZ have set up residence in this long-running club, bringing new ideas and pepping up the proceedings. The best night to go is Thursday, when the team from Yab (*see p196*) is enlisted to re-run its legendary Monday hip hop night, Smoove. Also worth a look-in is Friday's house night, B.fly, with live music from international bands. Saturday is an altogether more commercial affair with sounds from resident DJs Remo e Timmy. The club's flash VIP privé is unusual in that it often really does have celebrities (albeit minor ones) quaffing bubbly at its eight tables. Ring ahead to book if you're impressed by stardom.

Lochness

Via de' Benci 19r, Santa Croce (055 241464). **Open** 10pm-3am daily. Closed June-Aug. **Admission** free. **Credit** AmEx, MC, V. **Map** p335 C4.

A late-night studenty hangout with a spit 'n' sawdust style. Nessy is generally filled with foreign girls and Italians on the pull, though the hunky doormen seem to monopolise the girls' attentions (hence the constant crowd at the door). Out-of-luck boys can console themselves with pool or table footie.

Maracana Casa di Samba

Via Faenza 4, San Lorenzo (055 210298/www. maracana.it). **Open** *Restaurant* 8.30-11.30pm Tue-Sun. *Club* midnight-4am Tue-Sun. Closed June-Aug. **Admission** €10-€20. **Credit** (restaurant only) AmEx, DC, MC, V. **Map** p334 A3.

Give this place a wide berth if you can't stomach the sight of middle-aged suits drooling over wiggling Brazilian booties – after the restaurant stops serving South American fare, all decorum is shed. The main dancefloor is surrounded by poseur platforms and the balconies assure views of cleavages and bald patches. Exhibitionists will love the shots of themselves on the huge screen.

Meccanò

Viale degli Tigli 1, nr ponte di Vittoria, Outside the City Gates (055 331371). Bus 1, 9, 16, 26, 27. **Open** *Summer* 11.30pm-4am Tue-Sat. *Winter* 11.30pm-4am Mon-Sat. **Admission** €15-€20. **Credit** AmEx, MC, V.

Meccanò caters to the masses, who come out in force to play in its theme-park atmosphere. It's easy to play hide-and-seek in the labyrinthine tangle of bars and dancefloors, especially when the garden opens in summer. Music is mostly Latin, commercial party and trashy pop, with a sprinkling of hip hop and funky house. The best perch is in the Piccionaia – the quieter upstairs bar.

Tenax

Via Pratese 46, Outside the City Gates (055 308160/ www.tenax.org). Bus 29, 30. **Open** 10.30pm-4am Thur-Sat & for gigs. Closed mid May-Sept. **Admission** €20-€25. **Credit** AmEx, MC, V.

The most influential and international of the Florentine clubs is the warehouse-style Tenax in Peretola. Far enough outside the centre to make a night out an adventure, but not too far to be impractical without a car, it's best known as a live venue for hip international bands and for its DJ exchanges (Pete Tong, Deep Dish and Ashley Beedle have all hit the decks here). When it's closed in the summer, Tenax also organises one-off events, often in the Stazione Leopolda. Big-name DJ Alex Neri's Nobody's Perfect on Saturday is the hottest night in the city by a long shot, heaving with house, big beat, progressive and drum 'n' bass. There's free parking for Tenax punters in via Spini. *See also p192.*

Twice

Via Verdi 57r, Santa Croce (055 0517374/www. twiceclub.com). **Open** *Bar* 7.30-11pm Tue-Sun. *Club* 11pm-3am Tue-Sun. Closed mid May-Sept. **Admission** free. **Credit** AmEx, MC, V.

The main news at the latest incarnation of this long-running venue is the division of the night into early-evening wine bar and club, hence the name. The gimmicks don't stop there and while the wine bar's a safe stop-off for an *aperitvo*, the themed club nights become a tad tedious. Saturday is Hawaii house night complete with flower leis, while Tuesday is Lollipop Night (guess what's in the goody bag), with a hefty serving of old-school music. Hip hop and R&B Thursdays shed the tack and are worth a punt.

Yab

Via Sassetti 5r, Duomo & Around (055 215160). **Open** 9pm-4am Mon, Tue, Thur-Sat. Closed June-Sept. **Admission** free (€15 drinks minimum-spend Fri, Sat). **Credit** AmEx, DC, V. **Map** p334 B3.

Some refer to this large, trendy city-centre locale as a disco; others, a 'glamour club'. You Are Beautiful – popularly known as Yab – has existed since the late 1970s, and plays up to any narcissist tendencies, not only by its name but also its liberal use of mirrors,

Art Bar.

flattering lighting and on-tap female-focused compliments from the stalwarts. The powerful sound system has the mammoth dancefloor shimmying with dancers, while the wall-to-wall bar areas cater to those with tired feet. Monday hip hop nights are an institution among rowdy Americans, while Thursdays is deep house played to a young crowd letting it all hang out; the place is packed on Saturdays.

Pubs & bars

Art Bar

Via del Moro 4r, Santa Maria Novella (055 287661). **Open** 7pm-1am Mon-Thur; 7pm-2am Fri, Sat. Closed 3wks Aug. **No credit cards. Map** p334 B2.

Battered French horns hanging from the ceiling and sepia photos of blues and jazz musicians lend a beatnik air to this perennially popular bar. The ambience is cosy but animated, with student types holed up in the brick cellar sipping their potent piña coladas. During happy hour (7-9pm), drinks cost a bargain €5; on Mondays and Wednesdays, the happy 'hour' lasts all night.

Astor Caffè

For listings, *see p141*.

This huge, lively jazz bar draws an enthusiastic young crowd. The big skylight, soft red lighting and flash chrome bar are a clean backdrop for the regular art exhibitions, while internet points provide distraction from the busy socialising of the main bar.

Cabiria

For listings, *see p141*.

After a long history as the wildest and grungiest of the pre-club bars, Cabiria has grown up into a thirtysomething, along with its customers, a well-behaved, well-to-do genial crowd. The pretty candlelit terrace on piazza Santo Spirito is enjoyed on warm nights, while soft jazzy sounds emanate from the DJ sets inside.

Caffè la Torre

Lungarno Benvenuto Cellini 65r, Oltrarno (055 680643/www.caffelatorre.it). **Open** 10.30am-3am daily. **Credit** AmEx, DC, MC, V. **Map** p334 D6.

Caffè La Torre forms the central hub of eastern Oltrarno's bar-crawl itinerary, sandwiched as it is between Plasma in piazza Ferrucci, and Negroni and Zoe in piazza de' Renai. There are (almost) nightly live acts, and the place is also popular as a mercifully mellow post-clubbing stop-off; tapas and pasta are served till late.

Colle Bereto

For listings, *see p141*.

Perhaps because of its roots as a wine producer, this spin-off bar is one of the more grown-up of the central hangouts. Rivalling Noir (*see p198*) in popularity and location, it's packed with designer-clad model types till late, from Thursdays to Saturdays. Upstairs is the Attico, the VIP privé for which you have to book a table to enter, while the outside area is often booked for private parties for luxury car and fashion launches, especially during the Pitti shows. If you have no invite in your sticky paw, no amount of blagging will get you past the impassive bouncers.

Dolce Vita

For listings, *see p191*.

Despite the influx of trendy new bars, Dolce Vita is still going strong after years of hegemony in the summer nights-out stakes. Crowds spill out on to the medieval square during warm evenings. Inside, the cold metal and glass bar leads to a cosier salon, with sofas and soft lighting from beautiful crystal lamps, usually inhabited by those too weary to move on to the clubbing scene.

James Joyce

Lungarno Benvenuto Cellini 1r, Oltrarno (055 6580856). **Open** 6pm-2am Mon-Thur; 6pm-3am Fri-Sun. **No credit cards. Map** p335 D6.

The large enclosed garden with long wooden tables makes this one of the best of Florence's pubs in spring and summer. JJ has a high-spirited vibe, especially around happy hour (7.30-9.30pm). To go with the name, there's a small bookshop selling paperbacks, some of them in English.

Kikuya English Pub

Via dei Benci 43r, Santa Croce (055 2344879/ www.kikuyapub.it). **Open** 6pm-2am daily. **Credit** AmEx, MC, V. **Map** p335 C5.

Feeling homesick for something louty and lively? Here's a taste of British pub culture, with Guinness and John Bull English Ale, live footie on plasma screens and Tex-Mex cuisine. Allusions to authenticity stop there, though. Brazilian barmaids mix the

Colle Bereto.

Arts & Entertainment

drinks with panache and Kikuya's claim to fame is that it was voted one of the best pubs in Italy by *Playboy* magazine (draw your own conclusions). There's free Wi-Fi for anyone who cares to risk a pint down their laptop – this pub packs 'em in, especially during happy hour, from 7pm to 10pm.

Lido

Lungarno Pecori Giraldi 1r, Santa Croce (055 2342726). **Open** 12.30pm-2am Tue-Sat; 1pm-2am Sun. Lunch served 1-3pm daily. Closed Jan, Feb. **Admission** free. **No credit cards.**

Large glass doors open from this bar to a garden that extends to the riverbank, making it a good bet for hot summer nights, when queues inevitably form. The music is a thumping mix of drum 'n' bass, R&B and the like, though the dancefloor is entirely taken up by the queue for the bar. Fridays is stomping deep house.

Loonees

Via Porta Rossa 15r, Duomo & Around (055 212249/ www.loonees.it). **Open** 8pm-3am Tue-Sun. Closed Aug. **Admission** free. **No credit cards. Map** p334 C3.

A dark, sweaty underground hole, Loonees is popular with a young crowd from the international universities. There's a relaxed atmosphere, partly due to the very loud live music, which leaves you with little to do but take advantage of the free shot with every pint. *See also p192.*

Mayday Lounge Café

Via Dante Alighieri 16r, Duomo & Around (055 2381290/www.maydayclub.it). **Open** 8pm-2am Mon-Sat. Closed 2wks Aug. **Admission** free, membership required (free). **No credit cards. Map** p335 B4.

This wacky joint with odd art installations and hundreds of old Marconi radios hanging from the ceilings has earned itself something of a cult following. Somewhere between a beatnik refuge and something from *Lost in Translation*, Mayday is dark and edgy. There's a wildly diverse programme of events, with the only constant being a jazzy basis to the sounds.

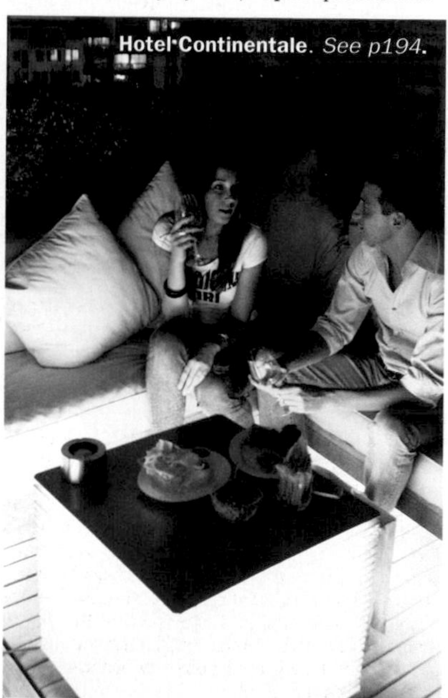
Hotel Continentale. *See p194.*

Moyo

Via de' Benci 23r, Santa Croce (055 2479738). **Open** 6pm-2am daily. **Admission** free. **Credit** AmEx, MC, V. **Map** p335 C5.

Being the first to have wireless internet in Florence is just one claim to fame for this buzzing bar. The cool wood decor and outdoor seating make for a welcoming year-round environment, and being on the edge of the no-drive zone means that parking is only a five-minute walk away. Come *aperitivo* time, it's packed out with hip Florentines.

Negroni

Via dei Renai 17r, Oltrarno (055 243647/www. negronibar.com). **Open** 8am-2.30am Mon-Sat; 6pm-2am Sun. Closed 2wks Aug. **Credit** MC, V. **Map** p335 D5.

Named after Signor Negroni himself – the man who invented the eponymous cocktail (gin, red vermouth, Campari) while sitting at a bar that used to be on this site – this is one of the coolest destinations in town. The streamlined, sleek, red and black interior is a backdrop for art and photography exhibitions, while the outside seating in the garden square is crowded on hot summer nights. The music works around CD promotions run in conjunction with Alberti record shop (*see p167*), and showcases the latest releases from progressive lo-fi bands.

Noir

For listings, *see p142.*

Impossibly hip Noir is the most desired of the city's central nightspots. The bar is busy on most nights of the year, but positively heaving during the week in summer, when you can join half of cool Florence outside blocking the traffic as you wait to get in. Entry accomplished, sit in the packed bar, people-watching and nursing a cocktail, or enjoy the clubby atmosphere with the DJ-set pumping out Latin jazz and big beats. Otherwise, chill out in the all black salon.

Plasma

Piazza Ferrucci 1r, Outside the City Gates (055 0516926/www.virtualplasma.it). **Open** 7pm-2am Wed-Sun. **Credit** AmEx, MC, V.

This spectacular bar on two floors, with LED-lit vaults, a backlit waterfall and a gallery of plasma screen art, is refreshingly ahead of its time in design-staid Florence. Indeed, the aesthetics alone might be enough reason to make the trek up the lungarno. But there are other draws: a cool repertoire of tunes played from a Bose music system and a 5m-long (16ft) glass bar where the polychromatic cocktails sit looking pretty. All in all, it's a sensory experience worthy of Miami, London or New York's best.

Porfirio Rubirosa

Viale Strozzi 38r, San Lorenzo (055 490965). **Open** 11am-2am Tue-Sun. Closed 2wks Aug. **Credit** MC, V.
A hedonist's haven, this bar is named after a Brazilian playboy and the locals flock here to do their best attempts at emulating the man himself. Weekend traffic restrictions in the city centre mean that the area is mobbed on Fridays and Saturdays – the outside bar here could easily be mistaken for a flash car showroom, so many motors pull up outside.

Rex Café

Via Fiesolana 25r, Santa Croce (055 2480331/ www.rexcafe.it). **Open** 6pm-2.30am daily. Closed June-Aug. **Credit** MC, V. **Map** 335 B5.
With more of a club than a bar vibe, Rex is king of the east of the city, filling up with loyal subjects who sashay to the sounds of the session DJs playing bassy beats and jungle rhythms. Gaudí-esque mosaics decorate the central bar, wrought-iron lamps shed a soft light while a luscious red antechamber creates welcome seclusion for more intimate gatherings. Tapas are served during the *aperitivo* happy hour (5-9.30pm), and the cocktails are especially good.

Il Rifrullo

For listings, *see p145.*
It's not unknown for people to wander in here for Sunday brunch and not emerge again until Apollo has well and truly left the building. Rifrullo has something of the hospitable friend's house vibe, what with the chatty bar staff, well-worn upholstered chairs, the continuous arrival of plates of homely food at *aperitivo* time, the fire in the grate in winter and the newly extended garden area with views of the old city walls. Don't bring the knitting, though – things liven up plenty as the night wears on.

Sky Lounge, Bar Continentale

Vicolo dell'Oro 6r, Duomo & Around (055 27262/ www.lungarnohotels.com). **Open** *Mar-Oct* 2.30-11.30pm daily. **Credit** AmEx, DC, MC, V. **Map** p334 C3.
In-the-know Florentines mix with hotel guests at sundown for aperitifs at the Hotel Continentale's swanky rooftop bar. The sides are lined with smart biscuit-coloured upholstered benches, and cocktails are served with crudités and mini brioches. The main attraction though is the 360-degree bird's eye view of the city. The bar is open in 'fine weather'; while officially closed in winter, it may be open or closed for a few weeks longer depending on the weather.

Slowly

Via Porta Rossa 63r, Duomo & Around (055 2645354). **Open** 7pm-2am Mon-Sat. **Credit** MC, V. **Map** p334 C3.
The ultimate chillout Bohemian-chic bar, Slowly is softly lit by candles in mosaic lanterns, with big soft sofas in alcoves, laid-back staff and mellow Buddha Bar sounds when the DJ gets stuck in. Even the inevitable crowds of pretty young things can't break the nice and easy spell. The restaurant overlooking the bar serves imaginative global cuisine.

Winter of content

The average Italian scuttles inside as soon as the night-time temperature drops below 'torrid' to just 'temperate', so most bars pile up the patio furniture come October only to dust it off in March or April. Despite the lack of local enthusiasm, though, hardier souls looking for a fix of out-of-season alfresco drinking holes still have a fair few options.

Dolce Vita (*see p197*) is the classic outdoor bar experience, and the canopied area and vases of box hedging keep out the worst of the wind and winter chills. The outside tables of **Cabiria** (*see p197*) are occupied year-round; though with only a few rope lights and candles dotting the tables for extra warmth, the secret to success in the colder months could have something to do with the blood alcohol content of the average punter.

Colle Bereto (*see p197*) has created a cosseting indoor-out oasis of sofas, cushions and bucket chairs to curl up in, and have added patio heaters, just in case. You half expect the waiters to bring you a cashmere wrap with your cocktail and tuck you in for the night. Also making use of the eco-enemies is next-door neighbour **Negroni** (*see p198*) and **Zoe** (*see p199*), while the incredibly popular **Noir** (*see p198*) relies on sheer numbers and the body heat of its winter faithfuls to keep each other warm.

I Visacci

For listings, *see p144.*
The daytime butter-wouldn't-melt style of this small bar hots up come night-time. On tap are a spicy mix of Latin and salsa beats, steaming coffee and liqueur concoctions, and the sort of regulars that make the holographic striped decor look boring in comparison.

Zoe

Via de' Renai 13r, Oltrarno (055 243111). **Open** 8am-1.30am Mon-Thur; 8am-2am Fri, Sat; 6pm-1am Sun. **Credit** AmEx, MC, V. **Map** p335 D5.
Zoe's red neon sign lures punters in with the promise of the sexiest atmosphere of the Oltrarno's many drinking holes. A long thin bar area functions as a proxy catwalk and bassy beats pump out from the DJ room at the back. Zoe also has the best red cocktails in town: there's the lethal Crimson Zoe with vodka, gin, Cointreau and the Red Caipiroska with crushed strawberries. Rule of thumb: if it's red, drink it.

Sport & Fitness

Sculpt your body into a work of art.

With health advice plastered on every TV channel, billboard and magazine, Florentines have become a lot more health and body conscious in recent years. Fitness enthusiasts, and those who want to work off that extra helping of *gelato*, can benefit from the huge resultant growth in the number of gyms in the city, offering a wide variety of services, including Pilates, step and yoga.

Spectator sports

Car & motorbike racing

Autodromo del Mugello

Nr Scarperia (055 8499111/www.mugellocircuit.it). **Open** Mar-Nov. **Tickets** phone for details.

Top-notch racing, including Formula 3 and motorcycle world championships, are held at this circuit 30km (20 miles) north of Florence. Bikers can live out their Carl Fogarty fantasies on the track (€50 for 20 minutes), but you have to bring your own Ducati. Call Paolo Poli at 055 480553 for reservations.

Stadio Artemio Franchi.

Football

Stadio Artemio Franchi

Campo di Marte, Outside the City Gates (055 503011/www.acffiorentina.it). Bus 11, 17. **Open** Aug-May. **Tickets** approx €20-€150; reduced prices for women and children. **No credit cards.**

ACF Fiorentina has had a tumultuous decade – what with its financial problems in 2002, and penalisation for involvement in the Calciopoli match-fixing scandal in 2006; but the club now seems to be largely back on form, re-establishing itself as one of the better Serie A teams and qualifying for the 2008 UEFA Cup.

The season runs from August to May; home matches are generally held every other Sunday, with kick-off at 3pm. You can buy tickets at the stadium, online (the website also has a list of authorised resellers) or up to three hours prior to a match at Chiosco degli Sportivi (via Anselmi, near piazza della Repubblica, Duomo & Around, 055 292363).

Horse racing

Ippodromo Le Cascine

Via delle Cascine 3, Parco delle Cascine, Outside the City Gates (055 422591/www.ippodromifiorentini.it). Bus 17C. **Open** Apr-May, Sept-Oct. **Admission** free. **No credit cards.**

Florence's *galoppo* (flat-racing) course. Keep an eye out for leading Tuscan jockeys such as Alessandro Muzzi and Claudio Colombi.

Ippodromo Le Mulina

Viale del Pegaso, Parco delle Cascine, Outside the City Gates (055 4226076/www.ippodromifiorentini.it). Bus 17C. **Open** Nov-Mar, June-July. **Admission** free. **No credit cards.**

Florence's racecourse for *il trotto* (trotting), where the driver sits in a carriage behind the horse. Enrico Bellei is the jockey to watch – he's notched up 47 wins and 37 placements in all of his 118 races, and took the top spot in 2007 with a win rate of nearly 40%. The Premio Duomo in June is among Tuscany's biggest equine events.

Active sports & fitness

Climbing & trekking

For books and information on trekking and mountaineering in the whole of Tuscany, visit Il Romito's **Libreria Stella Alpina** (via Corridoni 14, Outside the City Gates, 055 411688, www.stella-alpina.com).

Cave di Maiano

Via Cave di Maiano, Outside the City Gates (no phone). Bus 7.
If you're into free-climbing, the Cave di Maiano in Fiesole is the place to go – actually old mines, they make ideal climbing walls. You'll be on your own, without guides or instructors, so bring equipment.

Gruppo Escursionistico CAI (Club Alpino Italiano)

Via del Mezzetta 2, Outside the City Gates (055 6120467/www.caifirenze.it). Bus 6, 20. **Open** 4-7pm Mon-Thur; 9am-1pm, 4-7pm Fri. Closed Aug. **Rates** vary. **Credit** AmEx, MC, V.
Guided Sunday treks through the Tuscan countryside, mostly rated easy to moderate. Prices include transport to and from the city centre, but not lunch. In May, the Prato section of CAI organises 'Piazza to Piazza', an 84km (52-mile) two-day walk, including overnight arrangements. For more information, get in touch with the Associazione Sportiva Sci CAI Prato, via Altopascio, Prato (0574 29267).

Guide Alpine

338 9313444/www.ufficioguide.it.
These mountaineering experts organise courses throughout the summer. Phone Ufficio Guide on the above numbers for details, or check online.

Cycling

Florence by Bike

Via San Zanobi 120r-122r, San Lorenzo (055 488992/www.florencebybike.it). **Open** *Mar-Oct* 9am-7.30pm daily. *Nov-Feb* 9am-1pm, 3.30-7.30pm daily. **Credit** AmEx, DC, MC, V.
Bike rental and organised bike tours. Especially recommended is the one-day tour through Chianti (35km/22 miles) costing €70 per person and including bike and helmet rental, an English-speaking guide and lunch in a restaurant. Book in advance, as the maximum number in a group is 12.

Walking Tours of Florence

Via Sassetti 1, Duomo & Around (055 2645033/ 329 6132730 mobile/www.italy.artviva.com). **Open** *Office* 8am-6.30pm Mon-Sat; 8.30am-1.30pm Sun. *Mobile* 8am-8pm daily. **Credit** AmEx, MC, V. **Map** p334 C3.
Despite the name, this well-regarded company offers just about every kind of tour under the sun, including half-day bike tours of Tuscany. For €65, you'll get a guide, bike, helmet, equipment, snacks and wine. Tours leave from the office, tucked away on a little square off piazza Davanzati. *See also p74.*

Football

Tennis Carraia (*see p204*) has facilities for *calcetto* – a five-a-side, extremely fast-paced local variety of football. Most of the pitches there are outdoors and can be used by anyone. There's another, more popular football pitch behind piazzale Michelangelo, with floodlights at night, which is also open to outsiders. Whether you opt for a proper pitch or simply fancy a kickabout in a park, it is – as you'd expect – never hard to find a group of Italians eager to join in with you.

Golf

Circolo Golf Ugolino

Via Chiantigiana 3, Grassina (055 2301009/ www.golfugolino.it). Bus SITA. **Open** *Winter* 8.30am-6.30pm daily. *Summer* 8.30am-7.30pm daily. Closed Jan. **Rates** €70 Mon-Fri; €85 Sat, Sun. **Credit** AmEx, DC, MC, V.
This 18-hole course is the nearest to the city (about 20 minutes south by bus), but it's closed to non-members during the frequent weekend tournaments. It's best to phone or send an email (info@golfugolino.it) for reservations, at least a week in advance.

Poggio dei Medici

Via San Gavino 27, Scarperia (055 84350/www. poggiodeimedici.com). Bus SITA, then by taxi. **Open** 24hrs daily. **Rates** €52 Mon-Fri; €80 Sat, Sun; €30 club rental. **Credit** AmEx, DC, MC, V.
This 18-hole, par 72 course, built to USGA standards, opened in 1995 and was immediately recognised by *Il Mondo del Golf* as the best new course in Italy; a further nine holes are due to be constructed in the near future. Carts and clubs are available for rent and private lessons are also available.

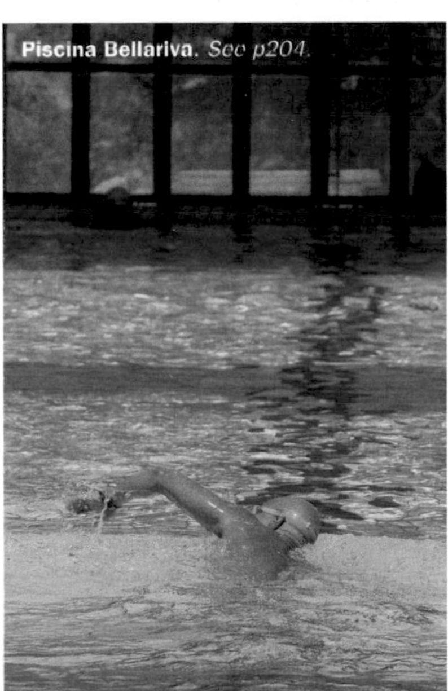
Piscina Bellariva. *See p204.*

Arts & Entertainment

Gyms

Fonbliù

Piazzale di Porta Romana 10r, Outside the City Gates (055 2335385/www.fonbliu.com). Bus 11, 36, 37. **Open** *Winter* 8.30am-9pm Mon-Fri; 8.30am-6pm Sat. *Summer* 8.30am-8.30pm Mon-Fri; 8.30am-1.30pm Sat. **Membership** €40/day; €120/mth. **Credit** AmEx, MC, V.

A small, high-tech spa at Porta Romana, which also has a fitness centre and indoor pool. Classes are normally limited to five people.

Klab Wellness Centers

Via de' Conti 7, Santa Maria Novella (055 7184300/ www.klab.it). **Open** 8.30am-10.30pm Mon, Wed; 8.30am-10pm Tue, Thur, Fri. Closed Aug. **Rates** €84/mth; call for info on day passes. **Credit** MC, V.

One of the biggest and best-equipped gyms in Florence, with three locations. Personal trainers, huge workout areas and a large pool are joined by a bio-sauna and massage and tanning facilities.

Palestra Ricciardi

Borgo Pinti 75, Santa Croce (055 2478444/ www.palestraricciardi.it). **Open** 9am-10pm Mon-Fri; 9.30am-6pm Sat; 10am-2pm Sun. Closed Aug. **Membership** €100/mth, then €20/day. **Credit** MC, V. **Map** p335 B5.

Staying fit in Florence generally requires exercising your wallet as much as your body, and this place proves no exception. There's a small garden outside where you can top up your tan after taking spinning, step or hip hop classes.

Tropos

Via Orcagna 20A, Outside the City Gates (055 678381/www.troposclub.it). Bus 14. **Open** 8am-10pm Mon-Fri; 8am-8pm Sat. **Membership** €30 trial visit, then various options. **Credit** AmEx, MC, V.

A luxurious (though correspondingly pricey) setting, whether you're splashing about in the aerobics pool, clocking up laps in the main pool or steaming yourself in one of the saunas.

Virgin Active

Via Generale Alberto dalla Chiesa, Outside City Gates (800 914555/www.virginactive.it). **Open** 8am-11pm Mon-Fri; 9am-7pm Sat, Sun. **Membership** call for details. **Credit** MC, V.

This complex has it all, with several pools and fitness areas, personal trainers, therapeutic services and even a babysitting facility.

Horse riding

Maneggio Marinella

Via di Macia 21, Outside the City Gates (055 8878066). Bus 28. **Open** 9am-1pm, 3-7pm daily. **Rates** €18/hr. **No credit cards**.

Phone ahead to book one of the daily rides at this stable in the northern suburbs. Lessons and special group trips are also organised on request.

Rendola Riding

Rendola, Montevarchi (055 9707045/www. rendolariding.it). **Open** 9am-1pm, 3-7pm daily. **Rates** €18/hr. **No credit cards**.

This stable – situated about 30 minutes' drive south of Florence, on the border with Chianti – offers respite from the busy city and an opportunity to enjoy the fabulous countryside. Various packages are offered, covering everything from one-hour rides through the countryside to two- to three-day trips (with lodging at a neighbouring *agriturismo*). Book at least a day in advance. There's a weight limit of 85kg (187lbs) because of the hilly tracks – which, for the same reason, are not recommended for children under ten.

Ice skating

Florence sets up a temporary ice-skating rink every winter from December to January. The venue tends to change every year, so contact the APT (055 23320) for the latest information. You pay by the session (there are three or four daily); the last ends at about 11pm.

In-line skating

Le Pavoniere

Viale della Catena 2, Parco delle Cascine, Outside the City Gates (335 5718547 mobile). Bus 17C. **Open** 5-8pm Tue-Wed; 10am-7.30pm Sat, Sun. Closed when raining. **Rates** €5/hr. **No credit cards**.

Hire in-line skates from this kiosk in the Parco delle Cascine and take advantage of miles of traffic-free paths along the banks of the river Arno.

Pool

Gambrinus

Via de' Vecchietti 16r, Duomo & Around (no phone). **Open** 1.30pm-1am daily. **Rates** €8/hr per table. **No credit cards. Map** p334 B3.

The only pool hall in Florence, Gambrinus offers nine pool tables and eight tables without pockets, where you can try your hand at *boccette* or *cinque birilli*. The clientele here is predominantly serious, though non-hostile, men.

Rowing

Canottieri Comunali

Lungarno Francesco Ferrucci 2, nr ponte Verazzano, Outside the City Gates (055 6812151/www.canottieri comunalifirenze.it). **Open** 8.30am-9pm Mon-Fri; 8.30am-7pm Sat; 8am-1pm Sun. **Membership** €620/3mths. **No credit cards**.

This rowing club enjoys a delightful location among the trees along the Arno – it's perfect in sunny weather. There's also a full range of lessons and activities on offer, including white-water rafting excursions in Tuscany.

The crying game

It's a familiar sight to football devotees (especially to fans of the World Cup-winning Italian team): a player rolls on the floor clutching an 'injured' body part. But in the local sport of *calcio storico*, if a player goes down, the likelihood is that he really is in pain. In fact, so violent is this hybrid of football, rugby and boxing, that tournaments over the past couple of years have been suspended. Within minutes of the starting whistle in the 2006 semi-finals (between Santa Croce and Santo Spirito), the violence was so sudden and so severe that the game was called to an end before it had barely begun, and the 2007 tournament was cancelled altogether.

Calcio storico (*see p173*) – also known as *calcio in costume*, or *calcio fiorentino* – traditionally takes place in piazza Santa Croce, with the final normally scheduled for 24 June. The 50-minute match involves two teams taken from the four ancient Florentine districts (and kitted out in appropriately coloured, medieval garb) attempting to land a ball in their opponents' wide goalmouth – while fending off and initiating brutal physical attacks. The game dates back to at least the early 16th century, and reportedly shocked the invading armies of Charles V.

Local Florentines, as well as fans around Italy, have been vocal about their disappointment regarding the cancelled games, with blogs and internet sites popping up by the dozen. While fans agree the game is violent, they also feel that this is an integral aspect of its heritage. However, economic motivation is also at play, with businesses counting on the surge of visitors who come to watch the spectacle.

After the cancellation, Ubaldo Nanucci, chief *procuratore* of Florence, said he was considering making the rules of *calcio storico* a little closer to those of rugby, where you can only tackle or attack the person with the ball. Further safety precautions will dictate that all players must be a resident of their *quartiere*, to prevent the hiring of professional boxers, rugby players and wrestlers. Furthermore, all players will need to have criminal background checks. A friendly match took place in October 2007 to test the 2008 rules, which include teams training together in order to foster 'a love for the sport and fair play'. Entirely in keeping with tradition, then.

Società Canottieri Firenze

Lungarno Luisa dei Medici 8, Duomo & Around (055 282130/www.canottierifirenze.it). **Open** 8am-8.30pm Mon, Sat; 8am-9.30pm Tue-Fri; 8am-1pm Sun. **Membership** €70/mth. **No credit cards**. **Map** p334 C3.

Tucked away in the caverns below the Uffizi (you enter the club through a tiny green door on the lungarno), this fairly exclusive club has boats that go out on the Arno. There's also a gym, indoor rowing tank, sauna and showers.

Running

Most joggers hit the **Parco delle Cascine** along the river, but you can also head for the hills. Your best bet is **viale Michelangelo**, where there's a wide pavement under trees. Small roads branch off and will have you in Tuscan countryside within minutes. Be particularly careful of cars on these back lanes; there are often no pavements.

Associazione Atletica Leggera

Viale Manfredo Fanti 2, Outside the City Gates (055 576616). Bus 10, 20. **Open** 1-6pm Mon, Wed; 9am-1pm Tue, Thur-Sat.

This is Florence's best source for running clubs and meets. Foreigners can only participate in amateur races – phone for further details.

Florence Marathon

Florence (055 5522957/www.firenzemarathon.it).

Normally held in late November, the increasingly popular Florence Marathon snakes through the centre of the city and the suburbs. It's open to anyone over the age of 18, providing they can show a certificate of health. *See also p174.*

Skiing

For the **Abetone** ski area in the province of Pistoia (an easy weekend or day trip from Florence), *see p220.*

Squash

Centro Squash Firenze

Via Empoli 16, San Quirico (055 7323055). Bus 1. **Open** 9.45am-9.45pm Mon-Fri; 9.30am-6pm Sat. Closed Sat June-Aug. **Rates** €8/hr Mon-Thur; €5/hr Fri, Sat. **No credit cards**.

If you're dying to get some squash practice in while you're in Florence, this is the place to go. It has a fully equipped gym and a sauna, as well as aerobics, spinning and step classes. Equipment rental is available.

Swimming

Many swimming pools are open only in the summer. During winter some pools require at least a month's membership and may limit access to a few occasions a week.

Costoli

Viale Pasquale Paoli, Outside the City Gates (055 6236027). Bus 10, 17, 20. **Open** *June-Aug* 2-6pm Mon; 10am-6pm Tue-Sun. *Sept-May* call for details. **Admission** €4.10/hr; free-€4.50/hr concessions. **No credit cards**.

Located near the football stadium, this is a swimmer's dream, with Olympic-size, diving and children's pools, surrounded by a lovely green park. Perfect for families. There's also an indoor pool for the winter months. Membership required.

FLOG

Via Mercati 24B, Outside the City Gates (055 484465/www.flog.it). Bus 4, 8, 14, 20, 28. **Open** *June, July* 10am-6.30pm Sat, Sun. *Aug* 10am-6.30pm daily. Closed Sept-May. **Admission** €6; €4 concessions. **No credit cards**.

This small outdoor pool in Poggetto is a great place to hang out on a baking hot day. Part of an 'afterwork club' of a metalworking factory, it has a sun terrace and refreshments stand.

Hotel Villa Le Rondini

Via Vecchia Bolognese 224, Outside the City Gates (055 400081/www.villalerondini.com). Bus 25. **Open** 10am-7pm daily. Closed Oct-Apr. **Admission** €17 Mon-Fri; €20 Sat, Sun. **No credit cards**.

A small outdoor pool beside a chic, hillside hotel at La Ruota just outside of town, surrounded by a lovely lawn and shady trees.

NUOTO+

Giovanni Franceschi (0571 993721/335 6172453 mobile/www.giovannifranceschi.it).

Through this organisation you can book week-long swim camps in locations across Italy. They run during the summer and are open to children, adults and whole families. Instruction at all levels is combined with a relaxing holiday. Give them a call or visit the website for enquiries.

Piscina Bellariva

Lungarno Aldo Moro 6, Outside the City Gates (055 677521). Bus 14. **Open** *May-Sept* 10am-6pm Mon, Wed, Fri-Sun; 10am-6pm, 8.30-11.30pm Tue, Thur. *Oct-Apr* 8.30-11pm Tue, Thur; 9.30am-12.30pm Sat, Sun. **Admission** €6.50; €4.50 concessions. **No credit cards**.

A lovely indoor Olympic-size pool in a beautiful green park to the east of town. There's a refreshments stand and a separate pool for small children, so it's a good option for a family trip. *Photo p201.*

Tennis

ASSI

Viale Michelangelo, Outside the City Gates (055 687858). Bus 12, 13. **Open** *Summer* 8am-11pm daily. *Winter* 8am-6pm daily. **Rates** *Before 6pm* €10/hr court for 2 people; €11/hr court for 4 people. *After 6pm* €11/hr court for 2 people; €12/hr court for 4 people. **No credit cards**.

Six clay courts beautifully situated overlooking the city on the south side of the Arno. There are three full-time pros and most of the instructors speak at least a little English.

Tennis Carraia

Via dell'Erta Canina 26, Outside the City Gates (055 7327047). **Open** phone for details. **Rates** phone for details.

Set in what feels like the countryside, the Carraia courts are just a ten-minute walk from Porta San Niccolò. There are only three courts, so reservations are needed. There are programmes for children, and several friendly pros can give private lessons.

Unione Sportiva Affrico

Viale Fanti Manfredo 20, Outside the City Gates (055 600845). Bus 17, 20. **Open** 9am-10.30pm Mon-Fri; 9am-7pm Sat; 9am-1pm Sun. Closed 2wks Aug. **Rates** €11.50/hr per court. **No credit cards**.

Near the football stadium in the east, this down-to-earth tennis club has eight courts. Non-members are allowed to reserve a court up to three days in advance, though this has to be done in person.

Theatre & Dance

Florence's theatres have banded together to deal with financial problems – and the move has paid off.

Tuscany is home to more than 200 active theatres, most of them running regular seasons, with more opening each year. A publishing entrepreneur is behind one of the next anticipated openings, after recently buying Florence's historic **Teatro Niccolini** on via Ricasoli, just steps from the Duomo. Dating from 1658 and closed since 1995, it should come back to life in 2009 as a state-of-the-art cultural centre.

Budget restraints are resulting in shorter seasons and cheaper stagings than in the theatre scene's heyday (with a high number of monologues being shown). Theatres have learnt the hard way that their only means of escape from this long-term crisis is networking. In Florence and neighbouring towns, 16 venues have joined forces and founded **Firenze dei Teatri** (055 2625903, www.firenzedeiteatri.it), giving themselves a better chance of public funding by submitting joint projects. Together with the **Teatri Aperti** festival (*see p207*), the association's most successful scheme is **Passteatri**, a voucher booklet that allows the holder to pick six performances out of a choice of 40, put on at over 14 different theatres, plus free bus transport to and from the venue. Priced at just €50, Passteatri has finally made theatre-going barely dearer than visiting the cinema – however, it mostly benefits Italian-speakers.

As a whole, the dance scene benefits from better public funding, and Tuscan dance companies have a far more solid international reputation than their theatrical counterparts. Full-length classical and contemporary productions by the **MaggioDanza** (*see p207*) are performed at the **Teatro del Maggio** (*see p206*), while modern work comes from ensembles such as the **Virgilio Sieni Dance Company**. Elsewhere in Tuscany, look out for groups such as **Company Blu** (Sesto Fiorentino), **Motus** (Siena), **Aldes** (Lucca), **Sosta Palmizi** (Cortona), **Micha Van Hoeke** (Castiglioncello), **Compagnia Xe** (San Casciano) and **Giardino Chiuso** (San Gimignano).

Theatre seasons run roughly from October to April, but the summer months offer an abundance of festivals (*see p207*) and open-air shows. As a rule, Sunday shows are matinées, and Monday is the day off. Unsold seats can be bought from the theatre's ticket office from an hour prior to the performance. Both in Florence and Tuscany, virtually all theatre productions – including Broadway musicals – are in Italian, but there's a fair amount of non-verbal theatre, and English-speaking companies like Festa and Fitc are tentatively entering the scene (*see p207*). Keep an eye out for details of upcoming events in the local press or look for the free monthly brochure issued by Firenze dei Teatri.

Venues

Cango Cantieri Goldonetta Firenze

Via Santa Maria 23-25, Oltrarno (055 2280525/ www.cango.fi.it). **Box office** 10am-5pm Mon-Fri. **Seasons** Sept-Dec, May-June. **No credit cards. Map** p334 D1.

The term *'cantiere'* (building site) refers to this venue's status as a project-in-progress. In addition to performances by the resident ensemble Virgilio Sieni (*see p207*), events include dance workshops, competitions and the Oltrarno Atelier festival in June.

Florence Dance Cultural Centre

Borgo della Stella 23r, Oltrarno (055 289276/ www.florencedance.org). **Box office** varies. Closed Aug. **Credit** MC, V. **Map** p334 C1.

Directed by former étoile Marga Nativo and American choreographer Keith Ferrone, this eclectic centre hosts a range of dance classes as well as a programme of visual art events called Etoile Toy. It also organises the Florence Dance Festival, which takes place in July and December (*see p207*).

Teatro Cantiere Florida

Via Pisana 111, Outside the City Gates (055 7131783/www.elsinor.net). Bus 6, 26, 27, 80. **Box office** 2-5pm Mon-Fri. **Season** Late Oct-Apr. **No credit cards**.

This bare-walled 288-seat theatre aims to promote young actors, directors and playwrights, and to appeal to young audiences. Productions range from reworks of Shakespearean classics to experimental pieces. Family shows are on Sunday afternoons.

Teatro Everest

Via Volterrana 4b, Galluzzo, Outside the City Gates (055 2321754/tickets 055 2048307/www. teatroeverest.it). Bus 36, 37. **Box office** 3.30-7.30pm Mon-Fri. **Season** Oct-Apr. **No credit cards**.

Launched in 2002, this refurbished 1950s parish hall belongs to Teatri Possibili, a national network of experimental theatres promoting emerging directors and actors, mixed in with a few established names.

MaggioDanza.

Teatro Goldoni

Via Santa Maria 15, Oltrarno (call Teatro del Maggio; see below). **Box office** contact relevant organising body. **Season** varies. **No credit cards**. **Map** p334 D1.

The diminutive 19th-century Teatro Goldoni is managed by the Teatro del Maggio Musicale Fiorentino (*see below*) on behalf of the Florence town council and is used primarily for dance and ballet performances, including the winter season of the Florence Dance Festival (*see p207*).

Teatro della Limonaia

Via Gramsci 426, Sesto Fiorentino, Outside the City Gates (055 440852/www.teatrodellalimonaia.it). Bus 2, 28A. **Box office** 3-6pm Mon-Fri; occasionally 4-7pm Sat. **Seasons** Dec-May, Sept-Oct. **No credit cards**.

The former lemon house of the Villa Corsi Salviati has been converted into a trendy 90-seater hosting alternative shows by up-and-coming Italian and international theatre and dance artists. Look out for the Intercity Festival in October (*see p207*).

Teatro del Maggio Musicale Fiorentino

Corso Italia 16, Santa Maria Novella (055 2779350/ tickets 055 213535/www.maggiofiorentino.com). **Box office** 10am-4pm Mon-Fri; 10am-1pm Sat. **Season** Sept-July. **Credit** AmEx, DC, MC, V.

Home to MaggioDanza (*see p207*), this theatre features mainstream ballet year-round. In late June, the Maggio Musicale festival (*see p207*) offers a dance jamboree in piazza della Signoria. *See also p187.*

Teatro della Pergola

Via della Pergola 18-32, San Marco (055 2264316/ www.pergola.firenze.it). **Box office** 9.30am-6.45pm Tue-Sat; 10am-12.15pm Sun. **Season** Oct-Apr. **Credit** AmEx, DC, MC, V. **Map** p335 B5.

Shakespeare, Pirandello and Goldoni feature regularly in the programme of ancient and modern classics presented by this historic theatre, which recently celebrated 350 years of activity. Watch out for guided visits on Sunday mornings (advance booking necessary). *See also p188.*

Teatro Puccini

Piazza Puccini, via delle Cascine 41, Outside the City Gates (055 362067/www.teatropuccini.it). Bus 17, 30, 35. **Box office** 3.30-7pm Mon-Sat; Sat also 10am-1pm. **Season** Oct-Apr. **No credit cards**.

Housed in a 1940s listed building, the Puccini focuses on comedy and satirical shows. The annexe Micrò room hosts an additional programme organised by Catalyst, one of the resident companies.

Teatro di Rifredi

Via Vittorio Emanuele 303, Outside the City Gates (055 4220361/www.toscanateatro.it). Bus 8, 14, 20, 28. **Box office** 4-7pm Mon-Sat. **Season** Oct-May. **No credit cards**.

Long-term residents Pupi e Fresedde (*see p207*) offer a varied programme devoted mainly to contemporary and fringe shows with an emphasis on emerging playwrights and directors. There's also the odd classic production, plus appearances by guest companies including acclaimed visual theatre artists.

Teatro Studio di Scandicci

Via Donizetti 58, Outside the City Gates (055 751853/757348/www.scandiccicultura.org). Bus 16, 26. **Box office** 1hr 30mins prior to show time only. **Season** Jan-May. *Special projects* Oct-Dec. **No credit cards**.

This unusual space (formerly a school gym) is one of the best spots to see alternative theatre. Artistic director Giancarlo Cauteruccio is a respected name with a strong vision, and his Compagnia di Krypton (*see p207*) is the principal resident here.

Teatro Verdi

Via Ghibellina 99, Santa Croce (055 212320/www.teatroverdifirenze.it). **Box office** 10am-1pm, 4-7pm Mon-Fri. **Season** Oct-Mar. **No credit cards. Map** p335 C5.

The city's largest theatre, Teatro Verdi hosts all the top-notch light comedies, musicals and dance shows whose more lavish sets and elaborate choreography would not fit in any of the smaller venues in town. *See also p188.*

Theatre companies

Compagnia di Krypton

055 2345443/krypton@dada.it.

This company, whose lighting, stage and sound techniques were considered to be avant-garde when the group started out in 1982, is resident at the Teatro Studio di Scandicci (*see p206*). It still experiments with projections, lasers, microphones and various other effects.

Elsinor, Teatro Stabile d'Innovazione

055 7131783/www.elsinor.net.

Elsinor manages the Teatro Cantiere Florida (*see p205*) as well as theatres further afield – in Milan, Bologna and Forlì. The company's productions encompass a repertoire of experimental shows and plays for children and young people.

Festa

334 8004624/www.festatheatre.com.

The Florence English Speaking Theatrical Artists (Festa) is a group of theatre professionals dedicated to providing English-language theatrical and interdisciplinary performances for English-speakers.

Fitc

055 2399949/www.florencetheatre.com.

Working primarily in English, the Florence International Theatre Company (Fitc) seeks to create a theatrical community in Florence reflecting the city's international status. Thearical performances, plus educational and outreach programmes, are held in a variety of venues around town, including theatres, libraries and bookshops.

Pupi e Fresedde

055 4220361/www.toscanateatro.it.

Founded in 1976, the managing company of the Teatro di Rifredi (*see p206*) is named after Peter Schumann's politically radical Bread & Puppet theatre. It has an eclectic repertoire of original titles about literature, science, current social issues and the Tuscan dialect.

Teatro delle Donne

055 8876581/www.donne.toscana.it/centri/teatrodonne.

Based at the Teatro Manzoni in Calenzano, this company promotes and performs plays by women and organises two festivals on the subject.

Dance companies

Compagnia Virgilio Sieni Danza

055 2280525/www.sienidanza.it.

Dancer/choreographer Virgilio Sieni directs one of the few local avant-garde dance companies to have achieved global recognition. Projects often involve musicians, visual artists and even fashion designers. The company is based at the Cango (*see p205*).

MaggioDanza

055 2779350/www.maggiofiorentino.com.

The work of the official ensemble of the Maggio Musicale Fiorentino (*see p206*) ranges from evergreens such as *Giselle* and the *Nutcracker* to contemporary works. Regrettably, financial worries and staff changes often tell on quality standards.

Versiliadanza

055 350986/www.versiliadanza.it.

Dancer/choreographer Angela Torriani Evangelisti founded this small company in 1993. Versiliadanza concentrates on contemporary pieces, but also has experience with Baroque and Renaissance dance. The group collaborates with the German choreographer Suzanne Linke.

Festivals

Fabbrica Europa

Stazione Leopolda, viale Fratelli Rosselli 5, Outside the City Gates (055 2480515/www.fabbricaeuropa.net). Bus 1, 9, 16, 26, 27. **Date** May.

The large space of this former railway station by Porta al Prato is well suited to an innovative festival of theatre, music, dance and multimedia arts.

Florence Dance Festival

Borgo Stella 23, Oltrarno (055 289276/www.florencedance.org). **Date** July & Dec.

The festival fuses some of the greatest names in contemporary, traditional and classical dance. The July 2007 event abandoned Fiesole's Teatro Romano and provisionally moved to the Cascine race course; this was considered unsuccessful, and a permanent venue was being negotiated as we went to press. A winter festival is held in the Teatro Goldoni (*see p206*).

Mese Mediceo

Florence and province (055 6120205/www.mesemediceo.it). **Date** May-July.

A programme of highly entertaining original plays about the lives and flaws of different members of the Medici family. Staged in various historic locations, the festival has become a favourite with visitors.

Teatri Aperti

Florence and metropolitan area (055 2779362/www.firenzedeiteatri.it). **Date** late Sept-early Oct.

Theatres in and around Florence (17 of them) offer about 60 shows and assorted events in this massive festival meant to disprove the notion of theatre-going as a stuffy, passive experience.

Tuscany

Getting Started	210
Florence & Prato Provinces	214
Pistoia Province	219
Pisa	222
Pisa & Livorno Provinces	230
Siena	235
Siena Province	247
Lucca	260
Massa-Carrara & Lucca Provinces	270
Arezzo	276
Arezzo Province	283
Southern Tuscany	290

Features

Spa-spangled manors	231
The Pallo	244
Gold comfort farm	250
Unter der toskanischen Sonne	254
Fine vines	258
Grand designs	265
Tuscany's Toontown	266
Market force	281
South park	297

Porto Ercole. *See p294.*

Getting Started

Look beyond the regional capital for hill towns, olive groves, vineyards and beaches... and lots more art.

Sand, sun and soil create a patchwork of colours in Southern Tuscany's **Maremma**. *See p290.*

Holiday hotspots and see-before-you-die sights the world over may come and go, but the enduring appeal of Tuscany always remains. Away from the tourist hordes in Florence, the pace of life relaxes and the countryside opens out into panoramic vistas of vineyards, olive groves, valleys and hills, cascading gently towards a coastline with its own highlights. Not that the culture starts and ends in the regional capital: Pisa, Siena, Lucca and Arezzo hold all manner of fabulous buildings, artworks and monuments, while smaller towns like Montepulciano, San Sepolcro and Montalcino maintain a sense of the spirit of another age.

Indeed, the only reason Florence has precedence over the destinations explored in the following chapters is because it emerged victorious after centuries of conflict – endless infighting that effectively ceased at the end of the 15th century, but can still be discerned in the conversation of any Tuscan. Tuscans class themselves according to their city district first, their city second and nationality third, defining themselves as 'Tuscan' only as a last resort to ensure you don't confuse them with a dastardly Pisano/Aretino/Sienese – not to mention a Florentine. This visceral sense of belonging is called *campanilismo*, and it's the Sienese, conscious of being frozen in their medieval glory, and most likely to attach themselves to a *contrada* (city district), who epitomise the idea of identification with place and history.

Tuscans (like Italians in general) are very fond of pigeonholing their regional neighbours. Prato commands respect for its wealth-generating entrepreneurial spirit, while Pistoia elicits the same for its sense of age. Montecatini also recalls the past, with its turn-of-the-19th-century parks and grandiose bathing establishments. Further west, Lucca, hermetically sealed by its chunky 16th-century walls, always managed to pay off would-be conquerors and now seems to have more friends – even in Tuscany – than enemies. Bourgeois Arezzo has also kept a high standard of living while falling under Florentine dominion, and working-class Livorno has always been open-minded, with loud-mouthed inhabitants and a pioneering spirit.

But it's not all about conflict. Tuscany's geography went a long way towards ensuring its overall unity amid constant internal squabbling: more than 90 per cent of its territory is mountainous or hilly, which leaves only small slivers of level ground along rivers and the coast to invade; the mountains to the north also prevented too many attacks from Europe. Taken in its entirety, Tuscany cradled an unmatched crop of poets, painters, scientists, explorers and architects, as well as creating a language so poetical the entire country adopted it. Its rulers also had the foresight to amass unprecedented artistic wealth: to this day, the region has the highest concentration of art in the country.

These attractions haven't escaped the notice of holiday-makers and their agents, and at times it can feel like areas of Tuscany (San Gimignano, for example) have turned into mini theme parks. Indeed, one of them practically has (*see p254* **Unter der toskanischen Sonne**). Yet, on the other hand, wandering the backstreets of a town like Volterra (*see p232*), it's not difficult to find yourself transported from the crowds entirely.

AN OVERVIEW

Tuscany's popular image is of sun-drenched and cypress-dotted rolling hills. While this isn't untrue, particularly for the areas south and south-east of Florence, it doesn't give the whole picture. The Apuan Alps and the Apennine peaks set the region apart, providing a plethora of giddy, winding roads (ideal for hardcore cyclists), as well as ski resorts and high-altitude trekking. These self-contained, forested areas – such as the Garfagnana and Lunigiana, and the Valtiberina valley – have provided the basic ingredients for Tuscany's culinary tradition and the backdrop for many of its paintings.

In the deep south is the Maremma, a large expanse of sparsely populated and previously malarial swampland that was once the region's poorest part but now houses a coastal playground for Italy's rich and famous. Etruscan remains are scattered all around here; inland, a series of small, ancient towns, including Pitigliano, cling precariously to hillsides. Towards the northern end of the coast is the modern port of Livorno, and the Versilia, with its beach umbrellas and nightspots. Mainland Tuscany is far from ideal for a seaside holiday, however: its coast is dominated by grey-brown sand, murky water and crowds. For better beaches, head to the Argentario peninsula or one of the islands; *see also p212* **Shingle belles**. To find out about Tuscany's underground draws (caves, mines, passageways), see www.toscanaunderground.it.

The chapters that follow don't aim to provide exhaustive information on the towns and provinces of Tuscany, so much as lead you in the direction of what we consider to be the area's very best elements.

WHERE, WHEN, HOW

The best overall advice, especially if you only have a week or two, is to concentrate on one or two provinces or parts of the region. Unless you want to dedicate your holiday to, say, wine tourism or art and architecture, Tuscany invites you to mix up your itinerary. Visit the ornate churches and galleries, but try not to saturate your days with hours spent driving around the countryside to see all the sights. Instead, spend a day walking and try to sit down once each day to a Tuscan meal. If you need to recuperate from sightseeing, spend a few hours at one of the region's many thermal spas (*see p231* **Spa-spangled manors**). Alternatively, build your holiday around a language, cookery or painting course (*see p212*).

In Easter and summer, many places get busy and you have to weigh up whether they're worth the effort. The gorgeous hill town of San Gimignano, for instance, is like honey to the tourist bees: visit in months either side of the rush, such as May or September/October. There

Don't miss Tuscany

Activities and events

The thermal spas of **Pisa Province** (*see p231* **Spa-spangled manors**); the heady pleasures of a day of **wine tasting** (*see p258* **Fine vines**); the adrenaline-stirring **Giostra del Saracino** in Arezzo (*see p276*) and **Palio** in Siena (*see p244* **The Palio**).

Aesthetic pleasures

Piero della Francesca's **Legend of the True Cross** (*see p276*); Pisa's **Leaning Tower** (*see p225*); **contemporary art** in Prato (*see p214*).

Wandering and relaxation

The walled-up privacy of **Lucca** (*see pp260-269*); marble and its meaty product lardo around **Colonnata** (*see p272*); hitting the **beaches** (and hopefully avoiding the crowds; *see p212* **Shingle belles**); the incomparable countryside of **Chianti** (*see pp247-249 and p258* **Fine Vines**).

Shingle belles

One glance at a map of Tuscany will reveal just how long its coastline is. Stretching from Marina di Carrara in the north to just south of Marina di Capalbio in the south, most of it is fringed with sand (and sometimes less-than-perfect water). Tuscans take full advantage of their natural holiday resource, finding any excuse to head '*al mare*' for a quick day or weekend trip from around early May to late September and, in many cases, relocating to the beach for much of the month of August.

A beach holiday Italian style is very different from the British version; swathes of Tuscany's sand is occupied by *stabilimenti balneari*, outfits who lay out row upon row of brightly coloured umbrellas and deckchairs for which you have to pay, often through the nose. When all these places are filled with bronzing bodies (which is likely at the weekends and in August), there's little room for manoeuvre and the noise level can be quite high.

There are alternatives, however, if you know where to go, although even the beaches listed below (which run from south to north) are crowded at the weekends from June until September, and are untenable in August.

La Feniglia

Just outside Porto Ercole, Grosseto; see p294.

These seven kilometres (4.3 miles) of fine pale sand are backed by a beautiful pine forest. Avoid the umbrellas and bars near the car park and walk from the car park along the beach to find your patch of solitude. Alternatively, hire a bike and cycle through the woods; there are plenty of footpaths that lead to the sand.

Marina di Alberese

South of Grosseto.

This strip of golden sand is part of the Parco Naturale della Maremma (*see p297* **South park**). In summer, buy a ticket for the car park (where space is limited) from the Visitor Centre at Alberese before driving the eight kilometres (five miles) to the beach.

Cala Violina

Between Follonica and Punta Ala, Grosseto.

The spectacular 'violin bay' is so called because of the sound emitted by the fine white sand (microscopic grains of white quartz) when you walk on it, a characteristic shared, apparently, by only one other beach in the world. The clear blue water is shallow and the beach is backed by *macchia*: Tuscan vegetation including wild juniper and myrtle.

La Sterpaia

Between Piombino and Follonica, Livorno Province/Grosseto.

Of the eight kilometres (five miles) of fine sand here, around 70 per cent is '*spiaggia libera*' (free beach). Part of a natural park, it's well organised, with parking spaces along its length. So avoid the *stabilimenti balneari* and try to ignore the power station at the northern end. The rest is gorgeous.

Golfo di Baratti

Between San Vincenzo and Piombino, Livorno Province.

This perfect half-moon of golden sand is fringed with pine trees and dominated by the ancient little town of Populonia (*see p234*).

are few crowds in winter, but many attractions and restaurants are either shut or open for limited hours, the more rural hotels and guesthouses sometimes put up their shutters off-season – and the weather won't be so good. In peak season, book rooms in advance. Prices given are for double rooms, unless otherwise stated.

TOURIST INFORMATION

The general tourist information website for Tuscany is www.turismo.toscana.it. Local tourist offices are listed under the individual towns and areas. Below we list a selection of the best touring and themed holidays. All phone numbers are in the UK unless otherwise stated.

Specialist holidays

Art history holidays

Prospect Art Tours

020 7486 5704/www.prospecttours.com.
Music and art history holidays, including a five-day trip to the Puccini Opera Festival (£995 including accommodation and most meals).

Cookery schools

La Bottega Del 30

Via Santa Caterina 7, 0577 359226 within Italy/ www.labottegadel30.it.
Popular five-day courses focusing on Chianti cookery. Classes (for up to ten) end with lunch and wine tastings. A wine cellar, library and *videoteca* are also at students' disposal.

Italian Cookery Weeks

020 8208 0112/www.italian-cookery-weeks.co.uk.
Excellent food and wine with daily tuition by an expert chef, accompanied by trips and excursions. Prices start at £1,599 per week, including flights.

Farming holidays

WWOOF (World-Wide Opportunities on Organic Farms)

01273 476286/www.wwoof.org.
Working holidays on organic farms, especially during the grape and olive harvests. Food and board are usually provided in exchange for about six hours work a day. It's wise to find out as much as you can about living and working conditions before you go. For a list of farms you need to join WWOOF.

Language schools

Italian Language Courses (www.italian-language-courses.net) and **Apple Languages** (www.applelanguages.com) are both reliable agencies with posts in Tuscany. *See also p312.*

Cooperativa 'Il Sasso'

0578 758311 within Italy/www.ilsasso.com.
Two- and four-week language courses based in Montepulciano for all levels, plus courses in art history. Rooms can be arranged in hotels, flats or with families. Prices start at €370 for a two-week course.

Italian Cultural Institute

020 7235 1461/www.icilondon.esteri.it.
The Italian Cultural Institute is a good source of information about language courses in Italy.

Painting courses

See also p212.

Simply Travel

0870 166 4979/www.simplytravel.co.uk.
Package holidays and city breaks to Florence and Tuscany, staying in private villas and hotels that are off the beaten track. A week-long holiday, including flights, transfers or car hire and accommodation in a villa, starts from £500 per person.

Verrochio Art Centre

020 8869 1035/www.verrocchio.co.uk.
Specialist painting and sculpture courses in a hill-top village. Prices start at £779 for a two-week course (accommodation, breakfast and dinner, excluding flights). The booking contact is Maureen Ruck.

Walking & cycling

Alternative Travel Group

01865 315678/www.atg-oxford.co.uk.
Escorted walking and cycling trips (from about £910, excluding flights) in small groups, plus customised unguided walking trips with rooms in family-run hotels (from £450 B&B per week, flights not included).

Ramblers Holidays

01707 331133/www.ramblersholidays.co.uk.
A variety of walking tours, including a week exploring the sights of Florence, from £513 half-board, including flights and accommodation.

Villa rentals & agriturismi

Many travel companies have a wide range of villas to rent across the region. Our favourites include **James Villas** (UK: 08700 556688, www.jamesvillas.co.uk), **Tuscan House** (US: 1-800 844 6939, 1-251 968 4444, www.tuscanhouse.com) and **Ville in Italia** (Italy: 055 412058, www.villeinitalia.com). Rates vary hugely according to the season and size of property, so call or browse the website.

Agriturismi – whereby farmers let out part of their property – are an increasingly common option. Check www.agriturismo.net for a wide range of properties online; for some of our favourites, *see p250* **Gold comfort farm.**

Florence & Prato Provinces

Homelands of Leonardo, Boccaccio, Giotto and the Medici.

Museo Leonardiano.

Heading out in any direction from Florence you'll find a multitude of delightful towns and villages ideal for a day trip. South-west are **Vinci**, Leonardo's hometown, **Certaldo Alto**, Boccaccio's birthplace, and **Montelupo**, with its colourful ceramics. To the north, the verdant **Mugello** deserves a visit for both its natural and artistic beauties. Between Florence and Pistoia stretches the recently created Prato Province, whose underrated provincial capital boasts Tuscany's best mix of historic and contemporary attractions. Nearby, **Poggio a Caiano**, **Carmignano** and **Artimino** stand guard to prime art treasures set in some of Tuscany's finest vineyards and olive groves.

Tuscany

Prato

Immediately to the west of Florence is Prato, created a province in its own right only in 1992. The town boasts Tuscany's highest per capita income, and the Pratesi joke that soon 'Prato will be Paris, and Florence its Versailles'. Prato is undeservedly considered little more than an industrial suburb of Florence, but the city council has spent squillions to upgrade Prato's attractions, and the improvements have led to a number of new restaurant, bar and club openings, and an enviable taste for contemporary art.

Prato was a thriving trading centre in the Middle Ages. The city's textile manufacturing heritage is celebrated by the **Museo del Tessuto** (via Santa Chiara 24, 0574 611503, www.museodeltessuto.it, closed Tue, admission €6). Prato's 13th-century **Cattedrale di Santo Stefano** (piazza del Duomo, 0574 26234) is a Romanesque-Gothic brick building with a 15th-century external pulpit designed by Michelozzo and carved with reliefs by Donatello (the originals are in the Museo dell'Opera del Duomo; *see below*). The city's religious icon, the Sacra Cintola (Holy Girdle) is shown here on festival days (*see p174*). Inside, the Cappella dell'Assunta has frescoes by Paolo Uccello. The choir was decorated by Filippo Lippi with beautiful frescoes. The visit is free except to the Holy Girdle and Lippi chapels (joint admission €3.50, including an audio guide; 10am-5pm Mon-Sat, 3-5pm Sun).

A €6 ticket covers three of the city's main museums: the **Museo dell'Opera del Duomo** (piazza del Duomo 49, 0574 29339, closed Tue

& Sun afternoon), housed in Palazzo Vescovile and exhibiting a fresco attributed to Paolo Uccello and works by both Filippo and Filippino Lippi; the **Museo di Pittura Murale** (piazza San Domenico, 0574 440501, closed Tue and all afternoons except Fri and Sat) displaying detached frescoes, sinopias and paintings; and the 13th-century **Castello dell'Imperatore** (piazza Santa Maria delle Carceri, 0574 38207, closed Tue). Outside the city walls, the **Centro per l'Arte Contemporanea Luigi Pecci** (viale della Repubblica 277, 0574 5317, www.centropecci.it, closed Tue, admission €5-€4), houses one of the country's most important collections of contemporary art.

Where to eat

At **Enoteca Barni** (via Ferrucci 22, 0574 607845, closed lunch Sat & all Sun, average €15 lunch, €50 dinner) lunch is informal and fairly inexpensive, while dinner is more elaborate and costly. For fish and seafood the best option is **Il Pirana** (via Valentini 110, 0574 25746, closed Sat & Sun lunch, average €55). If hearty Tuscan dishes are what you fancy, **La Vecchia Cucina di Soldano** (via Pomeria 23, 0574 34665, closed Sun, average €30) and **Osteria Cibbe** (piazza Mercatale 49, 0574 607509, closed Sun, average €23) are excellent and economical choices.

Where to stay

Prato's newest accommodation option, **Wallart** (viale della Repubblica 4/6/8, 0574 596600, www.wallart.it, €95-€150), is a hotel, convention centre, gallery, bookshop, restaurant and bar. Nearer the Pecci museum, **Art Hotel Museo** (viale della Repubblica 289, 0574 5787, www.arthotel-museo.it, €100-€150) is another luxury choice. A cheaper option in a prime location is **Hotel Flora** (via Cairoli 31, 0574 33521, www.hotelflora.info, €75-€140), offering parking and Wi-Fi.

Poggio a Caiano, Carmignano & Artimino

Heading west from Florence on the SS66 to Pistoia you reach the village of Poggio a Caiano, home to Lorenzo il Magnifico's country retreat, the impressive **Medici Villa Ambra** (piazza de' Medici 14, 055 8798779, closed 2nd & 3rd Mon of mth, admission free, escorted visits on the half hour). The second floor of the villa houses the **Museo della Natura Morta** (055 877012, admission free, escorted visits on the hour, reservation advised) with an impressive gallery of still lifes. Nearby **Scuderie Medicee** (via Lorenzo il Magnifico 5, 055 8701280) are set to house a permanent exhibition of works by Ardengo Soffici (1879-1964), the Futurist painter, writer and poet.

At Poggio a Caiano head south through pleasant countryside to **Carmignano**, whose pride and joy is the 1530 *Visitation* by Pontormo in **San Michele e San Francesco**. Nearby estates offering wines tastings and tours include **Capezzana** (via Capezzana 100, Seano, 055 8706005, www.capezzana.it, closed Sun) and **Fattoria di Bacchereto** (via Fontemorana, 055 8717191, closed 2wks Nov or Jan).

Not far away is the delightful walled village of **Artimino**, faced with the multi-chimneyed Medici villa known as **La Ferdinanda** (viale Papa Giovanni XXIII 1, 055 87151427, www.artimino.it, visits by arrangement), built in 1596. The surrounding countryside is rich in archaeological sites, and the villa houses the **Museo Archeologico Etrusco** (055 8718124, closed Wed, admission €4).

Where to eat & drink

In Carmignano, the excellent Tuscan dishes on the menu of **Osteria Su Pe' I Canto** (piazza Matteotti 25, 055 8712490, www.supeicanto.it, closed Mon & 3wks Aug, average €28) provide a perfect excuse to sample the fine wines. In Artimino, **Da Delfina** (via della Chiesa 1, 055 8718074, www.dadelfina.it, closed Sun evening, Mon and Aug, average €45) serves seasonal food such as rabbit with pine nuts and olives.

Vinci

A constant stream of visitors flocks to this quaint little hill town in search of Leonardo da Vinci's origins. The stone farmhouse where he was born (open daily, admission free) is in the hamlet of **Anchiano**, a three-kilometre (two-mile) drive or 1.5-kilometre (one-mile) walk out of Vinci. The bare rooms house educational panels with Leonardo's earliest known drawing. Back in Vinci, models of his machines and instruments are on display at the **Museo Leonardiano** (0571 933251, admission €6), split between **Palazzina Uzielli** on via Rossi and formidable **Castello dei Conti Guidi**. The panoramic piazza Guido Masi has a wooden statue of Leonardo's *Vitruvian Man* by Mario Ceroli (1987); piazza della Libertà houses a life-size equine monument by Nina Askamu (2001) inspired by Leonardo's drawings of horses.

Where to eat

In the town centre, **Il Ristoro del Museo** (via Montalbano 9, 0571 56516, closed Fri dinner, Sat lunch & Christmas holidays, average €30)

has a panoramic terrace and serves delicious traditional food. Nearby, the **Antica Cantina di Bacco** (piazza Leonardo da Vinci 3, 0571 568041, closed Mon, average €22) is a cute little wine bar that also serves food.

Montelupo

Montelupo has been known for its beautifully coloured glazed pottery since the Middle Ages. The main street of the town is lined with shops selling boldly patterned ceramics, and a week-long **Festa Internazionale della Ceramica** (*see p173*) is held in late June. A joint ticket of €5.50 admits to both of Montelupo's museums: the new **Museo Archeologico** (via Santa Lucia, 0571 541547, closed Mon, admission €3.50) and the **Museo della Ceramica** (via Sinibaldi 43, 0571 51352, www.museomontelupo.it, closed Mon, admission €3.50).

Certaldo Alto

This walled hilltop settlement's main claim to fame is that Giovanni Boccaccio (1313-75, author of the *Decameron*) was born, died and is buried here. In July the town is bathed in candlelight for the **Mercantia** festival of street arts (www.mercantiacertaldo.it), while **Boccaccesca** (*see p174*) in October celebrates Tuscan cuisine. **Palazzo Pretorio** (piazzetta del Vicariato 3, 0571 661219, closed Mon in winter, admission €3) is decorated with the coats of arms of past governors. A joint ticket of €6 also admits you to **Boccaccio's House** (via Boccaccio, 0571 664208, www.casaboccaccio.it, closed Oct-mid Jan, admission €2.50) and the **Museum of Sacred Art** (piazza SS Iacopo e Filippo, 0571 661219, closed Mon-Fri, admission €2.50).

Where to eat & stay

Set in a former 13th-century monastery, **Osteria del Vicario** (via Rivellino 3, 0571 668228, www.osteriadelvicario.it, closed Wed in winter, Sun in summer & mid Jan-Feb) has four rooms (€100) and a celebrated restaurant (average €55) often featuring the excellent local red onions. The new town down the hill is worth a visit for **La Saletta di Dolci Follie** (via Roma 3, 0571 668188, closed Tue and 2wks Aug, average €35).

Greve, Montefioralle & Panzano

Greve is a centre of the Slow Food movement and makes for an exceptionally pleasant base. A sliver of hairpin bends leads up from Greve's northern side to the ancient walled village of Montefioralle, a lovely spot for a quiet lunch. Further south is the fortified village of Panzano, overlooking the Conca d'Oro valley.

Where to eat & stay

In Greve itself, you can find delectable dishes at the tiny **Mangiando Mangiando** (piazza Matteotti 80, 055 8546372, closed Mon in winter and mid Jan-mid Feb, average €30). If you're looking for a room, the best option is **Albergo Verrazzano** (piazza Mattoetti 28, 055 853189, www.albergoverrazzano.it, closed mid Jan-mid Feb, €105), which has a charming restaurant.

Up in Montefioralle, family-run **La Taverna del Guerrino** is a rustic gem (via Montefioralle 39, 055 853106, closed Mon-Wed, 2wks Dec, average €35). In Panzano, try **Villa Sangiovese** (piazza Bucciarelli 5, 055 852461, www.villasangiovese.it, average €35, doubles €125, restaurant closed Wed, & both closed mid Dec-mid Mar).

The Mugello

The hilly Sieve valley north of Florence is known as the **Mugello**, while the mountainous **Alto Mugello** extends up the Apennine passes to the border with Romagna. This beautiful area of woods and pastures offers great walks, while the man-made **Lago di Bilancino** is popular for its beaches and watersports. The Medici went back to their homeland to build several mansions such as **Castello di Trebbio** and **Villa Cafaggiolo**, both near San Piero a Sieve.

Borgo San Lorenzo is the bustling commercial hub of the area. Just east of Borgo, sleepy little **Vicchio** was the birthplace of Fra Angelico and Giotto. A few kilometres north-west of Borgo is **Scarperia** (*photo p218*), founded in 1306 as the northernmost military outpost of the Florentine Republic. The crenellated **Palazzo dei Vicari** (055 8468165, admission €3) boasts a 1445 clock by Filippo Brunelleschi. For the Autodromo Internazionale del Mugello racetrack, *see p200.*

Where to eat & stay

For Mugello cuisine in Scarperia, try **Il Torrione** (via Roma 78-80, 055 8430263, closed Mon, average €22). Between Borgo and Vicchio, don't miss the area's best potato *tortelli* at the rustic **Trattoria Sagginale Da Giorgione** (via Belvedere 23, località Sagginale, 055 8490130, closed Thur and 2wks June, average €22) or enjoy refined versions of local dishes in Borgo itself, at the centrally located **Ristorante degli Artisti** (piazza Romagnoli 1, 055 8457707, www.ristorantedegliartisti.it, closed Wed, average €55). Next door, the **Locanda degli Artisti** (piazza Romagnoli 2, 055 8455359, www.locanda artisti.it, €100-€140) has pleasant art nouveau rooms. If the bill isn't a concern, the most stylish hotel in the area is **Villa Campestri** (via di Campestri 19-22, 055 8490107, www.villacampestri.it, closed mid Nov-mid Mar, €144-€210), a lovely Renaissance villa set in green hills just above Sagginale.

Resources

Tourist information

Carmignano *Piazza Vittorio Emanuele II 1-2 (055 8712468/www.carmignanodivino.it).* **Open** *Summer* 9.30am-12.30pm, 4-7pm Tue-Sun. *Winter* 9.30am-12.30pm Tue-Sun, 3-6pm Tue-Sat.

Certaldo *Nr Railway Station, piazza Masini (0571 656721).* **Open** *Easter-mid Oct* 9am-1pm, 3.30-7pm daily. *Mid Oct-Dec* 10am-12pm, 3.30-6pm daily. Closed Jan-Easter.

Greve *Piazza Matteotti 1, Greve (055 8546287/ www.chiantislowtravel.it).* **Open** 9am-1pm, 2.30-6.30pm Mon-Sat.

Montelupo Fiorentino *Museo della Ceramica, via Baccio da Montelupo 43, Montelup (0571 518993/www.museomontelupo.it).* **Open** 10am-6pm Tue-Sun.

The Mugello *Villa Pecori Giraldi, piazzale Lavacchini, Borgo San Lorenzo (055 845271/www.mugellotoscana.it).* **Open** 10am-1pm, 3-6pm Tue, Thur-Sun; 10am-1pm Wed.

Poggio a Caiano *Ex Scuderie Medicee, via Lorenzo il Magnifico (055 8798779/www.prolocopoggioa caiano.it).* **Open** 3-6.30pm Wed-Sun; 10am-1pm, 3-6.30pm Sat, Sun.

Prato *Piazza Santa Maria delle Carceri 15 (0574 24112/www.prato.turismo.toscana.it).* **Open** *Summer* 9am-1.30pm, 2.30-7pm Mon-Sat; 10am-1pm Sun. *Winter* 9am-1.30pm, 2.30-6.30pm Mon-Fri; 9am-1.30pm, 2-6pm Sat.

Vinci *Via della Torre 11 (0571 568012/www.terre delrinascimento.it).* **Open** *Summer* 10am-7pm daily. *Winter* 10am-3pm Mon-Fri; 10am-6pm Sat, Sun.

Getting there

By bus

For Prato, Poggio a Caiano and Carmignano check **Cap** (055 214637, www.capautolinee.it) and **Copit** (0573 3630, www.copitspa.it) services. Montelupo is served by **Lazzi** (055 363041, www.lazzi.it) and **Ataf** (800 424500, www.ataf.net). **Sita** (800 373760, 055 294955, www.sita-on-line.it) runs bus services to Borgo San Lorenzo and Vicchio (1hr).

By car

Head west on the A11 motorway from Florence. Montelupo is just off the Florence–Pisa–Livorno (Fi–Pi–Li) *superstrada*. For Certaldo, exit at Empoli Ovest and continue south on the SS429. For Vinci, exit at Empoli and head north for Pistoia. From Florence, Poggio a Caiano, Carmignano and Artimino are best reached via the SS66 (via Pistoiese). For Borgo San Lorenzo, take either the SS65 (via Bolognese) or the more windy SS302 (via Faentina). For Scarperia, take the SS65 and pick up the SS503 at San Piero a Sieve. For Vicchio, head for Borgo then take the SS551.

By train

Frequent trains from Florence stop at Prato Centrale (main line to Bologna) or Porta al Serraglio (local line to Lucca). Montelupo is on the Florence–Empoli–Pisa line (20-30mins). For Vinci, reach Empoli by train and catch a local bus (hourly, fewer in the weekends). Certaldo is on the Siena line; a train change may be necessary at Firenze Rifredi and/or Empoli (1hr). Borgo San Lorenzo is served by two routes from Florence, one via Pontassieve and Vicchio (1hr) and one via Vaglia and San Piero a Sieve (45mins) continuing through the Alto Mugello and Faenza. For information, call 892021 or visit www.trenitalia.com.

Scarperia. *See p217.*

Pistoia Province

Pistols, Pinocchio and pools for the pampered.

The province of Pistoia is deepest Tuscany, surrounded by cool, green Apennine scenery, spas and sleepy villages, as well as skiing in Abetone. The provincial capital of Pistoia is, for some incomprehensible reason, little known outside Tuscany, and remains very much off the tourist track. Perhaps this has something to do with its violent past – the city gave its name to the pistol – but it's an unadulterated gem, offering superb art to be savoured in the absence of the crushing crowds that can mar ventures in Florence and Siena. Foreign tourists in this province tend to head for the upmarket spa town of Montecatini Terme, where you can pamper yourself at one of the swish hotels.

Pistoia

The countryside for miles around Pistoia is characterised by neat rows of dwarf trees and small shrubs. The rich soil has given rise to a lucrative line in plant nurseries, which has become a multi-million-euro industry. The quiet old town itself is one of Tuscany's most enchanting cities, with an almost perfectly intact historic centre encircled by medieval walls and few fellow tourists to spoil your enjoyment. Despite its lovely ambience today, Pistoia's history is a bloody one: it was where the Catiline conspirators were rounded up after they failed to destroy the Roman Republic in 62 BC; it fought bitter wars with Renaissance rivals Florence and Lucca; and was birthplace of the brutal feud between Black and White Guelphs (a struggle often referred to in Dante's *Divine Comedy*, who was himself forced into exile by rival parties).

The **Ospedale del Ceppo**.

The architectural style of many of Pistoia's monuments combines Florentine and Pisan elements. The **Cattedrale di San Zeno** has an arcaded Pisan façade and a simple Romanesque interior; the fine campanile has a plain lower section and exotic tiger-striped arcades on top. It houses the famous gold and silver *Altar of St James* within the chapel of the same name (admission €2). Across the square is the octagonal 14th-century, green and white striped Baptistery. The **Museo Civico** (0573 371296, closed Mon, admission €3.50), behind the Duomo, has fine 14th-century paintings on the ground floor and some fairly dreadful late Mannerist works two floors above. The portico of the **Ospedale del Ceppo** (founded in the 13th century and still a functioning hospital) is decorated with a splendid ceramic frieze in the style of Giovanni della Robbia (1526-9). The nearby church of **Sant'Andrea** has a magnificent hexagonal stone pulpit (1298-1301) created by Giovanni Pisano.

Local events include the **Giostra dell'Orso** (Joust of the Bear) on 25 July and the popular **Pistoia Blues music festival** (May/June); for the latter, *see also p192*.

Where to eat & drink

La Bottegaia (via del Lastrone 17, 0573 365602, closed lunch Sun & all Mon, average €26) is a delightful wine bar/restaurant tucked away in a little square behind the Baptistery, which serves great food. The **Trattoria dell' Abbondanza** (via dell'Abbondanza 10, 0573 368037, closed Wed, lunch Thur, average €18) is even better, serving hearty Tuscan fare such as *baccalà alla Livornese*, superb fried chicken, tripe and rabbit. For civilised coffee and cakes, try **Caffè Pasticceria Valiani** (via Cavour 55, 0573 23034, closed Tue in winter and 1st 3wks Aug). Frescoed walls were uncovered in 1864 when its foundations were being laid.

Where to stay

One rural option is the five beautifully decorated rooms of *agriturismo* **Tenuta di Pieve a Celle** (Pieve a Celle, 0573 913087, www.tenutadipieveacelle.it, €120). More mainstream is the pleasant and central **Hotel Leon Bianco** (via Panciatichi 2, 0573 26675, www.hotelleonbianco.it, €85-€100). **Hotel Patria** (via Crispi 6, 0573 25187, www.patria hotel.com, €75-€90) is good value and central. There are over 100 farm-stays around Pistoia – call the tourist office for a brochure.

Montecatini Terme

At the start of the 20th century, Montecatini Terme was one of the most fashionable destinations in Europe for royalty, aristocracy and political and literary movers and shakers. The monumental thermal buildings, set around beautiful **Parco delle Terme** and constructed in a variety of OTT styles, date from this time. Today, the place still has a very civilised air of restrained if slightly faded elegance; thousands come each year to take the waters and enjoy the town. There are around 200 hotels, but in high season these can be packed. The place all but closes between late November and Easter.

The warm saline waters at Montecatini are supposed to be particularly beneficial for digestive complaints and are taken both internally and externally. The spas are modernising but many are still housed, at least partially, in the original buildings; grandest of all is **Terme Tettuccio**. For information about spas and the treatments on offer, contact the central Terme office at viale Verdi 41 (800 132538, www.termemontecatini.it).

On a balmy evening, a lovely diversion is to ride the funicular railway (viale Alfredo Diaz, €3 single, €5 return) up to charming Montecatini Alto and its panoramic views.

Where to eat & drink

There's a wide choice of places to eat in Montecatini Terme. **Il Cucco** (via del Salsero 3, 0572 72765, closed Tue, average €30) serves delicious local fare including pasta with fresh broad beans and courgette flowers. You can get good pizza (dinner only) and pasta at **Egisto's** (piazza Cesare Battisti 13, 0572 78413, closed Tue, average €23). If you want to try Tuscan wines, staff at **Il Chicco d'Uva Vineria** (viale Verdi 35, 0572 910300, closed Mon and Feb) are laid-back experts. **Enoteca Giovanni** (via Garibaldi 25-27, 0572 71695, closed Mon and Feb) claims to stock close to 1,000 different wines, many of them local; it serves good traditional Tuscan food too.

Where to stay

Most hotels insist on half or even full board in high season. If you want to stay near Montecatini Alto try the upmarket and tasteful **Casa Albertina** (via Fratelli Guermani 12, 0572 900238, www.casaalbertina.it, €100), which has glorious views over the Nievole valley from the garden. In town, the **Grand Hotel & La Pace** (via della Torretta 1, 0572 9240, www.grand hotellapace.com, €248-€436) is set in extensive grounds with two pools and has a sumptuous belle époque atmosphere. The revamped **Metropole** (via della Torretta 13, 0572 70092, www.hotel-metropole.it, €80) is situated in a turn-of-the-19th-century villa and has 40 rooms, while the spotless, family-run **Hotel Savoia & Campana** (viale Cavallotti 10, 0572 772670, www.hotelsavoiaecampana.com, €50-€82) has an old-fashioned air and 30 pleasant rooms.

Take a dip at **Montecatini Terme**.

Collodi

Collodi, on the SS435 just west of Pescia, is famous for being the birthplace of Pinocchio, Italy's most cherished fairytale character. This claim to fame brings the tourists to what is an otherwise minor, but not unattractive, town. There's no shortage of signs directing visitors to **Parco di Pinocchio** (via San Gennaro 3, 0572 429613, www.pinocchio.it, admission €10, €7 under-14s). Opened in 1956, it features a walk-through maze and Pinocchio statues, including one by Emilio Greco, and a colourful mosaic-lined courtyard by Venturino Venturi. Its delightful, tactile constructions are worlds away from the blizzard of distractions found at British and American theme parks. Just across the road from the park, **Giardino Garzoni** (piazza della Vittoria 1, 0572 429590, admission €12, €10 under-14; combined ticket with Parco di Pinocchio €18, €14 under-14s) is a Baroque garden designed by Romano di Alessandro Garzoni. There's a feeling of faded glory to it, although an ongoing restoration programme is sprucing up the fountains and statues.

Pescia

Pescia is the flower capital of Italy. Some three million blooms are exported from this attractive town every day in summer. Take in the kaleidoscopic colours and head-spinning perfumes between 6am and 8am Monday to Saturday at the vast flower market at via Salvo d'Acquisto 10-12 (0572 440502).

The Montagna Pistoiese

The Apennine mountains to the north of Pistoia, known as the Montagna Pistoiese, make a cool, escape from the heat of the plain in summer; at the top is **Abetone**, one of Tuscany's two ski destinations (the other is Monte Amiata in Grosseto Province; *see p293*). Beautifully situated **San Marcello Pistoiese** is a popular summer resort standing 820 metres (2,690 feet) above sea level, while a little further on is the attractive old town of **Cutigliano**, which also fills up in summer. Reached via a splendid and ancient forest, Abetone stands at nearly 1,400 metres (4,590 feet) above sea level. Just 85 kilometres (53 miles) from Florence, it's easily accessible for a weekend or even a day trip. It gets very crowded at weekends and from January to March, when parents take kids out of school for a week on the slopes; its wide runs are ideal for beginner and intermediate level skiers. On average, ski-boot hire costs €20 per day and ski passes are €25 per weekday, €29.50 at the weekend.

Where to stay & eat

In Cutigliano, the old-fashioned **Miramonte** (piazza Catilina 12, 0573 68012, €70 per person full board – obligatory in high season) occupies a 16th-century palazzo on the main square. Up in Abetone, the modest **Noemi** (via Brennero 244, località Le Regine, 0573 60168, €35-€52) has ten en suite rooms. Or there's the four-star **Bella Vista** (via Brennero 383, 0573 60028, www.bellavista-abetone.it, €80-€100). The best place to eat in Abetone is **Le Prunecce** (via Montaccolle 14, 0572 67301, closed Wed, average €25), which serves up brilliant rabbit dishes, and home-made pecorino. The rustic **L'Osteria** (via Roma 6, 0573 68272, average €25) in Cutigliano specialises in mushrooms; you can eat them in soups, risottos, pastas or deep fried. **La Vecchia Cantina** (via Risorgimento 4, località Maresca, 0573 64158, closed Tue, average €30) serves a great range of pasta dishes such as *ravioli verdi con ricotta*, and excellent juicy steaks.

Resources

Tourist information

Abetone *Tourist information 0573 60231. Ski information 0573 60001.*
Montagna Pistoiese APT *Via Marconi 70, San Marcello Pistoiese (0573 630145).* **Open** 8am-2pm Mon-Sat.
Montecatini Terme APT *Viale Verdi 66 (0572 772244).* **Open** 9am-1pm, 3-6pm daily.
Pistoia APT *Piazza del Duomo (0573 21622).* **Open** 10am-1pm, 3-6pm Sun daily.
Pistoia Province *www.pistoia.turismo.toscana.it.*

Getting there

By bus

LAZZI (055 363041, www.lazzi.it) runs regular buses from Florence to Pistoia (45mins) and Montecatini Terme (1hr). **CAP** (055 214637) links Pistoia with Florence. From Pistoia, **CAO** operates a service into the mountains (San Marcello, Cutigliano, Abetone). **CLAP** (0583 587897) buses connect Lucca with Pescia (45mins) and less regularly with Collodi. **COPIT/CAP** runs daily 'ski buses' from Florence to Abetone in season, but you must change in Pistoia. For timetables call 0573 3630 or 055 214637.

By car

Pistoia, Montecatini and the Montagne Pistoiese are accessible off the A11 *autostrada*.

By train

Regular trains on the Florence–Lucca line service Pistoia (35mins), Montecatini (50mins) and Pescia (60-75mins). For the Montagna Pistoiese, take the train to Pistoia then change to a CAP bus. See www.trenitalia.it or call 892021 for details.

Pisa

A city to be enjoyed from several different angles.

Writing in the 12th century, the monk Donizone wrote: 'Those who go to Pisa can see monsters coming from the sea: this town is full of pagans.' Almost 900 years later, we might rephrase this slightly to '…this town is full of tourists', a fact that's become even more pertinent since June 2007, when Pisa airport received its first direct flight from the United States. The **Campo dei Miracoli** – the ultimate Catholic theme park, where you'll find the **Duomo**, the **Baptistery** and the **Leaning Tower** (for all, *see p223*) – is the focus of this touristic onslaught, with groups of visitors herded in and around the square all through the summer. However, although it would be a travesty to completely ignore the Campo, there's a great deal more to Pisa than the sum of its most famous parts, with interesting restaurants, shops and clubs opening all the time, and providing plenty of opportunities to escape the crowds.

SOME HISTORY

Pisa is located in a broad flood plain surrounding a loop in the River Arno, ten kilometres (six miles) before it flows into the Tyrrhenian Sea. In ancient times, the estuary of the Arno was further inland, creating a lagoon inlet with easy landing for boats. The settlers there soon became traders, initially under the Etruscan sphere of influence, and then, from 27 BC, as a prosperous Roman colony. The chance discovery in 1998 of 18 2,000-year-old ships that had been preserved beneath layers of silt, bore tangible witness to such early clout. The **Arsenale Mediceo**, on lungarno Simonelli, is being restored and will house the boats and their cargos from 2009. You can arrange tours of the current site (off via Andrea Pisano, just south of Stazione San Rossore) by visiting www.navipisa.it or www.coidra.it – the website of the co-operative running the restoration project. Book at least five days before your visit.

During the Middle Ages, the wealth and power of Pisa increased, and by the 11th century it had established itself as a great maritime republic. The accrued wealth paid for urban expansion, including the Campo dei Miracoli, but by the 15th century the city was in decline. It didn't do well under the Medici grand dukes; their successor, Pietro Leopoldo of Lorraine, found it to be 'languid and poor, with insalubrious air, swampy lands and widespread misery'. So, in the late 1700s, he set about putting things right.

He did a pretty decent job (though much of downtown Pisa was destroyed when the Allies and Germans clashed during World War II). By 1844, Pisa was linked to Florence by rail, and had begun to develop the taste for intellectual advancement that it retains to this day. As well as its eminent university and the prestigious Scuola Normale Superiore, it is home to numerous research institutes. The academic population lends the streets a purposeful atmosphere, but also provide a youthful pulse: there are a good number of bars and nightclubs here, as well as events such as June's **Metarock** (www.metamusic.it). The two main local festivals, however, are a little more historic: the **Luminara di San Ranieri** (16 & 17 June) and **Il Gioco del Ponte** (last Sunday in June); for both, *see p172* Giugno Pisano.

An alternative way to see the city is by boat. The **Il Navicello** tour company (www.ilnavicello.it) operates two Pisan boat tours, a town-based itinerary and a Sundays-only excursion to the nearby **Parco Naturale di San Rossore** (050 530101), where north Italian racehorses spend their winter holidays.

Sightseeing

Campo dei Miracoli

The scale and elegance of the layout that encompasses the Duomo, the Baptistery, the Leaning Tower and the Camposanto is undeniable. The 13th-century court astrologer Guido Bonatti argued that the spatial design was symbolic of the cosmos, and of the theme of Aries in particular. Look carefully: the Duomo and Baptistry both lean as well, though less perceptibly.

There are now ticket offices in just two sites (in the **Museo delle Sinopie**, and just north of the Tower), with the tourist office in the **Museo dell'Opera del Duomo**. There are several varieties of ticket, including one that offers admission to all the sights (except the Leaning Tower, for which *see p223*) for €10.50. Call 050 3872210 for information, or visit www.opapisa.it.

Tuscany

Baptistery

050 3872210/www.opapisa.it. **Open** *Apr-Sept* 8.30am-8pm daily. *Mar, Oct* 9am-6pm daily. *Nov-Feb* 10am-5pm daily. **Admission** €5. **Credit** MC, V. **Map** p224 A1.

The marble Baptistery was designed by Diotisalvi (literally 'God-save-you') in 1152, with later decorative input by father and son Nicola and Giovanni Pisano. The magnificent pulpit by Nicola Pisano (1260) is still there to be admired in situ (compare it to his son's 1310 pulpit in the Duomo), though most of the precious artwork is now kept in the Museo dell'Opera del Duomo (*see p226*). The harmonious, onion-shaped dome was a later addition, from the mid 14th century. Every half-hour, singing attendants demonstrate the building's extraordinary acoustics.

Camposanto

Open *Apr-Sept* 8am-8pm daily. *Mar, Oct* 9am-6pm daily. *Nov-Feb* 10am-5pm daily. **Admission** €5. **Credit** MC, V. **Map** p224 A2.

The Camposanto (Holy Field), begun in 1277 by Giovanni de Simone, is a felicitous stylistic misfit, with elements of various styles, including Gothic and Romanesque, plus more than 100 Roman sarcophagi (stone coffins). Lining the Gothic cloisters around the edge of the field are the gravestones of VIP Pisans buried in holy soil. On the west wall hang two massive lengths of chain that were once strung across the entrance to the Pisan port to keep out enemy ships. Pisan legend has it that the soil in the middle of the Camposanto was imported from the Holy Land. In 1944, the roof collapsed as a result of Allied bombardment, destroying frescoes and sculptures, including a fabulous cycle by Benozzo Gozzoli. However, a few survived (including, appropriately enough, *Triumph of Death, Last Judgement* and *Hell*), and these are being painstakingly restored as part of an ongoing project.

Duomo

050 3872210/www.opapisa.it. **Open** *Mid Mar-Sept* 10am-8pm Mon-Sat; 1-8pm Sun. *Oct* 10am-7pm Mon-Sat; 1-7pm Sun. *Nov-mid Mar* 10am-1pm, 2-5pm Mon-Sat; 1-5pm Sun. **Admission** €2. **Credit** MC, V. **Map** p224 A2.

Begun in 1063 by Buscheto (who's buried in the wall on the left side of the façade), Pisa's cathedral is one of the finest examples of Pisan Romanesque architecture. The delicate, blindingly white marble four-tiered façade incorporates Moorish mosaics and glass within the arcades (there are more examples in the Museo dell'Opera del Duomo; *see p226*). The main entrance facing the Leaning Tower is called the Portale di San Ranieri and features bronze doors by Bonanno da Pisa (1180). The brass doors (touch the lizard for good luck) by the Giambologna school were added in 1602 to replace the originals, which were destroyed in a fire in 1595.

After the fire, the Medici family immediately came to the rescue, beginning restoration work; the ornate ceiling features their coat of arms for this reason. Sadly, at the time, nothing could be done to save Giovanni Pisano's superb Gothic pulpit (1302-11), which was incinerated and lay dismembered in crates until the 1920s. Legend has it the censer suspended near the now-restored pulpit triggered Galileo's discovery of the principles of pendular motion, but it was actually cast several years later. Crane your neck to admire the Moorish dome decorated by a vibrant fresco of the Assumption by Orazio and Girolamo Riminaldi (1631). Behind the altar is a mosaic by Cimabue of St John (1302); Giuliana Vangi's 2001 pulpit and altar are noticeably more modern in style, and kicked up something of a fuss locally.

Leaning Tower

050 3872210/www.opapisa.it. **Map** p224 A2.

The south-east corner of the Campo holds Pisa's most popular attraction, and one of the most famous curiosities on earth. Begun in 1173 (the commemorative plaque offering 1174 as the start date is based on the old Pisan calendar) by an unknown architect, the famous tower – the campanile for the Duomo – started to lean almost as soon as it was erected, and many years before the top level, housing the seven bells, was finally added in 1350. Architect Giovanni di Simone (architect of the Camposanto; *see above*), who worked on the tower in the 13th century, attempted to correct the tilt by building floors that had one side higher than the other. However, this only served to make the tower lean in the opposite direction (which is why it's now, in fact, curved). In

Leaning Tower.

Tuscany

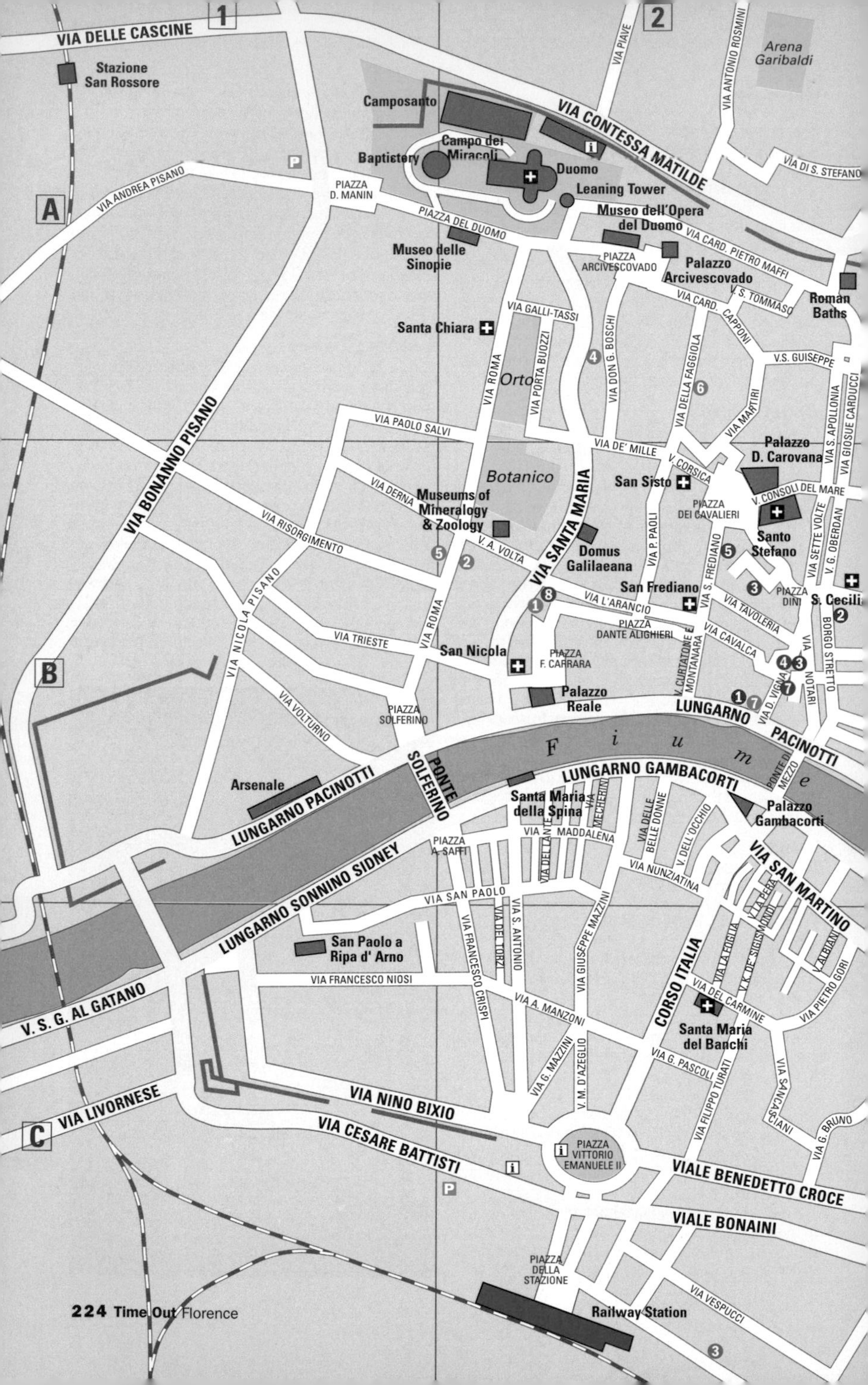
VIA DELLE CASCINE
Stazione San Rossore
Camposanto
Campo dei Miracoli
Baptistery
Duomo
Leaning Tower
VIA CONTESSA MATILDE
Arena Garibaldi
Museo dell'Opera del Duomo
PIAZZA D. MANIN
PIAZZA DEL DUOMO
Museo delle Sinopie
PIAZZA ARCIVESCOVADO
Palazzo Arcivescovado
Roman Baths
Santa Chiara
Orto
Botanico
VIA BONANNO PISANO
Museums of Mineralogy & Zoology
VIA SANTA MARIA
Domus Galilaeana
San Sisto
PIAZZA DEI CAVALIERI
Palazzo D. Carovana
Santo Stefano
San Frediano
S. Cecilia
San Nicola
PIAZZA DANTE ALIGHIERI
PIAZZA F. CARRARA
Palazzo Reale
LUNGARNO PACINOTTI
PIAZZA SOLFERINO
PONTE SOLFERINO
Fiume
Arsenale
LUNGARNO GAMBACORTI
Santa Maria della Spina
Palazzo Gambacorti
VIA SAN MARTINO
LUNGARNO SONNINO SIDNEY
San Paolo a Ripa d' Arno
CORSO ITALIA
Santa Maria dei Banchi
V. S. G. AL GATANO
VIA LIVORNESE
VIA NINO BIXIO
VIA CESARE BATTISTI
PIAZZA VITTORIO EMANUELE II
VIALE BENEDETTO CROCE
VIALE BONAINI
PIAZZA DELLA STAZIONE
Railway Station
VIA VESPUCCI

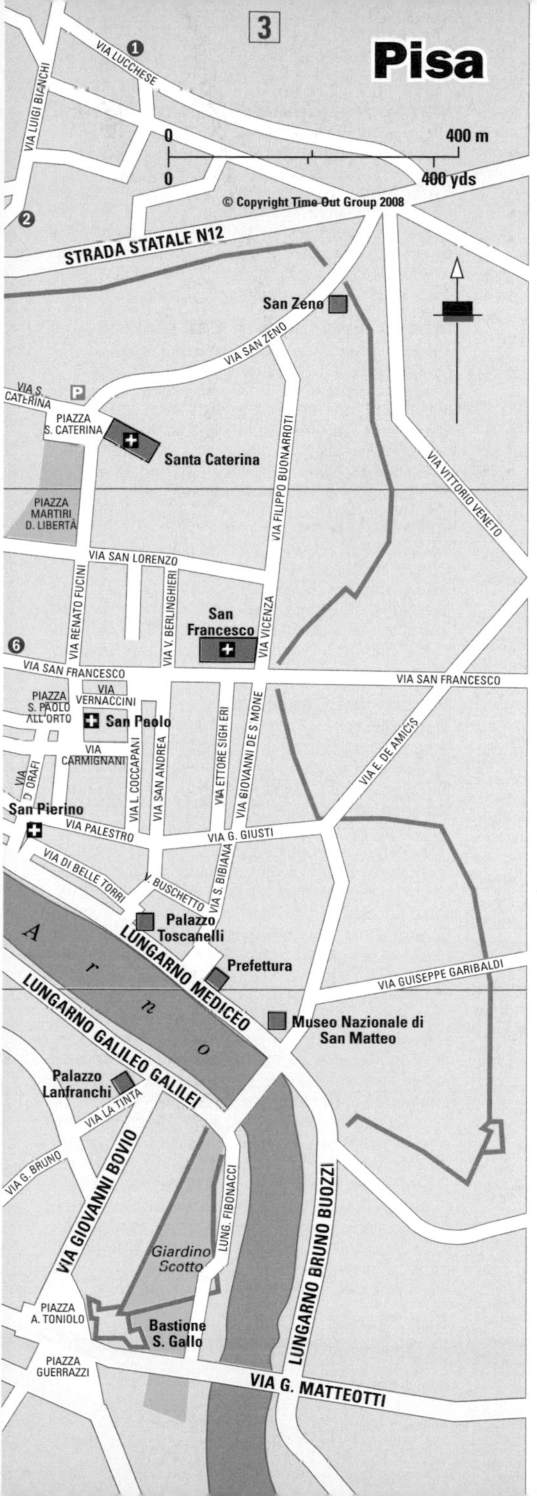

A. Volta, Via - B2
Albiani, Via - C2
Andrea Pisano, Via - A1
Antonio Rosmini, Via - A2
Belle Donne, Via Delle - B2
Benedetto Croce, Viale - C2
Berlinghieri, Via V. - B3
Bonaini, Viale - C2
Bonanno Pisano, Via - A1, B1
Borgo Stretto - B2
Buschetto, Via - B3
Card. Pietro Maffi, Via - A2
Card. Capponi, Via - A2
Carmignani, Via. - B3
Carmine, Via Del - C2
Cascine, Via Delle - A1
Cavalca, Via - B2
Cesare Battisti, Via - C1, 2
Consoli Del Mare, Via - B2
Contessa Matilde, Via - A2
Corsica, Via - B2
Corso Italia - B2, C2
Curtatone E Mont, Via - B2
D. Orafi, Via - B3
D. Vigna, Via - B2
De Amicis, Via E. - B3
Del Lante, Via - B2
Del Torzi, Via - C2
Dell' Occhio, Via - B2
Derna, Via - A2
Di Mezzo, Via - B2
Don G. Boschi, Via - A2
Ettore Sighieri, Via - B3
Faggiola, Via Della - A2
Filippo Buonarroti, Via - A3, B3
Filippo Turati, Via - C2
Francesco Crispi, Via - C2
Francesco Niosi, Via - C1, 2
G. Bruno, Via - C2
G. Giusti, Via - B3
G. Matteotti, Via - C3
G. Oberdan, Via - B2
G. Pascoli, Via - C2
Galli-Tassi, Via - A2
Giosue Carducci, Via - A2
Giovanni Bovio, Via - C3
Giovanni De Simone, Via - B3
Giuseppe Mazzini, Via - B2, C2
Guiseppe Garibaldi, Via -B3
K. De'Sigismondi, Via - C3
L. Coccapani, Via - B3
La Foglia, Via - C2
La Pera, Via - B2
La Tinta, Via - C3
L'arancio, Via - B2
Livornese, Via - C1
Lucchese, Via - A3
Luigi Bianchi, Via - A3
Lung. Fibonacci - C3
Lungarno Bruno Buozzi - C3
Lungarno Galileo Galilei - C3
Lungarno Gambacorti - B2
Lungarno Mediceo - B3, C3
Lungarno Pacinotti - B1/2
Lungarno R. Simonelli - B1, 2
Lungarno Sonnino Sidney - B1, C1
Maddalena, Via - B2
Martiri, Via - A2
Mecherini, Via - B2
Mille, Via De' - B2
Nicola Pisano, Via - B1
Nino Bixio, Via - C1,2
Notari, Via - B2
P. Paoli, Via - B2
Palestro, Via - B3
Paolo Salvi, Via - A1
Piave, Via - A2
Piazza A. Saffi - B2
Piazza A. Toniolo - C3
Piazza Arcivescovado - A2
Piazza D. Manin - A2
Piazza Dante Alighieri - B2
Piazza Dei Cavalieri - B2
Piazza Del Duomo - A1, 2
Piazza Della Stazione - C2
Piazza Dini - B2
Piazza F. Carrara - B2
Piazza Guerrazzi - C3
Piazza Martiri D. Libertà - B3
Piazza S. Caterina - A3
Piazza S. Paolo All'orto - B3
Piazza Solferino - B1
Piazza Vittorio Emanuele Ii - C2
Pietro Gori, Via - C2
Porta Buozzi, Via - A2
Renato Fucini, Via - B3
Risorgimento, Via - B1
Roma, Via - A2
S. Antonio, Via - B2, C2
S. Apollonia, Via - A2/B2
S. Bibiana, Via - B3
S. Frediano, Via - B2
S. G. Al Gatano, Via - C1
S. Stefano, Via - A2
S. Tommaso, Via - A2
San Andrea, Via - B3
San Francesco, Via - B3
San Lorenzo, Via - B3
San Martino, Via - B2
San Paolo, Via - B2
San Zeno, Via - A3
Sancasciani, Via - C2
Santa Maria, Via - A2, B2
Sette Volte, Via - B2
Solferino, Ponte - B1/2
Strada Statale N12 - A3
Tavoleria, Via - B2
Torri, Via Di Belle -B3
Trieste, Via - B1
V. M. D'Azeglio, Via - C2
Vernaccini, Via - B3
Vespucci, Via - C2
Vicenza, Via - B3
Vittorio Veneto, Via - A3, B3
Volturno, Via - B1

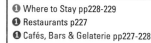

❶ Where to Stay pp228-229
❶ Restaurants p227
❶ Cafés, Bars & Gelaterie pp227-228

1989, the year before the tower was closed to the public, more than a million visitors scrambled up its 294 steps. After years of restoration work (external cleaning is still ongoing), it reopened in December 2001, but with some heavy restrictions: the tower is open only for guided tours, and then only to groups of 30 willing to pay €15 a head (plus €2 booking fee). You don't have to book, but to guarantee a time slot it's a good idea: visit www.opapisa.it, or go to one of the ticket offices (*see p222*). Under-eights aren't allowed; children aged eight to 12 must hold hands with an adult throughout; and those between 12 and 18 must be accompanied by a grown-up. In summer 2007, Pisan authorities experimented with opening the tower at night; it remains to be seen whether this will become a permanent part of the attraction. As we went to press, plans were being floated to introduce an online audio guide to download on to your iPod. *Photo p223.*

Museo dell'Opera del Duomo

050 3872210/www.opapisa.it. **Open** *Apr-Sept* 8am-8pm daily. *Mar, Oct* 9am-6pm daily. *Nov-Feb* 10am-6pm daily. **Admission** €5. **No credit cards. Map** p224 A2.

This museum contains works from the monuments of the Campo dei Miracoli. Among its more interesting exhibits is a series of sculptures from the 12th to 14th centuries, including a clutch of notable works by Giovanni Pisano. Bonanno's medieval bronze doors from the east entrance to the Duomo, fresh from recent restoration, are now on show.

Museo delle Sinopie

050 560547/www.opapisa.it. **Open** *Apr-Sept* 9am-8pm daily. *Mar, Oct* 9am-6pm daily. *Nov-Feb* 9am-5pm daily. **Admission** €5. **No credit cards. Map** p224 A2.

The 1944 bombings and subsequent restoration work uncovered the *sinopie* (preliminary sketches, made with a reddish-brown pigment composed of iron oxides) from beneath the frescoes in the Camposanto. They were meant to be hidden forever, after the artist covered the original *arriccio* (dry plaster on which the sketches were made) with a lime-rich plaster called *grassello*. The *sinopie* show what brilliant draftsmen the painters were, but also give the observer an intriguing sense of scale.

Torre di Santa Maria

Open 10am-6pm daily. **Admission** €2. **No credit cards. Map** p224 A1.

Head here for a good overview of the Campo dei Miracoli and access to a small part of the city walls.

Other sights

The **Domus Galileiana** (via Santa Maria 26, 050 23726, www.domusgalileiana.it) is the city's official tribute to its great former resident, but is not a visitor attraction as such; mainly used for archival work, it does, however, occasionally put on exhibitions.

Museo Nazionale di Palazzo Reale

Lungarno Pacinotti 46 (050 926539). **Open** 9am-3pm Mon-Fri; 9am-1.30pm Sat. **Admission** €5; €8 with Museo Nazionale di San Matteo. **No credit cards. Map** p224 B2.

Housed in a Medici palace dating from 1583, this museum shows many Medici-related works, donated by private collectors. Portrait paintings represent members of various European dynasties; there's also traditional Gioco del Ponte gear (*see p172*).

Museo Nazionale di San Matteo

Piazza San Matteo in Soarta, lungarno Mediceo (050 541865). **Open** 8.30am-7pm Tue-Sat; 8.30am-1pm Sun. **Admission** €5; €8 with Museo Nazionale di Palazzo Reale. **No credit cards. Map** p225 C3.

Once a convent, this 12th- to 13th-century building now contains Pisan and Islamic medieval ceramics, works by Masaccio, Fra Angelico and Domenico Ghirlandaio, and a bust by Donatello.

Orto Botanico

Via Luca Ghini 5 (050 560045/www.horti.unimore.it). **Open** 8.30am-1pm Mon-Fri; 8am-1pm Sat. **Admission** free. **Map** p224 A2/B2.

The oldest university garden to be found anywhere in Europe (it was started by Luca Ghini back in 1543), the Orto Botanico was originally used to study the medicinal values of plants.

Piazza dei Cavalieri

Map p224 B2.

A focal point of Pisa, this beautiful square houses the Palazzo dei Cavalieri, the seat of one of Italy's most prestigious universities, the Scuola Normale Superiore, established by Napoleon in 1810. In the 16th century, Giorgio Vasari designed most of the piazza's buildings, including the Chiesa dei Cavalieri, the Palazzo della Conventuale (opposite the church, erected as home to the Cavalieri of Santo Stefano), the Palazzo del Consiglio dell'Ordine and the Palazzo Gherardesca. The latter occupies the site of a medieval prison where, in 1288, Count Ugolino della Gherardesca, along with three of his male heirs, was condemned to starve to death for conducting covert negotiations with the Florentines. His sons and grandsons all died relatively quickly, but Ugolino lasted nine months, after he reputedly kept himself alive by eating his own children. Although that condemned him to Hell in Dante's *Inferno*, the poet ensured that Ugolino had a measure of revenge: the count spent eternity gnawing the head of Archbishop Ruggieri, the man who had betrayed him (Canto XXXIII).

You'll see the Maltese Cross everywhere in this piazza, but nowhere else in Pisa. Cosimo wanted to hammer home the parallel between his new Cavalieri of Santo Stefano and the crusading Knights of Malta. Elsewhere, you're likely to spot the Pisan cross with two balls resting on each point.

San Nicola

Via Santa Maria 2 (050 24677). **Open** 8.30am-11.30am, 5-6.30pm Mon-Sat; 9am-noon, 5.30-6.30pm Sun. **Admission** free. **Map** p224 B2.

Dating from 1150, this church is dedicated to one of Pisa's patron saints, San Nicola da Tolentino. In one chapel there's a painting showing the saint protecting Pisa from the plague in around 1400. Built on unstable ground, the campanile leans.

Santa Maria della Spina

Lungarno Gambacorti (050 3215446). **Open** *Mar-Oct* 10am-1.30pm, 2.30-6pm Tue-Fri; 10am-7pm Sat, Sun. *Nov-Feb* 10am-2pm Tue-Sun. Closed late Dec-early Jan. **Admission** €1.50. **No credit cards. Map** p224 B2.

This gorgeous, tiny Gothic church on the banks of the Arno was completely dismantled and moved to higher, drier ground in 1871. Originally an oratory, it took its present form in 1323 and gets its name from the fact that it used to own what was claimed to be a thorn (*spina*) from Christ's crown, brought back by the Crusaders. *Photo p229.*

Where to eat & drink

Restaurants

Cèe alla Pisana (eels), one of Pisa's culinary assets for centuries, are increasingly hard to find. When they are plucked from the Arno (they're a winter delicacy), the eels are tossed in warm oil, garlic and sage, then sautéed.

Aphrodite

Via Lucchese 33A (050 830248/www.ristorante aphrodite.com). **Open** 8pm-1am Tue-Sun. **Average** €35. **Credit** MC, V. **Map** p225 A3 ❶

This exciting restaurant offers innovative cuisine – and some interesting wines – in a cool, funky setting. Owner Emilio Traina and his chef create dishes that delight both palate and eye. The ample garden comes into its own in summer.

Bruno

Via Luigi Bianchi 12 (050 560818). **Open** noon-3pm, 7-10.30pm Mon, Wed-Sun. **Average** €35. **Credit** AmEx, DC, MC, V. **Map** p225 A3 ❷

Bruno concentrates on typical, good-value Tuscan cooking. Try the *ribollita*, supposedly the best this side of the Arno, or pasta with rabbit and wild boar.

Cagliostro

Via del Castelletto 26-30 (050 575413/www.cagliostro.cc). **Open** 7.45pm-1am Mon; 12.45-2.30pm, 7.45pm-1am Wed, Thur, Sun; 12.45-2.30pm, 8pm-2am Fri, Sat. **Average** €20. **No credit cards. Map** p224 B2 ❸

Cagliostro is named after a Sicilian count who masqueraded as an alchemist in France and Italy. The extensive wine list complements the menu, which draws on recipes from all over Italy. It's tricky to find – ask for the restaurant, not the street.

La Mescita

Via Cavalca 2 (050 957019/www.lamescita.org). **Open** 1-2.15pm, 8-10.30pm Tue-Fri; 1-2.15pm Sat, Sun. Closed 3wks Aug. **Average** €30. **Credit** AmEx, MC, V. **Map** p224 B2 ❹

Set in the heart of Vettovaglie market, La Mescita is pretty and tranquil. Try *brandade di stoccafisso* (salt cod) with tomatoes, but check the window for its calendar of *degustazioni* and creative cooking nights.

Osteria dei Cavalieri

Via San Frediano 16 (050 580858). **Open** 12.30-2pm, 7.45-10pm Mon-Fri; 7.45-10pm Sat. Closed late July-late Aug. **Average** €30. **Credit** AmEx, DC, MC, V. **Map** p224 B2 ❺

One of Pisa's best eateries, especially for the money. It serves typical Tuscan dishes with flair: steak with beans and mushrooms, perhaps, or *tagliolini* with rabbit and asparagus. The wine list is noteworthy.

Osteria La Grotta

Via San Francesco 103 (050 578105). **Open** noon-2.30pm, 8-11pm Mon-Sat. **Average** €25. **Credit** AmEx, DC, MC, V. **Map** p225 B3 ❻

Built to simulate a *grotta* or cave with rough stone walls and a cosy fire in winter, this fine spot serves hearty local soups, *maccheroncini* with sun-dried tomatoes, courgettes and pecorino, and excellent *baccalà* (salt cod). The wine list is good too.

Pizzeria Il Montino

Via del Monte 1 (050 598695). **Open** 10am-3pm, 5.30-10.30pm Mon-Sat. **Average** €25. **No credit cards. Map** p224 B2 ❼

Visit this small snack bar to try the unique taste of *cecina*, a bright yellow, very thin pancake made with chickpea flour from a 13th-century recipe; and *spuma*, a refreshing non-alcoholic beverage.

Re di Puglia

Via Aurelia Sud 7 (050 960157). **Open** 8-10pm Wed-Sat; 1-3pm, 8-10pm Sun. Closed 2wks Jan. **Average** €27. **No credit cards.**

Slabs of succulent meat are grilled in front of your eyes on the open fire at this rustic restaurant a few kilometres south of Pisa on the Livorno road. While meat (especially beef, lamb and rabbit) reigns supreme, the menu also includes five types of Tuscan antipasti. Eat outdoors in summer.

Ristoro Al Vecchio Teatro

Via del Collegio Ricci 3 (050 20210). **Open** 12.30-3pm, 8-10.30pm Mon-Sat. **Average** €20. **Credit** AmEx, DC, MC,V. **Map** p224 B2 ❽

Restaurant owner Giovanni displays pictures of Pisa all around the interior of his restaurant, which serves fine traditional fare like octopus and chickpeas, and has tables facing attractive, quiet piazza Dante.

Cafés, bars & gelaterie

De Coltelli

Lungarno Pacinotti 23 (050 541611/www.de coltelli.com). **Open** 1pm-1am daily. Closed Jan. **No credit cards. Map** p224 B2 ❶

Although the presence of some decidedly strange varieties – like *alle vongole* (clams) – might scare off some people, rest assured that the ice-cream dished up here is tremendous.

Pasticceria Salza

Borgo Stretto 46 (050 580144). **Open** 7.45am-8.30pm Tue-Sun. **Credit** MC, V. **Map** p224 B2 ❷
This distinguished *pasticceria*, the oldest in Pisa, is a real multitasker, with café tables in the front, a sweet shop inside and a restaurant at the back.

Pizzicheria Gastronomia Cesqui

Piazza delle Vettovaglie 38 (050 580269). **Open** 7am-1.30pm, 4-8pm Mon, Tue, Thur-Sat; 7am-1.30pm Wed. **Credit** MC, V. **Map** p224 B2 ❸
Stock up on cheeses, pastas, wines and snacks at this deli, while bantering and gossiping with the staff.

Shops & services

Pisa's main shopping drag is corso Italia, but across from the ponte di Mezzo is a funkier zone, starting at the loggia of borgo Stretto. The **Mercatino Antiquario** takes place where the two meet, on the second weekend of every month, offering modern arts and crafts as well as antiques. The **Mercato Vettovaglie**, a fruit and vegetable market, is held every morning. Look out too for **De Bondt**, one of Italy's foremost chocolate artisans (lungarno Pacinotti 5, 050 3160073, www.debondt.it).

Nightlife

For Pisa's best gay bar and sauna, *see p185*.

Borderline

Via Vernaccini 7 (050 580577/www.borderline club.it). **Open** 9pm-2am Mon-Sat. **Admission** free-€10.50. **No credit cards. Map** p225 B3.
Good for late drinks or the occasional live gig, with blues, roots and country music taking centre stage.

Dottorjazz

Via Vespucci 10 (339 8619298/www.drjazz.it). **Open** 9pm-2am Wed-Sun. Closed June-Sept. **Admission** €5-€10. **No credit cards. Map** p224 C2.
You'll need to look hard to find this jazz venue, which is located at the far end of what seems like a warehouse car park and with no sign to give it away. Once inside, though, it's an attractive place, with small candlelit tables and pictures of jazz greats on the walls. Thursday night is blues night.

Mississippi

Via Livornese 1313, località San Piero a Grado (339 1573877/www.mississippi.it). **Open** from 9.30pm Tue-Sat. **Admission** phone for details.
This out-of-town venue is popular with young people for beer and music (heavy metal, rock and blues).

Teatro Verdi

Via Palestro 40 (050 941111/542600/www.teatro dipisa.pi.it). **Open** *Box office* 4-7pm Mon, Tue, Thur, Sat; 11am-1pm, 4-7pm Wed, Fri; also 1hr before events. *Phone bookings* 2-4pm Mon-Fri. Closed Aug. **Credit** MC, V. **Map** p225 B3.
An enjoyable venue for dance, drama and music.

Where to stay

Accommodation in Pisa can be a bit hit or miss, with most of the latter in the budget categories. To ensure you get a decent room, reserve in advance during high season and for major festivals. The tourist information centre at the Campo dei Miracoli (*see p222*) has a list of hotels. You'll find the nearest camping in Marina di Pisa (*see p229*).

Albergo Galileo

Via Santa Maria 12 (050 40621). **Rates** €60. **Credit** AmEx, MC, V. **Map** p224 B2 ❶
Though it's illegal to employ Galileo Galilei's full name for commercial purposes in Pisa, this pensione manages to get away with using half of it. It's worth asking for one of the five (of nine) rooms that are decorated with 17th-century frescoes.

Amalfitana

Via Roma 44 (050 29000). **Rates** €70-€82. **Credit** AmEx, MC, V. **Map** p224 B2 ❷
A favourite of visiting Italians seeking central, two-star category accommodation.

Casa della Giovane

Via Filippo Corridoni 29 (050 43061). **Rates** €25/person double. **No credit cards. Map** p224 C2 ❸
This college, close to the station, contains a women-only boarding house. As you'd expect, it caters to students (though not exclusively) and is often packed in term-time. Note that there's an 11pm curfew.

Centro Turistico Madonna dell'Acqua

Via Pietrasantina 13 (050 890622). Bus 3. **Open** *Office* 6pm-midnight daily. **Rates** per person €21 double; €18 triple; €16 quadruple or bigger. **Credit** MC, V.
Located in a village a short distance outside the city, this is the only youth hostel that you'll find in the Pisa area. There's no point turning up before 6pm as the hostel doesn't open until then.

Grand Hotel Duomo

Via Santa Maria 94 (050 561894/www.grand hotelduomo.it). **Rates** €188. **Credit** AmEx, DC, MC, V. **Map** p224 A2 ❹
Hints of its previous opulence remain, but the Grand is now, sadly, getting somewhat frayed around the edges. But its location can't be faulted if you want somewhere central, especially if you land one of the fourth-floor rooms that have sweeping views over the Campo dei Miracoli from the terrace. If you arrive by car, make sure you ask for a parking permit for via Santa Maria.

Hotel Novecento

Via Roma 37 (050 500323/www.hotelnovecento.pisa.it). **Rates** €140. **Credit** AmEx, DC, MC, V. **Map** p224 B2 ❺
Conveniently placed for both Campo dei Miracoli and downtown Pisa, this impressive new opening

has pristine cream rooms and a pretty garden at the back. There's lots of fresh fruit for breakfast and a 12th-century well lies beneath reception.

Hotel Repubblica Marinara

Via Matteucci 81 (050 3870100/www.hotelrepubblica marinara.it). **Rates** €99-€144. **Credit** MC, V.
The rooms at this new hotel come with all manner of technological bells and whistles – internet access, orthopaedic mattresses and various lighting options. Take via Matteoti, passing the Congress Palace.

Relais dell'Orologio

Via della Faggiola 12-14 (behind piazza de' Cavalieri, 050 830361/www.hotelrelaisorologio. com). **Rates** €326-€340. **Credit** AmEx, DC, MC, V. **Map** p224 A2 ❻
Maria Louisa Bignardi's dream of turning her 13th-century house into a five-star hotel became a reality a few years back. The 21 rooms are individually decorated, so the place still has the feel of a private home. The Peli di Vaglio suite has exposed frescoes.

Royal Victoria

Lungarno Pacinotti 12 (050 940111/www.royal victoria.it). **Rates** €138. **Credit** AmEx, DC, MC, V. **Map** p224 B2 ❼
Situated on the Arno, this hotel was a popular stop back in the days of the Grand Tour and counts illustrious names, such as Charles Dickens, Theodore Roosevelt and Daryl Hannah, among its previous guests. The atmosphere still harks back to the 'old days', and though the bedrooms have lumbering old furniture, they're full of character.

Resources

Hospital

Santa Chiara, via Roma 67 (050 992111).

Internet

Via La Nunziatina (no phone).

Police

Questura, via Mario Lalli 3 (050 583511).

Post office

Piazza Vittorio Emanuele II 8 (050 5194).
Open 8.15am-7pm Mon-Sat.

Tourist information

Turistica APT *Campo dei Miracoli (no phone/ www.pisa.turismo.toscana.it).* **Open** 9am-6pm Mon-Sat; 10.30am-6.30pm Sun. **Map** p224 A2.
Other locations Galileo Galilei Airport (050 503700); piazza della Stazione 11 (050 42291); piazza Vittorio Emanuele II 16 (050 42291).

Getting there & around

By air

Galileo Galilei Airport (050 849300) is still Tuscany's major international airport. The airport handles flights from all around Europe and has recently started flights to and from the US. There are frequent buses and regular trains into Pisa and Lucca from here. For further information about the airport and its transport links, *see p300.*

By bus

LAZZI (piazza Sant'Antonio, 050 46288, www.lazzi.it) operates a regular service to Lucca (journey time 50mins), with onward connections to Florence (2hrs 30mins), as well as buses to Viareggio (50mins). **CPT** (piazza Sant'Antonio, 050 505511, www.cpt.pisa.it) covers the area around Pisa and runs buses to nearby areas such as Livorno and Marina di Pisa.

By taxi

You can find taxi ranks at piazza della Stazione (055 41252) and piazza del Duomo (050 561878). If you need to book a taxi in advance, call Radio Taxi on 050 541600.

By train

Pisa is on a main connecting line to Rome (journey time 3hrs on Intercity, otherwise 4hrs) as well as Genoa (2hrs). There are also frequent trains to Florence via Empoli (80mins), Lucca (25mins) and Livorno (15mins); some trains also stop at Pisa Aeroporto and San Rossore. The train station is Pisa Centrale, piazza della Stazione (information 892021, www.trenitalia.it).

Gothic **Santa Maria della Spina**. *See p227.*

Pisa & Livorno Provinces

Delve into Etruscan history – or into a thermal bath.

The Leaning Tower, fortunately, does not cast its shadow over the entirety of Pisa Province – or its regional neighbour, Livorno. Armed with a car and a robust road map, you can be glorying in the stunning countryside in no time – or relaxing on a beach, or having your cares steamed away in one of the many spa pools: the possibilities are many and varied.

Behind the scenes, there's a great deal of industrial activity going on; tucked-away boatyards produce some of the world's most luxurious yachts here. Meanwhile, between Bolgheri and Castagneto Carducci, a once poor farming area produces some of Tuscany's most prestigious wines. The coast is one attraction that draws the crowds (*see also p212* **Shingle belles**), but it's not the only reason to visit. Further inland, the northern section of the Maremma (known as the Maremma Pisana) runs between Cecina and Follonica on the coast and inland towards the Colline Metallifere.

San Giuliano Terme

The healing qualities of San Giuliano's local spa waters were known to Grand Duke Stephen of Lorraine, who ordered a magnificent 18th-century residence to be constructed here, which formed the nucleus of the town. Guests at the very comfortable **Bagni di Pisa** hotel (largo Shelley 18, 050 88501, www.bagnidipisa.com; *see also p231* **Spa-spangled manors**), the town's main building, can soak away the aches induced by too much sightseeing, before adjourning to the hotel's fine restaurant. Indeed, the town is so close to Pisa that it makes for a handsome alternative base to the city.

San Miniato

Snaking along the crest of a lofty hill, the town of San Miniato grew prominent on account of its strategic position above the Pisa–Florence road. It was fortified in the 12th and 13th centuries and was one of Tuscany's foremost imperial centres, but it succumbed to Florentine power in the mid 1300s. Unfortunately, the interiors of both the 13th-century Duomo and the later church of San Domenico were subjected to heavy-handed Baroque 'improvements'. The spacious loggia of San Domenico is used for an antiques fair on the second Sunday of each month (except July and August). The surrounding area is rich in truffles; November weekends are devoted to tasting them as part of the **Festa del Tartufo**.

Where to eat

Caffè Centrale (via IV Novembre 19, 0571 43037, closed Mon and late Aug/early Sept, average €12) serves simple pastas for lunch and has a great view, while just outside town there's **Il Convio** (via San Maiano 2, 0571 408114, closed Wed, average €30), with more Tuscan favourites, plus a truffle-laden vegetarian menu. As an alternative, try **La Trattoria dell'Orcio Interrato** in nearby Montopoli Valdarno (piazza San Michele 2, 0571 466878, closed all Mon, Sun dinner in winter, 2wks Aug, 1wk Feb, average €35), which has a summer terrace and interesting interpretations of Renaissance dishes. An alluring spot in the old town is **Pepenero** (via IV Novembre 13, 0571 419523, www.pepenerocucina.it, closed Wed), which is liberal with white truffle.

Casciana Terme

Tucked away in the Pisan hills and less crowded than Montecatini or Saturnia, this spa town, known as Castrum ad Aquas to the Romans, was destroyed in World War II and rebuilt in the 1960s. After taking the waters at **Terme di Casciana** (piazza Garibaldi 9, 0587 64461; *see also p231* **Spa-spangled manors**), relax out front with an espresso at the traditional café.

A kilometre east of Calci, the **Certosa di Pisa** (050 938430, closed Mon & Sun afternoon, admission €4) is a vast complex used as a monastery from 1366 until 1969, when it was abandoned by the Carthusian monks. Inside there's a 14th-century church, plus cloisters and gardens, while its former granaries, workshops and cellars now house the university's much-lauded **Natural History Museum** (via Roma

Spa-spangled manors

Heading to Tuscany in the winter? You'd better pack your swimming costume. No Italian region is as rich in spas as Tuscany: the waters are warm, if not hot, and naturally rich with minerals that should ease your aches and uplift your spirits. You can even factor in a massage for that little bit of extra luxury. Check the websites for opening/closing times, which vary from year to year.

Just north of Pisa, in San Giuliano Terme, is the very comfortable **Bagni di Pisa** hotel (*see p230*), recently upgraded to a four-star establishment. It's found a measure of fame for its decent restaurant, but also has a small hot pool, a Turkish bath in a natural grotto and a host of good masseurs. South of Pisa, meanwhile, is **Terme di Casciana** (0587 644655, www.termedicasciana.it), which has a large, luxurious modern pool and spa facilities fronted by a more traditional café.

At Bagno Vignoni, directly south of Siena, the recently revamped **Hotel Posta Marcucci** (0577 887112, www.hotelpostamarcucci.it) provides another great opportunity for aquatic indulgence. Set in pretty gardens with a magnificent view across the valley, the pool has a thundering cascade that provides a memorable hydro-massage. The water at **Bagni San Filippo** (0577 872982, www.termesanfilippo.it, closed Nov-1wk before Easter), a little further south, is hotter still and more sulphurous, with a scorcher of a cascade (the water is around 42°). Looking over the valley towards Monte Amiata at San Casciano dei Bagni, the **Terme di San Casciano** (0578 572405, www.fonteverde terme.com) offers upmarket facilities and a pool with a thundering hydro-massage. If it's salty rubs and seawater cures you pine for, head for Marina di Castagneto Carducci on the coast, where you'll find Tuscany's only thalassotherapy escape, the **Tombolo Talasso Resort** (via del Corallo 3, Maria di Castagneto Carducci, 0565 74530, www.tombolotalasso.it), which has five seawater pools and a wellness centre set in pleasant gardens, just a stone's throw from the beach.

Tombolo Talasso Resort.

103, 050 2212970, closed Mon, admission €5), founded in 1591 by Grand Duke Ferdinando I.

Where to stay & eat

Just down the road from the thermal waters is **La Speranza** (via Cavour 24, 0587 646215, www.hotel-lasperanza.com, €40), which has an attractive pool and gardens; not too far away is the spacious and inviting **Villa Margherita** (via Marconi 20, 0587 646113, www.margherita-hotel.it, closed 4 Nov-5 Dec & Jan-Easter, €74-€98). Restaurant-wise, go for **Il Merlo** (piazza Minati 5, 0587 644040, closed Mon & Jan), which has a handsome wine list. A few kilometres further on from Terricciola is the stately **Villa San Marco** (località San Marco 13, 0587 654054, €79-€85). The tourist office (via Cavour 9, 0587 646258) can give you more accommodation information.

Volterra

Volterra stands proudly on a 531-metre (1,742-foot) peak between the Cecina and Era valleys in Pisa Province. The surrounding area is rich in mineral deposits, which explains why it was settled as early as the Neolithic period. By the seventh century BC, the city known as Velathri had become one of the 12 Etruscan states, with a population of 25,000 and a prosperous trade in iron and alabaster artefacts. It put up a hearty resistance to the Romans and was the last Etruscan city to fall to the Empire. But fall it did in 260 BC, when it was renamed Volaterrae.

The town as it appears today was built in the 12th and 13th centuries; save for patches of the fortified walls, all traces of the Etruscans have been erased. Fortunately, the **Museo Etrusco Guarnacci** (via Don Minzoni 15, 0588 86347, €8) helps make up for this: among its exhibits is the celebrated 'evening shadow' statuette – a long, thin statue that was found by a local farmer and used as a fire stoker until someone recognised its importance. The ticket also admits you to Volterra's other two museums: the **Pinacoteca** (0588 87580, closed afternoons in winter), located in the late 15th-century Palazzo Minucci Solaini and worth a visit purely to see the astounding use of colour in the fabulous Mannerist *Deposition* by Rosso Fiorentino, and the **Museo d'Arte Sacra** (0588 86290, closed afternoons in winter), which boasts work by the same artist.

Where to stay & eat

A convent more than five centuries ago, **Hotel San Lino** (via San Lino 26, 0588 85250, www.hotelsanlino.com, €77-€105) now has its own pool and a shady cloister. Both offer relief from the bustle. Two kilometres outside of Volterra, the 15th-century **Villa Rioddi** (0588 88053, www.hotelvillarioddi.it, €68-€93; €520-€780 weekly for a two-room apartment) also has a pool and a lovely garden. Just outside town, **Il Vecchio Mulino** (via del Molino, località Saline, 0588 44060, closed Mon), features some new guestrooms as well as a restaurant specialising in inventive Tuscan cuisine. The town's eating options are led, though, by the cosy **Trattoria del Sacco Fiorentino** (piazza XX Settembre, 0588 88537, closed Wed, Jan & Feb, average €25); located near the Museo Etrusco Guarnacci, it serves seasonal goodies, such as gnocchi with spring vegetables, and a 100-strong wine list. An elegant alternative is **Del Duca** (via di Castello 2, 0588 81510, closed Tue, average €40), with its ancient wine cellar and secret garden.

Bolgheri. *See p234.*

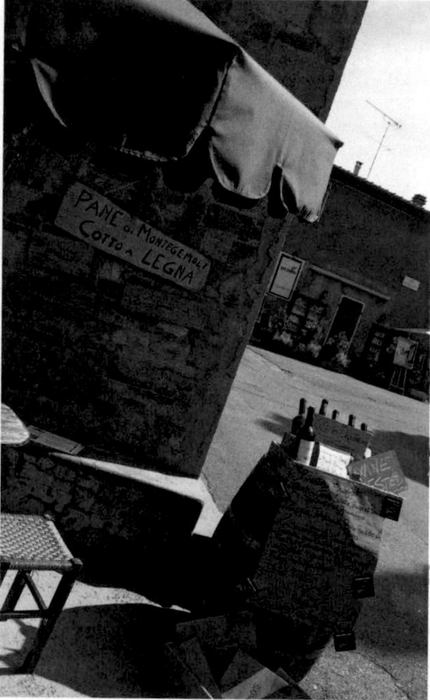

Tuscany

Livorno

By the 16th century, the Arno had silted up, leaving the maritime republic of Pisa shorn of its outlet to the sea. As a remedy, Cosimo I pounced on a tiny fishing village in 1571, with major designs for improving it. A far-sighted constitution set up in 1593 allowed foreigners to reside in the city regardless of nationality and religion, instantly endowing the place with a cosmopolitan mentality that has surivived over the centuries. In fact, Livorno (bizarrely translated as Leghorn in English) has a completely different feel from other Tuscan towns. With exotic hints of Marseille (sailors, immigrants, and a busy commercial port with all that entails), it's a fun place to pass a day and is blissfully tourist-free. There are also some fabulous fish restaurants in which to sample the town's speciality, *cacciucco*, a spicy fish soup that often has to be ordered in advance. Livorno is the hopping-off point for the islands of the Archipelago Toscano, Sardinia and Corsica.

The **Porto Mediceo**, with the red-brick bastion of the **Fortezza Vecchia**, designed by Sangallo the Younger in 1521, has long been the focus of city life. From here the charming canals of **Venezia Nuova** (or I Fossi) extend, tracing the pentagonal perimeter of Francesco I's late 16th-century plan for an ideal city. Look out for the concerts and food fest of the **Effetto Venezia**, which takes place in late July. Sadly, bombing during World War II destroyed most of Livorno's historic monuments, and post-war reconstruction finished them off. Buontalenti's piazza Grande was cut in two; all that remains of the 16th-century Duomo is Inigo Jones's fine portico. Located near the ferry port, piazza Micheli sports Livorno's only other artistic treasure, the superb **Quattro Mori** monument by Pietro Tacca (1623), consisting of four colossal bronze slaves who sit chained to the pedestal of an earlier statue of Ferdinand I.

Where to stay, eat & drink

Osteria da Carlo (viale Caprera 43-45, no phone, closed Sun & 3wks Sept, average €22) serves a decent *cacciucco*, while **La Corsara** (via Mentana 78, 0586 897208, closed Wed, average €25) is also good for fish. Other spots worth trying for local fare include **La Chiave**, across from the Fortezza Nuova (scali delle Cantine 52, 0586 888609, closed all Wed, average €45) and **Il Sottomarino** (via de' Terrazzini 48, 0586 887025, closed Mon, Tue & 2wks July, average €35). Located on a hill overlooking the coast at Castellaccio, just south of the town, **Ghiné & Cambrì** (via di Quercianella 263, 0586 579414, closed Mon, Tue Oct-May & 2wks Jan, average €25), has become something of a cult eaterie with the younger generation for its relaxed atmosphere and fine meat and vegetable dishes. For ice-cream, try **La Chiostra** (via Cecioni Adriano 8, 0586 813564, closed Mon in winter).

Livorno's youth tend to head for the disco-bars on the canals. The **Barge** (scali delle Anchore 6, 0586 888320) has a piano bar (live music Tue, Fri & Sat), an 'English' bar and canalside tables in the summer. If you need to stay overnight, the choices in town are rather grim, but you could try the central **Hotel Gran Duca** (piazza Micheli 16, 0586 891024, www.granduca.it, €98-€154). A more pleasant alternative is **La Vedetta di Montenero** (via della Leccetta 5, piazza Micheli, 0586 579957, www.hotellavedetta.it, €51-€130), located on a hillside in the suburb of Montenero.

Bolgheri, Castagneto Caducci & Suvereto

While **Marina di Cecina** is a pleasant enough seaside town with a popular windsurfing beach, the inland areas are more attractive. Heading south on the Aurelia (the SS1) and then inland,

Gambero Rosso. *See p234.*

Tuscany

you'll reach **Bolgheri** via its famous approach, a straight, five-kilometre (three-mile) road lined with tall cypress trees. This beautiful little medieval town has become synonymous with **Sassicaia**, one of Italy's most prestigious (and expensive) wines. Ludovico Antonori's Ornellaia is another hallowed local label, but if your wine budget doesn't run to such elevated figures (a bottle of either of these could cost hundreds of euros), look out for the much cheaper Rosso di Bolgheri. The town boasts an inordinate number of restaurants and wine bars. One of the best is **Enoteca Tognoni** (via Lauretta 5, 0565 762001, www.enotecatognoni.it, average €25), which is packed with bottles and cases of wine, where you can eat a full meal or choose from a menu of snacks; wine is also sold by the bottle. Bolgheri also has a WWF nature reserve.

Further south is **Castagneto Carducci**. It's also small and charming, attracting the sort of Italian glitterati who spurn the crowded coast in the summer months. There are many good opportunities for cyclists to stretch their legs in the area; after a day's pedalling, head to **Nettare degli Dei** (salita San Lorenzo, 0565 765118) to sample the morning's catch, or put your feet up at the **Hotel Ristorante Zì Martino** just outside town at San Giusto (0565 766000, closed Mon in winter & possibly in Nov (unconfirmed at press time)).

From here, proceed south to **Suvereto**, a lovely medieval town surrounded by wooded hillsides and dominated by an ancient *rocca* (hilltop castle). It has a splendid arcaded town hall dating from the 13th century and a set of circular walls that are almost intact. Around ten kilometres (six miles) from the coast is another medieval charmer – lively **Campiglia Marittima** has an arty subculture with great views over the Val di Cornia to the sea.

San Vincenzo

Back down on the coast, halfway between Livorno and Grosseto, is San Vincenzo, another family-oriented beach resort that once acted as a coastal watchtower for Pisa; the tower itself dates from 1304. The main attraction here is the Michelin-starred **Gambero Rosso** (piazza della Vittoria 13, 0565 701021, closed Mon & Tue, average €105), Fulvio Pierangelini's elegant yet unpretentious temple of food that overlooks the tourist port. Try the signature dish: *passatina di ceci con crostacei* (a cream of chickpeas with sweet shrimp tails).

Piombino & around

The only reason to visit sooty **Piombino** is to catch a ferry to **Corsica**, **Elba** (*see p296*) and the ex-prison island of **Pianosa**. Far more attractive is the stretch of coastline that runs north from here and up to the ruins of Etruscan Populonia. On the way you'll see mystifying rock formations, necropoli, beaches and clean, unspoilt waters.

Populonia, one of the most important trading ports in ancient Etruria, perches high above the golden arc of sand that fringes the **Golfo di Baratti** (*see p212* **Shingle belles**) with its little fishing port. There's a small archaeological museum within the village, but more worthwhile is the **Parco Archaeologico di Baratti e Populonia**, which covers the lush green hillside overlooking the bay, and which incorporates Etruscan burial chambers and other remains of the once-mighty settlement. The car park and visitor centre is behind the beach; allow several hours for a complete tour with one of the polyglot guides.

Resources

Tourist information

Livorno *APT, piazza Cavour 6 (0586 204611/ www.costadeglietruschi.it)*. **Open** 8.30am-5pm Mon-Fri.

Piombino *Ufficio di Turismo, Torre Comunale, via del Ferruccio (0565 225639)*. **Open** 9am-3pm, 5-11pm Mon, Wed-Sun. Closed mid Sept-May.

San Miniato *Ufficio di Turismo, piazza del Popolo (0571 42745/www.cittadisanminiato.it)*. **Open** *Summer* 8.30am-1pm, 3-7pm daily. *Winter* 9am-1pm, 3-6.30pm daily.

Volterra *Associazione Pro Volterra, via Giusto Turazza 2 (0588 86150/www.provolterra.it)*. **Open** *Spring-autumn* 9am-1pm, 3-7pm daily. *Winter* 9am-12.30pm, 3-6pm Mon-Sat.

Getting there

By bus

SITA (800 373760, www.sita-on-line.it) runs buses from Florence to Volterra (1hr 50mins). **LAZZI** (050 46288, www.lazzi.it) connects Livorno with Pisa, Lucca, Viareggio and Florence. Livorno is also a port, with services to Sardinia, Corsica, Capraia and Sicily.

By car

Driving is the easiest option. Livorno is just off the coastal SS1, a 20-minute drive south of Pisa along the same road. The A12 *autostrada* also runs past the city. The Poggibonsi exit of the Si–Fi (Siena–Florence) *autostrada* quickly gives access to Volterra.

By train

Livorno's main station (on piazza Dante) is on the Rome–Pisa train line, a 12-minute journey from Pisa. Trains also run to and from Florence (journey time 1hr 20mins) via Pisa and Empoli. National timetable information is available by calling 892021 or by logging on to www.trenitalia.it.

Siena

Architectural beauty, lively nightlife and a no-holds-barred horse race – Siena is a city that ignites passions.

Piazza del Campo.

The Sienese are fond of saying that theirs is the most perfect medieval city in the world, and it's easy to agree. Not only has Siena preserved its exquisite monuments, it has also maintained its traditions and its passion for local cuisine. Head for the centre and soak up the atmosphere of **piazza del Campo** (or just 'Il Campo'); it fans out in nine segments of herringbone paving, focusing on the grand council chambers of **Palazzo Pubblico** and the magnificent **Torre del Mangia** (for all, *see p239*).

Siena emerged from the Dark Ages as a robust centre of pilgrimage and trade, only to have a sequence of events – including savage attacks of plague – halt its development forever. What you see today is, virtually, Siena as it always has been. The historic centre of the city is divided into three sections. **Terzo di Città** was the original residential nucleus and includes the Duomo; **Terzo di San Martino** grew around the via Francigena, the pilgrim route heading south to Rome; and the **Terzo di Camollia** contains churches and basilicas to the north.

These three sections house the 17 *contrade* – city districts that largely define the citizens' perception of their own identity. During the summer, any citizen with a pulse commits their spirit to their *contrada* with a fervour unequalled anywhere else in Italy for the **Palio** (*see p173 and p244* **The Palio**), the world-famous horse race held in July and August, when district rivalry reaches its zenith.

While the crowded tourist corridor between the piazza and the **Duomo** has lots to offer, ambling through the quiet back alleys is the best recommendation for the idle traveller.

SOME HISTORY

The Sienese hills were inhabited in prehistoric times, and were later settled by the Etruscans, who created an important trading colony with Volterra. In 90 BC, the city became a Roman colony named Saena Julia, ruled by Emperor Augustus. However, development was slow.

What eventually put Siena on the map was the **via Francigena**, the pilgrim route leading south from France and spanning the whole of Tuscany. The road was heavily trafficked throughout the Middle Ages, bringing in its wake the trade that provided Siena with commercial and political clout.

The young city had amassed enough self-confidence by 1125 to pick fights with Florence. The hatred between Tuscany's sister cities over the following century was one of history's more malevolent rivalries. Things came to an explosive head on 4 September 1260, when Siena won the bloody Battle of Montaperti.

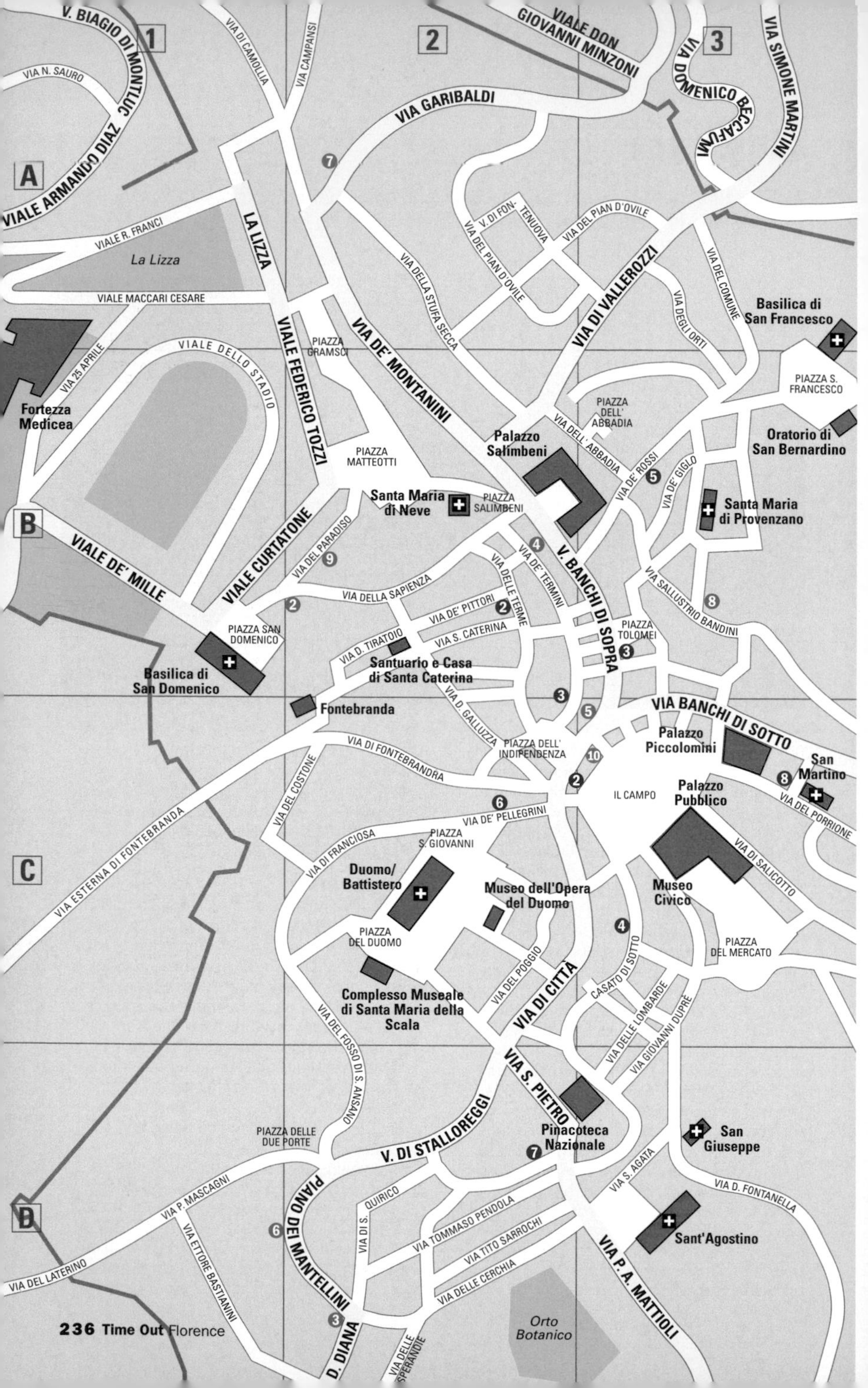
1
2
3
A
B
C
D
V. BIAGIO DI MONTLUC
VIA N. SAURO
VIALE ARMANDO DIAZ
VIA DI CAMOLLIA
VIA CAMPANSI
VIALE DON GIOVANNI MINZONI
VIA DOMENICO BECCAFUMI
VIA SIMONE MARTINI
VIA GARIBALDI
VIALE R. FRANCI
La Lizza
LA LIZZA
VIALE MACCARI CESARE
V. DI FONTENUOVA
VIA DEL PIAN D'OVILE
VIA DI VALLEROZZI
VIA DEL COMUNE
VIA DEGLI ORTI
VIA DELLA STUFA SECCA
Basilica di San Francesco
PIAZZA S. FRANCESCO
Oratorio di San Bernardino
PIAZZA GRAMSCI
VIA DE' MONTANINI
VIALE FEDERICO TOZZI
VIA 25 APRILE
VIALE DELLO STADIO
Fortezza Medicea
PIAZZA DELL' ABBADIA
VIA DELL' ABBADIA
Palazzo Salimbeni
PIAZZA MATTEOTTI
Santa Maria di Neve
PIAZZA SALIMBENI
VIA DE' ROSSI
VIA DE' GIGLO
Santa Maria di Provenzano
VIALE DE' MILLE
VIALE CURTATONE
VIA DEL PARADISO
VIA DELLA SAPIENZA
VIA DELLE TERME
VIA DE' TERMINI
V. BANCHI DI SOPRA
VIA SALLUSTRIO BANDINI
VIA DE' PITTORI
VIA S. CATERINA
VIA D. TIRATOIO
PIAZZA SAN DOMENICO
Basilica di San Domenico
Santuario e Casa di Santa Caterina
PIAZZA TOLOMEI
Fontebranda
VIA D. GALLUZZA
VIA BANCHI DI SOTTO
Palazzo Piccolomini
San Martino
VIA DI FONTEBRANDRA
PIAZZA DELL' INDIPENDENZA
IL CAMPO
Palazzo Pubblico
VIA DEL PORRIONE
VIA DEL COSTONE
VIA DE' PELLEGRINI
VIA ESTERNA DI FONTEBRANDA
VIA DI FRANCIOSA
PIAZZA S. GIOVANNI
Duomo/ Battistero
Museo dell'Opera del Duomo
Museo Civico
VIA DI SALICOTTO
PIAZZA DEL DUOMO
PIAZZA DEL MERCATO
CASATO DI SOTTO
VIA DEL POGGIO
VIA DI CITTÀ
Complesso Museale di Santa Maria della Scala
VIA DEL FOSSO DI S. ANSANO
VIA DELLE LOMBARDE
VIA GIOVANNI DUPRÈ
VIA S. PIETRO
Pinacoteca Nazionale
San Giuseppe
PIAZZA DELLE DUE PORTE
V. DI STALLOREGGI
VIA S. AGATA
VIA D. FONTANELLA
VIA P. MASCAGNI
VIA DI S. QUIRICO
VIA TOMMASO PENDOLA
VIA TITO SARROCHI
Sant'Agostino
VIA ETTORE BASTIANINI
PIANO DEI MANTELLINI
VIA DELLE CERCHIA
VIA P. A. MATTIOLI
VIA DEL LATERINO
Orto Botanico
D. DIANA
VIA DELLE SPERANDIE

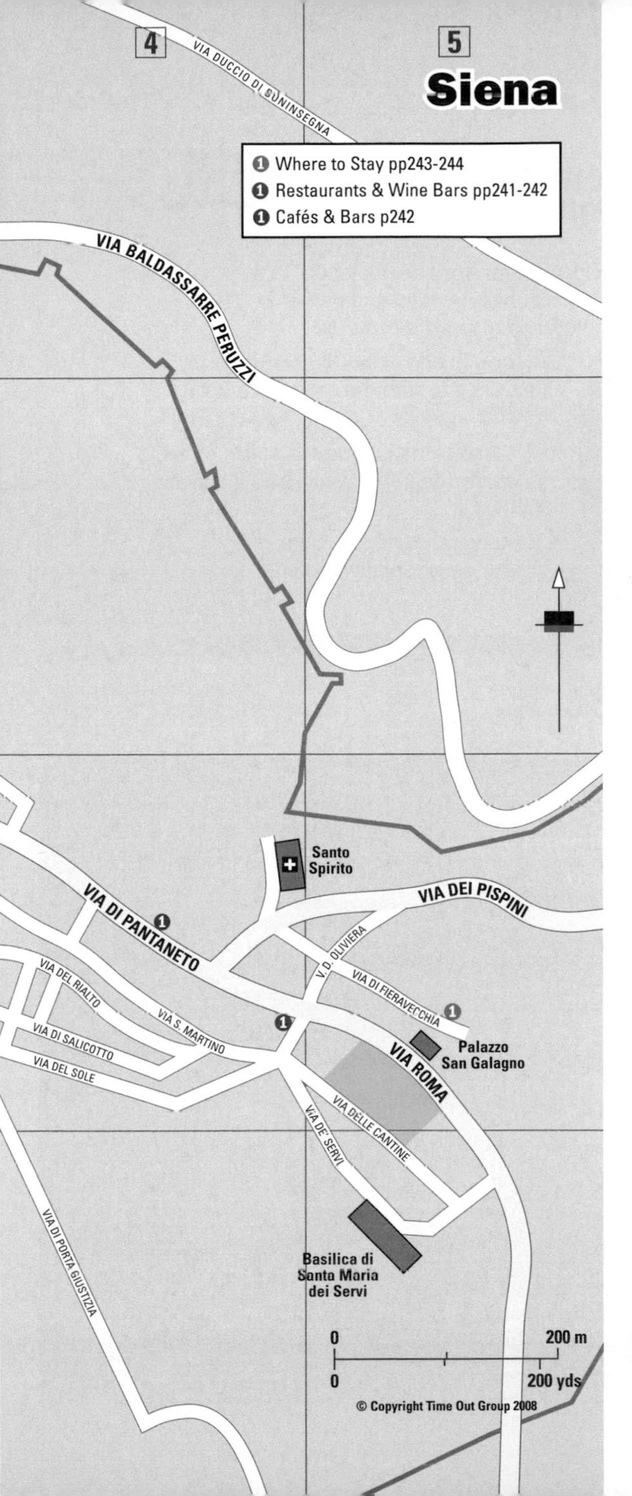

25 Aprile, Via - A1/B1
Abbadia, Piazza Dell' - B3
Abbadia, Via Dell' - B2/3
Armando Diaz, Viale - A1
Baldassarre Peruzzi, Via - A4/B4/5
Banchi Di Sopra, Via - B2/3
Banchi Di Sotto, Via - C3
Biagio Di Montluc, Via - A1
Camollia, Via Di - A1
Campansi, Via - A2
Cantine, Via Delle - C5/D5
Casato Di Sotto, - C3
Cerchia, Via Delle - D2
Città, Via Di - C2
Comune, Via Del - A3
Costone, Via Del - C2
Curtatone, Viale - B1/2
Diana, Via D. - D2
Domenico Beccafumi, Via - A3
Don Giovanni Minzoni, Viale - A2/3
Duccio Di Boninsegna, Via - A4/5
Duomo, Piazza Del - C2
Duprè, Via Giovanni - C3/D3
Esterna Di Fontebranda, Via - C1
Ettore Bastianini, Via - D1
Federico Tozzi, Viale - B2
Fieravecchia, Via Di - C5
Fontanella, Via D. - D3
Fontebrandra, Via Di - C2
Fontenuova, Via Di - A2
Fosso Di S. Ansano, Via Del - C2/D2
Franci, Viale R. - A1
Franciosa, Via Di - C2
Galluzza, Via D. - B2/C2
Garibaldi, Via - A2
Giglo, Via De' - B3
Gramsci, Piazza - A2/B2
Il Campo - C3
Indipendenza, Piazza Dell' - C2
La Lizza - A1
Laterino, Via Del - D1
Lombarde, Via Delle - C3/D3
Maccari Cesare, Viale - A1
Mantellini, Piano Dei - D2
Mascagni, Via P. - D1
Matteotti, Piazza - B2
Mattioli, Via P. A. - D3
Mercato, Piazza Del - C3
Mille, Viale De' - B1
Montanini, Via Dei - A2/B2
Oliviera, Via D. - C5
Orti, Via Degli - A3/B3
Pantaneto, Via Di - C4
Paradiso, Via Del - B2
Pellegrini, Via De' - C2
Pian D'ovile, Via Del - A2/3
Pispini, Via De' - C5
Pittori, Via De' - B2
Poggio, Via Del - C2
Porrione, Via Del - C3
Porta Giustizia, Via Di - D4
Porte, Piazza Delle Due - D1/2
Rialto, Via Del - C4
Roma, Via - C5/D5
Rossi, Via De' - B3
S. Agata, Via - D3
S. Caterina, Via - B2
S. Francesco, Piazza - B3
S. Giovanni, Piazza - C2
S. Martino, Via - C4
S. Pietro, Via - D2
S. Quirico, Via Di - D2
Salicotto, Via Di - C3/4
Salimbeni, Piazza - B2
Sallustrio Bandini, Via - B3
San Domenico, Piazza - B1
Sapienza, Via Della - B2
Sauro, Via N. - A1
Servi, Via De' - C5/D5
Simone Martini, Via - A3
Sole, Via Del - C4
Sperandie, Via Delle - D2
Stadio, Viale Dello - B1
Stalloreggi, Via Di - D2
Stufa Secca, Via Della - A2/B2
Terme, Via Delle - B2
Termini, Via De' - B2
Tiratoio, Via D. - B2
Tito Sarrochi, Via - D2
Tolomei, Piazza - B2/3
Tommaso Pendola, Via - D2
Vallerozzi, Via Di - A3

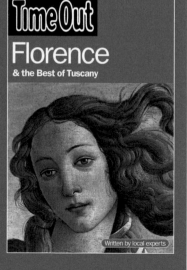

A 15,000-strong Sienese army killed 10,000 Florentine soldiers and captured 15,000 more. The jubilant Sienese danced on the bodies of the fallen Florentines with nails in their shoes. But nine years later the two cities clashed and this time Florence came out on top. This defeat marked a profound shift in Siena's social and political identity that paradoxically forged the way for its prosperous golden age.

The Sienese then channelled their creative juices into commerce. Gradually, successful merchants and bankers gave rise to a wealthy middle class, while trade with France and England brought in cash and nourished a flourishing wool industry. The city's most important public works – much of the Duomo, the Palazzo Pubblico, the Torre del Mangia and piazza del Campo, among others – were constructed under the Council of Nine, set up in 1287 in friendship with Florence.

Siena's golden age came to an abrupt halt in 1348 with the arrival of the Black Death, which slashed the population from 100,000 to 30,000 in less than a year. Internal fighting brought down the Council of Nine in 1355; in 1399 Siena fell under the control of Gian Galeazzo Visconti, Grand Duke of Milan, who was followed by the tyrannical Pandolfo Petrucci. Spain's Charles V besieged the city in 1552, but three years later a popular insurrection against the Spanish left Siena open to Cosimo I de' Medici. Reduced to 8,000 inhabitants, the city couldn't defend itself. The end of the Sienese Republic came in 1559.

In 1859, Siena became the first major Tuscan city to join a united Italy. It soon launched a lucrative tourist trade that endures to this day.

Sightseeing

Palazzo Pubblico

Piazza del Campo. **Map** p236 C3.

Work on this elegant example of Gothic architecture began in 1288, but the brick and stone building, which houses the town hall and the Museo Civico, wasn't completed until 1342. The palazzo is a symbol of medieval Siena's mercantile wealth; with its she-wolf and Medici balls, its striking façade reads like a history book of the city. Inside the *cortile* you'll find the excellent Museo Civico (*see p241*).

Piazza del Campo

Map p236 C3.

Piazza del Campo is often described as one of Italy's most beautiful squares. Beautiful it is, but square it isn't: the piazza is uniquely shell-shaped. Building commenced in 1293; its nine sections are said to represent both the ruling Council of Nine and the folds of the Madonna's cloak protecting the townsfolk. The Fonte Gaia (built 1408-19), designed by Jacopo della Quercia, sits on the north-east side of the piazza. The fountain's basin serves as a terminus for the city's network of underground wells and aqueducts (a total of 25km/16 miles throughout the province). According to legend, before the Fonte was built, workers uncovered a perfectly preserved antique marble statue of Venus. When the Black Death struck in the middle of the 14th century, the Sienese blamed the treasure, which was smashed to pieces and then buried in Florentine territory. *Photo p235.*

Piazza Salimbeni

Map p236 B2.

A beautiful square flanked by three of Siena's most glorious *palazzi*: Tantucci, Spannocchi and Salimbeni. The latter serves as the headquarters of the Monte dei Paschi di Siena, founded in 1472 by resolution of the General Council of the Sienese Republic; today with 1,900 branches, half the bank's profits are ploughed back into the community.

Santuario e Casa di Santa Caterina

Via Santa Caterina. **Open** 9am-12.30pm, 3-6pm daily. **Admission** free. **Map** p236 B2.

This small collection of buildings is highly revered as the house of St Catherine, Siena's patron saint.

Torre del Mangia

0577 292614. **Open** *Mid Mar-June, Sept, Oct* 10am-7pm daily. *July, Aug* 10am-11pm daily. *Nov-mid Mar* 10am-4pm daily. **Admission** €6 (from Museo Civico ticket office). **No credit cards. Map** p236 C3.

Asked to build their tower as high as possible, architect brothers Minuccio and Francesco di Rinaldo followed their instructions to the letter: when it was completed in 1348, the Torre del Mangia, next to the Palazzo Pubblico, was medieval Italy's tallest tower, checking in at 102m (335ft), with 503 steps, and affording views over Siena Province. It's named after one of its first bell-ringers: the pot-bellied *mangiaguadagni* ('eat-profits'). These days, only 15 visitors are allowed up at any one time, and tickets sell out quickly. At the foot of the tower is the Gothic Cappella di Piazza, finished in 1352 to commemorate the end of the plague.

Churches

Basilica di San Domenico

Piazza San Domenico (0577 280893). **Open** *Nov-Apr* 9am-1pm, 3-6pm daily. *May-Oct* 7am-1pm, 3-6.30pm daily. **Admission** free. **Map** p236 B1.

This soaring brick edifice was one of the earliest Dominican monasteries in Tuscany. Started in 1226, the building that remains today is mostly the result of an extensive mid 20th-century restoration. That said, a few historic features have survived intact. At the end of the nave is a *Madonna Enthroned* attributed to Pietro Lorenzetti, while halfway down on the right is the restored chapel of Siena's patron saint, St Catherine. The chapel itself is beautiful, with tromp l'œil pilasters, marble floors and works by Sodoma who also did the tabernacle. Inside it, in a container, is the relic of the saint's head.

Basilica di San Francesco

Piazza San Francesco (0577 289081). **Open** 7am-1.30pm, 3.30-7pm daily. **Admission** free. **Map** p236 A3.

The Franciscans built this grand, severe church of Gothic origins in 1326. Precious little of its original artwork survived a fire in 1655. However, one work that did is Pietro Lorenzetti's *Crucifixion* (1331), in the first chapel of the transept.

Battistero

Piazza San Giovanni (0577 283048). **Open** *May-Aug* 9.30am-8pm daily. *Sept-Nov, Mar-May* 9.30am-7pm daily. *Nov-Feb* 10am-5pm daily. **Admission** €3. **No credit cards. Map** p236 C2.

Squeezed under the apse of the Duomo (*see below*), the Baptistery is, unusually, rectangular, rather than octagonal. The unfinished Gothic façade includes three arches adorned with human and animal busts, while inside, colourful frescoes by various artists (mainly Vecchietta) fill the room. The focal point is the central font (1417-34): designed by Jacopo della Quercia and considered one of the masterpieces of early Renaissance Tuscany, it features gilded bronze bas-reliefs by Jacopo, Donatello and Lorenzo Ghiberti. In the same complex is the newly restored Crypt.

Duomo

Piazza del Duomo (0577 283048). **Open** *Summer* 10.30am-8pm Mon-Sat; 1.30-8pm Sun. *Sept, Oct, Mar-May* 10.30am-7.30pm Mon-Sat; 1.30-8pm Sun. *Nov-Feb* 10.30am-6.30pm Mon-Sat; 1.30-8pm Sun. **Admission** €3; €6 19 Aug-31 Oct. An all-inclusive (Duomo, Baptistery and Crypt) ticket is also available. **No credit cards. Map** p236 C2.

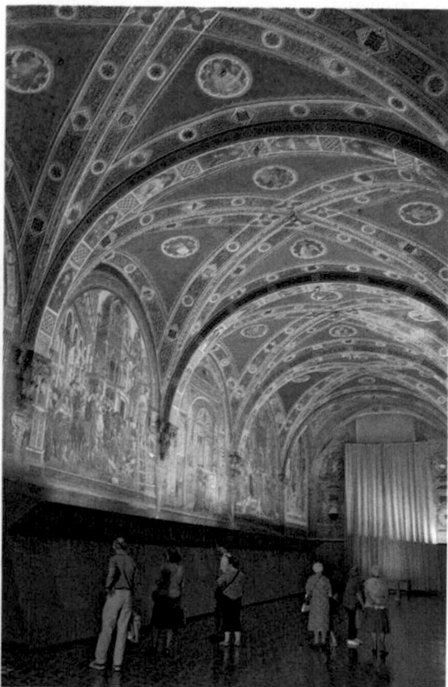

Complesso Museale di Santa Maria.

Construction on Siena's Duomo, one of Italy's first Gothic cathedrals, started in 1150 on the site of an earlier church, but plans for a massive cathedral had to be abandoned because of the Black Death of 1348. The resulting structure is Gothic in style but Romanesque in spirit. The black and white marble façade was started in 1226; 30 years later work began on the dome, one of the oldest in Italy. The lower portion of the façade and the statues in the centre of the three arches were designed by Giovanni Pisano and built between 1284 and 1296.

Inside, the cathedral's polychrome floors are its most immediate attraction; though the intricately decorated inlaid boxes are usually covered by protective planks, they are generally visible between mid August and the end of September. The most impressive are those beneath the dome, by Domenico Beccafumi, who created 35 of the 56 scenes from 1517 to 1547. In the apse is a splendid carved wooden choir, built between the 14th and 16th centuries. Above it, back in place after a restoration-enforced absence, is a stained-glass rose window (7m/23ft across) made by Duccio di Buoninsegna in 1288 – probably the earliest Italian example of a stained-glass window. The tabernacle has Bernini's *Maddalena* and *San Girolamo* statues.

Another highlight is the pulpit, completed in 1266 by Nicola Pisano with the help of his son Giovanni and Arnolfo di Cambio. The Piccolomini altar includes four statues by a young Michelangelo (carved 1501-04). At the far end of the left aisle, a door leads to the Libreria Piccolomini (admission €3), built in 1495 to house the library of Sienese nobleman Aeneas Silvius Piccolomini, who became Pope Pius II. This vaulted chamber was constructed at the behest of his nephew (who became Pope Pius III for 28 days) and frescoed by Pinturicchio (1502-09, his last work), reportedly assisted by a young Raphael, with scenes from Pius II's life.

Oratorio di San Bernardino

Piazza San Francesco (0577 283048). **Open** *Mar-Oct* 1.30-7.30pm daily. Closed Nov-Feb. **Admission** €3. **No credit cards. Map** p236 B3.

To the right of San Francesco lies this oratory, built in the 15th century on the site where St Bernard used to pray. On the first floor is a magnificent fresco cycle (1496-1518) by Beccafumi, Sodoma and their lesser contemporary, Girolamo del Pacchia.

Museums

Complesso Museale di Santa Maria della Scala

Piazza del Duomo 2 (0577 224811/www.santamariadellascala.com). **Open** 10.30am-6.30pm daily. **Admission** €6. **No credit cards. Map** p236 C2.

This is the site of Siena's newest museum, the brilliant Museo Archeologico, and various spectacular temporary exhibitions (on the upper floors, entered from the left-hand doorway). Founded in the ninth century, it was one of the earliest hospitals in Europe and one of the first to ensure disinfected medical equipment, and was still taking in patients until relatively recently: the author Italo Calvino died here in 1985. Entry to the museum is at the Pellegrinaio (Pilgrim's Hall), decorated by, among others, Domenico di Bartolo (1440-43), with elaborate frescoes depicting the history of the hospital. Underground you'll find passageways carved out of the tufa, now home to the archaeological museum in a brilliant labyrinth of corridors and chambers. Highly recommended for children.

Museo Civico

Palazzo Pubblico, piazza del Campo (council cultural office 0577 292226/ticket office 0577 292263/ www.comune.siena.it). **Open** *Mid Feb-mid Mar, Oct-late Nov* 10am-6.30pm daily. *Mid Mar-Oct* 10am-7pm daily. *Late Nov-mid Feb* 10am-5.30pm daily. **Admission** €7. **No credit cards**. **Map** p236 C3.

In the Anticappella of the Museo Civico you can admire a number of frescoes by Taddeo di Bartolo (1362-1422), which reflect his fascination with Greek and Roman antiquity and mythological heroes, plus a *Madonna and Child with Saints* by Sodoma at the altar of the Cappella del Consiglio. The Sala del Mappamondo was decorated by Ambrogio Lorenzetti around 1320-30; its barely visible cosmological frescoes depicting the universe and celestial spheres. This room also houses one of Siena's most cherished jewels: the *Maestà* fresco painted by Simone Martini in 1315. Thought to be one of his earliest works, if not his very first, it's also considered one of the first examples of political art, with the devotion to the Virgin Mary depicted said to represent devotion to the Republic's princes. Finally, in the Sala della Pace, is an extraordinary fresco cycle by Lorenzetti (1338-40), the *Allegory of Good* and *Effects of Bad Government* (severely damaged). This is the largest secular fresco since Roman times and was commissioned to remind the Council of Nine of their responsibilities. The fresco's details of daily life are of exceptional interest.

Museo dell'Opera del Duomo

Piazza del Duomo 8 (0577 283048). **Open** *Mid Mar-May, Sept* 9am-7.30pm daily. *June-Aug* 9.30am-8pm daily. *Oct* 9am-6pm daily. *Nov-mid Mar* 9am-5pm daily. **Admission** €6. **No credit cards**. **Map** p236 C2.

Occupying the never-completed nave of the Duomo, this museum displays works taken from the cathedral. On the ground floor is a large hall divided in two by a stunning 15th-century wrought-iron gate; along the walls, you can enjoy a better view of Giovanni Pisano's 12 magnificent marble statues (1285-97) that once adorned the façade of the Duomo. In the centre of the room is the bas-relief of the *Madonna and Child*

Opt for alfresco dining or the convivial interior space, at **Osteria Le Logge**. *See p243.*

Tuscany

with St Anthony by Jacopo della Quercia, commissioned in 1437 and probably not quite completed when the artist died the following year. On the first floor is the *Pala della Maestà* (1308-11) by Duccio di Buoninsegna, used as the high altar of the Duomo until 1506. The front has a *Madonna with Saints*; the back depicts 26 religious scenes in dazzling colours.

Palazzo delle Papesse

Via di Città 126 (0577 22071/www.papesse.org). **Open** 11am-7pm Tue-Sun. **Admission** €5. **No credit cards**. **Map** p236 C2.

This relatively new centre for contemporary art operates from within an edifice built in 1460 at the behest of Caterina Piccolomini, whose brother became Pope Pius II. The temporary exhibitions of intense modern-day works are often juxtaposed against the delicately frescoed ceilings.

Pinacoteca Nazionale

Palazzo Buonsignori, via San Pietro 29 (0577 286143). **Open** 8.30am-1.30pm Mon; 8.15am-7.15pm Tue-Sat; 8.15am-1.30pm Sun. **Admission** €4. **No credit cards**. **Map** p236 D2.

One of Italy's foremost art collections, this lovely 15th-century palazzo holds more than 1,500 works of art, and is particularly renowned for its Sienese *fondi d'oro* (paintings with gilded backgrounds). The second floor is devoted to Sienese masters from the 12th to the 15th centuries, including Guido da Siena and the Lorenzettis (don't miss *A City by the Sea*). The first floor houses works by the Sienese Mannerist school of the early 1500s, including pieces by Sodoma and Beccafumi, while the third floor holds the Spannocchi Collection, containing works by northern Italian and European artists of the 16th and 17th centuries.

Monuments, squares & gardens

Fortezza Medicea

Viale C Maccari. **Map** p236 B1.

This vast red-brick fortress just outside the city is a sore reminder of Siena's troubled past. Charles V of Spain forced the Sienese to build a fortress on this spot in 1552; as soon as his reign ended they celebrated by demolishing it, but when Cosimo I de' Medici annexed the city a few years later he demanded the fortress be rebuilt. These days, with its views over the city, it's a good place for an evening stroll or a glass of wine at the Enoteca Italiana (*see p245*), especially during the *settimana dei vini*, a week-long showcase of regional wines held here every year in early June.

Orto Botanico

Via Mattioli 4 (0577 235407). **Open** 8am-12.30pm, 2.30-5.30pm Mon-Fri; 8am-noon Sat. **Admission** free. **Map** p236 D2.

The botanical gardens belong to the university and are a haven of tranquillity.

Palazzo Chigi Saracini/ Accademia Musicale Chigiana

Via di Città 89 (0577 22091/www.chigiana.it). **Guided tours** 10am-7.30pm Sat; 10am-1.30pm Sun. **Admission** €7. **Map** p236 C2.

A must for classical music fans, this beautiful Renaissance *palazzo* has its own rococo-style concert hall, museum of instruments and library. It hosts a week of Sienese music in July, followed by a series of summer concerts until the end of August.

Where to eat & drink

Many recipes from the Siena region have survived since medieval times, including *pici* (thick, irregular spaghetti) and *panzanella* (dried bread soaked in water, and served in a salad with basil, onion and tomato). Popular desserts include *panforte* (slabs of nuts, candied fruits and honey) and *ricciarelli* (almond biscuits).

On a summer's night, piazza del Campo turns into a great eating bowl. There are a dozen establishments from *birrerie* to *pizzerie*, most mediocre: best bets are **Al Mangia** (no.43, 0577 281121, www.almangia.it) and **L'Osteria Bigelli** (no.60, 0577 42772), with an interesting menu. Wine bar **Liberamente Osteria** (no.27, 0577 274733, www.liberamenteosteria.it) has a short, tasty menu.

Restaurants & wine bars

Antica Trattoria Botteganova

Via Chiantigiana 29 (0577 284230/www.anticatrattoriabotteganova.it). **Open** 12.30-2.30pm, 7.30-10.30pm daily. **Average** €40. **Credit** AmEx, DC, MC, V.

Although this *trattoria* is just out of town on the north side, it's worth the short taxi ride. The enjoyable food is complemented by a strong wine list.

Cane e Gatto

Via Pagliaresi 6 (0577 287545). **Open** 8-10.30pm daily. **Average** €45. **Credit** AmEx, MC, V. **Map** p237 C4 ❶

The *menù degustazione* (€75) at this family-run restaurant can teach you everything you could ever wish to know about Sienese cooking. A decadent lunch is served for small groups by arrangement. Highly recommended.

Compagnia dei Vinattieri

Via delle Terme 79 (0577 236568/www.vinattieri.net). **Open** 11am-midnight daily. **Average** €30. **Credit** AmEx, DC, MC, V. **Map** p236 B2 ❷

Cinzia Certosini, who was previously a restaurateur in Chianti, established this excellent *enoteca* a few years ago, with an ambition to make wine more approachable. The admirable list includes a rich array of respectable Tuscan labels, in addition to products from other regions and countries. A food menu is also served.

Campo Regio Relais. See p245.

Enoteca I Terzi

Via de' Termini 7 (0577 44329). **Open** 1.30-3.30pm, 7-11pm Mon-Sat. **Credit** AmEx, MC, V. **Map** p236 C2 ❸

This wine cellar serves various light snacks, including cold cuts, cheeses and breads.

Hosteria Il Carroccio

Via del Casato di Sotto 32 (0577 41165). **Open** 12.30-2.30pm, 7.30-10pm Mon, Thur-Sun; noon-2.30pm Tue. **Average** €30. **Credit** V. **Map** p236 C3 ❹

Run by Renata Toppi and her children, Hosteria Il Carroccio is a real find. Try the *tegamate di maiale* (pork cooked in a ceramic bowl), based on an old Sienese recipe that's virtually extinct today.

Medio Evo

Via de' Rossi 40 (0577 280315). **Open** 12.30-2.30pm, 7.30-10pm Mon-Thur, Sat, Sun. **Average** €35. **Credit** AmEx, DC, MC, V. **Map** p236 B3 ❺

Typical Sienese cuisine served in a medieval dining hall decked out with *contrada* flags.

Da Mugolone

Via de' Pellegrini 8-12 (0577 283235). **Open** 12.30-3pm, 7.30 10pm Mon-Wed, Fri, Sat; 12.30-3pm Sun. Closed 3wks Jan. **Average** €40. **Credit** AmEx, DC, MC, V. **Map** p236 D2 ❻

Many residents consider this one of Siena's best eateries. It's simple yet elegant, and serves largely meat-based dishes using local ingredients, cooked and presented to unfussy perfection.

Osteria Castelvecchio

Via Castelvecchio 65 (0577 49586). **Open** 12.30-2.30pm, 7.30-10pm daily. Closed Sun in winter. **Average** €25. **Credit** AmEx, DC, MC, V. **Map** p236 D2 ❼

Just a few steps from the Pinacoteca Nazionale (*see p242*), in former horse stables, Castelvecchio offers vegetarian dishes at least twice a week from an inventive menu based on seasonal fare.

Osteria Le Logge

Via del Porrione 33 (0577 48013). **Open** noon-2.45pm, 7.15-10.30pm Mon-Sat. **Average** €35. **Credit** AmEx, DC, MC, V. **Map** p236 C3 ❽

A popular, well-established and central *osteria*, with great food and a charming setting. *Photo p241.*

Cafés & bars

Caffè Ortensia

Via Pantaneto 95 (0577 40039). **Open** 8am-1am Mon-Fri; 5pm-1am Sat. **No credit cards. Map** p237 C4 ❶

A bohemian student bar with a well-stocked bookcase, plus newspapers, magazines and games.

Fiorella

Via di Città 13 (0577 271255). **Open** 7am-7.30pm Mon-Sat. **No credit cards. Map** p236 C2 ❷

This *caffè-bar* serves up fabulous coffee, roasted on the spot. Standing only.

Nannini Conca D'Oro

Via Banchi di Sopra 24 (0577 236009). **Open** 7-10pm daily. **Credit** AmEx, MC, V. **Map** p236 B3 ❸

Sleek and modern, with something of a chain vibe, Nannini specialises in *panforte* and *ricciarelli*. You can sit at the back if you order a light lunch.

Other locations Via Massetana Romana 42-44.

Shops & services

The main shopping street in Siena is **via di Città**, which forks above the Campo: **banchi di Sotto** heads down and **banchi di Sopra** climbs up to **piazza della Posta**.

Strolling along via del Terme you'll find a number of modern interiors shops. Siena's fantastic, buzzy general **market** (8am-1pm Wednesday) stretches from piazza la Lizza to the Fortezza.The third Sunday of the month also sees an antiques market at **piazza del Mercato**, behind the Campo.

9 Farmacie

Various locations around the historic centre.
Still in their original 19th-century premises, these pharmacies preserve their wonderful original architecture while prescribing modern medication.

Antica Drogheria Manganelli

Via di Città 71-73 (0577 280002). **Map** p236 C2.
Trading since 1879, this shop's antique wooden shelves and glass cabinets display a scrumptious array of traditional sweets, condiments and herbs, as well as delicious slices of *panforte* and *riccarelli*.

The Palio

Siena's Palio is the explosive culmination of centuries-long neighbourhood rivalries, and the event that defines the social, cultural and political fabric of the city each year.

There's a singular objective: to win at all costs. Cheating, biting and dosing opponents' horses with laxatives have all been tried. No one seems to care very much when the hired bareback jockeys – often dismissed as mere mercenaries – fall off their horses. The horse, on the other hand, is adored, receiving special rites and banquets.

The *contrade* that contest the Palio are districts of Siena that trace their roots back to the 12th century and vaguely represent the military groups that once protected it. At the head of each was a mayor and a central governor (*podestá*) flanked by councillors. Originally, the city was divided into 42 *contrade*, but the numbers shrank to the current 17 in 1729, and of these ten are selected to participate, always including the seven who missed out last time round.

The Palio takes place in the piazza del Campo twice a year, commemorating the feast of the Virgin Mary on 2 July and the Assumption on 16 August. On the perimeter, there are balconies and stands for spectators (usually wealthy tourists) willing to shell out €300 to watch the race in comfort. Most Sienese – up to 30,000 of them – stand under the blazing sun in the centre of the square.

The Palio starts in the late afternoon with a parade of costumed drummers and flag carriers. The horses charge three times round the square; the first one over the line wins the Palio and earns a banner of the Virgin Mary as a trophy – not to mention adulation from fans. The event is normally over in a startlingly brief 90 seconds, as riders spur on their steeds (and attack enemy riders) with their *nerbo*, a whip made of dried ox penis.

The reactions of the Sienese, depending on their allegiance, range from weeping and hair-tearing to rapturous embracing; second place is considered a far worse way to lose than last place. Banquets and festivities sponsored by the winning *contrade* last into September, and animosity between the first- and second-placed teams lasts until the following year.

The actual event is preceded by three days of trials, every day at around 9am and 7.30pm in the Campo, plus dress rehearsals, banquets and horse blessing.

Tuscany

Book Shop

In the Galleria off via San Pietro 19 (0577 226594/ www.bookshopsiena.com). **Open** 10am-8pm Mon-Sat. **Credit** MC, V. **Map** p236 D2.
American-born owner Lisa Fallon runs this pleasant and relaxed English-language bookstore.

Dolci Trame

Via del Moro 4 (0577 46168). **Open** 3.30-7.30pm Mon; 10am-1pm, 3.30-7.30pm Tue-Sat. **Credit** AmEx, DC, MC, V. **Map** p236 B3.
Hip women's clothing at the back of piazza Tolomei.

Enoteca Italiana

Via Camollia 72 (0577 288497/www.enoteca-italiana.it). **Open** noon-8pm Mon; noon-1am Tue-Sat. **Credit** AmEx, MC, V.
Italy's only national wine cellar, located in the massive vaults of the fortress, stocks more than 1,000 wines from all over the country.

La Fattoria Toscana

Via di Città 51 (0577 42255). **Open** 9.30am-8pm daily. **Map** p236 C2.
La Fattoria Toscana offers an excellent selection of gastronomic goodies, including wines, oils, sweetmeats, local truffles and Val d'Orcia saffron.

Fioretta Bacci

Via San Pietro 7 (0577 282200). **Open** 10.30am-7pm Mon-Sat. **Credit** AmEx, MC, V. **Map** p236 D2.
Beautiful hand-loomed shawls and garments, with a giant loom in the shop.

Panificio il Magnifico

Via de' Pellegrini 27 (0577 281106). **Open** 7.30am-7.30pm Mon-Sat. **Credit** AmEx, DC, MC, V. **Map** p236 C2.
A busy bread shop and *salumeria* where you take a number and await your turn. Pannini and the like are sold, as well as marvellous *panforte*, well priced and packaged in sealed foil bags.

Where to stay

Siena doesn't have enough hotels to meet the demand, so booking in advance is advisable. It's worth contacting the **Hotels Promotion Service** (0577 288084, www.hotelsiena.com).

The huge Castello di Casole estate that lies 35 kilometres (22 miles) from Siena was being restored and converted into a boutique hotel as this guide went to press; **Hotel Castello di Casole** (www.castellodicasole.com), due to open in spring 2009, will feature 41 luxury suites and a world-class spa.

Antica Torre

Via di Fieravecchia 7 (0577 222255/www.anticato rresiena.eu). **Rates** €90-€120. **Credit** AmEx, DC, MC, V. **Map** p237 C5 ❶
Set in a nicely restored 16th-century tower, this eclectic and friendly hotel gets booked up well in advance: not surprisingly, as there are just two rooms on each floor. Those situated on the top two levels of the building boast views over the surrounding countryside.

Campo Regio Relais

Via della Sapienza 25 (0577 222073/www.campo regio.com). **Rates** €180-€250. **Credit** AmEx, MC, V. **Map** p236 B2 ❷
Just down the hill from San Domenico, this elegant little palazzo offers a surprising range of rooms and a high level of comfort. Despite its tiny entrance, it has two pleasant terraces and splendid views of the valley behind. The 1500s building was the dwelling of various noble Sienese families. *Photo p243.*

Certosa di Maggiano

Strada di Certosa 82 (0577 288180/www.certosa dimaggiano.com). **Rates** €490-€650. **Credit** AmEx, DC, MC, V.
Raised from the ruins of a 13th-century monastery, Certosa di Maggiano is located just south of the city and is renowned for its stunning garden and extensive amenities, including tennis courts, swimming pools and even a heliport.

Il Chiostro del Carmine

Via della Diana 4 (0577 223476/www.chiostrodel carmine.com). **Rates** €80-€500. **Credit** AmEx, MC, V. **Map** p236 D2 ❸
This beautifully refurbished religious building offers business-class accommodation. All rooms have internet LAN and wireless connections, while meeting rooms, conference facilities and breakfast rooms are in the highly decorated Friars Choir and the austere, vaulted Tinaia dei Frati.

Chiusarelli

Viale Curtatone 15 (0577 280562/www.chiusarelli.com). **Rates** (incl breakfast) €95-€119. **Credit** AmEx, MC, V.
This three-star hotel sits on the edge of the historic centre. Rooms are unfussy but comfortable – ask for a quiet one at the back.

Grand Hotel Continental

Via Banchi di Sopra 85 (0577 44204/www.royaldemeure.com). **Rates** €329-€429; €935 suite. **Credit** AmEx, DC, MC, V. **Map** p236 B2 ❹
The area's only five-star hotel is set amid the richly frescoed interiors of what was once Palazzo Gori Pannilini. If you can't afford to stay, pop in to admire the magnificently ornate first-floor reception.

Palazzo Fani Mignanelli – Residenza d'Epoca

Via Banchi di Sopra 15 (0577 283566/www.residenzadepoca.it). **Rates** €90-€200. **Credit** AmEx, DC, MC, V. **Map** p236 C3 ❺
A few minutes' walk from the piazza del Campo, this historic house offers charming rooms on the third floor of an old palazzo (with lift). The individually decorated rooms are priced according to size.

Pensione Palazzo Ravizza

Pian dei Mantellini 34 (0577 280462/www.palazzo ravizza.it). **Rates** (incl breakfast) €160-€230. **Credit** AmEx, DC, MC, V. **Map** p236 D1 ⑥

Owned by the same family for more than 200 years, this 17th-century palazzo still has its original furnishings, including lovely frescoes. Many of the 38 rooms overlook a charming, well-kept garden.

Piccolo Hotel Oliveta

Via Piccolomini 35 (0577 283930/www.oliveta.com). **Rates** €130. **Credit** AmEx, MC, V.

A stone's throw from Porta Romana, the Piccolo Hotel Oliveta offers pleasant rooms in what was once a stone farmhouse. In warm weather breakfast is served in the terraced garden, with wonderful views over the countryside.

Piccolo Hotel Il Palio

Piazza del Sale 18 (0577 281131/www.piccolo hotelilpalio.it). **Rates** €70-€108. **Credit** MC, V. **Map** p236 A2 ⑦

This pleasant, small hotel is housed in a former convent dating back to the 15th century. The location is convenient if you're arriving by train, and it's (unusually) accessible by car. Rooms are basic but clean, and a quad room is available.

Soggiorno Sabrina Hostel

Via Calzoleria 16 (0577 47237/www.dormisiena.it). **Rates** €75. **Credit** AmEx, MC, V. **Map** p236 B3 ⑧

Centrally located basic hotel rooms with access to common kitchen and shared facilities.

Villa Scacciapensieri

Via di Scacciapensieri 10 (0577 41441/www.villa scacciapensieri.it). **Rates** €185-€245. **Credit** AmEx, DC, MC, V.

As the name ('banish your thoughts') suggests, you can leave your worries behind as you check into this family-run hotel. It's 3km (two miles) north of the city: follow the signs up a private tree-lined drive to the crest of the hill. There's an excellent restaurant, a tennis court and a pool.

Apartments

Residence Paradiso

Via del Paradiso 16 (0577 222613/www.residence paradiso.siena.it). **Rates** €70. **Credit** AmEx, DC, MC, V. **Map** p236 B2 ⑨

Accommodation in 12 furnished mini-apartments in a historic building, with the use of cooking and laundry facilities. Reductions are offered for longer stays and in winter. There are ten more apartments in via del Porrione.

Siena Soggiorno

Via di Città 15 (368 7424871 mobile/www.siena soggiorno.it). **Rates** €40-€75. **Credit** AmEx, DC, MC, V. **Map** p236 C3 ⑩

Three mini-apartments with kitchen and spare period furniture. Two apartments overlook the Campo. There's a minimum three nights booking policy.

Resources

Hospital

Viale Bracci, north of the city (0577 586111).

Internet

Via Pantaneto 4 (0577 44946). **Map** p237 C4.

Police

Via del Castoro (0577 201111). **Map** p236 C2.

Post office

Piazza Matteotti 37 (0577 214295). **Map** p236 B2.

Tourist information

Centro Servizi Informazioni Turistiche Siena (APT) *Piazza del Campo 56 (0577 280551/www. terresiena.it).* **Open** 9am-7pm daily. **Map** p236 C3.

Getting there & around

By bike & moped

For bike hire, contact **DF Bike** (via Massetana Romana 54, 0577 271905). Mopeds are rented at **Automotocicli Perozzi** (via del Romitorio 5, 0577 223157).

By bus

Siena's major bus terminal is at the edge of the historic centre at piazza Gramsci; the main ticket office (0577 204225) is underground. Most buses leave from the adjacent viale Federico Tozzi or nearby piazza San Domenico. **Tra-in**, the principal bus company serving Siena and beyond (0577 204225), has departures every 30mins for Florence (direct service takes 75mins), as well as services to Arezzo, Grosseto and most regional towns of interest. The excellent www.comune.siena.it/train gives full timetable information on all services.

By car

The *raccordo* dual carriageway links Florence and Siena (45mins), or there's the more rural SS2. The centre of Siena is mainly traffic-free, so you'll have to park in one of nine big car parks around the city (several at the Stadio Comunale, one near the Fortezza Medicea, and the large underground Parcheggio Il Campo on via Fontanella 11); all can be busy at weekends and during public holidays. To hire a car, try **Avis** (via Simone Martini 36, 0577 270305) or **Hertz** (viale Sardegna 37, 0577 45085).

By taxi

Call **Radio Taxi** (0577 49222), or go to one of the taxi ranks at piazza Stazione (0577 44504) or piazza Matteotti (0577 289350).

By train

There are some direct trains to and from Florence, but you'll normally have to change at Empoli (journey time up to 2hrs); you always have to change there for trains to Pisa. Siena's train station is at the bottom of the hill on the east side of the city (piazza Fratelli Rosselli, tickets 0577 280115, national timetable information 892021, www.trenitalia.it). A local bus makes the journey up to piazza Gramsci.

Siena Province

Breathtaking landscapes, ancient villages, good food in abundance and some of the world's best reds.

Badia a Coltibuono. *See p248.*

It's no wonder that when people imagine rural Italy they conjure up thoughts of rolling hills defined by cypresses, tiny hamlets unchanged for centuries, eating alfresco or under vaulted ceilings, tables groaning with simple foods from the land and gentle, welcoming people. The province of Siena delivers the clichés with such charm and good humour that it's impossible not to feel the gentle bliss wash over you.

It's here that the 12th-century pilgrim route from France to Rome, the via Francigena, created a boom of medieval stone churches and villages, until a series of plagues decimated the population; gradually, after a struggle, the place came under Florentine dominion.

Now promoted as the **Terre di Siena** (www.terresiena.it), the province boasts some of the most popular tourist towns in Italy, which thrive on the hordes of travellers that visit each summer. Other, smaller towns, equally beautiful, retain their odd Italian hours, falling into sleepy oblivion for the three luncheon hours. The gourmet traveller will find the area dominated by its excellent wines: Chianti to the north-east, Vernaccia di San Gimignano, Brunello di Montalcino and Vino Nobile di Montepulciano, and a sophisticated culinary culture that will satisfy any palate. For tips on visiting wineries in the region, *see p258* **Fine vines**.

Chianti

If the words 'Chianti' and 'wine' are virtually synonymous, it's probably because good wine has been produced in the region for a very long time indeed. Renaissance, Roman, Etruscan – the story is a long one. The black cockerel logo of Chianti and the raffia-wrapped wine bottle both helped establish the wine long before the term 'wine buff' was invented.

The Chianti landscape is familiar through the art of the Renaissance – and doesn't appear to have changed much since then. Its gentle slopes are still clad with vines, olive groves abound and there's plenty of woodland, much of it inhabited by wild boar. The feeling of temporal petrification is hard to avoid.

But the region has changed, and the way people tend their land is quite unlike the methods of the past. Sunflower cultivation, for example, gives the farmland a short blast of yellow, or black when they've died off – colours that were absent from the landscape during the Renaissance. Yet changes such as these are subtle, and the area has become so desirable today there's hardly a barn that hasn't been renovated (*see p254* **Unter der toskanischen Sonne**).

Castellina & around

From Panzano, follow the SS222 to the hilltop town of **Castellina**. Originally an Etruscan settlement, its layout is essentially medieval: the imposing fortifications bear witness to the town's historic role as a bastion of Florentine dominion in its southward expansion towards Siena in the 15th and 16th centuries. The imposing **Torre** dominates the main square, piazza del Comune, and the medieval town around it. There are plenty of places to taste and buy wine; one of Chianti's top wineries, **Castello di Fonterutoli** (*see also p258* **Fine vines**), is nearby.

Gaiole, located on the steep eastern edge of Chianti, was a busy market town back in the Middle Ages, but it's quieter now and makes a pleasant stop on the way to the nearby castles and wineries (*see p258* **Fine vines**). One of the latter, **Badia a Coltibuono**, is an impressive spot for a decent meal or an overnight stay.

On the western side of Gaiole, taking the SS484 will lead you to the famous **Castello di Brolio**, a 19th-century rendering of a castle wrecked by Spanish troops in 1478 and finished off by the Sienese 50 years later. Baron Bettino Ricasoli, the so-called 'Iron Baron' who was responsible for pushing Chianti's wine industry into the major league, rebuilt the castle in the 19th century. The **Ricasoli** winery below the castle (*see p258* **Fine vines**) remains one of the region's best, along with nearby **Felsina**.

Abbazia di San Galgano. *See p253.*

Where to stay & eat

In Castellina, pleasant rooms are available at **Palazzo Squarcialupi** (via Ferruccio 22, 0577 741186, www.palazzosquarcialupi.com, closed Nov-mid Mar, €107-€160). For a verdant setting and a pool, head beyond **Fonterutoli** on the Siena road and stop at **Belvedere di San Leonino** (località San Leonino, 0577 740887, www.hotelsanleonino.com, closed Oct-Easter, €156); it has its own restaurant, **Il Cortile**. **Ristorante Albergaccio** (via Fiorentina 63, 0577 741042, closed Sun lunch & Wed, Thur lunch in winter & all Nov & 3wks Jan, average €40) offers two tasty fixed menus; **Antica Trattoria La Torre** (piazza del Comune 15, 0577 740236, closed Fri and last 2wks Feb, 1st 2wks Sept, average €30) is a classic eaterie.

In Radda, you can dine and stay at **Palazzo Leopoldo** (via Roma 33, 0577 735605, €150-€290). Another dining option is the elegant **Ristorante Vignale** (via Pianigiani 9, 0577 738701, closed Dec-late Feb, average €40). Accommodation is at the beautifully restored **Relais Vignale** (via Pianigiani 8, 0577 738300, closed 2mths in winter, €135-€300). The rates at the *agriturismo* **Podere Terreno** (via della Volpaia, 0577 738312, www.podereterreno.it, €35 per person) include an excellent dinner with wine. Near Gaiole, the restaurant at **Badia a Coltibuono** (0577 749031, closed Mon, Nov-Mar, average €38) specialises in game; in summer, eat at tables in the beautiful gardens; the old cloisters house some lovely guestrooms if you want to stay the night. South of Gaiole, in the hamlet of San Sano, just off SS408, the friendly **Hotel Residenza San Sano** (0577 746130, closed Nov-Mar, €135-€140) has a pool among old stone houses.

Resources

Tourist information

Castellina, Gaiole and Radda share a common website at www.chiantistorico.com.

Castellina *Ufficio Informazioni Turistiche, via Ferruccio 40 (0577 741392).* **Open** 9.30am-1pm, 2-6.30pm daily.

Radda *Piazza Castello 2 (0577 738494).* **Open** 10am-1pm, 3-7pm Mon-Sat; 10am-1pm Sun.

Gaiole *Pro Loco, via Antonio Casabianca (0577 749311).* **Open** 9.30am-12.30pm, 3-6pm Mon-Fri; 10am-1pm Sat. Closed Nov-Mar.

West of Siena

The Poggibonsi exit of the Si–Fi (Siena–Firenze) *autostrada* leads to the western Siena Province.

Colle di Val d'Elsa

The historic centre of this attractive, lively town spans the hilltop (Colle Alta) and the lower-lying Colle Bassa. The two points are joined by a very modern lift. The River Elsa was channelled for power here as early as the 13th century, giving rise to flourishing industries: wool, paper and, more recently, crystalware. The **Museo del Cristallo** (via dei Fossi 8a, 0577 924135, www.cristallo.org, closed Mon) is a beautiful underground glass museum in the lower part of town. There are a number of crystal outlets in the upper town. The best is **La Grotta del Cristallo** (via del Muro Lungo 20, 0577 924676). The **Museo Archeologico** (piazza del Duomo, 0577 922954, closed Mon, admission €3) is uncrowded and specialises in Etruscan and Roman remains from the area. Just down the road is the **Museo Civico e Diocesano d'Arte Sacra** (via del Castello, 0577 923888, closed Mon, admission €3).

Where to stay & eat

In town, **Hotel Arnolfo** (via F Campana 8, 0577 922020, www.hotelarnolfo.it, €80) is handily placed. On a hillside, a stone's throw from the centre, is **Relais della Rovere** (via Piemonte 10, località La Badia, 0577 924696, www.chiantiturismo.it, closed Nov-Feb, €180-€230), housed in a restored 11th-century abbey set in gardens with a pool.

Colle is a good place for food. **Da Arnolfo** (via XX Settembre, 0577 920549, www.arnolfo.com, closed Tue & Wed, average €75), carries two Michelin stars, well deserved for its superb ingredients, ingeniously combined. On the main square, **Il Frantoio** (via del Castello 40, 0577 923652, www.ristorante ilfrantoio.com, closed Mon, average €40) serves classic Tuscan fare in historic surroundings. **Dietro le Quinte** (vicolo della Misericordia 14, 0577 920458, www.dietrolequinteristorante.it, average €40, light lunch €22) is located on the town walls and has a lovely garden; it's hard to find, but worth the search. For an *aperitivo* (or, indeed, a handsome snack), head for the **14 in Canonica** wine bar (piazza Canonica 2, 0577 923444, closed Nov-Mar).

San Quirico's **Collegiata**: look out for the lions and dragons. *See p255.*

Gold comfort farm

Often misleadingly translated as 'farm holidays', agriturismi have long been viewed with suspicion by British holidaymakers, who shudder at the thought of mucking out on the farm when they could be quaffing Brunello di Montalcino. Technically, agriturismi are structures that make the bulk of their profits from agriculture rather than tourism – but more often than not, they're swanky country-house retreats set in acres of olive groves and vineyards, where the only agri-related duty is the arduous task of tucking into the organic produce grown on site.

The unspoilt Sienese countryside is fertile ground for the business of agritourism; the numerous farms and villas that dot its gentle, vine-clad slopes make tranquil places to stay – and feel appealingly remote, though Tuscany's sights are generally within easy reach (it certainly helps to have a car, though). The standard of accommodation varies enormously, from rustic farmhouses with spartan decor and budget rates, to luxury manor houses on chi-chi wine estates, with swimming pools, spas and all mod cons. The agriturismi detailed below are our favourites, but constitute just a tiny proportion of those to be found in the area; see www.agriturismo.it and www.agriturismo.net for a comprehensive list.

San Giovanni

Strada del Partagnone 12-14, Cetona (0578 238251/www.casagiovanni.it). **Rate** €85.

An unpretentious place set in the lush Val d'Orcia, San Giovanni is a no-frills *agriturismo* with an appeal altogether different to that of its glitzier rivals. The farm has been in the same family since the 18th century; Giovanni works the land, while Onelia is in charge of the food – made using home-grown produce, meals here are exceptional. Furnishings in the three farmhouse apartments were handmade using wood from the farm. For a *Good Life*-style experience in deepest Tuscany, you couldn't ask for much more.

Fattoria Vegi

Vegi 16, Castellina in Chianti (0577 743255/www.vegi.it). **Rate** €66.

Vegi's history dates to the 13th century, when it was a shooting lodge of the Squarcialupi, local lords. Perched on a hilltop overlooking a breathtaking sweep of olive groves, vineyards and cypresses, the accommodation is divided into two farmhouses: the 17th-century Fermentini, with brick-vaulted ceilings and a vast farmhouse kitchen, and the cosier, 19th-century Del Guardia. The houses share a garden with swimming pool; Chianti Classico, olive oil and grappa are made on site.

Il Rigo.

La Lodola

Strada delle Chiarne 3, Asciano (0577 726954/www.lalodola.it). **Rate** €70.
La Lodola's restored 19th-century stone farmhouse has been divided into seven lovely apartments; pick of the bunch is La Vite, which has a living room with stone fireplace and raftered ceiling, bedrooms with canopied beds, and marble bathrooms. You may be tempted to spend your days soaking up the sun by the tear-shaped pool, but the *agriturismo* is well placed for exploring – it's a short drive to the nearby thermal springs, 20 minutes to Siena – and temptingly close to the Chianti wineries.

Podere Salicotto

Salicotto 73, Buonconvento (0577 809087/ www.poderesalicotto.com). **Rate** €840/wk.
Set on a 280,000sq m farm, this friendly *agriturismo* is equipped with six wood-beamed rooms, all decorated in warm, Tuscan tones; the Belvedere apartment above the barn offers staggering views. The atmosphere is relaxed in the extreme; a sumptuous breakfast – made with organic goodies from the farm, naturally – merges into lunch for late-risers. The vivacious hosts Silvia and Paolo are full of information and advice, and will happily whisk you off on bike tours or for a day out on their fabulous six-berth boat.

Castello di Tornano

Gaiole in Chianti (0577 746067/ www.castelloditornano.it). **Rate** €85.
Tornano's fairytale hilltop tower may date back over 1,000 years, but this *agriturismo* is far from a museum piece: Chianti Classico, vin santo, grappa and olive oil are all produced here. Rooms are lavishly decorated, with swathes of wine-coloured drapery, chandeliers galore and travertine bathrooms; the seven simply decorated apartments in the farmhouse can feel a little like servants' quarters in comparison. The panoramic turret-top terrace and lovely pool carved out of the rock are further draws.

Il Rigo

Casabianca, San Quirico d'Orcia (0577 897291/www.agriturismoilrigo.com). **Rate** €55/person.
Set amid the rolling hills of the Crete Senesi, Il Rigo's simple, antique-furnished rooms, decorated in homely, country-house style, are distributed between two buildings 600m (1,968ft) apart. 'Casabianca', an ancient stone farmhouse at the end of a cypress-lined drive, is where meals are served; red-brick 'Poggio Bacoca' once housed the farmworkers. Owner Lorenza, an accomplished cook, serves up hearty Tuscan fare at lunch and dinner, on request, and shares her secrets of culinary greatness in on-site cookery courses.

Tuscany

San Gimignano.

Resources

Tourist information

Ufficio Turistico Pro Loco *Colle di Val d'Elsa, via del Campana 43 (0577 922791).* **Open** 9.30am-1pm, 3-7pm Mon-Sat.

San Gimignano

Of all the Tuscan towns, San Gimignano is the most easily recognisable, with its 14 towers defying the centuries, rising high above the terracotta roofs of this iconic village – whose historic centre has been a UNESCO World Heritage site since 1990. The silhouette of the town seems to draw you to it, as it may well have done to the pilgrims who passed this way from France on the via Francigena to Rome in the 12th century. They brought trade and prosperity and the families of San Gimignano flourished, commencing a peculiarly medieval practice of building ever-higher towers to assert their eminence; there were once as many as 72. But three waves of plague that sent San Gimignano into an enchantment-like sleep. The best way to appreciate the heritage is to scale the 218 steps of **Torre Grosso** (54m/ 180ft; 9.30am-7pm Mar-Oct, 10am-5.30pm Nov-Feb), the 'big tower' of the **Palazzo Comunale**. The €5 entrance fee also includes the **Pinacoteca** (0577 990312) with its collection of 12th- to 15th-century Florentine and Sienese art.

The 11th-century **Collegiata**, or cathedral (0577 940316, closed Sun morning and late Jan-early Mar except services, admission €3.50), which features astounding frescoes of the Old and New Testaments and a beautiful chapel dedicated to Santa Fina by Ghirlandaio. Walk down via San Matteo from the main square and you'll reach the **Museo Archeologico**, the **Spezzeria di Santa Fina** and the **Galleria d'Arte Moderna e Contemporanea Raffaele De Grada**, all located in what was once the **Convent of Santa Chiara** (via Folgore 11, 0577 940348, www.comune.sangimignano.si.it, 11am-6pm daily, admission €3.50). The archaeology is largely Etruscan, found locally but influenced by the culture of nearby Volterra (*see p232*). The ceramics in the Spezzeria were made for the convent's pharmacy.

Waves of day trippers now ply the streets but the increased human traffic has its benefits. San Gimignano has become a surprising new centre for contemporary art. **Galleria Gagliardi** (via San Giovanni 57, 0577 942196, www.galleriagagliardi.com) has a brilliant collection of contemporary sculpture, while **Galleria Continua** (via del Castello 11, 0577 943134, www.galleriacontinua.com) has a reputation for showcasing cutting-edge work.

Where to stay & eat

The classiest hotel in San Gimignano is **L'Antico Pozzo** (via San Matteo 87, 0577 942014, www.anticopozzo.com, closed 3wks Jan & 3wks Dec, €150); a pleasant alternative is the family-run **Hotel Bel Soggiorno** (via San Giovanni 91, 0577 940375, closed mid Nov-Dec, €80-€130), which has a tempting restaurant. For a cheap and charming alternative, try **La Casa di Giovanna** (via San Giovanni 58, 0577 940419, www.casagiovanna.com, €55); this place only has three rooms, but is conveniently located on the main street.

For regional cooking with a twist, try **Osteria delle Catene** (via Mainardi 18, 0577 941966, closed Wed, average €30-€45). One of San Gimignano's more elegant places, **Ristorante Dorandò** (vicolo dell'Oro 2, 0577 941862, www.ristorantedorando.it, closed Mon in winter, average €50) serves food based on a variety of Etruscan, medieval and Renaissance recipes. **Gelateria di Piazza** (piazza della Cisterna 4, 0577 942244, www.gelateriadi piazza.com, closed Nov-Feb) has achieved worldwide renown for its ice-cream, and has some unusual flavours on offer, like the infamous chocolate and saffron.

Resources

Tourist information

Pro Loco *Piazza del Duomo 1 (0577 940008/ www.sangimignano.com).* **Open** *Summer* 9am-1pm, 3-7pm daily. *Winter* 9am-1pm, 2-6pm daily. Audio guide to the town €5.

Abbazia di San Galgano

Located in the Valdimerse, on the SS73, heading to the south-west of Siena, this abandoned abbey is like something out of a fairy tale. Built between 1218 and 1288, it was a Cistercian powerhouse until the 14th century. Its monks devised complex irrigation systems and sold their services as doctors, lawyers and architects. But the abbey was sacked one time too many and eventually abandoned. Its monumental, roofless ruins retain an atmosphere of eerie spirituality.

St Galgano was a noble young knight, who renounced his warlike ways to become a Cistercian hermit. When fellow knights tried to persuade him to revert to his old self in 1180, he defiantly stabbed a stone and his sword slid in. The (alleged) sword in the stone is now on display in the **Cappella di Montesiepi**, next to the abbey. This curious circular Romanesque chapel, which has fading frescoes by Ambrogio Lorenzetti, is also worth a visit.

South-east of Siena

South of Siena, the landscape opens up to reveal rolling hills of open fields interspersed with solitary cypresses. Green in the spring with durum wheat that turns pale yellow in the summer, brown and beige in the autumn after ploughing, it's a simple but interesting landscape. To the south-east are the Crete Senesi or Sienese claylands. Throughout this apparently barren area there are a number of well-preserved hill towns to explore.

Buonconvento

On the SS2 south, stop off in the old walled town of Buonconvento. It has two excellent museums and a pleasant enclosed ambience. The **Museo d'Arte Sacra** (via Soccini 18, 0577 807190, closed Mon, and between 1-3pm daily, admission €4). Works by Duccio and others illustrate the strength of Siennese early Renaissance art. The **Museo della Mezzadria** (in the old walls, piazzale Garibaldi, 0577 8071812, admission €4) gives a detailed account of how hard life on the farm really was. The tourist information office (www.turismobuonconvento.it) is also in the foyer of the museum.

Monte Oliveto Maggiore

Up the winding road from Buonconvento, through forests of pine, oak and cyprus, lies the magnificent abbey of Monte Oliveto Maggiore. Founded in 1313, the monastery began as a solitary hermitage in an arid area. However, due to the devotion and wealth of its founder, Bernardo Tolomei, the place soon drew a large following – the Olivetan order was recognised by the pope in 1344 – and the place has survived the centuries with a well-preserved structure and with little deterioration to the marvellous fresco cycle in the cloister; the 36 exceptional frescoed panels, painted between 1495 and 1505 by Il Sodoma (27) and Luca Signorelli (9), portray *The Stories of St Benedict*. The library here, once one of the most famous in Europe, can now only be seen with a guide (since the theft of some volumes). The choir stalls in the church are by Giovanni di Verona and are considered among the best wood inlay work in Italy. Gregorian chant at vespers is very popular. There's also a café-cum-restaurant, and a Benedictine gift shop selling own-brewed drinks, honey and herbal medicines (0577 718 567, www.monteoliveto maggiore.it, 9.15am-noon, 3.15-5pm daily; 9.15am-noon, 3.15-6pm daily in summer).

San Giovanni d'Asso

The little Crete Sinese town of San Giovanni d'Asso has made a heady name for itself through its truffles. It holds two truffle festivals: one in the autumn, featuring the *tuber magnatum pico*, or precious white truffle, and another in March, when the less heralded but still delectable *marzuolo* variety ripens. In the town's castle there's even a multimedia **Truffle Museum** (piazza Gramsci 1, 0577 803268, www.museodeltartufo.it, Sat, Sun only, admission €3). At the rear of the castle sits the **Locanda del Castello** (piazza Vittorio Emanuele 4, 0577 802939, closed mid Jan-mid Mar, €110-€150), a pleasant little inn.

However, the most notable feature here is the **Bosco della Ragnaia** (www.laragnaia.com), a magical garden in a steeply sloping wood, where light flickers through foliage, trickling water provides a soothing background sound, and all formal geometries are quietly subverted. It's the creation of American painter Sheppard Craige. The garden is open daily from dawn to dusk, and admission is free.

Montalcino

Nearly everyone heading to Montalcino is doing so at least partly to try a glass of Brunello di Montalcino, one of Italy's most celebrated red wines. Once there, though, you'll discover a proud hilltown – neither tourist hotspot nor sleepy outpost, but with a gentle Tuscan quality. Under Siena's rule in the 13th century, four families dominated the town's political identity, and are represented these days in Montalcino's four *contrade* (districts). The **Fortezza** (*see below*) was built by the Sienese in 1362, and in 1555 became the last and short-lived stronghold of the Sienese Republic.

The decline that followed didn't abate until the late 1970s, when improved cellar techniques and far-sighted marketing put Brunello di Montalcino on the wine map (*see p258* **Fine vines**). Tourism came in its wake; and it's not just the Brunello estate that has benefited. Other estates, such as SIRO Pacenti, L'Ucceliera and Cupano, all make fine Rosso di Montalcinos.

All roads in Montalcino lead to **piazza del Popolo**, in the heart of the town. Here you'll find the shield-studded **Palazzo Comunale** (with its tall tower), modelled after Siena's Palazzo Pubblico in 1292. Around the corner, annexed to **Sant'Agostino church** (built in 1360, with superb frescoes by Bartolo di Fredi), is another admirable example of the Sistema Musei Senesi: the **Museo Civico e Diocesano** (via Ricasoli 31, 0577 846014, closed Mon, admission €4.50, €6 incl entrance to the Fortezza). Its collection includes works by Simone Martini, a brilliant altarpiece by Bartolo di Fredi and a worthy exhibit of early ceramics. Montalcino enjoys views that can extend all the way to Siena. Brace yourself for the climb up to the battlements of the **Fortezza** (0577 849211, admission €4). Reward yourself by sampling wines at the well-stocked *enoteca* inside the fortress walls.

Unter der toskanischen Sonne

It's usually the British who are accused of colonising Tuscany, but the scenic hilltop village of **Tenuta de Castelfalfi**, a highly desirable piece of real estate just north of Siena, has recently been snapped up by a German tour operator, TUI, for an estimated €250 million. The near-derelict settlement is to receive a dazzling makeover: by 2009, it will have been transformed into a self-contained holiday world, the glitzily titled 'Toscana Resort Castelfalfi', offering, TUI promises, 'a genuine rural experience' to upwards of 3,000 guests. Everything from the village's medieval castle to its olive groves and its charmingly crumbling villas was included in the job lot – except the village church, which remains in Italian hands, though the Germans are obliged to pay for its renovation. The ancient walls are to house a luxury hotel, spa and golf course, and faux-rustic trattorie will line the cobbled streets, serving fruit, vegetables and wine grown on site, alongside lorryloads of imported bratwurst.

Local media have launched a predictable campaign against the 'German invasion' – it doesn't help that the German army commandeered the village as their regional HQ in World War II – but residents themselves have taken a more pragmatic view. Castelfalfians have seen their numbers dwindle to just five in recent years, and the village is in dire need of renovation. Even at the risk of their rural idyll being transformed into a Tuscan-Teutonic theme park, villagers are preparing to welcome the coachloads of German holidaymakers with open arms; as 73-year-old Camillo Carli put it, 'It's a bit too quiet around here.' Not for much longer.

Where to stay, eat & drink

On the southern edge of town, the three-star **Hotel Vecchia Oliviera** (Porta Cerbaia, corner of via Landi, www.vecchiaoliviera.com, 0577 846028, €120-€190) has a pool, a terrace and lovely views over the valley. In Montalcino itself, the **Albergo Il Giglio** (via Soccorso Saloni 5, www.gigliohotel.com, 0577 846577, €110) is a family-run place with 12 frescoed rooms in its main building and an additional five (€75) next door. The **Castello Banfi** (Sant'Angelo Scalo, 0577 840111, www.castellobanfi.com, €400-€850), 20 minutes south-west, is a huge family-owned vineyard estate quite far off the beaten track – but it's comfortably self-contained, with two restaurants, a fitness centre, a pool, cooking and wine classes and even its own museum.

Montalcino's restaurants aren't really up to the fame of its wine. The best is the **Re di Macchia** (via Soccorso Saloni 21, 0577 846116, closed Thur, average €24), which has a small, well-thought-out menu. For well presented food and great views, head out of town towards **Torrenieri** until, on your right, you come to **Boccon di Vino** (località Colombaio Tozzi 201, 0577 848233, closed Tue, average €40). People-watch over a coffee or an *aperitivo* at the **Fiaschetteria Italiana** (piazza del Popolo 6, 0577 849043). **Bacchus** (via G Matteotti 15, 0577 847054, closed Mon, Tue, Thur & Sat in winter) is a decent spot for light meals.

Wine connoisseurs are well served with *enoteche* in Montalcino. The most imposing is **Enoteca Osteria Osticcio** (via G Matteotti 23, 0577 848271, closed Sun, average €20): your samplings may be pricey, but they come with a priceless view. If you want to buy a bottle or two to take away, try **Montalcino 564** (via Mazzini 25, 0577 849109, closed Sun in winter), where you'll also find fine glassware and table linens. For a winning location and a vast selection, stop at **Enoteca Fortezza** (inside the Fortezza's keep, www.enotecalafortezza.com); a light luncheon plate is also available.

Resources

Tourist information

Ufficio Informazioni *Costa del Municipio (0577 849331/www.prolocomontalcino.it).* **Open** 10am-1pm, 2-5.50pm daily. Closed Mon in winter.

Abbazia di Sant'Antimo

The lovely Benedictine abbey of Sant'Antimo lies quietly in a vale beneath the hamlet of **Castelnuovo dell'Abate**. Its founding is attributed to Charlemagne in 781, though what remains largely dates to the 12th century. The Romanesque interiors feature finely carved capitals, including one portraying Daniel in the lion's den (second column from the right of the nave). A group of French Premonstratensian monks (Cistercian branch) moved here in 1979 and salvaged it from decline. Gregorian chant (7am, 9am, 12.45pm, 1.45pm, 2.45pm, vespers 7pm, and 8.30pm; free admission) accompanies many of the day's religious functions, drawing audiences from far and wide.

San Quirico d'Orcia & Bagno Vignoni

San Quirico d'Orcia is one of the lesser-known treasures of Siena Province. This perfectly preserved town, snug within its ancient walls, was a major stopping point on the via Francigena. The 12th-century Romanesque church, the **Collegiata**, with its carved stone portals of lions and dragons, has a terrific altarpiece by Sano di Pietro. Next door is the splendid 17th-century **Palazzo Chigi**. Down the main street is the main square, piazza della Libertà, with a classic **Bar Central** (piazza della Libertà 6, 0577 897583) where you can have a plate of the local *pici* and order its own-made *semifredo* by the kilo. The 16th-century **Horti Leonini**, a lovely formal garden, is also accessed from the square; there's a delightful rose garden at the back. Like many towns in the area, San Quirico has its own traditional olive press, which becomes the focal point of the annual **Festa dell'Olio** (held around 10 December). It's a convivial, somewhat bibulous opportunity for gorging on bruschetta soaked in the excellent, freshly pressed local produce.

Just south of San Quirico is the tiny hamlet of **Bagno Vignoni**. In summer, the place has the feel of an exotic resort, with many restaurants with outdoor seating. Piazza delle Sorgenti, the main square, has a large pool of thermal water in its centre, flanked by houses and a low Renaissance loggia. St Catherine and, later, Lorenzo il Magnifico came here to ease their aching limbs. Though you can't swim in the historic baths, you can soak blissfully in the thermal pool at **Hotel Posta Marcucci** (*see also p231* **Spa-spangled manors**).

Where to stay & eat

Within San Quirico the **Palazzo del Capitano** (0577 89902, www.palazzodelcapitano.com, €90) is a smart option serving good-quality meals and running the odd cookery course. **Hotel Osteria Val d'Orcia** (0577 887111, www.hotelorcia.it, €120-€155), on the road rising toward Castiglion d'Orcia (turn right at the first bend), is a very pleasant country inn that also has an excellent restaurant.

At Bagno Vignoni, the **Hotel Le Terme** (piazza delle Sorgenti 13, 0577 887150, www.albergoleterme.it, €58-€75), built for Pope Pius II as a summerhouse, is right beside the antique baths in the centre. There's fine food and an interesting wine list at the newly renovated **La Terrazza** restaurant. The **Locanda del Loggiato** (piazza del Moretto 30, 0577 888925, www.loggiato.it, €130-€150) has six pleasant rooms and provides light meals.

Radicofani & Sarteano

Further south along the via Francigena from Bagno Vignoni, along the ancient via Cassia around Monte Amiata, lies the tiny town of **Bagni San Filippo**. Here, you can explore the forest that surrounds a natural thermal spa (*see also p231* **Spa-spangled manors**), where hot waters run in the stream with a spectacular white moat of limestone encrustations.

Further south, **Radicofani** can be viewed from quite a distance, with its stony stronghold built from the volcanic basalt that must have erupted from Monte Amiata in its fiery prehistoric youth. To reinforce the strategic nature of this location, a **Città Fortificata** (fortress) was built on the summit of the hill to which Radicofani clings. Once home to a vagabond knight, Ghinotto di Tacco, the restored site is now a museum (0578 55905, 10.30am-7.30pm, admission €3); an excellent adjoining picnic area affords amazing views during the summer months.

Further on, you'll come to **Sarteano**, a delightful, well-preserved and relatively untouristy town. With its collection of Etruscan funerary urns shaped like heads, the tiny **Museo Civico Archeologico** (0578 269261, closed Mon May-Sept, open winter by appt only, admission €2.50) is worth a peek.

Where to stay & eat

In Radicofani, **La Grotta** (piazza Santa Agata 12, 0578 55866, closed Tue, average €15) serves robust, no-frills local fare. In Sarteano, the **Residenza Santa Chiara** (piazza Santa Chiara 30, 0578 265412, closed Feb, €130), which was once a convent and is now a charming hotel overlooking the town, also has an excellent restaurant (average €30) and an impressive *enoteca* of its own. Down below, opposite the museum, you can eat well at the **Osteria da Gagliano** (via Roma 5, 0578 268022, closed lunch in winter & Tue year-round, average €20). It's small, though, so book ahead.

Pienza

Originally called Corsignano, this little town was remodelled – and consequently renamed – between 1458 and 1462 by Aeneas Silvius Piccolomini, who became Pope Pius II in 1458. If you stand in **piazza Pio II** and slowly turn around, you'll notice decorative themes and variations (the *tondo* and the garland) that lend a sense of unity to the different types of building and the materials used. It's pretty astounding to think that the whole project was accomplished in four years. The body of the Duomo is in tufa stone and, at the rear, deliberately Gothic in style, as if to fit into the existing urban context. The travertine façade, by contrast, is as Renaissance as it could be, for those days a bold declaration of modernity.

Palazzo Piccolomini (0577 286300, www.palazzopiccolominipienza.it, closed Mon mid-late Feb and mid-late Nov, admission €7), the pope's residence, was modelled after Alberti's Palazzo Rucellai in Florence (*see p94*). There's a delightful hanging garden that you can view from the gate. You need a ticket for tours of Pius II's lavish private apartments, but access to the courtyard is free.

Pienza's art collection is kept in the **Museo Diocesano** (corso Rossellino 30, 0578 749905, closed Tue & Mon-Fri Nov-Mar, admission €4.10).

Where to stay & eat

Those wanting to stay the night will enjoy the comfort and calm of **Hotel Relais Il Chiostro** (corso Rossellino 26, 0578 748400, closed early Jan-late Mar, €110-€169), housed in a 15th-century convent. It has an inviting swimming pool and its own restaurant (closed lunch Mon, average €50). **La Chiocarella** (via Chiocarella 9, 0578 748406, €60) has three pleasant rooms off the main street with a private garden, while the **San Gregorio Residence** (via della Madonnina 4, 0578 748059, €80-€120) is excellent for families with small children.

For dining, **Trattoria Latte di Luna** (via San Carlo 6, 0578 748606, closed Tue & mid Feb-mid Mar & July, average €25) is a good bet, while the best restaurant in the area is **La Pergola** (0578 748051, via dell'Acerto 2, closed Mon & Nov, average €25). Otherwise, head down to the hamlet of Monticchiello, a few miles away, and eat at **La Porta** (via del Piano 1, 0578 755163, closed Thur & early Jan-early Feb & late June-early July, average €30). Also in Pienza is **Enoteca di Ghino** (via delle Mura 8, 0578 748057, www.enotecadighino.it), an excellent, keenly priced wine shop with bottles from Tuscany and beyond.

Wheels of pecorino, rolling hills and solitary cypresses: Siena Province lives up to its image.

Resources

Tourist information

Ufficio Informazioni *Piazza Dante Alighieri 18 (0578 749071/www.ufficioturisticodipienza.it).* **Open** 9.30am-1pm, 3-6.30pm daily.

Montepulciano

Montepulciano was an early and important outpost for the Republic of Florence, and the town consequently has an elegant and stately presence in this otherwise medieval landscape. As early as 1685, a poem entitled 'Bacco in Toscana' declared that, 'Montepulciano of all wine is sovereign'. Though wine (Vino Nobile di Montepulciano) has been a mainstay of the local economy for centuries, the town owes its visible substance more to political nous than viticulture. Montepulciano swore allegiance to Florence as early as 1511, thereby defending itself from the designs of both Siena and Perugia.

The best way to see the town is by tackling the steep via di Gracciano del Corso, which starts near Montepulciano's northern entrance, Porta al Prato. Along the way, note the Roman and Etruscan marble plaques cemented into the base of **Palazzo Bucelli**: they were gathered by Pietro Bucelli, an 18th-century collector whose interest in antiquities helped supply the **Museo Civico** (0578 717300, closed Mondays, admission €3). A bit further up, on piazza Michelozzo, you can't help but notice the towering **Torre di Pulcinella**, a clock tower topped by a mechanical figure typical of the Neapolitan *Commedia dell'Arte*.

Your efforts will eventually be rewarded when you reach piazza Grande, the town's highest and most beautiful point. The spacious square paved with chunky stones is reminiscent of Pienza's 'ideal city' layout. The **Duomo** was never embellished with a proper façade, and the rough brick front belies the treasures of the interior: the fine Gothic *Assumption* by Taddeo di Bartolo (1401) above the altar; the *Madonna and Child* by Sano di Pietro towards the top of the left of the nave; the marble *Ciborium* sculpted by Vecchietta, one of the artists invited by Pius II to embellish the Duomo in Pienza with a painting; the delicately carved tomb of Humanist Aragazzi (1428) by Michelozzo.

Also in the square are Sangallo's **Palazzo Tarugi**, with loggia; the 13th-century **Palazzo Comunale**, which deliberately echoes the Palazzo Vecchio in Florence (visits to the roof €1.50); and **Palazzo Contucci**. Not far away and worth a look is the **Museo Civico** in Palazzo Neri Orselli (via Ricci 10, 0578 717300, closed Mon); its archaeology section is especially strong. Around 20 minutes' walk from Porta al

Fine vines

Treno Del Vino.

Wine-lovers have long known the joys that a visit to a vineyard can offer. Tastings – sometimes given for free if you look like the type to make a purchase – often take place in atmospheric vaults among large oak barrels, or beneath the sun beating down on the rows of vines spreading before you. Siena Province has the pick of the bunch when it comes to wineries, home as it is to some of Italy's foremost quality DOCG wine appellations: Chianti, Chianti Classico, Brunello di Montalcino and Vino Nobile di Montepulciano (*see also pp43-48*).

Most wineries are happy to show visitors around, but few are equipped with staff and tasting rooms for proper tours. It's always a good idea to call ahead. The most notable innovation in recent years has been the creation of the **Treno Del Vino** (Wine Train; www.winestation.it). Departing from Siena, this dinky 150-seater takes you through the beautiful countryside of the Val d'Orcia to Monte Amiata, then on to a vineyard. It makes a fun day out for curious non-experts or those without their own transport.

These are some of the more prominent and worthwhile wineries. The **Strada da Vino Nobile** (*see p259*) can give you more advice.

Chianti Classico

Castello di Fonterutoli

Fonterutoli, Castellina in Chianti (0577 73571/www.fonterutoli.it). **Open** 9.30am-6.30pm Tue-Fri; 9.30am-12.30pm, 1.30-6.30pm Mon, Sat. **Credit** DC, MC, V.
State-of-the-art cellars have recently been installed here; you'll need to book in advance.

Felsina

SS Chiantigiana 484, nr Castelnuovo Berardenga (0577 355117). **Open** *Mar-Oct* 8.30am-6pm Mon-Fri. *Nov-Feb* 8.30am-12.30pm, 1.30-5.30pm Mon-Fri. **Credit** MC, V.
Some of Siena Province's best wines are produced here, including Fontalloro.

Further information

Consorzio Chianti Classico (055 82285/www.chianticlassico.com).

Brunello di Montalcino

Fattoria dei Barbi

Podere Novi village 170, Montalcino (0577 841111/www.fattoriadeibarbi.it). **Open** 10am-1pm, 2.30-6pm Mon-Fri; 2.30-6pm Sat, Sun. **Credit** AmEx, DC, MC, V.
Dei Barbi has some fine old cellars selling a variety of wines.

Fattoria del Casato

Località Podere Casato 17 (0577 849421/ www.cinellicolombini.it). **Open** 9am-1pm, 3-6pm Mon-Fri; Sat, Sun by appointment. Credit MC, V.
Donatella Cinelli Colombini's tour is fun and instructive, and the wines promising.

Further information

Consorzio del Vino Brunello di Montalcino Costa del Municipio 1, Montalcino (0577 848246/www.consorzio brunellodimontalcino.it).

Vino Nobile di Montepulciano

Avignonesi

Via Colonica 1, Valiano di Montepulciano (0578 724304/www.avignonesi.it). **Open** 9am-6pm Mon-Fri. **Credit** MC, V.
Approximately 23km (14 miles) outside Montepulciano, Avignonesi has tastings and tours on weekdays.

Poliziano

Via Fontago 1, Montepulciano (0578 738171/www.carlettipoliziano.it). **Open** 8.30am-12.30pm, 2.30-6pm Mon-Fri. Closed Aug & 2wks Dec. **Credit** AmEx, DC, MC, V.
Three different types of Vino Nobile are produced here, two of which are single-vineyard crus.

Further information

Consorzio del Vino Nobile di Montepulciano *Piazza Grande 7, Montepulciano (0578 757812/ www.vinonobiledimontepulciano.it).*

Prato sits the pilgrimage church of **San Biagio**. Designed by Sangallo and built between 1518 and 1545, this Bramante-influenced study in proportion is a jewel of the High Renaissance.

Where to stay & eat

For lodgings, try the **Albergo Il Marzocco** (piazza Savonarola 18, 0578 757262, www.albergoilmarzocco.it, €90), just inside the Porta al Prato in a 16th-century palazzo. A few of its spacious rooms have terraces. A smaller residence, dripping in historical charm, is **Meublè Il Riccio** (via di Talosa 21, 0578 757713, www.ilriccio.net, €100).

Osteria dell'Acquacheta (via del Theatro 22, 0578 758443, www.acquachcta.eu, average €20) is a busy taverna with rustic tables; booking is recommended. For drinks or light snacks, don't miss **Antico Caffè Poliziano** (via di Voltaia nel Corso 27-29, 0578 758615, www.caffepoliziano.it), an art deco institution that's a great place to sample Vino Nobile. At San Biagio there's more substantial food at **La Grotta** (0578 757607, closed Wed, average €40), a former 14th-century staging post.

Resources

Tourist information

Pro Loco *Via del Corso 59a (0578 757341/ www.prolocomontepulciano.it).* **Open** *Summer* 9.30am 12.30pm, 3 8pm Mon Sat; 9.30am-12.30pm Sun. *Winter* 9.30am-12.30pm, 3-6pm Mon-Sat; 9.30am-12.30pm Sun.
Strada da Vino Nobile *Piazza Grande 7 (0578 717484/www.stradavinonobile.it).*
Gives tourist information and can organise tastings.

Getting there

By bus

There's a regular **SITA** bus service (800 373760, www.sita-on-line.it) from Florence to Greve (50mins) and Panzano (70mins). SITA also runs buses from Florence to San Gimignano (via Poggibonsi, 70mins) via Colle di Val d'Elsa (1hr). In addition, **Tra-in** (0577 204246) operates a service between Siena and Montalcino (1hr), and another service between Siena and Montepulciano (via Pienza, 90mins).

By car

Siena province is best experienced by car. From the A1 Milan–Rome motorway, exit at Firenze Certosa, Valdarno, Valdichiana or Chusi and follow the signs to Siena; check www.autostrade.it.

By train

There are regular trains from Siena to San Gimignano (25mins) and Montepulciano (1hr). For national train information, call 892021 or go to www.trenitalia.it.

Lucca

Within these walls.

The **ramparts**. *See p264.*

A conservative bastion in left-wing, progressive Tuscany, Lucca stands alone and slightly aloof behind its perfectly preserved 16th-century walls. Unlike Florence and Siena, Lucca has few must-see sights, though in many ways it's a more attractive proposition for the curious traveller. For Lucca's real attraction lies in its organic wholeness, its handsome *piazze*, its ample, tree-shaded fortifications and its ambience: cultured, reserved but welcoming to tourists, who rarely gather in numbers that overwhelm Lucca's *centro storico*. It's also one of the few cities in Europe whose relationship to the surrounding countryside remains that of a medieval city state, locked in a symbiotic relationship. Its pace is gentle too: much of the city is pedestrianised and the best way to discover it is on foot. Or do as the locals do: spend a day in the saddle.

The ornate white façades of the Romanesque churches – the fragile wedding-cake serenity of **San Michele in Foro**, truly one of the great sights of Tuscany; the glistening mosaic of **San Frediano**; and the hugely charming asymmetry of **Duomo di San Martino** – all appear unexpectedly. The colourful **piazza dell'Anfiteatro** (*photo p263*) still retains the oval shape of an ancient amphitheatre, while the tree-lined ramparts and the oak-topped **Torre Guinigi** afford splendid views of the tight cityscape. Another good starting point for a local exploration is the enormous **piazza Napoleone**, named after Napoleon's sister, and home to a carousel.

Lucca's flatness and relatively simple grid plan make everything easily accessible. One lovely way to get your bearings is to hire a bike (*see p269*) and cycle the four kilometres (2.5 miles) along the top of the city walls in the company of joggers, dog walkers and footballing youngsters (*see p264*).

SOME HISTORY

Possibly the site of a Ligurian and then an Etruscan settlement, Lucca came of age as a Roman municipium in 89 BC and hosted the signing of the first triumvirate between Pompey, Julius Caesar and Crassus in 56 BC. It was crucially positioned at the crossroads of the Empire's communications with its northern reaches and controlled the Appennine passes along the Serchio valley.

Despite Rome's fall, the city continued to maintain its supremacy in Tuscany, first as capital of Tuscia under Lombard rule and then as the seat of the Frankish Margravate from 774. By the turn of the first millennium, Lucca had grown into Tuscany's largest city. Wealth engendered commercial rivalry with its upstart neighbours. This soon turned into open military clashes with Pisa and a gradual loss of political dominance to Florence.

The 14th century was a turbulent time for Lucca. A short-lived heyday as the capital of a mini-empire under the helm of the condottiere Castruccio Castracani (1320-28) soon gave way to a series of setbacks leading to domination by Pisa from 1342. In 1369, Lucca was finally granted its autonomy and independence by Emperor Charles IV of Bohemia; this was to last, unbroken, until 1799.

Having renounced its claims to regional leadership, Lucca moved into relative obscurity. An oligarchy of ruling families controlled all public offices and private wealth and set about enlarging the medieval urban nucleus. In 1805,

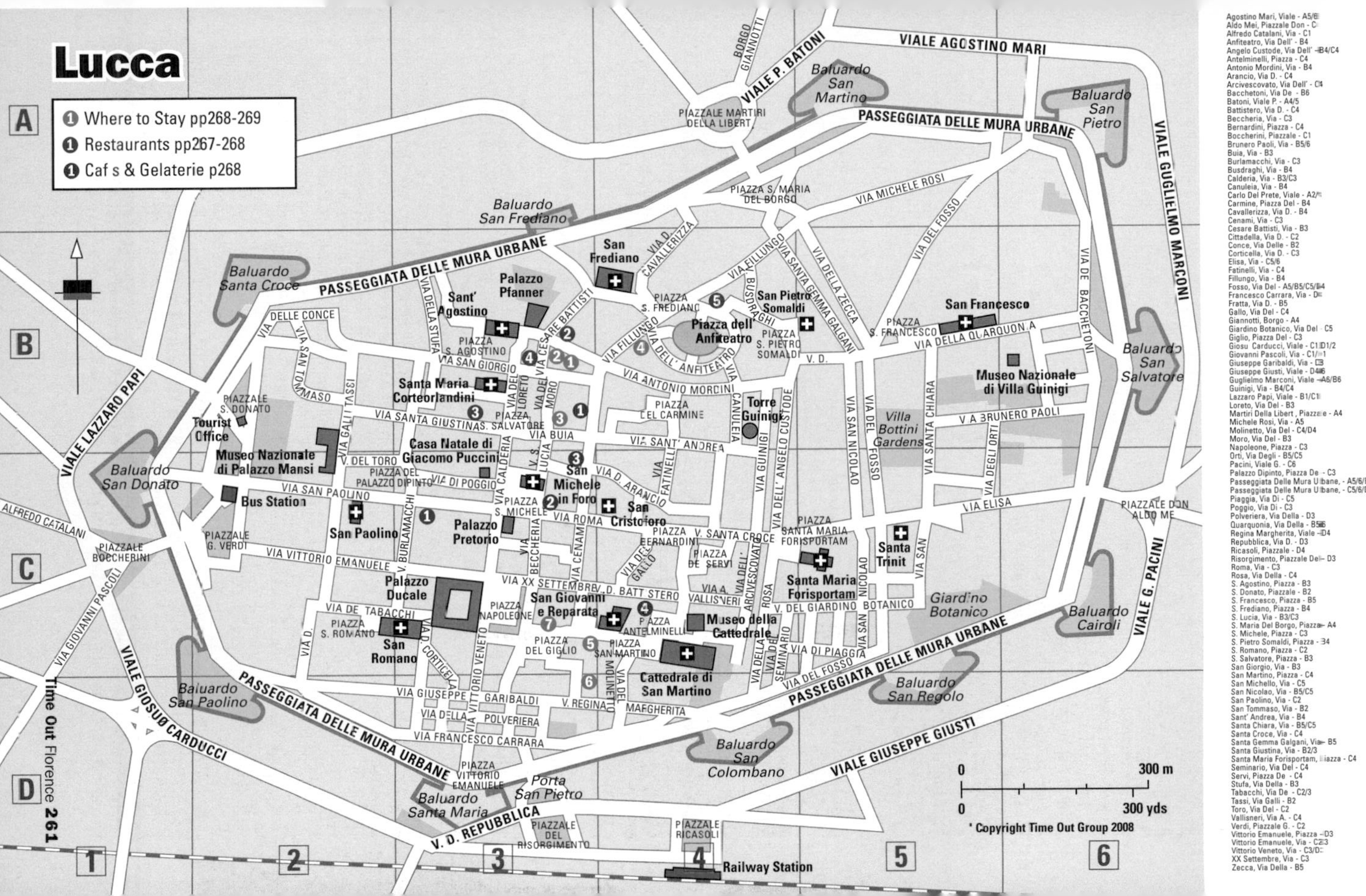
Lucca
Where to Stay pp268-269
Restaurants pp267-268
Caf s & Gelaterie p268
A
B
C
D
1
2
3
4
5
6
VIALE AGOSTINO MARI
VIALE GUGLIELMO MARCONI
VIALE G. PACINI
VIALE GIUSEPPE GIUSTI
VIALE GIOSUØ CARDUCCI
VIALE LAZZARO PAPI
VIALE P. BATONI
PASSEGGIATA DELLE MURA URBANE
Baluardo San Martino
Baluardo San Pietro
Baluardo San Salvatore
Baluardo Cairoli
Baluardo San Regolo
Baluardo San Colombano
Baluardo Santa Maria
Baluardo San Paolino
Baluardo San Donato
Baluardo Santa Croce
Baluardo San Frediano
PIAZZALE MARTIRI DELLA LIBERT
PIAZZALE DON ALDO ME
PIAZZALE RICASOLI
PIAZZALE DEL RISORGIMENTO
PIAZZALE BOCCHERINI
PIAZZALE G. VERDI
PIAZZALE S. DONATO
BORGO GIANNOTTI
V. ALFREDO CATALANI
VIA GIOVANNI PASCOLI
V. D. REPUBBLICA
San Frediano
Palazzo Pfanner
Sant' Agostino
Santa Maria Corteorlandini
Casa Natale di Giacomo Puccini
Museo Nazionale di Palazzo Mansi
Tourist Office
Bus Station
San Paolino
Palazzo Pretorio
San Michele in Foro
San Cristoforo
Palazzo Ducale
San Romano
San Giovanni e Reparata
Museo della Cattedrale
Cattedrale di San Martino
Santa Maria Forisportam
Santa Trinit
Torre Guinigi
Piazza dell' Anfiteatro
San Pietro Somaldi
San Francesco
Museo Nazionale di Villa Guinigi
Villa Bottini Gardens
Giardino Botanico
Porta San Pietro
Railway Station
0
300 m
0
300 yds
' Copyright Time Out Group 2008
Agostino Mari, Viale - A5/6
Aldo Mei, Piazzale Don - C
Alfredo Catalani, Via - C1
Anfiteatro, Via Dell' - B4
Angelo Custode, Via Dell' - B4/C4
Antelminelli, Piazza - C4
Antonio Mordini, Via - B4
Arancio, Via D. - C4
Arcivescovato, Via Dell' - C4
Bacchetoni, Via De - B6
Batoni, Viale P. - A4/5
Battistero, Via D. - C4
Beccheria, Via - C3
Bernardini, Piazza - C4
Boccherini, Piazzale - C1
Brunero Paoli, Via - B5/6
Buia, Via - B3
Burlamacchi, Via - C3
Busdraghi, Via - B4
Calderia, Via - B3/C3
Canuleia, Via - B4
Carlo Del Prete, Viale - A2/
Carmine, Piazza Del - B4
Cavallerizza, Via D. - B4
Cenami, Via - C3
Cesare Battisti, Via - B3
Cittadella, Via D. - C2
Conce, Via Delle - B2
Corticella, Via D. - C3
Elisa, Via - C5/6
Fatinelli, Via - C4
Fillungo, Via - B4
Fosso, Via Del - A5/B5/C5/D4
Francesco Carrara, Via - D
Fratta, Via D. - B5
Gallo, Via Del - C4
Giannotti, Borgo - A4
Giardino Botanico, Via Del - C5
Giglio, Piazza Del - C3
Giosu Carducci, Viale - C1/D1/2
Giovanni Pascoli, Via - C1/D1
Giuseppe Garibaldi, Via - D3
Giuseppe Giusti, Viale - D4/6
Guglielmo Marconi, Viale - A6/B6
Guinigi, Via - B4/C4
Lazzaro Papi, Viale - B1/C1
Loreto, Via Del - B3
Martiri Della Libert, Piazzale - A4
Michele Rosi, Via - A5
Molinetto, Via Del - C4/D4
Moro, Via Del - B3
Napoleone, Piazza - C3
Orti, Via Degli - B5/C5
Pacini, Viale G. - C6
Palazzo Dipinto, Piazza De - C3
Passeggiata Delle Mura Urbane, - A5/6/B2/3
Passeggiata Delle Mura Urbane, - C5/6/D2/3/4
Piaggia, Via Di - C5
Poggio, Via Di - C3
Polveriera, Via Della - D3
Quarquonia, Via Della - B5/6
Regina Margherita, Viale - D4
Repubblica, Via D. - D3
Ricasoli, Piazzale - D4
Risorgimento, Piazzale Del - D3
Roma, Via - C3
Rosa, Via Della - C4
S. Agostino, Piazza - B3
S. Donato, Piazzale - B2
S. Francesco, Piazza - B5
S. Frediano, Piazza - B4
S. Lucia, Via - B3/C3
S. Maria Del Borgo, Piazza - A4
S. Michele, Piazza - C3
S. Pietro Somaldi, Piazza - B4
S. Romano, Piazza - C2
S. Salvatore, Piazza - B3
San Giorgio, Via - B3
San Martino, Piazza - C4
San Michello, Via - C5
San Nicolao, Via - B5/C5
San Paolino, Via - C2
San Tommaso, Via - B2
Sant' Andrea, Via - B4
Santa Chiara, Via - B5/C5
Santa Croce, Via - C4
Santa Gemma Galgani, Via - B5
Santa Giustina, Via - B2/3
Santa Maria Forisportam, Piazza - C4
Seminario, Via Del - C4
Servi, Piazza De - C4
Stufa, Via Della - B3
Tabacchi, Via De - C2/3
Tassi, Via Galli - B2
Toro, Via Del - C2
Vallisneri, Via A. - C4
Verdi, Piazzale G. - C2
Vittorio Emanuele, Piazza - D3
Vittorio Emanuele, Via - C2/3
Vittorio Veneto, Via - C3/D
XX Settembre, Via - C3
Zecca, Via Della - B5

Lucca passed under the direct rule of Elisa Baciocchi, Napoleon's sister, and then in 1817 to the Infanta Maria Luisa di Borbone of Spain. Both did much to recast the city architecturally and patronised a brief but highly intense period of artistic ferment. In 1847, Lucca was ceded to the Grand Duchy of Tuscany and thereafter joined a united Italy in 1860. The city's almost uninterrupted history as a wildly opulent and free commune has left it largely unaffected by outside developments, both architecturally and in terms of the local psychology.

In so far as the timing of your own visit is concerned, some of the following dates may be worth bearing in mind: the **Santa Zita** flower show and market (four days at the end of April); a summer music festival in piazza dell' Anfiteatro (July); the **Luminara di San Paolino**, a torchlit procession celebrating Lucca's patron saint (11 July); the **Luminara di Santa Croce** procession of the *Volto Santo* (13 September); the many cultural, religious and sporting events of **Settembre Lucchese** (September, October); and the charming **Natale Anfiteatro** Christmas market.

Sights

Churches

Duomo (Cattedrale di San Martino)

Piazza San Martino (0583 957068). **Open** *Duomo* Summer 9.30am-5.45pm daily. Winter 9.30am-4.45pm daily. *Sacristy* Summer 9.30am-5.45pm Mon-Fri; 9.30am-6.45pm Sat; 9-9.50am, 11.20-1.50am, 1-5.45pm Sun. Winter 9.30am-4.45pm Mon-Fri; 9.30am-6.45pm Sat; 11.20-11.50am, 1-4.45pm Sun. No entry during services. **Admission** *Duomo* free. *Sacristy* €2.50; €6 incl Museo della Cattedrale & San Giovanni e Reparata. **No credit cards. Map** p261 C4.

At first glance, Lucca's Romanesque cathedral seems somewhat unbalanced. A closer look reveals why. The oddly asymmetrical façade has the arch and the first two series of *logge* on the right literally squeezed and flattened by the campanile. Nobody is really to blame (or commend) for this as the Lombard bell tower was erected before the rest of the church in around 1100 and completed just 200 years later. It predates the Duomo, on which work began in earnest only in the 12th century. The odd asymmetry of the façade, designed by Guidetto da Como, only adds to the overall atmosphere of wild exuberance and eccentricity.

San Martino's interior is so dimly lit that coin operated lights are on hand to illuminate paintings such as Tintoretto's *Last Supper*. Midway up the left nave is the underrated Matteo Civitali's octagonal marble *Tempietto* (1484), home to a dolorous wooden crucifix known as the *Volto Santo* (Holy Face). The effigy – what we see is a copy – was supposedly begun by Nicodemus and finished by an angel, set on a pilotless ship from the East in the eighth century and brought to Lucca on a cart drawn by steer. This miraculous arrival quickly spawned a cult following and the relic soon became an object of pilgrimage throughout Europe. Nowadays, it's draped in silk and gold garments and ornaments, and marched through Lucca's streets in highly dramatic nighttime processions on 13 September.

The Duomo's Sacristy contains the other top attraction: the tomb of Ilaria del Carretto (1408), a delicate sarcophagus sculpted by Sienese master Jacopo della Quercia. It represents the young bride of Paolo Guinigi – Lucca's strongman at the time.

San Francesco

Via della Quarquonia (0583 91175/338 9433388 mobile). **Open** 9-11am daily (phone in advance). **Admission** free. **Map** p261 B5.

Although the Franciscans left in November 2002, this beautifully simple church remains open to visitors in the morning, though you must let the church custodian know so he can let you in.

San Frediano

Piazza San Frediano (0583 493627). **Open** 8.30am-noon, 2.30-5.30pm Mon-Sat; 9-11.30am, 3-6pm Sun; 10.30am-5pm public hols. **Admission** free. **Map** p261 B4.

San Frediano's strikingly resplendent Byzantine-like mosaic façade is unique in Tuscany, rivalled only by that above the choir of San Miniato al Monte in Florence. A church was founded on this site by Fredian, an Irish monk who settled in Lucca in the sixth century and converted the ruling Lombards by allegedly diverting the River Serchio and saving the city from flooding. This miracle put the finishing touches on Christianity's hold on Lucca and earned Fredian a quick promotion to bishop, eventually leading to canonisation. A few centuries later, in the 1100s, this singular church was built for him.

Apart from its mosaic, an *Ascension* in which a monumental Jesus is lifted by two angels over the heads of his Apostles, the façade of San Frediano is in the Pisan-Romanesque style of many of Lucca's other churches and was the first to face east. Inside, immediately on the right, is a small gem: the *fonte lustrale* (or baptismal font) surrounded with scenes from the Old and New Testaments. Behind it is a glazed terracotta *Ascension* by Andrea della Robbia. In the chapel next to it is another of Lucca's revered relics, the miraculously conserved though somewhat shrivelled body of St Zita, a humble servant who was canonised in the 13th century and whose mummy is brought out for a close-up view and a touch by devotees on 27 April. Ongoing restoration projects care for San Frediano's frescoes, including those by Amico Aspertini.

San Giovanni e Reparata

Via del Duomo (0583 490530). **Open** *Mid Mar-Oct* 10am-6pm daily. *Nov-mid Mar* 10am-5pm Sat, Sun. **Admission** *San Giovanni* €2; *Museo della Cattedrale* €4; *sacristy* €2.50. **No credit cards. Map** p261 C4.

Originally Lucca's cathedral, the 12th-century basilica of San Giovanni, now part of the Duomo, is on the site of a pagan temple. Apart from its magnificently ornate ceiling, the church's main draw is the architectural remains uncovered by excavations in the 1970s (included in the ticket price), ranging from a second-century Roman bath to a Paleo-Christian church. For the most enjoyable experience of this enigmatic attraction, ignore the baffling floor plans and just wander at will.

Santa Maria Corteorlandini

Piazza Giovanni Leonardi (0583 467464). **Open** 9am-noon, 4.30-6pm daily; 8.30am-noon public hols. **Admission** free. **Map** p261 B3.

This overwhelming late Baroque church is Lucca's odd man out when it comes to the visual splendour of interior design. Its trompe l'œil frescoed roofs, abundance of coloured marble and the gilded and ornamented tabernacle by local artist Giovanni Vambre (1673) provide a break from the stark and grey interiors of the city's other churches.

Santa Maria Forisportam

Piazza Santa Maria Forisportam (0583 467769). **Open** 7.30am-noon, 3-6pm daily. **Admission** free. **Map** p261 C5.

Set on the square known to Lucchesi as piazza della Colonna Mozza (referring to the truncated column at its centre), Santa Maria takes its name from its location just outside Lucca's older set of walls. The unfinished marble façade dates mostly from the 12th and 13th centuries, and is a slightly toned-down version of the Pisan-Romanesque style present throughout the city.

San Michele in Foro

Piazza San Michele (0583 48459). **Open** 8am-noon, 3.30-6pm daily. **Admission** free. **Map** p261 C3.

Set on the site of the Roman forum, San Michele's Pisan-Romanesque façade is among the finest in Tuscany, and remains Lucca's most alluring sight. Every element in the church's elaborate interior lightly plays off against the other: the oddly knotted, twisted and carved columns with their psychedelic geometric designs and the fantastical animals, and fruit and floral motifs in the capitals. The façade culminates in a winged St Michael precariously perched while vanquishing the dragon. San Michele's façade contrasts sharply with its sombre interior. On the right as you enter is a *Madonna and Child* by della Robia – a copy of the original is on the church's right-hand outside corner. Further on, you'll find Filippino Lippi's gorgeously simple and serene *Saints Jerome, Sebastian, Rocco and Helena*, arguably Lucca's greatest artistic asset. *Photo p264.*

San Paolino

Via San Paolino (0583 53576). **Open** 8.15am-noon, 3.30-6pm daily. **Admission** free. **Map** p261 C2.

Giacomo Puccini received his baptism of fire here in 1881 with his first public performance of the *Mass for Four Voices*. San Paolino had, in fact, always been the Puccini family's second home, with five generations of them serving as its organists at one time or another. Built from 1522 to 1536 for Lucca's patron St Paulinus, the city's first bishop, who allegedly came over from Antioch in AD 65 and whose remains are buried in a sarcophagus behind the altar, it's Lucca's only example of late Renaissance architecture.

Piazza dell'Anfiteatro. *See p260.*

San Michele in Foro. *See p263.*

Museums

Casa Natale di Giacomo Puccini

Corte San Lorenzo 9, off via di Poggio (0583 469225/ www.casanatalepuccini.it). **Open** *Mar-May, Oct-Dec* 10am-1pm, 3-6pm Tue-Sun. *June-Sept* 10am-6pm daily. Closed Jan, Feb. **Admission** €3; €2 reductions. **No credit cards. Map** p261 C3.

Ongoing restorations at the birthplace of Lucca's most famous son, Giacomo Puccini, mean that this charming museum is closed until 2009, so phone ahead for more information (if you don't get through, phone the tourist office). If it is welcoming visitors, you'll be in for some interesting insights into the artist's sheltered youth, turbulent private life and artistic genius. The rooms of memorabilia include the original librettos of his early operas, his private letters on subjects both musical and sentimental, the piano on which he composed *Turandot* and the gem-encrusted costume used in the opera's American debut in 1926. *Photo p267.*

Museo della Cattedrale

Via Arcivescovado (0583 490530). **Open** *May-Oct* 10am-6pm daily. *Nov-Apr* 10am-6pm Mon-Fri; 10am-5pm Sat, Sun. **Admission** €4; €6 incl San Giovanni e Reparata. **No credit cards. Map** p261 C4.

Attractively laid out over various levels, this well-curated modern museum houses many treasures transferred from the Duomo di San Martino and from nearby San Giovanni (for both, *see p262*). Displays cover everything from the cathedral's furnishings, its gold and silverware to its sculptures, including Jacopo della Quercia's *Apostle*. The free English audio guides are excellent.

Museo Nazionale di Palazzo Mansi

Via Galli Tassi 43 (0583 55570). **Open** 9am-7.30pm Tue-Sat; 8.30am-2pm Sun. **Admission** €4; free reductions; €6.50 incl Villa Guinigi. **No credit cards. Map** p261 C2.

Beyond the impressive stagecoach at the entrance to this, Lucca's single most remarkable example of Baroque exaggeration, is a 16th- to 17th-century palazzo home to a collection of mostly Tuscan art. While the frescoed Salone della Musica (which hosts chamber music concerts) and the neoclassical Salone degli Specchi are light on the eye, over-indulgence climaxes in the Camera della Sposa, an OTT bridal chamber with a *baldacchino* bed. The largely uninspiring art includes pieces from the Venetian school with lesser-known works by Tintoretto and Titian. Perhaps best is Pontormo's Manneristic portrait of his fiercesome patron, Alessandro de' Medici.

Museo Nazionale di Villa Guinigi

Via della Quarquonia (0583 496033). **Open** 8.30am-7pm Tue-Sat; 8.30am-1.30pm Sun. **Admission** €4; €6.50 incl Palazzo Mansi; free reductions. **No credit cards. Map** p261 B6.

This porticoed pink-brick villa (1403-20), surrounded by tranquil gardens and medieval statues, houses art from Lucca and its surrounding region. The first floor of the museum has a selection of fascinating Roman and Etruscan finds along with some 13th- and 14th-century capitals and columns. Highlights from the upstairs rooms are Matteo Civitali's *Annunciation*, some ornate altarpieces by Amico Aspertini and Fra Bartolomeo, and intarsia panels by Ambrogio and Nicolao Pucci.

Monuments

Ramparts

On a good day you'll see Lucchesi of all ages strolling, jogging, picnicking, cuddling and enjoying the views from *le nostre mura* ('our walls'), as the ramparts are lovingly known. Built in the 16th and 17th centuries, Italy's best-preserved and most impressive city fortifications measure 12 metres (39 feet) in height and 30 metres (98 feet) across, with a circumference of just over four kilometres (2.5 miles). They are punctuated by 11 sturdy bastions, designed to ward off heavily armed invaders. A proper siege never happened, though in 1812 they enabled the city to seal itself hermetically from floodwaters. Soon after, Maria Luisa di Borbone turned the walls into a public park and promenade, dotting them with plane, holm-oak, chestnut and lime trees. Today, cyclists and pedestrians are still making the most of them, not to mention the families who populate the play areas found in almost every *baluardo* (rampart) across town.

Torre Guinigi

Via Sant'Andrea 14 (0583 316846). **Open** *Nov-Feb* 9.30am-6pm daily. *Mar* 9am-5pm daily. *Apr* 9.30am-9pm daily. *May, Oct* 10am-6pm daily. *June-Sept* 9am-midnight daily. **Admission** €3.50; €2.50 reductions. **No credit cards**. **Map** p261 B4.

It may be something of a slog, but it's well worth the climb to reach the tranquil and leafy summit of Torre Guinigi, with its distinctive cluster of oak trees. From the very top of this 14th-century, 44m (144ft) high tower, there are spectacular views over Lucca's rooftops to the countryside beyond.

Parks & gardens

Giardino Botanico

Via del Giardino Botanico 14 (0583 442160). **Open** *May, June* 10am-6pm daily. *July-Sept* 10am-7pm daily. *Oct, Mar, Apr* 10am-5pm daily. *Nov-Feb* 9.30am-12.30pm by appointment only. **Admission** €3; €2 reductions. **No credit cards**. **Map** p261 C5.

Nestling in the south-east corner of the city walls, the Giardino Botanico makes a relaxed spot for a romantic stroll or a quiet sit-down – as do the gardens of the Villa Bottini just a little further up via Santa Chiara. The greenhouse and arboretum are planted with a wide and impressive range of Tuscan flora, many of which are rare species.

Palazzo Pfanner

Via degli Asili 33 (340 9233085 mobile). **Open** *Mar-mid Nov* 10am-6pm daily. *Mid Nov-Feb* by appointment. **Admission** €3 for palace and garden; €2.50 for one or the other; free under-8s. **No credit cards**. **Map** p261 B3.

These peaceful gardens, overlooked by the tower of San Frediano and the city walls, are a lovely place to aimlessly stroll away an afternoon. The palace has been restored to its former glory, and features cabinets housing the surgical implements used by Pietra Pfanner (who rose to become mayor of the city and later Knight Commander of the Crown of Italy) beneath impressive frescoed ceilings. Film buffs might recognise the gardens as a backdrop from *The Portrait of a Lady*.

Nightlife

Bars & clubs

Don't come to Lucca for late nights and hedonism: the big nightspots are out towards the Versilia coast (*see pp270-273*). There are, however, a number of decent wine bars in town. Good choices include **Rewine** (via Calderia 6, 0583 48427, closed Sun), a red and black bar that also serves decent snacks; **Vinarkia** (via Fillungo 188, 0583 495336, closed Mon), a laid-back bar with regular wine tastings and free buffet at 6pm and 10pm every night; and **La Corte dei Vini** (corte Campana 6, 0583 584460, closed Sun), notable for its cheeses and wines.

Shopping

You'll find plenty of well-known designer and other high-street names on and around Lucca's main shopping artery, via Fillungo. The other main hubs are via Vittorio Veneto (leading off piazza San Michele) and via Santa Croce. Despite Lucca's staid reputation, there are several boutiques and shoe shops, in particular along via Fillungo and via Vittorio Veneto.

There are excellent food shops at each turn, stocked with everything from regional wines and olive oils to cheeses and honeys, and a locally produced salami made with pig's blood and raisins. Two of the best in town are **La Grotta** (via dell' Anfiteatro 2, 0583 467595) and **Delicatezze** (via San Giorgio 5, 0583 492633).

The town's general market is held on via de' Bacchettoni by the eastern wall on Wednesdays and Saturdays, selling clothes, food, flowers

Grand designs

The countryside around Lucca is smattered with elegant villas and gardens that were originally the country retreats of wealthy merchants from the city. Elisa Baciocchi, Napoleon's sister, once resided at the stunning 17th-century **Villa Reale** at Marlia (0583 30108, www.parcovillareale.it, closed Mon and Dec-Feb, admission €6). Although the house is closed, you can visit the lovely statue-filled garden, which also contains a little theatre. The garden of the 16th-century **Villa Oliva Buonvisi** at San Pancrazio (0583 406462, admission €6) is open from March until November, as is the large English-style park and orangery of the nearby **Villa Grabau** (0583 406098, closed Mon Easter-Oct & Mon-Sat Nov-Easter, admission €5 garden only, €6 villa and garden). The 17th-century **Villa Mansi** (0583 920234, closed Mon, admission €7), over at Segromigno, is another very fine house, with frescoes of the *Myth of Apollo* by Stefano Tofanelli in the salon. The statue-filled garden was laid out by the Sicilian architect Juvarra; it's partly Italian (geometric) and partly English (not geometric) in style. There are also musical concerts in summer. The **Villa Torrigiani** (0583 928041, closed Tue, admission €6 gardens only, €9 gardens and villa) and its fine park at Camigliano are open from March to November. Inside are 16th- to 18th-century paintings and an excellent collection of porcelain.

Tuscany's Toontown

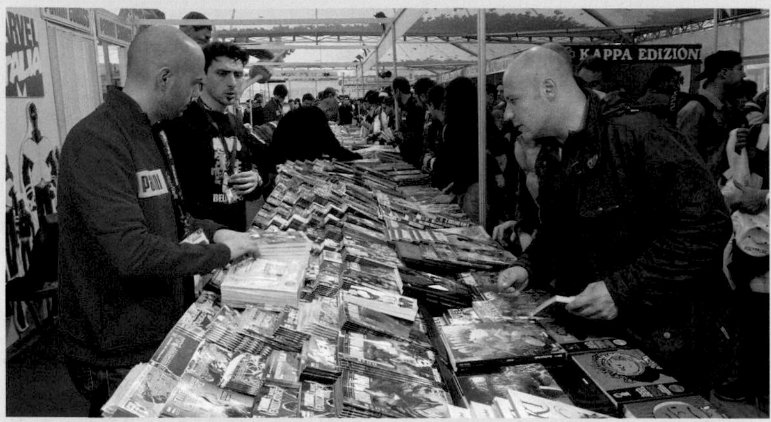

At most times of the year, you'd never guess that laid-back, old-fashioned Lucca has been Italy's capital city of comic art for over four decades. However, in 1966 Lucca inherited a cartoon fair from the Italian Riviera. The show grew steadily until 1993, when it moved to Rome. By then, however, the fondness for comics and cartoons had been etched into the city's consciousness, and **Lucca Comics & Games** was created in its stead. Recently, the fair has expanded to include two more sections – Lucca Junior and Lucca Multimedia – and attracts over 85,000 visitors and 360 exhibitors annually over an autumn weekend.

To coincide with this hugely popular event, half a dozen themed exhibitions are hosted in **Palazzo Ducale**. If, however, you can't time your visit to catch these colourful happenings, never fear: you can always visit the **Museo Nazionale del Fumetto** to find out about the greatest Italian comic characters of all time.

Lucca Comics & Games

0583 48522/www.luccacomicsandgames.com. **Dates** *Fair* 4 days late Oct/early Nov (admission charge). *Exhibitions* 2wks late Oct/early Nov (admission free).

Museo Nazionale del Fumetto e dell'Immagine

Piazza San Romano 4 (0583 56326/www.museonazionaledelfumetto.it). **Open** 10am-7pm Tue-Sun. **Admission** €4-€6. **No credit cards**. **Map** p261 C2.

and household goods. There's an antiques market in and around piazza San Martino on the third weekend of each month, with everything from coins to jewellery, and a crafts market (*arti e mestieri*) in piazza San Giusto on the last weekend of the month.

Cacioteca

Via Fillungo 242 (0583 496346). **Open** 7am-1.30pm, 3.30-8.30pm Mon, Tue, Thur-Sat; 7am-1.30pm Wed. **Credit** AmEx, MC, V. **Map** p261 B4.

An intense waft of seasoned cheese emanates from this shop. Give your taste buds a treat with the typical dairy products of the Garfagnana (*see p273*).

Mercato del Carmine

Off piazza del Carmine. **Open** 8am-noon, 4-8pm daily. **No credit cards**. **Map** p261 B4.

Between its fruit and vegetable stalls, fishmongers, butchers and delis, this superb colonnaded covered market offers the best of Lucca's regional produce: look out for the blood sausages, a local speciality. There's also a café where you can rest your weary feet and refuel along with the locals.

Vini Liquori Vanni

Piazza del Salvatore 7 (0583 491902). **Open** 4-8pm Mon; 9am-1pm, 4-8pm Tue-Sat. **Credit** AmEx, DC, MC, V. **Map** p261 B3.

This *enoteca*'s seemingly endless cellar is a treasure for those seeking out Lucca's better (and little-known) vintages. Probably also the least expensive place to get your hands on a bottle of the new range of Super Tuscan reds, as well as some of the more obscure varieties. Call ahead and book a wine lesson and *degustazione*, plus a mini-tour.

Where to eat

Restaurants

The neighbouring Garfagnana valley (*see p273*) contributes many prime ingredients to Lucca's cuisine, including chestnut flour, river trout, olive oil and above all *farro* (spelt grain), which pops up on every menu. The signature pudding is *buccellato* (a doughnut-shaped sweet bread flavoured with aniseed and raisins, and topped with sugar syrup).

La Buca di Sant'Antonio

Via della Cervia 3 (0583 55881/www.ristorantilucca.it). **Open** 12.30-2pm, 7.30-10pm Tue-Sat; 12.30-3pm Sun. Closed 2wks Jan. **Average** €26-€31. **Credit** AmEx, DC, MC, V. **Map** p261 C3 ❶

First stop on the tourist trail but an undeniably fine hostelry with a few outside tables amid plants and flowers, La Buca serves traditional Lucchese food – its mushroom dishes are superb – with the occasional innovative touch. You'll need to reserve in advance, but if it's fully booked, try sister restaurant Il Giglio (0583 494058) on piazza Napoleone.

Da Guido

Via Cesare Battisti 28 (0583 467219). **Open** noon-2.30pm, 7-10.30pm Mon-Sat. Closed 3wks Jan. **Average** €15. **Credit** AmEx, MC, V. **Map** p261 B3 ❷

Don't be put off by the appearance of this *trattoria*: at first glance it looks a bit down-at-heel, but step inside and you're treated to excellent home cooking from the friendly Guido and family. Rich, thick *zuppa di farro* is almost a meal in itself, while the choice of mains features roast meats, pastas and salads. Desserts are own-made and might include *crostate della casa* (jam tarts) or panna cotta.

Da Leo

Via Tegrimi 1 (0583 492236/www.trattoriadaleo.it). **Open** noon-2.30pm, 7.30-10.30pm daily. **Average** €20. **No credit cards**. **Map** p261 B3 ❸

The waiters sing and local families compete to be heard over the din of children, yet despite all this noise and bustle, Da Leo is one of Lucca's mellowest restaurants. You won't be hurried through your meal, which will inevitably be made up of hearty country dishes like roast chicken, grilled steak, *spaghetti alle vongole* and *pappardelle broccoli e salsiccia*. Remember to bring cash, though: in true country fashion, credit cards are not accepted.

Locanda di Bacco

Via San Giorgio 36 (0583 493136). **Open** 12.30-2.30pm, 7.30-10.30pm Mon, Wed-Sun. Closed 2wks Feb & 2wks Nov. **Average** €23. **Credit** MC, V. **Map** p261 B3 ❹

This spacious, stylish but friendly restaurant is a relative newcomer to the local restaurant scene, but already a hit with both locals and tourists. The wine list is extensive and includes a number of relatively rare northern Tuscan varieties. The starters include *crostini* with melted gorgonzola and honey; pasta dishes include *pappardelle al cinghiale* (with wild boar); and the desserts are irresistible. *Photo p268.*

Locanda Buatino

Borgo Giannotti 508, nr piazzale Martiri della Libertà (0583 343207). **Open** noon-2pm, 7.30-10pm Mon-Sat. Closed 2wks Aug. **Average** €20. **Credit** AmEx, MC, V.

Locanda Buatino is a gem in a busy street leading from the city walls. From the outside it looks little more than a bar, and the feel is low-key, with small wooden tables, strings of garlic and rustic paintings. But the food is terrific, perhaps the best in Lucca. On Mondays from October to May, it's jazz night (€25 including a meal with wine). Upstairs are basic rooms for €40 with shared bathrooms.

La Mora

Località Ponte a Moriano, via Sesto di Moriano 1748, Sesto di Moriano (0583 406402/www.ristorantelamora.it). **Open** noon-2.30pm, 7.30-10.30pm Mon, Tue, Thur-Sun. Closed 1st 2wks Jan & last 2wks June. **Average** €35. **Credit** AmEx, DC, MC, V.

Culinary heavyweight Sauro Brunicardi has turned this old post-house 10km (6 miles) north of Lucca into a regionally renowned *osteria* where you can eat outside in refined surroundings. Try *tagliolini all'anguilla* (with eel sauce), *piccione* (pigeon) and tip-top desserts. La Mora also has a good list of wines from the nearby Lucchese hills (look for '*colle lucchese*'), some of which, along with the olive oils, come from the proprietor's own estate.

Casa Natale di Giacomo Puccini. *See p264.*

Locanda di Bacco. See p267.

Ristorante Puccini

Corte San Lorenzo 1-2, off piazza Cittadella (0583 316116/www.ristorantepuccini.com). **Open** 12.30-2.30pm, 7.30-10.30pm Mon, Thur-Sun; 7.30-10.30pm Wed. Closed Dec-Feb. **Average** €35. **Credit** AmEx, MC, V.

Housed in a 15th-century palazzo with a quiet courtyard and secluded terrace, Puccini is widely regarded as Lucca's best fish restaurant. Prices aren't cheap – even a rocket and parmesan salad will set you back €10 – and the tasting menus (€40 for meat, €45 for fish) is the best bet. Alternatively, in summer you can order a dish at a time for €8.

Vineria I Santi

Via dell'Anfiteatro 29A (0583 496124). **Open** 11am-3pm, 7pm-1.30am Mon, Tue, Thur, Fri, Sun; 11am-3pm, 7pm-2am Sat. **Average** €20. **Credit** AmEx, MC, V. **Map** p261 B4 ❺

This superb little *vineria* oozes style – from its modern rustic furniture and delicate light fittings to the discreet wine paraphernalia dotted around its walls. Dishes are short in number but high in imagination; the likes of smoked sea bass with marinated fennel, orange and pine nuts, but simpler dishes (tomato and mozzarella lasagne) also get a look-in.

Cafés & gelaterie

Ice-cream parlours, cafés and pretty cake shops abound in Lucca. These are our favourites.

Caffè di Simo

Via Fillungo 58 (0583 496234). **Open** *Bar* 9am-7.30pm Tue-Sun. *Restaurant* 12.30-2.30pm Mon, Tue, Thur-Sun. Summer also 7-10pm Thur-Sat. **Average** €18. **Credit** DC, MC, V. **Map** p261 B3 ❶

Lucca's most celebrated belle époque café-*pasticceria* is surprisingly unsnobby: workmen mix amiably with upmarket tourists and civil servants. It's still mainly about pastries, ice-creams and posh chocolates, but more substantial dishes include the ubiquitous *zuppa di farro* and other regional fare.

Casali

Piazza San Michele 40 (0583 492687). **Open** *Apr-Oct* 7.30am-11.30pm daily. *Nov-Mar* 7am-8.30pm Mon, Tue, Thur-Sun. Closed 20 Jan-6 Feb. **Credit** MC, V. **Map** p261 C3 ❷

Casali's outside tables are the perfect spot for people watching with an ice-cream or an aperitif in hand.

Gelateria Veneta

Chiasso Barletti 23 (0583 493727). **Open** *Winter* 11am-8pm Mon, Wed-Sun. *Summer* 11am-midnight daily. Closed early Jan-mid Feb. **No credit cards. Map** p261 C3 ❸

Heavenly ice-creams are sold at this venerated *gelateria*. There are some good pavement tables for those who don't want to walk and lick.

Other locations Via Vittorio Veneto 74 (0583 467037).

Girovita

Piazza Antelminelli 2 (0583 469412). **Open** 8am-1am Tue-Fri, Sun; 8am-2am Sat. **Credit** AmEx, DC, MC, V. **Map** p261 C4 ❹

Directly opposite the cathedral, the terrace of this stylish café-bar is the perfect spot for a morning coffee and pastry or, come cocktail hour, a sundowner accompanied by a great spread of free nibbles.

Where to stay

Lucca is not really known for its abundance of accommodation – and there are no signs that this is going to change. The Lucchesi have no intention of overcrowding their civilised environs with tourists. That said, there are a number of B&Bs and a handful of decent hotels cropping up around town. It's always best to book ahead if possible, however. **Locanda Buatino** (*see p267*) also offers basic rooms.

Affittacamere San Frediano

Via degli Angeli 19 (0583 469630/www.sanfrediano.com). **Rates** €55-€70. **Credit** AmEx, DC, MC, V. **Map** p261 B3 ❶

A friendly, well-located B&B with cosy rooms featuring iron bedsteads and satellite TV. The top floor, which dates back to the 16th century, was recently turned into a lounge for guests.

Alla Corte degli Angeli

Via degli Angeli 23 (0583 469204/www.allacortedegliangeli.com). **Rates** €175. **Credit** AmEx, DC, MC, V. **Map** p261 B3 ❷

This place is a few notches up from Affitacamere San Frediano just two doors down (*see p268*), and is thus pricier as a result. The rooms are named after flowers and decorated to the highest quality, with bold colours, fine antiques and period furniture, and all come with their own minibars and luxurious whirlpool baths as standard.

La Bohème

Via del Moro 2 (0583 462404/www.boheme.it). **Rates** €90-€120; extra person €25. **Credit** MC, V. **Map** p261 B3 ❸

A nicely decorated B&B in the heart of town, La Bohème is a stylish choice if you're thinking of stopping in town, with richly coloured walls, dark wood furniture, chandeliers and a bright, airy breakfast room. Recommended. Cash payers with this guide get a 5% discount.

Locanda L'Elisa

Via Nuova per Pisa 1952, Massa Pisana (0583 379737/www.locandalelisa.com). **Rates** €210-€260. **Credit** AmEx, DC, MC, V.

In a league of its own, this elegant four-star hotel 4km (2 miles) south of Lucca is one of the area's best. The villa's current appearance dates back to 1805, when Napoleon's sister and Lucca's ruler, Elisa Baciocchi, had the interiors and gardens refashioned. Highlights include a restaurant modelled after an English conservatory, 18th-century furnishings, revamped gardens and a large swimming pool.

La Luna

Corte Compagni 12, off via Fillungo (0583 493634). Closed early Jan-early Feb. **Rates** €112. **Credit** AmEx, DC, MC, V. **Map** p261 B4 ❹

La Luna is well priced, given its location at the upper end of busy via Fillungo. Rooms, housed in two 17th-century *palazzi* facing each other across a courtyard, are comfortable (if plain), with the usual mod cons.

Piccolo Hotel Puccini

Via di Poggio 9 (0583 55421/www.hotelpuccini.com). **Rates** €85. **Credit** AmEx, MC, V. **Map** p261 C3 ❺

Just a baton's throw from Puccini's boyhood home, this discreet hotel is excellent value for money. The vibe is friendly and the staff speak good English.

San Martino

Via della Dogana 9 (0583 469181/www.albergo sanmartino.it). **Rates** €50-€160. **Credit** AmEx, DC, MC, V. **Map** p261 D3 ❻

This very friendly 16th-century hotel is centrally located yet far enough away from the main drag to be relaxing. Breakfast can be taken in the elegant courtyard and the two suites are perfect for families.

Universo

Piazza del Giglio 1 (0583 493678/www.universo lucca.com). **Rates** €170. **Credit** AmEx, DC, MC, V. **Map** p261 C3 ❼

Right beside the elegant piazza Napoleone, the Universo is the faded old queen of Lucca's hotels. Rooms have recently been given a facelift, but vary hugely in size and decor. The nicest (and priciest) are almost hip, with wooden beams, blonde wood, cream furnishings and rainfall showers.

Resources

Hospital

Campo di Marte hospital *Via dell'Ospedale (0583 9701).*

Police station

Viale Cavour 38, nr train station (0583 455487).

Post office

Via Vallisneri 2, nr Duomo (0583 43351).

Tourist information

Comune di Lucca Tourist Office *Piazzale Giuseppe Verdi, nr Vecchia Porta San Donato (0583 442944).* **Open** 9.30am-5.30pm daily. **Map** p261 B2.

Other locations Piazza Santa Maria, viale Luporini, Porta Elisa and inside Palazzo Ducale.

Getting there & around

By bike

Cycling is a nice way to get around the area, especially during warmer weather (but not too warm). There are several bike hire shops, with the largest concentration to be found in piazza Santa Maria; for daily or weekly rentals, try **Cicli Bizzarri** at no.32 (0583 496031) or **Poli Antonio** at no.42 (0583 493787, www.biciclettepoli.com).

By bus

The bus station is at piazzale Giuseppe Verdi. **CLAP** (0583 587897) operates buses to towns in Lucca Province. **LAZZI** runs buses to Florence, Pisa, Bagni di Lucca, Montecatini, La Spezia and Viareggio (0583 584876, www.lazzi.it). At least one bus an hour leaves Florence for Lucca (first 5.58am, last 8.15pm) and from Lucca to Florence (first 6.10am, last 7.45pm). The journey takes around 1hr 15mins.

By car

For car hire try **Europcar** (via Dante Alighieri 214, 0583 464590), **Hertz** (via Catalani 59, 0583 418058) or **Nolo Auto Pittore** (piazza Santa Maria 34, 0583 467960). Within the city walls parking is expensive, except for hotel guests, but there's a spacious free car park just outside the walls past Porta San Donato.

By taxi

There are radio taxi ranks at piazza Napoleone (0583 492691), the train station (0583 494989), piazza Verdi (0583 581305), piazza Santa Maria (0583 494190) and the hospital (0583 950623).

By train

Lucca's train station is at piazza Ricasoli, two minutes' walk from the southern gate, Porta San Pietro. Trains from Florence to Viareggio stop at Lucca (as well as Prato and Pistoia). The trip from Florence takes about 1hr 20mins, with trains leaving almost every hour from early until 10pm. For train information call 892021 or visit www.trenitalia.com.

Massa-Carrara & Lucca Provinces

Rivers deep, mountains high.

Embracing cool, sparsely populated, alpine landscapes and a sunburnt coast that's a summer magnet for hedonists and families alike, north-west Tuscany is little visited by foreign tourists. Though it holds few of the great Renaissance treasures of the region's celebrated cities, it was here that Michelangelo and his contemporaries came for their marble, and the massive quarries that surround **Carrara** remain a staggering sight. Those seeking peace and tranquillity should head for the **Alpi Apuane**, which divides into two regions: the Garfagnana, on the banks of the River Serchio, which links the Alps to the Apennine spine of central Italy; and the Lunigiana, dominated by huge pine forests. It's all a long way from the clichés of Chianti and olive oil; here, you're more likely to find chestnuts and lard on the menu, and these staples of the local cuisine are considered by many to be the best in Tuscany.

Running parallel to the heavy industry inland, the **Versilia Riviera** welcomes sun worshippers from the Ligurian border to Viareggio. The **Garfagnana** is a walkers' paradise of snowy peaks and river valleys. The **Lunigiana** is Tuscany's least-explored region, particularly the Cisa pass and the area surrounding Pontremoli and Aulla.

The Versilia Riviera

Viareggio

The main attractions of this seaside town are its beach and its palm-lined promenade. On hot summer nights Florence's clubbers trek here for the mega-clubs between Viareggio and the swanky resort town of **Forte dei Marmi**, ten kilometres (six miles) up the road. By day, the

Pietrasanta.

stabilimenti balneari (bathing establishments) are full of tourists topping up tans. One of Europe's first *stabilimenti*, the **Balena**, was founded in 1827. Long since modernised to include the B2K complex (www.balena2000.net), it offers five pools plus classes and treatments.

The 130-year-old **Carnevale**, held around February, is one of Italy's wildest (*see p174*). Head to the **Cittadella del Carnevale**, in the north of town on via Santa Maria Goretti (take the exit marked Viareggio Nord).

Some six kilometres (four miles) south of town is the reed-fringed **Lago di Massaciuccoli**. On its shore is the town of **Torre del Lago Puccini**, where Italy's last truly great composer spent his summers. His villa is open to visitors (0584 341445, closed Mon, admission €7). During July and August the town hosts a Puccini festival (*see p189* **Seasonal settings**). For the area's lively gay scene, *see p185* **Torre adore**.

Nightlife

Il Giardino (via IV Novembre 10, Forte dei Marmi, 0584 81462, closed Tue except July & Aug) is a good, though not cheap, spot for pre-club drinks. It's popular with twentysomething *figli di papa* (rich kids driving daddy's car), and is a good introduction to the painful snobbery of the Tuscan club scene. Slick club **Twiga** (viale Roma 2, Marina di Pietrasanta, 0584 21518, www.twigaclub.it, closed Oct, Nov & Mon-Thur & Sun Dec-June) is recognisable by its distinctive giraffe logo. **Seven Apples** (viale Roma 109, Marina di Pietrasanta, 0584 20458, www.sevenapples.it) draws a trendy crowd to its beachside bar with a pool and two dancefloors. Otherwise, **La Capannina** (viale Franceschi, Forte dei Marmi, 0584 80169, www.lacapanninadifranceschi.it), Versilia's oldest club, has two dancefloors that are packed all summer. **La Canniccia** (via Unità d'Italia 1, Marina di Pietrasanta, 0584 745685) has a huge garden, a lake and a dancefloor.

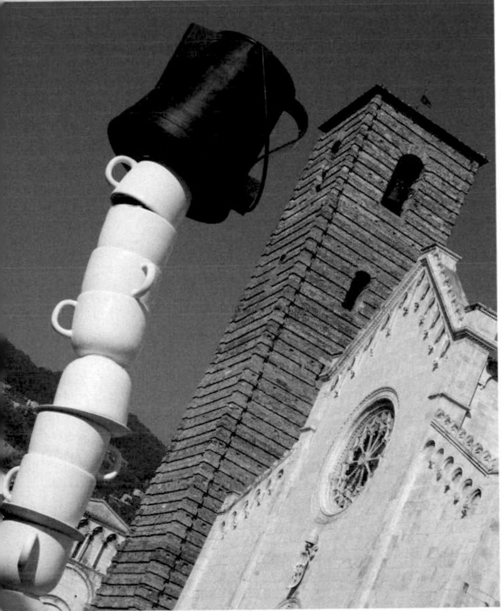

Where to stay & eat

Although Viareggio has more than 100 hotels, rooms can be hard to find in high season. Try via Vespucci, via Leonardo da Vinci and via IV Novembre, which run from the station down to the sea. Stand-outs include the newly renovated **Principe di Piemonte** (piazza G Puccini 1, 0584 4011, www.principedipiemonte.com, €250-€340), a glorious Liberty-style palazzo, and the swish **Hotel Plaza et de Russie** (piazza d'Azeglio 1, 0584 44449, www.plaza etderussie.com, €141-€272), which offers *fin-de-siècle* luxury in a 19th-century building.

On the other side of the marina, affordable fish restaurants such as **La Darsena** (via Virgilio 150, 0584 392785, closed Sun & late Dec-early Jan, average €35) attract locals to the backstreets behind the boatyards, while further south are the *stabilimenti* and modern bars and restaurants of viale Europa. Perhaps the best restaurant in Viareggio is **Romano** (via Mazzini 122, 0584 31382, closed Mon, average €50), though some consider it a bit passé. Another contender for the top spot is **Da Lorenzo** in Forte dei Marmi (via Carducci 61-63, 0584 89671, closed Mon, average €85), a superb restaurant with an emphasis on seafood.

Pietrasanta

Carrara is home to the raw material, but Pietrasanta (literally, 'holy stone') is where artists transform the famous marble. Wandering through this relaxed little town, you'll see modern-day Michelangelos with newspaper hats (which absorb sweat but filter marble dust) sculpting from marble, bronze and clay. Check out the two busy studios side by side on via Sant'Agostino (nos.51 & 53). Small groups wanting in-depth tours of the town's various studios and foundries or the nearby marble quarries should contact Barbara Paci (339 7780379 mobile, barbarapaci@inwind.it).

In summer, **piazza del Duomo** becomes an open-air exhibition space for artists against the splendid backdrop of the 13th-century cathedral and the citadel up the hill, **Rocca Arrighina**.

Where to stay & eat

Pietrasanta's accommodation options are fairly limited. The sumptuous 17th-century style of **Albergo Pietrasanta** (via Garibaldi 35, 0584 793726, www.albergopietrasanta.com, €220-€320) caters to the town's grander visitors, leaving two others – **Hotel Palagi** (piazza Carducci 23, 0584 70249, www.hotelpalagi.com, €150) and **Hotel Stipino** (via Provinciale 50, 0584 71448, www.hotelstipino.com, €62-€75) – to mop up the rest.

Of the bars and restaurants dotted among the modern art galleries and clothes shops, **Pizzeria Betty** (piazza del Duomo 32-33, 0584 71247, closed Mon, average €15) offers good-value food in cool surroundings, while **Enoteca Marcucci** (via Garibaldi 40, 0584 791962, closed all day Mon, lunch Tue-Sun & all Nov, average €35) manages to be both trendy and warmly welcoming, serving interesting food accompanied by an excellent array of wines.

Massa & Carrara

Set between the sea and the Apuan Alps, these twin cities are barely distinguishable from the dreary mesh of industry and traffic that congests the area. **Massa** is of little interest except for its two superb restaurants. **Trattoria Astolfo** (via Beatrice 58, 0585 44844, closed Sun, €20) is in the centre of town and serves *baccalà* marinaded in herbs, a divine spaghetti in pesto, and chestnut soup. Further out, in the direction of Forno, is **Trattoria Paradiso** (località Forno, via Giugno 13, 0585 315331, closed Mon, average €18), noted for its tortelli with herbs and fried rabbit.

Carrara, however, is fascinating. The steep ridges of the mountains flanking the town glow brilliant white with the world's largest concentration of pure marble. The ancient Romans built most of their imperial city with it, while Michelangelo considered Carrara's marble the purest and whitest in the world: it reflects light off its thinnest outer layer, giving the stone a translucent, wax-like lustre. Carrara mines less marble these days, but about 1.5 million tonnes are still extracted from the nearby hills each year.

If you want to visit the quarries, take the striking scenic route marked *strada panoramica* towards **Colonnata**, where every second house seems to make or sell the absolutely delicious but coronary clogging *lardo di Colonnata*. If you're peckish, try a meal at the **Locanda Apuana** (via Comunale 1, 0585 768017, closed Sun dinner & Mon, average €30), about seven kilometres (four miles) from town, which has been selling local produce since the 16th century, and where the owners cure their own lardo and make delicious *tordelli* (meat- and vegetable-stuffed ravioli). Around three kilometres (two miles) out of town, near the football stadium, is the **Museo Civico del Marmo** (viale XX Settembre 85, 0585 845746, closed Sun, admission €4.50), which documents marble history and production.

In Carrara itself, **piazza Alberica** is the most attractive square, lined with pastel-coloured buildings. Off the north-east end of the piazza, via Ghibellina opens up to reveal a seductive view of the 11th-century **Duomo** with its Pisan façade and 14th-century rose window carved from a single slab of marble.

Where to eat

For restaurants in Massa, *see above*. In Carrara, the retro **Caffeteria Leon d'Oro** (piazza Alberica 8, no phone, closed Sun) is a pleasant spot for a drink. The tiny **Enoteca Ninan** (via Bartolini 3, 0585 74741, closed lunch Mon, average €45) serves good food – its steaks are great – and wine.

Resources

Tourist information

Agenzia per il Turismo APT *Viale Carducci 10, Viareggio (0584 962233/www.versilia.turismo.toscana.it).* **Open** *Summer* 9am-2pm, 3-7.30pm Mon-Sat. *Winter* 9am-1pm, 3-6pm Mon-Sat (also Sun afternoons during Carnevale).

Getting there

By bus

CLAP buses (0584 30996, www.clapspa.it) service Viareggio and link the city several times a day with Pietrasanta and Lucca. **LAZZI** buses (0584 46234, www.lazzi.it) also make the longer journey between Viareggio and Florence (journey time 2hrs).

By car

Both the main A12 coastal *autostrada* and via Aurelia (SS1, very busy in summer) run through the entire Versilia area. Viareggio, Pietrasanta and Carrara are all accessible via the *autostrada*. Another *autostrada* (A11) in turn links Versilia with Lucca (about 45mins) and other cities inland.

By train

Viareggio is linked to Florence (2hrs) by regular trains on the Lucca (20mins) line. Trains between Pisa and Genoa also pass through the Versilia area, stopping at Viareggio (20mins from Pisa), Pietrasanta (35mins) and Carrara-Avenza (a bus ride from Carrara, 50mins from Pisa). For information, call 892021 or go to www.trenitalia.it.

The Garfagnana

Bagni di Lucca

A mood of faded gentility haunts this charming little spa village. Its renowned saline and sulphurous thermal waters have attracted many famous names over the decades, from the artistic elite (Shelley, Byron, Puccini) to Elisa Bonaparte Baciocchi (Napoleon's sister), whose summer home is now the Hotel Roma; *see below*.

For healthier indulgences, visit the **Terme Jean Varraud** (piazza San Martino 11, 0583 87221, www.termebagnidilucca.it), which offers a range of services, including mud treatments and hydro-massage. But don't go expecting 21st-century gloss: facilities are rather archaic.

On the SS12 from Lucca, six kilometres (four miles) south of Bagni, is a striking sight: the arched spine of the **ponte della Maddalena**. Nicknamed the Devil's Bridge, it was built in the 11th century by, they say, Beelzebub himself, in return for the soul of the first person who crossed it. The locals decided to send a dog.

Where to stay & eat

For central accommodation, try the beguiling **Hotel Roma** (via Umberto I 110, 0583 87278, closed mid Oct-Mar, €35-€45), where the surprisingly cheap, elegant rooms have parquet flooring and splendid antique furniture. For good eating there's **Circolo dei Forestieri** (piazza Varraud 10, 0583 86038, closed Mon & Tue lunch & Nov-Jan, average €25) or **Ristorante Antico Caffè del Sonno** (viale Umberto I, 146-148, 0583 805080, closed Thur and 4wks Jan or Feb, average €20).

Barga

With its well-preserved medieval streets and alleyways threading through the city and up to the 11th-century **Duomo**, Barga is as picturesque as they come. The cathedral's most striking feature is its pulpit, carved by Como sculptor Guido Bigarelli in the 13th century. But there's much more to this town than its history: Barga is a hotbed of culture. Its attractions during summer include **Barga Jazz** (via del Pretorio 23, www.bargajazz.com, admission €10) and an opera festival (*see p189* **Seasonal settings**). For more information, visit www.barganews.com.

Where to stay & eat

Caffè Capretz (piazza Salvo Salvi 1, 0583 723001, closed Mon and 2wks Nov) was founded in 1870; its outdoor tables are set under a wood-beamed loggia. Otherwise, there's **Alpino** (via Pascoli 41, 0583 723336, closed Mon in winter, Nov, average €18), where the Castelvecchi family serve up superb local fare (like the memorable crêpe of ricotta and honey).

Accommodation options vary; one of the best is the **Hotel Villa Libano** (via del Sasso 6, no phone, www.hotelvillalibano.com, €52), an 18th-century building with a lovely garden.

Ham it up at **Il Vecchio Mulino**. *See p274.*

Grotta del Vento

Seven kilometres (four miles) of hairpin bends from L'Eremo di Calomini lead to the semi-abandoned town of **Fornovolasco** and Tuscany's geological wonder, the **Grotta del Vento** or 'wind cave' (0583 722024, www.grottadelvento.com, admission €7.50-€17), packed with stalactites, stalagmites and underground lakes. The cold air that blows from the cave's entrance gave it its name and a practical purpose: it was used as a refrigerator until the 17th century. It wasn't until 1898, when bullies forced a little girl to go in and she came back out describing the wonders inside, that scientists became aware of its existence. There are one-, two- and three-hour tours.

Castelnuovo di Garfagnana

Garfagnana's capital makes a decent base from which to explore the area. Encased by ancient walls and dominated by a 13th-century castle, its historic centre is a lovely place to refuel.

For daytime and early-evening snacks **Il Vecchio Mulino** (via Vittorio Emanuele 12, 0583 62192, closed Mon, average €20, *photo p273*) is a characterful wine bar with top-notch salamis, cured meats and cheeses. For rooms try **Hotel-Ristorante Ludovico Ariosto** (via Francesco Azzi 28, 0583 62369, www.hotelludovicoariosto.com, €65-€72). **La Bottega del Fattore** (via Francesco Azzi 1a, 0583 62179, closed Mon) is a must for oenophiles, with a huge choice of regional and national wines by the glass and bottle. The best restaurant is probably **Da Carlino** (via Garibaldi 15, 0583 644270, closed Mon, average €18), offering chestnuts and porcini in season.

Parco Orecchiella

The **Parco Orecchiella** (0583 619098/65169, closed Nov-Easter, museum €1.50) may well be the loveliest part of the Apuan Alps. Abundant rain gives the area lush forests and meadows, and wildlife includes deer, boar, goats, predatory Apennine wolves and more than 130 species of bird, including the eagles that are Orecchiella's symbol. Hiking and biking paths of varying difficulty criss-cross the park.

The Lunigiana

Fosdinovo

For more than ten centuries, from prehistory and the Romans to the heyday of the traffic-heavy via Francigena trade route, the region was of utmost significance. And with prime location comes fortification. Lunigiana is dotted with scores of castles and towers, of which the **Castello Malaspina** (information 0187 688911, closed Tue, admission €5) in the idyllic feudal town of **Fosdinovo** is a prime example. There are five daily tours of the castle for a minimum of six people or you can simply wander through the pretty sloping streets that

Pontremoli is a popular stop off for cyclists crossing the border with Emilia-Romagna.

surround it and take in some breathtaking views of mountains and sea. Fosdinovo was built by local warlords the Malaspinas; some of their descendants still live here 800 years later. For eating, try **Il Cucco** (via Cucco 26, 0187 68907, closed Thur, average €15), which offers very basic but delicious Lunigiana cuisine. The gnocchi are superb.

Fivizzano

Even if it didn't boast gorgeous views and a sleepy pace of life, Fivizzano would be worth a visit just to spend a night in the family-run **Hotel Il Giardinetto** (via Roma 151, 0585 92060, closed Mon, €50). Elegant rooms creaking with antiques attract a similarly old-world clientele, while some seriously tasty Tuscan cooking is offered in the restaurant (closed Mon Nov-June & all Oct, average €20).

Just around the corner is **piazza Medicea** (also called piazza Vittorio Emanuele), where the main fountain sports four marble dolphins – a gift from Cosimo III in 1683, when the town served as the Medici government's Lunigiana capital. The bell tower belonging to the church of **San Jacopo e San Antonio** bristles with a Heath Robinson-style collection of giant cogs. On the perimeters of the piazza is **Caffè Elvetico** (0585 926657, closed Sun in winter).

North-east of town on the SS63, the **Castello della Verrucola** was also built by the Malaspinas, who controlled the area from here all the way to Carrara. About 15 kilometres (ten miles) out of town in the direction of Germalla lies one of the gems of Tuscan cuisine: **Al Vecchio Tino** (località Germalla 1, 0585 97733, closed Wed, average €25) is justly famous for its lard and rosemary gnocchi.

Pontremoli

Pontremoli (literally, 'trembling bridge') is the Lunigiana's biggest town, though only 11,000 people live here. Its wealth grew from its position as an important station on the via Francigena trade route and the Cisa pass. These days the route is more likely to be clogged with packs of ambitious cyclists.

Looking down over the pretty arched streets of Pontremoli's old town is the **Castello del Piagnaro**. It houses the **Museo delle Statue Stelle** (Castello di Piagnaro, 0187 831439, closed Mon in winter, admission €3.50), home to 19 prehistoric statues discovered in the area.

In the town itself, the **Duomo Santa Maria del Popolo** (piazza del Duomo) was designed in 1633 by the Cremonese architect Alessandro Capra. Finished in 1687, it's of interest for its aisleless nave and short transept, but most of all for its notably high, luminous dome. Also worth a look is the 14th-century **Torre del Campanone**, with its beautiful little park and picnic area by the burbling Magra river.

Where to stay & eat

There are plenty of restaurants and *trattorie* in Pontremoli, but one of the very best is the characterful **Da Bussé** (piazza del Duomo 31, 0187 831371, closed dinner Mon-Thur, all day Fri and 3wks July, average €27), a wonderfully old-fashioned place that makes fabulous *testaroli* (a pancake smothered in tangy pesto). **Il Caveau del Teatro** (piazza Santa Cristina, 0187 833328, www.caveaudelteatro.it, average €38) is an altogether more upmarket – but no less charming – option, where you can eat creative local dishes and drink fine wines from all over Italy. There are also seven delightful rooms (doubles €100) furnished with antiques.

Resources

Tourist information

Centro Visite Parco Alpi Apuane & Centro di Coordinamento del Turismo Rurale *Piazza delle Erbe 1, Castelnuovo di Garfagnana (0583 65169/ garfagnana@tin.it).* **Open** *June-Sept* 9am-1pm, 3-7pm daily. *Oct-May* 9am-1pm, 3.30-5.30pm daily.
The English-speaking staff have information on both the Garfagnana and the Lunigiana, including *agriturismo* accommodation, walking routes and sporting activities in the Apuan Alps.

Getting there

By bus

CLAP (0583 587897, www.clapspa.it) operates buses to Barga and Castelnuovo di Garfagnana from Lucca. **LAZZI** (0583 584876, www.lazzi.it) runs several buses a day from Lucca to Bagni di Lucca. Neither company runs services to the Lunigiana.

By car

Take the SS12 north out of Lucca; it follows the Serchio river valley and branches off towards Bagni di Lucca. At the same intersection you can take the winding hill road (SS445) towards Barga and Castelnuovo di Garfagnana. This is the main route through the Garfagnana region and smaller roads fan off from it towards highlights such as the Grotta del Vento (turn off near Barga to the south) and the Parco Orecchiella. It also leads, eventually, to the SS63 (and then the SS62), which goes through the Lunigiana region to the far north.

By train

An irregular but very scenic rail service (892021, www.trenitalia.it) goes through this area between Lucca and Aulla in the north, with stops at Bagni di Lucca (30mins), Castelnuovo di Garfagnana (60mins) and piazza al Serchio (75mins).

Arezzo

It's not just the men in tights that give this city a good name.

Medieval horseplay at the **Giostra del Saracino**.

Arezzo is now bearing the fruit of its hard work over the last few years, having recreated itself from a gold-orientated semi-backwater to a modern, welcoming tourist destination. Fortunately, not too many people have discovered this yet, so it's the ideal time to explore this town of art, antiques and… OK, the gold is still a big draw.

A decade or so ago, the Aretini (as the locals are known) were too busy manufacturing gold jewellery – which had turned a generation of peasants into millionaires – to devote much attention to their city. They kept to their factories in the suburbs, accruing great wealth and occasionally going out for a spin in their Ferraris. Little wonder, then, that tourists beat a retreat after admiring the frescoes. Happily, a lot has changed in a short time. Just as the city's gold and textile industries face leaner years (though they're undeniably still big businesses), a younger generation has decided to employ its own entrepreneurial acumen outside the confines of the factories. As a result, there's a real buzz about the place.

The annual local music festival Arezzo Wave, started in 1987, was becoming a highly popular, energetic affair – but, in 2007, the organisers moved the location of the festival to Sesto Fiorentino, in Florence Province, and renamed it Italia Wave, leaving Arezzo without one of its most forward-looking events. The excellent backward-looking ones make up for this loss, however, principally the **Giostra del Saracino** (*see p172*), a heady riot of medieval pageants, straight-faced tight-wearing and jousting. Besides this explosion of excitement, Arezzo's main pleasures are to be found in the town's shopping and in its artistic heritage. It's an essential stop on any Piero della Francesca trail, housing his *Legend of the True Cross* in the church of **San Francesco** (*see p279*), and a *Mary Magdalene* in the **Duomo** (*see p278*); anyone interested in Giorgio Vasari can visit the **Casa Vasari** (*see p279*) to get an insight into this prodigious artist.

SOME HISTORY

Strategically built at the intersection of four fertile valleys (the Casentino, Valdarno, Valtiberina and Valdichiana), Arezzo was a flourishing centre of Etruscan culture by the fourth century BC. It was later taken over by the Romans in their northward expansion, becoming a military stronghold and economic outpost. By 89 BC, its people were granted honorary Roman citizenship; an amphitheatre, an aqueduct and fortified walls followed.

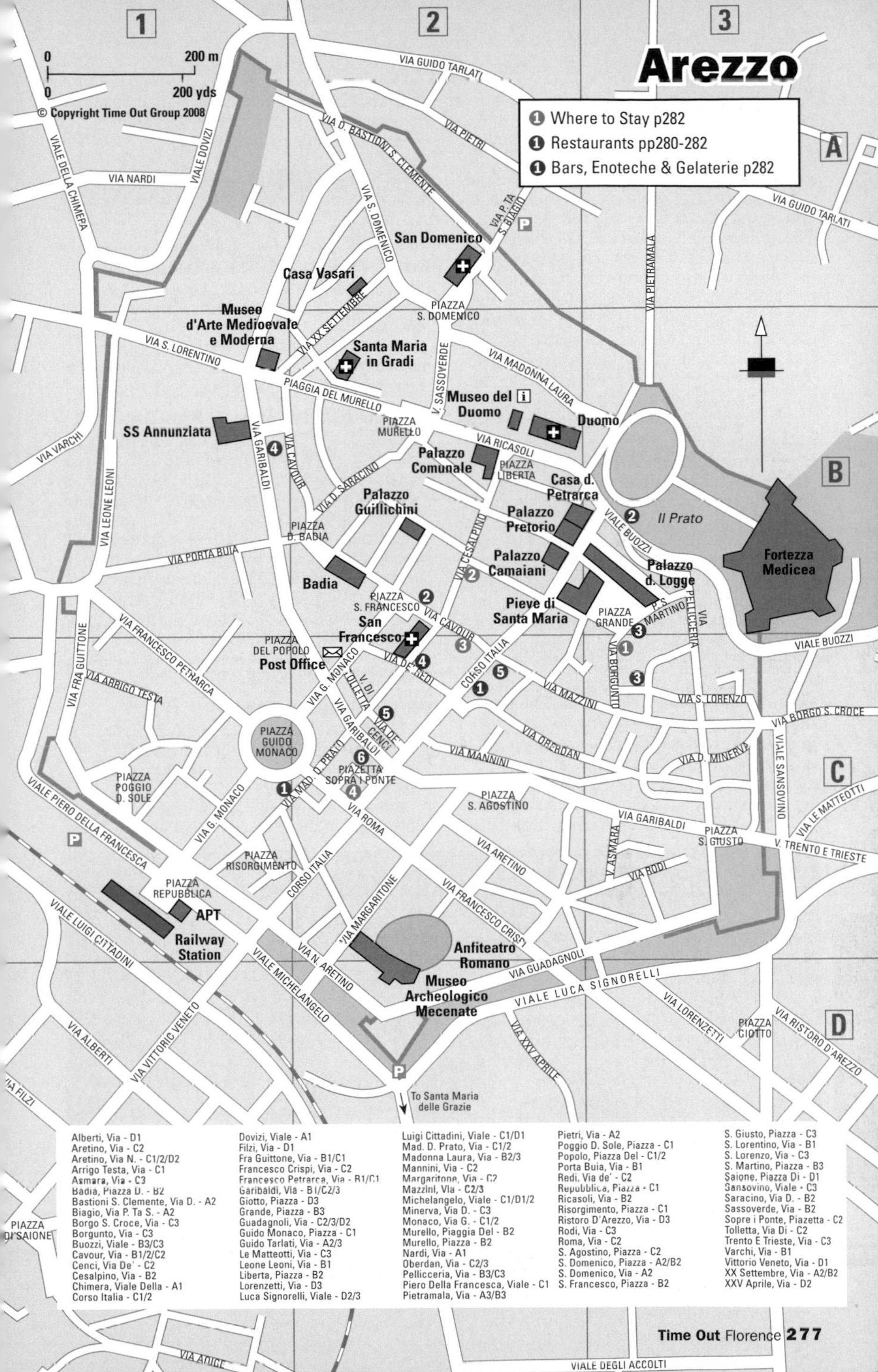
Arezzo
1
2
3
A
B
C
D
0
200 m
0
200 yds
© Copyright Time Out Group 2008
Where to Stay p282
Restaurants pp280-282
Bars, Enoteche & Gelaterie p282
San Domenico
Casa Vasari
Museo d'Arte Medioevale e Moderna
Santa Maria in Gradi
Museo del Duomo
Duomo
SS Annunziata
Palazzo Comunale
Casa d. Petrarca
Palazzo Pretorio
Palazzo Guillichini
Palazzo Camaiani
Palazzo d. Logge
Pieve di Santa Maria
Badia
San Francesco
Post Office
Il Prato
Fortezza Medicea
APT
Railway Station
Anfiteatro Romano
Museo Archeologico Mecenate
To Santa Maria delle Grazie
Piazza S. Domenico
Piazza Murello
Piazza Libertà
Piazza D. Badia
Piazza S. Francesco
Piazza del Popolo
Piazza Grande
Piazza Guido Monaco
Piazzetta Sopra i Ponte
Piazza Poggio D. Sole
Piazza S. Agostino
Piazza Risorgimento
Piazza Repubblica
Piazza S. Giusto
Piazza Giotto
Piazza di Saione
Via Guido Tarlati
Via D. Bastioni S. Clemente
Via Pietri
Via P. Ta S. Biagio
Via S. Domenico
Viale Dovizi
Via Nardi
Viale della Chimera
Via Pietramala
Via XX Settembre
Via S. Lorentino
Piaggia del Murello
V. Sassoverde
Via Madonna Laura
Via Ricasoli
Via Varchi
Via Leone Leoni
Via Garibaldi
Via Cavour
Via D. Saracino
Via Cesalpino
Viale Buozzi
Via Porta Buia
Via Pellicceria
P.S. Martino
Via Borgunto
Via Fra Guittone
Via Francesco Petrarca
Via Arrigo Testa
Via G. Monaco
Via de' Redi
V. di Tolletta
Via de' Cenci
Corso Italia
Via Mazzini
Via S. Lorenzo
Via Borgo S. Croce
Viale Sansovino
Via Oberdan
Via Mannini
Via D. Minerva
Via Mad. D. Prato
Via Roma
Viale Piero della Francesca
Via Garibaldi
Via Le Matteotti
V. Trento e Trieste
V. Asmara
Via Rodi
Via Aretino
Via Francesco Crispi
Via Margaritone
Viale Luigi Cittadini
Via N. Aretino
Viale Michelangelo
Via Guadagnoli
Viale Luca Signorelli
Via Lorenzetti
Via Ristoro d'Arezzo
Via XXV Aprile
Via Alberti
Via Vittorio Veneto
Via Filzi
Via Adige
Viale degli Accolti
Alberti, Via - D1
Aretino, Via - C2
Aretino, Via N. - C1/2/D2
Arrigo Testa, Via - C1
Asmara, Via - C3
Badia, Piazza D. - B2
Bastioni S. Clemente, Via D. - A2
Biagio, Via P. Ta S. - A2
Borgo S. Croce, Via - C3
Borgunto, Via - B3
Buozzi, Viale - B3/C3
Cavour, Via - B1/2/C2
Cenci, Via De' - C2
Cesalpino, Via - B2
Chimera, Viale Della - A1
Corso Italia - C1/2
Dovizi, Viale - A1
Filzi, Via - D1
Fra Guittone, Via - B1/C1
Francesco Crispi, Via - C2
Francesco Petrarca, Via - B1/C1
Garibaldi, Via - B1/C2/3
Giotto, Piazza - D3
Grande, Piazza - B3
Guadagnoli, Via - C2/3/D2
Guido Monaco, Piazza - C1
Guido Tarlati, Via - A2/3
Le Matteotti, Via - C3
Leone Leoni, Via - B1
Liberta, Piazza - B2
Lorenzetti, Via - D3
Luca Signorelli, Viale - D2/3
Luigi Cittadini, Viale - C1/D1
Mad. D. Prato, Via - C1/2
Madonna Laura, Via - B2/3
Mannini, Via - C2
Margaritone, Via - C2
Mazzini, Via - C2/3
Michelangelo, Viale - C1/D1/2
Minerva, Via D. - C3
Monaco, Via G. - C1/2
Murello, Piaggia Del - B2
Murello, Piazza - B2
Nardi, Via - A1
Oberdan, Via - C2/3
Pellicceria, Via - B3/C3
Piero Della Francesca, Viale - C1
Pietramala, Via - A3/B3
Pietri, Via - A2
Poggio D. Sole, Piazza - C1
Popolo, Piazza Del - C1/2
Porta Buia, Via - B1
Redi, Via de' - C2
Repubblica, Piazza - C1
Ricasoli, Via - B2
Risorgimento, Piazza - C1
Ristoro D'Arezzo, Via - D3
Rodi, Via - C3
Roma, Via - C2
S. Agostino, Piazza - C2
S. Domenico, Piazza - A2/B2
S. Domenico, Via - A2
S. Francesco, Piazza - B2
S. Giusto, Piazza - C3
S. Lorentino, Via - B1
S. Lorenzo, Via - C3
S. Martino, Piazza - B3
Saione, Piazza Di - D1
Sansovino, Viale - C3
Saracino, Via D. - B2
Sassoverde, Via - B2
Sopre i Ponte, Piazzetta - C2
Tolletta, Via Di - C2
Trento E Trieste, Via - C3
Varchi, Via - B1
Vittorio Veneto, Via - D1
XX Settembre, Via - A2/B2
XXV Aprile, Via - D2

A century later, Arezzo's first industry was born: embossed pottery, traded far and wide.

Following the decline of the Roman Empire, the city was overrun by Barbarians. The darkest days came under the Lombards in the sixth century. Yet, gradually, a feudal economic system began to pull the city from its slump. The turning point arrived in 1100, when the emerging merchant class started to question its subservience to Arezzo's clerical-feudal overlords. Secular power began to shift to the budding bourgeoisie, and, in 1192, the *commune* was established. There was extensive building and Arezzo began to take on its current urban contours. However, another foreign power, this time Florence, set its sights on the city. The two clashed in the Battle of Campaldino in 1289, from which Arezzo never fully recovered. The city eventually succumbed to Florence in 1384.

Luckily, political submission didn't equal artistic or cultural paralysis: Medici patronage in Florence provided wider scope for those with talent. Foremost among the creative spirits of the time was Giorgio Vasari (1511-74), a painter, architect and historian, whose *Lives of the Artists* has enlivened our perception of the Renaissance. However, the boost to local creativity didn't last: the city had become a conservative backwater by the 17th century. And so it remained, until recently, when the parochial outlook began to be supplanted by more progressive policies. Today, a younger, better-educated generation of entrepreneurs and local administrators seems set on increasing the city's appeal. To those ends, the city centre has been largely pedestrianised, and a new parking area just outside the walls on the north side, behind the church of San Domenico, makes access to the city centre far easier and more attractive.

Sights

Churches

Badia di Santi Fiora e Lucilla

Piazza di Badia (0575 356612). **Open** 8am-12pm, 4-7pm Mon-Sat; 7am-12.30pm Sun. **Admission** free. **Map** p277 B2.

As well as a giant *Crucifixion* by de Segna and a marble-effect altar by Vasari, Arezzo's Badia boasts an ingenious illusory drawn dome by Andrea Pozzo.

Duomo (Cattedrale di San Donato)

Piazza del Duomo (0575 23991). **Open** 7am-12.30pm, 3-7pm daily. **Admission** free. **Map** p277 B2.

Construction on Arezzo's Gothic Duomo began in 1277, but the finishing touches weren't made until the early 1500s, and it was a further 300 years before its campanile was erected. The overall effect of its size and the vertical thrust of its ogival vaulted ceilings are inspiring, as are the exquisite stained-glass windows (c1515-20) by Guillaume di Marcillat. But the Duomo's real attractions are along the left aisle: Piero della Francesca's *Mary Magdalene* (c1465), and the Cappella della Madonna del Conforto, screened off from the rest of the church.

Pieve di Santa Maria

Corso Italia (0575 22629/www.santamariadella pieve.it). **Open** *Oct-Apr* 8am-1pm, 3-6pm daily. *May-Sept* 8am-1pm, 3-7pm daily. **Admission** free. **Map** p277 B2.

A striking example of Romanesque architecture built mostly in the 12th and 13th centuries. Santa

The **Legend of the True Cross**. *See p276.*

Tuscany

Maria's pale stone façade is harmonious, with five arcades surmounted by three increasingly busy orders of *logge*. The ornate columns holding them up, all 68 of which have an eccentric motif, reach a climax in the bell tower *delle cento buche* (of the 100 holes). As you enter, look above the doorway: the colour on the calendar statues beneath the arch has survived from the 13th century.

San Domenico

Piazza San Domenico 7 (0575 23255). **Open** 8.30am-1pm, 3.30-7pm daily. **Admission** free. **Map** p277 A2.

San Domenico was started by Dominicans in 1275, around the same time as their Franciscan brothers were getting under way with San Francesco (*see below*). Facing a simple, open square, it has an attractive quaintness about it that's accentuated by its uneven Gothic campanile, which comes complete with two 14th-century bells. Inside you'll find a magnificent crucifix by Cimabue.

San Francesco

Piazza San Francesco (0575 20630/3527270 to reserve tickets). **Open** 8.30am-7pm daily. **Admission** free. **Map** p277 C2.

The interior of San Francesco, begun by Franciscan friars in the 13th century, was adorned with frescoes, chapels and shrines during the 1500s, thanks to Arezzo's merchant class. By the 19th century, it was being used as a military barracks. Happily, however, *The Legend of the True Cross* (*see also p27*), Piero della Francesca's magnum opus, survived, and was unveiled in an opening ceremony in 2000 after a meticulous, decade-long restoration. Considered to be one of the most important fresco cycles ever produced, it was begun in 1453, the year Constantinople fell to the Ottoman Turks, and portrays the fear this induced in the Christian world. A separate ticket (€6) gains you an audio guide and access to the chapels (it's best to book in advance in high season), but note that some of the frescoes are too high to be properly appreciated by the naked eye: take a pair of binoculars if you can, and be prepared for some neck-craning.

Santa Maria delle Grazie

Via Santa Maria (0575 323140/www.abd.it/santa maria). **Open** 8am-7pm daily. **Admission** free.

On the site of an ancient sacred spring, the Fonte Tecta, as the religious complex built around Santa Maria delle Grazie is known, houses the Renaissance's first porticoed courtyard. Started in 1428, the religious buildings were imposed by San Bernardino of Siena on the recalcitrant Aretini, who proceeded to march from San Francesco, brandishing a wooden cross, to destroy the spring site, replacing it with a *Madonna della Misericordia* by local artist Parri di Spinello. The enlightened Antonio da Maiano, one of the Renaissance's foremost architects and the man who created the loggia, reconciled the church's late Gothic, essentially medieval design with the then-emergent classical style.

Museums

Casa Museo Ivan Bruschi

Corso Italia 14 (0575 354126/www.fondazione bruschi.it). **Open** *Summer* 10am-6pm Tue-Sun. *Winter* 10am-1pm, 2-6pm Tue-Sun. **Admission** €3. **No credit cards. Map** p277 B2.

Located opposite the Pieve (*see p278*), this was the home of the founder of the Arezzo antiques fair. Today, it's full of antiquarian delights, with archaeological pieces, Egyptian artefacts, musical instruments, books, stamps and more. There are tours every hour, the only way to ensure access.

Casa Vasari

Via XX Settembre 55 (0575 409040). **Open** 9am-7pm Mon, Wed-Sun; 9am-1pm Sun. **Admission** €2. **No credit cards. Map** p277 A2.

Medici favourite Giorgio Vasari bought and decorated this house in extravagant style before taking up an important post in Florence in 1564. Today, the museum houses the Archivio e Museo Vasariano and proudly exhibits a number of Vasari frescoes and other late Mannerist paintings.

Museo Archeologico Mecenate

Via Margaritone 10 (0575 20882). **Open** 8.30am-7.30pm daily. **Admission** €4. **No credit cards. Map** p277 D2.

This estimable collection of Etruscan and Roman artefacts is located just beside the Roman amphitheatre (*see p280*). The Etruscan bronze votive figurines and jewellery are particularly splendid, as is the Attic bowl decorated by Euphronios (AD 500-10) and the coralline pottery.

Museo d'Arte Medioevale e Moderna

Via San Lorentino 8 (0575 409050). **Open** 8.30am-7.30pm Tue-Sun. **Admission** €4. **No credit cards. Map** p277 B1.

Once you realise that *moderna* does not mean 'contemporary', this museum reveals itself to be an interesting, if uneven, collection of sculpture and painting from the Middle Ages to the 19th century. The Baroque vestibule on the first floor is dominated by Vasari's *Wedding Feast of Ahasuerus and Esther* (1548); past it are rooms containing one of Italy's finest collections of 13th- to 17th-century glazed ceramics from the della Robbia school. Among the later works are pieces belonging to the Macchiaioli school (the name that has been given to the Tuscan Impressionists). The museum hosted a hugely successful Piero show in 2007.

Museo dell'Oro

Via Fiorentina 550 (0575 925953/925403/www. unoaerre.it). **Open** 9am-6pm Mon-Fri; 9am-1pm Sat. **Admission** free.

Run by Uno A Erre, one of the world's foremost producers of gold jewellery, this museum includes a unique collection of pieces dating from the 1920s to the present day.

Landmarks

Anfiteatro Romano

Accessible from via Margaritone or via Crispi (0575 20882). **Open** 8.30am-7pm daily. **Admission** free. **Map** p277 C2.

In the second century, this amphitheatre drew crowds of up to 10,000 people, but its travertine and sandstone blocks were plundered by Cosimo I for the Fortezza Medicea (*see below*) in 1531. You can still make out its elliptical shape and stage, plus parts of what were probably the stands.

Fortezza Medicea

No phone. **Open** *Summer* 7am-8pm daily. *Winter* 7.30am-6pm daily. **Admission** free. **Map** p277 B3.

When the Medici finally decided to turn Arezzo into a duchy in 1531, they set about improving the city's defences, and the introduction of cannons prompted them to embark on another (the eighth) stint of wall building. The perimeter is visible in sections around the city and dominated by the architecturally revolutionary Fortezza Medicea (1538-60). Its pentagonal form was designed by Antonio da Sangallo the Elder and required the razing of towers, alleys and medieval *palazzi* in the hills of San Donato.

Piazza Grande

Map p277 B3.

A bonanza of architectural irregularity, thanks to its growth from peripheral food market to political heart of the city. The jumble of styles includes the arcaded, rounded back of the Romanesque Pieve di Santa Maria at the square's lowest point, the Baroque Palazzo del Tribunale and, next to it, Palazzo della Fraternità dei Laici, designed mostly by Bernardo Rossellino. Vasari also had a hand in the piazza Grande: his is the typically arcaded Palazzo delle Logge, which presides over the assortment of medieval homes around the rest of the square. Arezzo holds its main historic event, the Giostra del Saracino (*see p172*), in this main square.

Parks & gardens

Il Prato

Map p277 B3.

Arezzo's only park – located between the Duomo and the Fortezza Medicea – has views over the town and nearby countryside. Locals flock to La Casina del Prato (*see p282*) on summer nights.

Shopping

As you climb corso Italia, mainstream shops give way to a proliferation of antique vendors around piazza Grande, with some interesting finds to be had on via Cavour. On Saturdays, a general market sells clothes, food, flowers and household goods, but on the first Sunday of the month (as well as the day before) the city centre is taken over by a huge and important antiques fair (*see p281* **Market force**). The APT (*see p282*) has a handy Italian-English glossary and a map to guide you around the place.

There are more than 1,600 gold factories in Arezzo Province, so it's surprising there aren't more outlets in the town itself. Look along corso Italia, and check out the store at the Museo dell'Oro (*see p279*).

Boutique del Pane

Via Garibaldi 74 (0575 354992). **Open** 7.30am-1pm, 5.30-8pm Mon-Sat. **No credit cards**. **Map** p277 C2.

A wide selection of breads and baked goods.

Busatti

Corso Italia 48 (0575 355295/www.busatti.com). **Open** 3.30-7.30pm Mon; 9am-1pm, 3.30-7.30pm Tue-Sat. **Credit** AmEx, DC, MC, V. **Map** p277 C2.

Upholstery fabrics and household linens.

Macelleria-Gastronomia Aligi Barelli

Via della Chimera 22B (0575 357754). **Open** 8am-1pm, 4-7pm Mon, Tue, Thur, Fri; 8am-1pm Wed, Sat. *Winter* also Sat pm. Closed 3wks Aug. **Credit** AmEx, DC, MC, V. **Map** p277 A1.

This renowned *macelleria* (butcher) has salamis from the Casentino and a range of ready-made dishes largely based around, you guessed it, meat.

Pasticceria de' Cenci

Via de' Cenci 17 (0575 23102). **Open** 9am-1pm, 4-8pm Tue-Sat; 9am-1pm Sun. Closed Aug. **No credit cards**. **Map** p277 C2.

This *pasticceria* is full of elegant delights like *bigné al limone* (lemon cream puff) or fluffy *budini do riso*.

Where to eat & drink

Restaurants

Among Arezzo's favoured pasta dishes are *funghi porcini* (ceps) and *tartufo nero* (black truffle); local Chianina steak crops up on many a menu. Lunch is a serious business here – most shops and many sights shut from 1pm to 3.30pm.

Il Cantuccio

Via Madonna del Prato 76 (0575 26830/www.il-cantuccio.it). **Open** noon-2.30pm, 7.30-10.30pm Mon, Tue, Thur-Sun. **Average** €20. **Credit** AmEx, DC, MC, V. **Map** p277 C1 ❶

The vaulted cellar here is arguably the city's most rustic. Own-made pasta dishes include *tortelloni alla Casentinese* (with a potato filling).

Gastronomia Il Cervo

Via Cavour 38-40 (0575 20872). **Open** 7.30am-9pm Tue-Sun. Meals served 11am-3pm, 5-9pm Tue-Sun. **Average** €20. **Credit** AmEx, DC, MC, V. **Map** p277 B2 ❷

This deli prepares a whole range of goodies that you can eat at tables upstairs. Ideal for a light meal.

Market force

In 2008, one of Italy's most successful antique's market celebrates its 40th birthday. Splayed around Arezzo, over 500 vendors – and up to 30,000 customers – arrive from all over the country to deal in everything from ornate candlesticks to collectable junk.

The brainchild of the antique dealer Ivan Bruschi (whose house is now a museum, *see p279*), this was the first monthly fair of its kind in Italy and claims to be the biggest. Now well and truly established, you'll find the market buzzing on the weekend that encompasses the first Sunday of the month. In the piazza Grande, the big traders are to be found selling a fascinating array of jewellery, delicate lace, traditional linen and small sculptures. The Fiera houses many furniture sellers plus everything from copper vessels to palazzo chandeliers; replacement ornaments for incomplete items can be found in corso Italia.

Some collectors scoff that the market is too expensive and offers little for the serious buyer; others will be found poking around the tables month in month out. There's plenty to take in – but it's advisable to refrain from heedlessly rifling through that pile of old tea towels, or photographing a load of old war junk. You may get a frosty 'hands off' or 'no photo'.

Though a Baroque bedroom set from Puglia might stretch the luggage allowance, there are plenty of charming little things to buy – you just have to rummage. Under the Logge Vassari (piazza Grande), an enticing choice of exquisite taste is put on display by some of the region's most important antiquaries, including Bottegantica. We succumbed to temptation in the cloister of Petrach's house (via dei Pileati) where the jewellers assemble, and on corso Italia Alessandra Tizzoni had one fewer of her fine kilims to carry home.

Fiera Antiquario di Arezzo

Between piazza Grande, piazza San Francesco, piazza della Badia (www.arezzofieraantiquaria.com). **Dates** 1st Sun of mth and preceding Sat. **Admission** free.

Miseria e Nobiltà

Via Piaggia di San Bartolomeo 2 (0575 21245/www.miseriaenobilta.com). **Open** 7-11.30pm Tue-Sun. **Average** €30. **Credit** AmEx, DC, MC, V. **Map** p277 C3 ❸

A universe of culinary creativity in a medieval vault. The meats, pastas and fish are all recommended.

Sbarbacipolle

Via Garibaldi 120 (0575 299154). **Open** 7.30am-8pm daily. Closed 3wks Aug. **Average** €9. **No credit cards**. **Map** p277 B1 ❹

A colourful corner deli with a good choice of panini and cold dishes. No surprise that it's immensely popular with the locals.

Trattoria Il Saraceno

Via Mazzini 6A (0575 27644/www.ilsaraceno.com). **Open** noon-3pm, 7-10.30pm Mon, Tue, Thur-Sun. Closed 2wks Jan. **Average** €25. **Credit** AmEx, DC, MC, V. **Map** p277 C2 ❺

Il Saraceno does decent, reliable food, including lamb with rosemary, own-made pasta dishes and some wood-oven pizzas.

I Tre Bicchieri

Piazzetta Sopra i Ponti 3-5 (0575 26557). **Open** 12.30-2pm, 7.45-10pm Mon, Tue, Thur-Sun. **Average** €45. **Credit** MC, V. **Map** p277 C2 ❻

In an inner courtyard behind corso Italia, this excellent restaurant is run by two brothers who opted out of the gold business to indulge their passion for innovative cuisine. There's also a great wine list.

Bars, enoteche & gelaterie

Canto de' Bacci

Corso Italia 65 (0575 355804/www.cantodebacci.com). **Open** 8am-2pm, 3-8pm Mon-Sat. *Winter* also 1st Sun of mth. **Credit** AmEx, DC, MC, V. **Map** p277 C2 ❶

A good selection of wines (some quite unusual), plus other products of local gastronomy.

La Casina del Prato

Via Palagi 1, Il Prato park (0575 299757). **Open** *Summer* 10am-1am daily. *Winter* 10am-1am Mon, Wed-Sun. Closed Dec. **No credit cards**. **Map** p277 B3 ❷

An open-air summer hotspot overflowing with a hip crowd. Some snacks are available.

Enoteca La Torre di Gnicche

Piaggia San Martino 8 (0575 352035). **Open** noon-3pm, 6pm-1am Mon, Tue, Thur-Sun. Closed 2wks Jan. **Credit** MC, V. **Map** p277 B3 ❸

A tastefully decorated bar with a superb selection of local wines. The hot food is also worth a try.

Fiaschetteria de' Redi

Via de' Redi 10 (0575 355012). **Open** noon-3pm, 7.30-11.30pm Tue-Sun. **Credit** MC, V. **Map** p277 C2 ❹

A cosy bustling wine bar just off corso Italia, with a good wine selection. *Osteria*-style food is served.

Il Gelato

Via Madonna del Prato 24 (0575 300069). **Open** *Summer* 11am-midnight Mon, Tue, Thur-Sun. *Winter* 11am-8pm Mon, Tue, Thur-Sun. **No credit cards**. **Map** p277 C2 ❺

An unassuming *gelateria* with great-tasting ice-cream. Try *pinolata* (with pine nuts) or *arancello al liquore* (liqueur orange).

Where to stay

La Corte del Re

Via Borgunto 5 (0575 401603/348 6959100/www.lacortedelre.com). **Rates** €680-€1,000/wk. **Credit** AmEx, MC, V. **Map** p277 C3 ❶

Six fully equipped mini-apartments just a stone's throw from piazza Grande.

La Foresteria

Via Bicchieraia 32 (0575 370474). **Rates** €60-€75. **No credit cards**. **Map** p277 B2 ❷

A dozen simple rooms in a former 14th-century convent. Many of the rooms are frescoed and, although simple, are stylishly furnished. A bargain.

Hotel Patio

Via Cavour 23 (0575 401962/www.hotelpatio.it). **Rates** €165. **Credit** AmEx, DC, MC, V. **Map** p277 C2 ❸

A delightful small hotel featuring comfortable rooms designed with real flair. Original and friendly.

I Portici

Via Roma 18 (0575 403132/www.hoteliportici.com). **Rates** €130-€155; €185-€235 with terrace. **Credit** AmEx, DC, MC, V. **Map** p277 C2 ❹

Once a private house, I Portici is now a small upmarket hotel run by the scions of the original owners.

Resources

Hospital

Ospedale San Donato *Viale Alcide de Gasperi 17 (0575 255003).*

Internet

Phone Centre *Piazza Guido Monaco 8B (0575 371245).* **Open** 9am-1pm, 3-8.30pm Mon-Fri; 9am-1pm Sat. Closed 2wks Aug.

Police

Via Poggio del Sole (0575 3181602).

Tourist information

Azienda di Promozione Turistica (APT) *Piazza della Repubblica 28 (0575 377678/www.apt.arezzo.it).* **Open** *Oct-Mar* 9am-1pm, 3-7pm Mon-Sat; 9am-1pm 1st Sun of mth. *Apr-Sept* 9am-1pm, 3-7pm Mon-Sat; 9am-1pm Sun. **Map** p277 C1.

Getting there & around

By bus

Bus services from Florence are slow and irregular. **LFI** (La Ferrovia Italiana, 0575 39881, www.lfi.it) has direct buses to Siena (90mins) and Cortona (1hr). **SITA** (for Sansepolcro; 0575 74361/743681, www.sita-on-line.it) also covers the region. The bus terminal is opposite the train station. For local routes, call ATAM Point (0575 382651).

By car

Arezzo is off the A1 (Florence–Rome) *autostrada*. Journey time from Florence is an hour. The SS73 links to Siena to the west (about 1hr) and Sansepolcro to the north (30mins). Parking can be difficult and expensive in Arezzo. The APT (*see above*) has a list of free spots. The new car park on the north side is the best. For car hire, you could try Avis (piazza della Repubblica 1, 0575 354232) or Hertz (via Calamandrei 97D, 0575 27577).

By taxi

Radio Taxi (0575 382626).

By train

Intercity and InterRegionale (892021, www.trenitalia.it) trains link Arezzo with Florence (50-60mins) and Rome (90mins). The train station is located at piazza della Repubblica (0575 20553).

Arezzo Province

Quintessential Tuscan hill towns rub shoulders with industrial centres and tranquil monastic retreats.

The hermitage at **La Verna**. *See p285.*

The province of Arezzo spreads itself over several wide, fertile valleys hemmed in by the Apennines to the east. From busy tourist towns to centuries-old monastic retreats, the valleys offer diverse pleasures for the enquiring traveller. Dawdling through tranquil Tuscan hill towns, you'll chance upon opportunities to indulge in truffles, porcini mushrooms, local salami and the delicious feasts created from the impoverished peasant culture of times gone by; other towns give you the chance to snap up designer bargains at factory outlets or indulge in traditional linens and woollens.

Between Florence and Arezzo lies the **Valdarno**. Industry predominates, but to the north, the imposing Pratomagno Apennine range shelters early Romanesque churches that speak of quiet and reflection. By contrast, nature prevails in the **Casentino** area to the north-east of Arezzo. The steep slopes are clad with tall forests, creating the sort of isolation sought by hermits and monks, who chose this area for their sanctuaries. Lower down in the foothills, traditional wood and stonework has survived, as has the production of the thick, rough, hard-wearing Casentino cloth.

The **Valtiberina**, Tuscany's easternmost fringe, is now more easily accessible than it used to be, due to the completion of the *autostrada dei Due Mari* ('motorway of the two seas'). The area takes its name from the River Tiber, which flows down from the Apennine peaks past the gentle town of Sansepolcro.

Finally, in the south, is the **Valdichiana**, nestled between the Appenines and the hills of Chianti. In previous times, this area was a swamp first drained and made passable by the Etruscans, only to revert to its previous state following the decline of the Roman Empire. A thousand years passed before the Chiana valley was reclaimed again by the Lorraine Grand Dukes, by which time a layer of humus had formed to create a fertile agricultural plain. Its name today is synonymous with Chianina beef – large, greyish, white-horned creatures, raised organically. To the west of Valdichiana are outposts such as Monte San Savino and Lucignano, while the eastern ridge is dominated by Foiano della Chiana, Castelfiorentino and the lovely sandstone town of Cortona.

Valdarno

Loro Ciuffena & Castelfranco di Sopra

The ancient **Setteponte** ('seven bridges') pilgrim route along the Pratomagno foothills crosses the Arno's tributaries amid olive and chestnut groves. It's much less direct than the *autostrada*, but provides access to historic towns with artistic legacies. (If you're more intent on bagging a few designer bargains at the outlet stores around the industrial towns of Pontassieve, Incisa, San Giovanni Valdarno and Montevarchi, you'll need to take the S69, often referred to as the 'Aretino'.) From Arezzo, take the road north in the direction of Bibbiena, then take a left turn for **Quarata**, and on to **ponte a Buriano**, a 13th-century bridge – the Arno's oldest. Miraculously surviving the last war, it's said to be the bridge that's just visible over the left shoulder of Leonardo's *Mona Lisa*; a small visitor centre nearby details its history. The area is notable for its wetlands and provides excellent walking and cycling trails.

Continue through Castiglion Fibocchi to **Loro Ciuffena**, set on the edge of a gorge over the roaring Ciuffenna torrent, once used to power flour mills. Loro grew up around an ancient *borgo* (hamlet) and has its own ponte Vecchio. Just before Loro, take a right turn to see the stark and very simple Romanesque church of **San Pietro a Gropina**, dating from the ninth century.

Here the Setteponte rises over a heavily eroded landscape known as **Le Balze**, made up of ravines and pinnacles of barren earth shaped over millions of years; the shapes and forms are said to have inspired Leonardo in his painting. Above is **Castelfranco di Sopra**, founded as a Florentine military outpost in the late 13th century. Just outside it is the **Badia di San Salvatore a Soffena**, a 12th-century abbey with a bright interior sporting an *Annunciation* and other pastel-coloured frescoes.

Where to stay & eat

Relais Villa Belpoggio (via Setteponti Ponente 40a, Loro Ciuffenna, 055 9694411, www.villabelpoggio.it) is a pleasant country house-cum-boutique hotel with two apartments.

Trattoria del Pescatore (ponte a Buriano 19b, near Quarata, 0575 364096) specialises in fresh fish, while **Il Canto del Maggio** (055 9705147, www.cantodelmaggio.com) in the centre of the medieval village of Penna Alta (known as 'La Penna') near Loro Ciuffena, is a high-quality *osteria-enoteca*, with a beautiful garden and pleasant apartments for hire.

Museo Civico.

Casentino

Poppi, Bibbiena & Pieve a Socana

A delightful small town, **Poppi** slopes down through arcaded streets from the 13th-century **Castello dei Conti Guidi** (0575 520516, closed Mon-Wed Oct-Mar, admission €4 castle plus €2 tower, incl audio guide) high above the valley. The castle is worth visiting, not only for its frescoed rooms, but also for the fabulous view of the Casentino. Dante is said to have stayed here, and there's a statue of him outside.

Heading out of Poppi, the road leading to **Camàldoli** takes you to the small **Parco Zoo della Fauna Europa** (via del Parco 16, 0575 504541, www.parcozoopoppi.it, admission €6, €5 concessions), home to European species including wolves, lynx, deer and birds of prey; the ample parkland has designated picnic spots, and there's an on-site restaurant (fixed menu €15). On the S70 heading towards Pratovecchio, meanwhile, you'll see signs for the **Pieve di San Pietro di Romena**, a 12th-century baptismal church. Inside there are sculpted stone capitals and some remarkable pieces of art by the local priest; you can call him if it's closed (0575 58725, 9am-noon, 3-7pm).

In the opposite direction, south of Poppi, lies **Bibbiena**, a gentle walled town still largely undiscovered by tourists and the capital of the Casentino. In the historic centre are some fine old *palazzi* to admire, including the elegant Renaissance **Palazzo Dovizi**, while in the church of **San Lorenzo** you'll find a magnificent della Robbia glazed terracotta *Adoration of the Shepherds*. A food market takes place on Thursday mornings and every fourth Saturday of the month.

Around 25 kilometres (18 miles) south of Bibbiena, west of the main Bibbiena–Arezzo road, lies **Pieve a Socana**. The town embodies 2,600 years of history and the votive aspirations of three civilisations: Etruscan, Roman and Christian. Excavation has brought to light a magnificent sacrificial altar and the staircase of a temple dating back to the Etruscan period as well as a cylindrical wall and pilaster strips of Roman origin. The Christians subsequently built three separate churches in addition to the Etruscan temple.

Where to stay & eat

In Poppi, a good bet for a bed is homely **Albergo Casentino** (piazza della Repubblica 6, 0575 529090, €65), which has its own little enclosed garden and a restaurant (closed Wed, average €24). Otherwise, in the country just beyond Bibbiena you'll find the **Agricola Casentinese** (località Casanova 63, 0575 594806, www.agricolacasentinese.it, from €70), offering comfortable rooms and an evening meal in the middle of a huge working farm, where you can also ride and trek.

It's not hard to find decent cuisine in these parts, but many restaurants close for the month of November. In Poppi, head for the **Antica Cantina** (via Lapucci 2, 0575 529844, www.anticacantina.com, closed Mon and in winter Tue, average €25), housed in a 12th-century cellar, for its excellent selection of wine. In Bibbiena, **Il Tirabusciò** (via Borghi 73, 0575 595474, www.tirabuscio.it, 7.30pm-midnight, closed Tue, €30 average) has friendly service, a range of interesting dishes and a list of fine wines to complement them.

Camaldoli & La Verna

In the hills north-east of Poppi lies the extremely beautiful **Foreste Casentinesi** national park (www.parcoforestecasentinesi.it), a protected area of ancient woodland, streams and nature reserves home to deer, wild boar, wolves and a plethora of birdlife. Hiking and mountain bike trails weave through the park, and it's a popular place for horse riding, or cross-country skiing in winter. The visitor centre at **Badia Prataglia** (via Nazionale 14r, 0575 559477, www.parks.it, closed Mon-Thur winter), in the midst of the park, is a good source of information and advice.

Close to Badia Prataglia lie the monastery and hermitage of **Camaldoli**. The latter was founded in 1012 by St Romuald. Surrounded by fir trees, the monks' individual cells are visible only through a gate, though Romualdo's original cell, with its wooden panelling and cot, is open to visitors. Three kilometres (two miles) downhill is the 16th-century monastery that links the Camaldolite monks to the outside world. Its church contains some early Vasaris, including a *Madonna and Child* and a *Nativity*. The young artist took refuge here from 1537 to 1539, following the murder of his patron, Alessandro de' Medici.

A little further south, close to the town of Chiusi, an even more important monastic complex dominates the surrounding landscape from a rocky outcrop at 1,129 metres (3,670 feet). In 1214, St Francis's vagabondage brought him to this isolated peak, where he and some followers were inspired to build cells for themselves. Ten years later, Italy's patron saint received the stigmata here and, ever since, **La Verna** has been an important stop on the Franciscan trail. The basilica contains a reliquary chapel with the saint's personal effects. The sanctuary also contains a great number of Andrea della Robbia's glazed terracottas. This hugely impressive religious compound of interconnected chapels, churches, corridors and cloisters attracts large numbers of visitors, but on a quiet weekday the sunset over the Casentino inspires meditative silence.

Where to eat

Ristorante Camaldoli (via Camaldoli 0575 556091, open daily, closed in winter Tue, average €28) is just near the monastery, with a roaring fire inside or cooling trees outside. Try the *acquacotta* (soup with toasted bread) or *ravioli all'Ortica* (ricotta and nettle ravioli).

Valtiberina

Sansepolcro

The Valtiberina's largest town, Sansepolcro gives meaning to the expression 'quality of life'; it's both tranquil and culturally alive, off the beaten track yet welcoming to visitors.

Sansepolcro is best known as the birthplace of the early Renaissance maestro of perspective and proportion, Piero della Francesca, some of whose works are prominently displayed in the town's **Museo Civico** (via Aggiunti 65, 0575 732218, admission €6.20). Sansepolcro is the centre of the so-called 'Piero Trail' (with Arezzo, Monterchi and Urbino) where the cognoscenti can view his work in situ. Works include the important *Madonna della Misericordia* (c1445), in which Piero overturns the laws of proportion by depicting an all-encompassing, monumental Madonna dwarfing the faithful and protecting them with her mantle. The artist can't resist placing himself among the Virgin's followers, facing us from the Madonna's left. Another self portrait appears in *The Resurrection* (c1460), where a muscular Christ steps from his tomb, awakening the somnolent soldiers at his feet. Among them, to the left, is Piero. Aldous Huxley referred to the work as 'the greatest painting in the world' – a tag that helped save Sansepolcro from bombing in World War II.

The 14th-century Romanesque **Duomo** contains on its left altar an imposing wooden crucifix known as the *Volto Santo* (Holy Face), thought to have been brought to Sansepolcro from the Orient during the crusades, and bearing a strong similarity to its better-known equivalent in Lucca's Duomo di San Martino (*see p262*). Local events include a torch-lit procession on Good Friday and a crossbow tournament, the Palio della Balestra, on the second Sunday in September – the culmination of a festive medieval week. The place is also a food lover's paradise: weekly food markets take place every Tuesday and Saturday, plus there's a special gourmet market held on every third Saturday of the month.

Where to stay, eat & drink

Albergo Fiorentino (via L Pacioli 56, 0575 740350, www.albergofiorentino.com, €62), on the corner of via XX Settembre, offers a very acceptable accommodation option, while the **Ristorante da Ventura** (via Aggiunti 30, 0575 742560, closed dinner Sun, all Mon, average €30) is the best of the classics. For sampling fine wine together with good food, **Enoteca Guidi** (via L Pacioli 44, 0575 741086, closed Wed, Sat, lunch Sun, average €23) is the place. The popular **Osteria in Aboca**, past Sansepolcro, on the road to Rimini (Fraz Aboca 11, 0575 749125, www.losteriainaboca.it, closed Mon, average €22) is a good bet.

Monterchi

This tiny hilltop village on the road between Arezzo and Città di Castello is synonymous with Piero della Francesca's *Madonna del Parto*, the famous painting of a pregnant Madonna, and the prized possession of the eponymous **Museo Madonna del Parto** (via Reglia 1, 0575 70713, admission €3.10). Two angels lightly drawing back a canopy reveal the exquisite and melancholy young Madonna – the only one of its kind in Renaissance art.

Where to stay & eat

Driving three minutes east towards Città di Castello is restaurant and pizzeria **La Pieve Vecchia** (0575 709053, www.lapievevecchia.com, lunch €12, evening €29). The daily fixed lunch menu is always interesting, and outdoor tables are available on summer evenings; the large complex also has three ensuite rooms in a newly restored barn.

Anghiari

Perched on a hill overlooking the Valtiberina and Sansepolcro, Anghiari's dominant position and impressive walls made it a stronghold from which Florence controlled the far east of Tuscany, following victory over the Milanese Visconti family in the Battle of Anghiari in 1440. The battle is commemorated by Leonardo da Vinci in his famously unfinished and long-lost work, thought by some to be hidden behind a Vasari fresco in Florence's Palazzo Vecchio. For more information, *see pp32-35*.

Today, with its maze of vaulted alleys and flower-strewn doorways, the town is a peaceful, well-preserved town, renowned for wood-based crafts and antique furniture restoration. It hosts the annual Valtiberina crafts market in late April and an antiques fair on the third Sunday of every other month. The **Museo Statale di Palazzo Taglieschi** (piazza Mameli 16, 0575 788001, closed Mon, admission €2) displays various local artefacts, a polychrome terracotta by della Robbia and a singularly striking wooden sculpture of the Madonna by Jacopo della Quercia.

Anghiari's other major traditional and commercial draw is its woven and naturally dyed textiles, exemplified by the **Busatti** store-cum-factory (via Mazzini 14, 0575 788013, www.busatti.com, closed Mon morning & Sun). Its deafening shuttle looms, some of them almost a century old, continue to produce a range of linens from natural fibres.

Where to eat

One of the great treats of the valley is **Da Alighiero** (via Garibaldi 8, 0575 788040, www.daalighiero.it, closed Tue, average €30), where regional porcini mushrooms often feature on the menu.

Valdichiana

Monte San Savino

Circular and enclosed, Monte San Savino is a prominent provincial town. Its Renaissance heyday, however, was brief, coinciding with the commercial patronage and religious power exercised by the Di Monte family in the 15th and 16th centuries. The main architectural attractions, both bearing the family's imprint, face each other along corso Sangallo.

The quintessentially Renaissance Palazzo di Monte, now the **Palazzo Comunale**, contains an arcaded courtyard, through which you reach the hanging gardens and an open-air theatre overlooking a cypress-dotted landscape. Across from it is the **Loggia dei Mercanti**, attributed to architect and sculptor Andrea Sansovino, the town's most eminent son.

Castiglion Fiorentino.

Monte San Savino is known for engraved pottery designed in delicate floral motifs, with examples on display at the **Museo del Cassero** (piazza Gamurrini, 0575 843098, free admission). The products at **Ceramiche Artistiche Lapucci** (corso Sangallo 8-10, 0575 844375, closed Sun, ring bell for entry) still reflect this tradition.

Where to stay & eat

For a pleasantly relaxed meal, try the *enoteca-osteria* **La Pecora Nera** (via Zanetti 4, Monte San Savino, 0575 844647, www.pecoranera.it, closed Thur, average €25), nearby to the Porta San Giovanni. The medieval **Castello di Gargonza** (0575 847021, www.gargonza.it, €101-€171), six kilometres (3.5 miles) west of town, has rooms on a bed & breakfast basis as well as several mini-apartments with modern facilities.

Lucignano

An urban time capsule still artfully encased within its old walls, tiny Lucignano has managed to preserve its medieval character and its rather eccentric town planning. Walk round and up its spiral layout and you find yourself at the steps of the church of the **Collegiata di San Michele**. Behind it is the 13th-century church of **San Francesco**, barn-like in its simplicity and breathtaking in its humble beauty.

Inside the Palazzo Comunale, the **Museo Civico** (piazza del Tribunale 22, 0575 838001, closed Tue, admission €3) exhibits Lucignano's symbol, the *Albero di San Francesco*, a late Gothic reliquary representing a plant-like cross, along with panels by Signorelli and a Bartolo di Fredi triptych.

Where to eat

Lucignano has two good restaurants: **Il Goccino** (via G Matteotti 90, 0575 836707, closed Mon in winter, average €25), which has a good wine list and space for eating outside in the summer; and **La Rocca** (via G Matteotti 15-17, 0575 836775, closed Tue, average €25), which serves an excellent *zuppa dei tarlati* (chicken soup made with wild fennel, served with croutons). Paradise on a plate here is fried eggs topped with plenty of fresh truffle shavings.

Foiano della Chiana

Foiano's buildings and steeples are largely distinguished by the warm, reddish tones of their *cotto* bricks. Its oval shape centres on piazza Cavour, dominated by Palazzo delle Logge, formerly a Medici hunting lodge. Today, it houses the **Fototeca Furio del Furia**, an engrossing display of early 20th-century photographs of rural life in Italy.

Outside the walls is Foiano's other main draw, the neoclassical **Collegiata di San Martino**. It houses an Andrea della Robbia terracotta, the *Madonna of the Girdle*, and Signorelli's last work, *Coronation of the Virgin* (1523), influenced by Piero della Francesca.

Castiglion Fiorentino

On the other side of the valley, the old town of Castiglion Fiorentino still sits behind its walls on a small hill at the very foot of the Apennines, while new developments have spilled downwards and on to the plain. It's still dominated by the impressive **Torre del Cassero**. The Etruscan origins were reaffirmed by excavation works several years ago, while

Cortona.

the early Christian building in the crypt of the Chiesa di Sant'Angelo al Cassero confirms continuous habitation of the site. The **Museo Civico Archeologico** displays a range of early artefacts and building materials. Above this is the **Pinacoteca Comunale** (via del Cassero, 0575 657466, closed Mon, admission €3), with paintings by Giotto's godson and follower, Taddeo Gaddi, and by 15th-century artist Bartolomeo della Gatta.

The main piazza (just keep walking up hill) has a splendid loggia by Vasari overlooking the Apennine valley. In the corner of the loggia is the bar **Café degli Ignoranti**.

Where to stay & eat

For a friendly, reasonably priced hotel in the country, go for **Villa Schiatti** (località Montecchio 131, 0575 651440, www.villaschiatti.it, €38-€42), which also serves a pleasant evening meal. It has a pool and plenty of room for children to scamper. In the old town you can have a meat eater's feast at **Da Muzzicone** (piazza San Francesco 7, 0575 658403, closed Tue, average €30-€35).

Cortona

Cortona is without doubt the signature Tuscan hill town. Since finding fame through *Under the Tuscan Sun* – Frances Mayes's idealised memoir on the good life in Tuscany, made into a film in 2003 – the town has rather predictably gained its fair share of tacky gift shops and hordes of Mayes devotees, who dutifully troop to this town to see her paradise with their own eyes. Yet even these more touristy elements cannot totally obliterate the beauty of the town itself or diminish its unique architectural and elemental charms: a jumble of irregular, angular buildings, windswept Etruscan city walls and layered urban development distinguishes it from central Italy's historic cities.

Its strategic position dominating the Valdichiana meant that Cortona grew into an important Etruscan outpost around the eighth century BC and then passed under Roman rule. The recently restored **Museo dell'Accademia Etrusca e della Città di Cortona** (0575 637235, admission €7), in piazza Signorelli's Palazzo Casali, recounts the town's early history through imaginatively laid-out exhibits, including some truly magnificent Etruscan items.

Following depredation by the Goths, Cortona thrived as a free community from the 11th century. Sacked by Arezzo in 1258, it bounced back and was taken over and quickly sold by the King of Naples to Florence in 1411. Since then it has prospered, and today it's the quintessential provincial *città d'arte* with plenty going on: from concerts as part of the Umbria Jazz Festival in late July to the convivial Sagra della Bistecca feast in mid August (along with August's Tuscan Sun Festival; *see p189* **Seasonal settings**).

To soak up the atmosphere of the place, head for the steps leading up to the crenellated clock tower of the heavy-set **Palazzo Comunale**, overlooking the small and uneven piazza della Repubblica – the elegant central square that's home to a restaurant, bar, *gelateria* and bespoke hat shop. Adjacent is the slightly larger piazza Signorelli, honouring Cortona's foremost son, High Renaissance artist Luca Signorelli (c1445-1523). The arcaded Teatro Signorelli sits neatly within the square, along with the stunning Museo dell'Accademia Etrusca (*see above*).

The nearby piazza del Duomo opens on to a picture-postcard view of the valley, while opposite the bland Duomo lies the **Museo**

Diocesano (0575 62830, admission €5), home to Fra Angelico's glorious *Annunciation* and impressive works by Signorelli and Pietro Lorenzetti. For more of Cortona's rewarding sights, climb steep via Berrettini towards the Fortezza Medicea. Here you'll find the 15th-century church of **San Nicolò**, with its delicate courtyard and Baroque-roofed interior containing a Signorelli altarpiece (you'll need to ring the doorbell to enter). Also worth the schlep is the **Chiesa di Santa Margherita**, a little further on, with its vivid ceilings; reach the fort above and you'll be rewarded with views to Lake Trasimeno, and a peaceful, tourist free sense of tranquility.

Where to eat

The **Osteria del Teatro** (via Maffei 2, 0575 630556, closed Wed, average €30) serves very good food in an operatic setting. **Preludio** (via Guelfa 11, 0575 630104, closed Mon & lunch Nov-May, average €20) serves highly individual pasta creations. **La Loggiata** (piazza Pescheria 3, 0575 630575, closed Wed, average €30) has a few tables with a balcony view over piazza della Repubblica. **Trattoria Dardano** (via Dardano 24, 0575 601944, closed Wed, average €16) is a locals' haunt that serves home cooking. **La Grotta** (piazzetta Baldelli 3, 0575 630271, closed Tue) serves excellent own-made pasta dishes.

Where to stay

Hotel Italia (via Ghibellina 7, 0575 630254, €105) offers good quality and value for money, while **Hotel San Luca** (piazza Garibaldi 1, 0575 630460, www.sanlucacortona.com, €120) is more generic and modern, but with spectacular views over the valley. If you're after something central and classy, consider the **Hotel San Michele** (via Guelfa 15, 0575 604348, www.hotelsanmichele.net, €165-€250), which boasts an 18th-century ceiling in the breakfast room. The spoil-yourself option comes in the form of the four-star **Hotel Villa Marsili** (via Cesare Battisti 13, 0575 605252, €132-€310), a beautifully restored 18th-century private residence with its own gardens.

Alternatively, three kilometres (two miles) from Cortona, **Relais Villa Baldelli** (località San Pietro a Cegliolo 420, 0575 612406, www.villabaldelli.it, €220-€330) offers nice rooms in an 18th-century residence. The luxurious **Il Falconiere** is about the same distance from town (località San Martino a Bocena, 0575 612679, www.ilfalconiere.com, €260-€560) and has its own Michelin-starred restaurant (average €65).

Resources

Tourist information

Cortona

Via Nazionale 42 (0575 630352/www.apt.arezzo.it). **Open** *May-Sept* 9am-1pm, 3-7pm Mon-Sat; 9am-1pm Sun. *Oct-Apr* 9am-1pm, 3-6pm Mon-Sat.

Sansepolcro

Piazza Garibaldi (0575 740536). **Open** 9.30am-1pm, 3.30-6.30pm daily.

Getting there

By bus

LAZZI (055 9199922, www.lazzi.it) has regular buses linking Montevarchi, Terranuova Bracciolini and Loro Ciuffenna with Arezzo. Irregular LFI buses (0575 39881) serve Camaldoli and Chiusi Verna from Bibbiena station. They run more regular buses between Cortona (from piazzale Garibaldi) and Arezzo, which also stop in Castiglion Fiorentino. **SITA** (0575 74361, www.sita-on-line.it) runs buses between Arezzo and Sansepolcro (journey time 1hr) that also stop in Anghiari (45mins) and, sometimes, in Monterchi.

By car

There are several driving routes through the Valdarno, including the Florence–Rome *autostrada* (A1), the slower SS69, which runs through San Giovanni and Montevarchi and on to Arezzo, or the Setteponti route through the country. The region's main arteries are the SS70 and SS71. To explore the Valtiberina, take the SS73 out of Arezzo, heading north-east towards Sansepolcro. Monterchi, Citerna and Anghiari are signposted off this road, a few kilometres before Sansepolcro. The A1 *autostrada* passes right through the Valdichiana, with exits for Monte San Savino and Valdichiana (for Cortona, off the main SS75 to Perugia). From Arezzo, Castiglion Fiorentino and Cortona are reached via the SS71.

By train

Local trains on the Florence–Arezzo line stop at Montevarchi (45mins from Florence, 25mins from Arezzo). Timetable information for this and all other routes is available by calling 892021 or by visiting www.trenitalia.it. A tiny train line run by **La Ferroviaria Italiana** (LFI) links Pratovecchio (journey time 1hr), Poppi (40mins) and Bibbiena (30mins) to Arezzo, with departures per hour by day. Cortona has two train stations: Camucia-Cortona, 5km (3 miles) away, and Terontola-Cortona, 11km (7 miles) from town. Castiglion Fiorentino is on the same line. Trains from Arezzo take 15mins to Castiglion, 22mins to Camucia and 27mins to Terontola. Slow trains between Florence (journey time to Terontola 90mins) and Rome (Terontola 80mins) also pass through all three stations. A regular bus service links Cortona with its two stations. Sansepolcro is also linked to Città di Castello and Perugia on a local Umbrian train service (use www.trenitalia.it or www.fcu.it).

Southern Tuscany

Escape the crowds in this relatively undiscovered corner of Italy.

Southern Tuscany looks towards the coast, enjoying a milder climate than the more inland reaches of the region. As the area lacks both the reputation and the popularity of other parts of Tuscany, development here has been slower; for most of the year, it's a delightfully low-key destination. However, the area can get crowded at Easter and in the height of summer, especially around the islands of Elba and Giglio. Grosseto is the provincial capital and no great attraction, but there are plenty of charming small towns to explore on the mainland too, to say nothing of good food and wine, extraordinary wildlife reserves and rich Etruscan archeological sites.

Grosseto Province & the Maremma

The coastal and inland area south of Piombino, stretching down to the Tuscan border with Lazio, is known as the **Maremma**. The word probably derives from the Spanish *marisma*, or marsh, the linguistic legacy of 200 years of Spanish rule. Until they were definitively drained in the mid 20th century, these marshlands were poor and malarial, which explains why the area got off to a late start as a tourist destination. Farming in the area is still relatively small-scale and mixed. The resulting landscape creates a glorious patchwork of textures and colours. Here and there are patches of grazing land for the sheep, whose milk becomes pecorino cheese, and the long-horned, dark-eyed Maremma breed of cattle. For the Maremma's natural park, *see p297* **South park**.

Grosseto

The largest Tuscan town south of Siena, Grosseto has had to contend with a lot over the centuries. Though it gained city status in 1138, the surrounding area was so wretched that the population never thrived. The city was eventually annexed by Siena in 1336, and became part of the Grand Duchy of Tuscany in 1559. Apart from fortifying their new outpost, the Medici clearly didn't feel that Grosseto had much scope, and by 1745 the population had dwindled to a mere 648.

Things didn't pick up until the Lorraine Grand Dukes began reclaiming the surrounding marshlands in the 18th and 19th centuries, before further agricultural improvements came under the Fascist regime in the 1920s and '30s. The strips of pinewood that stretch north and south along the coast are largely the product of this period. Planted to curb the encroaching sea, they also ensured salt-water didn't permeate areas now devoted to fish farming.

Although Grosseto got a pasting in World War II, a central area, enclosed by high walls, was partially spared. Other attractions include the **Museo Archeologico** (piazza Baccarini 3, 0564 488750, closed Mon, admission €5), with information on the local topography and the important Etruscan settlements in the area.

Where to stay & eat

In the pedestrianised part of town, the **Bastiani Grand Hotel** (piazza Giberti 64, 0564 20047, €146) is pleasant and slightly old-fashioned. Not far away is one of the town's best eating options: **Il Canto del Gallo** (via Mazzini 29, 0564 414589, closed Sun, average €35). Located in the Medici fortified walls, space is at a premium, but the food is good, and largely organic in origin. Otherwise, visit the neighbouring seaside hamlet of Castiglione della Pescaia, and stay and eat at the attractive **Locanda La Luna** (via del Podere 8, 0564 945854, www.locanda-laluna.it, average €30).

Massa Marittima

Massa dominates the high southern ranges of the Colline Metallifere, a rich source of the iron, copper and other minerals that contributed to its flourishing economy in the Middle Ages. The area's prosperity began to decline when it lost its status as an independent city-state, and it was taken over by Siena in 1337. Half a millennium of neglect followed the plague years of 1348-50, until a small-scale return to mining, along with the draining of the surrounding marshes, turned the tide in the middle of the 19th century. Today, Massa boasts one of the best-preserved and most uniform examples of 13th-century Tuscan town planning. The **Duomo** (via Giro del Duomo 6, 0566 902237) harmoniously blends Romanesque and Gothic details and its bare stone interior includes a baptistery, famous for its 13th-century bas-reliefs by Giroldo da Como.

The fountain – named **Le Fonti dell' Abbondanza** ('fountains of abundance') – was the hub of town life in the second half of the 13th century. Among the town's other diversions are the **Museo Civico Archeologico** in the 13th-century Palazzo del Podestà on piazza Garibaldi (0566 902289, closed Mon, admission €3), which has an Etruscan collection and a marvellous 1330 *Maestà* by Ambrogio Lorenzetti, and the **Città Nuova** ('New Town', built in the 14th century) up via Moncini. There's a fine Sienese arch here: climb it for a few euros, or walk around the side (for free) to take in equally excellent views over the town and countryside.

Another draw is the **Balestro del Girifalco** festival on the fourth Sunday in May – the feast day of San Bernardino of Siena, who was born here. The *sbandieratori* (flag throwers) are faultless and the final contest, when teams attempt to shoot down a mechanical falcon with their crossbows, is fascinating. The town stages concerts in the square in August and a week-long photography festival in July (www.toscanafotofestival.it).

Where to stay & eat

If you fancy staying the night, opt for the three-star **Sole** (corso Libertà 43, 0566 901971, closed mid Jan-mid Feb, €80), in an old palazzo.

Foodwise, good local dishes such as stewed wild boar with black olives can be had at **Enoteca Grassini** (via della Libertà 1, 0566 940149, closed Tue and Jan-mid Mar, average €17). Even more atmospheric is **Da Tronca** (vicolo Porte 5, 0566 901991, closed lunch, all day Wed and mid Dec-mid Mar, average €18), a nearby *osteria* that serves distinctive regional fare. For more inventive cuisine, drive a couple of kilometres north to Ghirlanda for **Bracali** (via di Perolla 2, 0566 902318, closed Mon, Tue & lunch Wed, Thur, average €130).

Scansano

The little town of Scansano dates back to the 12th century, but only came into its own in the early 1800s, when Grand Duke Leopoldo II decreed that all public offices should move here from pestilent Grosseto for the summer months.

Though local government no longer summers here, the air is still sweet and fresh when it's excessively hot on the coast. Don't be put off by the nondescript buildings outside the centre – this is a friendly town with a rural heart. People love to stop for a chat, especially on Friday mornings (market day).

Scansano is home to the Morellino di Scansano DOCG wine, a red with depth and structure that relies more on fresh fruit than muscle. In August and September, tasting events are held in the Dentro to showcase local wines, pecorino and cold cuts from the tasty local *cinta senese* pig.

Where to stay & eat

Outside Scansano, in the hamlet of Montorgiali, there's an attractive inn with a good restaurant: **La Tana dei Lupi** (via del Corso 10-16, 0564 580221, closed Thur, dinner only Fri-Sun, average €24). Another nice place to stay is **Agriturismo Casa Nova**, an organic farm located at Montepò (località Montepò 42, 0564 580317, casanova@agriturismo.com, €90-€150). The **Antico Casale di Scansano** (0564 507219, www.anticocasalediscansano.com, €80-€130), just out of town at Castagneta, offers board and lodging, plus opportunities for horse riding and spa facilities. In Scansano itself, try **Osteria Rifrullo** (via Marconi 3, 0564 507183, www.osteriarifrullo.it, closed Sun, average €30) for local fare, just up from piazza Garibaldi. **La Cantina** (via delle Botte 1-3, 0564 507605, closed Sun eve & Mon) has a fine cellar to accompany a thoughtful approach to

Massa Marittima's **Duomo.** *See p290.*

Saturnia.

Maremma cuisine. For creative cooking, try the more expensive **Pane e Tulipani** (via Diaz 3, 0564 507531) near the old hospital. Ten minutes outside town on the SP9 towards Montiano lies **Le Mandorlaie** (0564 507149), where Graziella provides good food using produce from the family farm.

Roccalbegna & Santa Fiora

A number of the towns on the slopes that embrace **Mount Amiata** (the highest mountain in Tuscany, at 1,738 metres/5,702 feet) are well worth a visit for the magnificent scenery, good hiking and excellent food. Relatively removed from Grosseto and the main highways because of the steep, winding roads leading up to them, these communities offer a glimpse of rural Tuscany as it was several decades ago.

Roccalbegna is a walled medieval town that seems to grow out of the chalky rock of Monte Labbro. A monolithic stony peak defends the back of the town, while limestone outcrops feature like giant statues in the olive groves below the walls, where the view opens up to embrace a glorious landscape. Walk through the atmospheric narrow streets, and take a look at the Ambrogio Lorenzetti triptych (1340) in the central church of **SS Pietro e Paolo**, a rare example of a painting of such importance still to be found in a parish church.

In the immediate vicinity of Raccalbegna are three WWF-protected nature reserves with mapped-out paths: the **Monte Labbro** reserve is due north; **Pescinello** is just outside the town; while **Bosco di Rocconi** can be found heading due south.

While in the area, it's worth visiting **Santa Fiora**, which overlooks the source of the River Fiora; the whole hamlet reverberates with the sound of rushing water. The hillside town features some fine old houses and a certain grandeur deriving from its history as a stronghold of the powerful Aldobrandeschi family. The **Pieve delle Santa Fiora e Lucilla** church houses some fine glazed terracotta works by Andrea della Robbia. Visit in July/August to coincide with the **Santa Fiora in Musica** festival (www.santafiorainmusica.com).

Where to stay & eat

In Roccalbegna, **Antica Locanda La Pietra** (via XXIV Maggio 69B, 0564 989019, www.locandalapietra.it, €75-€115) has been run by the same family for six generations and offers old-fashioned rooms, home-made bread for breakfast and one of the best restaurants in the area. In Santa Fiora, a good meal can be had at **Il Barilotto** (via Carolina 24, 0564 977089, closed Wed, €28-€38).

Saturnia, Montemerano & Manciano

According to legend, Saturn once sent down a thunderbolt that split open the earth, in order to punish those who thought only of war. Steamy water poured forth from the gash; earthlings found solace in it and became calm. That was a while ago; these days, the road to **Saturnia** is well worn by tourists seeking regeneration in the small, sulphurous tributary of the Albenga.

The **Hotel Terme** (*see below*) offers mud treatments and massages, as well as its own mineral-rich pool, while the **Terme di Saturnia** (0564 602934, www.termedisaturnia.com, closed 2 wks mid Jan, €200-€310) has a park full of different pools, and cascades to give you a good pummelling. For a cheaper choice, head down the road and bathe for free in the pretty **Cascate del Gorello** falls and pools, where the rocks are stained green. It can get crowded, but on a warm, clear and quiet night, it's magical.

Six kilometres (four miles) away sits **Montemerano**, a well-preserved hillside town with a medieval castle. Beyond is **Manciano**, the main municipality. Though its outskirts have not been enhanced by modern buildings, the old centre is pleasant and quite lively.

Where to stay & eat

Saturnia's **Hotel Terme** (0564 600111, www.termedisaturnia.it, €360) is pretty pricey, but fitted out with a gym, a golf driving range and tennis courts to go with the mineral-rich pool. Much more reasonable is the family-run **Villa Clodia** (via Italia 43, 0564 601212, www.hotelvillaclodia.com,€95-€115), in a country house two kilometres (1.2 miles) from the spa.

For lunch or dinner, Saturnia's **Bacco e Cerere** (via Mazzini 4, 0564 601235, closed Wed and 2wks Jan or Feb, average €40) is great for meat. If you've cash to splash, make for Montemerano and the renowned **Da Caino** (via Canonica 4, 0564 602817, closed all day Wed, lunch Thur and mid Jan-mid Feb, average €90), which also has three guestrooms. Otherwise, there's **Passaparola nell'Antico Frantoio** (via delle Mura 21, 0564 602835, closed Thur, 2wks July, and 2wks Feb, average €30). In Manciano, **Da Paolino** (via Marsala 41, 0564 629388, closed Mon, average €26-€36) is a good, traditional *trattoria* with an interesting wine list and very reasonable prices.

Pitigliano

Perched high on a rocky outcrop, Pitigliano is an awesome sight from afar, appearing to grow from the sheer golden tuff limestone cliffs that fall away on all sides. The dramatic drop into the valley below is accentuated by an immense aqueduct, built in 1545, that connects the lower and upper parts of town. The 1527 church of **Madonna delle Grazie**, on an opposite hill as you approach, provides a vantage point over the town and countryside. During the Middle Ages, Pitigliano was one of the foremost centres of power of the Aldobrandeschi family, who were succeeded by the Orsinis in the 14th century. Both coats of arms are on display in the Orsini family's palace courtyard on piazza Orsini.

The Jewish community that was attracted here by increasing Medici tolerance in the 16th century either left or was forced out during World War II. There's a small **Museo Ebraico**, housed in the former synagogue in vicolo Marghera (0564 616006, closed Sat, admission €3), once part of the ghetto. It comprises caves once used for ritual bathing and another area in which bread was baked. There's a *pasticceria* just around the corner that still makes a local Jewish pastry called *sfratti* ('the evicted'). Elsewhere, the **Museo Civico Archeologico** (piazza Orsini, 0564 614067, closed Mon, admission €3) has a small but well-presented collection of Etruscan artefacts.

Today, Pitigliano is home to a number of interesting craft shops: for colourful leather goods made on the spot, visit Rodolfo Cilento's **Bottega Artigiana** (via Roma 87, 0564 616218); for olive-wood kitchenware, head for **L'Albero dell'Olivo** (via Zuccarelli 90, 0564 615676); for unusual handwoven clothes and jewellery, try **Animaglia** (piazza San Gregorio VII 104, 340 8671628 mobile).

Where to eat

Good food and an interesting wine list can be found at **Il Castello** (piazza della Repubblica 92, 0564 617061, €30), which marries modernity with tradition. Otherwise, try a local *trattoria* such as **Il Grillo** (via Cavour 18, 0564 615202, closed Tue and July, average €17).

Sovana & Sorano

The Etruscans controlled the middle reaches of the Fiora river between the sixth and seventh centuries BC, thus also controlling the main communications route between the coast and the mineral rich areas of Monte Amiata. This accounts for the development of **Sovana**, which continued to grow and prosper in Roman times and during the Middle Ages.

Today, it's a charming little town, and a good place to stay when visiting the Etruscan necropolises in the immediate vicinity. There's a small museum of local history in the 13th-century **Palazzo Pretorio** (0564 633099, closed Mon, admission €2.50), next door to the arched **Loggetta del Capitano**; nearby is the church of **Santa Maria** (0564 616532), with its magnificent pre-Romanesque ciborium (altar canopy).

Perched high above the Lente river as you head north-east from Sovana is the town of **Sorano**. Though less restored and touristy than Sovana, it's actually the municipal centre. It was a defence post under the Orsini empire, but at times its geology proved more dangerous than rampaging enemies, and a series of landslides encouraged a slow but steady exodus. **Masso Leopoldino**, a giant terraced tufa cliff, peers down on the town. Sorano hosts a good crafts fair in mid August.

Where to stay & eat

Albergo Scilla (via R Siviero 1-3, 0564 616531, €80) has 20 nice, fairly priced rooms and a restaurant, the excellent **Ristorante dei Merli** (0564 616531, closed Tue, average €25). Otherwise, it's worth considering the **Sovana Hotel & Resort** (via del Duomo 66, 0564 617030, €120), which also owns the fine **Taverna Etrusca** (piazza del Pretorio 16, 0564 616183, closed Wed, Jan & Feb, average €28). If you want to stay in a medieval Tuscan fortress, head to Sorano's comfortable **Della Fortezza** (piazza Cairoli, 0564 632010, closed Jan & Feb, €100-€130), which has amazing views. For thoughtful local cuisine try **Hostaria Terrazza Aldobrandeschi** (via del Borgo 44, 0564 638699, www.hostaria-aldobrandeschi.com, closed Tue & Wed lunch, average €32).

Monte Argentario & Orbetello

A mountain rising abruptly and dramatically from the sea, **Monte Argentario** is the Tuscan coast at its most rugged. If it looks as though it should be an island, that's because it was – until the 18th century, when the two long outer sand-spits created by the action of the tides finally reached the mainland. They created and enclose the **Orbetello** lagoon. With the smaller Lago di Burano just to the south, these shallow waters are a prime and protected birdwatching area. They are also the breeding ground for eels and grey mullet whose roe becomes *bottarga*, a local gastronomic delicacy.

Orbetello itself sits in the middle of the most central of the three isthmuses connecting Monte Argentario to the mainland. It has remnants of Spanish fortifications dating from the 16th and 17th centuries, when it was the capital of the Stato dei Presidi, a Spanish enclave on the Tuscan coast. There's a small antiquarium you can visit, with some rather uninspiring Etruscan and Roman exhibits, and the cathedral has a Gothic façade, but Orbetello is more about atmosphere than sightseeing.

Two nice beaches make up the sand-spits that join Monte Argentario to the mainland. To the north, access to **La Giannella** is from the main Talamone-Argentario road (look for any of the little pathways through the pines), while to the south, **La Feniglia** is accessible by parking at the western end. You can hire a bicycle and cycle through the protected pine woods behind La Feniglia. Both beaches have the odd paid *bagno*, but the rest is free.

On the south-east corner of Argentario lies the exclusive town of **Porto Ercole**, where Caravaggio died drunk on the beach in 1610. Easter and August holidays see this small bay packed to the gills. **Porto Santo Stefano** is another atmospheric port – you'll almost certainly find fishermen mending nets on the quay – although the vibe is more upmarket during the holidays when the yachting crowd arrives. You can catch a ferry for the **Isola del Giglio** here (*see p296*).

Where to stay & eat

In Orbetello, join the evening *struscio* (along the corso Italia promenade) before dining on a plate of eels fished from the lagoon at one of the town's simple *trattorie*. A top choice in these parts for fish is **I Pescatori** (via Leopardi 9, 0564 860611, closed Mon-Wed in winter & Mon-Sat lunch in winter, average €20). The best of the town's less expensive hotels is **Piccolo Parigi** (corso Italia 169, 0564 867233, €68).

In Porto Ercole, the best views are available at the three-star **Don Pedro** (via Panoramica 7, 0564 833914, www.hoteldonpedro.it, closed Oct-Mar, €100-€110). The charismatic two-star **Hotel Marina** (lungomare Andrea Doria 23, 0564 833055, €120) is more central. There are several seafood restaurants to be found along the Porto Ercole harbour, plus a pizzeria. But the best place to eat fish in town is the **Osteria dei Nobili Santi** (via del Ospizio 8-10, 0564 833015, closed Mon & lunch Sun, average €40).

In Porto Santo Stefano, the **Hotel Vittoria** (via del Sole 65, 0564 818580/1, www.hvittoria.com, €67-€95) is a nice place to stay. Good dining can be found at **Dal Greco** (via del Molo 1-2, 0564 814885, closed Tue and Nov or Jan, average €45), a seafood restaurant with a harbour terrace, and at the slightly cheaper **Il Moletto di Amato & Figli** (via del Molo, 0564 813636, closed Wed and mid Jan-Feb, average €26), fantastically located at the end of the quay. The seafront is lined with a string of bars, including the overwhelmingly fashionable **Il Buco** (lungomare dei Navigatori 2, 0564 818243, closed Tue in winter, average €34).

Capalbio & Ansedonia

Close to the Lazio border, **Capalbio** is a magnet for Rome's poets, politicians and musicians, especially during August's **Grey Cat Jazz Festival**. The main attraction for tourists is **Il Giardino dei Tarocchi** (0564 895122, closed late Oct-mid May, admission €6.20-€10.50), an amazing walled garden to the south-east of the town. Founded in 1976, it contains around 20 huge sculptures (some of which house four-storey buildings) that represent characters from the tarot deck.

Due west on the coast is **Ansedonia**, on whose rocky promontory lie the remains of Cosa, a Roman colony founded in 273 BC. Remains of walls, a gate and residential areas are still visible. The **Museo di Cosa** (via delle Ginestre 35, 0564 881421, admission €2) displays artefacts from the area.

Daily trains from Grosseto stop at Capalbio station, from where it's three kilometres (two miles) to the beach alongside the picturesque **Lago di Burano lagoon** (now a WWF reserve). The coastline stretching southwards from Ansedonia offers 18 kilometres (11 miles) of beach, but there's an industrial plant looming through the haze at the far south end, so you're better off on the beaches north of Argentario or heading straight for an island.

Where to stay & eat

La Locanda di Ansedonia (via Aurelia Sud km140.5, 0564 881317, www.lalocandadiansedonia.it, €105), situated in an old farmhouse, has 12 rooms and a restaurant. Breakfast includes all sorts of home-made goodies. In Capalbio, the **Hotel Valle del Buttero** (via Silone 21, 0564 896097, €40-€120) is a large three-star structure. **Ghiaccio Bosco** (via della Sgrilla 4, 0564 896539, €85-€95) is a nice *agriturismo* with pool. **Trattoria La Torre da Carla** (via Vittorio Emanuele 33, 0564 896070, closed Mon-Fri in winter & all Thur, average €26) serves a good selection of robust Tuscan cuisine.

Resources

Tourist information

Grosseto *Agenzia Promozione Turismo (APT), viale Monterosa 206 (0564 462611).* **Open** 8.30am-1.30pm, 2.30-6.30pm Mon-Fri; 8.30am-1.30pm Sat.
Massa Marittima *Ufficio Turistico, via Todini 3 (0566 904756).* **Open** *Summer* 9.30am-12.30pm, 3-7pm Mon-Sat; 10am-1pm, 4-7pm Sun. *Winter* 9.30am-12.30pm, 3-6pm Mon-Sat; 10am-1pm Sun.
Pitigliano *Ufficio Turistico, piazza Garibaldi 51 (0564 617111).* **Open** 10.30am-1pm, 3-7pm Tue-Sun.
Porto Santo Stefano *Corso Umberto 55a (0564 814208).* **Open** 9am-1pm, 2-4pm Mon-Sat.
Saturnia *Consorzio L'Altra Maremma, piazza Vittorio Veneto 10 (0564 601280/www.laltramaremma.it).* **Open** *Summer* 10.20am-1pm, 3-7pm Mon-Sat. *Winter* 10.20am-1pm, 2-6pm Mon-Sat.

Getting there & around

By bus

There are about ten buses a day connecting Grosseto and Siena (journey time 90mins). Buses leave from in front of Grosseto's train station. For further information on buses serving regional towns such as Piombino and Pitigliano call **Rama** on 0564 25215.

By car

The main coast road (E80/SS1) links Grosseto with Livorno to the north and the Maremma to the south. The SS223, currently being widened, is the main route down from Siena. The region's most scenic road is the SS74, which branches inland off the SS1, north of Orbetello, and winds towards Manciano and Pitigliano.

By train

Grosseto is on the main train line between Rome and Pisa (90mins from Rome, 80mins from Pisa). Trains on this line also stop at Capalbio and Orbetello (for Monte Argentario) to the south, and San Vincenzo and Cecina to the north. A local train links Grosseto with Siena (2hrs). For national train information, call 892021 or go to www.trenitalia.it.

On the lagoon at **Orbetello**.

The Islands

The islands of the Tuscan archipelago are a welcome antidote to the area's largely unremarkable coast, particularly tiny, tranquil **Isola del Giglio** west of the Argentario peninsula. Both **Elba** and **Giglio** get crowded during Easter, July and August, and their idyllic sands and scenery are best enjoyed in May, June and September. The islands and the sea in which they're set make up the **Parco Nazionale Arcipelago Toscano**, Europe's biggest protected marine park. For information, call 0565 919411 or visit www.islepark.it.

Isola del Giglio

A steep and winding road connects the three villages on this beautiful little island: **Giglio Porto**, where the ferry docks; **Campese**, on the other side; and **Giglio Castello**, on the ridge between the two, with its medieval walls and steep narrow lanes. The main beach is at Campese, but there are other, smaller beaches dotted around elsewhere. The two great pleasures here are exploring the virtually uninhabited south and indulging at one of the many good restaurants on the quayside in Porto. Most of the hotels on the island are in Porto; there are also rooms to let in local homes.

Porte Ercole. *See p294.*

Where to stay & eat

Overlooking Giglio Porto, the three-star **Castello Monticello** (via Provinciale, 0564 809252, closed Oct-Mar, €80-€130) occupies a crenellated folly. For a fantastic meal book at **Arcobalena** (via Vittorio Emanuele 58, 0564 806106, average €32) up at the Castello. The menu depends on freshly caught fish and whatever's in the veg patch. The **B&B Airone** (contrada Santa Maria 12, 0564 806076, €40-€70) has good views. For more sun and sea, head to **Pardini's Hermitage** (Cala degli Alberi, 0564 809034, www.hermit.it, closed Nov-Mar, €200-€350 full board) in a secluded cove accessible only by foot or by boat (staff will fetch you).

While on the beach in Campese, you can have anything 'from a cappuccino to a lobster' at local stalwart **Tony's** (via della Torre 13, 0564 806453, closed Nov, average €24), on the north end of the beach below the tower.

Resources

Tourist information

Via Provinciale 9 (0564 809400/www.isoladelgiglio ufficioturistico.com). **Open** 9am-12.30pm, 4-6pm daily. Closed Nov-Easter.

Elba

Part of the Tuscan archipelago, Elba is Italy's third largest island, with 142 kilometres (88 miles) of coastline. Due to its wealth of mineral deposits, it was inhabited in prehistoric times, and later by the Greeks and the Etruscans. The **Museo dei Minerali Elbani** at **Rio Marina** (via Magenta 26, 0565 962088, www.parco minelba.it, closed Mon and Nov-Feb, admission €2.50) provides an interesting alternative to lolling on the beach, where things can get a bit crowded at Easter and in summer – the resident population of 30,000 swells to almost a million at peak season. Go in May or late September if you want to catch the island at its best.

Portoferraio is the island's capital and the focus of Napoleonic interest. The **Palazzo dei Mulini**, Napoleon's town residence, is worth a visit for its views and Empire-style furnishings. His summer retreat, the neoclassical **Villa Napoleonica di San Martino**, is roughly six kilometres (four miles) south-west of town.

Choosing between Elba's many village resorts can be tricky. Tiny **Viticcio** overlooks a pretty, secluded bay with some rock and shingle; **Biodola** has a terrific beach, but is dominated by large hotels and parasols; **Poggio** has a good portion of free beach but can get very busy; while **Marciana Marina** is an attractive port town.

South park

The beautiful, WWF-protected nature reserve of Parco Naturale della Maremma stretches from Principina Mare to Talamone, taking in the Monti dell'Uccellina. The strip – a coastal wilderness – offers miles of sandy beach, mostly unencumbered by resorts.

A train service runs from Grosseto to Marina di Alberese; from here, head for the **Visitors' Centre** at Alberese (via Bersagliere 7-9, 0564 407098, closed afternoons Nov-Apr) for information about trails, wildlife and activities such as canoeing and horse riding. Then, take a bus or walk (cars aren't allowed in the park) the four kilometres (2.5 miles) to the park entrance (open 9am-an hour before sunset daily, admission €5.50-€8).

Birds thrive in the reserve, including ospreys, falcons, kingfishers, herons and the rare Knight of Italy. The terrain ranges from the mudflats and umbrella pines of the estuary to the woodland of the hills.

There are two lodges, which must be booked via the **Poiana Viaggi** travel agent on 0564 412000. Otherwise, head to the charming town of Magliano in Toscana to the **Locanda delle Mura** (piazza Marconi 5, 0564 593057, €80-€100), a classy B&B, or to Talamone, near the southern entrance to the park. Options around here include **Hotel Capo d'Uomo** (via Cala di Forno 5, 0564 887077, closed Nov-Mar, €110-€130), a three-star hotel that overlooks the bay, and **Telamonio** (piazza Garibaldi 4, 0564 887008, www. hotelcapoduomo.com, closed Oct-Mar, €90-€130), in the town. Note that camping is not allowed within the park.

Up the hill, **Marciana** itself and **Sant' Andrea** are good starting points for an ascent of **Monte Capanne**. The national park in the north-west is a walker's paradise. The tourist office has a good booklet with a list of trails.

Many of the villages on the south and south-western side of the island have good beaches; the pick of them is at **Fetovaia**.

Where to stay & eat

Affrichella, on Marciana Marina's via Santa Chiara (no.7, 0565 996844, closed Wed in winter, early Nov-early Dec & early Jan-early Mar, closed Sun-Thur, average €31) offers local fish dishes. In Poggio, head to **Publius** (piazza del Castagneto 11, 0565 99208, closed Mon in winter and Jan-Feb, average €25), which has fantastic views, the best cellar on the island and a menu that isn't limited to the usual fish dishes. Nearby is **Luigi** (località Lavacchio, 0565 99413, closed all Tue & Mon mid June-Aug and Nov-Apr, average €20), offering fresh rustic dishes. As you leave Porto Azzurro heading for Portoferraio you'll find **La Botte Gaia** (viale Europa 5-7, 0565 95607, closed Mon & mid Jan-mid Mar, average €28), which focuses on fish and has a good wine list. Just out of Portoferraio, towards Bagnaia, is **La Carretta** (locandia Magazzini 92, 0565 933223, closed Wed and mid Oct-mid Jan); don't be put off by its low-key exterior – the owners pride themselves on their Elban cuisine.

Accommodation-wise, at Capo Sant'Andrea, **Hotel Ilio** (via Sant'Andrea 5, 0565 908018, www.hotelilio.com, €50-130/person) has 20 nice rooms overlooking lovely gardens, and a good restaurant. Otherwise, **Casa Lupi**, on the outskirts of Marciana Marina (Ontanelli, 0565 99143, closed Jan & Feb, €30-€70), is one of the best one star hotels on Elba. In Viticcio, stay at two-star **Scoglio Bianco** (0565 939036, www.scogliobianco.it, closed Oct-Easter, €42-€170 half-board). In Fetovaia, **Lo Scirocco** is clean, smart and well located (località Fetovaia, 0565 988033, closed Oct-Mar, €85-€120).

Ottone is home to the huge **Rosselba le Palme** (località Ottone, 0565 933101, www. rosselbalepalme.it, bungalows €125, tents €13), one of the best camping and bungalow sites on Elba, and **Villa Ottone** (località Ottone, 0565 933042, www.villaottone.com, €87-€202 half-board per person), a swish hotel with a restaurant open only to hotel guests. Alternatively, the **Monte Fabbrello** winery (Schiopparello, 0565 933324) has rooms for €45 to €60.

Resources

Tourist information

Azienda Promozione Turismo Elba, calata Italia 43, Portoferraio (0565 914671/www.aptelba.it). **Open** 8am-8pm Mon-Sat; 9.30am-12.30pm, 3.30-6.30pm Sun.

Getting there

By boat

Toremar (0564 810803, www.toremar.it) has services from Piombino (*see p290*) to Elba and from Porto San Stefano to Giglio. **Maregiglio** (0564 812920, www.maregiglio.it) runs just the latter service.

Directory

Getting Around 300
Resources A-Z 304
Vocabulary 317
Glossary 318
Further Reference 319

Features

Travel advice 305
Average monthly climate 314

Mercato Nuovo. *See p84.*

Directory

Getting Around

Arriving & leaving

By air

Amerigo Vespucci Airport at Peretola is by far the easiest way to reach Florence, but only Meridiana flies here from London Gatwick. Pisa's **Galileo Galilei Airport** has frequent flights to and from the UK, and increasingly the US, but is a train or coach journey away. A third choice is Bologna's **Guglielmo Marconi Airport**.

Florence Airport, Peretola (Amerigo Vespucci)

055 3061300/flight information 055 3061700 /www.aeroporto.firenze.it.
About 5km (3 miles) west of central Florence, Amerigo Vespucci is linked to the city by the **Volainbus**, a bus shuttle service that runs half-hourly 6am-11.30pm, costs €4.50 and stops in the SITA station at via Santa Caterina da Siena 15 (*see p301*). Buy tickets on the bus, at the airport bar or wherever bus tickets are sold (*see p301*). Bus season ticket holders don't have to buy an extra ticket. A taxi to Florence costs from €20 (*see also p301*) and takes about 20 minutes. For coaches to Pisa Airport, *see below*.

Pisa International Airport (Galileo Galilei)

050 849111/flight information 050 849300/www.pisa-airport.com.
The direct train to Florence's Santa Maria Novella (SMN) station from Pisa Aeroporto takes just over an hour. Buy tickets (€5.50 each way) at the desk to the right of arrivals in the main airport concourse. Trains run roughly every hour from 6.40am to 1am, though in the evening you'll need to change at Pisa Central. The service via Lucca is less frequent and takes longer. A taxi into Pisa from the airport costs about €10, and the CPT bus 5 leaves for Pisa city centre and train station every 15 minutes.

There are very few direct trains from Florence to Pisa Aeroporto, with most in the morning and the last at 22.35. Most trains during the day will mean changing at Pisa Centrale where the trains to Pisa Aeroporto generally leave from Platform 14 (via an underpass) or take the CPT bus.

A coach service from Pisa airport to Florence SMN train station is run by **Terravision** (050 26080, www.terravision.eu). It leaves from outside the arrivals area and from the steps of Florence SMN train station. Tickets can be bought from the kiosk in the airport, from the hotel reservations booth at the top of platform 16 of Florence SMN, from several travel agencies (see website for details), online or by phone. Tickets cost €8 each way and the journey takes 70 minutes. The coach also goes on to Florence Airport for no extra charge.

To get to Florence by car, take the Firenze–Pisa–Livorno road, which goes to the west of the city.

Bologna Airport (Guglielmo Marconi)

051 6479615/www.bologna-airport.it.
An airport bus stops outside terminal A (arrivals) and leaves for Bologna train station every 15 minutes between the hours of 6am to 11.40pm. Tickets cost €5 from the machine in the terminal building or on board. The trip takes about 30 minutes in total. A taxi costs about €18.

From Bologna Centrale, trains to Florence are frequent and take between 50-90 minutes; prices vary. The fastest trains are the Eurostars, which run frequently 6am-9.45pm daily (7.15am-10.20pm in the other direction). A single ticket is €15. Reservations are recommended as trains are often sold out. Intercities are less regular and cost €11.50. Another downside of flying in to Bologna is that you may find some trains into Florence fully booked, unless you've bought a ticket in advance (which means changing your ticket if the plane is delayed).

Travelling by car, the journey to Florence takes about 90 minutes, south on the A1.

Major airlines

Alitalia *06 2222/www.alitalia.it*
British Airways *199 712266/ www.britishairways.com*
Easyjet *Customer service 899 234589/bookings 899 678990/ www.easyjet.co.uk*
Meridiana *892928/+39 0789 52692 from outside Italy/www.meridiana.it*
Ryanair *899 678210/ www.ryanair.com*

By rail

Train tickets can be bought from the ticket desks, vending machines in the station, **Ticket Point LAZZI** (*see p301*), from www.trenitalia.com, or travel agents with the **FS** logo (Ferrovie dello Stato, state railways).

Before boarding any train, stamp (*convalidare*) your ticket and any supplements in the yellow machines at the head of the platforms. Failure to do this will get you a €50 fine payable on the train, unless you go immediately to the train guard and ask him to validate your ticket. Bear in mind that there is also a €50 fine for boarding without a ticket.

Taxis serve Florence's main **Santa Maria Novella** station on a 24-hour basis; many city buses also stop there. It's a 5- to 10-minute walk into central Florence. Some services go to **Campo di Marte** station to the north-east of the city, where buses 67 and 70 also stop. Note that train strikes are still fairly common. Details on train services in Italy can be obtained by calling the central information line on 892021 (7am-9pm daily; some English is spoken) or visiting www.trenitalia.com/en/index.html. Information on disabled access is available at the disabled assistance desk on platform 5 at Santa Maria Novella or on 055 2352275 or by calling the national line 199 303060. Both are open 7am-9pm daily and English is spoken.

Campo di Marte

Via Mannelli, Outside the City Gates (disabled assistance 055 2352275). Bus 12, 70 (night).
Florence's main station when SMN is closed at night. Many long-distance trains stop here. The ticket office is open 6.20am-9pm daily.

Santa Maria Novella

Piazza della Stazione, Santa Maria Novella. **Open** 4.15am-1.30am daily. *Information office* 7am-9pm daily. *Ticket office* 5.50am-10pm daily. **Map** p334 A2.

By road

By coach, you'll probably arrive at either the **SITA** or the **LAZZI** coach stations, both near Santa Maria Novella station (*see above*).

Ticket Point LAZZI
Piazza Adua, Santa Maria Novella (055 215155/www.lazzi.it). **Open** 9am-7pm Mon-Sat. **Credit** (train tickets only) AmEx, DC, MC, V. **Map** p334 A2.
Tickets for LAZZI, Eurolines coaches and Ferrovie dello Stato.

SITA
Via Santa Caterina da Siena 15, Santa Maria Novella (055 4782870/ www.sitabus.it). **Map** p334 A2.
See also p303 Transport in Tuscany.

Public transport

While the new tram system is under construction, the city's only public transport is still the comprehensive **ATAF** bus network. Strikes are unfortunately still fairly frequent; weekend and evening waiting times can be long. Regular train services run between the city's three train stations, which can be particularly useful for getting nearer your destination, if there's a bus strike.

Bus services

ATAF
Piazza della Stazione, opposite north-east exit of train station, Santa Maria Novella (800 424500/199 104245 from mobiles/www.ataf.net). **Open** 7am-1.15pm, 1.45-7.30pm Mon-Fri; 7.15am-1.15pm Sat.
The main ATAF desk has English-speaking staff, but on the phone you may not be so lucky. At this office, you can buy a variety of bus tickets, and also get a booklet with details of major routes and fares.

Fares & tickets
It's cheaper to buy tickets before boarding buses, but you can now get tickets on board at €2 for 70mins. Tickets are available from the ATAF office in piazza della Stazione (except for season tickets), a few machines, *tabacchi*, newsstands and any bars displaying an orange ATAF sticker. When you board, stamp the ticket in one of the validation machines. If you are using a ticket for two consecutive journeys, stamp it on the first bus only, but keep it till you complete your journey, and if you go beyond the time limit, make sure that you stamp another to cover it.

Be aware that local plain-clothes inspectors regularly board buses for spot checks; anyone without a valid ticket is fined €50, payable within 30 days at the main information office or in post offices.

70min ticket (*biglietto 60 minuti*) €1.20; valid for 70mins of travel on all city area buses.
Multiple ticket (*biglietto multiplo*) €4.50; 4 tickets, each valid for 70mins.
3-hour ticket (*biglietto tre ore*) €1.80.
AGILE card €10; electronic card with 10 x 70min tickets (swipe once over validating machine for each traveller).
AGILE card €20; electronic card with 21 x 70min tickets (swipe once over validating machine for each person travelling).
24-hour ticket (*biglietto ventiquattro ore*) €5; one-day pass that must be stamped at the start of the first journey.
3-day ticket (*biglietto tre giorni*) €12.
7-day ticket (*biglietto sette giorni*) €16.
Monthly pass (*abbonamento*) €34; €23 students. The ordinary pass can be bought from the ATAF office at Santa Maria Novella station, or from any outlet with an 'Abbonamenti ATAF' sign. For the student pass, go to the Ufficio Abbonamenti in piazza della Stazione (open 7.15am-1.15pm, 1.45-7.45pm Mon-Fri; 7.15am-1.15pm Sat) with ID and two passport photos.

A special 24-hour sightseeing bus ticket, **Firenze Passepartour**, costs €22.

Daytime services
Most ATAF routes run from 5.30am to 9pm with a frequency of 10-30 minutes. Don't take much notice of the timetables posted on many bus stops: they're over-optimistic, to say the least. After 9pm, there are four night services in operation (*see below*). The orange and white *fermate* (bus stops) list the main stops along the route. Each of the stops has its name indicated at the top.

Night services
Four bus routes operate until 12.30am/1am (67, 68, 71 and 304). One more, the 70, runs all night: it leaves Santa Maria Novella every hour and passes through the centre of town before heading north, calling at Campo di Marte station and returning to Santa Maria Novella. Tickets are available on board for €2; you'll need the correct change.

Disabled travellers
Most buses across Florence are now of the newer design (grey and green) and are fully wheelchair accessible via an electric platform at the rear door. The city's remaining orange buses are sadly not.

Useful tourist routes
7 from Santa Maria Novella station, via piazza San Marco to Fiesole.
10 to and from Settignano.
12, 13 circular routes via Santa Maria Novella station, piazza della Libertà, piazzale Michelangelo and San Miniato.

ATAF also runs a network of electric buses, which covers four central routes: **A**, **B** and **C**, plus a smaller version of the diesel buses, the **D**. Normal bus tickets or season tickets are valid. These routes are detailed in ATAF's booklet and marked on our map (*pp334-35*).

As the best way of getting around the city centre is on foot, we only give bus numbers in listings when the venue/sight is located outside the city gates.

Rail services

Trenitalia
There are regular local train services from the central Santa Maria Novella station to Campo di Marte in the east and Rifredi in the west (892021/www.trenitalia.com/en/index.html). Tickets can be bought online or at the station ticket offices (*see also p300*). For lost property, *see p308*.

Tram services

The new **Tramvia** tram system is under construction, with completion projected for 2010. The first line, central Florence to Scandicci, is expected to be finished in 2008. For updates, visit www.tramvia.fi.it.

Taxis

The taxi situation has improved over the last couple of years but finding a cab can still be tough, especially during rush hour, at night, when it's raining and during trade fairs.

Licensed cabs are white with yellow graphics, with a code name of a place plus ID number on the door; 'Londra 6', for example. If you have problems, make a note of this code. You can only get a cab at a rank or by phone: they can't be flagged in the street. For important appointments, book by phone several hours ahead, although this isn't a guarantee of getting a cab, as you may be told the pre-booking 'quota' has been filled and you'll have to call when you need one.

Fares & surcharges

Taxis in Florence are expensive. When the taxi arrives, the meter should read €3.20 during the day, €5.10 on Sundays and on public holidays, and €6.40 at night. The fare increases at a rate of €1/km. Lone women pay 10% less after 9pm, but only if they request the discount when booking. There is an overall minimum fare of €5. Phoning for a cab carries a surcharge of €1.90; each item of luggage in the boot is €1, and destinations beyond the official city limits cost a lot more. For details, see the tariff card that cabs are required to display. Taxis between the airport and anywhere in the city centre have a fixed tariff of €20 in the day, €26.40 at night.

Phone cabs

When your call is answered, give the address where you want to be picked up, specifying if the street number is *nero* or *rosso* (for an explanation, *see p304*). If you've called before, the operator will just ask you to confirm your address. If a cab is available, you'll be given its code and a time; for example, 'Londra 6 in tre minuti'. Otherwise, a pre-recorded message or the operator will tell you to call back.
Taxi numbers 055 4390; 055 4798; 055 4242; 055 4499.

Taxi ranks

Ranks are indicated by a blue sign with TAXI written in white, but this is no guarantee that any cars will be waiting, or will arrive during your lifetime. Try piazza della Repubblica, piazza della Stazione, piazza Santa Maria Novella, piazza del Duomo, piazza San Marco, piazza Santa Croce and piazza di Santa Trinità.

Driving

The centre of Florence is easily walkable and the electric bus service is a good back-up so it's usually best to leave cars at home. Apart from the clogged traffic on the ring roads, whole parts of the centre are off limits, parking is difficult and quite expensive, and when local pollution reaches a certain level, cars on diesel or leaded fuel are banned from within a large radius of the city, though hire cars and cars with foreign plates are allowed access to hotels. Digital notices above the main roads into town give notice of these bans, which are also announced on local radio and in the local papers. You can also check on www.poliziamunicipale.fi.it/blocchiinq2007.htm (Italian only).

In addition, there are the permanent Traffic-Free Zones (ZTL). These areas (lettered A-E) include the old city centre and are expanding. Only residents or permit-holders can enter from 7.30am to 7.30pm, Monday to Saturday. This is usually extended in the summer to exclude cars from the centre in the evenings from Thursday or Friday to Sunday. On top of this, the city is frequently bringing in new restrictions then revoking them, so if you're in any doubt, your best bet is to check in the local press or with the municipal police (*see p310*).

Speed limits in the city are currently 50km/h (45km/h on motorbikes and mopeds), on the *superstrada* the limit is 90km/h and on the motorway (*autostrada*) 130km/h.

Anyone driving is strongly advised not to drink any alcohol. Legal drink drive limits are 0.5g/litre, which as a guide are generally reached or passed with less than a quarter litre of wine or a half litre of beer.

If you do decide to drive, remember that in Italy you drive on the right.

In a traffic emergency eg accidents or situations of immediate danger call 055 3285 (055 328 3333 for less urgent situations that still require swift intervention). *See also p306* Emergencies. For general traffic or parking information, call 800 055055 (8am-8pm Mon-Sat).

Breakdown services

It's advisable to join a national motoring organisation such as the AA or RAC in Britain or the AAA in the US before taking a car to Italy. They have reciprocal arrangements with the Automobile Club d'Italia (ACI), which will tell you what to do in case of a breakdown. Even for non-members, the ACI is the best contact if you have a breakdown, though you will, of course, be charged.

Automobile Club d'Italia (ACI)

Viale Amendola 36, Outside the City Gates (055 24861/24hr info in English 166 664477/24hr emergencies 803116). Bus 8, 12, 13, 14, 31. **Open** 8.30am-1pm, 3-5.30pm Mon-Fri.
The ACI has English-speaking staff, and charges reasonable rates. Members of associated organisations are entitled to free basic repairs, and to other services at preferential rates.

Car hire

Most major car hire companies are near the station, on or near borgo Ognissanti. Shop around for the best rates, which vary according to season (as do opening times).

If you don't want to rent a car, there are other motoring options operating across the city. One of these is **Sunny Tuscany** (055 286199/335 8020304/www.sunnytuscany.com), which provides chauffeur-driven cars for tours of Florence/Tuscany. And in Florence itself, consider renting an electric car, a very practical option as you can drive electric vehicles throughout the historic city centre. One conveniently central company with electric car hire is **Firenze by Car** (055 22825/333 1816919/www.firenzebycar.com).

Avis *Borgo Ognissanti 128r, Santa Maria Novella (055 213629/www.avis.it). Bus B.* **Open** 8am-7pm Mon-Sat; 9am-1pm Sun. **Credit** AmEx, DC, MC, V. **Map** p334 B1.
Other locations Peretola Airport (055 315588); Pisa Airport (050 42028).

Europcar *Borgo Ognissanti 53-55, Santa Maria Novella (055 290438/www.europcar.it). Bus B.* **Open** 8am-1pm, 2.30-7pm Mon-Fri; 8am-1pm Sat. **Credit** AmEx, DC, MC, V. **Map** p334 B1.
Other locations Peretola Airport (055 318609); Pisa Airport (050 41081).

Hertz *Via Maso Finiguerra 33, Santa Maria Novella (055 2398205/www.hertz.com). Bus B.* **Open** 8am-8pm Mon-Fri; 8am-7pm Sat; 8am-1pm Sun. **Credit** AmEx, DC, MC, V. **Map** p334 B1.
Other locations Peretola Airport (055 307370); throughout the city.

Maxirent Car & Scooter Rental *Borgo Ognissanti 133r, Santa Maria Novella (055 2654207/www.maxirent.com).* **Open** 9am-6pm Mon-Fri; 9am-1pm Sat; by appt Sun. **Credit** AmEx, DC, MC, V. **Map** p334 B1.

Car pooling

Car pool members pick up a car from one of the car points, and drop it back or to any of the other car points. Annual membership is €120, plus a €60 enrolment fee; you then pay between €2.05 and €2.60 an hour, plus 24¢-65¢ per kilometre. Call 055 241618 or see www.carsharingfirenze.it (Italian only).

Car pounds

If your car's not where you left it, chances are it's been towed. Call 055 4224142 with the car's registration number to confirm. The central car pound, Depositeria SaS (open 24hrs daily), is in via Allende, behind the Novoli fruit and veg market. The car owner must take proof of ownership and ID to regain possession. There's an initial charge for the towing (it varies depending on where it was towed from), plus a daily charge for the time left at the pound. In the unlikely event your car was stolen and found (check first that it has not been towed), it will be taken to the Ufficio Depositeria Comunale in piazza Artom 13-14 (055 3283660). The office is open 8am-12.45pm Mon-Fri, and Thur till 6pm.

Fuel stations

All petrol stations sell unleaded fuel (*senza piombo*). Diesel fuel is *gasolio*. Many offer a discount for self-service. Attendants don't expect tips.

There are stations on most main roads leading out of town. Normal hours are 7.30am-12.30pm and 3-7pm daily except Sundays. There are no permanently staffed 24-hour petrol stations in Florence: the nearest are on the motorways. AGIP stations on via Bolognese, via Aretina, viale Europa, via Senese and via Baracca have 24-hour self-service machines for overnight drivers.

Parking

Car hire is easily organised and driving yourself around during your trip is certainly an attractive option in theory, but beware that parking in Florence is a major problem and is severely restricted in the centre of town and cars are towed or clamped without pity (*see p302* Car pounds).

Most main streets are no-parking zones. Parking is forbidden where you see *passo carrabile* (access at all times) and *sosta vietata* (no parking) signs. In unrestricted areas, parking is free in most side streets. Blue lines denote pay-parking; there will be either meters or an attendant to issue timed tickets, which you should return to them when you get back. Disabled spaces are marked by yellow stripes and are free. *Zona rimozione* (tow-away area) signs are valid for the length of the street, while temporary tow zones are marked at each end. Most streets are cleaned every one or two weeks, and vehicles either have to be removed or will be forcibly towed away to allow this to happen. Signs tell you when cleaning takes place, so if parking seems suspiciously easy in a street empty of cars then be sure to check.

The safest place to leave a car is in one of the underground car parks (*parcheggi*), such as **Parterre** and **Piazza Stazione**, which both have surveillance cameras.

Parcheggio Oltrarno *Piazza della Calza, Oltrarno (055 2232744/ www.firenzeparcheggi.it).* **Open** 24hrs daily. **Rates** €1.50/hr; €15/ 24hrs; €52/wk.

Parcheggio Parterre *Via Madonna della Tosse 9, just off piazza della Libertà, Outside the City Gates (055 5001994/www.firenze parcheggi.it). Bus 8, 17, 33.* **Open** 24hrs daily. **Rates** €1.50/hr; €18/ 24hrs; €65/wk.

Parcheggio Piazza Stazione *Via Alamanni 14/piazza della Stazione 12-13, Santa Maria Novella (055 2302655).* **Open** 24hrs daily. **Rates** €2/hr for 1st 2hrs, then €3/hr; 5 days €140. **Map** p334 A2.

Parcheggio S Ambrogio *Piazza Annigoni, Santa Croce (055 244641/ www.firenzeparcheggi.it).* **Open** 24hrs daily. **Rates** €1-1.50/hr for 1st 2hrs, then €3/hr.

Roads

There are three motorways in Tuscany that you have to pay a toll to use: the *autostrade* **A1** (Rome–Florence–Bologna), **A11** (the coast–Lucca–Florence) and **A12** (Livorno–Genova). *Autostrade* are indicated by green signs. As you drive on to one, pick up a ticket from one of the toll booths; hand it in, and pay when you come off. You can pay with a Viacard (a swipecard available from newsagents and the ACI; *see p302*), cash or credit cards. As an idea of price, it costs €15-€20 to drive the 270km (168 miles) from Rome to Florence, at a rate of 5¢ or 6¢ per kilometre.

Cycling

Cycling in Florence is essentially a form of Russian roulette. There are cycle lanes on the main *viali*, but that's no guarantee they'll only be used by bikes. Watch for doors being opened suddenly from cars parked on the side of the road.

Moped & bike hire

Mille e Una Bici is a council scheme to encourage the use of bikes. There are hire points all around the city including at the three main train stations, piazza Cestello, piazza Tasso and Parterre. Bike hire costs either €1.50/hour or €8/day and for residents and those with train or bus passes, it's 50¢ per hour, €1 a day or €15 a month. The companies below also rent out bikes.To hire a scooter or moped (*motorino*), you need a credit card, ID and cash deposit. Helmets must be worn on all mopeds. Cycle shops normally ask you to leave ID rather than a deposit. In addition to the following examples, *see p302* Maxirent.

Alinari

Via Guelfa 85r, San Lorenzo (055 280500/www.alinarirental.com). **Open** 9.30am-1pm, 3-7.30pm Mon-Sat; 10am-1pm, 3-7pm Sun. **Credit** MC, V. **Map** p334 A4.
Rental of a 50cc moped for use of one person only is €30/day; 125cc for one or two people is €55/day. A current driver's licence is required.

Florence by Bike

Via San Zanobi 120r, San Lorenzo (055 488992/www.florencebybike.it). **Open** 9am-7.30pm daily. Closed Nov-Feb. **Credit** AmEx, MC, V.
Bike hire costs either €2.70/hour or €14/day. Moped hire for two is from €65 a day. Guided tours are also available, and the majority of staff speak good English.

Walking

Even if you're in a hurry, walking is the quickest way to get around central Florence, and parts of the historic centre (*centro storico*) are totally pedestrianised. Still, watch out for bicycles and mopeds zooming up behind you, and don't be surprised if you meet two-wheeled vehicles coming the wrong way up a one-way street. What's more, don't expect cars to stop instantly at lights, and do expect them to ignore red lights when making right turns from side streets.

Our street maps (*see p334-35*) cover most of the centre. In addition, a good street map is available free from APT offices. If you need a more detailed map, check out the TuttoCittà, a detailed street atlas covering the whole urban area supplied by Telecom Italia with the phone book (most bars and hotels keep one). For an overview map of the city, *see p332-33.*

Transport in Tuscany

Driving is the best way of getting around Tuscany. If you don't have a car, it's possible to reach many parts of Tuscany by bus, though they can be few and far between. Companies such as **Tra-in** (out of Siena) and **LAZZI** (out of Florence) operate around major towns. In most villages, buses are timed to coincide with the school day, but combining bus and rail services can make things easier.

Information

For train information, *see p300.* Major Tuscan bus companies include the following:

CAP *Largo Fratelli Alinari 9, Santa Maria Novella, Florence (055 214637/www.capautolinee.it).* **Map** p334 A2.

LAZZI *Piazza della Stazione 4, corner of piazza Adua, Santa Maria Novella, Florence (055 351061/055 283878/www.lazzi.it).* **Map** p334 A2.

Rama *Via Topazo 12, Grosseto (0564 454169/www.rama mobilita.it).*

SITA *Via Santa Caterina da Siena 15, Santa Maria Novella, Florence (055 4782870/www.sitabus.it).* **Map** p334 A2.

Tra-in *Piazza San Domenico, Siena (0577 204111/www.comune. siena.it/train or www.trainspa.it).*

Resources A-Z

Addresses

Addresses in Italy are numbered and colour-coded. Residential addresses are 'black' numbers (*nero*), while most commercial addresses are 'red' (*rosso*). This means that on any one street, there can be two addresses with the same number but different colours and these properties can sometimes be quite far apart. Some houses are both shops and flats and could have two different numbers, one red and one black. Red numbers are followed by an 'r' when the address is written, a practice we have followed throughout this guide.

Note that the name on a business's shopfront or awning is quite often different from its official, listed name. We have used the former name wherever possible.

Age restrictions

In Italy, there are official age restrictions on a number of goods and activities. However, it's extremely rare for anyone to be asked to show ID in bars or elsewhere, other than in gay bars and clubs. The age of consent for heterosexual sex is 16, for gay sex 18. Beer and wine can be legally drunk in bars and pubs from the age of 16; spirits can be drunk by those 18 and over. It's an offence to sell cigarettes to children under 16. Mopeds (50cc) can be driven from the age of 14; cars from 18; only those over 21 can hire a car.

Attitude & etiquette

In churches, women are expected to cover their shoulders and not wear anything skimpy. Shorts and vests are out for anyone. Most major museums and galleries forbid the taking of photos with flashes; many even ban non-flash cameras. It's best to check at the ticket desk.

Queues are a foreign concept, but in a crowded shop, customers know who is before them and who's after, and usually respect the order. In shops, say *buongiorno* or *buona sera* on entering and leaving, and bear in mind that it's generally considered rude to walk in, look around and leave without asking for what you are looking for or at least greeting the shop assistant.

When addressing anyone except children, it's important to use the appropriate title: *signora* for women, *signorina* for young women, and *signore* for men.

Business

Conventions & conferences

Firenze Fiera *Via Leone X 3, Outside the City Gates (055 49721).*
This centre includes the Palazzo dei Congressi in the Fortezza da Basso and the Centro degli Affari Firenze. It specialises in hosting international meetings and can accommodate parties of up to 1,000 people.

Couriers & shippers

All major shipping companies will collect from Florence.

DHL *199 199345/www.dhl.com.* **Open** 24hrs daily. **Credit** AmEx, DC, MC, V.

Federal Express *800 123800/ www.fedex.com.* **Open** 8am-7pm Mon-Fri. **Credit** AmEx, DC, MC, V.

Mail Boxes Etc *Via della Scala 13r, Santa Maria Novella (055 268173/www.mbec.om).* **Open** 9am-1pm, 3.30-7pm Mon-Fri; 10am-1pm Sat. **Credit** AmEx, MC, V. **Map** p334 B2.

Oli-Ca Packing *Borgo SS Apostoli 27r, Duomo & Around (055 2396917).* **Open** 9am-1pm, 3.30-7.30pm Mon-Fri; 9am-1pm Sat. **Map** p334 C3.

SDA *199 113366/www.sda.it.* **Open** 8am-5pm Mon-Fri. **Credit** AmEx, MC, V.

TNT *803 868/800 019951/ www.tnt.it.* **Open** 8am-6pm Mon-Fri. **Credit** AmEx, MC, V.

UPS *800 877877/www.ups.com.* **Open** 8am-7pm Mon-Fri; 8.30am-1pm Sat. **Credit** AmEx, MC, V.

Office services

See also p311 Postal services.

Emynet *Lungarno Soderini 5/7/9r, Oltrarno (055 219228/emynet@ emynet.com).* **Open** 9.30am-1.30pm, 3-7pm Mon-Fri. **Map** p334 C1.
Full written and spoken translations in most languages.

Interpreti di Conferenza *Via Guelfa 116, San Lorenzo (055 475165/www.interpreti.net).* **Open** 9am-1pm Mon-Fri. **Map** p334 A2.
Interpreters for business meetings.

Useful organisations

Camera di Commercio Industria, Artigianato e Agricoltura (Chamber of Commerce) *Piazza Giudici 3, Duomo & Around (055 27951/ www.fi.camcom.it).* **Open** 8am-3.30pm Mon-Fri. **Map** p335 C4.
Provides information on all elements of import/export and business in Italy, and on Italian trade fairs.

Commercial Office, British Consulate *Lungarno Corsini 2, Duomo & Around (055 289556).* **Open** 9.30am-12.30pm, 2.30-4.30pm Mon-Fri. *Telephone enquiries* 9am-1pm, 2-5pm Mon-Fri. **Map** p334 C2.
Provides business advice and information to British nationals. Call for an appointment.

Commercial Office, United States of America Consulate *Lungarno A Vespucci 36/38/40, Outside the City Gates (055 211676/ 283780). Bus B.* **Open** 9am-12.30pm, 2-3.30pm Mon-Fri.

Consumer

Most shops are unlikely to take back purchases for a refund, unless the goods are faulty. The best you can hope for is an exchange or credit note. There is a desk at the tourist office for tourist consumer omplaints: via Cavour 1r, 055 2760382.

Customs

EU nationals don't have to declare goods imported into or exported from Italy for their personal use, as long as they arrive from another EU country. Personal use is considered to be within the limits of 800 cigarettes (and limits on cigars), 10 litres of spirits, 90 litres of wine (and limits on other alcoholic drinks). US citizens should check their duty-free allowance on the way out. Random checks are made for drugs (*see right* Drugs). For non-EU citizens, the following import limits apply:

- 200 cigarettes or 100 small cigars or 50 cigars or 250g of tobacco
- 1 litre of spirits (over 22% alcohol) or 2 litres of fortified wine (under 22%)
- 50 grams of perfume
- 500 grams of coffee

There are no restrictions on the importation of cameras, watches or electrical goods. Visitors are also allowed to bring in up to €10,329 (or equivalent) in cash without declaring it.

Disabled

Disabled facilities in Florence are improving. Recent laws stipulate that all new public offices, bars, restaurants and hotels must be equipped with full disabled facilities. Currently, the standard of access still varies greatly, though most museums are wheelchair-accessible, with lifts, ramps on steps and toilets for the disabled.

Pavement corners in the centre of town are now sloped to allow for wheelchair access. New buses are equipped with ramps and a wheelchair area (*see p301*). Trains that allow space for wheelchairs in the carriages and have disabled loos have a wheelchair logo on the outside, but there is no wheelchair access up the steep steps on the south side of the station: use the east or north entrance, or call the information office for assistance (*see p300*). Taxis take wheelchairs, but tell them when you book.

There are free disabled parking bays all over Florence, and disabled drivers with the sticker have access to pedestrian areas of the city. There are wheelchair-accessible toilets at Florence and Pisa airports and Santa Maria Novella station, as well as in many of Florence's main sights and at several public loos (*see p314* Toilets).

The Provincia di Firenze produces a booklet (also in English, available from tourist offices) with disabled-aware descriptions – how many steps on each floor, wide doorways and so on – of venues across Florence Province. For more information, call 800 437631 (some English spoken). The official council website (www.comune.fi.it) also has useful sightseeing itineraries suitable for disabled visitors.

Wheelchair hire is free of charge both from the Misericordia (055 212222) and the Fratellanza Militare (055 26021). If they don't have any available they can refer to paid hire services.

Drugs

Drug-taking is illegal in Italy and a new law has increased the severity of sentencing and put all drugs, from cannabis to heroin, on the same level from a legal standpoint. If you're caught in possession of drugs of any type, you may have to appear before a magistrate. If you can convince him or her that your stash was for purely personal use, then you may be let off with a fine, have your passport or driving licence confiscated, have your movements restricted or be ordered to leave the country. Trafficking or dealing can land you in prison for up to 20 years. It is an offence to buy or sell drugs, or to give them away. Sniffer dogs are a fixture at most ports of entry into Italy; customs police are vigilant about visitors entering with even the smallest quantities of any banned substances, and you could be refused entry or arrested.

Electricity

Most wiring systems work on one electrical current, 220V, compatible with British and US-bought products. A few systems in old buildings

Travel advice

For up-to-date information on travel to a specific country – including the latest news on safety and security, health issues, local laws and customs – contact your home country government's department of foreign affairs. Most have websites packed with useful advice for would-be travellers.

Australia
www.dfat.gov.au/travel

Canada
www.voyage.gc.ca

New Zealand
www.mft.govt.nz/travel

Republic of Ireland
www.irlgov.ie/iveagh

UK
www.fco.gov.uk/travel

USA
www.state.gov/travel

are 125V. With US 110V equipment, you'll need a current transformer: buy one before you travel as they can be hard to find. Adaptors, on the other hand, can be bought at any electrical shop (look for *elettricità* or *ferramenta*).

Embassies & consulates

There are no embassies in Florence. However, there are some consular offices, which offer limited services.

Australian Embassy *Via Antonio Bosio 5, Rome (06 852721/www.italy.embassy.gov.au).*

British Consulate *Lungarno Corsini 2, Duomo & Around (055 284133/www.britishembassy.gov.uk).* **Open** 9.30am-12.30pm, 2.30-4.30pm Mon-Fri. *Telephone enquiries* 9am-1pm, 2-5pm Mon-Fri. **Map** p334 C2.
Out-of-hours, a message will tell you what to do if you need urgent help.

Canadian Embassy *Via Zara 30, Rome (06 854441/www.dfait-maeci.gc.ca/canada-europa/italy/menu-en.asp).*

Irish Embassy *Piazza Campitelli 3, Ghetto, Rome (06 6979121/www.europeanirish.com/Embassies).*

New Zealand Embassy *Via Zara 28, Rome (06 4417171/www.nzembassy.com).*

South African Consulate *Piazza dei Salterelli 1, Duomo & Around (055 281863/www.dfa.gov.za/foreign/sa_abroad/sai.htm).* **Map** p334 C3.
No office. You have to call to make an appointment.

US Consulate *Lungarno A Vespucci 38, Outside the City Gates (055 2398276/www.florence.usconsulate.gov/english). Bus B.* **Open** 9am-12.30pm, 2-3.30pm Mon-Fri.
In case of emergency call the above phone number and a message will refer you to the current emergency number.

Emergencies

See also Health: Accident & emergency, Helplines and Police.

Emergency services & state police *Polizia di Stato 113.*
Police *Carabinieri (English-speaking helpline) 112.*
Fire service *Vigili del Fuoco 115.*
Ambulance *Ambulanza 118.*
Car breakdown *Automobile Club d'Italia (ACI) 116/803 116.*
City traffic police *Vigili Urbani 055 3285.*
Pet health emergencies *800 029 449.*

Gay & lesbian

For more HIV and AIDS services, *see p307*.

ArciGay *199 444 592.*
Advice line.

Azione Gay e Lesbica *Circolo Finisterrae, via Pisana 22, Outside the City Gates (055 220250).* **Open** 6-8pm Mon-Wed. Closed 3wks Aug.
As well as organising parties, this group maintains a library and archive, facilitates HIV testing and provides general community information.

IREOS-Queer Community Service Center *Via de' Serragli 3, Oltrarno (055 216907/www.ireos.org).* **Open** 5-8pm Mon-Thur, Sat. **Map** p334 C1/D1.
Ireos hosts social open houses, and offers HIV testing, and referrals for psychological counselling and self-help groups. It also organises hikes and outings and has free internet access most evenings and Saturday mornings. See website for details of timetable.

LILA *055 2479013.*
Not-for-profit gay health advice line.

Queer Nation Holidays *Via del Moro 95r, Santa Maria Novella (055 2654587/www.queernationholidays.com).* **Open** 9.30am-7.30pm Mon-Fri; 10am-6pm Sat. **Credit** MC, V. **Map** p334 B2.
Queer Nation Holidays can organise individual and group travel. It can also make referrals to other gay and lesbian organisations.

Health

Emergency healthcare is available for all travellers through the Italian national health system. EU citizens are entitled to most treatment for free, though many specialised medicines, examinations and tests will be charged for. To get treatment, you'll need a European Health Insurance Card (*see p308*). From the UK this is available by phoning 0845 606 2030 or online from www.ehic.org.uk (you need to provide name, date of birth and National Insurance number). The EHIC has replaced the E111, which is no longer valid. The card will only cover partial costs of medicines. In non-emergency situations, citizens from countries with a reciprocal agreement with Italy (eg Australia) should go to the state health centre (Azienda Sanitaria di Firenze, or ASF, www.asf.toscana.it) on the second floor of borgo Ognissanti 20 (open 8am-1pm Mon-Fri plus 2.30-6pm Tue). Other non-EU visitors are charged for health care.

For hospital treatment, go to one of the casualty departments listed below. If you want to see a GP, go to the ASL for the district where you are staying, taking your EHIC with you. The ASLs are listed in the phone book and they usually open 9am-1pm and 2-7pm Monday to Friday.

Consulates (*see above*) can provide lists of English-speaking doctors, dentists and clinics. *See also p307* Doctors.

Non-EU citizens will need to take out private health insurance before visiting to be covered for healthcare.

Accident & emergency

If you need urgent medical care, it's best to go to the *pronto soccorso* (casualty) department of one of the hospitals listed below; they're open 24 hours daily. Alternatively, call 118 for an ambulance (*ambulanza*).

To find a doctor on call in your area (emergencies only), phone 118. For a night (8pm-8am) or all-day-Sunday emergency home visit, call the Guardia Medica for your area (quartiere 1: 055 2339456; Oltrarno: 055 215616).

Ospedale di Careggi *Viale Morgagni 85, Outside the City Gates (055 7949644/www.ao-careggi.toscana.it). Bus 2, 8, 14C.*
The main hospital and the best place to go to for most emergencies.

Ospedale Meyer (Children) *Via Luca Giordano 13, Outside the City Gates (055 56621/www.ao-meyer.toscana.it). Bus 11, 17.*

Ospedale Santa Maria Annunziata (known as Ponte a Nicchieri) *Via Antella 58, Bagno a Ripoli, Outside the City Gates (055 24961). Bus 32.*

Ospedale Torregalli *Via Torregalli 3, Outside the City Gates (055 71921). Bus 83.*
Ospedale Palagi (eye hospital) *Viale Michelangiolo 41, Outside the City Gates (055 65771).* **Open** 8am-8pm daily. Bus 12, 13. For eye emergencies; outside these opening hours go to Careggi.
Santa Maria Nuova *Piazza Santa Maria Nuova 1, Duomo & Around (055 27581).* **Map** p335 B4.
The most central hospital in Florence. There's also a 24-hour pharmacy directly outside.

One of the obvious anxieties involved with falling ill when abroad is the language problem. If you need a translator to help out at the hospital, contact.

AVO (Association of Hospital Volunteers) *Via G Carducci 8, Outside the City Gates (24hrs 055 2344567).* **Open** *Office hours* 4-6pm Mon, Wed, Fri; 10am-noon Tue, Thur.
AVO is a group of volunteer interpreters who help out with explanations to doctors and hospital staff in 22 languages. They also give support and advice.

Complementary medicine

Most pharmacies sell homeopathic and other complementary medicines, which are quite commonly used in Italy. Herbalists sell herbal but not homeopathic medicines; some can refer you to alternative health practitioners. *See also p163.*

Contraception & abortion

Condoms and other forms of contraception are widely available in pharmacies and some supermarkets. If you need further assistance, the Consultorio Familiare (family planning clinic) at your local ASL state health centre (*see p306*) provides free advice and information, though for an examination or prescription, you'll need an EHIC (*see p306*) or insurance. An alternative is to go to a private clinic like those run by AIED.

The morning-after pill is sold legally in Italy; it must be taken within 72 hours, and to obtain it, you'll need to get a prescription (*see below*). Abortion is legal in Italy and is performed only in public hospitals, but the private clinics that are listed below are able to give consultations and references.

AIED *Viale dei Mille 9, Outside the City Gates (055 582833).* **Open** 3-7pm Mon-Fri.
The clinics run by this private organisation provide help and information on contraception and related matters, and medical care at low cost. Treatment is of a high standard and service is often faster than in state clinics. An examination will usually cost something in the region of €40 plus €15 compulsory membership, payable on the first visit and then valid for a year.
Santa Chiara *Piazza Indipendenza 11, San Lorenzo (055 496312/ 475239).* **Open** 8am-7pm daily by appointment.
This clinic offers gynaecological examinations and general health check-ups. Call for an appointment.

Dentists

The following dentists speak English. Always call ahead for an appointment.

Dr Marcello Luccioli *Via de' Serragli 21, Oltrarno (055 294847).* **Open** 9am-1pm, 2.45-7pm Mon-Fri. **Map** p334 C1.
Dr Sandro Cosi *Via Pellicceria 10, Duomo & Around (055 214238/ 0335 332055).* **Open** 9am-1pm, 3-6pm Mon-Wed; 9am-1pm Thur, Fri. **Map** p334 C3.

Doctors

For a comprehensive list of English-speaking doctors in Florence, by specialisation, see www.italy.usembassy.gov/acs/professionals/doctors-florence.asp.

Dr Stephen Kerr *Via Porta Rossa 1, Duomo & Around (055 288055/ 0335 8361682/www.dr-kerr.com).* **Open** *Surgery* by appointment 9am-1pm Mon-Fri. Drop-in clinic 3-5pm Mon-Fri. **Credit** AmEx, MC, V. **Map** p334 C3.
This friendly, knowledgable English GP practises privately in Florence. He charges €40-€70 (standard charge €50) for a consultation in his surgery.
Medical Service *Via Lorenzo il Magnifico 59, Outside the City Gates (24hr line 055 475411/ www.medicalservice.firenze.it). Bus 8, 13.* **Open** *Clinic* 11am-noon Mon-Sat, 5-6pm Mon-Fri.
A private medical service that organises home visits by doctors. Catering particularly to foreigners, it promises to send an English-speaking GP or specialist out to you in the city of Florence within an hour for between €80 and €150. Clinic visit €50.

Hospitals

See p306 Accident & emergency.

Opticians

For eye tests, prescription glasses and contact lenses, *see p165*.

Pharmacies

Pharmacies (*farmacia*), which are identified by a red or green cross hanging outside, function semi-officially as mini-clinics, with staff able to give informal medical advice and suggest non-prescription medicines. Normal opening hours are 8.30am-1pm and 4-8pm Mon-Fri and 8.30am-1pm Sat, but many central pharmacies are open all day. At other times, there's a duty rota system. A list by the door of all pharmacies indicates the nearest one open outside normal hours, also published in local papers. At duty pharmacies, there's a surcharge of €2.60 per client (not per item) when only the special duty counter is open – usually midnight-8.30am. Prescriptions are required for most medicines. If you require regular medication, make sure you know their chemical (generic) rather than brand name, as they may be available in Italy only under a different name.

The pharmacies listed on page 165 provide a 24-hour service without a supplement for night service.

STDs, HIV & AIDS

Clinica Dermatologica *Via della Pergola 64, San Marco (055 2758684).* **Open** 8am-noon Mon, Wed, Thur, Fri; 8-11am Tue, Sat. **Map** p335 A5.
Clinica Dermatologica carries out examinations, tests, treatment and counselling for all sexually transmitted diseases, including HIV and AIDS. Some services are free, while others are state-subsidised. Some staff speak English.
Ambulatorio Malattie Infettive *Ospedale di Careggi Viale Morgagni, Outside the City Gates (055 4279425/6). Bus 2, 8, 14C.* **Open** 9am-12.30pm, 3-6pm Mon-Fri; 9am-12.30pm Sat.
AIDS centre with information, advice and testing. Call ahead for an appointment. Basic English spoken.
Infoline per la Salute Omosessuale *(199 444592, 4-8pm Fri).*
Run by the ArciGay organisation, this infoline provides help about services relating to AIDS and HIV.

Helplines

AIDS helpline *800 571661*
Alcoholics Anonymous *055 294417*

Regular AA and Al Anon meetings are held at St James Church (*see p311* Religion for details).
Drogatel *800 016600*. **Open** 9am-8pm daily.
A national help centre for drug-related problems. It also gives advice on alcohol-related problems.
Samaritans *800 860022*.
Some English-speakers.
Voce Amica *055 2478666*.
The local Italian version of the Samaritans. Some English spoken.
Women's Rights & Abuse *800 001122*.

ID

In Italy, you're required by law to carry photo ID at all times. You'll be asked to produce it if you're stopped by traffic police (who will demand your driving licence, which you must have on you whenever you are in charge of a motor vehicle). ID will also be required when you check into a hotel.

Insurance

EU nationals are entitled to reciprocal medical care in Italy, provided they have in their possession a European Health Insurance Card (EHIC). *See p306* for details of how to obtain the card.

Despite this provision, short-term visitors from all countries are advised to get private travel insurance to cover a broad number of eventualities (from injury to theft). Non-EU citizens should ensure that they take out comprehensive medical insurance with a reputable company before leaving home.

Visitors should also take out adequate property insurance before setting off for Italy. If you rent a car, motorcycle or moped, make sure that you pay the extra for full insurance and sign the collision damage waiver before taking off in the vehicle. It's also worth checking your home insurance first, as it may already cover you.

Internet

It's very easy to find internet access in Florence. Even most budget hotels will allow you to plug your modem into their phone system; the more upmarket hotels will probably have wireless in the public areas and bedrooms. Some Italian phone plugs are different from US and UK versions: most have the square plug, though in modern hotels the US Bell socket is often used. As usual, it's best to check in advance with your hotel.

A number of Italian providers offer internet access. These include Libero (www.libero.it), Tiscali (www.tiscalinet.it), Kataweb (www.kataweb.com), Telecom Italia (www.tin.it) and Wind (www.inwind.it).

As we went to press local government announced plans for free Wi-Fi hotspots in several prominent *piazze* around town, due to be fully operative by the end of 2008. Some cafés also provide Wi-Fi access.

There are internet points in all areas of the city centre. Most of them charge around €5/hour, and there are often discounts for students. Remember to take ID, though: you'll need it to register, even as a guest user.

Internet Train *Via de' Benci 36r, Santa Croce (055 2638555/ www.internettrain.it)*. **Open** 10am-midnight Mon-Sat; 3-11pm Sun. **Credit** MC, V. **Map** p335 B5.
Internet Train was the first internet shop in Italy: it started off with four PCs, but now has nine shops in Florence. The chain has helpful English-speaking staff and 30 PCs. The company can also organise shipping and museum tickets for visitors.
Other locations *Via Porta Rossa 38r, Duomo & Around (055 2741037)*. **Open** 10am-midnight Mon-Sat; 3-11pm Sun. **Credit** MC, V. **Map** p335 B5.
Intotheweb *Via de' Conti 23r, San Lorenzo (055 2645628)*. **Open** 10am-midnight daily. **Credit** MC, V. **Map** p334 B3.
This friendly centre has 10 PCs and 10 Macs, and also sells international phone cards, sends and receives faxes and rents out mobile phones.
The Netgate *Via Sant'Egidio 10r, Santa Croce (055 2347967/ www.thenetgate.it)*. **Open** *Summer* 11am-9.45pm Mon-Sat. *Winter* 11am-9pm Mon-Sat; 2-8pm Sun. **Map** p335 B5.
A spacious centre with 35 computers.

Language

English is spoken in many central shops and all main hotels and restaurants, though in some small businesses, and in more out-of-the-way Tuscan villages, it may be trickier to communicate. Taking a phrase book is a good idea. For basic Italian vocabulary, *see p317*.

Left luggage

There's a left luggage point in Santa Maria Novella train station on platform 16 (055 2352190).

Legal help

Your first stop should be your embassy or consulate (*see p306*). Staff will be able to supply you with a list of English-speaking lawyers.

Libraries

Biblioteca Marucelliana *Via Cavour 43-47, San Marco (055 2722200/www.maru.firenze.sbn.it)*. **Open** 9am-7pm Mon-Fri; 9am-1pm Sat. **Map** p335 A4.
A diverse range of books, including some in English. ID will be needed to register.
British Institute Library & Cultural Centre *Lungarno Guicciardini 9, Oltrarno (055 26778270/www.britishinstitute.it)*. **Open** 10am-6.30pm Mon-Fri. **Map** p334 C3.
The British Institute's library requires an annual membership fee (€65, students €50), but offers a reading room that overlooks the Arno, an extensive collection of art history books and Italian literature, and well-informed staff.
Kunsthistorisches Institut in Florenz *Via G Giusti 44, Santa Croce (055 249111/www.khi.fi.it/en)*.

Open 9am-8pm Mon-Fri.
Map p335 A6.
One of the largest collections of art history books in Florence is held by the German Institute and is available to students. Books are in various languages and there's also an extensive photo library of Italian art, You'll need a letter of presentation and a summary of your research project.

Lost property

For property lost anywhere other than in planes, trains and taxis, contact the Ufficio Oggetti Ritrovati, the council's lost property office in via Circondaria 17b (Outside the City Gates, 055 3283942/ 3283943, bus 23, 33, open 9am-noon Mon-Sat). There's also a search option online for lost property: www. comune.firenze.it/comune/ oggettitrovati.htm.

For lost passports, contact the police (*see p311*).

Airports

Aeroporto di Firenze
055 3061302.
Pisa International Airport
050 849538.
Aeroporto di Bologna: two companies depending on the airline *051 6479443/051 6479647* (see www.bologna-airport.it for details).

Buses

Check at the council's lost property office (*see above*).

Taxis

If you leave something in a cab, call the taxi company and quote the car's code (place name and number), if you can remember it. Otherwise, contact the council's lost property office (*see above*), where anything left in cabs will be taken by the drivers.

Trains

FS/Santa Maria Novella (SMN) *Interno Stazione SMN, Santa Maria Novella (055 2356120).*
Open 6am-midnight daily.
Map p334 A2.
Articles found on state railways in the Florence area are sent to the Assistenza Clienti office at Santa Maria Novella station (located on platform 5). Minimal English.

Media

Magazines

Many newsstands in the centre of town sell *Time*, *Newsweek*, *The Economist* and other glossy English-language magazines. For Italian-speakers, Italian magazines worth checking out include *Panorama* (www.panorama.it) and *L'Espresso* (http://espresso.repubblica.it), weekly current affairs and general interest rags, the full-frontal style covers of which do little justice to the high-level journalism and hot-issue coverage found within. There are also some useful booklets with listings of events in Florence:

Firenze (www.firenzemagazine.it) Plush glossy running interviews with local indigenous and foreign celebrities, fashion stories, the odd cultural review and *Tatler*-style self-congratulatory party pics.
Firenze Spettacolo (www.firenzespettacolo.it) A monthly listings and local interest magazine that has an English-language section.
Florence Concierge Information (www.florence-concierge.it) Found at tourist offices and most hotels, this freebie gives events, useful information, timetables and suchlike in English.
Florence & Tuscany News Available around town, this booklet is useful for concerts and temporary exhibitions in Florence and Tuscany.

Newspapers

Foreign dailies

Many news-stands sell foreign papers, which usually arrive the next day (though sometimes the same evening in summer). The widest range are around piazza del Duomo, piazza della Repubblica, via de' Tornabuoni and SMN station.

Local English-language papers

The Florentine (www.the florentine.net) is a free English-language newspaper distributed every Thursday in restaurants, bars, hotels, language schools and the main squares. As well as news and events, it includes articles on culture, politics, travel and food.

Italian dailies

Only one Italian in ten buys a daily newspaper, so the press has little of the clout of other European countries, and the paper is generally a simple vehicle for information rather than a forum of pressure for change. Most papers publish comprehensive listings for local events. Sports coverage in the dailies is extensive, but if you're not sated, the sports papers *Corriere dello Sport* (www.corrieredellosport.it) and *La Gazzetta dello Sport* (www. gazzetta.it) offer even more detail.

Corriere della Sera (www.corriere.it) Serious and relatively neutral newspaper.
Il Giornale (www.ilgiornale.it) Owned by the brother of Silvio Berlusconi, *Il Giornale* takes the expected centre-right line. The Florence edition has a section dedicated to local news.
Libero (www.libero-news.it) Decidedly right-leaning newspaper launched in 2000, with a pull-no-punches, politically incorrect style.
La Nazione (http://qn.quotidiano.net) Selling some 160,000 copies daily, this is the most popular newspaper in Tuscany. Founded in the mid 19th century by Bettino Ricasoli, it's also one of Italy's oldest. Basically right-wing and gossipy, it consists of three sections (national, sport and local). Each province has its own edition.
La Repubblica (www.repubblica.it) Politically centre-left, with strong coverage of the Mafia and Vatican issues. The Florence edition has about 20 pages dedicated to local and provincial news.
Il Manifesto (www.ilmanifesto.it) A solidly left-wing intellectual paper.
L'Unità The media voice-piece for the far left.

Radio

BBC World Service Piggybacks live on FM on various Italian broadcasts (for a schedule see www.bbc.co.uk/cgi-bin/worldservice/ psims/ScheduleSDT.cgi) and can also be found on shortwave (SW); details of how to listen can be found on www.britishembassy.gov.uk.

Controradio (93.6 MHz/www.contro radio.it) Dub, hip hop, progressive drum 'n' bass and indie rock feature heavily on this station.
Nova Radio (101.5 MHz/www. novaradio.it) Run by volunteers and committed to social issues, Nova Radio broadcasts a very good mixture of jazz, soul, blues, reggae, world music, hip hop and rap. Best of all, there are no ads.
Radio Diffusione Firenze (102.7 MHz/www.rdf.iy) This radio station plays mainstream pop, house and club music.
Radio Montebeni (108.5 MHz/ www.firenzemedia.com/montebenicla ssica.html) Classical music only.
Radio Montecarlo (106.6 MHz/ www.radiomontecarlo.net) Best at night with Monte Carlo Nights hosted by Scottish DJ Nick the

Nightfly playing smooth jazzy sounds and world music.
Virgin Radio Italia (107.2MHz/89.1MHz/www.virginradioitaly.it) The newest mainstream radio station with very little chat and an emphasis on British and US rock.

Television

Italy has six major networks. Of these, three are Berlusconi-owned Mediaset channels: **Italia 6** shows familiar US series, Brazilian soaps, Japanese cartoons and adventure films; **Rete 4** spews out an awful lot of cheap game shows and *Columbo* repeats but also shows decent nature documentaries; and **Canale 5** is the top dog, with the best films, quiz programmes, live shows and the most popular programme on Italian TV, the scandal-busting, satirical *Striscia la Notizia*. Programmes are riddled with ad breaks and promotions.

RAI, the state-run channels, are known for their better-quality programming but generally much less slick presenting, and there is still a relentless stream of quiz shows and high-kicking bikini-clad bimbettes. When these have bored you, there are numerous local stations featuring cleaning demos, dial-a-fortune-teller (surprisingly popular), prolonged adverts for slimming machines and trashy late-night soft porn.

Of the many satellite and cable TV subscription channels, the best are **Stream** and **Telepiù**. Some of their packages include BBC and major US channels. The French channel **Antenne 2** is also accessible in Tuscany.

Money

Italy is in the euro (€) zone. There are euro banknotes for €5, €10, €20, €100, €200 and €500, and coins worth €1 and €2, plus 1¢, 2¢, 5¢, 10¢, 20¢ and 50¢ (cents). Credit cards are widely accepted, though AmEx and Diners Club slightly less so than Visa and MasterCard. Travellers' cheques can be changed at all banks and bureaux de change but are only accepted as payment (in any major currency) by larger shops, hotels and restaurants.

Banks & ATMs

Expect long queues even for simple transactions, and don't be surprised if the bank wants to photocopy your passport or driving licence as proof of ID. Many banks no longer give cash advances on credit cards, so check for the signs, or ask before queuing. Branches of most banks are found around piazza della Repubblica.

Most major banks have 24-hour cashpoint (Bancomat) machines, and the vast majority of these also accept cards with the Maestro and Cirrus symbols. To access the cashpoint lobby of some banks, you have to insert your card in the machine outside. Most machines will dispense a daily limit of €250. Your home bank will make a charge.

Bureaux de change

Changing your money in a bank usually gets you a better rate than in a private bureau de change (*cambio*) and will often be better than in your home country. However, if you need to change money out of banking hours, there's no shortage of bureaux de change (*cambi*). Commission rates vary considerably: you can pay from nothing to €5 for each transaction. Watch out for 'No Commission' signs; the exchange rate at these places will almost certainly be worse. Main post offices also have bureaux de change, where commission is €2.50 for all cash transactions (maximum €1,000). Some large hotels also offer an exchange service, but again, the rate is almost certainly worse than in a bank. Always take ID for any financial transaction.

American Express *Via Dante Alighieri 14r, Duomo & Around (055 50981).* **Open** 9am-5.30pm Mon-Fri; 9am-12.30pm Sat. **Map** p335 B4.
AmEx also has a travel agency.
Thomas Cook *Lungarno Acciaiuoli 4/8r, Duomo & Around (055 290278).* **Open** 9am-7pm Mon-Sat; 9.30am-5pm Sun. **Map** p334 C3.
One of the few exchange offices open on a Sunday. No commission for cash withdrawal via MasterCard or Visa.

Chip & PIN

The Chip and PIN system is up and running in Italy, though it's not available everywhere.

Credit cards

Italians have an enduring fondness for cash, but nearly all hotels of two stars and above, as well as most shops and restaurants (though still surprisingly few museums), now accept at least some of the major credit cards. The credit cards we list in this guide are American Express (AmEx), Diners Club (DC), MasterCard (MC) and Visa (V).

Lost/stolen

Most lines are freephone (800) numbers, have English-speaking staff and are open 24 hours daily.

American Express card emergencies 06 72900347.
Diners Club 800 864064.
CartaSì 800 151616.
MasterCard 800 870866.
Visa 800 819014.

Tax

Sales tax (IVA) is applied to all purchases and services at 1%, 4% and 20% in an ascending scale of luxury, but is almost always included in the price stated. At some luxury hotels, tax will be added on to the quoted rates, but prices will be clearly stated as escluso IVA.

By law, all non-EU residents are entitled to an IVA refund on purchases of €155 and over at shops participating in the 'Tax-free shopping' scheme, identified by a purple sticker. On presentation of your passport, they will give you a 'cheque' that can be cashed at the airport desk on your way home at the Tax Free Cash Refund desk at the airport. You'll need to show your passport and the unused goods, and there's a three-month time limit. IVA paid on hotel bills cannot be reclaimed.

Natural hazards

The sun can be fierce in spring, summer and even autumn, so remember sunscreen, wear a hat and take to the shade during the hottest parts of the day (*see p315*). Mosquitoes are a major nuisance in warm weather, so bring repellent.

Opening hours

Bank opening hours are generally from 8.20am to 1.20pm and from 2.35pm to 3.35pm Monday to Friday. All banks are closed on public holidays. Most post offices open from 8.15am to 1.30pm, closing an hour earlier on Saturdays; the main post office stays open Monday to Saturday from 8.15am to 7pm (*see also below*). Food shops generally open early morning and close for lunch from 1pm to 3.30pm (though some stay closed till 5pm), then are open again until 7.30pm. They are generally closed on Wednesday afternoons (Saturday afternoons in the summer). Other shops tend to open later in the morning and are closed on Monday mornings. Many shops now stay open all day (*orario continuato*). *See also p148* for shop opening info.

Police

Italian police forces are divided into four colour-coded units. The *vigili urbani* and *polizia municipale* (municipal police) wear navy blue. The *vigili* deal with all traffic matters within the city, and the *polizia municipale* with petty crime. The two forces responsible for dealing with crime are the *polizia di stato* (state police), who also wear blue jackets but have pale grey trousers, and the normally black-clad *carabinieri*, part of the army. Their roles are essentially the same. The *guardia di finanza* (financial police) wear grey and have little to do with tourists.

In an emergency, go to the tourist aid police or the nearest *carabinieri* post or police station (*questura*); we have listed central ones below, but others are found in the phone book. Staff will either speak English or be able to find someone who does. If you have had something stolen, tell them you want to report a *furto*. A statement (*denuncia*) will be taken, which you'll need for an insurance claim. Lost or stolen passports should also be reported to your embassy or consulate. *See also p306* Emergencies.

Comando Provinciale Carabinieri *Borgo Ognissanti 48, Santa Maria Novella (055 2061).* **Open** 24hrs daily. **Map** p334 B1.
A *carabinieri* post near the town centre; the best place to report the loss or theft of personal property.

Ufficio Denuncie *Via Duca D'Aosta 3, San Lorenzo (055 49771).* **Open** 24hrs daily. Ufficio Stranieri 8.30am-12.30pm Mon-Fri.
To report a crime, go to the Ufficio Denuncie, where you will be asked to fill in a form.

City Police *Via Pietrapiana 50r, Santa Croce (055 203911).* **Open** 8.30am-7.30pm Mon-Fri; 8.30am-1.30pm Sat. **Map** p335 B6.
Interpreters are on hand to help report thefts, lost property and any other problems.

Postal services

Improvements have been made to Italy's postal service, and you can now be more or less sure that the letter you sent or were sent will arrive in reasonable time.

Stamps (*francobolli*) can be bought at *tabacchi* or post offices. Most post boxes are red and have two slots, Per la Città (for Florence) and Tutte le Altre Destinazioni (everywhere else).

A letter takes about five days to reach the UK, eight to the US. There is now only one class of post (*posta prioritaria*), which generally fulfils its delivery promise of within 24 hours in Italy, three days for EU countries and four or five for the rest of the world. A small letter or postcard weighing 20 grams or less sent to addresses in Italy costs 60¢. To any EU country, it costs 65¢; to the US, it'll cost 85¢; sending mail further afield will cost €1. Special stamps can be bought at post offices and *tabacchi*.

Mail (20 grams or less) can be sent *raccomandata* (registered) for €2.80 for Italy, €3.45 or the EU and €3.65 for the US. *Assicurata* (insured) for up to €50 costs €5.95 in the EU; €6.15 to the US, from post offices only.

Heavier mail is charged according to weight. To send a parcel weighing a kilogram to the UK costs €9.20 (*posta prioritaria*), €16.70 to the US.

Italian postal charges are complicated, so be prepared for variations. For guaranteed fast delivery, use a courier or the SDA Italian post office courier service (*see p304*).

The Italian post call centre number is 803160 (officially Italian only, though you may strike lucky).

Post offices

Local post offices (*ufficio postale*) in each district generally open from 8.15am to 1.30pm Monday to Friday, and from 8.15am to 12.30pm on Saturdays. The main post office (Posta Centrale) has longer opening hours and a range of additional services.

Posta Centrale

Via Pellicceria 3, Duomo & Around (055 2736481). **Open** 8.15am-7pm Mon-Sat. **Map** p335 A4.
This is Florence's main post office.

Other post offices

Via Cavour 71A, San Marco (055 463501). **Open** 8.15am-1.30pm Mon-Fri; 8.15am-12.30pm Sat. **Map** p334 C3.
Via Pietrapiana 53, Santa Croce (055 2674231). **Open** 8.15am-7pm Mon-Fri; 8.15am-12.30pm Sat. **Map** p334 C3.
Via Barbadori 37r, Oltrarno (055 288175). **Open** 8.15am-1.30pm Mon-Fri; 8.15am-12.30pm Sat. **Map** p334 C3.

Poste restante

Poste restante (general delivery) letters (in Italian, *fermoposta*) should be sent to the main post office (*see above*), addressed to Fermoposta and the code and address of the post office you wish to pick up your mail from (a list is available at www.poste.it/online/cercaup/elenco_dati.php). You need a passport to collect mail and you may have to pay a small charge if sent from outside Italy (if sent from Italy a charge of 26¢ is added to the postage). Mail can also be sent to any Mail Boxes Etc branches (*see p304*).

Religion

There are Roman Catholic churches all over the city,

and a few churches still sing mass. Catholic mass is held in English at Santa Maria del Fiore (the Duomo) on Saturday afternoons at 5pm and at the Chiesa dell'Ospedale San Giovanni di Dio (borgo Ognissanti 20) on Sundays and public holidays at 10am.

American Episcopal Church (St James's Church) *Via Rucellai 9, Santa Maria Novella (055 294417/ www.stjames.it).* **Services** (in English) 9am, 11am Sun. **Map** p334 A1.
Anglican *St Mark's Church, via Maggio 16, Oltrarno (055 294764/ www.stmarksitaly.com).* **Services** 9.30am (Low Mass), 10.30am (Sung Mass) Sun; 6pm (Low Mass) Thur; 8pm (Low Mass) Fri. **Map** p334 C2.
Islamic *Associazione Islamica, via Tagliamento 3a, Outside the City Gates (055 65030331). Bus 23, 31.*
Jewish *Comunità Ebraica, via Farini 4, Santa Croce (055 245252/ www.firenzebraica.net).* **Services** 8.30/8.45am Sat. Call for details of Fri & Sat evening services; times vary. **Map** p335 B6.
Methodist *Chiesa Metodista, via de' Benci 9, Santa Croce (055 288143).* **Services** 11am Sun. **Map** p335 C4.

Safety & security

Crime has unfortunately been on the increase in Florence though serious street crime is rare, and it remains a relatively safe city to walk in. Take care at night, when lone women in particular should stick to the main well-lit streets. For visitors to the city, the main risk comes from the numerous pickpockets and bag-snatchers. Buses, shops, bars and other crowded areas are petty criminals' hunting grounds. As you would in any major city, take common-sense precautions:

- Don't keep wallets in back pockets. This is a pickpocket's favourite swipe, especially on buses and public transport.
- Wear shoulder bags diagonally and facing away from the road to minimise the risk of *scippi* – bag-snatching from mopeds, which is still common in the city.
- Never leave bags on tables or the backs of chairs in bars.
- Keep an eye on your valuables while trying on clothes and shoes.

Also, watch out for 'baby-gangs' of children or teenagers who hang around the tourist spots and create a distraction by flapping a newspaper or card while trying to slip their hands into bags or pockets. If you are approached, keep walking, keep calm and hang on to your valuables.

For emergency numbers, *see p306*. For information on the police, *see p311*.

Smoking

A law banning smoking in all public places came into force in 2005 and is scrupulously respected and enforced. This includes bars, restaurants and clubs, although there is a clause that allows some venues to set aside a smoking room, as long as it is separated by double doors and adequately ventilated and filtered. Owners who allow customers to smoke are fined heavily, the smoker can also be fined. Cigarettes are on sale at *tabacchi* and *bar-tabacchi*; both are recognisable by the blue/black and white sign outside.

Study

With over 20 US university programmes and countless language schools and art courses, many of which have international reputations, the city's student population rivals that of its residents at some times of the year. The courses listed in this section are all generally in English. However, if you don't speak any Italian, double-check before you enrol.

To study in Florence, you will need a *permesso di soggiorno per studio*. The same requirements apply as for the *permesso di soggiorno* (*see p316*), plus a guarantee that your medical bills will be paid (an EHIC card will do for UK students), evidence that you can support yourself and a letter from the educational institution. To study alongside Florentine undergraduates, contact an Italian consulate to apply to do a *corso singolo*, or one year of study at the University of Florence. You need to register at the Centro di Cultura per Stranieri at the beginning of November. The fees for a *corso singolo* (maximum five subjects) are approximately €1,200. To complete a degree course, you must have studied to university level. For details, see www.unifi.it. There are also exchange programmes for EU students.

Several US universities, including Georgetown, Sarah Lawrence, New York, Gonzaga and Syracuse, have Florence outposts open to students from any US university for the semester and summer courses.

Università di Firenze: Centro di Cultura per Stranieri *Via Francesco Valori 9, Outside the City Gates (055 5032701/2/3/ www.unifi.it/ccs). Bus 8, 10, 11, 13, 17, 20, 33.* **Open** 9am-noon Mon-Fri.
Offers language and cultural courses.

Art, design & restoration courses

Il Bisonte *Via San Niccolò 24, Oltrarno (055 2347215/ilbisonte.it).* **Map** p335 D5.
Located among the artisans' workshops in the former stables of Palazzo Serristori, Il Bisonte has specialist courses and theoretical/ practical seminars in the techniques of etching and printmaking.
Charles H Cecil Studios *Borgo San Frediano 68, Oltrarno (055 285102/www.charlescecilstudios.com).* **Map** p334 C1.
The church of San Raffaello Arcangelo was converted into a studio complex in the early 19th century. It now houses one of the more charismatic of Florence's art schools, Charles H Cecil Studios, which is heavily frequented by Brits. It gives a thorough training in the classical techniques of

drawing and oil painting, and runs classes for the general public.

L'Istituto per l'Arte e il Restauro *Palazzo Ridolfi, via Maggio 13, Oltrarno (055 282951/www.spinelli.it).* **Map** p334 D2.
Widely considered one of the best art restoration schools in Italy, the Institute offers a multitude of courses in the restoration of frescoes, paintings, furniture, gilt objects, ceramics, stone, paper and glass. They last between one and three years. One-month courses are held from July to September in the same disciplines.

Oro e Colore *Via Toscanella 18r, Oltrarno (055 289415/www.oroecolore.com).* **Map** p334 D2.
Month- to year-long courses in art restoration, gold leaf restoration and other techniques. No previous experience is needed; however, places on courses are limited and are taught only in Italian.

Studio Art Centers International (SACI) *Via Sant'Antonino 11, San Lorenzo (055 289948/www.saci-florence.org).* **Map** p334 A3.
SACI offers five specific credit programmes for graduates and undergraduates. These include both academic and practical courses in the arts, ranging from museology to batik design. There is an entry requirement for certain courses.

Università Internazionale dell'Arte *Villa il Ventaglio, via delle Forbici 24-26, Outside the City Gates (055 570216/www.uiafirenze.com). Bus 7.*
Based in a fabulous villa, courses cover restoration and preservation, museum and gallery management and art criticism.

Language classes

There are no end of language and culture courses in Florence, including many intensive one- or two-month courses, which should provide an adequate everyday grasp of the language. Prices refer to a standard four-week course with four hours' tuition a day.

ABC Centro di Lingua e Cultura Italiana *Via de' Rustici 7, Santa Croce (055 212001/www.abcschool.com).* **Price** €566. **Map** p335 C4.
ABC offers language teaching at six levels, as well as preparatory courses for the entrance exam to the University of Florence.

British Institute Language Centre *Piazza Strozzi 2, Duomo & Around (055 26778200/www.britishinstitute.it).* **Price** €630. **Map** p334 B3.
Short courses in Italian language, history of art, drawing and cooking. For the British Institute's Library & Cultural Centre, *see p178*.

Centro Linguistico Italiano Dante Alighieri *Piazza della Repubblica 5, Duomo & Around (055 210808/www.clida.it).* **Price** €595, plus €100 enrolment fee. **Map** p335 D4.
Eleven language levels; opera and literature courses too.

Istituto Lorenzo de' Medici *Via Faenza 43, San Lorenzo (055 283142/www.lorenzodemedici.it).* **Price** €600. **Map** p334A3.
Four different courses in Italian as well as classes in cooking, Italian cinema and art history.

Scuola Leonardo da Vinci *Via Bufalini 3, Duomo & Around (055 294420/www.scuolaleonardo.com).* **Price** €600, plus €70 enrolment. **Map** p335 B4.
Versatile language courses, plus classes in history of art, fashion, drawing, design, cooking and wine.

Scuola Machiavelli *Piazza Santo Spirito 4, Oltrarno (055 2396966/www.centromachiavelli.it).* **Price** €480, plus €30 enrolment fee. **Map** p335 D1.
This small co-op offers Italian, pottery, fresco, mosaic, trompe l'œil and book-binding classes.

Useful organisations

Council of International Education Exchange (CIEE) *300 Fore Street, Portland, Maine, ME 04101, USA (+1 207 553 4000/www.ciee.org).*

Institute of International Education *809 UN Plaza, New York, NY 10017-3580, USA (+1 212 883 8200/www.iie.org).*

Italian Cultural Institute *39 Belgrave Square, London SW1X 8NX, UK (+44 (0)20 7235 1461/www.italcultur.org.uk).*

Telephones

Competition has led to price cuts for telephone customers, with Telecom Italia, the biggest and most commonly used Italian phone company, in direct competition with newer phone companies, such as Tele 2 and Infostrada. Tariffs are higher if you're calling from a public phone and usually higher still from a hotel: you're generally better off buying an international phone card, though they don't offer anything approaching the same level of discounts as in the UK or US. Calling from a phone centre costs the same as from a payphone, but it's more convenient as you pay at the end for the call.

Dialling & codes

The international code for Italy is 39. To dial in from other countries, preface it with the exit code: 00 in the UK and 011 in the US. All normal Florence numbers begin with the area code 055. The code for Siena is 0577, for Pisa 050. As with all Italian codes, these must always be used in full, even when you are calling from within the same area, and when dialling internationally. For mobile phone numbers there is no initial zero.

To make an international call from Florence, dial 00, then the country code (Australia 61; Canada 1; Irish Republic 353; New Zealand 64; United Kingdom 44; United States 1), followed by the area code (for calls to the UK, omit the initial zero) and individual number. The same pattern works to mobile phones.

All numbers beginning 800 are free lines (*numero verde*). For numbers that begin 840, you'll be charged one unit only, regardless of where you're calling from or how long the call lasts. These numbers can be called from within Italy only; some only function within one phone district. Phone numbers starting 3 are mobile numbers; those with 199 codes are charged at local rates; 167 numbers are billed at premium rates.

Faxes

Faxes can be sent from most large post offices (*see p311*), which charge per sheet (€1.30 in Italy, €5.09 for Europe). Faxes can also be sent from some photocopying outlets and internet points, and at most hotels.

Mobile phones

Pay-as-you-go mobiles can be bought from many phone shops from around €80, including the SIM card and €5 of calls. Top-up cards are available from all *bar-tabacchi* and some newsstands; either call the number given on the card, or, if the bar has the electronic top-up facility, tap in your phone number and the amount requested will be credited automatically. One top-up has to be made at least every 11 months to keep the number active. SIM cards can also be bought without having to buy a phone; prices vary.

Some internet points hire out phones: try Intotheweb or Internet Train (*see p308*). Italian mobile phone numbers begin with 3 (no zero).

The mobile phone shops listed below are located in central Florence.

TIM, Telecom Italia Mobile *Via de' Lamberti 12-14, Duomo & Around (055 2396066).* **Open** 9am-7pm Mon-Fri; 9am-1pm Sat. **Credit** AmEx, MC, V. **Map** p334 C3.
Vodafone *Via de' Martelli 25-31r, Duomo & Around (055 2670121).* **Open** 9am-7pm Mon-Fri; 9am-1pm Sat. **Credit** AmEx, MC, V. **Map** p334 A4.

Operator services

To make a reverse-charge (collect) call, dial 170 for the international operator in Italy. To be connected to the operator in the country you want to call, dial 172 followed by a country code (so 172 00 44 for the UK and 172 00 1 for the US) and you'll be connected directly to an operator in that country. The following services operate 24 hours daily (calls are charged):

Operator and directory enquiries *1254* (option 1 for Italian directory enquiries 24hrs; option 2 for international enquiries 7am-midnight).
International operator *170.*
Problems on national calls *182.*

Public phones

Since the popular mobile phone revolution and the opening of so many small internet point/call centres (*see p308*), public phones in Florence have all but disappeared, especially in less central areas. However, some bars still have payphones as do a few of the city's squares, the stations and airport. Public phones only accept phone cards with magnetic strips (*schede telefoniche*), not coins; some also accept major credit cards. *Schede telefoniche* are available from *tabacchi*, some newsstands and some bars, as are the pre-paid phone cards offering access via an 800 number to both domestic and international calls. To use a card phone, lift the receiver and wait for the tone, then insert the card (with the perforated corner torn off) and dial.

Phone centres

There are now phone centres throughout the city centre, very often combining phone services with internet services and faxes. For a full list check in the *Yellow Pages* under 'Telecomunicazioni'.

New Communication *Via della Scala 63r, Santa Maria Novella (055 2645992).* **Open** 9am-11pm Mon-Sat. **No credit cards. Map** p334 A1. Conveniently close to the station.
Londra Internet *Piazza Sauro 5r, Oltrarno (055 210631).* **Open** 10am-midnight daily. **No credit cards. Map** p334 C1 Also has internet access and basic office services.

Telephone directories

All hotels and most restaurants and bars have phone books and *Yellow Pages* (if they're not obviously on display, ask to see the *elenco telefonico* or *pagine gialle*). Telecom Italia has a useful website (www.1254.alice.it) with an online directory enquiries service.

Telegrams

Telegrams can be sent from main post offices. The telegraph office at the Posta Centrale (*see p311*) is open 8.30am-7pm Mon-Sat. Alternatively, dictate telegrams over the phone. Dial 186 from a private or hotel phone and a message in Italian will tell you to dial the number of the phone you're phoning from. You will then be passed to a telephonist.

Time

Italy is one hour ahead of London, six ahead of New York and eight behind Sydney. Clocks go forward an hour in spring and back in autumn, in line with other EU countries.

Tipping

The 10-15 per cent tip customary in many countries is considered generous in Florence. Locals sometimes leave a few coins on the counter when buying drinks at the bar and, depending on the standard of the restaurant, will drop €1-€5 for the service after a meal. That said, some larger restaurants are now starting to add a 10-15 per cent service charge on the bill automatically. Tips are not expected in small restaurants, although they are always appreciated. Taxi drivers will be surprised if you do more than add a euro or two.

Toilets

A network of public toilets has been opened over the last few years, most with disabled access and nappy-changing tables. The cost is 50-60¢. See www.comune.fi.it/servizi_pubblici/turismo/bagnipubblici.htm for the full list with facilities symbols. Most are slightly outside the very central area, but bars are also obliged by law to let you use their loos. Ask for *il bagno*; in some bars you'll be given the key. Unfortunately, so many bars were reluctant to let people use their loos that the council has introduced the Courtesy Point initiative; bars and restaurants displaying this symbol have undertaken to welcome visitors politely and let them use their toilet facilities without making a fuss. The current list can be found at www.comune.firenze.it/servizi_pubblici/turismo/c_p/cpesterno.pdf

Tourist information

To be sent an information pack in advance of your visit, get in touch with ENIT, the Italian tourist board (UK: 0800 00482542/020 7408 1254, www.enit.it; US: 212 245 4822, www.enit.it/www.italiantourism.com). Tell staff where and when you're travelling, and whether or not you have any special interests.

Florence's provincial tourist board, the Azienda Promozionale Turistica (APT; www.firenzeturismo.it), and the council-run Ufficio Informazioni Turistiche have helpful, multilingual staff who do their best to supply reliable information: not easy, since museums and galleries tend to change their hours without telling them. There's no central information service for the Tuscany region; you have to contact the APT in each area. There is a head office in each provincial capital, then local offices in various towns within the province. Details of tourist offices are listed in this guide under the relevant area.

For info on maps, *see p303.*

Tourist information offices

Via Cavour 1r, San Lorenzo (055 290832). **Open** 8.30am-6.30pm Mon-Sat; 8.30am-1.30pm Sun. **Map** p335 A4.
Borgo Santa Croce 29r, Santa Croce (055 2340444). **Open** *Summer* 9am-7pm Mon-Sat; 9am-2pm Sun. *Winter* 9am-5pm Mon-Sat, 9am-2pm Sun. **Map** p335 C5.
Piazza della Stazione 4A, Santa Maria Novella (055 212245). **Open** 8.30am-7pm Mon-Sat; 8.30am-2pm Sun. **Map** p334 A2.
Run by the city of Florence, these offices provide maps and info. There are also offices in Florence and Pisa airports. Hotel bookings can be made by emailing Florence Promhotels on info@promhotels.it (website: www.promhotels.it), a free hotel-booking service available by email or through the tourist office.

Tourist help

Open *Easter-Sept* 8am-7pm daily.
Some years a special service is run by the *vigili urbani* from three vans: one in piazza della Repubblica, one in via Calzaiuoli and one just south of the ponte Vecchio in via Guicciardini. APT personnel and the municipal police provide help and information. You can also register any complaints you might have about restaurant or hotel charges.

Visas & Immigration

Non-EU citizens and Britons require full passports to travel to Italy. EU citizens are permitted unrestricted access to Italy to travel (*see also p316* Working in Florence); citizens of the USA, Canada, Australia and New Zealand should check about visa requirements at an Italian embassy or consulate in their own country before setting off for Italy.

Weights & measures

Italy uses only the metric system; remember that all speed limits are in kilometres. One kilometre is equivalent to 0.62 mile, with 1 mile converting to 1.6 kilometres. Petrol, like other liquids, is measured in litres: one UK gallon = 4.54 litres; 1 US gallon = 3.79 litres. A kilogram is equivalent to 2.2 pounds (one pound = 0.45 kilos). Food is often sold in *etti* (sometimes written hg); 1 etto = 100 grams (3.52 ounces). In delicatessens, you should ask for multiples of *etti* (*un etto, due etti*, etc).

What to take

Any prescription medicines should always be obtained before leaving. Make sure you have enough to cover the entire period of your stay, as not all US and UK medicines are available in Italy.

When to go

Climate

The hills surrounding Florence mean that it can be cold and humid in winter and very hot and humid in the summer. Between late June and August, temperatures often soar to 40°C (104°F) and rarely fall below 30°C (86°F). During the summer, you should be sure to take the sun seriously: every year, local doctors issue warnings about the number of visitors who are hospitalised with serious burns from spending too much time in the sun and going out in the middle of the day. (Italians stay indoors whenever they can during the hottest hours.) The short spring and autumn in Florence and Tuscany can be very warm. They're not without risk of rain, though, especially in March, April and September. Between November and February, you can't rely on good weather: you could find anything from a week of rain to crisp, bright and sometimes even warm sunshine.

Public holidays

On public holidays (*giorni festivi*) virtually all shops, banks and businesses are shut, though most bars and restaurants stay open so you will be able to eat and drink. Public holidays are as follows:

New Year's Day (Capodanno) 1 Jan
Epiphany (La Befana) 6 Jan
Easter Monday (Lunedi di Pasqua)
Liberation Day (Venticinque Aprile/Liberazione) 25 Apr
May Day (Primo Maggio) 1 May
Republic Day (Festa della Repubblica) 2 June

Average monthly climate

Month	High temp	Low temp	Rainfall	Relative humidity
January	10°C (50°F)	–1°C (30°F)	64mm (2.5in)	75%
February	12°C (54°F)	1°C (34°F)	61mm (2.4in)	72%
March	15°C (59°F)	5°C (41°F)	69mm (2.7in)	72%
April	20°C (68°F)	8°C (46°F)	71mm (2.8in)	72%
May	24°C (75°F)	11°C (52°F)	73mm (2.9in)	71%
June	29°C (84°F)	14°C (57°F)	56mm (2.2in)	64%
July	34°C (93°F)	18°C (64°F)	34mm (1.3in)	66%
August	32°C (90°F)	14°C (57°F)	47mm (1.8in)	71%
September	28°C (82°F)	13°C (55°F)	84mm (3.3in)	76%
October	23°C (73°F)	11°C (52°F)	99mm (3.9in)	81%
November	16°C (61°F)	4°C (39°F)	103mm (4.1in)	81%
December	13°C (55°F)	4°C (39°F)	79mm (3.1in)	73%

Florence Saint's Day (San Giovanni) 24 June
Feast of the Assumption (Ferragosto) 15 Aug
All Saints' (Tutti i Santi) 1 Nov
Immaculate Conception (Festa dell'Immacolata) 8 Dec
Christmas Day (Natale) 25 Dec
Boxing Day (Santo Stefano) 26 Dec

There is limited public transport on 1 May and Christmas afternoon. Holidays falling on a Saturday or Sunday are not celebrated the following Monday, but if a holiday falls on a Thursday or Tuesday, many locals also take the intervening day off and make a long weekend of it; such a weekend is called a *ponte* (bridge). Beware of the *rientro* or homecoming, when the roads are horrendously busy.

Many people also disappear for a large chunk of August, when *chiuso per ferie* (closed for holidays) signs appear in shops and restaurants detailing dates of closure. These closures are co-ordinated on a rota system by the city council, so there should be something open in each area at any given time. However, if you should find yourself in Florence, or many other Tuscan towns, on the Ferragosto (Feast of the Assumption; 15 August), the chances are that your only company will be other tourists wandering the baked streets in search of something to do or somewhere to eat. The Florentines desert the city like rats from a sinking ship, and are likely to stay away for several days either side. You'll find the exceptions to this rule are holiday resorts such as coastal towns where, although shops and public offices may close, the infrastructure doesn't completely collapse. For a calendar of Tuscany's traditional and modern festivals throughout the year, *see pp170-174*.

Women

Although it's not one of the worst places for women travellers, Tuscany still has its hassles. Visiting women can feel daunted by the sheer volume of attention they receive, but most of it will be friendly; men are unlikely to become pushy or aggressive if given the brush-off. It's normally a question of all talk and no action, but be aware of who's around you: it's quite common to be followed. If things get too heavy, go into the nearest shop or bar and wait or ask for help. The notorious bum-pinching is uncommon but not unknown, especially on buses. As in Anglo-Saxon countries, it's a criminal offence, and recent prosecutions and convictions show that it's taken seriously.

Tampons (*assorbenti interni*) and sanitary towels (*assorbenti esterni*) can be bought in supermarkets, pharmacies and some *tabacchi*. For info on contraception, abortion and other health matters, *see p307*.

See also p306 Health and *p307* Helplines.

Artemesia

Via del Mezzetta 1/int, Outside the City Gates (055 602311/children's line 055 601375). Bus 10, 11, 70. **Open** 10am-6pm Mon-Fri.

A voluntary association for women and children who have suffered from abuse. Provides legal advice, social and psychological support, group therapy and has two safe houses.

Clinica Ostetrica

Reparto Maternità, Ospedale di Careggi, Viale Morgagni, Outside the City Gates (055 794111). Bus 2, 8, 14C. **Open** 24hrs daily.

Female victims of sexual assault should go to the Clinica Ostetrica for medical attention.

Network

Villa Rossa, piazza Savonarola 15, Outside the City Gates (contact Jane Fogarty). Bus 10, 11, 13, 17.

A professional women's organisation geared mainly towards residents whose first language is English. It aims to improve communication, exchange ideas and information among the English-speaking community. Meetings are generally on the second Wednesday of the month. Annual fees are €40, which includes newsletters and mailings.

Working in Florence

Finding a job in Italy is not simple. The jobs market isn't known for being mobile and unemployment is fairly high, especially for graduate positions. Most of the jobs that are available are connected to tourism in some way, although there are a few multinationals that occasionally advertise for native English-speakers. The classified ads paper *La Pulce* has job listings; it's also worth checking the local English-language press.

The bureaucracy involved is not easy but has been simplified by recent changes, at least for EU citizens. Since April 2007, EU citizens no longer need to apply for a *permesso di soggiorno* (permit to stay). For stays of over three months, EU citizens should sign up at their local *anagrafe* (Register Office) presenting proof of their work, study or training activities, or providing proof of adequate financial means to support themselves (this is judged by the number of people in the family, from just over €5,000 for single applicants, to just over €15,000 for those with four or more extra family dependents).

Citizens from outside the EU should check about visa requirements at an Italian embassy or consulate in their own country before setting off for Italy. All non-EU citizens who are planning to stay for more than three months should register with the police within eight days of arrival and then apply for their permits. More details are on the Polizia di Stato website: www.poliziadistato.it/pds/ps/immigrazione/soggiorno.htm (Italian only).

Administration & permit offices

Comune di Firenze (Florence town hall), Palazzo Vecchio & Piazza Signoria, Duomo & Around (switchboard 055 27681/800 831133). **Open** 8.30am-1.30pm Mon-Wed, Fri, Sat; 8.30am-6.30pm Thur. **Map** p335 C4.

For residency enquiries, ask for the Ufficio Circoscrizione. Given your address, they will then give you the number you need to call to progress further with your application.

Permits to stay

Immigration Office Via della Fortezza 17, San Lorenzo (055 4977057). **Open** 8.15-10am Mon-Thur.

To apply for your documents go here (English-speaking staff are usually available to help).

Vocabulary

Any attempt at speaking Italian will always be appreciated. Indeed, it may well be necessary: away from services such as tourist offices, hotels and restaurants popular with foreigners, the level of English is not very high. The most important thing is making the effort, not whether or not your sentences are perfectly formed with an authentic accent. The key is to take the plunge and not be shy.

It's a myth that you can get by in Italy with Spanish: true, you may well understand some Italian (both written and spoken), but try speaking it and Italians generally won't understand you (unless, of course, they speak Spanish).

Italian is a phonetic language, so most words are spelled as they're pronounced (and vice versa). Stresses usually fall on the penultimate syllable. There are three forms of the second person: the formal *lei* (used with strangers), the informal *tu*, and the plural form *voi*. Masculine nouns are usually accompanied by adjectives ending in 'o', female nouns by adjectives ending in 'a'. However, there are many nouns and adjectives that end in 'e' that can be either masculine or feminine.

Pronunciation

Vowels

a – as in **a**pple
e – like **a** in **a**ge (closed e), or **e** in s**e**ll (open e)
i – like **ea** in **ea**st
o – as in h**o**tel (closed o) or in h**o**t (open o)
u – like **oo** in b**oo**t

Consonants

c – before a, o or u: like the **c** in **c**at; before e or i: like the **ch** in **ch**eck
ch – like the **c** in **c**at
g – before a, o or u: like the **g** in **g**et; before e or i: like the **j** in **j**ig
gh – like the **g** in **g**et
gl – followed by 'i': like **lli** in mi**lli**on
gn – like **ny** in ca**ny**on
qu – as in **qu**ick
r – is always rolled
s – has two sounds, as in **s**oap or ro**s**e
sc – followed by 'e' or 'i': like the **sh** in **sh**ame
sch – like the **sc** in **sc**out
z –has two sounds, like **ts** and **dz**

Double consonants are sounded more emphatically.

Useful words & phrases

hello and goodbye (informal) – *ciao*
good morning, good day – *buongiorno*
good afternoon, good evening – *buona sera*
I don't understand – *non capisco/non ho capito*
do you speak English? – *parla inglese?*
please – *per favore*
thank you – *grazie*
you're welcome – *prego*
when does it open? – *quando apre?*
where is... ? – *dov'è…?*
excuse me – *scusi (polite), scusa (informal)*
open – *aperto*
closed – *chiuso*
entrance – *entrata*
exit – *uscita*
left – *sinistra*
right – *destra*
car – *macchina*
bus – *autobus*
train – *treno*
bus stop – *fermata dell'autobus*
ticket/s – *biglietto/i*
I would like a ticket to... – *vorrei un biglietto per…*
postcard – *cartolina*
stamp – *francobollo*
glass – *bicchiere*
coffee – *caffè*
tea – *tè*
water – *acqua*
wine – *vino*
beer – *birra*
the bill – *il conto*
single/twin/double bedroom – *camera singola/a due letti/ matrimoniale*
booking – *prenotazione*

Days of the week

Monday – *lunedì*
Tuesday – *martedì*
Wednesday – *mercoledì*
Thursday – *giovedì*
Friday – *venerdì*
Saturday – *sabato*
Sunday – *domenica*
yesterday – *ieri*
today – *oggi*
tomorrow – *domani*
morning – *mattina*
afternoon – *pomeriggio*
evening – *sera*
night – *notte*
weekend – *fine settimana, weekend*

The come-on

do you have a light? – *hai da accendere?*
what's your name? – *come ti chiami?*
would you like a drink? – *vuoi bere qualcosa?*
where are you from? – *di dove sei?*
what are you doing here? – *che fai qui?*
do you have a boyfriend/ girlfriend? – *hai un ragazzo/una ragazza?*

The brush-off

I'm married – *sono sposato/a*
I'm tired – *sono stanco/a*
I'm going home – *vado a casa*
I have to meet a friend – *devo incontrare un amico/ una amica*

Numbers & money

0 *zero*; **1** *uno*; **2** *due*; **3** *tre*; **4** *quattro*; **5** *cinque*; **6** *sei*; **7***sette*; **8** *otto*; **9** *nove*; **10** *dieci*; **11** *undici*; **12** *dodici*; **13** *tredici*; **14** *quattordici*; **15** *quindici*; **16** *sedici*; **17** *diciassette*; **18** *diciotto*; **19** *diciannove*; **20** *venti*; **21** *ventuno*; **22** *ventidue*; **30** *trenta*; **40** *quaranta*; **50** *cinquanta*; **60** *sessanta*; **70** *settanta*; **80** *ottanta*; **90** *novanta*; **100** *cento*; **1,000** *mille*; **2,000** *duemila*; **100,000** *centomila*; **100,000** *un milione*.

how much does it cost/is it? – *quanto costa?/quant'è?*
do you have any change? – *ha da cambiare?*
can you give me a discount? – *mi puó fare uno sconto?*
do you accept credit cards? – *si accettano le carte di credito?*
can I pay in pounds/dollars/ travellers' cheques? – *posso pagare in sterline/dollari/ con i travellers?*
can I have a receipt? – *posso avere una ricevuta?*

Glossary

Annunciation depiction of the Virgin Mary being told by the Archangel Gabriel that she will bear the son of God.
Attribute object used in art to symbolise a particular person, often saints and martyrs.
Baldacchino canopied structure; in paintings holding an enthroned Madonna and child.
Banderuola small forked flag bearing an inscription, held in Renaissance art by angels or *putti*.
Baptistery building for baptisms, usually octagonal to symbolise new beginnings, as seven is the number of completion and eight the start of a new cycle.
Baroque sumptuous art and architectural style from the 17th to mid 18th centuries.
Byzantine spiritual and religious art of the Byzantine Empire (fifth-15th centuries).
Campanile bell tower.
Cartoon full-scale sketch for painting or fresco.
Cenacolo depiction of the Last Supper.
Chiaroscuro painting or drawing technique using shades of black, grey and white to emphasise light and shade.
Classical ancient Greek and Roman art and culture.
Corbel brackets jutting from a roof.
Cupola dome-shaped structure set on a larger dome or a roof.
Deposition depiction of Christ taken down from the Cross.
Diptych painting made of two panels.
Fresco technique for wall painting where pigments bind with wet plaster.
Golden mean Renaissance art theory with division of proportions by a ratio of 8:13. Considered to create perfect harmony.
Gothic architectural and artistic style of the late Middle Ages (from the 12th century) characterised by the integration of art forms, with pointed arches and an emphasis on line.
Grotesque ornate artistic style derived from Roman underground painted rooms (*grotte*).
Hortus conclusus garden around Madonna and child symbolising their uncontaminated world of perfection and contentment.
Iconography study of subject and symbolism of works of art. For example, in Renaissance art: a **dog** symbolises faithfulness to a master, usually the Medici; an **egg** is a symbol of perfection; a **peacock** symbolises the Resurrection; a **giglio** (lily of Florence) is often found in Annunciations to symbolise the purity of the Madonna; a **sarcophagus** (stone or marble coffin) symbolises the death of an important person; and the colour **blue** sometimes symbolises divine peace.
Illumination miniature painted as an illustration for manuscripts.
Loggia covered area with one or more sides open, with columns.
Lunette half-moon painting or semicircular architectural space for decoration or window.
Madonna of Mercy Madonna with her cloak open to give protection to those in need.
Maestà depiction of the Madonna on a throne.
Mandorla almond-shaped 'glory' surrounding depiction of holy person.
Mannerism 15th-century art movement in Italy, defined by exaggerated perspective and scale, and complex compositions and poses.
Medieval relating to the Middle Ages (from the fall of the Roman Empire in the west, in the 5th century, to the 1453 fall of Constantinople).
Modernist (Modernism) the movement away from classical and traditional forms towards architecture that applied scientific methods to its design.
Palazzo (*palazzi*) large and/or important building, not necessarily a royal palace.
Panel painting on wood.
Panneggio style of folded and pleated drapery worn by figures in 15th- and 16th-century painting and sculpture.
Pietà depiction of Christ lying across the Madonna's lap after the Deposition.
Pietra dura inlaid gem mosaics.
Polyptych painting composed of several panels.
Putto (*putti*) small angelic naked boys, often depicted as attendants of Venus.
Relief sculpted work with three-dimensional areas jutting out from a flat surface.
Renaissance 14th- to 16th-century cultural movement based on the 'rebirth' of classical ideals and methods.
Romanesque architectural style of the early Middle Ages (c500-1200), drawing on Roman Byzantine influences.
Secco the finishing-off or retouching of a fresco, done on dried plaster (*intonaco*).
Sinopia preparatory drawing for a fresco made with a red earth mix or the red paint itself.
Tempera pigment bound with egg, the main painting material from 12th to late 15th centuries.
Tondo round painting or relief.
Triptych painting composed of three panels.
Trompe l'œil painting designed to give the illusion of a three-dimensional reality.
Vanitas objects in art symbolising mortality, such as skulls and hourglasses.
Votive offering left as a prayer for good fortune or recovery from illness, usually as a painting or a silver model of the limb/organ to be cured.

Further Reference

Books

Non-fiction

Luigi Barzini *The Italians*
A dated yet hilarious portrait.
Julia Conaway Bondanella & Mark Musa *Introduction to the Major Italian Writers & Influential Thinkers of the Renaissance*
Famous names and a few surprises.
Thomas Campanello
A Defence of Galileo, the Mathematician from Florence
The life, times and influence of Florence's most famous heretic.
Paul Ginsborg
A History of Contemporary Italy: Society and Politics 1943-1988
Comprehensive modern history.
Frederick Hartt *The History of Italian Renaissance Art*
The definitive work.
Tobias Jones
The Dark Heart of Italy
Fantastic introduction to contemporary Italy.
Ross King *Brunelleschi's Dome: The Story of the Great Cathedral*
A fascinating account of the building of Florence's magnificent dome.
Monica Larner & Travis Neighbor *Living, Studying and Working in Italy*
Everything you need to know.
Mary McCarthy
The Stones of Florence
A portrait of Florence and its arts.
Caroline Moorhead *Iris Origo*
Biography of the writer who helped protect Allies and refugee children during the war.
Iris Origo *Images and Shadows; The Merchant of Prato*
Autobiographical and biographical accounts of Florence and Tuscany.
Thomas Paloscia
Accadde in Toscana (Vol III)
A beautifully illustrated who's who of Tuscany's contemporary artists.
Laura Raison
Tuscany: An Anthology
A collection of writings and illustrations, classic to contemporary.
Leon Satkowski *Giorgio Vasari: Architect & Courtier*
A biography of the most famous Italian art chronicler.
Dava Sobel *Galileo's Daughter*
A study of Galileo's life in the context of his relationship with his daughter.
Matthew Spender *Within Tuscany*
A witty account of growing up in an unusual family in Tuscany.
Paul Strathern *The Medici: Godfathers of the Renaissance*
A most enjoyable exposition of the remarkable influence of the Medici in Florence and throughout Europe.

Fiction

Italo Calvino *The Florentine*
One of Calvino's 'folktales' collections of short stories. Tells of the misery of a Florentine who longs to travel.
Jack Dann *The Memory Cathedral: A Secret History of Leonardo da Vinci*
Mystery and intrigue in Florence.
Michael Dibdin *A Rich Full Death*
An amusing thriller with insight into 19th-century Florence.
Sarah Dunant *The Birth of Venus*
Gender and art in Medici Florence.
EM Forster *A Room with a View; Where Angels Fear to Tread*
Social comedy from the master.
Robert Hellenga *The 16 Pleasures*
A young American woman goes to Florence and feels obliged to act out 16 'pleasures' from a book of erotica.
Christobel Kent *Late Season*
Past and present collide for a group of friends and family on holiday in a Tuscan farmhouse.
Christobel Kent
A Party in San Niccolò; *A Florentine Revenge*
An eventful week leads up to the 75th birthday party of an English expat; a tour guide becomes involved in a gruesome murder.
W Somerset Maugham
Up at the Villa
Temptation and fate in '30s Florence.
Frances Mayes *Under the Tuscan Sun, Bella Tuscany*
Year in Provence-style expat dreams.
Magdalen Nabb *Death of an Englishman; The Monster of Florence*
Murder in the secretive world of Florentine antiques dealers; thriller based on a serial killer who murdered 16 campers in the 1980s.
Michael Ondaatje
The English Patient
Booker-winning novel turned Oscar-winning film, partly set in Tuscany.
Sally Stewart
An Unexpected Harvest
London yuppie moves to Tuscany to help grandparents save family estate.

Food & wine

Giancarlo and Katie Caldesi
Return to Tuscany
Recipes, lessons and culture.
Leslie Forbes *A Table in Tuscany*
A personal account of Tuscan food, with recipes from local restaurants.
Claudia Roden *The Food of Italy*
A wonderful book of Italian recipes, with a section on Tuscany.
Slow Food & Gambero Rosso
Italian Wines Guide
The English edition of reliable annual guide to Italian wines.

Film

The English Patient (1996)
Tragic World War II story starring Ralph Fiennes and Juliette Binoche.
Hannibal (2000)
Anthony Hopkins serial killer travels to Florence.
Life is Beautiful (La Vita è Bella) (1997)
Roberto Benigni's bittersweet comedy about wartime Arezzo.
Much Ado about Nothing (1993)
Kenneth Branagh's fun interpretation of Shakespeare's comedy.
Portrait of a Lady (1996)
Nicole Kidman stars in this version of Henry James's story about a New World woman in Old World Italy.
A Room with a View (1985)
Helena Bonham Carter learns of love and loss in 19th-century Florence.
Stealing Beauty (1995)
Bernardo Bertolucci's Tuscan-based film brought us Liv Tyler.
Tea with Mussolini (1998)
Judy Dench and Maggie Smith form part of an eccentric group of expats.
Up at the Villa (2000)
Sean Penn's cynical American proves innocent in comparison to his European companions.

Music

Puccini *Gianni Schicchi*
This delightful one-act opera is set in medieval Fucecchio, west of Florence.
Tchaikovsky *Souvenir of Florence*
The composer wrote this string sextet while living in via San Leonardo in Florence.

Websites

www.boxol.it
Information and online booking for concerts and shows.
www.cultura.toscana.it
The official Regione Toscana site has information on museums, exhibitions and libraries in Tuscany. Italian only.
www.firenze.net
The best local site; has info on cinemas, nightlife, music, art, traffic and weather in Florence and Tuscany, plus a booking service.
www.firenzespettacolo.it
The monthly listings mag website has what's-on information, reviews and plenty more.
www.fol.it
Plenty of links relating to health, travel, sports, hotels and business.
www.intoscana.net
Regional updates in five languages .
www.lapulce.it
Online small ads mag. Italian only.

Index

Note: Page numbers in **bold** indicate section(s) giving key information on a topic; *italics* indicate photographs.

a

Abbazia di San Galgano *248*, 253
Abbazia di Sant'Antimo 255
abortion 307
accident & emergency 306
accommodation 50-69
best, the 53
by price: luxury 53-54, 57-59, 63, 64-65, 66; expensive 54, 59, 61-63, 66; moderate 55-56, 65, 60-61, 63-64, 67-68; budget 56-57, 59-60, 64, 65
campsites 69
hostels 68-69
villa rentals 213
see also p324 Accommodation index
addresses 304
age restrictions 304
agriturismi 250-251
AIDS 307
airlines 300
airports 300
Alberti, Leon Battista 39, 95
Alexander VI, Pope 16
Alighieri, Dante 14, 15, 75
Allori, Cristoforo 31
Amico Museo 172
Amidei family 11
Ammannati 40, 83
Anghiari 286
Ansedonia 295
Arezzo 276
accommodation 282
Anfiteatro Romano 280
Badia di Santi Fiora e Lucilla 278
Casa Museo Ivan Bruschi 279
Casa Vasari 279
Duomo 278
Fiera Antiquario di Arezzo 281
Fortezza Medicea 280
Museo Archeologico Mecenate 279
Museo d'Arte Medioevale 279
Museo dell' Oro 279
piazza Grande 280
Pieve di Santa Maria 278
Prato, Il 280
restaurants 280-282
San Domenico 279
San Francesco 279
Santa Maria delle Grazie 279
shopping 280
Arezzo province 283-289
architecture 36-46
best, the 37
art 26-31, 56
art history holidays 213
Art Park 31, *31*
Artigianato e Palazzo 172
Artimino 215
Associazione Musei dei Ragazzi 83, **85**

b

Badia Fiesolana 114
Badia Fiorentina 84, **85**
Bagni di Lucca 273
Bagno Vignoni 255
bakeries 159
Bandinelli, Baccio 29
banks 310
Barga 273
Bargello 84, 103, **104**, *104*
Barni, Roberto 31
Battistero de San Giovanni 37
beaches 212
Befana, La 174
Bellosguardo 115
Benigni, Roberto 180
Bibbiena 284
Biblioteca Nazionale 103
Bicci, Giovanni di 16
Boboli Gardens 40, 107, 109
Boccaccesca 174
Boccaccio 15
Bolgheri *232*, 234
Bonfire of the Vanities 16, **27**
books 319
bookshops 149
Botticelli, Sandro 26, 30
Brancacci Chapel 107
Bravio delle botti 173
Brozzi 112
Brunelleschi, Filippo 27, 38, 99
Buonarroti, Michelangelo *see* Michelangelo
Buonconvento 253
Buondelmonti, Buondelmonte dei 11
Buontalenti 40
bureaux de change 310
buses 301
business services 304

c

cafés, bars & gelaterie 140-147
best, the 141
with views 146
see also p325 Cafés, Bars & Gelaterie index
Calcio Storico 173, 203
Calici di Stelle 173
Camaldoli & La Verna 285
Cambio, Arnolfo di 38
Campi Bisenzio 112
Canossa family 11
Canossa, Matilde di 11
Cantine Aperte 172
Capalbio 295
Capella dei Pazzi 38
Capelle Medicee 40, **96**
Capella Rucellai 93
car & motorbike racing 200
car hire 302
Cardi, Ludovico 31
Carmignano 215
Carnevale di Viareggio 174
Carrara 272
Carrara marble 37
Casa Buonarroti 103, **104**
Casa Guidi **107**, **108**
Casa Museo Rodolfo Siviero 107, **108**
Casciana Terme 230
Casentino 284-285
Castagneto Caducci 234
Castellina 248
Castelnuovo di Garfagnana 274
Castiglion Fiorentino 287
Cellini, Benvenuto 31, 84, **87**
Cenacolo del Conservatorio di Fuligno 96, **97**
Cenacolo di Ognissanti 94
Cenacolo di Sant'Apollonia 97
Cenacolo di Santo Spirito 108
Certaldo Alto 217
Certosa del Galluzzo 115
Charlemagne 11
Charles V 17
Charles VIII 16
Chianti 247-248
Chiesa di Dante 84
children 175-177
bookshops 175-176
clothes shops 151
gardens & parks 176
play centres 176-177
restaurants 176
theatre 177
toy shops 176
Chiostro dello Scalzo 97
Christmas 174
Christmas Market 174
Cimabue 26
Cimitero degli Inglesi *112*, 113
cinemas 178-179
classical music & opera 186-189
festivals 189
groups & promoters 188-189
venues 186-188
Clement VII, Pope 17

climate 315
climbing & trekking 200-201
coffee 142
Colle di Val d'Elsa 249
Collezione Contini-Bonacossi 84, **85**
Collodi 221
complementary medicine 307
consulates 306
consumer rights 304
contraception 307
cookery schools 213
Corridoio Vasariano 84
Cortona 288
Cortona, Pietro da 31
cosmetic shops 165
credit cards 310
Cronaca, Il 39
Crypt of Santa Reparata 78
customs 305
cycling 201, 303
  holidays 213

d

Dante, *see* Alighieri
David 29, *29*, **99**
dentists 307
department stores 148
designer shops 164
directory 299-319
disabled 305
doctors 307
Dolci, Carlo 31
Donatello 27, 28
driving 300-301, 302-303
drugs 305
Duomo 37-38, 75, **77**, *77*, *80-81*
  baptistery 79
  campanile 79, 81
  crypt of Santa Reparata 78
  cupola 79, 80
Duomo & Around 75-91
  accommodation 53-57
  cafés & bars 141-142
  restaurants and wine bars 121-123

e

Effetto Venezia 173
Elba 296
electricity 305
electronics shops 151
embassies 306
emergencies 306
Estate Fiesolana 172
etiquette 304
Etruscans, the 10

f

Farmacia Santa Maria Novella 93
farming holidays 213
fashion 153-155
Fattori, Giovanni 31
Festa del Grillo 172
Festa della Donna 170
Festa di San Giovanni 173
Festa Internazionale della Ceramica 173
festivals & events 170-174
  music festivals 189
  theatre and dance festivals 207
Fiesole 36, 112, 114
film 178-180, 319
  festivals 179-180
Firenze Nova 112
Fivizzano 275
flat rental 69
flood of 1966 *20-21*, 22
Florence Marathon 174
Florence province 214-218
florists 166
Foiano della Chiana 287
food 43-45
  books 319
  glossary 134-135
  shops 159-161
football 200, 201
Forte di Belvedere 107, **108**
Fortezza da Basso 96, 113
Fosdinovo 274
Foster, Sir Norman 42
Fra Angelico 26, 27, 100
Francesca, Piero della 27
Fratini family 67

g

Galilei, Galileo 34-35
Galleria d'Arte Moderna 108
Galleria dell'Accademia 99
Galleria Palatina & Appartamenti Reali 109
galleries 181-182
Garfagnana, the 273-274
gay & lesbian 183-185, 306
gelaterie 146-147
Genio Fiorentino 172
Ghibellines, the 11, 14
Ghiberti, Lorenzo 27
Giambologna 28, 31, 83
Giardini di Boboli *see* Boboli Gardens
Giardino Bardini 107, 108
Giardino dei Semplici 99, **100**
gift shops 162-163
Giostra del Saracino 172
Giostra dell'Orso 173
Giotto 26, 38
Giugno Pisano 172
Giuliano, Duke of Nemours 17
golf 201
Goths, the 11
Greve 217
Grosseto 290
Grosseto province & the Maremma 290-296
Grotta del Vento 274
Guelphs, the 11, 14
gyms 202

h

hairdressers 164
health 306
helplines 307-308
Hercules and Cacus 29, *29*, 84
history 10-22
holidays 315-316
Holy Week 170
homeware shops 166
horse racing 200
horse riding 202
hospitals 307

i

ice skating 202
ID 308
immigration 24
in-line skating 202
insurance 308
Interactive Museum of Medieval Florence 96
internet 308
islands, the 296-297
Isola del Giglio 296
Isozaki, Arata 42
Istituto degli Innocenti 102

j

jewellery shops 157
Jewish Florence 22

l

La Specola 107, **111**
language 308
left luggage 308
Lega, Silvestro 31
legal help 308
Leo X, Pope 17
Leopold II, Grand Duke 19-20
libraries 308-309
Lippi, Filippo 30, **98**
literature 101, 319
Livorno 233
Loggia dei Lanzi 84
Loggia del Pesce 77, 104
Loggia di San Paolo 93
Lorenzo, Duke of Urbino 18
Lorenzo, Piero di 17
lost property 309
Lucca 260-269
  accommodation 268-269
  Casa Natale di Giacomo Puccini 264, *267*
  Duomo 262
  Lucca Comics & Games 266
  Museo della Cattedrale 264
  Museo Nazionale del Fumetto e dell'Immagine 266
  Museo Nazionale di Palazzo Mansi 264
  Museo Nazionale di Villa Guinigi 264
  nightlife 265
  parks & gardens 265
  ramparts 264
  restaurants 267-268
  San Francesco 262
  San Frediano 262
  San Giovanni e Reparata 262
  San Michele in Foro 263, *264*
  San Paolino 263
  Santa Maria Corteorlandini 263
  Santa Maria Forisportam 263
  shops 265-266
Lucignano 287
luggage shops 157
Lunigiana, the 274-275

Index

m

Macchiaioli, the 31
Madonna of the Trumpet 85
magazines 309
Maggio Musicale Fiorentino 170
malls 149
Manciano 292
Mannerism 30-31
Marini, Marino 31
markets 150
Mary Magdalene 28, *28*
Masaccio 27
Masolino 27
Massa 272
Massa-Carrara & Lucca provinces 270-275
Massa Marittima 290
Medici, Alessandro de' 18
Medici, Anna Maria 19
Medici, Cosimo de' (il Vecchio) 14, 15
Medici, Cosimo I de' 18
Medici, Cosimo II de' 19
Medici, Cosimo III de' 19
Medici, Ferdinando I de' 19
Medici, Ferdinando II de' 19
Medici, Francesco I de' 19
Medici, Gian Gastone 19
Medici, Lorenzo de' (il Magnifico) 14, 15, *16*, **17**
Medici, Piero de' (il Gottoso) 16
Medici villa 39
Medieval Festival 173
Mercato Nuovo 84, 150
Michelangelo 26, 29, 30, 33-34, 39-40
Michelozzo 38
Mille Miglia 172
money 310
Montagna Pistoiese, the 221
Montalcino 254
Monte Argentario 294
Monte Oliveto Maggiore 253
Monte San Savino 286
Montecatini Terme 220, *220*
Montefioralle 217
Montelupo 217
Montemerano 292
Montepulciano 257, 259
Monterchi 286
Mostra Mercato di Piante e Fiori 170
Mugello, The 217
Museo Archeologico 99, 100, 114
Museo Bandini 114
Museo Bardini 107
Museo Casa di Dante **85**
Museo degli Argenti 109
Museo del Calcio 177
Museo del Cenacolo di Andrea del Sarto 113
Museo del Costume 109
Museo dell'Antica Casa Fiorentina 90
Museo dell'Opera del Duomo 42, *78*, **82**
Museo dell'Opera di Santa Croce & Cappella dei Pazzi 103, **105**
Museo delle Carrozze 109
Museo delle Porcellane 109
Museo di Antropologia e Etnologia 103, **104**
Museo di Bigallo 75, **82**
Museo di Firenze com'era 103, **105**
Museo di Orsanmichele 86
Museo di San Marco 99, 100
Museo di Storia della Scienza 84, **86**
Museo di Storia Naturale 99, **102**
Museo Diocesano di Santo Stefano al Ponte 84, **86**
Museo Ferragamo 90
Museo Fiorentino di Preistoria 103, **105**
Museo Horne 39, 103,**105**
Museo Leonardo da Vinci 99, 100
Museo Marino Marini 93, **94**
Museo Nazionale Alinari della Fotografia 93, **94**
Museo Stibbert 113
museums
  anthropology: Museo di Antropologia e Etnologia 103, **104**
  archaeology; Museo Archeologico 99, 100, 114
  art: Bargello 84, 103, **104**, *104*; Cenacolo di Santo Spirito 108; Collezione Contini-Bonacossi 84, **85**; Forte di Belvedere 107, **108**; Galleria d'Arte Moderna 108; Galleria dell'Accademia 99; Galleria Palatina & Appartamenti Reali 109; Museo Bandini 114; Museo Bardini 107; Museo dell'Opera del Duomo 42, *78*, **82**; Museo dell'Opera di Santa Croce & Cappella dei Pazzi 103, **105**; Museo di Bigallo 75, **82**; Museo Horne 39, 103, **105**; Museo Marino Marini 93, **94**; Palazzo Strozzi 35, 90, **91**; Spedale degli Innocenti 99, **102**; Uffizi 26, *36*, 40, **88**
  carriages: Museo delle Carrozze 109
  ceramics: Museo delle Porcellane 109
  children: Associazione Musei dei Ragazzi 83, **85**
  costume: Museo del Costume 109
  famous figures: Casa Buonarroti 103, **104**; Casa Museo Rodolfo Siviero 107, **108**Museo Casa di Dante **85**; Museo Leonardo da Vinci 99, 100
  fashion: Villa Bardini 111
  football: Museo del Calcio 177
  historic buildings: Museo dell'Antica Casa Fiorentina 90
  history: Interactive Museum of Medieval Florence 96; Museo di Firenze com'era 103, **105**; Museo Fiorentino di Preistoria 103, **105**; Museo di San Marco 99, 100
  Jewish: Sinagoga & Museo di Arte e Storia Ebraica 103, **106**, *106*
  miscellaneous: Museo Stibbert 113; Serial Killer & Death Penalty Museum 96
  natural history: La Specola 107, **111**
  photography: Museo Nazionale Alinari della Fotografia 93, **94**
  religion: Museo del Cenacolo di Andrea del Sarto 113; Museo di Orsanmichele 86; Museo di San Marco 99, 100; Museo Diocesano di Santo Stefano al Ponte 84, **86**;
  science: Museo di Storia della Scienza 84, **86**
  shoes: Museo Ferragamo 90
  silver: Museo degli Argenti 109
music 319
  shops 167-168
  see also classical & opera and rock, pop & jazz

n

Nativities 174
Neptune 83
New Year's Eve 174
newspapers 309
nightlife 193-199
  clubs 195-197
  pubs & bars 197-199

o

Ognissanti 94, **95**
Oltrarno 107-111
accommodation 64-65
cafés & bars 144-145
restaurants 130-137
On the Road Festival 173
opening hours 74, 310
Opificio delle Pietre Dure 99, **102**
opticians 165, 307
Oratorio dei Vanchetoni 93
Orbetello 294, *295*
Orcagna, Andrea 26
Orsanmichele 38, 85, **86**
Ospedale degli Innocenti 38
Ostensione della Sacra Cintola & Corteggio Storico 174
Outside the City Gates 112-115
accommodation 66-68
cafés & bars 145
restaurants & wine bars 137-139

p

painting courses 213
Palagio di Parte Guelfa 90
Palazzo Antinori 90
Palazzo Bartolini-Salimbeni 90
Palazzo d'Antella 103
Palazzo Davanzati 38, *39*, 90
Palazzo dell'Arte della Lana 85
Palazzo Medici Riccardi 38, 96, **97**
Palazzo Pitti 40, 107, 108
Palazzo Rucellai 38, 93
Palazzo Spini Feroni 90
Palazzo Strozzi 35, 90, **91**
Palazzo Vecchio 83, 86, *84*
Palio delle Contrade 173
Panzano 217
Parco delle Cascine 113
Parco Naturale della Maremma 297
Parco Orecchiella 274
pâtisseries 160
Pazzagli, Enzo 31
Perseus 84, 87, *87*
Pescia 221
Petrarch 15
pharmacies 164, 165, 307
photography shops 151-153
piazza Beccaria 113
piazza de'Ciompi 103
piazza del Duomo 75
piazza della Libertà 113
piazza della Repubblica 42, 77
piazza della Santissima Annunziata 99
piazza della Signoria 83, *88*
piazza Ghiberti 104
piazza Mino 114
piazza San Firenze 103
piazza Santa Croce 103
piazza Santa Maria Novella 93
piazza Santa Trinità 90
piazza Santo Spirito 107
piazzale Michelangelo 40, 107, 114
Pienza 256
Pietrasanta *270*, 271
Pieve a Socana 284
Piombino 234
Pisa 222-229
accommodation 228
baptistery 223
Campo dei Miracoli 222
Camposanto 223
Duomo 223
Leaning Tower 223, *223*
Museo dell'Opera del Duomo 226
Museo delle Sinopie 226
Torre di Santa Maria 226
Museo Nazionale di Palazzo Reale 226
Museo Nazionale di San Matteo 226
nightlife 228
Orto Botanico 226
piazza dei Cavalieri 226
restaurants 227
San Nicola 226
Santa Maria della Spina 227, *229*
shops 228
Pisa & Livorno provinces 230
Pistoia 219-220
Pistoia province 219-221
Pitigliano 293
pizza 119
Poggi, Giuseppe 40
Poggio a Caiano 215
police 311
ponte alle Grazie 103
ponte Santa Trinità 40, 42, 90
ponte Vecchio 84
Pontremoli 275
pool 202
Poppi 284
Porta al Prato 112
Porta alla Croce 113
post 311
Prato 214-215
Prato province 214-218

q

Quartieri Monumentali 83

r

Radicofani 256
radio 309
rail travel 300
Rape of the Sabine Women 28, *28*
religion 310-312
Renaissance **15**, 26-30, **32-35**
restaurants & wine bars 118-139
best, the 120
pizzerie & rosticcerie 125, 130, 137, 139
snacks 123, 125, 130
see also p325 Restaurants & Wine Bars index
Rificolona, La 174
Robbia, Luca della 27
Roccalbegna & Santa Fiora 292
rock, pop & jazz 190-192
best venues 191
festivals 192
Romans, the 11
rowing 202
running 203
Russian Orthodox church 113

s

safety 312
Sagra del Tordo 174
San Firenze 103
San Frediano 107
San Gimignano 252-253, *252*
San Giovanni Batista 42
San Giovanni d'Asso 254
San Giuliano Terme 230
San Lorenzo (area) 96-98
accommodation 60-61
cafés & bars143
restaurants & wine bars 125
San Lorenzo (church) 38, **98**
San Lorenzo market 96, *97*
San Marco (area) 99-102
accommodation 61-63
cafés & bars 143-144
restaurants 126
San Marco (church) 99, 102
San Michele *see* Orsanmichele
San Miniato 230
San Miniato al Monte 37, 115, *115*
San Niccolò 107
San Quirico d'Orcia 255
San Remigio 37
San Vicenzo 234
Sangallo, Giuliano da 39
Sansepolcro 285
Santa Croce (area) 103-106
accommodation 63-64
cafés & bars144
restaurants & wine bars 126-130
Santa Croce (church) 26, 38, 103, 105, *105*
Santa Felicità 107, **110**
Santa Fiora 292
Santa Maria del Carmine 107, **110**
Santa Maria del Fiore *see* Duomo
Santa Maria Maddalena dei Pazzi 103

Santa Maria Novella (area) 93-95
accommodation 57-60
cafés & bars 142-143
restaurants and wine bars 123-125
Santa Maria Novella (church) 37, 38, 93, **95**, *95*
Santa Maria Novella station 93
Santa Trinità 90, **91**
Santissima Annunziata 99, *100*, **102**
Santissimi Apostoli 37, 90, **91**
Santo Spirito 38, 39, 107, **110**
Sarteano 256
Sarto, Andrea del 31
Saturnia 292, *292*
Savonarola, Girolamo 16, 27
Scansano 291
Scoppio del Carro 170, *171*
Serial Killer & Death Penalty Museum 96
Sesto Fiorentino 112
Settignano 112, 114
Settimana dei Beni Culturali 172
shoe shops 159
shops 148-168
best, the 149
department stores 148
malls 149
shrines 74
Siena 235-246
accommodation 245-246
Basilica di San Domenico 239
Basilica di San Francesco 240
Battistero 240
Complesso Museale di Santa Maria della Scala 240, *240*
Duomo 240
Fortezza Medicea 242
Museo Civico 241
Museo dell'Opera del Duomo 241
Oratorio di San Bernardino 240
Orto Botanico 242
Palazzo Chigi Saracini/Accademia Musicale Chigiana 242
Palazzo delle Papesse 242
Palazzo Pubblico 239
Palio, the 244, *244*
piazza del Campo 23
piazza Salimbeni 239
Pinacoteca Nazionale 242
restaurants 242-243
Santuario e Casa di Santa Caterina 239
shops 243-245
Torre del Mangia 239
Siena province 247-259
sightseeing 72-74
best, the 73
Signorini, Telemaco 31
Sinagoga & Museo di Arte e Storia Ebraica 103, **106**, *106*
Sixtus IV, Pope 15
skiing 204
smoking 120, 312
Sorano 293
Southern Tuscany 290-297
Sovana 293
spas 165-166
in Tuscany 231
Spedale degli Innocenti 99, **102**
sport & fitness 200-204
active sports 200-204
spectator sports 200
sports shops 168
squash 204
Staccioli, Paolo 31
Stadio Artemio Franchi 42, 113
statues 28-29
STDs 307
study 312
Suvereto 234
swimming 204

t

taxis 301-302
Teatro Romano 114
telephones 313-314
television 310
tennis 204
Tenuta de Castelfalfi 254
theatre & dance 205-207
venues 205-207
companies 207
festivals 207
tickets 74, 168
time 314
tipping 314
toilets 314
Torre del Lago Puccini 185
Torrigiani, Pietro 94
tour buses 74
tourist information 74, 314-315
tours 74
trains 300
trams 24-25
transport 300-303
travel advice 305
travel agents 168
tripe 124
Tuscan Sun Festival 173

u

Uccello, Paolo 27
Uffizi 26, *36*, 40, **88**
bomb 22, 89, *91*

v

Valdarno 283-284
Valdichiana 286-289
Valtiberina 285-286
Vasari, Giorgio 31, 33-34, 40
Verrocchio, Andrea del 27, 30
Versilia Riviera 270-272
via de' Tornabuoni 90
via Maggio 107
Viareggio 270-271
Villa Bardini 111
Villa Bellosguardo 115
Villa della Petraia 113
Villa di Castello 114
Villa Medici 114
Villa Michelangelo 114
Vinci 215
Vinci, Leonardo da 15, 26, 30, 33
vintage clothes shops 158
visas 315
Vitruvius 38
vocabulary 317
architectural glossary 318
food glossary 134-135
Volterra 232
Volterra AD 1398 173

w

walking 303
holidays 213
walks
Boboli Gardens 110
fictional Florence 101
weather 315
websites 319
weights & measures 315
wine 45-48, 119
shops 160
Treno del Vino 258-9
wine bars *see* restaurants & wine bars
women 316
chefs 131
working 316
World War I 21
World War II 22

z

Zuccari, Federico 31

Accommodation

Abaco 59
Annalena 65
Antica Dimora Johlea 60
Antica Torre Tornabuoni Uno 59
B&B Novecento 55, *55*
Beacci Tornabuoni 59
Camping Michelangelo 69
Camping Panoramico 69
Casa Howard 59
Casa Pucci 65, *66*
Casa Roval *61*, 63
Casci 60
Cestelli 56
Classic Hotel 67
Dalí 64
Dei Mori 55
Ferretti 60
Florence & Abroad 69
Gallery Hotel Art 53
Grand Hotel 57
Grand Hotel Minerva 59
Helvetia & Bristol *51*, 53
Hermitage 54
Hostel Archi Rossi 68
Hotel Continentale 54
Hotel Santa Maria Novella 57
Il Guelfo Blanco 60
Istituto Gould 65

JK Place 57
Locanda degli Artisti 60
Loggiato dei Serviti 61
Lungarno 64
Lungarno Suites 54
Ostello Monaco 34 69
Ostello per la Gioventù 69
Palazzo Galletti 63, *64*
Palazzo Magnani Feroni 65
Pensione Bencistà 68
Perseo 55
Relais degli Uffizi 55
Relais Grand Tour 61
Relais Marignolle 66
Relais Santa Croce 63, *63*
Residence Hilda 61
Residenza d'Epoca in Piazza della Signoria
Residenza del Moro *56*, 57
Riva Lofts 67, *68*
Savoy 54
Scaletta, La 65
Scoti 60
Stanze di Santa Croce, Le 64
Torre Guelfa 55
Una Hotel Vittoria 66
Villa Poggio San Felice 68
Villa San Michele 66
Westin Excelsior 57
Your Agency in Florence (YAIF) 69

Cafés, Bars & Gelaterie

Amerini 142
Area 51 *143*, 145
Astor Caffè 141
Bar Perseo 141
BZF (Bizzeffe) 143
Cabiria 144
Caffè Cibrèo 144
Caffè degli Artigiani 144
Caffè Florian *140*, 142
Caffè Megara 142
Caffè Ricchi 144
Caffè Rivoire 141
Caffè San Carlo 142
Caffè Vitali 142
Caffellatte 144
Carabé 146
Caruso Jazz Café 141
Chiaroscuro 141
Colle Bereto 141
Gelateria dei Neri 147
Giacosa Roberto Cavalli 142
Gilli 141
Gold/La Carrozza 147
Grom 147, *147*
Hemingway *144*, 145
I Visacci 144
Il Rifrullo 145
Libreria Café La Cité 145, *145*
Loggia degli Albizi, La 144
Nabucco 143
Nannini Coffee Shop 143
Noir 142
Nuove Poste 144
Perchè No! 147
Porfirio Rubirosa 143
Procacci 141
Robiglio 143
Rose's 142
Terrazza, La 142, *146*
Vestri 147
Vivoli 147
Zona 15 143

Restaurants & Wine Bars

Accademia, L' 126
Al Tranvai 136
All'Antico Vinaio 129
Alla Vecchia Bettola 137
Amon 125
Arte Gaia, L' 137
Baldovino 126
Bar Galli 125
Beccofino 130
Bibe 137
Boccadama 126
Borgo San Jacopo 132
Caffè Italiano 130
Canova di Gustavino 121
Cantinetta Antinori 123
Cantinetta dei Verrazzano 121
Casa del Vino 125
Casalinga, La 132
Cavolo Nero 132
Cibreino 127
Cibrèo 127
Coquinarius 121
Da Camillo 132
Da Mario 125
Da Rocco 130
Da Ruggero 138
Da Sergio 125
Dei Frescobaldi Ristorante & Wine Bar 121
Del Fagioli 127
Enoteca Pinchiorri 127
Filipepe *126*, 133
Fuori Porta 139
Fusion Bar 121
Garga 123
Giostra, La 127
I Fratellini 121
Il Guscio 133
Il Latini 124
Il Pizzaiuolo 130
Il Santo Bevitore 136
Il Vegetariano 126
'Ino 119, 123
Kome 129
Mangiatoia, La 137
Napoleone 132, 133
Nerbone 125
Olio e Convivum 133
Oliviero 121
Omero 138
Ora d'Aria 123, 129
Osteria de' Benci 129
Pane e Vino 133
Pitti Gola e Cantina 137
Portofino 138
Povero Pesce 138, 139
Ricchi 133
Rosticceria della Spada 125
Rosticceria Giuliano Centro 130
Ruth's 129
Salaam Bombay 138
Sant'Agostino 23 136
Santa Lucia 139
Targa 138
Trattoria 4 Leoni 136
Trattoria del Carmine 136, 136
Trattoria I Fratellini 130
Vico del Carmine 139
Vie en Rose, La 129
Volpi e l'Uva, Le 137, 138
Zibibbo 139

Advertisers' Index

Please refer to the relevant pages for contact details

Consorzio Turistico Volterra Cecina and Valdera Valleys IFC

In Context

BBC Active 8
Adler Thermae Spa Resort 12-13

Where To Stay

Serristori Palace & Country 52
Hotel Casci 58
Hotel il Perseo 58
Hotel Kursal 62
Hotel Europa 62

Sightseeing

Castello di Pratelli 70

Restaurants & Wine Bars

Vestri 122
Koine' Centre 122
Sei Divino Wine Bar 128

Shops & Services

BM Bookshop 152
The Florentine 152

Tuscany

Bagni di Pisa 208
Grotta Giusti 216
Tenuta di Ricavo 238

Directory

Fonteverde 298

Maps

Angels Restaurant & American Bar 330

Doris Music & Drink IBC

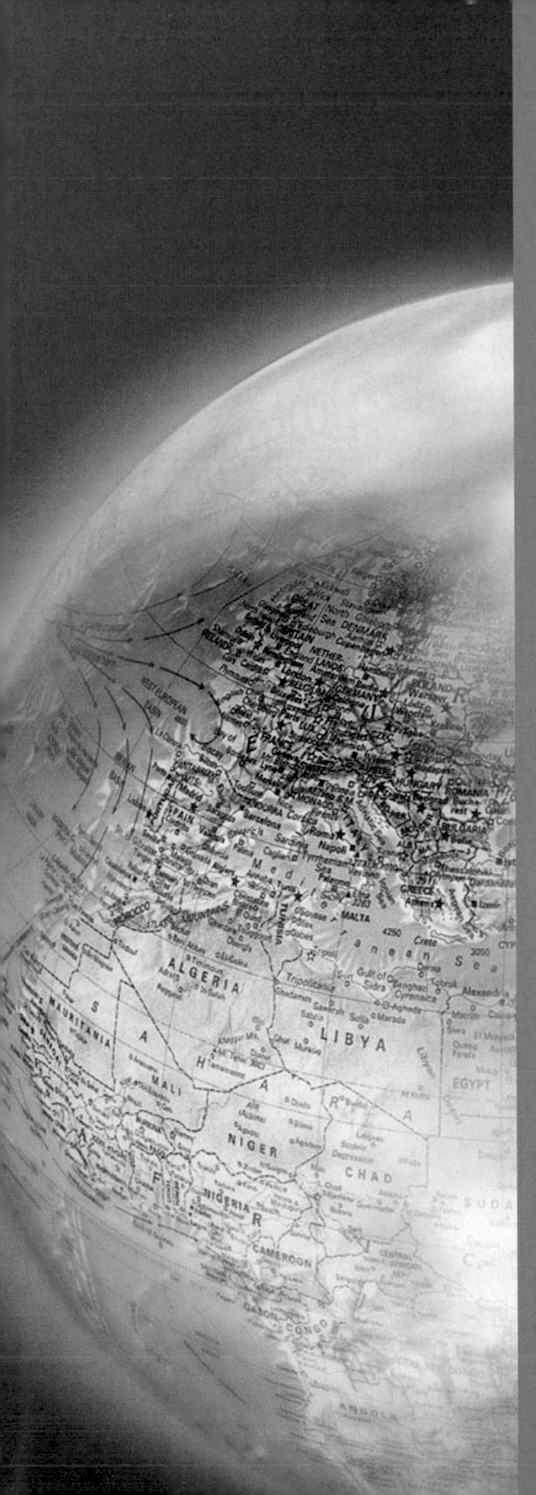

Regional border

Province border

Autostrada

City wall

Place of interest and/or entertainment

Railway station

Park

Hospital/university

Ancient site

Car park P

Tourist information *i*

Pedestrianised area

Electric bus route A

Maps

Tuscany 328

Greater Florence 331

Florence Overview 332

Street Maps 334

Street Index 336

LIGURIA
EMILIA-
ROMAGNA
Lunigiana
Pontremoli
Massa-
Carrara
(pp270-275)
A15
63
12
Fivizzano
Aulla
Parco dell'
Orecchiella
Garfagnana
445
1
Fosdinovo
LA SPEZIA
Castelnuovo
di Garfagnana
Abetone
Carrara
Colonnata
Isolasanta
Alpi Apuane
Barga
Massa
Fornovolasco
Val di Lima
Pistoia
(pp219-221)
Riviera della Versilia
Bagni di
Lucca
Forte dei Marmi
Pietrasanta
Lucca
(pp252-257)
PISTOIA
A12
Pescia
Montecatini
Terme
Collodi
Viareggio
LUCCA
(pp260-269)
Torre del
Lago Puccini
A11
Monsummano
Terme
Vinci
San Giuliano
Terme
PISA
(pp222-229)
Empoli
San Miniato
Cascina
67
Tirrenia
Montopoli
in Val D Ano
Terricciola
LIVORNO
Casciana
Terme
439
Pisa
(pp230-234)
Rosignano
Volterra
Vada
68
Cecina
Bolgheri
TOS
(TUS
1
Castagneto
Carducci
San Vincenzo
Suvereto
Massa
Marittima
Golfo di
Baratti
Livorno
(pp212-216)
Populonia
Piombino
Vetulonia
Portoferraio
Elba
(p297)
322
Ligurian
Sea
Capraia
Bastia
Corse
(Corsica)
Pianosa
Montecristo
Giglio
(p296)
0
40 km
0
20 miles
' Copyright Time Out Group 2008
AUSTRIA
SWITZERLAND
HUNGARY
SLOVENIA
CROATIA
Milan
Venice
Bologna
BOSNIA AND
HERCEGOVINA
SERBIA
Genoa
Firenze
(Florence)
Rimini
Pisa
Livorno
Siena
MONTENEGRO
ITALY
Bastia
CORSICA
ROME
ALBANIA
Naples
SARDINIA
SICILY

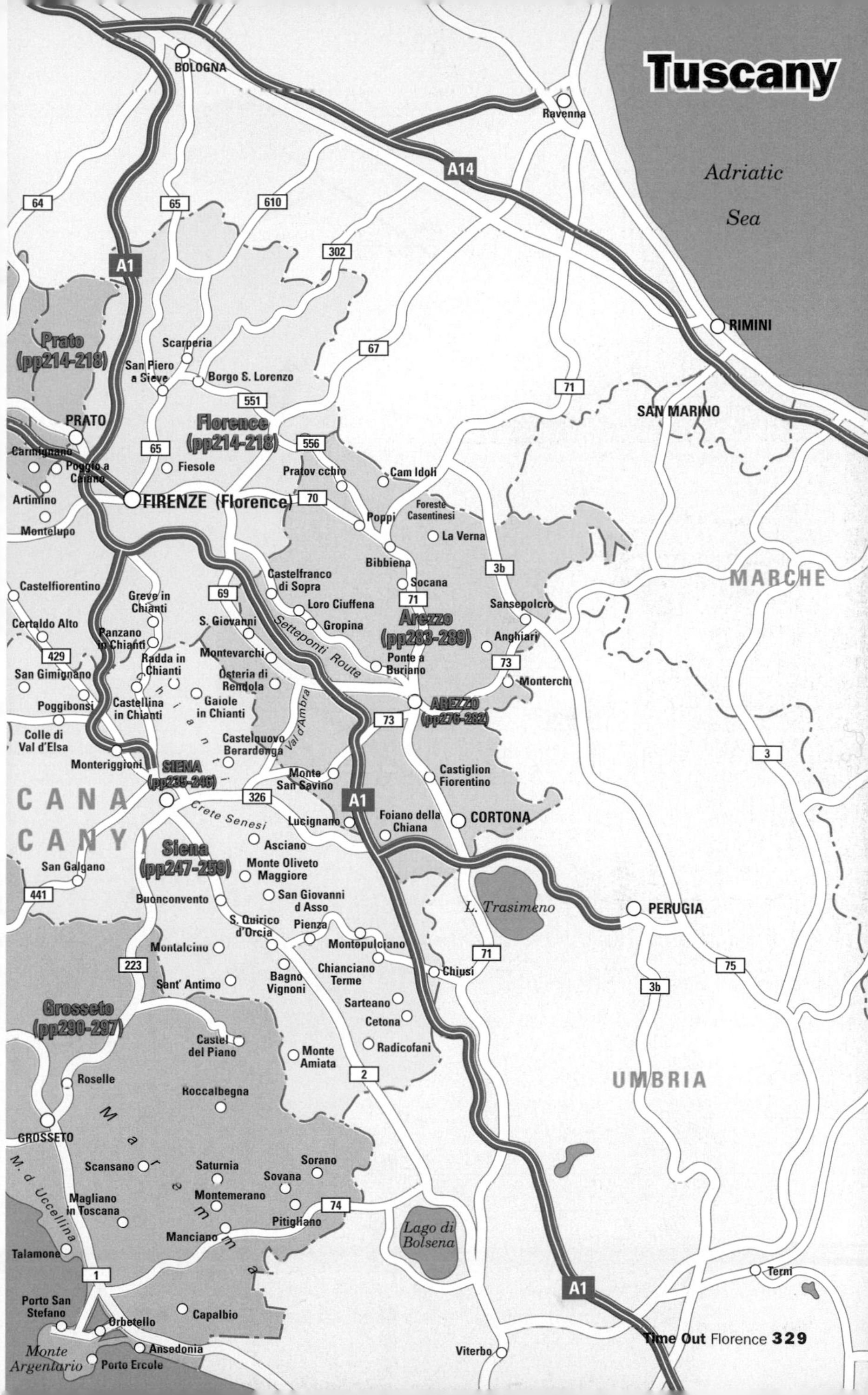

Tuscany
Adriatic Sea
BOLOGNA
Ravenna
A14
RIMINI
SAN MARINO
MARCHE
UMBRIA
A1
64
65
610
302
67
71
551
556
70
3b
69
73
429
326
441
223
2
74
1
3
75
Prato (pp214-218)
PRATO
Carmignano
Poggio a Caiano
Artimino
Montelupo
Scarperia
San Piero a Sieve
Borgo S. Lorenzo
Florence (pp214-218)
Fiesole
FIRENZE (Florence)
Pratov cchio
Cam Idoli
Foreste Casentinesi
Poppi
La Verna
Bibbiena
Socana
Castelfiorentino
Greve in Chianti
Castelfranco di Sopra
Loro Ciuffena
Gropina
Arezzo (pp283-289)
Sansepolcro
Anghiari
Certaldo Alto
Panzano in Chianti
S. Giovanni
Setteponti Route
Montevarchi
Ponte a Buriano
Monterchi
San Gimignano
Radda in Chianti
Osteria di Rendola
Poggibonsi
Castellina in Chianti
Gaiole in Chianti
AREZZO (pp276-282)
Colle di Val d'Elsa
Chianti
Castelnuovo Berardenga
Val d'Ambra
Monteriggioni
SIENA (pp235-246)
Monte San Savino
Castiglion Fiorentino
Crete Senesi
Lucignano
Foiano della Chiana
CORTONA
Asciano
Siena (pp247-259)
San Galgano
Monte Oliveto Maggiore
San Giovanni d Asso
Buonconvento
L. Trasimeno
PERUGIA
S. Quirico d'Orcia
Pienza
Montepulciano
Montalcino
Chianciano Terme
Chiusi
Sant' Antimo
Bagno Vignoni
Sarteano
Cetona
Grosseto (pp290-297)
Castel del Piano
Monte Amiata
Radicofani
Roselle
Roccalbegna
Maremma
GROSSETO
M. d Uccellina
Scansano
Saturnia
Sorano
Sovana
Magliano in Toscana
Montemerano
Pitigliano
Manciano
Lago di Bolsena
Talamone
Porto San Stefano
Capalbio
Orbetello
Ansedonia
Monte Argentario
Porto Ercole
Viterbo
Terni

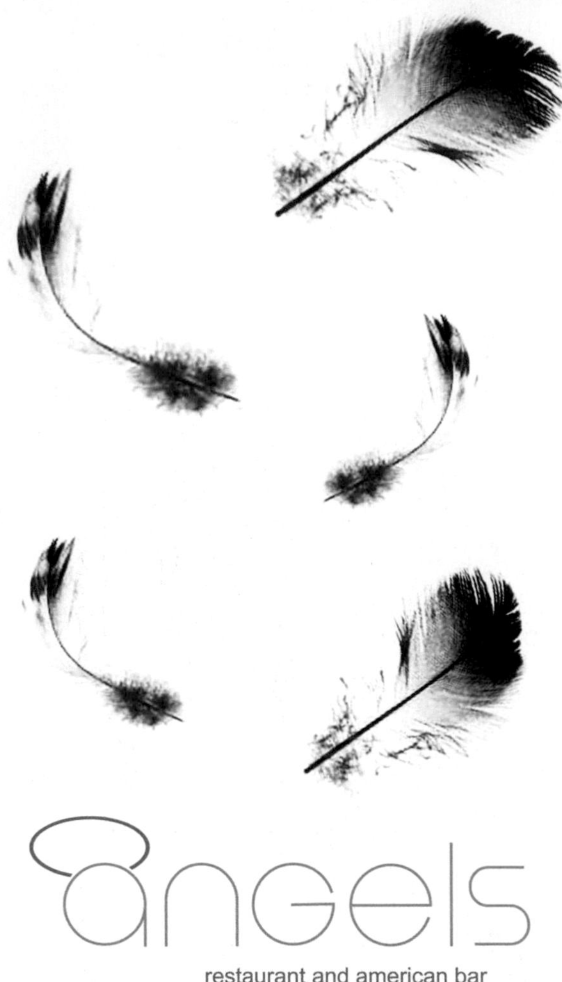

Greater Florence

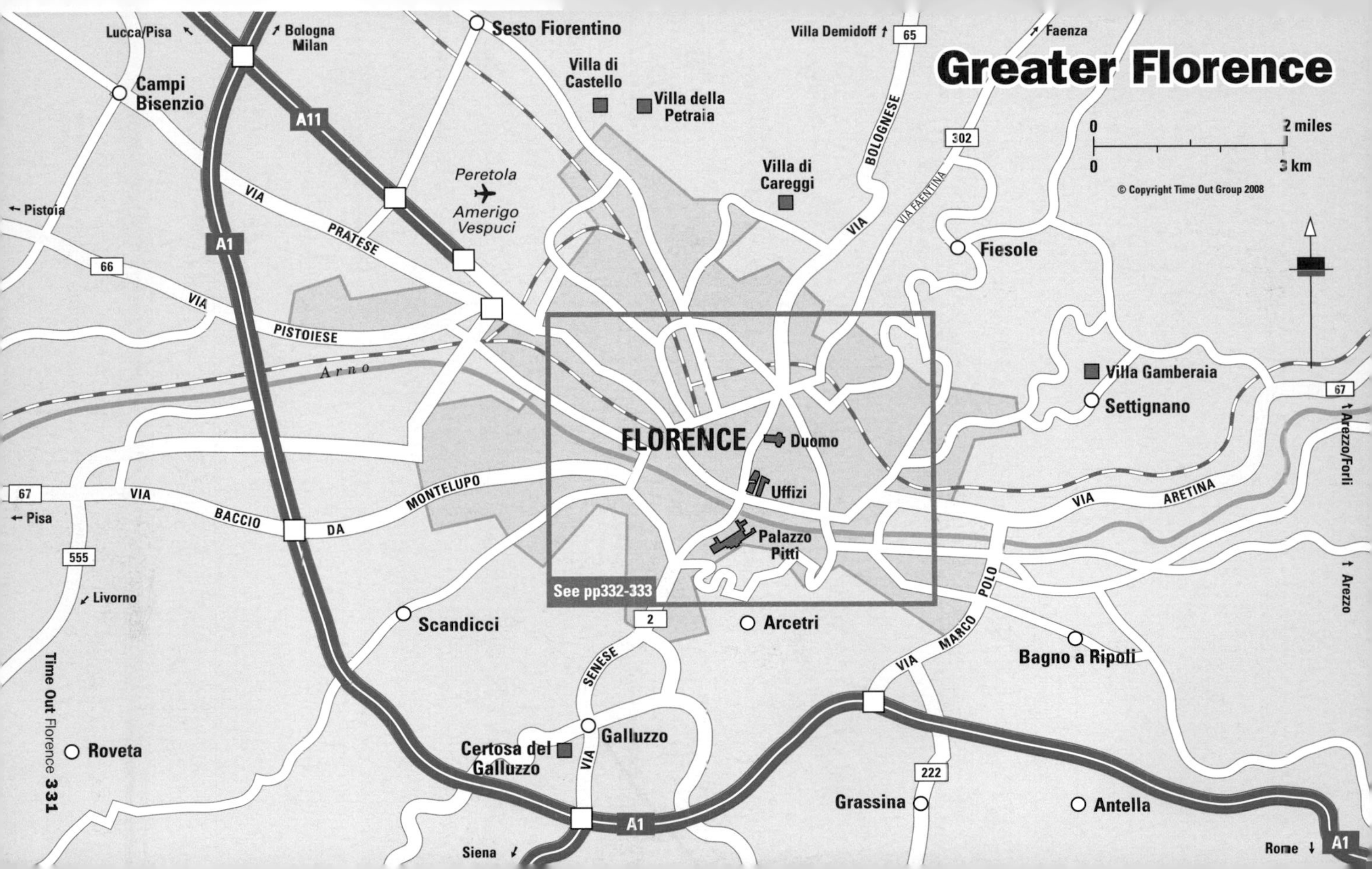

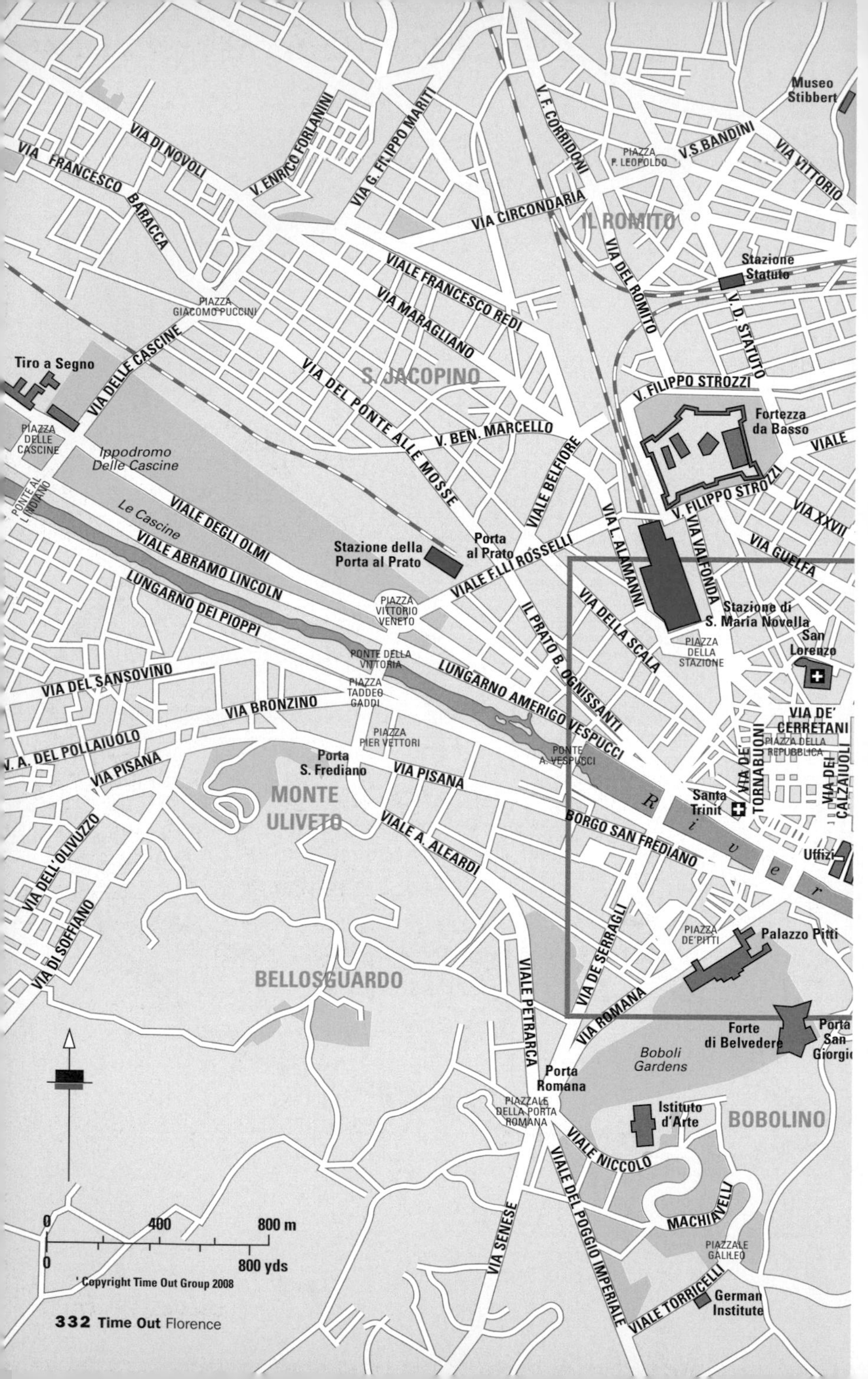
Museo Stibbert
VIA DI NOVOLI
VIA FRANCESCO BARACCA
V. ENRICO FORLANINI
VIA G. FILIPPO MARITI
V.F. CORRIDONI
PIAZZA F. LEOPOLDO
V.S.BANDINI
VIA VITTORIO
VIA CIRCONDARIA
IL ROMITO
Stazione Statuto
VIALE FRANCESCO REDI
VIA DEL ROMITO
V. D. STATUTO
PIAZZA GIACOMO PUCCINI
VIA MARAGLIANO
VIA DELLE CASCINE
Tiro a Segno
VIA DEL PONTE ALLE MOSSE
S. JACOPINO
V. FILIPPO STROZZI
Fortezza da Basso
PIAZZA DELLE CASCINE
V. BEN. MARCELLO
VIALE
Ippodromo Delle Cascine
PONTE AL L'INDIANO
Le Cascine
VIALE DEGLI OLMI
VIALE BELFIORE
V. FILIPPO STROZZI
VIA XXVII
VIALE ABRAMO LINCOLN
Stazione della Porta al Prato
Porta al Prato
VIALE F.LLI ROSSELLI
VIA L. ALAMANNI
VIA VALFONDA
VIA GUELFA
LUNGARNO DEI PIOPPI
PIAZZA VITTORIO VENETO
VIA DELLA SCALA
Stazione di S. Maria Novella
San Lorenzo
PONTE DELLA VITTORIA
IL PRATO
B. OGNISSANTI
PIAZZA DELLA STAZIONE
VIA DEL SANSOVINO
LUNGARNO AMERIGO VESPUCCI
PIAZZA TADDEO GADDI
VIA BRONZINO
VIA DE' CERRETANI
V. A. DEL POLLAIUOLO
PIAZZA PIER VETTORI
PIAZZA DELLA REPUBBLICA
VIA PISANA
Porta S. Frediano
VIA PISANA
PONTE A. VESPUCCI
VIA DE' TORNABUONI
VIA DEI CALZAIUOLI
MONTE ULIVETO
Santa Trinit
River
VIALE A. ALEARDI
BORGO SAN FREDIANO
Uffizi
VIA DELL'OLIVUZZO
VIA DI SOFFIANO
VIA DE SERRAGLI
PIAZZA DE' PITTI
Palazzo Pitti
BELLOSGUARDO
VIALE PETRARCA
VIA ROMANA
Forte di Belvedere
Porta San Giorgio
Boboli Gardens
Porta Romana
PIAZZALE DELLA PORTA ROMANA
Istituto d'Arte
BOBOLINO
VIALE NICCOLO
MACHIAVELLI
VIALE DEL POGGIO IMPERIALE
VIA SENESE
PIAZZALE GALILEO
VIALE TORRICELLI
German Institute
0
400
800 m
0
800 yds
© Copyright Time Out Group 2008

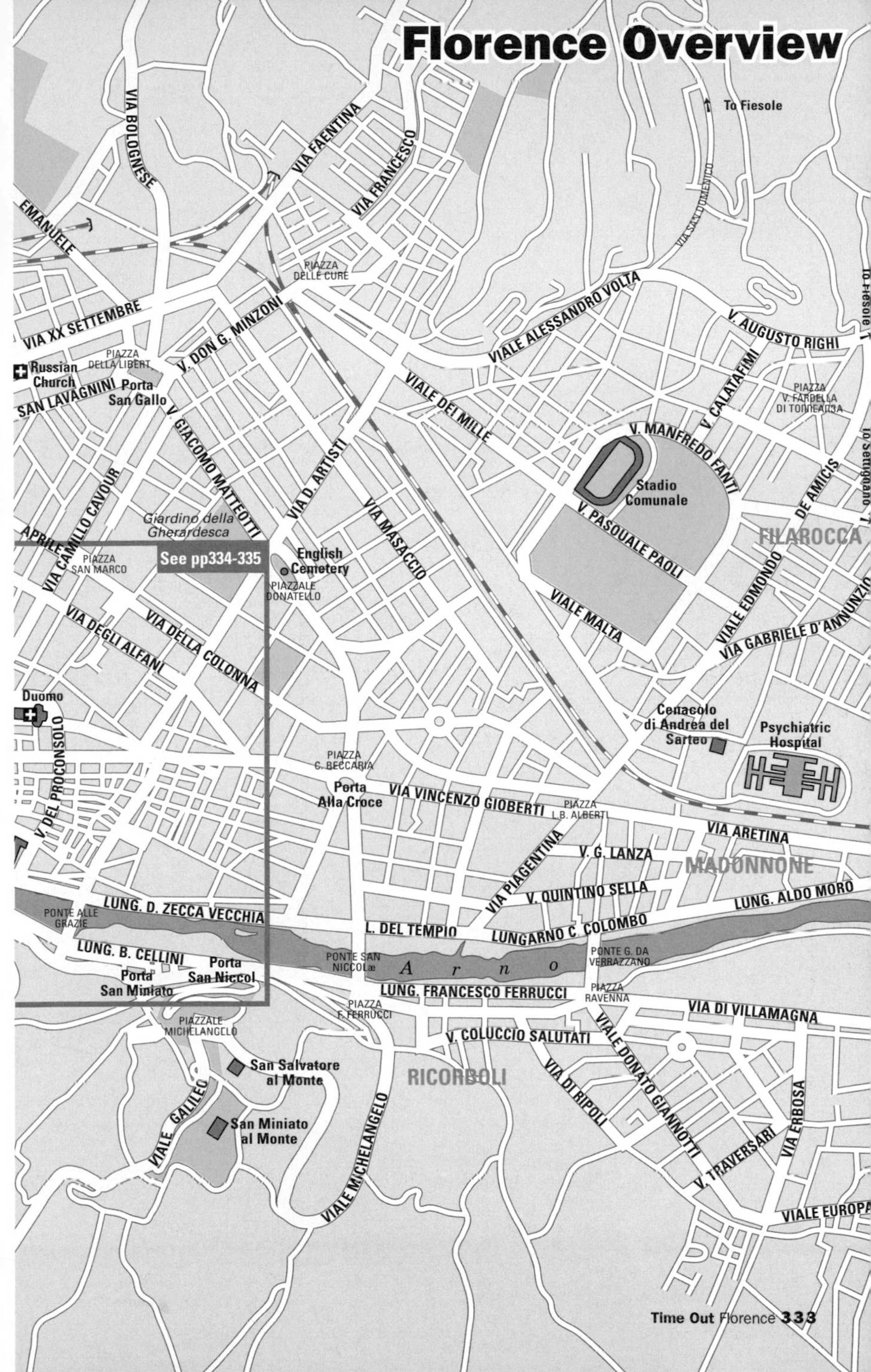
Florence Overview
To Fiesole
VIA BOLOGNESE
VIA FAENTINA
VIA FRANCESCO
EMANUELE
PIAZZA DELLE CURE
VIA SAN DOMENICO
To Fiesole
VIA XX SETTEMBRE
V. DON G. MINZONI
VIALE ALESSANDRO VOLTA
V. AUGUSTO RIGHI
Russian Church
PIAZZA DELLA LIBERTÀ
Porta San Gallo
SAN LAVAGNINI
VIALE DEI MILLE
V. CALATAFIMI
PIAZZA V. FARDELLA DI TORREARSA
To Settignano
V. GIACOMO MATTEOTTI
VIA D. ARTISTI
V. MANFREDO FANTI
Stadio Comunale
DE AMICIS
VIA CAMILLO CAVOUR
VIA MASACCIO
V. PASQUALE PAOLI
Giardino della Gherardesca
FILAROCCA
APRILE
PIAZZA SAN MARCO
See pp334-335
English Cemetery
PIAZZALE DONATELLO
VIALE EDMONDO
VIALE MALTA
VIA GABRIELE D'ANNUNZIO
VIA DEGLI ALFANI
VIA DELLA COLONNA
Duomo
V. DEL PROCONSOLO
Cenacolo di Andrea del Sarteo
Psychiatric Hospital
PIAZZA C. BECCARIA
Porta Alla Croce
VIA VINCENZO GIOBERTI
PIAZZA L.B. ALBERTI
VIA ARETINA
VIA PIAGENTINA
V. G. LANZA
MADONNONE
V. QUINTINO SELLA
LUNG. ALDO MORO
LUNG. D. ZECCA VECCHIA
PONTE ALLE GRAZIE
L. DEL TEMPIO
LUNGARNO C. COLOMBO
LUNG. B. CELLINI
Porta San Niccol
Porta San Miniato
PONTE SAN NICCOLÆ
Arno
PONTE G. DA VERRAZZANO
LUNG. FRANCESCO FERRUCCI
PIAZZA RAVENNA
VIA DI VILLAMAGNA
PIAZZA F. FERRUCCI
PIAZZALE MICHELANGELO
V. COLUCCIO SALUTATI
VIALE DONATO GIANNOTTI
San Salvatore al Monte
RICORBOLI
VIA DI RIPOLI
VIALE GALILEO
San Miniato al Monte
VIALE MICHELANGELO
VIA ERBOSA
V. TRAVERSARI
VIALE EUROPA

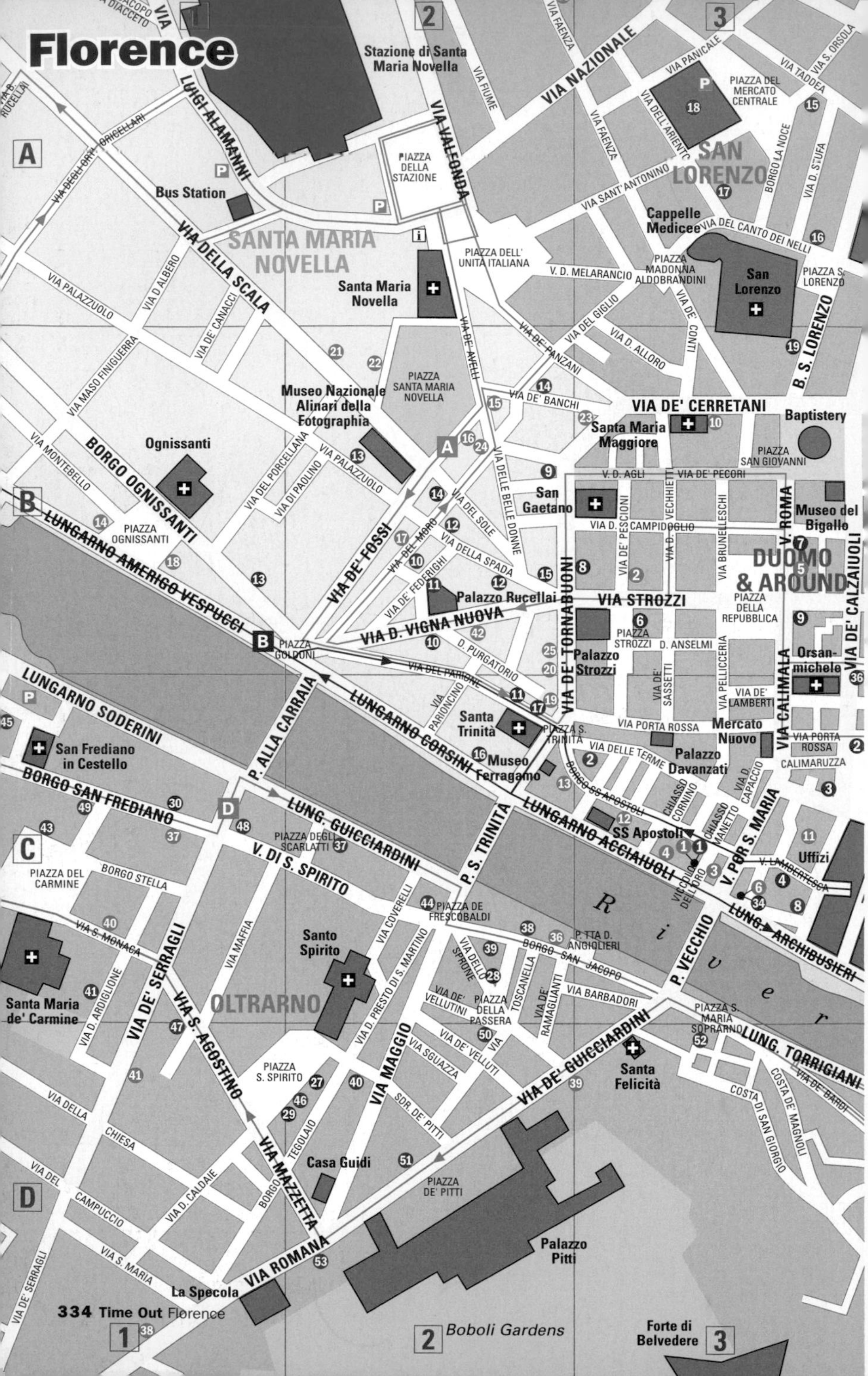

Florence
Stazione di Santa Maria Novella
Piazza della Stazione
Bus Station
Santa Maria Novella
Piazza dell' Unità Italiana
Piazza Santa Maria Novella
Museo Nazionale Alinari della Fotographia
Ognissanti
Piazza Ognissanti
San Lorenzo
Cappelle Medicee
Piazza Madonna Aldobrandini
Piazza del Mercato Centrale
Piazza S. Lorenzo
Santa Maria Maggiore
Baptistery
Piazza San Giovanni
San Gaetano
Museo del Bigallo
Duomo & Around
Palazzo Rucellai
Piazza Strozzi
Palazzo Strozzi
Piazza della Repubblica
Orsanmichele
Piazza Goldoni
Santa Trinità
Piazza S. Trinità
Museo Ferragamo
Mercato Nuovo
Palazzo Davanzati
SS Apostoli
Uffizi
San Frediano in Cestello
Piazza del Carmine
Santa Maria de' Carmine
Piazza degli Scarlatti
Piazza de Frescobaldi
P. tta d. Angiolieri
Santo Spirito
Oltrarno
Piazza della Passera
Piazza S. Maria Soprarno
Santa Felicità
Piazza S. Spirito
Casa Guidi
Piazza de' Pitti
Palazzo Pitti
La Specola
Boboli Gardens
Forte di Belvedere
River
Via Nazionale
Via Valfonda
Luigi Alamanni
Via della Scala
Borgo Ognissanti
Lungarno Amerigo Vespucci
Via de' Fossi
Via de' Cerretani
Via Strozzi
Via de' Tornabuoni
Via D. Vigna Nuova
Via Roma
Via Calimala
Via de' Calzaiuoli
Lungarno Soderini
Lungarno Corsini
Borgo San Frediano
P. alla Carraia
Lung. Guicciardini
V. di S. Spirito
P. S. Trinita
Lungarno Acciaiuoli
P. Vecchio
V. Por S. Maria
Lung. Archibusieri
Lung. Torrigiani
Via de' Serragli
Via S. Agostino
Via Maggio
Via de' Guicciardini
Via Mazzetta
Via Romana
B. S. Lorenzo

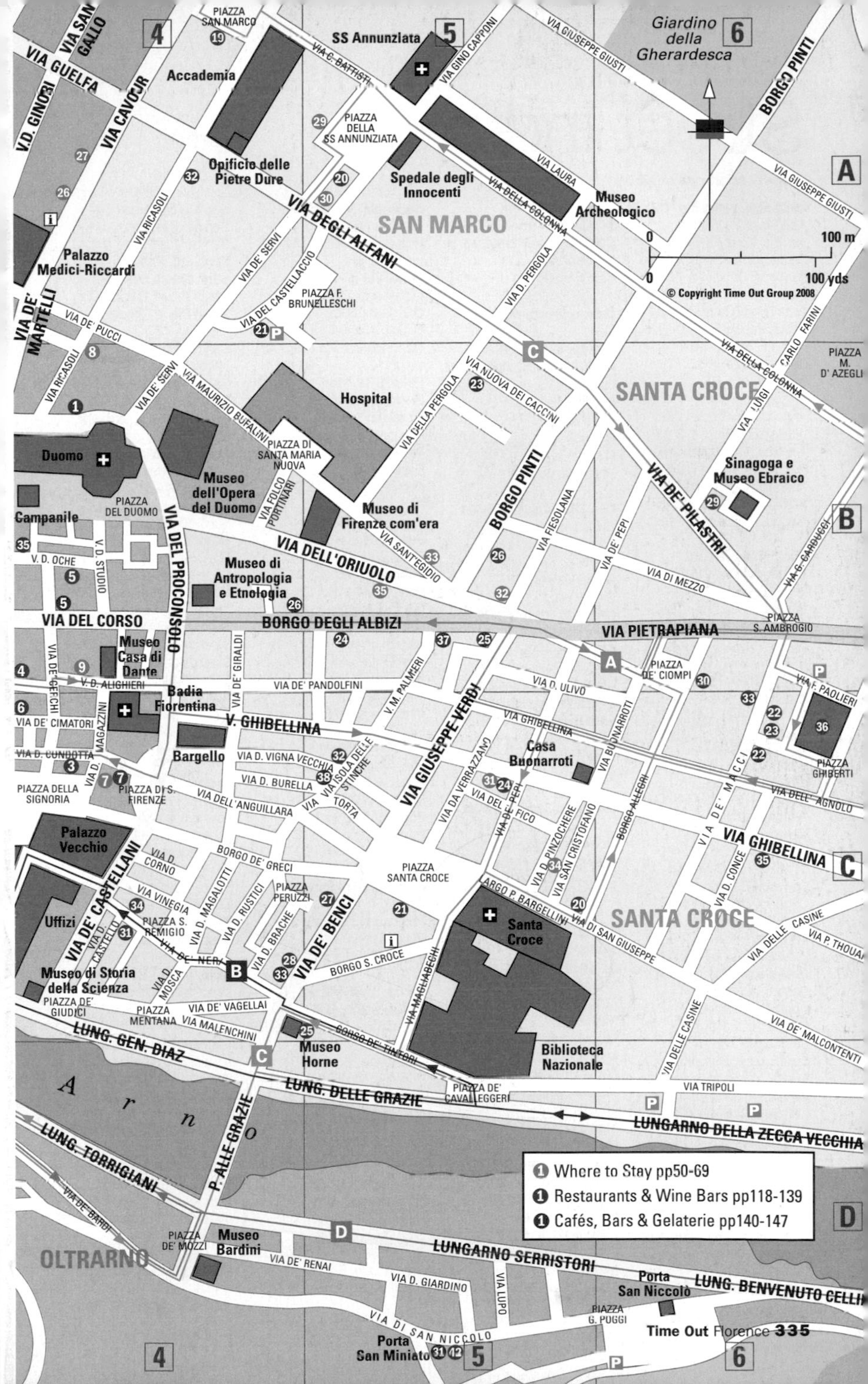

4
5
6
A
B
C
D
Piazza San Marco
SS Annunziata
Giardino della Gherardesca
Via San Gallo
Via Guelfa
Via Cavour
V.D. Ginori
Accademia
Via C. Battisti
Via Gino Capponi
Via Giuseppe Giusti
Borgo Pinti
Piazza della SS Annunziata
Opificio delle Pietre Dure
Spedale degli Innocenti
Via Laura
Via della Colonna
Museo Archeologico
Via Ricasoli
Via degli Alfani
San Marco
Via de' Servi
Via del Castellaccio
Piazza F. Brunelleschi
Via D. Pergola
0
100 m
100 yds
© Copyright Time Out Group 2008
Palazzo Medici-Riccardi
Via de' Martelli
Via de' Pucci
Via Maurizio Bufalini
Hospital
Via Nuova dei Caccini
Via della Pergola
Santa Croce
Via Luigi Carlo Farini
Piazza M. D'Azeglio
Duomo
Piazza di Santa Maria Nuova
Via Folco Portinari
Museo dell'Opera del Duomo
Piazza del Duomo
Campanile
Museo di Firenze com'era
Borgo Pinti
Via Fiesolana
Via de' Pepi
Via de' Pilastri
Sinagoga e Museo Ebraico
Via G. Carducci
Via del Proconsolo
V. D. Oche
V. D. Studio
Via dell'Oriuolo
Via Sant'Egidio
Museo di Antropologia e Etnologia
Via di Mezzo
Via del Corso
Borgo degli Albizi
Via Pietrapiana
Piazza S. Ambrogio
Museo Casa di Dante
Via de' Cerchi
V. D. Alighieri
Via de' Giraldi
Via de' Pandolfini
V. M. Palmieri
Via D. Ulivo
Piazza de' Ciompi
Via F. Paolieri
Badia Fiorentina
Via de' Cimatori
V. Ghibellina
Via Ghibellina
Via Giuseppe Verdi
Via Buonarroti
Via de' Macci
Via D. Condotta
Bargello
Via Magazzini
Via D. Vigna Vecchia
Via Isola delle Stinche
Casa Buonarroti
Piazza Ghiberti
Piazza della Signoria
Piazza di S. Firenze
Via D. Burella
Via Torta
Via da Verrazzano
Via de' Pepi
Via dell' Agnolo
Via dell'Anguillara
Via del Fico
Borgo Allegri
Via D. Pinzochere
Via San Cristofano
Palazzo Vecchio
Via D. Corno
Borgo de' Greci
Piazza Santa Croce
Via Ghibellina
Via de' Castellani
Via D. Magalotti
Via D. Rustici
Piazza Peruzzi
Via de' Benci
Via D. Conce
Via Vinegia
Argo P. Bargellini
Santa Croce
Via di San Giuseppe
Via delle Casine
Via P. Thouar
Uffizi
Piazza S. Remigio
Via D. Castello
Via de' Neri
Via D. Brache
Borgo S. Croce
Via Magliabechi
Via D. Mosca
Museo di Storia della Scienza
Piazza de' Giudici
Piazza Mentana
Via de' Vagellai
Via Malenchini
Corso de' Tintori
Museo Horne
Biblioteca Nazionale
Via de' Malcontenti
Lung. Gen. Diaz
Arno
Lung. delle Grazie
Piazza de' Cavalleggeri
Via Tripoli
Lungarno della Zecca Vecchia
Lung. Torrigiani
P. alle Grazie
Via de' Bardi
Where to Stay pp50-69
Restaurants & Wine Bars pp118-139
Cafés, Bars & Gelaterie pp140-147
Piazza de' Mozzi
Museo Bardini
Oltrarno
Via de' Renai
Lungarno Serristori
Via D. Giardino
Via Lupo
Porta San Niccolò
Lung. Benvenuto Cellini
Piazza G. Poggi
Via di San Niccolò
Porta San Miniato

Street Index

See street map, pp334-335.

Acciaiuoli, Lungarno - C2/3
Agli, Via d. - B3
Agnolo, Via dell' - C6
Agostino, Via Sant' - C1/D1
Alamanni, Via Luigi - A1
Albero, Via d. - A1
Albizi, Borgo degli - B4/5
Alfani, Via degli - A4/5
Alighieri, Via d. - B4
Allegri, Borgo - C6
Alloro, Via d. - B3
Anguillara, Via dell' - C4/5
Annunziata, Piazza della SS - A5
Anselmi, Via d. - B3
Ardiglione, Via d. - C1/D1
Ariento, Via dell' - A3
Avelli, Via de' - A2/B2
Azeglio, Piazza M. d' - B6

Banchi, Via de' - B2
Barbadori, Via - C2/3
Bardi, Via de' - D3/4
Battisti, Via C. - A5
Belle Donne, Via delle - B2
Benci, Via de' - C4/5
Brache, Via d. - C4
Brunelleschi, Via - B3
Buonarroti, Via - C6
Burella, Via d. - C4

Caldaie, Via d. - D1
Calimala, Via - B3/C3
Calimaruzza - C3
Calzaiuoli, Via de' - B3/C3
Campidoglio, Via d. - B3
Campuccio, Via del - D1
Canacci, Via de' - A1/B1
Canto De' Nelli, Via del - A3
Capaccio, Via d. - C3
Capponi, Via Gino - A5
Carducci, Via G. - B6
Carmine, Piazza del - C1
Casine, Via delle - C6/D6
Castellaccio, Via del - A4
Castellani, Via de' - C4
Castello, Via d. - C4
Cavalleggeri, Piazza de' - D5
Cavour, Via - A4
Cellini, Lung. Benvenuto - D6
Cerchi, Via de' - B4/C4
Cerno, Via d. - C4
Cerretani, Via de' - B3
Chiesa, Via della - D1
Cimatori, Via de' - C4
Ciompi, Piazza de' - B6
Colonna, Via della - A5/6/B6
Conce, Via d. - C6
Condotta, Via d. - C4
Conti, Via de' - A3/B3
Cornino, Chiasso - C3
Corsini, Lungarno - C2
Corso de' Tintori - C5/D5
Corso, Via del - B4
Costa de' Magnoli - D3
Costa di San Giorgio - D3
Coverelli, Via - C2
Croce, Borgo La - C5

Duomo, Piazza del - B4

Faenza, Via - A2/3
Farini, Via Luigi Carlo - A6/B6
Federighi, Via de' - B2
Fico, Via del - C5
Fiesolana, Via - B5
Finiguerra, Via Maso – B1
Fiume, Via - A2
Fossi, Via de' - B2

Gen. Diaz, Lung. - C4/D4
Ghibellina, Via - C4/5/6
Ghiberti, Piazza - C6
Giardino, Via d. - D5
Giglio, Via del - A3
Ginori, Via d. - A4
Giraldi, Via de' - B4/C4
Giuseppe Giusti, Via - A5/6
Giuseppe Verdi, Via - B5/C5
Goldoni, Piazza - B2
Grazie, Lung. delle - D4/5
Grazie, Ponte Alle - D4
Greci, Borgo de' - C4/5
Guelfa, Via - A4
Guicciardini, Lung. - C2
Guicciardini, Via de' - D2/3

Jacopo da Diacceto, Via - A1

La Noce, Borgo - A3
Lambertesca, Via - C3
Lamberti, Via de' - C3
Laura, Via - A5/6

Macci, Via de' - C6
Maffia, Via - C1
Magalotti, Via d. - C4
Magazzini, Via d. - C4
Maggio, Via - C2/D2
Magliabechi, Via - C5
Malcontenti, Via de' - C6/D6
Malenchini, Via - C4
Manetto, Chiasso - C3
Marttelli, Via de' – A3/4/B3/4
Maurizio Bufalini, Via - B4
Mazzetta, Via - D1/2
Melarancio, Via d. - A2/3
Mentana, Piazza - C4
Mercato Centrale, Piazza del - A3
Mezzo, Via di - B6
Montebella, Via - B1
Moro, Via del - B2
Mozzi, Piazza de' – D4

Nazionale, Via - A2/3
Neri, Via de' - C4
Nuova de' Caccini, Via - B5

Oche, Via d. - B4
Ognissanti, Piazza - B1
Ognissanti, Borgo - B1
Oriuolo, Via dell' - B4/5
Orti Oricellari, Via degli - A1

Palazzuolo, Via - A1/B1/2
Palmieri, Via M. - B5/C5
Pandolfini, Via de' - B4/5
Panicale, Via - A3
Panzani, Via de' - B2/3
Paolieri, Via F. - B6/C6
Paolino, Via di - B1/2
Parioncino, Via - C2
Parione, Via del - B2/C2
Passer, Piazza della - C2
Pecori, Via de' - B3
Pellicceria, Via - B3/C3
Pepi, Via de' - B6/C5
Pergola, Via d. - A5
Pergola, Via della - B5
Peruzzi, Piazza - C4
Pescioni, Via de' - B3
Pietrapiana, Via - B6
Pilastri, Via de' - B6
Pinti, Borgo - A6
Pinti, Borgo - B5
Pinzochere, Via d. - C5
Pitti, Piazza de' - D2
Poggi, Piazza G. - D6
Ponte Alla Carraia - C1/2
Por S. Maria, Via - C3
Porcellana, Via del - B1/2
Porta Rossa, Via - C3
Portinari, Via Folco – B4
Presto di S. Martino, Via D. - C2/D2
Proconsolo, Via del - B4
Pucci, Via de' - A4
Purgatorio, Via d. - B2/C2

Ramaglianti, Via de' - C2
Renai, Via de' - D4/5
Repubblica, Piazza della - B3
Ricasoli, Via - A4
Roma, Via - B3
Romana, Via - D1
Rossa, Via Porta – C3
Rucellai, Via B. - A1
Rustici, Via d. - C4

San Cristofano, Via - C5
San Egidio, Via - B5
San Frediano, Borgo - C1
San Gallo, Via - A4
San Giovanni, Piazza - B3
San Giuseppe, Via di - C5/6
San Jacopo, Borgo - C2/3
San Lorenzo, Borgo - A3/B3
San Marco, Piazza - A4
San Niccolo, Via di - D4/5
San Spirito, Piazza - D1/2
Sant' Antonino, Via - A3
Sant' Orsola, Via - A3
Santa Croce, Piazza - C5
Santa Maria Novella, Piazza - B2
Santa Maria Nuova, Piazza di - B4/5
Santa Maria, Via - D1
Santa Monaca, Via - C1
Santa Trinità, Piazza - C2
Santo Spirito, Via di - C1/2
Sassetti, Via de' - B3/C3
Scala, Via della - A1/B2
Serragli, Via de' - C1/D1
Serristori, Lungarno - D5
Servi, Via de' - A4
Sguazza, Via - D2
Signoria, Piazza della - C4
Soderini, Lungarno - B1/C1
Sole, Via del - B2
Sprone, Via dello - C2
SS Apostoli, Borgo - C3
Stazione, Piazza della - A2
Stella, Borgo - C1
Stinche, Via Isola delle - C5
Strozzi, Piazza - B3
Strozzi, Via - B3
Studio, Via d. - B4
Stufa, Via d. - A3

Taddea, Via - A3
Tegolaio, Borgo - D1/2
Terme, Via delle - C3
Thouar, Via P. - C6
Tornabuoni, Via de' - B2/C2
Torrigiani, Lung. - C3/D3/4
Torta, Via - C5
Toscanella, Via - C2/D2
Trinità, P. S. - C2
Tripoli, Via - D6

Ulivo, Via d. - B5
Unita Italiana, Piazza dell' - A2

Vagellai, Via de' - C4
Valfonda, Via - A2
Vecchio, P. - C3
Vechhietti, Via d. - B3
Velluti, Via de' - D2
Vellutini, Via de' - C2
Verrazzano, Via da - C5
Vespucci, Lungarno Amerigo - B1
Vigna Nuova, Via d. - B2
Vigna Vecchia, Via d. - C4/5
Vinegia, Via - C4

Zecca Vecchia, Lungarno della - D6